A COUNSELOR'S GUIDE TO
CAREER ASSESSMENT INSTRUMENTS
FOURTH EDITION

A Counselor's Guide to Career Assessment Instruments

Fourth Edition

Edited by:
Jerome T. Kapes
Texas A & M University

Edwin A. Whitfield
Ohio Department of Education

National Career Development Association
in Cooperation with the
Association for Assessment in Counseling

he United States of America
 bound by Royal Printing & Copy, Tulsa, OK 74103, USA

ibrary of Congress Cataloging-in-Publication Data

's guide to career assessment instruments / edited by Jerome T.
Edwin A. Whitfield.--4th ed.
. cm.
s bibliographical reference and index
 -885333-072-2 (pbk.)
cupation aptitude tests--Evaluation 2 Vocational interests--Testing--
ion. I. Kapes, Jerome T. II. Whitfield, Edwin A.

1.7.C68 2001
'000296--dc21

                                                    2001018003

Table of Contents

ABOUT THE EDITORS xi

FOREWORD xii

ACKNOWLEDGEMENTS xiii

CHAPTER 1: A COUNSELOR'S GUIDE: INTRODUCTION
TO THE FOURTH EDITION 1
Jerome T. Kapes A. and Edwin A. Whitfield

CHAPTER 2: TRENDS AND ISSUES IN CAREER ASSESSMENT 15
Edwin L. Herr

CHAPTER 3: SELECTING A CAREER ASSESSMENT INSTRUMENT 27
William A. Mehrens

CHAPTER 4: USING ASSESSMENT FOR PERSONAL, PROGRAM, AND
POLICY ADVOCACY 35
Norman C. Gysbers and Richard T. Lapan

CHAPTER 5: COMPUTER-ASSISTED CAREER ASSESSMENT 47
James P. Sampson, Jr., Jill A. Lumsden, and Darrin L. Carr

CHAPTER 6: ASSESSMENT AND COUNSELING COMPETENCIES AND
RESPONSIBILITIES 65
Nancy J.Garfield and Thomas S. Kriesbok

CHAPTER 7: APTITUDE/ACHIEVEMENT AND COMPREHENSIVE
MEASURES 73

Ability Explorer 74
Christopher Borman, Reviewer

Adult Basic Learning Examination (ABLE) 82
Eunice N. Askov and Juliet Smith, Reviewers

Adult Measure of Essential Skills (AMES) 87
Victor L. Willson and Jesus Tanguma, Reviewers

Armed Services Vocational Aptitude Battery Career Exploration Program
(ASVAB) 93
Jeff E. Rogers, Reviewer

Ball Aptitude Battery (BAB) 102
Donald Thompson and John Patrick, Reviewers

Career Planning Survey (CPS) 109
Robert C. Reardon and Stacie H. Vernick, Reviewers

CareerScope Assessment and Reporting System (CareerScope) 116
Clarence D. Brown, Reviewer

Differential Aptitude Test (DAT) and Career Interest Inventory (CII) 123
Lin Wang, Reviewer

Employability Competency Scale (ECS) 132
Patricia K. Freitag and Ralph O. Mueller, Reviewers

Explore and Plan 139
Patricia Henderson, Reviewer

Occupational Aptitude Survey and Interest Schedule. Second Edition 150
(OASIS-2),
Robert J. Miller and Candice Hollingsead, Reviewers

PESCO 2001 158
Jay W. Rojewski, Reviewer

PSI Basic Skills Test (BST) 164
Bruce Thompson, Reviewer

Tests of Adult Basic Education (TABE) 170
Bruce G. Rogers, Reviewer

Wonderlic Basis Skills Test (WBST) 178
Gerald S. Hanna and Kenneth F. Hughey, Reviewers

Work Keys 183
John Townsend, Reviewer

CHAPTER 8: INTEREST AND WORK VALUES INVENTORIES 193

Campbell Interest and Skill Survey (CISS) 194
Kathleen R. Boggs, Reviewer

Career Assessment Inventory (CAI) 202
Claire Usher Miner and Steven M. Sellers, Reviewers

COPSystem (CAPS, COPS, and COPES) 210
Pat Nellor Wickwire, Reviewer

Career Values Card Sort (CVCS) 218
Richard T. Kinnier and Jerry L. Kernes, Reviewers

Chronicle Career Quest (CCQ) 222
Larry G. Daniel, Reviewer

Harrington-O'Shea Career Decision-Making System, Revised (CDM) 228
Vicki L. Campbell and Gretchen W. Raiff, Reviewers

Interest Explorer 235
Sharon A. Sackett, Reviewer

Interest Determination, Exploration and Assessment System (IDEAS) 242
Tammi Vacha-Hasse and Lydia P. Buki, Reviewers

Jackson Vocational Interest Survey (JVIS) 250
Robert E. Shute, Reviewer

Kuder General Interest Survey, Form E (KGIS-E) 257
Mark Pope, Reviewer

Kuder Occupational Interest Survey, Form DD (KOIS-DD) 265
and Kuder Career Search with Person Match (KCS)
Kevin R. Kelly, Reviewer

Self-Directed Search, Fourth Edition (SDS) 276
Joseph C. Ciechalski, Reviewer

Strong Interest Inventory (SII) and Skills Confidence Inventory (SCI) 288
Nicholas A. Vacc and Deborah W. Newsome, Reviewers

Values Scale (VS) 298
Patricia Schoenrade, Reviewer

Vocational Interest Inventory, Revised (VII-R) 303
William D. Schafer, Reviewer

CHAPTER 9: CAREER DEVELOPMENT/CAREER MATURITY
MEASURES 309

Career Attitudes and Strategies Inventory (CASI) 310
Michael B. Brown, Reviewer

Career Beliefs Inventory (CBI) 316
Michael E. Hall and Jack R. Rayman, Reviewers

Career Development Inventory (CDI) 323
Donna L. Sundre, Reviewer

Career Factors Inventory (CFI) 331
Darrell A. Luzzo, Reviewer

Career Maturity Inventory (CMI) 336
Patricia Jo McDivitt, Reviewer

Career Thoughts Inventory (CTI) 343
Rich Feller and Joe Daly, Reviewers

CHAPTER 10: PERSONALITY ASSESSMENTS 349

Comprehensive Personality Profile (CPP) 350
Gary W. Peterson and Stephen R. Hill, Reviewers

Jackson Personality Inventory-Revised (JPI-R) 357
David A. Jepsen, Reviewer

Myers-Briggs Type Indicator (MBTI) 363
Charles C. Healy, Reviewer

Sixteen Personality Factor (16PF) Questionnaire 369
Timothy R. Vansickle, Reviewer

Student Styles Questionnaire (SSQ) 377
James Rounds and Molly C. McKenna, Reviewers

CHAPTER 11: INSTRUMENTS FOR SPECIAL POPULATIONS 385

Arc's Self-Determination Scale (Arc-SDS) 386
Pamela J. Leconte, Reviewer

Brigance Life/Employability Skills Inventories (LSI/ESI) 393
Linda H. Parrish and Ellen Blair, Reviewers

Learning/Working Styles Inventory (LWSI) 399
Patricia L. Sitlington and Jennifer McGlashing, Reviewers

Life-Centered Career Education Competency Assessment:...........................405
Knowledge and Performance Batteries(LCCE)
Patricia S. Lynch, Reviewer

Reading-Free Vocational Interest Inventory:2 (R-FVII:2) 412
Stephen W. Thomas, Reviewer

Street Survival Skills Questionnaire (SSSQ) 418
Gary M. Clark, Reviewer

Transition Planning Inventory (TPI) 425
Karl F. Botterbusch and Jeffery C. Lund, Reviewers

CHAPTER 12: ADDITIONAL CAREER ASSESSMENT INSTRUMENTS .433
Jerome T. Kapes, Linda Martinez, and Tammi Vacha-Haase

Multiple Aptitude, Achievement, and Comprehensive Measures 436

Specific Aptitude and Achievement Measures 443

Interest Inventories 448

Measures of Work Values 455

Card Sorts 458

Career Development/Maturity Measures 460

Personality Assessments..463

Instruments for Populations 468

APPENDIX A: SOURCES OF INFORMATION ABOUT TESTING
AND CAREER ASSESSMENT 475
David A. Jepsen and Jerome T. Kapes

APPENDIX B: PUBLISHER ADDRESSES, PHONE NUMBERS,
AND WEB PAGES 489
Edwin A. Whitfield and Linda Martinez

APPENDIX C: TESTING STANDARDS AND CODES 503

Responsibilities of Users of Standardized Tests 503

Code of Fair Testing Practices in Education 517

Rights and Responsibilities of Test Takers 523

APPENDIX D: A COUNSELOR'S GUIDE USER'S MATRIX 535
Jerome T. Kapes and Linda Martinez

INDEX 559

About the Editors

Jerome T. Kapes is Professor Emeritus of Educational Psychology at Texas A&M University. He has taught courses in career assessment, measurement, research and career development education for which he has been recognized with several teaching awards. His professional experience includes faculty positions at Penn State and Lehigh University. He is a graduate of Penn State with a B. S. and Ph.D. in Vocational-Industrial Education and an M.Ed. in Counselor Education. Dr. Kapes has been a member of ACA (AACD/APGA) since 1967 with divisional membership in NCDA and AAC. He has also been a Nationally Certified Counselor (NCC) and Career Counselor (NCCC). Additionally, he holds membership in the Association for Career and Technical Education (ACTE), American Educational Research Association (AERA), American Vocational Education Research Association (AVERA), and National Association for Industrial and Technical Teacher Educators (NAITTE) as well as other national, regional and state professional associations. He is the author or co-author of over 200 articles, books, chapters, monographs and papers presented at professional association meetings. In 1995, he was named a Distinguished Research Fellow in the College of Education at Texas A&M University. Much of his research and publication has been in the area of career development and related measurement topics.

Edwin A. Whitfield is an Associate Director with the Ohio Department of Education. His responsibilities include providing leadership and coordination for school guidance and counseling programs and assessment initiatives in the state of Ohio. Prior to his current position, he served as a coordinator of guidance and counseling in California, and as a teacher and counselor in Iowa and Ohio. He received his a B.A. from Loras College, his M.Ed. from Ohio University, and a Ph.D. from the University of Iowa. Dr. Whitfield has been actively involved in professional associations serving as NCDA president as well as president of NCDA state divisions in California and Ohio. He served as editor of the Vocational Guidance Quarterly (now the Career Development Quarterly) for six years, as coordinator of NCDA publications, and as chairperson of the ACA Council of Journal Editors. He has received the NCDA Merit Award twice. Dr. Whitfield has published works addressing career development, assessment, evaluation, and guidance program planning and implementation.

Foreword

The three previous editions of this outstanding resource have been widely used by counselors, educators, and researchers in the field of career development. Work on the four editions of this Guide, beginning in 1979, represents many years of professional commitment by Jerome T. Kapes and Edwin A. Whitfield, as well as Majorie M. Mastie who was co-editor of the three previous editions of this important resource. We are grateful for their outstanding contribution to the improvement of the career assessment field. We realize that over the years, literally hundreds of professionals have committed their time and expertise through various roles such as advisory committee members, chapter authors, instrument reviewers, and test publishers. Their cooperation has been outstanding.

Several improvements have been made in this edition including the entirely new material in Chapters 2, 4, and 5 as well as revisions to the other chapters. The Additional Instruments Section has been extensively revised and expanded both by eliminating out-of-date instruments and adding new instruments. This fourth edition of *A Counselor's Guide to Career Assessment Instruments* is an example of the many productive, collaborative efforts between the National Career Development Association (NCDA) and the Association for Assessment in Counseling (AAC), divisions of the American Counseling Association (ACA).

Gerald A Juhnke
President, 2000-2001
Association for Assessment
in Counseling

Diane Kjos
President, 2000-2001
National Career Development
Association

Acknowledgements

This fourth edition of *A Counselor's Guide* is the latest result of approximately 22 years of effort on the part of many contributors. From the beginning, the *Guide* has been developed under the auspices of the National Career Development Association (NCDA) with support from the Association for Assessment in Counseling (AAC). While the primary contributors are the authors of the chapters and reviews, there were many others who deserve recognition for the advice and support they provided.

As with this and previous editions of the *Guide*, the editors benefited from the input of an advisory committee. Although we did not convene this committee for group meetings, we sought and received their advice on many occasions by mail, phone, email and, when possible, in personal conversations. Those advisory committee members who have served for all four editions are Chris Borman, Dave Jepsen, and Linda Parrish. Additional advisors for this edition, some of whom also served as advisors to previous editions, were Ed Herr, Tim Vansickle, and Bruce Thompson.

In addition to the above named committee members, the editors are grateful for the continued advice and support of Marjorie M. Mastie, who was co-editor for all three previous editions of the *Guide*. Marge was extensively involved in planning the fourth edition, but was unable to continue as co-editor due to family circumstances that required her full attention. Her insight and extensive knowledge of the field helped to make the *Guide* the invaluable resource it has become.

Beginning with the first edition, The *Guide* has paid particular attention to assessments used with individuals who are members of special populations, particularily those with disabilities and disadvantages. In order to ascertain the state-of-the-art of career assessment with special populations, the editors relied on the input from 16 professionals from across the nation who have expertise in this area. Members of this advisory group responded to two rounds of a survey designed to ascertain which instruments were most used, or most likely to be used in the future. They are Eleanor Bicanich, Karl Botterbusch, Arden Boyer-Stephens, Clarence Brown, Jim Brown, Gary Clark, Pamela Leconte, Jean Lehmann, Patricia Lynch, Carolyn Maddy-Bernstein, Robert Miller, Debra Neubert, Linda Parrish, Michelle Sarkees Wircenski, Patricia Sitlington, and Donnalie Stratton.

Much of the day-to-day work of producing the fourth edition of the *Guide* was conducted at Texas A&M University with the support of the Dean of the College of Education, Jane Conoley, and the Head of the Department of Educational Psychology, Douglas Palmer. However, the Texas A&M staff person who was most indispensable to the success of the project was Linda Martinez, who served as project graduate assistant. She has been responsible for library research, word processing, communications, co-authoring several sections of the *Guide*, and other activities required to keep the project on track. If one person was indispensable to the completion of this fourth edition, it was Linda.

Some of the work of planning and producing the *Guide* was undertaken when the senior editor, Kapes, was on sabbatical at Penn State during the summer and fall of 1988 and summer of 1999. The Workforce Education and Development Program at Penn State provided office space as well as phone, copy, mail and computer support to the project. For their invaluable help, we are grateful to Eunice Askov, Department Head, Edgar Farmer and Ken Gray, Professors-in-Charge, and the secretarial staff of the Workforce Education and Development Program.

Support from NCDA was provided by Juliet Miller, Executive Director, and Linda Griffin, Administrative Assistant. They were responsible for converting our computer files into a polished manuscript. We also thank the various officers of NCDA and AAC who supported our efforts over the past three years in whatever way they could.

Also important to the success of the fourth edition of the *Guide* are Buros Institute at the University of Nebraska-Lincoln and Pro-Ed of Austin, Texas, publishers of the *Mental Measurement Yearbooks* and *Test Critique* respectively. As with previous editions, they again agreed to allow their reviewers to adapt their previously published reviews for inclusion in the *Guide*.

Many others, too numerous to mention here, also contributed to the *Guide*. Most notable among these are the authors of the reviews and chapters who contributed their time and effort to produce quality manuscripts. The instrument publishers also contributed by providing the information included preceding the reviews as well as complementary copies of the instruments selected for review. We encourage our readers to acknowledge their contributions personally, whenever the opportunities arise.

There are others who have contributed to this project over the past 22 years in an indirect way through their support and influence. Reflecting on our own career development, we want to acknowledge those individuals who have had a major influence on our personal and professional lives.

Personally, one's family serves as an integral and inseparable part of career, providing both reason and reward for our career efforts and accomplishments. For their unconditional support of our career pursuits over many years, we thank Evelyn and Becky Kapes and Marjorie Whitfield and Shauna, Hallie and Eric.

Professionally, although there are many to whom we owe our gratitude for their positive impact on our lives, we each would like to mention several of the most important. Kapes acknowledges Edward Gundy, scoutmaster, who instilled a curiosity about nature and an achievement motivation in the many youth entrusted to him; Richard McKinstry, psychology professor at Penn State, who encouraged his students to consider the practice of psychology as a career; and Joseph Impelletter, doctoral advisor, who nurtured the career development of his students both by serving as an example and through mentoring with patience and kindness.

Whitfield acknowledges appreciation to colleagues who provided continuous improvement opportunities over the years. The privilege of working with quality people has improved both his career satisfaction and success. In particular, the leadership and caring skills of two administrators, Glen Pierson and Roger Trent provided models and a goal for career growth. A special thanks to both of them.

JTK
EAW

CHAPTER 1

A Counselor's Guide: Introduction to the Fourth Edition

Jerome T. Kapes
Professor Emeritus of Educational Psychology
Texas A&M University

Edwin A. Whitfield
Associate Director
Ohio Department of Education

Background

Fourth Edition Development

The first edition of *A Counselor's Guide* was published in 1982, the second edition in 1988 and the third edition in 1994. Given the rapid changes that continue to occur in career assessment instruments and in the professions that use them, it appears that approximately six years is the maximum time between revisions if this work is to remain current. The time needed to plan and produce the Guide is approximately three years, with decisions about topics and instruments to include made relatively early in the process, while other content such as the additional instruments chapter and appendices continues to evolve until press time. All of the decisions concerning what to include were influenced by an advisory committee whose members are listed in the acknowledgements. However, the ultimate responsibility for the content of the fourth edition rests with the editors.

The first edition of the Guide contained 259 pages, the second 351 pages and the third 496 pages. For this edition, the decision was made to increase the size to approximately 550 pages with content similar to the third edition. The Additional Career Assessment Instruments chapter has been expanded to include 270 instruments, and a User's Matrix is again provided that lists all 326 instruments included in this edition. Several of the chapters and all of the reviews have different authors from any of the previous editions. Overall, there are 56 separate instruments included in 49 reviews by 68 authors and co-authors using a standard format that includes Description, Use in Counseling, Technical Considerations, Computer-Based Version (if applicable), Overall Critique, and References. The reviews include 30 instruments that were not reviewed in any of the previous editions and many other instruments that have been extensively revised or updated since the third edition.

Reviews and Reviewers

The decisions as to what instruments to include for review were based on input from the advisory committee, a review of the literature and publisher catalogues, and, for instruments for special populations, on the results of a survey of national experts. The principles underlying the decisions to select instruments for review were to include –

- Major instruments identified by a consensus of the advisory committee
- Previously reviewed instruments that have undergone extensive revision or update
- New instruments that appear to have promise of extensive use
- Instruments, not otherwise included, that could be used by employers to make hiring or advancement decisions or facilitate career development
- Instruments with proven utility for persons with disabilities or disadvantages based on the survey
- National experts

Given the rapid expansion of computer-based versions of career assessment instruments, it was decided to again include a section in each review to cover these versions. Also, Chapter 5 discusses the rapidly evolving developments in computer-assisted career assessment.

The process of selecting instrument reviewers was similar to that followed for the previous three editions. As was the case for previous editions, permission was obtained from the respective publishers for use of reviewers who had previously published reviews in either the Mental Measurements Yearbooks or in Test Critiques. Typically, these reviewers made extensive revisions in their previously published manuscripts both to update the information and to accommodate the *Counselor's Guide* format. Other members of AAC and NCDA, or professionals who publish in the journals of these associations, were recruited to write reviews for new or revised instruments for which no previous reviews were available. Lastly, other reviewers with unique expertise and experience with a particular instrument were also used. As before, all reviews published in *A Counselor's Guide* were subjected to an external evaluation by the editors or members of the advisory committee. However, the opinions expressed by the reviewers are their own.

Context Information for Users

Before deciding to employ psychometric instruments for career assessment, the user needs prerequisite contextual information. This includes a knowledge of the instruments available for the particular intended use, access to sources of good information about the available instruments, and awareness of the various legal, ethical, and social considerations that have an impact on the career assessment process. A brief discussion of each of these context considerations follows.

Instrument Availability and Use

Trustworthy information about what career assessment instruments are most used for career counseling and related purposes is difficult to obtain. The primary reason for this difficulty is that most users are familiar with only a few of the many instruments available. When users are asked to rate or rank the usefulness or applicability of a large number of instruments, they tend to place the ones they use at the top and then rank others by name recognition only somewhere below these choices. Several surveys conducted in the past have included instruments that were no longer available, yet they still received relatively large numbers of nominations for use, presumably because their names were familiar. In previous editions of *A Counselor's Guide*, the editors have reported such surveys conducted by others (Engen, Lamb & Prediger, 1982; Zytowski & Warman, 1982), by themselves (Kapes & Mastie, 1988, p. 7), and by Watkins, Campbell and Nieberding (1994). Given the dated and somewhat unreliable nature of this information, especially at the lower end of the rankings, these rankings are not included here. It may be useful, however, to know that in the lists cited above the most used measures (in alphabetical order) for aptitude were the Armed Services Vocational Aptitude Battery (ASVAB), Differential Aptitude Tests (DAT), and General Aptitude Test Battery (GATB) whereas the most used interest measures were the Kuder Occupational Interest Survey (KOIS/ Kuder DD), Self Directed Search (SDS) and Strong Interest Inventory (SCII/SII). Ranked below these were a number of other interest, values, and career development measures.

Although various surveys of career assessment instrument use have been reported, these surveys have typically not covered use with special populations. In preparation for the third edition of this Guide, a survey was conducted in Texas concerning the most used career assessments with special populations (Kapes, Parrish, & Funderburg, 1993). The results of that survey, which can be found in Chapter 1 of the third edition, were used to select instruments for the special populations sections of the third edition.

In order to obtain use information to plan the fourth edition of the Guide, a survey of 16 national experts was conducted to identify the most prominent and promising career assessment instruments for use with special instruments (Kapes & Martinez, 1999). This survey yielded a list of 93 instruments with some reported use. Of these, 26 instruments received at least three nominations. Many of the instruments on the list were also being used with typical populations and are reviewed in the appropriate sections of the Guide. These include the following: Career Occupational Preference System (COPS), Career Ability Placement Survey (CAPS), Self Directed Search (SDS), Occupational Aptitude Survey and Interest Schedule (OASIS), Career Assessment Inventory (CAI), Harrington-O'Shea Career Decision Making System (CDM), and Interest Determination, Exploration and Assessment System (IDEAS). Instruments that ranked high on the list of use and that are specifically intended for special populations included several learning styles inventories, the Life Centered Career Education Batteries, Transition Planning Inventory (TPI), Wide Range Interest-Opinion Test (WRIOT), Street Survival Skills Questionnaire (SSSQ), ARC Self-Determination Scale, Brigance Life Skills Inventory, Reading-Free Vocational Interest Inventory (RFVII), and Judgment of Occupational Behavior-Orientation (JOB-O). Of these, only the WRIOT and the JOB-O are not included for review in this fourth edition because they were reviewed in previous editions and have not been significantly revised since those reviews.

Sources of Information about Available Instruments
When the first edition of *A Counselor's Guide* was published in 1982, there was only one comprehensive source of information about career assessment instruments available. That source was the Buros Institute's publication, *Test in Print II* and its companion set of reviews, the *Eighth Mental Measurements Yearbook* (MMY), which was published in 1978. Since that time, the Buros Institute has published *Tests in Print III, IV,* and *V* (1983, 1994, 1999), and the *Ninth, Tenth, Eleventh, Twelfth,* and *Thirteenth Mental Measurements Yearbooks* (1985, 1989, 1992, 1995, 1999). Also, the Institute has established an online database through Bibliographic Retrieval Service (BRS) that makes reviews for subsequent yearbooks available as they are received.

A second major source of test information and reviews became available in 1983 when Test Corporation of America released its first volume of *Tests*, which was subsequently updated in 1987, 1991, and 1997. Also, the corporation began publication of *Test Critiques* (TC) in 1984. Since that time, 10 volumes have been released, the last four of which were published by PRO-ED in 1988, 1990, 1992, and 1994. The reviews in TC differ somewhat from those provided by the MMY in that more coverage is given to a description of the test, and information in addition to the traditional technical evaluation covered by the Buros reviews is provided. The MMY, however, usually provides reviews from more than one reviewer, while TC publishes only one review of each test. Also, each edition of the MMY is comprehensive and covers most published tests in the U.S. and other English-speaking countries, whereas TC is selective and cumulative and includes the most-used instruments in psychology, education, and business.

In addition to these two major providers of test information and reviews, there are other, more focused sources of information that the career counselor may find useful. Included among these are Educational Testing Service's (ETS) *Test Collection Catalogues*, several volumes of which describe instruments relevant to career assessment. The publications of the Stout Vocational Rehabilitation Institute-Materials Development Center at the University of Wisconsin-Stout specialize in assessments for persons with disabilities. Other sources that focus on special populations include several publications by PRO-ED, and more recently, handbooks dealing with multicultural assessment.

The professional journals continue to publish reviews. Those likely to contain reviews or articles about the use of career assessment instruments are the *Journal of Counseling and Development*, the *Career Development Quarterly*, the *Journal of Career Assessment*, and the *Measurement and Evaluation in Counseling and Development Journal*. Also, the Association for Assessment in Counseling (AAC) publishes test reviews in its organization newsletter, AAC *Newsnotes*, many of which deal with career assessment instruments.

Those desiring additional information about the sources described here as well as other sources of information about testing and career assessment are encouraged to consult Appendix A, which contains an annotated bibliography of available sources.

Legal, Ethical, and Social Considerations

Today's user of career assessment instruments needs to consider many more external factors than did those who pioneered the field. Very few laws existed almost 50 years ago when the post-World War II expansion of the use of tests in career counseling began. Since that time, both state and federal laws have been enacted that either govern, promote, or sometimes even require their use. Federal legislation that has promoted the use of tests for career counseling programs can be traced back to 1958 when the *National Defense Education Act* was passed with its emphasis on counseling and guidance in the public schools. This law was followed by *The Elementary and Secondary Education Act of 1965* and its later amendments that continued to promote school guidance and counseling activities, including testing and assessment.

A second stream of federal legislation that at first promoted vocational or career guidance and eventually required the use of tests in the public schools began with the *Vocational Education Act of 1963* and was expanded by its subsequent amendments in 1968 and 1976. The *1984 Carl D. Perkins Vocational Education Act* included in section 204 (c) a specific requirement for handicapped and disadvantaged students that stated:

> Each student who enrolls in a vocational education program and to whom subsection (b) applies shall receive (1) assessment of interests, abilities, and special needs of such student with respect to completing successfully the vocational education program . . .

The decade of the 1990s has produced several pieces of federal vocational education legislation with implications for career assessment as part of guidance and counseling services. In 1990, the *Carl D. Perkins Vocational and Applied Technology Education Act* replaced the earlier Perkins act; eight years later it was superseded by the *Carl D. Perkins Vocational and Technical Education Act of 1998*. Although these acts have not explicitly required the use of career assessment instruments, they included extensive provisions for career guidance and counseling services. Both Perkins acts have also required performance standards that have increased the use of applied achievement assessments.

This increased attention to student achievement assessment was stimulated by the first SCANS report *(Secretary's Commission on Achieving Necessary Skills*, 1991). In the middle of the decade, Congress also enacted the *School to Work Opportunities Act of 1994*, which was intended to provide all students with salable skills upon leaving high school. The major focus of the act was to integrate school- and work-based learning using connecting activities that include many career guidance services.

Parallel to federal vocational education legislation, which has focused on public schools and community college/postsecondary institutions, were the several acts directed at adults in the labor force who were unemployed or underemployed and who were economically disadvantaged. These include *the Manpower Development Training Act of 1962, Comprehensive Employment Training Act of 1973, Job Training Partnership Act of 1982* and the recent *Workforce Investment Act of 1998*. Many of the programs developed by the states to implement these acts included various career counseling and assessment services.

Operating alongside federal vocational education legislation have been *The Education of All Handicapped Children Act of 1975* and its subsequent amendments including the *Individuals with Disabilities Act of 1990* (IDEA) and its amendments of 1997. These laws have required the use of tests and other assessment devices as input to constructing Individualized Education Plans (IEPs) for individuals with disabilities through age 21 in the public schools. In addition, the IDEA Amendments of 1997 require transition planing beginning at age 14 to enable students to participate "… in advanced placement courses or a vocational education program" [Sec. 614 (d) (1) (A) (vii)]. Since students with disabilities in the public secondary schools are served in vocational education programs, tests targeted to this group have expanded greatly in quantity, if not in quality, over the past two decades.

Emerging over somewhat the same period as vocational education and handicapped/disability legislation, the Career Education movement also contributed to the use of tests in career guidance and counseling. Beginning in 1971, this movement was promoted by separate legislation in 1974, 1976, and 1977. The major impact this movement has had on career assessment is the development and use of instruments in the schools, including at the elementary and middle school level.

Although the above-described legislation promoted the use of assessment as part of the career guidance *and* counseling function of schools and agencies, other laws were passed that regulated its use. In 1979, the Department of Health, Education, and Welfare's Office of Civil Rights issued federal *Vocational Education Programs Guidelines for Eliminating Discrimination and Denial of Services on the Basis of Race, Color, National Origin, Sex, and Handicap*. These guidelines, based on three previous civil rights laws (*Civil Rights Act of 1964, Title IX of the Education Amendments of 1972*, and section 504 of the *Rehabilitation Act of 1973*), prohibit the use of tests in ways that would limit a person's options to pursue training in vocational education programs. The *1974 Family Educational Rights and Privacy Act* (The Buckley Amendment) and the National Institute of Education (NIE) (1978) *Guidelines for Assessment of Sex Bias and Sex Fairness in Career Interest Inventories* also govern or influence the use of tests.

Professional associations have also provided guidance for the use of tests in career counseling as well as in other areas. The *Standards for Educational and Psychological Testing* (1999) published by the American Psychological Association (APA) on behalf of a joint committee of APA, the American Educational Research Association (AERA), and the National Council for Measurement in Education (NCME), govern the development and use of all career assessment instruments. The National Board for Certified Counselors (NBCC) has also produced a code of ethics that includes a section on Measurement and Evaluation.

In 1980, the American Personnel and Guidance Association (now the American Counseling Association-ACA) published its policy statement *Responsibilities of Users of Standardized Tests* (RUST). This document, which contains much information relevant to the use of career assessment instruments, was revised in 1992. A similar publication, *Code of Fair Testing Practices in Education* (APA, 1988), was developed by a Joint Committee on Testing Practices, which involved six professional associations including ACA and AAC. Recently, this committee has also published *Rights and Responsibilities of Test Takers: Guidelines and Responsibilities* (APA, 1999). These last three documents are included in their entirety in Appendix C. An abbreviated checklist based on the standards and guidelines described above is included as Chapter 6.

Using the Guide

This fourth edition of *A Counselors Guide to Career Assessment Instruments* reviews or describes well over 300 career assessment instruments. To choose wisely from this array of assessment instruments, it is helpful to reflect on the purpose of career assessment and its role in enhancing career and human development.

The choice and use of career assessments can be based on three basic beliefs. First, career development is an integral and inseparable part of learning and human development; second, career guidance and career development programs should be a part of the total instructional program in schools, colleges, and training divisions of business and industry; and third, all assessment enhances learning as well as personal and career development.

It is also important to note certain principles that apply to all assessment:

- Assessment is something that is done with learners, not something that is done to them. It is much more than taking a test, regardless of purpose. Assessment is a process, a part of instruction, not an event.
- All assessments must complement and supplement each other. Assessment of achievement, aptitudes, interests, values, career development, and personality traits are a part of learning.
- All assessment should promote self-assessment, the involvement of the learner, and his/her ownership of the process and the results.
- Two major purposes of assessment are to improve and to prove: To improve learning and development and the programs provided to learners, and to prove the effectiveness of such programs.
- Assessment is inseparable from instruction, learning and development.

Although all assessments of learners contribute to their overall growth and development, career assessment provides additional information for the enhancement of career development and career success. In the third edition of *A Counselor's Guide to Career Assessment Instruments*, Herr (1994) described four main uses of career assessments:

1. Prediction: What is the probability of a learner's success in an educational program, occupation, or career?
2. Discrimination: How similar is a learner to those who are successful in a given program or occupation?

3. Monitoring: What is the status of a learner's career maturity, decision-making skills, or planning skills?
4. Evaluation: How effective are career interventions or program activities? What is the success of the program in terms of learner improvement or achievement of the intended results of the program?

The first three of Herr's uses of assessment results seek to improve the choices and career success of individuals; the last purpose adds the dimension of program accountability by using assessment data in aggregate.

Mastie (1994), also in the third edition of this Guide, described four uses of assessment in career counseling and discussed the appropriateness of each. She labeled these career assessments as Compass, Credential, Process, and Empowerment.

Career assessment as Compass is the process of amassing information about an individual (interests, aptitudes, values, skills, etc.) in order to improve the accuracy of a decision. In light of the limitations of available assessment instruments, Mastie cautioned of the dangers of using such information to find a right career path.

Career assessment as Credential was seen as limiting access and opportunity for those tested. She cautioned that if assessment is used to qualify learners for intended training opportunities and career paths, counselors must be aware of these hurdles and incorporate them into ongoing career development programs and provide interventions for counselees to prepare for them.

Career assessment as Process is based on the view of career development as an ongoing process, a series of choices. Thus, any particular career decision is merely a single instance in a lifetime of career choice points. Career assessment can assist learners to approach career choice points as times to reevaluate opportunities; to reassess their skills, interests, and values; to seek assistance if needed; and to use the information to create career plans and initiate action.

Career assessment as Empowerment is based on the premise that career planning is the work of learners, and not the work of the counselor. Career assessments are seen as questions for the learner, not answers. Using assessment results helps learners take control and to inform and enrich their own explorations of possible choices.

It is clear that choosing assessment instruments is neither a simple nor an isolated decision. Career assessment is both process and product. It is a vital ingredient in the process of planning and choosing and an important source of information about how learners are progressing in their career development. It provides information on career knowledge, self-knowledge, and career planning skills, all of which are necessary for the learner to enhance his/her career development and career success. It complements other assessments and instructional processes and draws from these to enhance career development. At the same time it allows for the benchmarking of learner progress singularly and in aggregate to enhance intervention techniques and allow us to assess and improve program effectiveness. Career assessment, used properly, can provide form and focus to a career development program. Inappropriate, misused, or unconnected to other program efforts, it offers little and has the potential to interfere with career development and career success.

This fourth edition of *A Counselors Guide,* while providing a plethora of career instruments from which to choose, also provides advice on choosing appropriate assessment strategies and using the assessment results to best serve the learner. Chapters 2 through 6 lead the reader through discussions of recent trends and concerns in the use of career assessment and the competencies needed to choose and use assessment wisely. Edwin Herr (Chapter 2) addresses the transformation of the roles and functions expected of assessment. Current issues as well as emerging trends and issues and the challenges they bring are discussed. William Mehrens follows in Chapter 3 with a review of factors that must be considered in selecting career instruments. Factors such as the intended purpose, technical information, and other practical issues are discussed.

In Chapter 4, Norman Gysbers and Richard Lapan look at societal changes and the challenges they represent for assessment. They envision three roles for assessment in responding to these challenges: personal advocacy, program evaluation, and formulating public policy. They conclude with an example of a policy brief to consider. James Sampson, Jill Lumsden, and Darrin Carr (Chapter 5) provide an authoritative and challenging look at how computer-assisted career assessment is affecting the counselors' and clients' roles in career assessment. Integrating computers into career assessment and the use of personal computers and the Internet as well as other issues influencing computer-assisted career assessment are covered.

Nancy Garfield and Thomas Krieshok (Chapter 6) provide an informal self-evaluation method for users to assess their own competencies, responsibilities, and practices in career assessment. Basic concepts covered include counseling skills, assessment skills, types of instruments, score reporting procedures, technical considerations, use, and interpretation.

A total of 56 instruments in 49 test reviews comprise the heart of this fourth edition. These are divided into five categories to facilitate location and selection of appropriate instruments: Chapter 7-Aptitude/Achievement and Comprehensive Measures, Chapter 8-Interest and Work Values Inventories, Chapter 9-Career Development/Maturity Measures, Chapter 10-Personality Assessments, and Chapter 11-Instruments for Special Populations.

Reviews begin with publisher-provided descriptive information in a standardized format, followed by a brief critical review of the instrument's strengths and limitations by one or two professionals of acknowledged expertise.

Users will find in these entries the answers to daily application questions such as–

> For what ages in this test appropriate? Who publishes it? What is the date of this inventory? Is there a new edition? Can it be given within one of our class periods? Can it be hand-scored? How expensive would it be for me to test an entire group? What kinds of scores would we get from this instrument?

Beyond these factual answers, users will find here the kind of practical information that they need for evaluating instruments for potential use:

> Are there reasons to believe this instrument may not be appropriate for the use I have in mind? Does this test really measure what we want to measure? What other instruments of this type are there for me to consider? Is there an entire category of measures we have overlooked?

In the final chapter (12), Jerome Kapes, Linda Martinez, and Tammi Vacha-Haase provide an extensive overview of 270 additional career assessment instruments that are available to the practitioner. Where available, readers are referred to more complete reviews. In total, 326 instruments are reviewed or described throughout this guide.

The Guide concludes with the appendices provided to facilitate the use of this, as well as other, career assessment resources:

- David Jepsen and Jerome Kapes provide an annotated bibliography (Appendix A) that contains a manageable number of current references in testing and career assessment.
- Publishers' full addresses, phone numbers, e-mail addresses, and web pages, when available, are provided in Appendix B to simplify requests for specimen sets or other assistance and to facilitate ordering.
- Appendix C provides the complete text of professional association position statements on the responsibilities of test users, code of fair testing practices, and the rights and responsibilities of test takers.
- The user's Matrix created by Jerome Kapes and Linda Martinez (Appendix D) lists all 326 instruments included in the guide and should help the reader to find instruments appropriate for selected purposes.

Once the reader has an overall picture of what is available here, thoughtful consideration should be given to perspective. Fairness and balance in the treatment of reviewed instruments drove all deliberations by the editors, advisory committee, and authors. We have made this reference as dependable, honest, and accurate as it was in our power to achieve. Nevertheless, limitations of length, technical documentation, and occasional divided professional opinion suggest that serious readers will need to undertake additional investigation, using the technical manuals and the sources referenced. This guide can neither teach a measurement course nor make a selection decision for a busy practitioner. The user must assume his or her own responsibility to achieve full professional competency through ongoing professional development programs and by gaining a great deal of experience with the instruments described here.

With this perspective in mind, however, we are pleased to offer this tool to assist in clarifying and making manageable the complex body of knowledge about career assessment available to today's career development practitioner.

References

American Counseling Association. (1992). *Responsibilities of users of standardized tests*. Alexandria, VA: Author.

American Educational Research Association, American Psychological Association, National Council on Measurement in Education. (1999). *Standards for educational and psychological testing*. Washington, DC: American Psychological Association.

American Psychological Association. (1988). *Code of fair testing practices in education*. Washington, DC: Author.

American Psychological Association. (1999). *Rights and responsibilities of test takers: Guidelines and responsibilities*. Washington, DC: Author.

Department of HEW, Office of Civil Rights. (1979, March 21). Vocational education programs guidelines for eliminating discrimination and denial of services on the basis of race, color, national origin, sex, and handicap. Washington, DC: *Federal Register* 44(6).

Engen, H. B., Lamb, R.R., & Prediger, D. T. (1982). Are secondary schools still using standardized tests? *Personnel and Guidance Journal*, 60, 287-290.

Herr, E. L., (1994). The counselor's role in career assessment. In J. T. Kapes, M. M. Mastie, & E. A. Whitfield (Eds.), *A counselor's guide to career assessment instruments* (3rd ed.) Alexandria, VA: National Career Development Association.

Kapes, J. T., & Martinez, L. (1999, February). Career assessment with special populations: Current instruments. Paper presented at the annual Vocational Education for Special Populations Statewide Conference, College Station, TX.

Kapes, J. T., & Mastie, M. M. (1982). *A counselor's guide to vocational guidance instruments*. Falls Church, VA: National Vocational Guidance Association.

Kapes, J. T., & Mastie, M. M. (1988). *A counselor's guide to career assessment instruments* (2nd ed.) Alexandria, VA: National Career Development Association.

Kapes, J. T., Mastie, M. M., & Whitfield, E. A. (1994). *A counselor's guide to career assessment instruments* (3rd ed.) Alexandria, VA: National Career Development Association.

Kapes, J. T., Parrish, L. H., & Funderburg, D. L. (1993). Vocational assessment for students with special needs: A survey of Texas public schools. *Occpational Education Forum*, 21(2), 31-44.

Mastie, M. M. (1994) Using assessment instruments in career counseling: Career assessment as compass, credential, process and empowerment. In J. T. Kapes, M. M. Mastie, and E. A. Whitfield (Eds.). (1994) *A counselor's guide to career assessment instruments* (3rd ed.) Alexandria, VA: National Career Development Association.

Secretary's Commission on Achieving Necessary Skills. *What work requires of schools: A SCANS report for America 2000.* Washington, DC: SCANS, U.S. Department of Labor, 1991. (ERIC Document Reproduction Service No. ED 332 054)

Watkins, C. E., Jr., Campbell, V. L., & Nieberding, R. (1994). The practice of vocational assessment by counseling psychologists. *The Counseling Psychologist*, 22(1), 115-128.

Zytowski, D. G., & Warman, R. E. (1982). The changing use of tests in counseling. *Measurement and Evaluation in Guidance*, 15(2), 147-152.

CHAPTER 2

Trends and Issues in Career Assessment

Edwin L. Herr
Distinguished Professor of Education
Counselor Education and Counseling Psychology Programs
The Pennsylvania State University

Background

Over the course of the development of the four editions of *A Counselor's Guide to Career Assessment Instruments*, assessment in the United States has changed in its acceptance as a significant tool in career counseling, as an intervention in its own right, and in the scope of the educational, occupational, and career issues to which it has been applied. Indeed, the status of assessment has changed during the 20th century in terms of how it is viewed by federal and state policies, criticisms of assessment methods, the social or economic climate related to assessment, the role of testing in counseling, and the effects of technology on assessment. As such themes interact, they provide the context for the role of assessment and, more specifically, career assessment in the next several decades.

Policy Perspectives on Assessment

At the present time in the United States, assessment, including career assessment, is being expected to perform roles and functions that are unprecedented in its history, and in combination with such expectations, criticisms of assessment contents and processes are also taking on new forms. Terwilliger (1997) has observed:

> It is obvious to even the most casual reader of the literature on educational assessment that the field is currently undergoing a fundamental and profound transformation. The traditional concepts and methodologies associated with assessment are being questioned by a variety of critics including school reform advocates, subject matter experts, cognitive theorists and others. (p. 24)

Similar criticisms have been raised about career assessment related to perceived disparities between theory and practice, excessive use of paper and pencil rather than performance assessments, and a variety of validity issues.

Whether such criticisms are justified or not, implications for assessment pervade the language of federal and state policies directed to the health care industry, to manufacturing and financial processes, to both basic and higher education, and to the classification, certification, and allocation of human resources. Terms such as competency standards, data driven, performance indicators, continuous quality improvement, total quality management, benchmarking, strategic initiatives and strategic actions, certification, accreditation, and licensure have become standard vocabulary that defines the professional existence of those employed in basic and higher education, community mental health services, one-stop career centers, human resource management, government, and independent practice. Each of these terms, as they are implemented, embodies some form of assessment, measurement, or testing. This national emphasis on accountability has caused one anonymous wag to suggest that in the Constitution of the United States we have replaced the creed of the Founding Fathers that "We hold these truths to be self-evident" with the words "We hold these truths to be statistical."

Assessment in the United States is still young in its historical sense, dating, in operational terms, only to the first two decades of the 20th century. It was then that Binet brought his intelligence test from France to the United States, the Army Alpha tests were developed for use in World War I, and the first vocational interest measure was given preliminary attention at what was then called Carnegie Tech in Pittsburgh in 1915. Assessment in the United States has achieved much and grown as a science during the last eight decades. But throughout the 20th century, assessment has tended to be used for rather specific purposes and within restricted contexts. Even though there are exceptions to this point in the armed forces classification systems, in such legislation as the National Defense Education Act, or in enabling legislation for employment or rehabilitation counselors, assessment has not been consistently defined by government policy as a sociopolitical instrument of national importance. Nor has it been the focus of federal policy debate.

In some contrast to the history of assessment in the earlier years of the 20th century, there currently appears to be a national love-hate climate surrounding assessment, as such processes have become partisan political grist for public policy debates. Examples of these issues are reflected in the headlines about creating national academic standards in reading and mathematics or other subject areas and voluntary national testing to determine whether these standards are being met versus views that federal money should not be focused on testing, but on better education (Hoff, 1997; Lawton, 1997b). Although there have been compromises on federal initiatives related to testing, other federal and state legislation continues to elevate assessment as a major strategy. For example, in 1999-2000 Massachusetts (White, 1997) began to require statewide learning standards and assessment in core subjects and has advocated a mandatory high school graduation examination such as the GED. New Jersey is in the process of linking funding levels for schools to statewide academic standards and their assessment (Johnson, 1997b). Rhode Island (Archer, 1997) is using criterion-referenced tests in selected academic subjects to measure how students do when compared against a state goal for performance. Rhode Island's approach to assessment, particularly in math achievement, is related to the efforts of the New Standards Project, a collaborative effort of more than a dozen states that developed standards and related assessments for student performance as these standards are benchmarked against national and international standards of what students should know and should be able to do.

Texas (Lawton, 1997a) has developed the Texas Assessment of Academic Skills that uses standardized tests as gatekeepers to high school graduation. North Carolina (Hoff & Manzo, 1997) has intensified its focus on teaching a state curriculum around which assessments were designed to hold schools and school districts accountable for student achievement. Michigan (Johnson, 1997a) has passed a bill to revise its high school testing program to grant "state endorsements" in math, science, social studies, and communication arts. The endorsements, which would be graded by student performance level (e.g., basic, above average, or outstanding), would appear on transcripts instead of on diplomas.

The Individuals with Disabilities Education Act (IDEA) (Sack, 1997) proposed rules that provide new requirements for an individualized education plan that each disabled student must have and the inclusion of disabled students in academic assessments. These rules require that all students with disabilities must be included in state or district assessments, or be given an alternative examination. Further, these roles require that states must set performance standards, similar to those for nondisabled students, for students receiving special education services.

However these state and federal initiatives are viewed, assessment has become a high stakes mechanism in the United States affecting the life chances of many young people and substantially defining the curriculum that teachers will teach in order to have their students perform as well as possible in state or national assessments.

One can argue that current policy debates about and implementation of educational testing for different purposes have little, if anything, to do with career assessment. But, in rebuttal, it can be argued that exit testing of students to determine whether they can graduate from high school, and with what academic competencies, has much to do with students' career development. These assessments are reflective of the skill sets that students need to acquire to build a secure career future. Indeed, in a society where knowledge work and knowledge workers are rapidly becoming the norm, educational achievement becomes an important element of one's career development and a significant factor in the types of career pathways one can gain access to and pursue. Many technical careers, not only those requiring college and university education, require a strong foundation in basic academic skills—English and communication skills, advanced mathematics and science—as the base on which to build technical skills. In this context, educational assessment overlaps and interacts with career assessment.

Issues in Assessment

Embedded in educational assessment trends at federal and state levels are a large array of issues and challenges that either revisit continuing and recurring questions or identify emerging and future challenges. Many of these have implications for career assessment as well.

Among the major issues in assessment that continue to occur are explicit or implicit concerns about test bias and gender differences. One of the perspectives on these issues come from studies by Supovitz (1997) and his colleagues at the Consortium for Policy Research in Education at the University of Pennsylvania which showed that standardized tests using a multiple-choice format are the predominant form of assessing the achievement of America's children. Supovitz argued that a diverse society deserves a more diverse assessment system. He contended that "of course standardized tests are biased. But it is not just standardized tests—any single testing method is biased because it applies just one approach to getting at student knowledge and achievement" (p.37). According to Supovitz,

> What we need are more experiments employing combinations of assessment approaches to arrive at an appropriate melding of test forms both economically feasible and robust enough to minimize the bias inherent in any single measure alone . . . In the end, the larger more intractable sources of disparities in student performance stem from broad social and educational inequities. But within the realm of assessment, the challenge for educators and policy makers is to find the appropriate balance of a variety of assessment forms, so that students of different genders, from different backgrounds, and with different affinities can demonstrate their capabilities. (p. 37)

The perspectives of Supovitz and his colleagues about test bias lead to related perspectives that are inherent if not explicit in the debates about specific uses of assessment by parents, minority groups, politicians and, indeed, testing experts. Arising from a multicultural perspective is the continuing concern of many observers that testing is gender or racially biased and, indeed, penalizes rather than facilitates the growth of specific groups of students or clients. Although some of the recommendations of Supovitz would be helpful in ameliorating such matters, still others argue that the reasons for testing during this century have changed and that purposes and uses of testing and assessment must change accordingly. The debates in Washington and in the states about assessment seem to be contemporary affirmations of the important insights of Gordon and Terrel (1981) nearly two decades ago. They stated:

> Critics of testing argue from a sociopolitical context, and thus challenge the very purpose as well as the developed technology of standardized testing. Defenders of testing argue from a traditional psychometric context, with little or no concern for political and social issues. The arguments of the two parties cannot be understood and appreciated without reference to those contexts. (p. 1167)

Although this chapter has lingered on current federal policy in basic education as a contemporary crucible for questions and challenges to assessment, many of the same concerns apply to the use of testing and assessment in other contexts (e.g., universities and workplaces) and also raise additional questions of particular relevance to counselors.

Career Assessment

Emerging Issues

Although many of the questions that arise from current national and state debates about assessment in education are the content of media headlines, many less publicized but similar questions arise as career assessments are being applied to particular groups of adolescents and adults. The latter include those moving from school or welfare to work; dislocated homemakers or women attempting to reenter paid employment; the use of assessments for military applicants in an increasingly technological environment and one that is changing rapidly in proportion of males and females; assessment, including literacy audits, of the competencies of current members of the American work force in their basic academic skills and their teachability relative to learning new industrial, manufacturing, or business processes; the need to ensure that persons with disabilities are able to use their talents and skills in educational and work settings without discrimination and bias; and the assessment of immigrant populations and cross-national populations being assimilated into or recruited for American jobs for which there are skill shortages.

Although space does not permit an extended analysis of the issues and challenges that relate to the assessment of the populations just cited, suffice it to say that among the assessment issues are the use of standardized, multiple-choice, knowledge-based tests versus performance-based assessment; new forms of functional analysis for persons with disabilities; and a lack of knowledge about the characteristics and lived experiences of lower socioeconomic level men and women, their learning styles, their inexperience with assessment processes and how these factors affect their scores. As a more pluralistic and culturally diverse population translates into a more culturally diverse work force, questions arise about how to create a more diverse assessment system for adults that accommodates language differences, differences in educational backgrounds in immigrants' countries of origin, and how responses to these issues should be incorporated into the training and the career assessment tools for employment and career counselors engaged in career assessment in different settings.

Counseling and Career Assessment
          Against the backdrop of issues just described, the historic alliance between counseling and career assessment has ebbed and flowed depending upon what counseling and personality theories were in vogue at particular times in our history, the types of training provided counselors at different points in the past century, and the degree to which assessment has been seen as a legitimate and useful complement to counseling. Contemporary issues have to do with a range of process concerns such as the following: are assessment processes being used effectively in counseling; are career assessments really interventions in their own right; do assessments effectively bridge the gap between theory and practice; who should test; are counselors and therapists being effectively trained to test and use the results appropriately; and what is our evidence regarding these questions?
          To a large degree, changes in counseling and in assessment have coincided with emerging theories of life span psychological development, client-centered or cognitive behavioral counseling, and, particularly, the expanding models of career development of John Holland, Donald Super, John Krumboltz, among others, and the attempts of these theorists to make their theories accessible to counselors through the use of career assessment instruments. For these theorists, career assessment has been the bridge to practice; theoretical constructs have been operationalized by reflecting them in the content of career interventions and, in particular, in tests and measurements.
          For example, Holland's 1985 theoretical constructs have stimulated the design and the content of the Vocational Preference Inventory, My Vocational Situation, and the Self-Directed Search; Holland's theoretical framework (the RIASEC model) is used as the organizing and interpretive structure for the recent iterations of the Strong Interest Inventory, the Career Assessment Inventory, and the Career Interest and Skills Survey. Holland's three-letter coding system of major personality types and occupational environments is widely used as a way of organizing U.S. government educational and occupational information through such sources as the *Dictionary of Holland Codes* and as the basis for some of the

self-assessment and informational components of the DISCOVER computer-mediated career guidance system.

Similarly, Super, from the beginning of his conceptual work, has used assessment instruments to operationalize and to evaluate his theoretical constructs. Like Holland, he has made his theory accessible to practitioners by using assessment to bridge theory and practice. Relevant examples include the Career Development Inventory, the Adult Career Concerns Inventory, the Work Values Inventory, the Values Scale, and the Salience Inventory. Each of these instruments attempts to describe or to measure individual career behavior in ways that are useful in defining goals for counseling, and in explicating individual career maturity, career adaptability, levels of career planfulness, knowledge and attitudes about career choice, intrinsic and extrinsic life-career values, and the relative importance to the client of major life roles beyond those of occupation or career.

Super's theoretical work has spawned the development of career assessments by others (e.g., Crites' *Career Maturity Inventory*, 1974); and models of career counseling (Super, 1957) including the recent Career Development, Counseling and Assessment (C-DAC) model (Super, Osborne, Walsh, Brown & Niles, 1992) in which career assessment and counseling are designed to be interactive as interventions.

There are many other examples, in career theory, of instances in which assessment has been used to bridge theory and practice and, indeed, been conceived as an intervention in its own right. A further illustration is that of Krumboltz's (1979) theoretical concepts, his development of innovative techniques and assessment devices during his earlier emphases on behaviorism and as he has articulated his social learning theory; and, more recently, his application of cognitive behavioral theory to such issues as faulty self-observation generalizations or inaccurate interpretations of environmental conditions and his development of the *Career Beliefs Inventory* (Krumboltz, 1994) as a counseling tool by which to identify irrational beliefs that may block people from achieving their goals.

In each of these theoretical contexts, assessment instruments have been derived from theory and used as important interventions alone and as stimuli to creating the content which career counseling explores, clarifies, and incorporates in individual plans of action.

Emerging Trends in Career Assessment

Beyond either the history of career assessment or the role of assessment in bridging career theory and counseling practice, there are other trends likely to be of importance in the early years of the 21st century. They include –

- The systematic development, planning, implementation, and evaluation of comprehensive career counseling *programs* in schools, colleges and universities, and workplaces. Rather than being a random collection of services, functions, or by-products of other activities, career counseling programs are increasingly expected to identify the results for which they are accountable and to provide evidence of their effectiveness for accountability purposes. Career assessments are seen as major tools to evaluate the outcomes of the integration of institutional missions, the deployment of career counseling resources and purposes, and as interventions within such programs.

- Cost-benefit ratios relative to career counseling programs increasingly will be an issue in the decades ahead. In the United States, cost-benefit issues have rarely been raised, but researchers in Europe have addressed them, and it is likely that such issues will be an emerging concern in schools, workplaces, and higher education in the near future. Assessment strategies will be critical as they relate to producing relevant measures of *productivity* by counselors in different environments, measures of their *effectiveness,* as well as the *costs* of producing the units of productivity measured in relation to, for example, effective decision making, successful transition to jobs, the use of goal-directed, time-limited interventions, or the use of technology.

- Attention to crisis intervention and to addressing the needs of persons at risk (e.g., those who experience chemical dependence or are violence prone, likely to be an academic or work failure) will be a pervasive theme in the 21st century. Related will be new approaches to early identification, prevention, and treatment; shared approaches by counselors and others to intervention for different populations and purposes, and more inclusion of career counseling and assessment in a total program of interventions aimed at the multiple problems experienced by most people at risk.

- More uses of technology (e.g., computer-assisted career guidance programs, testing and test interpretations by computers, self-directed planning and decision-making, distance learning, electronic information processes) will increase the need for career assessment to be used to evaluate both individuals and programs in outcomes and in differential treatment terms.

- An increased emphasis on training career counselors in the use of competency-based assessment formats is likely, with different mixes of didactic and hands-on supervision, to increase their ability to work in different settings and with different populations, including increasingly multicultural populations (Prediger, 1993).

Such a litany of potential trends is in no way exhaustive, but it suggests what would appear to be a growing need for more clarity about how career counseling and assessment need to be interactive. Such trends acknowledge that external forces—political, legal, economic, social—will likely modify and/or add to what has been said here about emerging trends describing the roles of career counselors and their needs for effective and comprehensive training. External forces will create other issues and challenges with which career counselors will need to grapple in the immediate future.

One of the growing political and economic challenges for counselors, either directly or indirectly, is the current national rhetoric about certifying competencies. As the United States continues to engage in school reform, redefinition of workplace education and development, school-to-work transitions, and workplace reorganization, the nation will place an increasing priority on the certification of competencies possessed by students in schools and universities and by workers. Employers are no longer satisfied to accept program completion as evidence of employability or occupational skill. Instead, new paradigms of competency certification of skills at various levels of achievement will be expected and assessment measures will be sought to provide such certification.

Applications of career and related assessments to questions of individual competence and program accountability are going to be major issues far into the 21st century. And, within such perspectives, career counselors are not likely to be exempt from such assessment concerns. The notions of certifying competencies noted above will extend to counselors as well. To date, most counselor certification approaches have been knowledge based, not performance based, at least as they relate directly to the impact of the counselor on clients. New methods of evaluating career counselors' ability to function effectively will be designed to use direct performance, simulation, and virtual reality for such purposes.

As the comprehensiveness of issues affecting career counseling and career assessment ensues there are several final challenges that are noteworthy-

- The use of tests as diagnostic instruments to identify developmental deficits, psychological traits or states, different forms of maximum behavior as in aptitude tests, or typical behavior as found in attitudes or interests has a long and important history. However, the scores from these assessments are sometimes treated as fixed effects by which to classify persons into static categories of performance. Instead they should be treated as fixed effects in some cognitive or behavioral areas but, in other areas, as measures of more malleable individual characteristics that are susceptible to learning on the part of the individual. The latter can be facilitated by teaching persons why their answers to the tests they took were wrong and what is implied for them in learning or relearning certain types of behavior or knowledge. In such cases, depending upon their uses, tests need to be more fully understood as interventions. In this context, Healy (1990) and others focus on helping clients to develop self-assessment skills and to being true collaborators in the appraisal process. The intent of such a process is to strengthen the client's self-confidence and insight by giving him or her the assessment skills that can be strengthened by teaching the test and by using the content to encourage client self-evaluation and decision making in ways by which the relationship between testing and career counseling can be enhanced, not fragmented (Kapes, Mastie, & Whitfield, 1994; Prediger, 1994; Zytowski, 1994).

• A further challenge, although not necessarily a new one, has to do with computer applications to testing. Computer applications to testing include the self-assessments embedded in computer-assisted career guidance programs, but they go beyond such applications to the administration, scoring, and interpretation of tests. Computers are increasingly being used for self-help programs of all kinds, including those purporting to provide personal counseling, as expert systems modeling counselor behavior in responding to a client's descriptions of his or her psychological dilemmas are being adapted to the computer. In general, however, the use of computers in testing, statistical analysis, or fostering individual decision making typically occurs in immediate conjunction to the process of career counseling, not simply as administrative procedures unconnected to counseling. As a result, there are continuing and, in some ways, increasingly complex ethical questions involved in the application of computers to testing, to self-appraisal, to personal and career counseling, and to the variations on these themes, whether they are done in conjunction with or independent of career counseling.

Of increasing importance are the challenges to assessment and to the ethics of assessment that are now inherent in the Internet. We have, as a nation, embraced the Internet with a passion that belies the reality that there has been virtually no research done about the effects of the Internet on learning, mental health, career decision making, or other related outcomes. More than 50,000 pages are being added to the World Wide Web each day; some of this content is directly relevant to career counseling and assessment. Other content purports to be relevant to what career counselors do and purports to offer self-directed assessment about which serious and comprehensive studies need to be undertaken. Just as is true in computer-assisted career guidance systems, studies of the role of career counselors prior to, during, and after students or clients participate on the Internet need to be undertaken (Sampson, Peterson, & Reardon, 1989); so do studies of Internet sites that offer accurate and reliable career information and assessment and how these can be incorporated into career counseling programs.

Conclusion

In conclusion, there are likely to be new trends, issues, and challenges associated with assessment in the 21st century. But, as these are identified, what is apparent is the reality that during the 20th century both career assessment and career counseling have sunk their roots deep into the American social fabric and both have matured in their conceptual and methodological processes. Both will be extremely important in the 21st century as they build on the important legacy of the 20th century and continue to broaden their contributions to national goals of mental health, career development, productivity, and individual purpose.

References

Archer, J. (1997, October 29). New test in Rhode Island sends shock waves through state. *Education Week, 17,* 15.

Crites, J. O. (1974). Career development processes: A model for vocational maturity. In E. L. Herr (Ed.), *Vocational guidance and human development* (pp. 296-320). Boston, MA: Houghton Mifflin.

Gordon, E. W., & Terrel, M. D. (1981). The changed social context of testing. *American Psychologist, 36,* 1167-1171.

Healy, C. C. (1990). Reforming career appraisals to meet the needs of clients in the 1990s. *The Counseling Psychologist, 18,* 214-226.

Hoff, D. J. (1997, November 5). Latest testing compromise appears doomed. *Education Week, 17,* 22.

Hoff, D. K. and Manzo, K.K. (1997, October 22). High stakes: Test truths or consequences. *Education Week, 17,* 1, 9.

Holland, J. L. (1985). *Making vocational choices: A theory of vocational person-alities and work environments* (2nd ed.). Englewood Cliffs, NJ: Prentice-Hall.

Johnson, R. C. (1997a, October 22). Michigan House passes bill to revise high school testing program. *Education Week, 17,* 11.

Johnson, R. C. (1997b, October 29). Education prominent in NJ. governor's race. *Education Week, 17,* 15, 17.

Kapes, J. T., Mastie, M. M., & Whitfield, E. A. (1994*). A counselor's guide to career assessment instruments* (3rd ed.). Alexandria, VA: National Career Development Association.

Krumboltz, J. D. (1979). Social learning theory of career decision making. In A. M. Mitchell, G. B. Jones & J. D. Krumboltz (Eds.), *Social learning and career decision making* (pp. 19-49). Cranston, RI: Carroll Press.

Krumboltz, J. D. (1994). The career beliefs inventory. *Journal of Counseling and Development, 72,* 424-428.

Lawton, M. (1997a, October 22). Discrimination claimed in Texas exit-exam lawsuit. *Education Week, 17,* 3.

Lawton, M. (1997b, December 3). State board leaders call for assessments bearing consequences. *Education Week, 17,* 7.

Prediger, D. J. (1994). Tests and counseling: The marriage that prevailed. *Measurement and Evaluation in Counseling and Development, 26,* 227-234.

Prediger, D. J. (Ed.). (1993, March). *Multicultural assessment standards for counselors.* Alexandria, VA: Association for Assessment in Counseling.

Sack, J. L. (1997, October 29). Proposed IDEA rules target testing, accountability. *Education Week, 17,* 19, 24.

Sampson, J. P., Jr., Peterson, G. W., & Reardon, R. C. (1989). Counselor intervention strategies for computer-assisted career guidance: An information-processing approach. *Journal of Career Development, 16,* 139-159.

Super, D. E. (1957). *The psychology of careers.* New York: Harper & Row.

Super, D. E., Osborne, W. L., Walsh, D. J., Brown, S. D. & Niles, S. G. (1992). Developmental career assessment and counseling: The C-DAC Model. *Journal of Counseling & Development, 71,* 74-83.

Supovitz, J. A. (1997, November 5). From multiple-choice to multiple-choices. A diverse society deserves a more diverse assessment system. *Education Week, 17,* 34, 37.

Terwilliger, J. (1997). Semantics, psychometrics, and assessment reform: A close look at 'authentic' assessments. *Educational Researcher, 26*(8), 24-27.

White, K. A. (1997, November 5). Duty-bound. *Education Week 17,* 28-32.

Zytowski, D. G. (1994). Tests and counseling: We are still married and living indiscriminant analysis. *Measurement and Evaluation of Counseling and Development, 26,* 219-223.

CHAPTER 3

Selecting a Career Assessment Instrument

William A. Mehrens
Professor of Educational Measurement
Michigan State University

Purpose

Many readers of this book are likely involved in making a decision regarding what instrument to select for their clients (or students). The purpose of this chapter is to remind you of several important factors in instrument selection and to assist you in systemizing your task. It is assumed that you are a qualified counselor who has had the necessary professional training in counseling, including the required (and much loved) course(s) in assessment.

In making a decision about whether to use any assessment instrument, and if so, which specific instrument, you need information. That information includes knowing the specific purpose of the assessment, recognizing who should be involved in instrument selection, obtaining information about the practical and technical qualities of various instruments, and making a final selection.

In its broadest sense, the purpose of any assessment is to gather data to facilitate decision making. But there are many kinds of decisions and many kinds of information that may facilitate such decisions. The decision to be made may relate to further education and/or career plans. The purpose may be to encourage the client to engage in further career exploration, to obtain information regarding scholastic ability, or to obtain information about the client's interests. Prior to selecting an instrument, it is necessary to specifically determine what information is desired and why and how that information would be useful.

In selecting an instrument, one must compare the intended purpose with the stated purpose of the instrument. The descriptions of the instruments in this book include statements of purpose. For other instruments you may be reviewing, the test manual should include such a statement. The *Standards for Educational and Psychological Testing* (AERA/APA/NCME, 1999) has several standards related to the purpose of the test. One of these standards is as follows:

Note: This chapter is a revision of the author's original chapter published in the 3rd edition of this Guide.

Standard 11.2: When a test is to be used for a purpose for which little or no documentation is available, the user is responsible for obtaining evidence of the test's validity and reliability for this purpose. (p. 113)

Who Should Be Involved in Instrument Selection

The proposed assessment may be intended for a specific client or for a large group of individuals (e.g., all 10th graders). If the assessment is to assist a specific individual, it is useful to involve the client in the process. Generally, the client would not select the *specific* test, but he/she might be involved in discussions about what types of instruments can provide the most useful information for whatever decisions are to be made. Client involvement should increase the motivation while completing the instrument and also make the clients more likely to accept the results and their interpretations (Hood and Johnson, 1997).

If the instrument to be selected is to be administered to a large group of individuals (for example, if it is to be a component of a school testing program), the selection procedure should be a cooperative venture. Teachers, administrators, counselors, and, to some extent, parents and students, can all contribute to determining purposes of assessment and in assisting in the *general* stages of instrument selection. This should lead to a more complete set of purposes and more enthusiastic test use than if the program is determined by a single individual. Typically, the final specific instrument selections should be the responsibility of the professional staff.

Sources of Information About Specific Instruments

After the purpose of assessment and the individuals who will be involved in the selection process have been determined, how can one ascertain which instruments will provide the needed information? This is accomplished by gathering data from many different sources. This book is one good source of information. As mentioned, the instruments' purposes are described as well as much other practical information. Although this book provides well-written reviews by prominent individuals, those reviewers would all agree that prior to a final selection, one would want to gather additional data about the instrument. The introductory chapter of this book as well as Appendix A provide appropriate information about various sources.

After one has determined the purpose of assessment and identified several instruments that seem to match that purpose, it is wise to obtain examination kits (and the technical manuals if not a part of the examination kits) of the instruments, read all information with care, and *actually take the instrument*.

Technical Information Regarding Instruments

The major technical characteristics to be concerned with are the adequacy of the norms, the reliability and validity of the instrument, the types of scores provided, and the instrument's appropriateness for various groups (e.g., various ethnic groups).

Norms

One can add meaning to a test score through norm referencing and/or through criterion referencing. It has been argued that at times the validity of the inference of interest is not enhanced through norm referencing. However, for most of the inferences one is interested in making (e.g., level of academic aptitude or level of interest in a particular career) it is important to add meaning to a score by comparing it to the scores of others or norm referencing. If one does norm referencing, it is important that the norm group is clearly defined and that it be both representative and relevant. It is often an advantage if the norms are recent.

A norm group is typically a *sample* of individuals from a larger *population*. If one is making an inference regarding how an individual compares to the population it is important that the sample be *representative* of that population. One consideration is the size of the sample. It should be large enough so that it provides reasonably stable values. A value is stable in a sampling sense if another sample would have produced a similar value. However, a large sample alone is not sufficient. If the sample is non-representative, making it larger will only increase the stability of the non-representative value. The sampling procedure must be correct. Most readers are not sampling statisticians and cannot be expected to delve into the sampling process extensively. In general, however, one should look to see whether the publisher considered relevant variables in the sampling procedure (such as age, gender, socioeconomic status, ethnicity, size of community, and geographic location). The publisher should explain in at least a general fashion how the relevant variables were considered in the sampling design and how the sample proportions compare with the population values.

In addition to providing information regarding the sampling design, the publisher should report the cooperation rate of the sample chosen. If the proportion of the original sample from which scores are obtained is too low, then the obtained scores may be from a biased sample.

The *relevance* of the norm group depends upon the degree to which the population sampled is comparable to the group with which users of the instrument wish to compare their clients. For example, suppose an individual client (who is a high school senior) is interested in making a decision about which college to attend and wishes to consider his/her academic ability (e.g., the SAT score) in making the choice. Knowing how his/her ability compared with a representative sample of high school seniors or even the set of all high school seniors in the nation who took the particular test would be useful. However, it would be even more useful to know how the SAT score compared to individuals attending the colleges under consideration. Hood and Johnson (1997) report, for example, that an SAT-V score of 540 would place one at the 3rd percentile at a particular Ivy League University and at the 99th percentile at a particular Southern State College.

An area where there remains some controversy in interest assessment is whether there should be separate gender norms or combined gender norms. The answer as to which norm group is more relevant may depend upon the particular inference to be made from the score.

Because one may reasonably desire different norm groups for different decisions (inferences), publishers frequently furnish a variety of norms. The important point in instrument selection is that the relevant norms for particular purposes are available.

Reliability

Technically speaking, reliability is a characteristic of the scores, not the instruments. The scores are reliable if they are consistent, that is, if they do not fluctuate due to random errors. Reliability indices of the scores may be estimated through an internal consistency analysis (e.g., K-R 20), through equivalent forms analysis, or through a measure of stability across time. Sometimes a coefficient of stability and equivalence is computed (correlating two different forms across a time period). Which estimate is of interest depends upon the purpose of the assessment. Typically, if one uses a total score (or subscore) in interpretation, then one wishes to know if the score represents a homogenous characteristic and so internal consistency reliability information is useful. (It should be noted that internal consistency estimates are inappropriate for speeded tests.) If the purpose of the assessment is to encourage career exploration and enhance current self-understanding, evidence regarding the long-term stability (or instability) of the scores may be unimportant. If one is using an interest inventory to assist in making a decision about a career, one should also be interested in evidence regarding the stability of the scores. If one is interested in assessing change across some period of time and wishes to use two different forms of the instrument, then one would need information regarding the equivalence of the forms.

At times, it is not the reliability of the scores, but rather the reliability of a decision made from the scores that is important. For example, some instruments are used to make "pass/fail" decisions and a criterion-referenced score is reported. For those decisions where one is interested in a dichotomous classification of individuals, the reliability of the set of scores is not nearly as important as the reliability of the classification. In those cases, the publisher should provide some evidence of the decision reliability.

Although the technical manual of an instrument should report reliability data, such data are not particularly useful to the *client*. The standard error of measurement should also be reported and this is the statistic that is best used to communicate to the client something about the consistency of the score. Typically, one reports a band of scores one standard error of measurement above and below the obtained score. If the manual does not report the standard error of measurement, it can easily be determined so long as the reliability estimate and the standard deviation of the scores are reported.

Readers may wonder how high the coefficient of reliability should be before adopting a test. There is no simple answer to such a question. It depends upon the purpose of the assessment and the availability of other data to assist in making a decision. For example, one needs more reliable data to make a decision about a single individual than to make an inference about a group characteristic. One should have more reliable data if the decision to be made is very important and/or irreversible than if the decision is of minor importance and is easily reversible. Thus, although no single guideline can be satisfactory, one should expect to find reliability estimates above .80 for almost all well-developed instruments; often the estimates are in the low .90s.

Validity

This statement and *Standard* 11.2 quoted earlier make the point that there must be validity evidence for the specific use intended, or the user must be responsible for gathering such evidence.

> Validity refers to the degree to which evidence and theory support the interpretations of test scores entailed by proposed uses of tests (AERA/APA/NCME, 1999, p. 9).

Thus, in judging validity, one must have in mind just what specific inferences are intended to be drawn from the scores and must look for (or gather) evidence to support such inferences.

It is useful to think of two general types of inferences: (1) making inferences about performance other than that measured; and (2) making inferences about a characteristic (construct) of the person measured. The first is a statistical inference and what is commonly referred to as criterion-related validity evidence is needed. The second is a measurement inference which requires content and/or construct validity evidence.

Information regarding validity may be obtained from any of the common sources of information (e.g., critical reviews in the *Mental Measurements Yearbooks* or the technical manual for the instrument). What about anecdotal (clinical) evidence from fellow counselors? Such "evidence" should not be discounted. Clinicians often have accurate perceptions regarding the usefulness of an instrument. However, such evidence should *not* be considered sufficient. Further, you need to remember that there is a concept called "face validity," which simply means that "on the face of it" the instrument appears to measure what it claims to measure. Face validity is *not* validity in a technical sense and should *not* be taken as evidence supporting "the interpretation of test scores entailed by the proposed use of tests."

Types of Scores and Interpretative Materials

Publishers frequently provide a variety of score types (e.g., percentiles, T scores, stanines). However, in communicating norm-referenced scores to clients, it is typically preferable to use a type of score that is easily understood by them. The percentile (or percentile rank) is typically the score easiest for clients to understand.

If the publisher provides a cut-off score for a criterion-referenced interpretation, it is important that "the rationale and procedures used for establishing cut scores should be clearly documented" (AERA/APA/NCME, 1999, p. 59).

In most situations, counselors are using assessment instruments to assist clients in making decisions about their own lives. Because the decision is the client's, it is important that he/she not only understand the score, but also its technical quality and the implications of that score for the decision to be made. As mentioned earlier, one way to communicate the reliability of a test score is to use a band interpretation (typically, the band is one standard error of measurement above and below the score).

Clients may understand the particular score and the meaning of the band interpretation and still not have a good understanding of how the information is useful to them. Other things being equal, one should choose an instrument that has available good interpretative materials that can be shared with clients. However, the responsibility of interpreting a score always lies with the counselor. It *cannot* be delegated to some computerized interpretation or publisher's handout.

Appropriateness for Various Groups

At times one may be interested in obtaining information from an instrument about a particular client (or group of clients) who is a member of a particular group (for example non-English speaking, physically disabled, ethnic minority). Attention should be paid to the appropriateness of an instrument for that group. The instrument may be inappropriate because the items are offensive or biased, or because the total scores are not valid for making the particular inference of interest for that particular group.

Major publishers are quite alert to the importance of these issues and generally take steps to maximize the value of the instrument for a variety of groups. For example, publishers typically have sensitivity reviews of the items, they do statistical analyses to detect items that function differently for different groups, and they obtain separate validity evidence for various groups. Nevertheless, it is safe to say that no publisher can possibly gather evidence on the appropriateness of the instrument for *all* possible groups, and some publishers do not gather sufficient data for any groups. It is incumbent upon those selecting instruments to determine whether data exist relating to the appropriateness of the instrument for the particular group that represents their clients.

Practical Issues in Instrument Selection

The most important practical issue in instrument selection is to select only those instruments that one is qualified to administer and/or interpret. For example, counselors are generally not trained to give individual intelligence tests and hence such an instrument should not be selected. Counselors are generally not trained as clinicians and should not choose instruments that require such a background.

Other practical issues include the time it takes to administer and score an instrument, the costs involved, the availability of alternate forms (primarily of importance for achievement tests), and the availability of a publisher's representative to assist should questions arise concerning any aspect of the administration or interpretation of the instrument. These practical issues are typically considerably less important than the technical issues discussed earlier.

Test Evaluation Outline

In the task of evaluating tests for selection purposes, it may be useful to follow an outline. The one presented here has been adapted from Mehrens, Lehmann, Eberly, and Denny (1991).

- Purpose for testing
- Group that will be tested (for example, age or grade)

- Name of test
- Author(s)
- Publisher
- Copyright date(s)
- Purpose and recommended use as stated in the manual
- Grade/age levels for which the instrument was constructed
- Forms: Are equivalent forms available? Is there evidence of equivalence of forms?
- Format: comment on legibility, attractiveness, and convenience
- Cost
- Content of test and types of items used
- Administrative and timing requirements
- Scoring processes available (e.g., machine scoring)
- Types of derived scores available
- Types and quality of norms
- Adequacy of reliability evidence presented in the manual
- Validity evidence
- General quality of administrative, interpretative, and technical manuals
- Comments about the instrument by outside reviewers

References

American Educational Research Association, American Psychological Asociation, & National Council on Measurement in Education. (1999). *Standards for educational and psychological testing*. Washington, DC: American Educational Research Association. (ERIC Document Reproduction Service No. ED 436591).

Hood, A. B. and Johnson, R. W. (1997). *Assessment in counseling: A guide to the use of psychological assessment procedures* (2nd ed.). Alexandria, VA: American Counseling Association.

Mehrens, W. A., Lehmann, I. J., Eberly, C. G., & Denny, G. S. (1991). *Instructor's manual to accompany Measurement and Evaluation in Education and Psychology*. Fort Worth, TX: Holt, Rinehart and Winston, Inc.

CHAPTER 4

Using Assessment for Personal, Program, and Policy Advocacy

Norman C. Gysbers
Professor

Richard T. Lapan
Associate Professor

Educational and Counseling Psychology Department
University of Missouri-Columbia

Rationale

The nature, shape, and substance of career development and the practice of guidance and counseling including assessment are not separate and independent from the economic, occupational, industrial, and social environments and structures in which they take place. Our understanding of career guidance and counseling and how we practice it including the use of assessments is closely related to what happens in these environments and the changes that have occurred and will occur in the future. Not only are the changes within environments important, but so also are the interactive effects that occur across environments as a result of change.

What do we anticipate some of these changes will be? In the 21st century, the United States will continue to undergo substantial changes in its occupational, social, and economic structures. Occupational and industrial specialization will continue to increase dramatically. Increasing size and complexity will be the rule rather than the exception. This will continue to create job invisibility and make the transition from school to work, and from work to further education and back to work again, more complex and difficult.

Social structures and social and personal values also will continue to change and become more diverse. Emerging social groups will continue to challenge established groups, asking for equality. People will continue to be on the move too, from rural to urban areas and vice versa, and from one region of the country to another in search of economic, social, and psychological security. Our population will be increasingly diverse.

All of these changes are creating substantial challenges for children, young people, and adults as they anticipate the future. A rapidly changing work world and labor force; globalization; violence in homes, schools, and communities; divorce; teenage suicide; substance abuse; and sexual experimentation are just a few examples of the challenges individuals face. These challenges are not abstract aberrations. They are real and have, and will continue to have, substantial impact on the personal/social, career and academic development of children, young people, and adults in the 21st century (Gysbers & Henderson, 2000).

Given societal changes such as these and the challenges they represent, what roles can assessment play in assisting children, young people, and adults to respond directly and positively to them? We envision three roles. First, assessment can be used to help individuals become personally empowered. Through the use of aptitude, achievement, interest, values, and personality and career development measures, valuable information can be provided as "tools of discovery" assisting them to explore, consider options, and make informed personal, academic, and career decisions. Thus, there is a personal advocacy role for assessment. Second, assessment instruments can be used to measure the effectiveness of guidance and counseling programs and their activities and services. In turn, such data can be used to advocate for and expand and extend these services and activities to the benefit of individuals of all ages and circumstances. Third, assessment data from personal advocacy and program effectiveness can be used to help formulate public policy to guide and direct guidance and counseling programs at the national, state, and local levels. Thus, assessment data can play a vital role in supporting and enhancing guidance and counseling programs through public policy advocacy. This chapter focuses on each of these roles that assessment plays beginning with personal advocacy followed by program effectiveness advocacy and ending with public policy advocacy.

Personal Advocacy

In such challenging and opportune times what role does assessment play in the empowerment of individuals? Mastie (1994) argued:

> Selected, administered and interpreted appropriately, then career assessment instruments: OPEN avenues to explore, ENCOURAGE investigation, FACILITATE follow-up, and AFFIRM a process. They do not stop the process and give an answer. They REASSURE that the answers are within the client and EMPOWER that client to find them. Such is "best practice," to the limits of our ability to define it today. (p. 40)

In an historical era when young adults need to develop a more proactive, self-directed approach to career management (Claes & Ruiz-Quintanilla, 1998), the use of assessment tools can substantially assist individuals to identify issues and learn essential lifelong skills. Used as "tools of self-discovery," assessments can improve the chances that all young adults will be able to create more satisfying career options, effectively respond to possibilities and challenges, take advantage of unanticipated events (Mitchell, Levin, & Krumboltz, 1999), and find greater satisfaction in one's life and adult roles (Super, Savickas, & Super, 1996). Viewed in this way, assessment instruments stand in direct opposition to arbitrary barriers that prematurely limit vocational aspirations and force unnecessary compromises in occupational decisions (Gottfredson & Lapan, 1997). The use of assessment instruments is a potent strategy that can advocate for disenfranchised groups (Betz & Hackett, 1987).

Super (1954) suggested that guidance and counseling services would be greatly improved if theory and research could identify those "traits and trends of development observed in adolescence" that predicts more successful career patterns in young adulthood (p. 18). Drawing upon career development research, Lapan and Kosciulek (in press) argued that to increase their chances of success in the future, adolescents should develop an orientation to the world-of-work characterized by growth in (1) purpose and direction (Marko & Savickas, 1998), (2) perceived opportunities and choice (Gottfredson & Lapan, 1997), (3) personal agency and empowerment (Richardson, 1998; Betz & Hackett, 1987), (4) perseverance and an ability to overcome obstacles (Lent, Brown, & Hackett, 1994), (5) commitment and maturity (Vondracek, 1994; Super, 1983), and (6) motivation and hopefulness (Markus & Nurius, 1986; Farmer & Associates, 1997).

Further, Lapan and Kosciulek (in press) identified six career constructs that promote either growth or constriction in such adaptive orientations to the world-of-work. First, now more than ever before, to succeed after high school, individuals must achieve academically. Second, efficacy expectations, outcome expectations, coping efficacy, and attribution processes have been shown to play critical roles in educational and career attainment (e.g., Lent, Brown, & Hackett, 2000; Luzzo & Jenkins-Smith, 1998). Third, active exploration and pursuit of personally valued, autonomously chosen goals have been found to facilitate the development of direction, meaning, social connectedness, and subjective well-being in life (Robbins & Kliewer, 2000; Cantor & Sanderson, 1999). Fourth, to be successful in the workplace adolescents need to better develop a wide range of work readiness behaviors and pro-social skills (e.g., Bloch, 1996; the Secretary's Commission on Achieving Employability Skills, 1991). Fifth, young people need to be extensively engaged in systematic exploration of those "career-related aspects" (Gati, 1998) that promote better person-environment fit (Swanson & Fouad, 1999). Sixth, adolescents should be actively engaged in the process of crystallizing and beginning to implement vocational preferences (Super, 1983). For a more in-depth discussion of the relationships between these constructs, their connection to more adaptive orientations toward the world of work, and their interface with surrounding demographic, social, economic, and political contexts, see Lapan and Kosciulek (in press).

In advocating for individuals, assessment instruments would be used to measure the extent to which development of these six constructs is occurring and to identify potential barriers to such growth. For example, recently a high school senior participated in a school-to-work evaluation study. She is a very strong student, ranking in the upper 10 percent of her class, and possesses a clear sense of efficacy about her ability to master a wide range of academic subjects. Unfortunately, her father died last year. In talking about her future plans, it was clear that she had a good sense of her talents and self-confidence. However, as she talked her concerns about finances surfaced. She very articulately spoke of the financial challenges currently being faced by her mother. From her perspective, finances for her future educational and career plans would now not be available. Finances had become a perceived barrier to her post-high school plans. She has quickly developed attributions around this issue that interpreted finances as a stable and permanent barrier that she would not be able to overcome (Luzzo & Jenkins-Smith, 1998). Without an assessment procedure that took a "wide lens" in addressing the range of critical career constructs necessary for developing a more adaptive orientation to the world of work (Savickas, 1999), these negative attributions would not have surfaced. Because of this assessment process, this young woman is now receiving emotional support from her school counselor.

Assessment instruments facilitate advocacy for individuals when they offer vantage points that highlight critical aspects of a person's experiences. These are perspectives that may be missed without the use of such assessment instruments. As "tools of self-discovery," assessment instruments provide a medium though which critical issues can be identified, explored, and eventually reintegrated. They improve a counselor's ability to empower individuals to make more informed choices.

Advocating for Effective Program

Herr (1995) has stated that policy makers need empirically supported arguments to pass legislation and policy directives to support effective workforce education programs. In his chapter in this guide, Herr argues that an important emerging trend in assessment will be the use of instruments to establish the effectiveness of comprehensive guidance and counseling programs that occur in a variety of different settings (e.g., schools and workplaces). Counseling practitioners will more likely be called on to justify results of their interventions. Assessment instruments will become one of the major tools by which counselors will attempt to evaluate outcomes for their programs. The role of counselors as advocates for effective guidance and counseling programs based on evaluation research activities has significant consequences for both the tests used and the test users (Gysbers & Henderson, 2000).

Assessment instruments used in program evaluation research will likely face a skeptical audience. Policy makers and those who try to influence legislation, especially those who demand results-based program accountability, will ask critical questions of the research results. Counselors will not be able to answer these questions adequately unless the assessments used address program content and meet rigorous psychometric standards. Counselors choosing tests to evaluate program outcomes may need to ask different questions about the psychometric adequacy of the tests than might typically be asked when working with individuals. For example, a test-retest reliability question might focus on whether or not there is enough reliable variance in the range of possible test scores to show change over time. Some scales may be more vulnerable to ceiling effects that would create a restricted range of test scores, thus reducing variability and ultimately co-variability or possible mean changes over time. Finding significant differences may elicit a "so what" reaction from those who control the budget. Counselors will need to answer this validity question by arguing that the significant effect size changes measured by instruments robustly predict outcomes of concern to policy makers. Normative samples must include the perspectives of the diverse population living in the United States. Test makers will need to justify construct validity by demonstrating that their tests are not confounded by unmeasured background variables.

In addition to asking different questions of the psychometric property of assessment instruments, counselors need a model of the developing person around which a program evaluation framework can be built. For example, Lapan and Kosciulek (in press) proposed a framework counselors could use to evaluate community career system partnerships. Measurement of the six constructs described in the personal advocacy section of this chapter served as the formative K-12 evaluation framework. Drawing on Life Career Development Theory (Gysbers, Heppner, & Johnston, 1998), Lapan and Koseiulck identified post-high school summative outcomes linked to career development occurring during the K-12 years. Outcomes were conceptualized within three life settings (i.e., school, work, and the community), three life roles (i.e., learner, worker, and citizen) and personal well-being. Possible post-high school benefits related to participation in community career system partnership activities were identified for students, employers and trade unions, and the community. Such a model can help to identify outcome targets around which practitioners can develop program activities and facilitate concerted actions across partnerships.

Some counselors will likely experience a certain amount of anxiety in expanding their role to include program advocacy through evaluation research. This reaction could be due to a number of factors. For example, graduate training for many counselors is likely not to have included a course teaching students how to evaluate program interventions. Counselors may have been required to take introductory statistics courses but such coursework likely did not instruct them in practical program evaluation strategies. From our experience teaching counselors at the graduate level, many experience a significant amount of anxiety in subject matter related to mathematics. Most counselors would identify with Holland's Social theme (i.e., wanting to promote individual growth and development by helping others) and not with the Investigative theme (i.e., analyzing and questioning) (Holland, 1997). These feelings and self-definitions may interact to make program evaluation appear much more daunting than is warranted.

We offer the following as an example of the positive benefits that can accrue to counselors who participate in program evaluation activities. Recently, a regional school-to-work coordinator went to a school board meeting at one of the schools that he was working with through funding from the School-to-Work Opportunities Act (1994). The school board wanted to know how school-to-work efforts were going, as budget finalization for next year was approaching. The coordinator's description of some of the activities met with a fair amount of interest from the board. One school board member asked if there were any data to substantiate possible gains for students and if the coordinator could return to the next meeting to present it. Fortunately, the coordinator had been involved in some cooperative student data collection activities. At the next school board meeting, he presented basic correlations between student satisfaction, their post-high school educational plans, and the six career constructs outlined in the personal advocacy section of this paper. This was enough to win additional school board funding for school-to-work activities for the following year. Also, this school recently had undergone a state accreditation review. Having these data aligned with their comprehensive guidance and counseling program improved their overall accreditation rating.

Advocacy Through Policy

A policy is "any plan or course of action adopted by a government, political party, business organization, or the like, designed to influence and determine decisions, actions, and other matters" (Morris, 1969, p. 104).

Currently, there is no one national, state, or local policy that guides and directs guidance and counseling programs across the age span. Policies emanate from various sources. Federal and state agencies, professional associations, and many other groups shape and influence policy content and direction. As a result, there is a diffuse set of policies in operation that influence and determine decisions and actions regarding the nature, structure, and content of guidance and counseling programs and the activities and services they provide.

Given our system of government at the local, state, and national levels and the many and various groups vying for attention and influence, it is highly unlikely that there ever will be one overall policy at any level that will guide and direct guidance and counseling programs. This, however, should not stop us from using our professional expertise to influence and shape policy at all levels. Unfortunately, our profession has attended to this important area only sporadically. Our professional associations, working alone or in concert, have worked hard to develop and influence legislation at state and national levels. In fact, the American Counseling Association has an "Office of Public Policy and Legislation." Various documents emphasizing preferred roles and functions of professional personnel including school counselors, vocational rehabilitation counselors, and mental health counselors have been disseminated, as have professional association position statements on topics of national, state, and local importance.

Although efforts such as these by professional organizations and others have had some impact on shaping and influencing national, state, and local policy formulation and legislation, much more needs to be done. We propose that a concerted effort be made to gather and organize student assessment and program evaluation data for the expressed purpose of shaping and influencing policy and legislation at all levels. We further propose that policy briefs be developed for local, state, and national decision makers and policy analysts that make the connection between the effects of guidance and counseling programs on individuals of all ages and circumstances, and the needed policies and legislation that will promote and sustain such programs. To accomplish these proposals will require that we "build a constantly evolving knowledge base about what works and what is promising" (Schorr, Sylvester, & Dunkle, 1999, p. 27). Unfortunately, much that we do as professionals still is fragmented and disconnected across the age span, as are the assessment data that we collect. Also, current "public policy often tends to segment problems artificially by age group or subject matter" (Research and Policy Committee of the Committee for Economic Development as cited in Herr & Gysbers, 2000). In addition to building a knowledge base, in part derived from assessment data, there is a need to connect and coordinate policies on guidance and counseling based on such data across all levels of government. As Herr & Gysbers (2000) recommended:

> there is the need for co-ordination and integration of career services across settings and government levels. Public policy at the federal level must connect with public policy at state and local levels and vice versa. Similarly, as voids in public policy are identified and life-cycle approaches are considered, counselors

must be made available and their services must be coordinated. In any locale, counselors in schools, employment services, rehabilitation agencies and other settings must take each other into account, and public policy must support the systematic integration of the skills each of these counselors have, rather than divide and isolate these professionals. In this regard, employers and workplaces need to be seen as part of a continuum of career guidance and counseling programs and services, not separate from and unrelated to such provisions. (p. 274)

Formulating and adopting coordinated policies for guidance and counseling programs and services across all levels of government, based in part on assessment data, require substantial and sustained work, but it is work that we must undertake. To begin, we can use currently available assessment data to develop "policy briefs" to be used with decision makers and legislators. A format for a two-page "policy brief" might look something like the following:

- *Statement of Need.* The guidance and counseling needs of a particular group or groups are described briefly.

- *A Response.* The work of professional counselors that responds to the needs is outlined. Assessment data and research studies that demonstrate the effectiveness of this work are highlighted.

- *The Keys.* The necessary organization, structure, resources, and staffing to carry out the effective guidance and counseling work are discussed briefly.

- *Problem.* Any problems in developing and implementing effective guidance and counseling programs are presented.

- *Recommendations.* Recommendations for policy formulation and legislation, if required, are presented. Helping the children, young people, and adults of our country face the challenges of today and tomorrow will require the strongest overall system of guidance and counseling programs and services that our nation can provide. We believe this will occur only if policies that guide and direct guidance and counseling programs and services for individuals of all ages and circumstances arc based in part on sound assessment data. Thus we urge professionals to take assessment data beyond their offices in school buildings, public or private agencies, and colleges and universities into the world of policy makers at all levels. Only then will we realize one of the most important but often neglected uses of assessment data, policy advocacy.

References

Betz, N. E., & Hackett, G. (1987). Concept of agency in educational and career development. *Journal of Counseling Psychology, 34,* 299-308.

Bloch, D. P. (1996). Career development and workforce preparation: Educational policy versus school practice. *The Career Development Quarterly, 45*, 20-40.

Cantor, N., & Sanderson, C. A. (1999). Life task participation and well-being: The importance of taking part in daily life. In D. Kahneman, E. Diener, & N. Schwarz (Eds.), *Well-being: The foundations of hedonic psychology.* New York: Russell Sage Foundation.

Claes, R., & Ruiz-Quintanilla, S. A. (1998). Influences of early career experiences, occupational group, and national culture on proactive career behavior. *Journal of Vocational Behavior, 52*, 357-378.

Farmer, H. S. & Associates. (1997). *Diversity and women's career development* Sage Publications, Inc.

Gati, I. (1998). Using career-related aspects to elicit preferences and characterize occupations for a better person-environment fit. *Journal of Vocational Behavior, 52.* 343-356.

Gottfredson, L. S., & Lapan, R. T. (1997). Assessing gender-based circumscription of occupational aspirations. *Journal of Career Assessment, 5,* 419-441.

Gysbers, N.C. & Henderson, P. (2000). *Developing and managing your school guidance program (3rd ed.).* Alexandria, VA: American Counseling Association. (ERIC Document Reproduction Service No. ED 4315974)

Gysbers, N. C., Heppner, M. J., & J ohnston, J. A. 1998). *Career counseling: Process, issues, and techniques.* Needham Heights, MA. Allyn and Bacon.

Herr, E.L. & Gysbers, N.C. (2000). Career development services and related policy issues: The U.S. experience. In B. Hiebert & L. Bezanson (Eds.) *Making waves: career development and public policy. Proceedings from the international symposium, May 2-4, 1999.* Ottawa, Canada: Canadian Career Development Foundation.

Herr, E. L. (1995). *Counseling employment bound youth.* Greensboro, NC: ERIC Clearinghouse on Counseling and Students Services, University of North Carolina.

Holland, J. L. (1997). *Making vocational choices: A theory of vocational peronalities and work environments* (3rd ed.). Odessa, FL: Psychological Assessment Resources.

Lapan, R. T., & Kosciulek, J. F. (2001). Toward a community career system program evaluation framework. *Journal of Counseling and Development, 79,* 3-15

Lent, R. W., Brown, S. D., & Hackett, G. (2000). Contextual supports and barriers to career choice: A social cognitive analysis. *Journal of Counseling Psychology, 47,* (1) 36-49.

Lent, R. W., Brown, S. D., & Hackett, G. (1994). Toward a unifying social cognitive theory of career and academic interest, choice, and performance. *Journal of vocational behavior, 45,* 79-122.

Luzzo, D. A., & Jenkins-Smith, A. (1998). Development and initial validation of the Assessment of Attributions for Career Decision-Making. *Journal of Vocational Behavior, 52,* 224-245.

Marko, K. W. & Savickas, M. L. (1998). Effectiveness of a career time perspective intervention. *Journal of Vocational Behavior, 52,* 106-119.

Markus, H., & Nurius, P. (1986). Possible selves. *American Psychologist, 41,* 954-969.

Mastie, M. M. (1994). Using assessment instruments in career counseling: Career assessment as compass, credential, process and empowerment. In

Kapes, J. T., Mastie, M. M., & Whitfield, E. A., (eds.), *A counselor's guide to career assessment instruments* (3rd ed, pp. 31-40). Alexandria, VA: National Career Development Association.

Mitchell, K. E., Levin, A. S., & Krumboltz, J. D. (1999). Planned happenstance: Constructing unexpected career opportunities. *Journal of Counseling and Development, 77,* 115-124.

Morris, W. Ed. (1969). *The American dictionary of the English language.* Boston: Houghton Mifflin Company.

Richardson, M. S. (1998). Counseling in uncertainty: Empowerment through work and relation practices. *Educational and Vocational Guidance, 62,* 2-8.

Robbins, S. B., & Kliewer, W. L. 2000). Advances in theory and research on subjective well being. In S. D. Brown & R. W. Lent (Eds.), *Handbook of counseling psychology* (3rd. ed, pp. 310-345). New York: Wiley.

Savickas, M. L. (1999). The transition from school-to-work: A developmental perspective. *The Career Development Quarterly, 47,* 326-336.

Schorr, L., Sylvester, K., & Dunkle, M. (1999). *Strategies to achieve a common purpose: Tools for turning good ideas into good policies.* Washington DC: Institute for Educational Leadership.

Secretary's Commission on Achieving Necessary Skills. (1991). *What work requires of schools: A SCANS report for America 2000.* Washington, DC: U.S. Department of Labor. (ERIC Document Reproduction Service No. ED 332 054).

School-to-Work Opportunities Act. (1994). P.L. No. 103-289.

Super, D. E., Savickas, M. L., & Super, C. M. (1996). The life-span, life-space approach to careers. In D. Brown, L. Brooks, & Associates (Eds.), *Career choice and development.* (3rd ed., pp. 121-178). San Francisco: Jossey-Bass.

Super, D. E. (1983). Assessment in career guidance: Toward truly developmental counseling. *Personnel and Guidance Journal, 61*, 555-562.

Super, D. E. (1954). Career patterns as a basis for vocational counseling. *Journal of Counseling, 1*. 12-20.

Swanson, J. L., & Fouad, N. A. (1999). Applying theories of person-environment fit to the transition from school-to-work. *The Career Development Quarterly, 47*, 337-347.

Vondracek, F. W. (1994). Vocational identity development in adolescence. In R. K. Silbereisen & E. Todt (Eds.), *Adolescence in context: The interplay of family, school, peers, and work in adjustment* (pp. 283-303). New York: Springer-Verlag.

CHAPTER 5

Computer-Assisted Career Assessment

James P. Sampson, Jr.
Professor, Department of Human Services and Studies, and
Co-director of the Center for the Study of Technology
in Counseling and Career Development

Jill A. Lumsden
Career Development Coordinator
The Career Center

Darrin L. Carr
Career Advisor
The Career Center

Florida State University

Background

Computer applications in career assessment have evolved to become an established feature of assessment. However, computer-assisted career assessment presents a mixture of assets and limitations, with much of the potential of the technology yet unrealized. In an effort to help counselors contribute more effectively to the design and use of this technology, this chapter will examine the roles of the computer, the counselor, and the client/individual in computer-assisted career assessment, current personal computer-based and Internet-based assessment applications, and issues influencing the effective design and use of this technology.

Note: Appreciation is expressed to Robert Reardon and Sandra Sampson for their comments on initial drafts of this chapter. The senior author may be reached at the University Center, Suite A4100, Florida State University, Tallahassee, Florida 32306-2490, (850) 644-2490, jsampson@admin.fsu.edu, http://www.career.fsu.edu/techcenter/

Optimizing Roles in Computer-Assisted Career Assessment

The ultimate effectiveness of computer-assisted career assessment is predicated upon optimal division of labor in the assessment process. The following sections examine the key roles of the computer and two primary kinds of users, the counselor and the client or individual. Although many practitioners may focus on the role of the professional counselor in the assessment process, Anastasi and Urbina (1997) note that "the test user is anyone who uses test scores as one source of information in reaching practical decisions" (p. 11). Thus, it is also important to consider the role of the client/individual in computer-assisted career assessment.

Role of the Computer in Career Assessment

Computer technology can be used to enhance the career assessment process. In particular, humans and computers can be assigned tasks that best suit their capabilities. The computer can be used as an addition, not a replacement, to the counselor, to improve delivery of services. The computer is better suited to perform computational and repetitive tasks (like administering items, scoring scales, and constructing interpretive reports), whereas practitioners can focus their time and energy on helping clients integrate assessment results from multiple sources into their existing knowledge about themselves and formulate a plan for action to meet their needs. Another way that computer technology can enhance the career assessment process is by improving the quality of test instruments and procedures through the development of previously unavailable techniques. For example, computer technology has resulted in the development of adaptive devices that allow individuals with disabilities to complete assessments independently (Sampson, 2000a). In self-help situations, the computer can be programmed to suggest that the user seek counseling when potential problems are identified by the user or the computer system (Offer & Sampson, 1999).

Role of the Counselor in Career Assessment

The role of the counselor is to ensure, to the best of his or her ability, that clients are given access to, or referred to, assessments that are valid and reliable for the purposes to which they are being used. During the counseling process, counselors must also ensure that (1) the assessments selected support identified goals; (2) clients are given access to, or referred to, an assessment that they can benefit from given their characteristics and career decision-making readiness; (3) clients are properly oriented to assessments; (4) clients are offered tentative interpretations and hypotheses based upon assessment results; (5) higher-order problem-solving skills are modeled for clients; and (6) clients have the opportunity to give the counselor feedback on the assessment process. Furthermore, to meet ethical obligations counselors must ensure that (1) assessments do not have any systematic bias with regard to gender, race, ethnicity, age, sexual orientation, or disability; (2) adequate steps are taken to maintain confidentiality of any client assessment records that are transmitted or stored on a computer; and (3) lack of financial resources does not pose an unreasonable barrier for individuals to gain access to computer-assisted career assessments. Finally, counselors should conduct regular evaluations to determine the effectiveness of the computer application in service delivery and that its implementation results in a full realization of its potential benefits (Campbell, 2000; Mastie, 1994; Reile & Harris-Bowlsbey, 2000; Sampson 1998; Sampson, Peterson, & Reardon, 1989; Sampson & Pyle, 1983; Walz, 1984; Watts, 1986).

Role of the Client/Individual in Career Assessment

Career assessments can be used by either "clients" involved in a counseling relationship or by "individuals" using self-help resources such as Internet-based interest inventories. The role of the client/individual includes (1) seeking counseling assistance if prompted to do so by self-help career assessments; (2) following the directions provided by the counselor or the software to keep test use congruent with the standardization procedures that contribute to assessment reliability and validity; (3) responding to test items in an honest and complete manner; (4) confirming and expanding upon interpretations offered by the counselor based upon assessment data (Mastie, 1994); (5) evaluating whether the goals of assessment were accomplished (Campbell, 2000); (6) following through with the application of assessment results in developing a plan of action to meet their needs; and (7) being a self-advocate for good assessment by reporting fraudulent assessment practices associated with software and practitioners to appropriate regulating entities, such as state attorney offices, licensure boards, certification boards, and professional association ethics committees.

Integrating Computers into Career Assessment

Computer technology has provided many contributions to the assessment process. In the area of test administration, clients can input answers via keyboard. Test scoring can be completed by the computer, providing quick and consistent results. The computer can also generate test score profiles customized for both the client and the practitioner, as well as narrative interpretive reports. In addition, clients can be provided with multimedia-based generalized test interpretation that reviews basic concepts and general test results before they receive a specific test interpretation from a counselor (Sampson, 2000a). The following sections examine the use of personal computer-based and Internet-based career assessment in more detail.

Use of the Personal Computer in Career Assessment

Two sources of data can be used to examine the use of PC-based career assessment: the book in which this chapter is published and a study by Sampson et al. (1998) of PC-based computer-assisted career guidance systems. This fourth edition of *A Counselor's Guide to Career Assessment Instruments* (Kapes & Whitfield, 2001) includes numerous assessments that have computer components in one or more of the five aspects of assessment identified above. Since this book aims to describe the most popular assessments in use today, this data source should provide some insights about the current state of the art in computer-assisted career assessment. Criteria for the selection of instruments were based on input from an advisory committee, a review of the literature and publisher cata-logues, and, for instruments for special populations, on the results of a survey of national experts. For instruments reviewed, the percentage of assessments in each aspect of computer-assisted assessment are 48 percent for test administration, 50 percent for test scoring, and 54 percent for test interpretation. Test score profiles are often included with interpretive reports. The availability of multimedia-based generalized test interpretation cannot be determined from the information pre-sented in the *Guide*.

Data from the fourth edition of the *Guide* do show that test scoring, pro-filing, and narrative report generation often occur simultaneously, if computer applications are available at all. Several assessments allow dual methods of com-puter-assisted test administration, e.g., clients inputting responses to items on a computer keyboard or clients completing a paper-and-pencil answer sheet that is subsequently optically scanned for computer input. Even with the availability of relatively inexpensive PCs, group test administrations appear to still be most cost-effectively completed by optically scanning answer sheets rather than ad-ministering tests on computer. Although multimedia-based generalized test inter-pretation appeared promising in better preparing clients for subsequent specific interpretations with a counselor (Hansen, 1986, 1987), the high development costs of instruction relative to other computer applications in testing and the ini-tially higher multimedia hardware costs for the service delivery organization may have restricted the availability of this innovative type of test interpretation.

Another source of data on the availability of PC-based testing is the de-scription of features of computer-assisted career guidance systems (CACG). Sampson et al. (1998) conducted a differential feature-cost analysis of 17 com-puter-assisted career guidance systems. In reviewing the assessment components of these systems, 9 of the 17 systems administered a standardized assessment online. Thirteen of the 17 systems allow the user to input scores from paper-and-pencil administrations of standardized assessment instruments. Although interests were the most common construct assessed, values, temperaments, abilities, aptitudes, and transferable skills were also included. Most of the career assessments administered online were direct adaptations of paper-and-pencil tests. Two innovative assessment procedures included the use of a card sorting technique for values clarification and the use of pictures to accompany text in the presentation of interest assessment items.

Use of the Internet in Career Assessment

Three sources of data can be used to examine the use of Internet-based career assessment: the fourth edition of *A Counselor's Guide to Career Assessment Instruments*; (Kapes & Whitfield, 2001), a study of career assessment on the Internet, and a study of Internet-based computer-assisted career guidance systems. From an examination of the reviewed instruments in this *Guide*, 18 percent of the tests were available directly on the Internet.

Oliver and Zack (1999) completed a comprehensive review of career assessments available on the Internet. The five aspects of computer-based assessment identified earlier – test administration, test scoring, score profile generation, narrative interpretive report generation, and multimedia-based generalized test interpretation (Sampson, 2000b) – can be used to further examine the Oliver and Zack (1999) data. Through using common search methods (e.g., search engines and gateway sites) Oliver and Zack identified 24 Internet sites that offered no-cost career assessments. Each site was then subjectively rated using a descriptive form covering ease of use, informative interpretation, fit of the assessment into a career planning schema, and the application of guidelines and standards. The findings for each Web site were summarized in a table and the overall implications discussed.

Test administration via keyboard or alternative device (e.g., mouse, trackball, or eye movement tracker) is basically inherent in the nature of the World Wide Web. However, Oliver and Zack did find some Internet-based self-assessments that relied on paper-and-pencil administration of career assessments that the user printed from a Web site. One of the benefits of distributing assessments on the Internet is the relatively small learning curve that one must overcome to navigate any given World Wide Web page. This is due to the generalizability of the navigation elements (e.g., check boxes, pick lists, and buttons) from one page to another. Thus, most modestly Web savvy clients would find it easy to use an Internet-based assessment, unless they encounter a Web page with poor design or one that does not conform to basic Web conventions. However, relatively new technologies such as Dynamic HTML and Javascript offer greater flexibility and creativity in interface design but increase the danger of confusing the client.

Test scoring via the computer used three types of scoring mechanisms in the Oliver and Zack study sites. The first type of scoring mechanism involved either open-ended or rating scale questions that encouraged user reflection as opposed to scoring items that build to a scale. The second type of Internet-delivered career assessment was printed out, taken by the user and then objectively self-scored. The third type of assessment offered both online item or scale scoring and some form of interpretation.

Test score profile generation via the computer typically includes profiles printed for the client and practitioner as appropriate. The generation of a score profile assumes the existence of a standardized assessment where a given client's scores are graphically compared to the scores of a norm group. The presence of standardized assessments on the Internet that provide such a profile is unclear from the data provided in the Oliver and Zack survey. It may be possible that those assessments that are normative in nature may simply skip the generation of a profile for the user and provide only an interpretive report, or that this type of assessment is not available on free Web sites.

In terms of the generation of narrative interpretive reports via the computer, Oliver and Zack found that the complexity of interpretation varied for each assessment instrument. From the sites included in the Oliver and Zack study, three levels of interpretive reports can be construed. The simplest level of interpretation was characterized by *categorization* (e.g., labels such as "highly promotable") and screening suggestions (e.g., "You would benefit from reading our book."). A second, more complex level of interpretation was *narration*, where the instrument generated a possible categorization with an additional narrative explaining the meaning of the categorization. The third level of interpretation provided *integration*, offering categorization, a narrative context, and referral to/guidance on additional information resources and services based upon specific user results. These three levels of interpretive complexity reside on a continuum that is analogous to the functions performed by a counselor. It appears that the majority of Oliver and Zack sites resided on the lower end of this continuum. Furthermore, Oliver and Zack found interpretation to be "inadequate in many cases" (p. 330). Thus, even those assessments using the most complex interpretation scheme may need to be approached with caution by clients, individuals, and counselors.

Given the Oliver and Zack data, it is not surprising that there is little evidence for Internet-based assessments that provide multimedia-based generalized test interpretation, despite the capability of the Internet to deliver this type of resource. Instead there appear to be many text-based interpretations that provide simple categorizations or narrations without reference to specific user needs. An example of multimedia-based generalized test interpretation would be an audio/video presentation explaining the theoretical constructs that undergird an instrument (e.g., the Holland hexagon or the five factor model of personality) and where the person generally relates to these constructs. These types of generalized multimedia interpretations have several advantages. The first is the alleviation of the counselor from routine communication of basic information. These routine duties often become tedious for the busy practitioner and this tedium can be perceived by the client as boredom with the client's case. A second reason is that different clients have different learning styles. Providing the same interpretive information in different ways (e.g., text, audio, and pictorial) allows the client to select a learning mode that best meets his or her needs. Furthermore, presenting generalized interpretive information in a multimedia format can be beneficial to those clients with cognitive or sensory disabilities as more than one channel of communication is used. The potential outcome of multimedia interpretation is that clients may come to the counselor better prepared to participate in a discussion about their assessment results, thus maximizing client-counselor time.

Another source of data about career assessments available on the Internet can be found in a differential feature-cost analysis of seven Internet-based career information delivery systems (Sampson, Lumsden, Carr, & Rudd, 1999). To be included in this study, sites were required to meet the definition of a career information delivery system specified by the Association of Computer-based Systems for Career Information (1999). This definition requires the presence of an assessment component that is integrated with search capabilities and occupation/education information. Although six of the seven systems in this study provided for the sorting of information based on self-assessment of variables, only one of these seven systems administered a standardized assessment. Five of the seven systems allowed for the searching of information by the results of assessments administered external to the system (e.g., a paper-and-pencil interest assessment). It is important to note that none of the systems was found to include information on the validity of the assessments and only two systems stated the limits of user confidentiality. Sampson et al. state that information on validity and confidentiality is necessary to allow practitioners to discharge their responsibilities ethically and for users to determine if the assessment will meet their needs.

A Comparison of PC-Based and Internet-Based Career Assessments

Computer applications in career assessment vary in terms of practitioner intervention, quality, and cost recovery. The PC can be used to deliver self-assessment or practitioner-assisted assessment of career constructs. In self-assessment, the results in the form of a score profile and narrative interpretation are provided to the individual after the test is completed and immediately scored. In practitioner-assisted assessment, the client completes the test and the results are immediately scored and profiled, and a narrative interpretive report is created and provided to the practitioner to review and provide a subsequent interpretation for the client. Currently, most PC-based career assessments are designed to include interpretation of test results by a practitioner, whereas Internet-based career assessments are predominately self-help in nature. The quality of PC-based career assessments (with the exception of interpretation validity) is fairly good, as the reviews in this book would attest. By comparison, most Internet-based assessments provide little or no data on the quality (reliability, validity, and utility) of career assessments (Oliver & Zack, 1999). Currently, PC-based assessments are available most often on a fee basis to fund the development and availability of tests, with a practitioner or organization purchasing multiple administrations at one time. In comparison, Internet-based career assessment is currently available most often at no cost, with the cost recovery for development and delivery supported by advertising or supported by public sector organizations or the government as a public good. Internet-based career assessment is also currently most often unvalidated and available primarily on a self-help basis. Figure 1 shows the relationships among access options, quality, and cost recovery for development and delivery of career assessment, with the most common kinds of assessments shaded in gray.

Issues Influencing Computer-Assisted Career Assessment

Personal computers have contributed to the reliability and validity of career assessment, improved client integration of assessment data in counseling, and enhanced staff efficiency and cost-effectiveness of career assessment (Sampson, 2000a). Internet-based career assessment adds the potential benefit of improving access to career assessment and counseling for persons with disabilities, for persons living in remote locations, or for persons who have traditionally been reluctant to seek career services (Robinson et al., 2000; Sampson & Lumsden, 2000; Sampson, 2000b). For both PC- and Internet-based applications, the availability of generalized, computer-based interpretations of assessment results can better prepare clients for subsequent individualized test interpretations with counselors (Gore & Leuwerke, 2000; Sampson, 2000a; 2000b). Also, the use of visual images may improve the effectiveness of career assessment for various multicultural groups (Sampson, 1990). The potential benefits of using computer-assisted career assessment, however, may be compromised by a variety of issues related to determining the appropriate application of testing standards and the quality, ethics, and funding of career assessment.

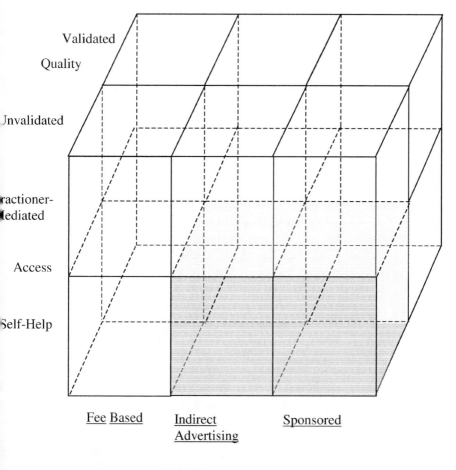

Cost Recovery

Figure 1. Organizational Schema for Internet-Based Career Assessment

Determining the Appropriate Application of Assessment Standards

The Joint Committee on Testing Practices (American Educational Research Association, American Psychological Association, & National Council on Measurement in Education, 1999) has recently updated the *Standards for Educational and Psychological Testing*, which are the most often used standards in testing. However, there may be confusion as to which assessments these standards apply. Although there appears to be general agreement that PC-based assessments from test publishers should abide by the standards, there is less agreement about Internet-based tests. One problem has to do with terminology. On the Internet, the terms test, instrument, scale, measure, questionnaire, and checklist appear to be used interchangeably. One position is that the standards apply only to assessments developed by members of the professional associations who approved the standards. Another position is that if individual items build to a scale or if individuals rate themselves on a particular construct that leads to the development of insight, then assessment is taking place and the standards apply irrespective of professional association membership. In the first position, the focus is on the nature of the assessment developer, whereas in the second position the focus is on the outcome of using the assessment. In the second position, if it works like a scale or a self-assessment of constructs, then it is assessment. In other words, "If it walks like a duck and quacks like a duck, then it's a duck." We endorse this second position that focuses on the nature of assessment outcomes rather than the association membership of the assessment developer. The problem, however, is that some assessments on the Internet have been developed by individuals who are either ignorant of the standards or who are aware of standards, but choose to ignore them to save time and cut costs. This may be due to a lack of awareness of the potential harm that unvalidated assessments may cause to unsuspecting users. In court cases, judges are increasingly using testing standards to establish an appropriate "standard of care" for assessment practice. As a result, providers and users of assessments need to become more aware of, and consistently apply, appropriate standards to ensure quality in computer-assisted career assessments and related services they offer and use. An important first step is clarifying whether or not assessments authored by non-AERA, APA, or NCME members (and affiliated groups) are required to abide by the 1999 Joint Committee Standards. The second step is to clearly communicate this understanding in preservice training, inservice training, and Web sites used by the general public.

Quality Issues

The quality of career assessments available on the Internet varies in terms of validity and reliability (Robinson et al., 2000). "Ethically and scientifically sound material coexists on the Internet with shoddy work that has not been evaluated at any level" (Clark, Horan, Tompkins-Bjorkman, Kovalski, & Hackett, 2000, p. 87). Oliver and Zack (1999) found few career assessment sites to provide evidence of the psychometric quality of the assessments available. The fact that no fee was charged to individuals who accessed the career assessments reviewed does not absolve developers from the responsibility of documenting the quality of their assessments.

Three distinct quality issues are associated with computer-assisted career assessment. First, new career assessments are being delivered exclusively by computer that provide little or no evidence of quality. A likely assumption is that a "caveat emptor" ("buyer beware") environment exists on the Internet similar to the magazine publishing environment that has regularly printed unvalidated psychological self-assessments in the guise of "quizzes" or "checklists." Individuals using the Internet without assistance from a counselor may be unable to differentiate valid and invalid software, especially given the general positive perceptions among the public concerning the inherent accuracy of computer-based resources. Prince, Chartrand, and Silver (2000) provide an example of how psychometric evidence can be presented on the quality of new career assessments developed for the Internet.

Second, some test manuals and assessment Web sites fail to provide evidence of the equivalency of the results obtained from traditional paper-and-pencil assessments that are subsequently available in computer-based versions. Enough evidence of score differences in administration modes for the same instrument exists to necessitate studies to establish the equivalence of paper-and-pencil and computer-based versions (Sampson, 2000a). Oliver and Chartrand (2000, pp. 98-99) stated: "no matter how well standardized, widely used, and highly regarded the instrument is, researchers and counselors cannot automatically assume that the measure will perform on a website as it does in the usual environment for test administration." The most recent *Standards for Educational and Psychological Testing* (AERA/APA/NCME, 1999) require that developers provide evidence of the equivalence of various test administration modes (standards, 4.10, 6.11, and 13.8). Prince, Chartrand, and Silver (2000) also provide an example of how evidence of administration mode equivalency can be presented on career assessments developed both for paper-and-pencil delivery and for Internet delivery.

Third, establishing the validity of a computer-based test interpretation is as important as establishing the validity of the instrument. Even in cases where well-established instruments provide substantial evidence of the validity of the measure, little evidence is often provided on the validity of the computer-based test interpretation. It may be that a "halo effect" exists where counselors and clients assume that a "good" test must have a "good" interpretation. The *Standards for Educational and Psychological Testing* (AERA/APA/NCME, 1999) require that developers describe the basis of any interpretation (standard 5.11) and evidence supporting the interpretation given (standard 6.12).

Ethical Issues

Numerous ethical issues have been raised related to computer-assisted assessment. In addition to the quality issues raised above, the confidentiality of assessment data transmitted and stored on PCs and computer networks can be compromised if appropriate security measures are not consistently followed. Individuals who need counseling along with using self-help computer software may be unaware of the potential value of counseling or they may be unable to locate an appropriate professional. Counselors may misuse or become dependent on computer-based test interpretation software as a result of being inadequately trained or overworked. Inadequate awareness of important location-specific circumstances may cause a counselor in a remote location to misinterpret client data or fail to recognize relevant issues. Clients with limited financial resources may have difficulty gaining access to computer resources, especially the Internet. Also, gaining access to the Internet from a residence that is shared with other persons may not allow the auditory and visual privacy necessary for test administration and related counseling. It is also uncertain how state counselor licensure laws will apply to a counselor delivering career assessment and related counseling services across state and national boundaries (Bartram, 1997; Bloom, 2000; Offer & Watts, 1997; Peterson, Murray, & Chan, 1998; Reile & Harris-Bowlsbey, 2000; Robinson et al., 2000; Robson & Robson, 1998; Sampson, 1998; Sampson et al., 1997; Sampson & Lumsden, 2000; Wilson, Jencius, & Duncan, 1997). Standards for PC-based assessment are included in ethical statements of the American Association for Counseling and Development (1988), the National Board for Certified Counselors (1997), and the National Career Development Association (1991). Relevant Internet-based ethical standards have been developed by the Association of Computer-Based Systems for Career Information (1999), National Board for Certified Counselors and the Center for Credentialing and Education (1997), and the National Career Development Association (1997).

Funding Issues

Although the cost of delivering career assessments on the Internet is relatively low, the cost of developing valid assessments and interpretive reports remains high irrespective of the delivery method. In the past, the costs associated with developing tests and interpretive reports were recovered through royalties paid to publishers by organizations delivering services or by clients receiving counseling. Oliver and Chartrand (2000) noted that numerous assessments are available at no charge on the Internet. Reile and Harris-Bowlsbey (2000, p. 82) noted that, "since most Websites can be used without a fee, their developers are not receiving income that can be continually reinvested to maintain and improve the site." It may be increasingly difficult to meet professional standards if adequate funding is not available for research and development (Harris-Bowlsbey, 1998). Stable public and private sources of funding for developing Internet-based computer applications are needed to avoid a reduction in the quality of assessments available. It is an irony that the Internet may result in improved user access to inferior assessments (Sampson, 1999).

Conclusion

With the exception of a few assessments created to support the searching for options feature of computer-assisted career guidance systems, the vast majority of computer applications in career assessment involve creating computer versions of previously developed paper and-pencil tests. Developers in general have not taken advantage of the unique features of the computer that would allow for the development of new assessment techniques as well as better integration of career assessment into the counseling process. The Internet in particular offers unique opportunities to improve test selection, orientation, administration, scoring, and interpretation. Career assessment is clearly in a transition phase from being paper and pencil based to being computer based. This transition will occur gradually as the costs of developing Internet-based assessment resources decline, as test developers gain more experience in developing computer-based assessments that take better advantage of computer capabilities, and as a greater proportion of the population gains easier access to computers that can deliver assessment resources and services. Our success in developing and delivering cost-effective computer-assisted career assessments will depend on keeping the best of past psychometric rigor and counseling integration, while exploring future uses of computer-based media to deliver innovative assessments and provide new opportunities for interaction among counselors and clients.

References

American Association for Counseling and Development. (1988). Ethical standards. *Journal of Counseling and Development, 67*, 4-8.

American Educational Research Association, American Psychological Association, & National Council on Measurement in Education. (1999). *Standards for educational and psychological testing*. Washington, DC: American Educational Research Association. (ERIC Document Reproduction Service No. ED 436 591).

Anastasi, A. & Urbina, S. (1997). *Psychological testing* (7th ed.). Upper Saddle River, NJ: Prentice Hall.

Association of Computer-Based Systems for Career Information. (1999). Hand book of standards for the operation of computer-based career information systems. Alexandria, VA: Author, ACSCI Administrative Office. Available: http://www.acsci.org/standards2.htm

Bartram, D. (1997). Distance assessment: Psychological assessment through the Internet. *Selection and Development Review, 13*, 15-19.

Bloom, J. W. (2000). Technology and web counseling. In H. Hackney (Ed.), *Practice issues for the beginning counselor.* Needham Heights, MA: Allyn and Bacon.

Campbell, V. L. (2000). A framework for using tests in counseling. In C. E. Watkins, Jr. & V. L. Campbell (Eds.), *Testing and assessment in counseling practice* (2nd ed). Mahwah, NJ: Lawrence Erlbaum Associates.

Clark, G., Horan, J. J., Tompkins-Bjorkman, A., Kovalski, T., & Hackett, G. (2000). Interactive career counseling on the Internet. *Journal of Career Assessment, 8,* 85-93.

Gore, P. A., Jr., & Leuwerke, W. C. (2000). Information technology for career assessment on the Internet. *Journal of Career Assessment, 8,* 3-19.

Hansen, J. C. (1986). Computers and beyond in the career decision-making process. *Measurement and Evaluation in Counseling and Development, 19,* 48-52.

Hansen, J. C. (1987). Computer-assisted interpretation of the Strong Interest Inventory. In J. N. Butcher (Ed.), *Computerized psychological assessment: A practitioner's guide* (pp. 292-321). New York: Basic Books.

Harris-Bowlsbey, J. (1998). Overview: Websites in support of career planning. In J. Harris-Bowlsbey, M. Riley-Dikel, & Sampson, J. P., Jr. (Eds.). *The Internet: A tool for career planning* (pp. 1-9). Columbus, OH: National Career Development Association.

Kapes, J. T., & Mastie, M. M. (Eds.) (1982). *A counselor's guide to vocational guidance instruments.* Washington, DC: National Vocational Guidance Association.

Kapes, J. T., & Mastie, M. M. (Eds.). (1988). *A counselor's guide to career \ assessment instruments* (2nd ed.). Alexandria, VA: National Career Development Association.

Kapes, J. T., Mastie, M. M., & Whitfield, E. A. (Eds.). (1994). *A counselor's guide to career assessment instruments* (3rd ed.). Alexandria, VA: National Career Development Association.

Kapes, J. T. & Whitfield, E. A. (Eds.). (2001). *A counselor's guide to career assessment instruments* (4th ed.). Columbus, OH: National Career Development Association.

Mastie, M. M. (1994). Using assessment instruments in career counseling: career assessment as compass, credential, process, and empowerment. In J. T. Kapes, M. M. Mastie, & E. A. Whitfield (Eds.), *A counselor's guide to career assessment instruments* (3rd ed., pp. 31-40). Alexandria, VA: National Career Development Association.

National Board for Certified Counselors. (1997). *Code of ethics* [Online]. Alexandria, VA: Author. Available: http://www.nbcc.org/ethics/nbcc-code.htm

National Board for Certified Counselors and the Center for Credentialing and Education. (1997). *Standards for the ethical practice of webcounseling* [Online]. Greensboro, NC: Author. Available: http://www.nbcc.org/ethics/wcstandards.htm

National Career Development Association. (1991). Ethical standards. [Online]. Alexandria, VA: Author.Available: http://www.ncda.org/about/poles.html

National Career Development Association. (1997). *NCDA guidelines for the use of the Internet for provision of career information and planning services* [Online]. Alexandria, VA: Author. Available: http://www.ncda.org/about/polnet.html

Offer, M., & Sampson, J. P., Jr. (1999). Quality in the content and use of information and communications technology in guidance. *British Journal of Guidance and Counselling, 27*, 501-516.

Offer, M., & Watts, A. G. (1997). The Internet and careers work. *NICEC Briefing*. Cambridge, United Kingdom: National Institute for Careers Education and Counselling, (ERIC Document Reproduction Service No. ED 414 451).

Oliver, L. W., & Chartrand, J. M. (2000). Strategies for career assessment research on the Internet. *Journal of Career Assessment, 8*, 95-103

Oliver, L. W., & Zack, J. S. (1999). Career assessment on the Internet: An exploratory study. *Journal of Career Assessment, 7*, 323-356.

Peterson, D., Murray, G., & Chan, F. (1998). Ethics and technology. In R. R. Cottone & V. M. Tarvydas (Eds.), *Ethical and professional issues in counseling* (pp. 196-235). Upper Saddle River, NJ: Merrill.

Prince, J. P., Chartrand, J. M., & Silver, D. G. (2000). Constructing a quality career assessment site. *Journal of Career Assessment, 8*, 55-67.

Reile, D. M., & Harris-Bowlsbey, J. (2000). Using the Internet in career planning and assessment. *Journal of Career Assessment, 8*. 69-84.

Robinson, N. K., Meyer, D., Prince, J. P., McLean, C. & Low, R. (2000). Mining the Internet for career information: A model approach for college students. *Journal of Career Assessment, 8*, 37-54.

Robson, D., & Robson, M. (1998). Intimacy and computer communication. *British Journal of Guidance & Counseling, 26*, 33-41.

Sampson, J. P., Jr. (1990). Computer-assisted testing and the goals of counseling psychology. *The Counseling Psychologist, 18,* 227-239.

Sampson, J. P., Jr. (1998). The Internet as a potential force for social change. In C. C. Lee & G. R. Walz (Eds.). *Social action: A mandate for counselors* (pp. 213-225). Greensboro, NC: University of North Carolina at Greensboro, ERIC Clearinghouse on Counseling and Student Services. (ERIC Document Reproduction Service No. ED 417 372)

Sampson, J. P., Jr. (1999). Effective design and use of Internet-based career resources and services. *IAEVG (International Association for Educational and Vocation Guidance) Bulletin, 63,* 4-12.

Sampson, J. P., Jr. (2000a). Computer applications. In C. E. Watkins, Jr. & V. L. Campbell (Eds.), *Testing and assessment in counseling practice* (2nd ed) (pp. 517-544). Matwah, NJ: Lawrence Erlbaum Associates, Inc.

Sampson, J. P., Jr. (2000b). Using the Internet to enhance testing in counseling. *Journal of Counseling and Development, 78,* 348-356.

Sampson, J. P., Jr., Kolodinsky, R. W., & Greeno, B. P. (1997). Counseling on the information highway: Future possibilities and potential problems. *Journal of Counseling and Development, 75,* 203-212.

Sampson, J. P., Jr., & Lumsden, J. A. (2000). Ethical issues in the design and use of Internet-based career assessment. *Journal of Career Assessment, 8,* 21-35.

Sampson, J. P., Jr., Lumsden, J. A., Carr, D. L., & Rudd, E. A. (1999). *A differential feature-cost analysis of Internet-based Career Information Delivery Systems (CIDS): (technical report No. 24).* Tallahassee, FL: Florida State University, Center for the Study of Technology in Counseling and CareerDevelopment [Online]. Available: http://www.career.fsu.edu/techcenter/tr24.html

Sampson, J. P., Jr., Peterson, G. W., & Reardon, R. C. (1989). Counselor intervention strategies for computer-assisted career guidance: An information processing approach. *Journal of Career Development, 16,* 139-154.

Sampson, J. P., Jr., & Pyle, K. R. (1983). Ethical issues involved with the use of computer-assisted counseling, testing and guidance systems. *Personnel and Guidance Journal, 61*(5), 283-287.

Sampson, J. P., Jr., Reardon, R. C., Reed, C., Rudd, E., Lumsden, J., Epstein, S., Folsom, B., Herbert, S., Johnson, S., Simmons, A., Odell, J., Rush, D., Wright, L., Lenz, J. G., Peterson, G. W., & Greeno, B. P. (1998). *A differential feature-cost analysis of seventeen computer-assisted career guidance systems: (technical report no. 10)* (8th ed.). Tallahassee, FL: Florida State University, Center for the Study of Technology in Counseling and Career Development [Online]. Available: http://www.career.fsu.edu/techcenter/tr10.html

Walz, G. R. (1984). Role of the counselor with computers. *Journal of Counseling and Development, 63,* 135-138.

Watts, A. G. (1986). The role of the computer in careers guidance. *International Journal for the Advancement of Counseling, 9,* 145-158.

Wilson, F. R., Jencius, M., & Duncan, D. (1997). *Introduction to the Internet: Opportunities and dilemmas.* Denver, CO: Love Publishing Co.

Assessment and Counseling Competencies and Responsibilities: A Checklist for Counselors

Nancy J. Garfield
Performance Improvement Administrative Executive
Veterans Affairs Medical Center Eastern Kansas Health Care System
Topeka, Kansas

Thomas S. Krieshok
Department of Psychology and Research in Education
University of Kansas
Lawrence, Kansas

Introduction

This checklist provides a practical means for counselors to evaluate their testing and counseling competencies and practices. It is intended to cover the basics and should not be viewed as a comprehensive statement of all responsibilities and competencies involved in assessment. Because each item is considered to be important, there is no pass-fail score.

As used here, the terms "test" or "assessment" subsume the various types of instruments covered by this Counselor's Guide—single tests, test batteries, inventories, card sorts, and various self-report scales. The term "counselee" is meant to include anyone to whom assessment instruments are administered (e.g., a sixth grader, college senior, or adult). Items in the Interpretation section of the checklist refer to the use of tests in individual counseling. Relevance of items to the use of tests with groups and in consultation with other professionals or parents should be evident. Some checklist items address computer-based assessment. Counselors interested in computer applications should consult the *Guidelines for Computer-Based Tests and Interpretations* (American Psychological Association, 1986) and *Standards for Educational and Psychological Testing,* (American Educational Research

Note: This chapter is a revision of a previous chapter by Nancy J. Garfield and Dale J. Prediger, which appeared in the third edition of this book.

Association, American Psychological Association, National Council Measurement in Evaluation, 1999).

Much of the content of this revised checklist was adapted from resources cited at the end of this chapter. Standards for Educational and Psychological Testing (AERA/APA/NCME, 1999), Test Interpretation and Diversity (APA, 1998), and ACA Code of Ethics and Standards of Practice (American Counseling Association, 1995) were major resources for this chapter.

Counselors wishing to improve their assessment skills in general will find Appendix A, (Sources of Information about Testing and Career Assessment) to be helpful. Although a number of test selection and interpretation responsibilities are cited in this checklist, Chapter 3 (Selecting a Career Assessment Instrument) and Chapter 4 (Using Assessment for Personnel, Program, and Polict Advocacy) provide more extensive suggestions.

Counseling Skills

Basic counseling skills are critical to providing effective career counseling. This section provides a review of these skills.

Use the following key in responding to the statements:

3 = I am able to apply the concept.
2 = I have some knowledge, but little experience in applying the concept.
1 = I have little or no knowledge of this concept.

Enter the appropriate number in the blank at the left of each statement.

___ 1. Build rapport with counselee.
___ 2. Be sensitive to diversity, including socioeconomic status, culture, and differing abilities.
___ 3. Consider developmental differences (e.g., be certain the instrument is age appropriate).
___ 4. Be responsive to the needs of the client.
___ 5. Attend to the counselee throughout the counseling process, asking for feedback as the process unfolds.
___ 6. Be knowledgeable of career theories and be able to integrate career development and personal counseling.
___ 7. Be knowledgeable of a repertoire of assessment instruments, both quantitative and qualitative (e.g., genogram, timeline).
___ 8. Be knowledgeable of self-help materials and outside resources for further reading.
___ 9. Help counselee balance strengths and opportunities for improvement.
___ 10. Give feedback in language counselee will understand.

_____ 11.   Relate results of assessments to the real world of work.

_____ 12.   Write reports that provide thorough, concrete, and useful recommendations.

_____ 13.   Practice ethically, attending to matters such as confidentiality and counselor competence with instruments used.

_____ 14.   Provide feedback in a manner that does not convey that the instruments say a counselee may not choose an educational or career path.

_____ 15.   Take the initiative to stay current in the fields of career and personal counseling.

Assessment Skills

Concepts important to the use of tests are listed below. Persons with final responsibility for evaluating and selecting assessment instruments will require knowledge beyond these basic concepts.

Use the following key in responding to the statements:

3 = I am able to apply the concept and explain it to others.

2 = I have some knowledge, but little experience in applying the concept.

1 = I have little or no knowledge of this concept.

Enter the appropriate number in the blank at the left of each statement

Statistics Used in Testing and Test Manuals

_____ a.   Measures of central tendency (mean, median, mode)

_____ b.   Measures of variability (range, variance, standard deviation)

_____ c.   Distributions (frequency, normal)

_____ d.   Scales of measurement (nominal, ordinal, interval, ratio)

_____ e.   Correlation coefficients (Pearson product-moment, point biserial)

Types of Instruments

_____ a.   Measures of maximum performance

_____ b.   Measures of typical performance

_____ c.   Similarities and differences among measures of intelligence, aptitude, ability, and achievement

_____ d.   Similarities and differences among self-reports, self-ratings, inventories, and tests

Score Reporting Procedures

_____ a.   Percentile ranks

_____ b.   Standard scores (including stanines)

_____ c.   Grade placement (equivalent) scores

_____ d.   Score profiles and profile analysis

____ e.   Group similarity indices ("Your scores are similar to the scores of people who...")
____ f.   Expectancy (experience) tables
____ g.   Estimates of probability of success and/or level of success; standard error of estimate

Standardization and Norms
____ a.   Standardized administration and scoring
____ b.   Limitations of raw scores
____ c.   Types of norms (e.g., local, national, gender, grade); their applications and limitations
____ d.   Norm-based vs. criterion-referenced interpretation

Reliability
____ a.   Meaning of test reliability
____ b.   Sources of measurement error
____ c.   Types of test reliability (test-retest, parallel forms, internal consistency – including split-half, inter-rater)
____ d.   Standard error of measurement and error bands

Validity
____ a.   Meaning of test validity
____ b.   Implications of test use for validation procedures
____ c.   Types of test validity (content, criterion-related, construct)
____ d.   Factors affecting test validity (e.g., the "criterion problem")
____ e.   Differential validity of test batteries for diverse criteria
____ f.   Potential sources of bias affecting validity

Responsibilities/Competencies

Test user responsibilities and competencies are listed in the next three sections. Use the following key in responding to the statements:

    3 = I do this routinely—as a regular practice.
    2 = I have done this on occasion.
    1 = I do not do this—but should give it consideration.
    NA = not applicable to the assessment instruments I am using.

Enter the appropriate number in the blank at the left of each statement.

Preparing for Test Use
____ 1.   Avoid unnecessary testing by determining whether existing information can meet the needs of your counselees and institution.

____ 2. Review advertisements for tests, promotional brochures, catalog descriptions.

____ 3. Read professional reviews of the test—for example, in the *Journal of Counseling and Development,* the *Mental Measurement Yearbooks, Test Critiques.* (See Appendix A for more information.)

____ 4. Obtain and review up-to-date copies of the administration, interpretation, and technical manuals for any test you are seriously considering. If not qualified to evaluate the instrument, obtain help from a qualified supervisor or consultant.

____ 5. Determine whether the test's reading level is appropriate for your counselee.

____ 6. Determine if the language in which the test is written is appropriate for the counselee you will be assessing.

____ 7. Verify that the test items, norms, and score-reporting procedures minimize bias due to gender race, sexual orientation, ethnic and cultural background, disability, or age. Bias can occur if an instrument does not retain its psychometric properties across different groups.

____ 8. Ensure that if there are special administration circumstances (e.g., large-print tests, which take longer to read; English is the second language; a counselee needs more time due to individual needs), you will still be able to use the results with confidence.

____ 9. Determine whether test-takers are fluent in English or establish that the instrument reliability and validity will not be compromised by language difficulties.

____ 10. Make necessary modifications to the administration or interpretation of the instruments for counselees whose differing abilities will affect their test taking. Modifications may involve instrument presentation, response format, timing, time setting, etc.

____ 11. Be aware of the complexity of culture, understanding that a counselee may belong to several different cultures simultaneously.

____ 12. Know whether you possess the qualifications (e.g., specific training and/or experience) required for use of a given assessment instrument. Apply the same criteria to anyone with delegated responsibility for assessing counselees.

____ 13. Determine whether research shows that the instrument measures what you want it to measure; evaluate the basis for any cutoff scores or decision rules advocated for interpretation.

____ 14. Avoid an instrument that requires the comparison of a counselee's raw scores unless research shows that equal raw scores for each of the test's scales (e.g., interest type) indicate equal amounts of the characteristic being measured.

___ 15.   Determine that computer-administered instruments meet the same standards (have been normed and determined to be reliable and valid for this mode of administration) as paper-and-pencil instruments.

___ 16.   Examine the basis for occupational attribute descriptions (e.g., relevant abilities, work activities) used to link counselee characteristics (e.g., abilities, interests) to occupations. Determine whether the descriptions and links are justified.

___ 17.   Before final adoption of an instrument, evaluate usability by administering and interpreting it to a small number of counselees. (See subsequent checklist items.) If possible, arrange to take the instrument yourself.

Administration and Scoring

___ 1.   Acquire the training necessary to administer the instrument. Study the directions for administration and know whether additional materials (e.g., timer, scratch paper) are needed.

___ 2.   Provide appropriate training for test administrators and proctors.

___ 3.   Ensure that reasons for testing are understood and accepted by counselees—why the instrument is being given, what it can and cannot do, who will receive the test results, how they will be used.

___ 4.   Maintain the security of assessment materials before, during, and after administration.

___ 5.   Provide a testing room and psychological climate that will allow each counselee to achieve optimal performance.

___ 6.   Plan for special circumstances affecting the administration of an assessment instrument (e.g., late arrivals, persons with disabilities, left handers).

___ 7.   Ensure that test administration directions are followed explicitly and completely.

___ 8.   Determine, in advance, appropriate answers to questions about guessing, skipping questions, and using time efficiently.

___ 9.   Note unusual behavior by any person(s) being tested. If the test results are not invalidated, consider whether a report of the unusual behavior should accompany the scores.

___ 10.   Periodically rescore a sample of "self-scored tests" to verify scoring accuracy. Routinely rescore the tests of counselees who, in your judgment, may have difficulty with self-scoring.

___ 11.   Develop a system for dating, recording, maintaining the confidentiality of, and scoring test results.

___ 12.   If the instrument is computer administered, ascertain the counselee's computer literacy. For those unfamiliar with computers, provide training about how to take a computer-administered instrument.

Interpretation

___ 1. Provide test interpretations based on documented bridges between scores and their real-world implications. Be sure your interpretations, including those provided on the score report and/or a computer terminal, are warranted by research conducted on the instrument.

___ 2. Initially, and periodically thereafter, discuss your interpretations with a qualified colleague.

___ 3. Review, with the counselee, the purpose and nature of the assessment—why it was given (e.g., its relevance to counselee goals); what the test can and cannot do; who will receive the results.

___ 4. Obtain the consent of the counselee before using assessment results for purposes other than those described prior to the testing.

___ 5. Consider whether a counselee's reading level, primary language, race, sexual orientation, ethnic and cultural background, disability, computer literacy, or age may have influenced the test results. Take such information into account in any report of results.

___ 6. Encourage counselees to discuss how they felt about the testing experience in general (e.g., did they see potential personal benefit?), their performance, and any problems encountered (e.g., nervousness, fatigue, language difficulty, and distractions).

___ 7. Provide a simple explanation of measurement error and its implications, especially for score differences and profiles.

___ 8. Help the counselee to think of assessment interpretations as hypotheses to be checked against past experience, compared with other information, tested via mutually planned activities, and periodically reviewed and modified.

___ 9. Apply good counseling techniques to test interpretation by attending to the counselee first and the results second (e.g., by listening attentively and encouraging feedback and discussion); allowing sufficient time for the counselee to assimilate information and ask questions; checking the counselee's understanding from time to time; and correcting any misconceptions.

___ 10. Help the counselee begin (or continue) the career planning process by cooperatively identifying career options, steps for exploring the options, and criteria for evaluating the options.

___ 11. Monitor and encourage career planning activities through informal contacts, scheduled progress reports, or follow-through counseling sessions.

___ 12. In general, observe the Golden Rule of Assessment: "Administer and interpret unto others as you would have them do unto you."

Resources

American Counseling Association. (1995*). ACA code of ethics and standards of practice.* Alexandria, VA: Author.

American Educational Research Association, American Psychological Association, National Council on Measurement in Education. (1999). *Standards for educational and psychological testing.* Washington, DC: Author.

American Psychological Association. (1988). *Code of fair testing practices in education.* Washington, DC: Author.

American Psychological Association Committee on Professional Standards and Committee on Psychological Tests and Assessment. (1986). *Guidelines for computer-based tests and interpretations.* Washington, DC: Author.

Biles, L. W. (1977) Competency based preparation programs for counseling psychologists, counselor educators, and counselors. In American Psychological Association (APA), *Division 17 Committee on Competency-Based Licensure in the Academic Psychology Setting: A report.* Washington, DC: American Psychological Association.

Engels, D. W., & Dameron, J. D. (Eds.).(1990). *The professional counselor: Competencies, performance, guidelines and assessment* (2nd ed.). Alexandria, VA: American Personnel and Guidance Association. (ERIC Document Reproduction Service No. ED 402 541)

Eyde, L. D., Robertson, G. J., Krug, S. E., & Associates (1993). *Responsible test use: Case studies for assessing human behavior.* Washington, DC: American Psychological Association.

Prediger, D. J. (Ed.). (1993). *Multicultural assessment standards: A compilation for counselors.* Alexandria, VA: Association for Assessment in Counseling/American Counseling Association.

Sandoval, J., Frisby, C. L., Geisinger, K. F. & Associates. (1999). *Test interpretation and diversity: Achieving equity in assessment.* Washington, DC: American Psychological Association.

Westbrook, B. W., & Mastie, M. M. (1983). Doing your homework: Suggestions for the evaluation of tests by practitioners. *Educational Measurement: Issues and Practice,* 2(1), 11-14, 26.

CHAPTER 7

Aptitude/Achievement and Comprehensive Measures

- Ability Explorer

- Adult Basic Learning Examination (ABLE)

- Adult Measure of Essential Skills (AMES)

- Armed Services Vocational Aptitude Battery Career Exploration Program (ASVAB)

- Ball Aptitude Battery (BAB)

- Career Planning Survey (CPS)

- CareerScope

- Differential Aptitude Test (DAT) and Career Interest Inventory (CII)

- Employability Competency Scale (ECS)

- Explore/Plan

- Occupational Aptitude Survey and Interest Schedule, 2nd edition (OASIS-2)

- PESCO 2001

- PSI Basic Skills Test (BST)

- Tests of Adult Basic Education (TABE)

- Wonderlic Basic Skills Test   (WBST)

- Work Keys

Ability Explorer

Thomas F. Harrington and Joan C. Harrington
Riverside Publishing
425 Spring Lake Drive
Itasca, IL 60143
630-467-7000
www.riverpub.com
rpewebmaster@hmco.com

Target Population: Level 1 is for middle school or junior high students, grades 6-8. Level 2 is for high school students, grades 9-12 and adults.

Statement of the Purpose of the Instrument: The Ability Explorer is a self-reported measure that provides students and adults with information about their abilities as they relate to the world of work and career and educational planning. Aligned with the National Career Development Guidelines and the National Standards for School Counseling Programs, and linked to publications of the Department of Labor, including the *Guide for Occupational Exploration* (GOE) and the *Occupational Outlook Handbook* (OOH), the Ability Explorer is designed to help students and adults discover and determine their potentials.

Titles of Subtests, Scales, Scores Provided: Shows ability self-ratings, as well as past activity and course performance, for 14 life and workplace abilities: Artistic; Clerical; Interpersonal; Language; Leadership; Manual; Musical/Dramatic; Numerical; Mathematical; Organization; Persuasive; Scientific; Social Spatial; Technical/Mechanical.

Forms and Levels Available, with Dates of Publication/Revision of Each: Level 1 (middle school/junior high) and Level 2 (high school and adult); published in 1996.

Date of Most Recent Edition of Test Manual, User's Guide, Etc.: Preliminary Technical Manual, 1996

Languages in Which Available: Available in English (machine-scored, hand-scored, and computer) and Spanish (hand-scored only).

Time: Actual Test Time: Interest Inventory: Approximately 40-45 minutes (Instrument untimed). Total Administration Time: Approximately 50-55 minutes.

Norm Group(s) on Which Scores Are Based: Norms for Level 1 are based on students in grades 6-9 (N=4893). Norms for Level 2 are based on students in grades 9-12 (N=3532), with separate Level 2 norms for adults (N=1531).

Manner in Which Results Are Reported for Individuals

Types of Scores: On the report to the individual, the ability self-ratings are represented in graphical format from highest to lowest according to percentile rank for the norm group (High 67-99; Medium 34-66; Low 1-33). The Counselor's Report for the Individual provides this percentile information in numerical format. The Individual Report graph also plots past performance on activities (in terms of percentile rank) and school courses (in terms of grade point average) for comparison with the ability self-ratings.

Report Format/Content:

Basic Service: On the Individual Report, narrative paragraphs beneath the graph of ability self-ratings provide information on the two highest rated abilities, including activities to try and courses to take that can help develop the abilities. The Level 2 report provides several career group recommendations based on all of the ability self-ratings. Each Individual Report also has narrative information on the Reading, Language, and Numerical/Mathematical self-ratings, with discussion of the information of these abilities for future success in school or the workplace. (The Reading self-rating is derived from a single question on the Ability Explorer asking the individual to rate his or her reading ability.) The individual's future plan and career goal, as noted on the Ability Explorer, also are discussed.

The Counselor's Report for the Individual has more detailed information about these results, including item-level information that allows the counselor to discuss specific items on the Ability Explorer with the individual.
Options: None.

Report Format/Content for Group Summaries:

Basic Service: The Counselor's Report for a Group (class or building) provides individual information in list format, and the Planning Summary provides a summary of class or building results, including a graph showing ability self-ratings from highest to lowest.
Options: None.

Scoring

Machine Scoring Service:

Cost of basic service per counselee: $2.10 for Individual Report.
Cost of options: (if any) $0.25 for extra copy of Individual Report, per student.
$0.60 for Counselor's Report for the Individual.
$0.65 for Counselor's Report for a Group.
$0.30 for Planning Summary.
Time required *for scoring and returning (maximum):* 15 working days.

Hand Scoring:

Scored by: Counselee; Clerk; Counselor.
Time required for scoring: 5 minutes.
Local Machine Scoring: Not available.

Computer Software Options Available: Standard administration online.

Other: Internet version is also available. For this version, score report is interactive, with score results linked to a careers database, allowing exploration of careers based on ability self-ratings. With user ID, user can revisit score report and career database at any time. User also has the option of taking only Part One of Ability Explorer to see report of ability self-ratings; Parts Two and Three, which show activity and course performance, can be taken at a later date.

Ways in Which Computer Version Differs: Both the standard administration online (part of the Guidance Information System, GIS) and the Internet version link score results directly to a careers database to allow for career exploration based on ability self-ratings.

Cost of Materials:
  Specimen Set: No specimen set, but samples available upon request.
  Counselee materials: Reusable Assessment Booklets for machine-scored version (Level 1 or Level 2), package of 25, including booklets and Directions for Administration, $30. Machine-Scorable Answer Folders (Level 1 or Level 2), package of 25, $15. Hand-Scorable assessment Booklets (English or Spanish), package of 25, including booklets and directions for Administration and Scoring, $35. Cards (with ID codes) for administration of Internet version, package of 25, $125.

Additional Comments of Interest to Users: Counselor's manual for interpreting the Ability Explorer available in 1999. The manual will include sample score reports and case studies, with suggested interventions. The final Technical Manual includes all relevant technical information.

Published Reviews: None Listed

Reviewed by

Christopher Borman
Professor
College of Education and Human Development
The University of Texas at San Antonio

Description

The Ability Explorer is a self-report measure designed to provide students with information about their abilities and the relationships between their abilities and school subjects as related to the world of work. This instrument consists of two levels (Level 1-middle school and/or junior high school; and Level 2-high school students as well as adults). The authors report that both levels are written at a grade 5 or below reading level. The intent of this instrument is to guide rather than predict because the authors believe that a person's potential talents need to be identified and explored before a prediction of success or failure is made. According to the test manual, clinical and educational psychologists have traditionally identified a small number of abilities (i.e., six to eight), vocational psychologists have favored a larger number of ability areas. To meet this need for more ability areas, the Ability Explorer was created and designed to easily assess 14 major work and career-related abilities. These 14 abilities areas, originally identified by Harrington and O'Shea in 1974 in U.S. Department of Labor publications, including the *Guide for Occupational Exploration* (Harrington & Harrington, 1996), are as follows: artistic, clerical, interpersonal, language, leadership, manual, musical/dramatic, numerical/mathematical, organizational, persuasive, scientific, social, spatial, and technical/mechanical. Directions for administration of the Ability Explorer and the student reports give extensive explanations for each ability, including associated activities, courses, and careers.

Levels 1 and 2 of the Ability Explorer are machine scorable and consist of three parts. In Part One, students are asked to read 140 statements and think about how good they are at doing the activity or how well they could do the activity if given a chance. Part Two is a list of 112 activities that the students may have tried with the following response options: 3 = tried activity and did it very well; 2 = tried activity and did it well; 1 = tried activity but did not do it well; and NT = never tried. Part Three is a list of school subjects (Level 1 has 28, Level 2 has 92) that students may have taken, and the students are asked to bubble-in their grades. Administration time of the Ability Explorer is between 35-45 minutes.

The hand-scorable version of the Ability Explorer uses the 140 items from Part One of the Level 1 version. There is not a Level 2 version that is hand scorable. The directions for taking and scoring this version of the instrument are included in the test booklet and in a test administrator's manual. Students are expected to hand score their own tests. After identifying their highest-rated abilities, students are asked to rate activities related to these abilities. Another activity in the test booklet has the students identifying courses that they have taken and did well in and courses that they have not taken but would like to take. The hand-scorable version of the Ability Explorer is also available in Spanish.

Use in Counseling

In addition to the technical manual for the Ability Explorer, a counselor's manual is planned, which will include information about how to help students use the results to make educational and career decisions. For both the machine-scorable and hand-scorable versions, there are instruction booklets that are clear, complete, and attractive. These booklets include an introduction and brief overview, a description of the structure of the instrument, a description of the 14 abilities, and a three-page orientation that can be distributed to students.

For the machine scorable versions (Levels 1and 2) students receive a five-page report that includes an introductory letter, list of directions for the report, a page including a table indicating results across the 14 ability areas and written explanations of the two highest ability areas, a page mapping out a career planning activity, and a page that includes a chart with the 14 abilities and brief listings of activities, courses and careers related to each ability. Reports for both levels of the instrument are similar with the exception of the career planning activity being more sophisticated for Level 2. For both Levels 1 and 2 of the Ability Explorer, students are asked to rate their reading ability (high, medium, low). Students are reminded of their self-ratings on reading ability and what these mean in terms of their career plans.

The counselor receives an individual report for each student that gives details on the student's responses and suggestions for relating high-ability areas to career groups. This report is an excellent resource for assisting a counselor in doing career planning with a student. The counselor and student directions for use of the hand scorable version seem clear and easy to follow. The career planning activities using the results seem appropriate for junior high or high school students. The authors claim that this instrument is aligned with the *National Career Development Guidelines* and that it fits well with other important movements in career guidance such as the career portfolio movement.

Technical Considerations

Individual results for the Ability Explorer are reported as high, medium, or low for each of the 14 ability areas for abilities, activities, and grades. Information was not available on normative data or how these rankings were calculated. However, the technical manual does give frequency distributions of responses to the ability statements by grade for both the Level 1 and 2 versions. The counselor report for each student gives percentile ranks for a student on each of the 14 ability areas with high (67-99), medium (34-66), and low (1-33). The assumption is that raw scores are converted to percentiles and then student results are reported as high, medium, or low.

Descriptive statistics (mean, standard deviation, range, minimum, maximum, N) are given for each scale by grade level for Levels 1 and 2 for both the ability and activity statements. The means for the ability statements are generally around 40 with minimum and maximum scores of 10 and 60. For the activity statements, the means are in the 10 to 12 range with minimum and maximum scores of 0 to 24.

Cronback alpha reliability coefficients are given in the test manual for both Levels 1 and 2 of the Ability Explorer. For Part One-Ability Statements, coefficients are given for each of the 14 ability scales, and these coefficients, attained from large samples (N = 3,100 to 4,400), range from .83 to 91. Alpha coefficients are also given for male and female subjects for both Levels 1 and 2, and the reliability coefficients are very similar to those for the combined sample. Alpha reliability coefficients for Part Two-Activity Statements range from .55 to .82 for the 14 scales (N = 2,600 to 3,900) for Levels 1 and 2 of the instrument. The coefficients are similar for female and male subjects. Overall, the reliability for the Ability Explorer is within acceptable standards, especially for Part One-Ability Statements.

Additional data given in the test manual include ability scale intercorrelations for both levels of the instrument with the correlations for Level 1 ranging from .23 to .83 and Level 2 ranging from .14 to .82. This information indicates considerable overlap between several of the scales and considerable difference among other scales. According to the authors, "The intercorrelation tables convey that no ability area is exclusively measuring a single domain, but instead a constellation of related skills which can be best described by the scale name" (Harrington & Harrington, 1996, p. 194). Sample information includes distribution by gender, grade level and race/ethnic groups. It is difficult to judge whether the test sample is representative of a national sample because information is not given on how the sample was drawn.

A series of tables in the manual indicates how ability self-reports on the Ability Explorer by employed workers and students in training for specified fields compared with the listings of abilities for various jobs in the *Guide for Occupational Exploration* (GOE) (Harrington & O'Shea, 1984; U.S. Department of Labor, 1979). This concurrent validity study included 5,643 participants (2,935 males and 2,708 females) from 114 samples (54 occupations, 39 college majors, and 21 vocational/technical programs). There was a match rate of 64%. The authors of the Ability Explorer believe that this rate underreports the reality of actual abilities used in jobs because ability descriptions were abbreviated in the second edition of the *Guide for Occupational Exploration* (1984).

The second source of validity information presented in the manual is a sample of 121 adults who were asked to complete the Ability Explorer and the *General Aptitude Test Battery* (GATB). A table is presented showing the correlations of selected GATB and *Ability Explorer* scales. The correlations are low to very low, with some of the similar-named scales having low correlations. An explanation given is that some of the scales have similar names, but are measuring different constructs. The authors state, "In sum, the *Ability Explorer* represents a broader understanding of abilities than the older ability measures that have been used traditionally by school and vocational counselors" (Harrington & Harrington, 1996, p. 188). Earlier in the manual, the authors state that through several years of research they have found that some self-report measures have comparable validity with more traditional measures, implying aptitude tests. Given this information, one would expect the correlations between the Ability Explorer and the GATB to be much higher.

Finally, the *Ability Explorer* manual describes how the items selected for each of the 14 ability scales in Part One were drawn primarily from the skills and abilities section of the *Guide for Occupational Exploration*. The authors seem to have used sound psychometric practices in selecting these items for the ability scales.

Computer-Based Version

Another option for taking the Ability Explorer is on the Internet. The Web site address(http://www.abilityexplorer.com/demo/) leads to initial information about the instrument and allows an individual to log on to take the test and receive a report for $10.00 each. Estimated testing time is 30 minutes, but the length of time depends on how many careers or career areas the individual wants to explore after receiving the results online. For any reason, an individual can stop the test at anytime and return to complete the instrument. After completing the instrument, the individual receives a report similar to the one received when taking the machine-scorable version. In addition to a chart showing results in the 14 ability areas and a narrative describing careers, activities to try, and courses to take for the two highest-rated ability areas, a section of the report lists the "best fit" career groups recommended for exploration. By clicking on a career group, the test-taker can get a listing of abilities most important for the career group and a list of occupations. If desired, an individual can browse the complete database of over 600 careers related to the 14 ability areas on the Ability Explorer. Of course, all of this information can be printed from the computer and used for future reference and career decision making. There are several advantages to taking the computer-based version of the test including immediate feedback and the opportunity to explore so many different careers. Separate reliability and validity data for the Web-based version are not currently available.

Overall Critique

The Ability Explorer offers a number of advantages as a career counseling tool. First, it is one of a growing number of self-report instruments that guides students in educational and career planning. In fact, the test manual says that the intent of the instrument is to guide rather than predict. Another advantage is the 14 ability areas assessed as compared to the six to eight abilities measured by a traditional aptitude test battery. Having two levels of the test for middle/junior high school students or high school students/adults and having machine-scorable, hand scorable, and computer versions provide considerable flexibility in using the Ability Explorer. This instrument seems very appropriate for middle to high school students, but the test items and career planning activities may not be as appropriate for many adults.

In looking at the technical information for the Ability Explorer, evidence for reliability of the instrument seems sufficient, but some of the validity data is questionable, especially when comparing results to a traditional aptitude test battery such as the GATB. Westbrook, Buck, Sanford, and Wynne (1994) found that the correlations between self-rated abilities and measured abilities ranged from the .30s to the .60s with medians in the .50s. If a counselor is interested in using this instrument for guiding students in the career planning process, instead of using the results to predict success in various careers, then the lack of validity data should not be too troubling. Therefore, the Ability Explorer is recommended as a useful guidance tool for career exploration with middle school and high school students.

References

Harrington, J. C. & Harrington, T. F. (1996). *Ability Explorer.* Chicago, IL: The Riverside Publishing Company.

Harrington, T. & O'Shea, A. (Eds.) (1984). *Guide for occupational exploration* (2nd ed.). Circle Pines, MN: American Guidance Services

U.S. Department of Labor, Employment and Training Administration. (1979). *Guide for occupational exploration.* Washington, DC: U.S. Government Printing Office.

Westbrook, B. W., Buck, R. W., Sanford, E. & Wynne, D. C. (1994). Career maturity in adolescence: reliability and validity of self-ratings of abilities by gender and ethnicity. *Journal of Career Assessment, 2,* 125-161.

Adult Basic Learning Examination (ABLE)

Bjorn Karlsen & Eric F. Gardner
The Psychological Corporation
555 Academic Court
San Antonio, TX 78204
www.hemweb.com

Target Population: Adults.

Statement of the Purpose of the Instrument: ABLE is a battery of tests designed to measure the achievement levels of adults who have had varying amounts of formal schooling.

Titles of Subtests, Scales, Scores Provided: (1) Vocabulary, (2) Reading Comprehension, (3) Spelling, (4) Language, Total Language (3 & 4), (5) Number Operations, (6) Problem Solving, Total Mathematics (5 & 6).

Forms and Levels Available, with Dates of Publication/Revision of Each: Forms E, F, Level 1, Level 2, Level 3, ©1986.

Date of Most Recent Edition of Test Manual, User's Guide, Etc.: 1986.

Languages in Which Available: English, Spanish edition of Level 2, Form E.

Time: Actual Test Time: Untimed.
        Total Administration Time: Approximately 3 hours.

Manner in Which Results Are Reported for Individuals: Profile/Score form.
    Types of Scores: Raw scores, percentile ranks, stanines, grade equivalents.

Report Format/Content for Group Summaries:
    Basic Service: Group record is completed by counselor. The same scores as on individual reports can be accommodated.
    Options: Item-Response Summary Report.

Scoring
    Machine Scoring Service: Not available.
    Hand Scoring:
        Scored by: Clerk; Counselor.
        Time required for scoring: 10 minutes.

Computer Software Options Available: Not available.

Cost of Materials:
    Specimen Set: $59.50 (valid to 10/31/01)
    Counselee Materials: Hand scorable or reusable test booklets, package of 25 - $84; Ready Score answer sheets, package of 25 - $75; Norms Booklets - $49 each level, Handbook of Instructional Techniques and Materials - $41 (prices valid to 10/31/01).

Published Reviews:
Fitzpatrick, A. R. (1992). Review of Adult Basic Learning Examination, (2nd ed.). In J. J. Kramer
& J. C. Conoley (Eds.), *Eleventh mental measurements yearbook.* Lincoln, NE: Buros
Institute University of Nebraska-Lincoln.
Thornton, G. C. (1984). Review of Adult Basic Learning Examination. In D. J. Keyser & R. C.
Sweetland (Eds.). *Test critiques II.* Kansas City, MO: Test Corporation of America.
Williams, R. T. (1992). Review of Adult Basic Learning Examination, (2nd ed.). In J. J. Kramer
& J. C. Conoley (Eds.), *Eleventh mental measurements yearbook.* Lincoln, NE: Buros
Institute University of Nebraska-Lincoln.

Reviewed by

Eunice N. Askov
Professor of Education

Juliet Smith
Doctoral Student

Adult Education Program
The Pennsylvania State University

Description

Karlsen and Gardner (1986a) state that in developing the most recent
edition of the Adult Basic Learning Examination (ABLE) they followed five
general guidelines: adult-oriented content; measurement of a wide range of
achievement; nonthreatening format; coverage of basic skills in reading, mathematics, and the language arts; and ease of administration. A review of the ABLE
and its accompanying materials (*ABLE: Directions for Administering* and *ABLE:
The Norms Booklet*) reveals that for the most part Karlsen & Gardner were successful in adhering to these principles.

The counselor may begin the testing process by asking his or her client to
take the SelectABLE; this is a screening device to help determine the level of the
ABLE that is most appropriate. There are three levels of the ABLE: Level 1 is for
adults who have no more than four years of schooling, Level 2 is intended for
adults who have completed five to eight grades; and Level 3 is for those who attended high school but did not graduate. Additionally two forms for each level
(Forms E and F) are available, making pre- and post-testing convenient.

All three levels include subtests in vocabulary, reading comprehension,
spelling, number operations, and problem solving. Additionally, Levels 2 and 3

have a language section that involves proofreading sentences and making necessary punctuation, capitalization, or grammatical changes. A difference among the levels is that the vocabulary, spelling, and problem-solving sections on Level 1 are dictated to the examinee, and he or she writes the answer in the test booklet. Obviously, this takes more time and supervision on the part of the counselor.

ABLE: Directions for Administering is clearly and thoroughly written, providing step-by-step directions for how to conduct the testing sessions and what to say to the examinee. Other than the dictated sections, all questions on the ABLE exam are multiple choice, and the test taker uses a separate bubble answer sheet to mark his or her answer.

The ABLE is not a timed exam although the *ABLE: Directions for administering* provides the approximate administration times (130 minutes for Level 1 and about 175 minutes for Levels 2 and 3). There is a total of 142 questions on Level 1: 32 items in the vocabulary section, 40 in reading comprehension, 30 in spelling, 20 for number operations, and 20 for problem-solving. Level 2 tests have a total of 206 questions: 32 for vocabulary, 48 for reading comprehension, 30 for spelling, 30 for language, 36 for number operations, and 30 for problem solving. Level 3, with a total of 220 questions, has slightly more items in number operations and problem-solving sections .

The expressed purpose of the ABLE is to "measure the level of *educational* achievement among adults [our emphasis]" (Karlsen & Gardener, 1986, p. 4). Yet as one continues to read in the *ABLE: Directions for Administering*, one finds conflicting notions concerning the content of the ABLE. The vocabulary section, for example, is intended to assess the knowledge of words that adults would come across in day-to-day activities. Yet, it is also includes words that come from the social and physical/natural sciences (p. 6). Thus, in the Level 1, Form F exam, one finds definitions for "toxic" and "fire extinguisher" alongside definitions for "shale" and "dorsal."

Similarly, the reading comprehension subtest contains "material of a functional and an educational nature" (p. 6). For example Level 3, Form E, contains questions on an Oliver Wendell Holmes poem, right after answering questions regarding a newspaper ad for a hardware store sale.

Use in Counseling

Individual counselors would be wise to heed Karlsen & Gardner's (1986b) instruction that one must "determine the validity of ABLE for measuring their own objectives"(p. 54). If the counselor wants to measure both functional and educational achievement, then the ABLE would be a good choice. If one wants a tool that strictly measures functional literacy, Comprehensive Adult Student Assessment System (CASAS) might be an appropriate choice. If one wants an exam that strictly measures educational academic achievement, perhaps for measuring scholastic knowledge retained from years of formal education, the Test of Adult Basic Education (TABE) might be a better choice.

Numerous tables appear at the end of the norms booklet providing all the objectives covered by each question and the corresponding p-values. For example, the objective of item 8 on the language subtest on Level 3 is "use a comma to set off an introductory adverbial phrase." This analysis of each test question is very useful for the counselor. When he or she goes over the results with the examinee, the counselor can discuss the particular skills that the client needs to improve.

Jackson (1990) points out that the reading section of Level 1 (Form E) may be flawed by reliance on background knowledge to answer the questions correctly. As a result, the counselor does not know whether reading comprehension or background knowledge is being measured.

Another important point to consider is that none of the items on the ABLE makes reference to computers or other technology. At the beginning of the 21st century, where everyday activities such as banking, working, and shopping are increasingly automated and computerized, this omission is glaring and seriously undercuts the functional literacy aspect of the exam.

Technical Considerations

ABLE: Norms Booklet is written so that even a novice statistician can grasp the gist of the differences among the types of scores and the limitations of each. A table is included that categorizes each type of scoring and gives the appropriate application of each.

All the normative data are based upon a research program conducted over a three-month period in the winter of 1984. The purpose of this research was to determine "statistical characteristics of the items and the appropriateness and difficulty of the various items types," to develop norms to equate the forms and levels of the ABLE, and to establish test reliability (Karlsen & Garnder, 1986b, Level 3, p. 48). From this research, the final two forms for each level of ABLE were developed. Samples were drawn from state mailing lists for adult education and vocational programs and penal institutions. In total 4,000 adults in 132 programs in 41 states took the ABLE during this tryout period. There is a demographic breakdown of this sample, and there is fair representation according to race, gender, age, and geographic location. Tables are included providing the percentile ranks, stanines, and grade equivalents corresponding to the different levels and forms of the tests.

The Kuder-Richardson Formula 21 was used to determine reliability (internal consistency). As Williams (1994) points out in his review of the ABLE exam in the third edition of this guide, most of the reliability coefficients are acceptable since they are $\geq$ .80. Williams does find the reliability of Level 1 vocabulary, number operations, and problem solving subtests among the prison population questionable on both Form E and F. Fitzpatrick (1992), in evaluating the ABLE in the *Eleventh Mental Measurement Yearbook*, notes that the test-retest and/or alternate form reliabilities should have been reported since the ABLE is used to demonstrate growth in evaluating program effectiveness.

Validity was established by intercorrelations among ABLE subtests and by correlations of the ABLE subtests and the Stanford Achievement Test Series given to children of comparable reading abilities. Both methods indicated that the ABLE subtests are valid. Content validity should be evaluated by reviewing the ABLE subtest objectives (Karlesen & Garnder, 1986b, Level 3, Table 10, p. 45)

Overall Critique

There are many reasons to recommend the ABLE: the material is clearly presented, it is easy to administer, the content is adult, it has been normed with a large and diverse population, and the explanation of the scores is helpful. If the counselor wants a measurement of a wide variety of objectives – both functional and academic – ABLE is a good choice. Otherwise, as mentioned earlier CASAS proves to be a better choice for measuring purely functional skills and the TABE is more appropriate for measuring academic skills. Moreover, this 1986 edition does show its age in that it lacks any items pertaining to computers or other technology.

References

Fitzpatrick, A.R. (1992). Review of Adult Basic Education Examination (2nd ed.). In J. J. Kramer & J.C. Conoley (Eds.), *Eleventh mental measurements yearbook*. Lincoln, NE: Buros Institute, University of Nebraska-Lincoln.

Jackson, G. (1990). Adult Basic Learning Examination (2nd ed.). In *Measures for adult literacy programs*. Washington, DC: ERIC Clearinghouse on Tests, Measurements, and Evaluation American Institutes for Research.

Karlsen, B. J. & Gardner, E. F. (1986a). *ABLE: Directions for administering.* San Antonio, TX: The Psychological Corporation.

Karlsen, B. J. & Gardner, E. F. (1986b). *ABLE: Norms booklet.* San Antonio, TX: The Psychological Corporation.

Williams, R. T. (1994). Review of Adult Basic Learning examination 2nd Edition (ABLE). In J. Kapes, M. Mastie, and E. Whitfield (Eds.). *A counselor's guide to career assessment instruments,* (3rd ed., pp. 57-63). Alexandria VA: National Career Development Association.

Adult Measure of Essential Skills™ (AMES)™

Shirley A. Biggs and Jo Smith
Steck-Vaughn Company
4515 Seton Center Parkway, Suite 300
Austin, TX 78759
www.steckvaughn.com

Target Population: Adults

Statement of the Purpose of the Instrument: AMES is a battery of authentic assessments designed to measure the necessary workplace and educational basic skills of adults who may or may not have graduated from high school. The assessment was designed to reflect the most current philosophies regarding adult education literacy curriculum and pedagogy.

Titles of Subtests, Scales, Scores Provided: Reading, communication, computation, applied problem solving, total mathematics.

Forms and Levels Available, with Dates of Publication/Revision of Each: Forms 1 and 2, Levels A, B, C, D, E. All forms and levels published in 1997.

Date of Most Recent Edition of Test Manual, User's Guide, Etc.: Directions for Administration, 1997; Technical Manual, 1999; A Guide for Interpreting Scores, 1999; Administrator's Reference Manual, 1998.

Languages in Which Available: English only.

Time: Actual Test Time: Locator Test 25 min., Level A only 40 min., Levels B-E 2 hours.
Total Administration Time: 2.5 hours.

Norm Group(s) on Which Scores Are Based: Adult Basic Education N=3,242. Corrections N=1,726. Community College N=768. Vo-Tech N =471.

Manner in Which Results Are Reported for Individuals
   Types of Scores: Scale scores, grade equivalents, stanines, normal curve equivalents, percentile ranks
   Report Format/Content:
      Basic Service: Using computerized scoring and reporting software: individual performance profile—shows all score types for a single student and includes performance status on each test objective. Individual longitudinal profile – compares one student's scores over multiple administrations.

Report Format/Content for Group Summaries:
      Basic Service: Using computerized scoring and reporting software: program/school performance summary—shows all score types for an administrator—selected group and includes performance status on each test objective. program/school narrative summary—

narratively and graphically summarizes average learner performance in an administrator-selected group compared to the selected norm group. Group longitudinal profile—compares a group's average score over multiple administrations.

Scoring
   Machine Scoring Service: Not available.
   Hand Scoring:
      Scored by: Clerk; Counselor.
   Local Machine Scoring:
      Provisions/conditions/equipment required: AMES scoring and reporting software PC (486 or higher) with Windows 95/98/NT and 16 MG RAM. "Scanner must have dual-head read" NCS or scan 2, 3, 5, 7 with scan tools. Scantron 8000, Scanmark 2000, 2250, 2500, 4000, 5000 with Scanbook. Laser printer.

Computer Software Options Available: Not available.

Cost of Materials:
   Specimen Set: AMES Preview Kit $10.
   Counselee Materials: Reusable test books $24/10 (Level A Consumable) Reusable Locator/practice Test Books $12.50/10. Reusable Directions for Administration $10. Reusable Directions and Key for Locator $5. Hand-scorable answer sheets $32/50. Machine-scorable answer sheets $35/50. Instant-Score Answer Sheets $40/50. Reusable Scoring Templates $10 each. Group record forms $15/10.Technical Manual $12.50. Norms Book (Level A) $4.95. Norms Book (Levels B-E) $12.95. Administrators. Reference Manual $99. Scoring and reporting software $995. Batch Header Sheets $12.95/25.

Published Reviews: None cited.

Reviewed by

Victor L. Willson
Professor of Educational Psychology
Texas A & M University

Jesus Tanguma
Assistant Professor of Education
University of Houston-Clear Lake

Description

The Adult Measure of Essential Skills (AMES) consists of five levels (A, B, C, D, and E), each with two forms, a Locator Test and a Practice Test. Level A focuses on basic print awareness, word knowledge, and computational skills, and is to be used with adults who have had from one to two years of schooling, who may be limited English proficient, or for whom English may not be the primary language. Levels B, C, D, and E assess reading, communication, computation, and applied problem solving. Level B is to be used with adults who have had from three to four years of schooling; Level C, five to six years of schooling; Level D, seven to eight years of schooling; and Level E, nine or more years of schooling. The technical manual provides item by objective linkage for content coverage and evidence for form parallelism in content and difficulty. Thus, either form may be used as a pretest and the other form as a posttest for instructional or program evaluation. The purpose of the Locator Test is to assist the adult educator or test administrator in determining which level of AMES (B, C, D, or E because some reading is required) should be most appropriately administered to an examinee. The purpose of the Practice Test, included with the AMES Locator, is to provide examinees with a brief orientation to the AMES assessment. Since the Practice Test requires reading, it is intended to be used with levels B, C, D, or E.

The tests include different types of visual representation for concepts, including pictures, tables, graphs, and diagrams. All of these visual representations, as well as the narratives, are large enough to be easily seen and interpreted. All pictures are done in shades of gray, and should be discernible to those with color limitations or moderate visual impairment.

An administrator's reference manual, in a three-ring binder (Steck-Vaughn, 1998), can easily be expanded and modified to suit the needs of the administrator or educator. The manual links individual or group test scores to specific instructional strategies. These can form the basis for specific study sessions or courses. A general classification for each content section of each Level test is provided: below average, average, and above average scoring. For each classification a suggested instructional activity is given.

The AMES package also includes various hand Scoring Key templates. These templates make it possible for the tests to be scored locally by hand. A scanning-scoring system is available for users with the required hardware configurations. This option is attractive for large-scale users.

Use in Counseling

The AMES is intended to be used by workplace personnel, prison counselors, and postsecondary counselors in placement and selection. The five levels (A-E) and leveling assessment will allow the user to estimate quickly the general level of functioning of a respondent in the areas of reading, communication skills, and mathematics, at least with respect to a comparable population (for all areas but the Northeast – see the norms discussion below). If the counselor or employer has good information about the relationship between general level of functioning and intended placements, the AMES will be a reasonable adult as sessment. Since no evidence is provided by the authors for any particular uses, it is left to the user to determine adequacy for a particular placement or selection.

Technical Considerations

The developers of the AMES (Steck-Vaughn, 1999b) selected 6,207 persons aged 19 and over for the norms. This sample included adult basic education course attendees (3,248), prisoners (1,726), community college students (768), and vocational/technical school students (471). The sample was split approximately equally among males and females, but tended to overrepresent Blacks (31.4%), properly represent Hispanics (19.5%), and underrepresent Whites (28.4%) for the U.S. population. For some norm groups, however, those proportions perhaps better represent the actual proportions, but no census information is given to support this. The Northeast is represented by only 7.6% of the sample, although it is the most populous region in the U.S. population. The distribution discrepancies can be expected to result in misinterpretation of scores for a number of groups. For example, Northeastern Whites, who are least represented, are the highest scoring group on most educational achievement tests. Effectively, the test may be most interpretable for the adult groups in the South, Midwest, and West.

Norm tables are provided for adult basic education, prison, community college, and vocational/technical classifications. Raw scores, continuous scaled score, percentile rank, stanine, and grade equivalent scores are provided for each classification (Steck-Vaughn, 1999a). NCE scores can be estimated using the percentile rank score using a table. The grade equivalent scores were estimated by equating scores on the AMES with the *Learning Progress Assessment* (LPA), a school achievement battery, based on about 1,500 adults who took both tests. Correlations between AMES and LPA tests (reading, communication, mathematics) were typically about .5, not exceptional but supportive of criterion-related validity.

The other deficiency in the norming is the small sample size for vocational/technical students. A total of only 471 students took forms C, D, and E, split among the three tests. With only about 160 students to provide the norms per form, it is clearly inadequate for that purpose given convenience samples.

The authors do a good job describing content for the different subject areas and levels by objectives and items measuring the objectives. If counselors are willing to take the time to examine a test-taker's responses carefully, the tables can be quite useful, and the authors are encouraged to develop interactive, computer-based interpretation programs that could aid this task greatly. Difficulty values for items are provided, allowing interpretation of achievement of objectives by a respondent in terms of typical norm group performance.

Internal consistency reliability coefficients are provided for each subject area in each level for each norm group (Steck-Vaughn, 1999c). This detail is to be complimented. Most coefficient values are reasonable and adequate for the length of the tests, all in the .80s or higher.

Content validity was reasonably established through a series of reviews and interviews discussed in the Technical Manual. Item analysis procedures appear to be adequate using Rasch modeling. Item bias was addressed through review by a panel of minority educators.

Criterion-related validity is addressed only indirectly through the linkage to the LPA. Although minimal, it is insufficient to have confidence that AMES scores can be used by employers or educators for purposes other than estimation of general functioning. It would be of use to employers to develop and provide data with the AMES and occupational functioning. Since onsite validation for the use of tests such as the AMES is required for all but small companies, users should consider including it in such studies at the beginning of use of the AMES.

The authors might have done some basic measurement analyses, such as confirmatory factor analysis of the scales to demonstrate reasonable unity of scales and discriminate analysis on the various norm groups to demonstrate differences within level if they exist, and perhaps linking the differences to educational levels. Such analyses would strengthen the validity evidence at quite modest expenditure.

Overall Critique

The AMES battery of tests is an adequate set of assessments of adult learning. It can be improved, particularly by increasing the norm sample with representation from the Northeast and by increasing the size of the vocational/technical student group. Costs do not appear to be exorbitant. Scoring can be done onsite either manually or with scanning hardware and software. For small-scale use there is no reason to purchase such equipment, but for large-scale use potential users should investigate the cost in hand scoring versus investing in the equipment for automated scoring.

The inclusion of the Administrator's Reference Manual, with its instructional support, is potentially a real advance in such tests. Its potential for effective intervention appears great. Although the instructional approach appears to be generally top-down direct instruction, there is good evidence in more general learning literature for its efficacy.

Employers and educational users will need to develop local validity evidence for use of the AMES, since no occupational or educational validity studies were presented by the authors. For employers at small companies this is a distinct disadvantage, although large companies will need to perform the studies in any case.

References

Steck-Vaughn Company (1998). *Adult Measure of Essential Skills: Administrator's reference manual.* Itasca, IL: The Riverside Publishing Company.

Steck-Vaughn Company (1999a). *Adult Measure of Essential Skills: Guide for interpreting scores.* Itasca, IL: The Riverside Publishing Company.

Steck-Vaughn Company (1999b). *Adult Measure of Essential Skills: Norms book a guide to interpreting scores.* Itasca, IL: The Riverside Publishing Company

Steck-Vaughn Company (1999c). *Adult Measure of Essential Skills: Technical manual.* Itasca, IL: The Riverside Publishing Company

Armed Services Vocational Aptitude Battery Career Exploration Program (ASVAB)

Defense Manpower Data Center
Personnel Testing Division
400 Gigling Road
Seaside, CA 93955
http://www.dmdc.osd.mil/asvab/CareerExplorationProgram/

Target Population: High school sophomores, juniors, and seniors; postsecondary students.

Statement of the Purpose of the Instrument: To provide a comprehensive, state-of-the-art career exploration and development program for use in high schools and postsecondary institutions. Individuals complete a multi-aptitude test battery, an interest inventory based on Holland's theory, a work values exercise, and questions assessing their future plans. Based on this information, participants find careers and occupations that fit their aptitudes, interests, and future plans and choices. By completing the assessments and exercises, participants also gain valuable skills in the career exploration and development process that can help them in the future.

Titles of Subtests, Scales, Scores Provided: ASVAB (General Science, Arithmetic Reasoning, Word Knowledge, Paragraph Comprehension, Numerical Operations, Coding Speed, Auto and Shop Information, Math Knowledge, Mechanical Comprehension, Electronics Information, Academic Ability, Math Ability, Verbal Ability; ASVAB Score Code, Military Careers Score); Interest-Finder (Realistic, Investigative, Artistic, Social, Enterprising, Conventional).

Forms and Levels Available, with Dates of Publication/Revision of Each: ASVAB 18/19 (1995); Interest-Finder (1995).

Date of Most Recent Edition of Test Manual, User's Guide, Etc.: Counselor's Manual (1995); Technical Manual (2000); Military Careers (2000); Student/Parent Guide (1995); Educator's Guide (1995); Basic Skills of Career Exploration (1995); Exploring Careers–The ASVAB Workbook (1995); The OCCU-FIND (1995).

Languages in Which Available: English only.

Time: Actual Test Time: ASVAB (3.5 hours); Interest-Finder (.5 hours).
Total Administration Time: 5.0 hours.

Norm Group(s) on Which Scores Are Based: National probability sample of representative 17–24 year-olds collected in 1980. New norms available for academic year 2002 based on national probability sample of 17–24 year-olds collected in 1997-1999.

Manner in Which Results Are Reported for Individuals
Types of Scores: ASVAB–norm-based standard scores and percentile scores based on same grade/same sex and on same grade/ opposite sex. Interest-Finder–raw scores and same sex/ opposite sex percentile scores.

Report Format/Content:

> **Basic Service:** Participants receive a summary sheet that lists their ASVAB scores and a brief summary of the meaning of the scores. All participants receive a posttest interpretation from trained CEP personnel. In this interpretation, participants ask questions; complete and self-score the Interest-Finder, work values inventory, and personnel preference questions; complete the OCCU-FIND exercise which shows them occupations that match their ability, interest, and values profiles; and learn the basics of career exploration. This service is without cost to schools or individual participants.

Report Format/Content for Group Summaries:

> **Basic Service:** Counselors receive ASVAB summary scores for all participants. This contains a synopsis of the scores for each participant, as well as a group summary.

Scoring

> **Machine Scoring Service:**
> **Cost of basic service per counselee:** There is no cost either to participating schools or individuals.
> **Cost of options: None.**
> > *Time required for scoring and returning (maximum):* One week.
> **Hand Scoring:** Not available.
> **Local Machine Scoring:** Not available.

Computer Software Options Available: Not available.

Cost of Materials:
Specimen Set: Free of charge to schools and potential qualified users.
Counselee Materials: All materials are free of charge.

Additional Comments of Interest to Users: A shortened version of the ASVAB will be available for the 2001-2002 school year. New national norms will be available for the ASVAB and for the Interest-Finder for the 2002 school year. An Internet version is also being planned.

Published Reviews:

Elmore, P. B., & Bradley, R. W. (1994). Armed Services Vocational Aptitude Battery (ASVAB) Career Exploration Program. In J. T. Kapes, M. M. Mastie, & E. A. Whitfield (Eds.), *A counselor's guide to career assessment instruments* (3rd ed. pp. 71-77). Alexandria, VA: National Career Development Association.

Jensen, A. R. (1988). Review of the Armed Services Vocational Aptitude Battery. In J. T. Kapes, & M. M. Mastie (Eds.), *A counselor's guide to career assessment instruments* (2nd ed. pp. 59-62). Alexandria, VA: National Career Development Association.

Jensen, A. R. (1985). Test reviews: Armed Services Vocational Aptitude Battery. *Measurement and Evaluation in Counseling and Development, 18,* 32-37.

Rogers, J. E. (1996). Review of the Armed Services Vocational Aptitude Battery (ASVAB) Career Exploration Program. *Measurement and Evaluation in Counseling and Development, 29,* 176-182.

Welsh, J. R., Kucinkas, S. K., & Curran, L. T. (1990). *Armed Services Vocational Aptitude Battery (ASVAB): Integrated review of validity studies.* Brooks Air Force Base, TX: Air Force Human Resources Laboratory.

Reviewed by

Jeff E. Rogers
Community Mental Health Services
Account Manager
ProtoCall Services, Inc.

Description

The heritage of the ASVAB, a multiple aptitude battery designed to be administered to individuals in grades 10-12 and in two-year postsecondary schools in a group setting, can be traced directly back to the earliest military screening test, the Army General Classification Test (U.S. Department of Defense, 1995). The ASVAB's primary purpose, as was its predecessors', is to provide the armed services with the necessary aptitude information on potential inductees to allow accurate occupational classifications to be made. The ASVAB Forms 18f, 18g, 19f, and 19g, published in 1992, represent the latest iteration of one of the most highly developed instruments of its kind available.

The newest ASVAB, however, adds a dimension that is evident from its complete title – the ASVAB Career Exploration Program (CEP). The new program attempts to provide students with occupational guidance for both military and civilian careers. Using a special chart called the OCCU-FIND, students integrate ASVAB results with personal educational goals and work values, along with results from the newly developed Interest Finder, a 240-item measure that parallels and replaces the previously used and widely known Self-Directed Search (Wall & Baker, 1997). The result is a listing of military and civilian occupations that match the students' aptitudes and interests. This element moves the ASVAB program far beyond its traditional purpose as a military classification tool to that of a true career guidance instrument.

The ASVAB itself consists of 334 items arranged in 10 homogeneous subtests, each of which yields a percentile rank score. The 10 subtests are word knowledge (WK/35 items), paragraph comprehension (PC/15 items), arithmetic reasoning (AR/30 items), mathematics knowledge (MK/25 items), general science (GS/25 items), auto and shop information (AS/25 items), mechanical comprehension (MC/25 items), electronics information (EI/20 items), numerical operations (NO/50 items), and coding speed (CS/84 items). The NO and CS subtests are speeded; the remaining eight are power tests. In addition to the ten subtest scores, three composite scores are yielded. Verbal ability (VA) is a composite of the WK and PC scores. Similarly, math ability (MA) is a composite of

Note: Portions of this review were adapted from the author's original review in *Meaurement and Evaluation in Counseling and Development* with permission of the Association for Assessment in Counseling.

the AR and MK scores. Academic ability (AA), described in the *ASVAB Counselor Manual* (U.S. Department of Defense, 1995) as the ASVAB's measure of potential for further formal education, is a composite of the VA and MA scores. Although the VA and MA composites were derived through factor analysis, the AA composite was derived using the logic that combining VA and MA should yield a measure of overall intelligence. Jensen (1988), moreover, cites factor analytic studies supporting this logic. This measure of overall intelligence is central to the contention that CEP results generalize to civilian occupations.

Each student is provided with a primary and secondary ASVAB Code for use with the OCCU-FIND. These one-digit codes (1-5) are translations of a student's percentile ranking for the AA composite score. Students also receive a three-digit military careers score to use in determining enlisted military career fields for which they may qualify.

Use in Counseling

All of the materials comprising the ASVAB CEP are of outstanding quality. Attractive and durable test booklets and manuals, color pictures, easily readable text, and a common-sense approach to layout and design show an extraordinary level of attention to the needs of the user. Particularly praiseworthy is how each manual is designed for a specific user. The *ASVAB Counselor Manual* (U.S. Department of Defense, 1995) provides high-school counselors with extensive information on test content, reliability, validity, and norms, in addition to containing practical sections on testing arrangements, sample counseling outlines, and the history and usage of the ASVAB by the military. An abbreviated version, the *ASVAB Educator and Counselor Guide* (U.S. Department of Defense, 1997), is an excellent quick reference. The *ASVAB Student and Parent Guide* (U.S. Department of Defense, 1997) answers a wide variety of probable questions that might arise and provides the students with a practice test containing elements of all 10 ASVAB subtests. The centerpiece of the program, *Exploring Careers. The ASVAB Workbook* (U.S. Department of Defense, 1997), is superbly suited for its purpose. Designed in an integrated comic book and narrative format, it guides students through an interpretation of their ASVAB scores, helps them administer the Interest Finder, and then narratively and graphically depicts how to analyze the results using the OCCU-FIND. Finally, using the Military Careers Score, students can determine the military careers for which they might qualify by referring to another visually appealing manual, *Military Careers* (1995), containing pictures and general descriptions of a variety of enlisted and officer career fields. A comprehensive *Technical Manual for the ASVAB 18/19 Career Exploration Program* was still in draft form at the time of this review; however, the draft *Technical Manual* appears to adhere to the same high standards of the other ASVAB materials and provides the test user with a wealth of validity, reliability, and normative data on the various components of the Career Exploration Program.

Results are provided to students on a large, easily understood *ASVAB Student Results Sheet*. The upper portion of the sheet is the student summary, and the bottom portion is the counselor summary. Both report subtest and composite scores in score-band format for same grade/sex. Students are also provided simple percentile rank scores for same grade/sex and for same grade/opposite sex. Counselors are provided an additional simple percentile rank score for same grade/combined sex. Both portions of the score report also contain the ASVAB Codes and Military Careers Score. The scoresheet itself is a model for other tests to follow. It not only reports score information, but also provides simple, yet comprehensive, instructions to the student and counselor to help them interpret the scores.

The ASVAB may be administered only by specially-trained examiners from the DOD or the U.S. Office of Personnel Management. Testing dates and times are arranged by contacting either the local military recruiter or the nearest Military Entrance and Processing Station (MEPS). Schools are responsible for scheduling students, arranging for sufficient proctors (one per 40 students), and providing actual facilities for testing. Administration of the test takes approximately three hours. Scoring may only be done by the MEPS which returns the results to the school within 30 days.

School officials must also inform the military service representative prior to testing which of eight options they choose for posttest recruiter contact of students. Only two of these options forbid outright the release of test data to local recruiters. This is perhaps the element of the ASVAB program most subject to criticism, in that schools are allowed to make a decision to release test information to military recruiters who then can use testing lists and results to contact students in the 11th grade and higher. This could result in students being subject to unwanted solicitation by military recruiters.

Technical Considerations

Taken by itself, the ASVAB represents the highest level of development for tests of its kind (Jensen, 1988). The ASVAB Form 8a served as the reference form for the current Forms 18/19. Anchor norms for the current form were obtained from approximately 12,000 individuals ages 16-23 who took the Form 8a in 1980. This sample, referred to as the Profile of American Youth, provided a statistically equivalent profile of the American population stratified by race (Black, White, and Hispanic) and gender. Scores on the new forms are referenced to the 1980 anchor norms and reported as percentile scores.

As would be expected, the ASVAB composite scores are highly reliable, whereas subtest scores are somewhat less reliable. The reliability analyses are based on the vast data available from the administration of the parallel Form 8a and all intermediary forms leading up to the Form 18/19, all of which are also parallel. The *ASVAB Counselor Manual* states that over 900,000 students from over 14,000 schools now take the ASVAB annually. By grade, the ASVAB composite scores yielded internal consistency reliability coefficients of between .93 and .94 for MA, .92 to .94 for VA, and .96 for AA. Internal consistency reliability for the eight power subtests was lower, ranging from .71 to .91 with the lowest reliability found for Electronics Information and Paragraph Comprehension. Alternate-form reliability coefficients were computed for the two speeded subtests, with coefficients of .77 and .85 for NO and CS, respectively.

Given the ASVAB's primary purpose, effective classification of military recruits, it is not surprising that much effort was invested in criterion-related validity studies. Military studies show the ASVAB composite scores correlate highly with success in military training school (.60) and eventual job performance (.23 to .73) (ASVAB 18/19 Counselor Manual, 1995). Reviewers differ, however, on how predictive ASVAB scores are for civilian job selection and performance.

In contrast to Jensen (1988), Prediger and Swaney (1992) argue that the AA composite, the "g" measure, used to generate the ASVAB codes and complete the OCCU-FIND is not the best criteria for use in career exploration. Claudy and Steel (1990), using extant data from the National Longitudinal Survey of Youth, conducted a study of the predictive ability of the ASVAB for civilian careers. They support Prediger and Swaney (1992) in that they found ASVAB composite scores were not as predictive as ASVAB subtest scores of actual membership in civilian occupational groups. Analysis based on subtest scores successfully predicted 12 % of occupational membership, as opposed to 7 % that would have been expected due to chance. When composite scores were used, however, successful prediction dropped to 7.4 %.

Welsh, Kucinkas, and Curran (1990) provided an excellent review of validity studies relating to the ASVAB. They concluded that research to date showed the ASVAB to be a valid predictor of success in military careers and was likely to be a valid predictor of success in civilian careers. However, they went on to state that results were inconclusive concerning whether "g" is the predominant factor that is at work in prediction. Elmore & Bradley (1994) did, however, argue that the new CEP is superior to the ASVAB alone for counseling purposes because it considers interest and values along with ability.

The ASVAB is considered to have both content and construct validity by Welsh et al. (1990). Good test construction methodology and factor analysis are reported as reasons for content validity. The draft *Technical Manual* cites a study by Streicher and Friedman (1983) that demonstrated the high positive relationships between ASVAB subtest scores and composite scores and similar scores on the California Achievement Test, the Differential Aptitude Test, and the Flanagan Industrial Tests/Flanagan Aptitude Classification Tests. Further information is provided that shows similar correlations between the ASVAB and the General Aptitude Test Battery. All of these comparisons are designed to demonstrate that the ASVAB results parallel those of more widely used aptitude measures.

Elmore and Bradley (1994) have raised questions about ethnic bias in the ASVAB. The draft *Technical Manual* acknowledges this concern and cites studies that do, in fact, show that composite scores of Black test takers fall statistically below those of White participants, while also overpredicting the successful performance of Blacks in training. Other reviewers of the full CEP have also expressed reservations about the ethnic fairness of the program. Prediger & Swaney (1992) found a high percentage of African-Americans and Hispanics scored below the mean, which might limit them in their career search based on CEP results. For example, they predicted that 13 % of Whites would receive the highest ASVAB Code of 1, as opposed to only 1 % of Blacks and 2 % of Hispanics. These results indicated that a disproportionately low percentage of Blacks and Hispanics would be directed toward professional and highly technical careers. Partially as a result of this finding, Elmore & Bradley (1994) recommended against the use of the CEP for all high school students pending further research. In their integrative review, Welsh et al. (1990) argued strongly that the ASVAB was relatively free of subgroup bias. They did agree, however, that there were statistically significant mean differences between African-Americans and Whites on ASVAB aptitude composite scores, with African-Americans scoring consistently lower.

Computer-Based Version

Discussions with MEPS personnel and with Manpower Data Center representatives confirmed that a computerized adaptive testing (CAT) version of the ASVAB is currently in use. This enables faster administration of the ASVAB with supposedly equivalent reliability and validity. Due to concerns over test security, however, the CAT ASVAB is used only at the MEPS and is not available for distribution to schools or other institutions. Although there is some consideration of more widespread use of the CAT ASVAB, at present no further distribution of the test is foreseen.

Overall Critique

There is general agreement among all reviewers that the ASVAB itself is one of the finest examples available of a multiple-aptitude battery based on its superb psychometrics, extensive norming data, and excellent materials. Weitzman (1985), Jensen (1988), and Elmore & Bradley (1994) comment positively on the instrument for its utility in its primary role, classification of military recruits, and its use as a general aptitude battery.

The ASVAB Forms 18/19 represent the state of the art in multiple aptitude batteries. The Department of Defense has devoted a great number of skilled individuals and considerable time to developing an instrument that will allow effective and accurate classification of military recruits. The recent military force reductions mean every person entering the military must be assigned according to his or her best use. The ASVAB, perfected over many years, seems an ideal tool for this task.

Though all reviewers comment positively on the military use of the ASVAB, there appears to be disagreement between external reviewers and the DOD reviewers about ASVAB's predictive validity when applied to civilian occupations. The question of whether or not the ASVAB is biased against African-Americans and Hispanics, and whether it should be used in high schools as a counseling tool has also been debated.

In this reviewer's opinion, there are adequate data to support other reviewers' concern over the predictive validity of the ASVAB CEP when applied to civilian careers. The same may be said concerning the potential impact of the ASVAB on African-Americans, Hispanics, and other minority students whose results may limit their potential career choices. These issues are important enough to require further discussion and research. This is particularly salient, given that the ASVAB CEP is administered to high school students at a critical time in their career selection process. Thus, the ASVAB has the potential to have a strong influence on their choice of an occupation. Its administration to over 900,000 students annually is indicative of the potential scope of that influence.

Given the disagreement over the ASVAB CEP's predictive validity for civilian careers, high school counselors should pay particular attention to incorporating ASVAB CEP results into a comprehensive counseling model, using all available data for each individual student to help guide them toward potential careers. Counselors should be particularly aware of students' propensity to interpret test results literally and encourage them not to limit their career search solely to those options identified in the ASVAB CEP results. This is particularly true in the case of minorities, whose results may indicate they are more limited in the pursuit of civilian occupations than may be found through full examination of their record and potential. To the credit of the ASVAB CEP, it strongly promotes just such an approach and provides counselors with many recommendations and examples to assist them in carrying out such a program.

References

Claudy, J. G. & Steel L. (1990). Armed Services Vocational Aptitude Battery: Validation for civilian occupations using national longitudinal survey of youth data. Final report for period August 1988-March 1990. (Report No. AFHRL-TR-90-29). Brooks Air Force Base, TX: Air Force Human Resources Laboratory (ERIC Document Reproduction Service No. ED 347 284).

Elmore, P. B., & Bradley, R. W. (1994). Review of the Armed Forces Vocational Aptitude Battery (ASVAB) Career Exploration Program. In J. T. Kapes, M. M. Mastie, & E. A. Whitfield (Eds.), *A counselor's guide to career assessment instruments (3rd ed.)* pp. 73-77. Alexandria, VA: National Career Development Association.

Jensen, A. R. (1988). Review of the Armed Services Vocational Aptitude Battery (ASVAB) Career Exploration Program. In J. T. Kapes & M. M. Mastie, (Eds.), *A counselor's guide to career assessment instruments* (2nd ed., pp. 59-62). Alexandria, VA: National Career Development Association.

Prediger, D. J., & Swaney, K. B. (1992). *Career counseling validity of Discover's job cluster scales for the revised ASVAB score report* (Report No. 92-2). Iowa City, IA: The American College Testing Program. (ERIC Document Reproduction Service No. ED 353 318).

Streicher, A. H., & Friedman, D. (1983). *Armed Services Vocational Aptitude Battery (ASVAB Form 14): Comparison with CAT, DAT and FIT/FACT tests. Unpublished report.* Rockville, MD: Research Applications, Inc.

U.S. Department of Defense. (1995). *ASVAB 18/19 counselor manual: The ASVAB career exploration program.* (1995). North Chicago, IL: United States Military Entrance Processing Command.

U.S. Department of Defense. (1997). *ASVAB educator and counselor guide.* North Chicago, IL: Department of Defense, United States Military Entrance Processing Command.

U.S. Department of Defense. (1997). *ASVAB student and parent guide.* North Chicago, IL: Department of Defense, United States Military Entrance Processing Command.

U.S. Department of Defense. (1997). *Exploring careers: The ASVAB workbook.* North Chicago, IL: Department of Defense, United States Military Entrance Processing Command.

U.S. Department of Defense. (1995) *Military careers.* North Chicago, IL: United States Military Entrance Processing Command.

Wall, J. E. & Baker, H. E. (1997) The Interest-Finder: Evidence of validity. *Journal of Career Assessment*, 5, 255-273.

Weitzman, R. A. (1985). Review of the Armed Services Vocational Aptitude Battery. In J. V. Mitchell, Jr. (Ed.), *The ninth mental measurements yearbook* (pp. 83-84). Lincoln, NE: Buros Institute, The University of Nebraska-Lincoln.

Welsh, J. R., Jr., Kicinkas, S. K. & Curran, L. T., (1990). *Armed Services Vocational Aptitude Battery (ASVAB): Integrative review of validity studies* (Report No. AFHRL-TR-90-22). Brooks Air Force Base, TX: Air Force Human resources Laboratory.

Ball Aptitude Battery (BAB)

The Ball Foundation
800 Roosevelt Road, C-120
Glen Ellyn, IL 60137
www.ballfoundation.org

Target Population: 9th and 10th grade high school students (Level 1A), and 11th and 12th grade students and adults (Level 2).

Statement of the Purpose of the Instrument: Objective aptitude assessment to provide students with important self-knowledge that will assist them in their career planning.

Titles of Subtests, Scales, Scores Provided: Analytical Reasoning, Associative Memory, Auditory Memory Span, Clerical, Idea Generation, Inductive Reasoning, Numerical Computation, Numerical Reasoning, Paper Folding, Vocabulary, Word Association, Writing Speed.

Forms and Levels Available, with Dates of Publication/Revision of Each: Form M Level 1A – 1998, Form M Level 2A – 1998.

Date of Most Recent Edition of Test Manual, User's Guide, Etc.: Examiner's Manual (1998). Test Administration Manual (1998). Technical Manual (1995-under revision).

Languages in Which Available: English only.

Time: Actual Test Time: 12 tests, 1-13 minutes each.
    Total Administration Time: 2 hours 10 minutes.

Norm Group(s) on Which Scores Are Based: 9th and 10th grade students (Level 1A-1997) and 11th and 12th grade students and adults (Level 2A-1979, provisional norms).

Manner in Which Results are Reported for Individuals: Ball Career System
    Types of Scores: Raw scores, percentile ranks and verbal labels (high, moderate or mid-range, low).
    Report Format/Content:
        Basic Service: Ball Career System includes three reports: (1) Profile Report (percentile ranks and raw scores), accuracy, memory, reasoning, academic, spatial, creativity, and orientation); (2) Narrative Report, a companion to the Profile Report, provides each user with an interpretive paragraph about each score shown in their profile; (3) Ball Aptitude Pattern Indicator (API) (verbal labels—suggests career areas, work groups to explore and provide crosswalk to GOE); and (4) Ball Career System Guide (provides description of reports, aptitudes, and work groups).
        Options: Additional copies for counselor file at additional cost.

Report Format/Content for Group Summaries: Not available.
    Basic Service: Group summary available upon request (listing of students and scores and/or total group scores).

Scoring

    Machine Scoring Service: $145 for one test administration manual and 20: BAB (battery of 12 tests), scoring, three reports (Profile, Narrative, Aptitude Pattern Indicator), and Ball Career System Guide. Cost of $7.25 per student(minimum of 10 orders) for tests, scoring, and reporting.

    Time required for scoring and returning (maximum): Two weeks per 100 batteries.

    Hand Scoring: Not available.

    Local Machine Scoring: Not available.

Computer Software Options Available: Available for 2002.

Cost of Materials:

    Specimen Set: $15 (includes Examiner's Manual and sample test items and reports).

    Counselee Materials: Audiocassette tapes ($7.50 per student), Technical Manual ($25), Examiner's Manual ($15), Counselor's Manual ($25), Counselor training session ($600 per group), Counselor Training manual ($25). All items are reusable.

Additional Comments of Interest to Users: Technical and counselor's manuals currently under revision, addition of interest inventory to Ball Career System, further research on API, revision and testing of Form M Level 2 into Form N, moving to computer and Internet administration.

Published Reviews:

Benson, P. G., (1989). The Ball Aptitude Battery (Test Review). In J.C. Conoley & J.J. Kramer (Eds.). *Tenth mental measurements yearbook*, Lincoln, NE: Buros Institute, University of Nebraska-Lincoln.

Hall, A. E. (1985). The Ball Aptitude Battery (Test Review). *Journal of Educational Measurement, 22*, 167-172.

Layton, W. L. (1989). The Ball Aptitude Battery (Test Review). In J.C. Conoley & J.J. Kramer (Eds.). *Tenth mental measurements yearbook*, Lincoln, NE: Buros Institute, University of Nebraska-Lincoln.

Reviewed by

Donald Thompson
Professor and Dean
Division of Counseling, Education, and Psychology

John Patrick
Associate Professor of Counseling and Human Development

Troy State University Montgomery
Montgomery, AL

Description

In 1948, the Psychological Corporation provided the following definition of aptitude: "Nothing inherent in the concept assumes that aptitudes are hereditary; aptitude is the result of the interaction of heredity and environment. It includes intelligence, achievement, personality, and interests, as well as other abilities and skills. Aptitude is best summarized as a capacity to learn" (p. 2). Research indicates that aptitudes tend to be highly stable over long periods of time (Goldman, Bizot, & Rischall, 1994).

The Ball Aptitude Battery (BAB) is a paper-and-pencil, and performance-based, multiple aptitude battery that was developed primarily for use in career planning and counseling (Sung & Dawis, 1981). The test publisher, the Ball Foundation, has been involved in long-term, intensive research concentrating on the identification and development of human potential and aptitudes since 1975. One outgrowth of this research is the Ball Aptitude Battery (BAB) originating from work sample tests developed by Johnson O'Connor. The BAB is a set of multiple-ability tests designed specifically to increase individuals' knowledge of their aptitudes that are needed for successful performance in a wide variety of education and work settings (Ball Foundation, 1998a).

Although the full battery BAB consists of 18 tests, including several individually administered apparatus measures, only 12 aptitude tests are normally used in Form M of the BAB. The 12 tests are grouped into seven broad categories for ease of interpretation. These categories include Speed and Accuracy, Memory, Reasoning, Academic, Spatial, Creativity, and Orientation. Specific aptitude tests used in Form M of the BAB include the following: Clerical (compare pairs of numbers quickly and accurately), Writing Speed

---

Note: Portions of this review were adapted from the first author's original review in the *Thirteenth Mental Measurements Yearbook* with permission of the Buros Institute.

(write words rapidly), Associative Memory (recall number-letter pairs), Auditory Memory Span (recall a series of numbers presented aloud), Analytical Reasoning (understand relationships between ideas and organize them in a logical manner), Inductive Reasoning (find relationships among seemingly unrelated pieces of information), Vocabulary (identify the accurate meaning of English words), Numerical Computation (solve arithmetic problems), Numerical Reasoning (find a pattern in a series of numbers), Paper Folding (visualize three-dimensional figures in two-dimensional space), Idea Generation (generate a rapid and abundant flow of ideas), and Word Association (cognitive orientation). There are five tests that are not included in Form M, but may be used as supplemental.

They include Idea Fluency (generate creative and clever ideas), Shape Assembly (assemble a structure from three-dimensional shapes), Finger Dexterity (manipulate small objects quickly and with precision), Grip Strength (hand and arm strength) and Karma Music Test (recognize and separate out patterns of sound) (Ball Foundation, 1998a).

Both levels of the BAB may be administered individually or in groups. The time required for the administration of each level, including time for introduction, instructions, and the completion of a biographical questionnaire is approximately 2 hours and 10 minutes (Ball Foundation, 1998a). The primary factors for success on all the tests are based on the test subject's speed and accuracy in responding to test items. The tests are designed such that nearly everyone could do each test given enough time. However, those who have the strongest aptitudes in each test area can respond most quickly and with the higher degree of accuracy.

Each test taker receives the Ball Career System after taking the BAB. This includes the BAB Narrative, the BAB Profile, the Ball Aptitude Pattern Indicator (API), and the Ball Career System Guide. The BAB Narrative and Profile provide information regarding the test takers' scores on the 12 aptitudes. The API recommends career areas to explore based on the BAB scores. The Ball Career System Guide is a folder in that the three reports are inserted. It describes each report and provides instruction on how to interpret them.

Use in Counseling

Perhaps every aspect of living, and especially every occupation or type of work, whether it be medicine, engineering, bricklaying, carpentry, law, or management, requires certain aptitudes. The work that people are most likely to be successful at will usually be work that uses their aptitudes. Aptitude testing that helps students/clients identify their relative strengths and weaknesses is an important tool in career counseling and selection.

According to the descriptive material provided in the Administration Manual, the BAB is designed to measure aptitudes related to successful work behavior. A variety of reported studies support the contention that it is an effective tool for this purpose (Dawis, Goldman, & Sung, 1992; Dohm & Sung, 1982). As a valid and reliable measure of aptitudes, the BAB can be used effectively for a variety of career counseling and development purposes. It can be used as a tool in school-based career guidance programs with children starting in grade nine as either a career exploration tool or for making initial career choices related to educational/vocational programs. It has also been used successfully in outplacement counseling to help displaced adult workers choose various occupational or educational options.

The Examiner's Manual is concise and well written, and provides explicit information on how to administer the test in a manner that counselors will find easy to understand and use. There are two other supplemental manuals that counselors will find useful to purchase with the BAB, including the Ball Career System Administration Manual and the Ball Career System Counselor Training Manual. The Counselor Training Manual and the accompanying training audiotape provide an overview of aptitudes and their relevance to career planning, how aptitudes fit into the context of a career counseling model, and how to interpret the BAB profile. Also included in the manual are "overheads for use in presenting feedback to students and accompanying handouts including sample test items, sample reports, and other interpretive materials" (Ball Foundation, 1998c, p. 1).

Technical Considerations

The standardization sample (obtained in 1998) for BAB Form M, Level 1 provides norms for 9th and 10th grade test takers. The description of this sample (N=2,688) suggests that the standardization group had appropriate representation geographically, ethnically, and by gender. For the BAB Form M, Level 2, the current version uses provisional norms from the 1980's (although the test was renormed in 1995 based on this earlier data). A standardization study is currently underway for a complete renorming, and those results are to be available in spring, 2000. This norm study should provide a very solid basis for interpreting test results.

Both test-retest and internal consistency studies of reliability have been conducted on Form M of the BAB. The authors indicate that test-retest estimates of reliability have ranged from .50 to .94 with a median of .79 when employing a time interval of 2 to 6 weeks. They also report a study that examined the long-term stability of aptitudes measured by the BAB (between 9th and 12th grade), that yielded correlations ranging from .38 to .82, with a median of .50. Reported internal consistency reliability estimates range from .52 to .88, with a median of .80. Several of the tests that comprise the BAB are not amenable to internal consistency measurement as they are either speeded tests or do not provide meaningful and independent scores for individual items (Ball Foundation, 1998a).

Several studies reported by the authors provide evidence of the construct validity of the BAB. Dong, Goldman, & Sung (1986) employed a multimethod-multitrait approach to compare the BAB with the Comprehensive Ability Battery, the Differential Aptitude Tests, and the General Aptitude Test Battery. They found correlations between similar constructs generally ranged from .26 to .87 with a median of .63 thus supporting the convergent and discriminant validity of the BAB. Information is also provided on the criterion-related validity of the BAB. Authors found the BAB subtests to be moderately predictive of high school grade point average (.06 to .53), and performance on several standardized achievement tests (.10 to .40). The Examiner's Manual reports that validation studies examining the relationship of BAB subtest scores and on-the-job performance indicate that the BAB is effective in predicting success in more than 25 occupations (no statistical data were provided however) (Ball Foundation, 1998a).

Test subjects (college level adult students) who took Form M Level 2 as a part of this review reported that they found the test easy to understand and complete. They found it easy to interpret and were impressed with the information provided in the BAB narrative, profile, API and the Ball Career System Guide. Several students indicated that they would have preferred to take this test via computer administration if it were available in that format. They were interested in immediate feedback on their performance (J. Patrick, personal communication, June 5, 1999).

Overall Critique

The Ball Foundation continues to work on improving the BAB. They are reportedly working on incorporating an interest inventory and providing a computer-administered version of the BAB. It is presumed that the computer-based version will provide local and immediate scoring for several of the aptitude subtests and local report generation. This will be a significant improvement over the current scoring and report process, that require the test to be returned to the Foundation.

The BAB is a fine example of an aptitude test, and the Ball Foundation is to be commended for the quality of their empirical work in developing and refining the test. There have been reviews of earlier versions of the BAB that have been critical of various psychometric limitations. However, it appears that the Foundation has taken the criticisms into account and addressed them in this latest version.

Both the Technical Manual and the Examiner's Manual are very well written and appear to include all necessary and appropriate information. The instructions for administering the test are clear and precise. Although the BAB may not have the longevity and the wealth of research of some other comprehensive aptitude batteries such as the DAT and GATB, it is a well-conceived test that continues to be refined and developed. It is a good choice for aptitude assessment as a part of the overall career planning and choice process.

References

Ball Foundation (1998a). *Ball Career System examiner's manual.* Glen Ellyn, IL: Author.

Ball Foundation (1998b). *Ball Career System administration manual.* Glen Ellyn, IL: Author.

Ball Foundation (1998c). *Ball Career System counselor training manual.* Glen Ellyn, IL: Author.

Ball Foundation (1998d). *Ball Aptitude Battery technical manual.* Glen Ellyn, IL: Author.

Dawis, R. V., Goldman, S. H., & Sung, Y. H., (1992). Stability and change in abilities for a sample of young adults. *Educational and Psychological Measurement, 52,* 457-465.

Dohm, T. E. & Sung, Y. H., (1982). *The construct validity of the Ball Aptitude Battery.* Technical Report. Glen Ellyn, IL: Ball Foundation, (ERIC Reproduction Service No. ED 253 546)

Dong, H-K., Goldman, S. H., & Sung, Y. H., (1986). The validity of the Ball Aptitude Battery (BAB): Relationship to CAB, DAT, and GATB. *Educational and Psychological Measurement, 46,* 245-250.

Goldman, S. H., Bizot, E. B., & Rischall, R. Y. (1994, July). *Three year test-retest shows stability of aptitudes in adolescence.* Paper presented at the annual meeting of the American Psychological Society, Washington, DC.

Psychological Corporation (1948). What is an aptitude? *Test Service Bulletin. 36,* 2-3.

Sung, Y. H. & Dawis, R. V. (1981). *Technical manual: Ball Aptitude Battery.* Glen Ellyn, IL: Ball Foundation.

Career Planning Survey (CPS)

ACT Staff Members
ACT, Inc.
2201 N. Dodge Street
Iowa City, IA 52243

Target Population: Grades 8-10

Statement of the Purpose of the Instrument: The Career Planning Survey helps students gain self-awareness, learn how the world of work is structured, begin to explore personally relevant career options, and develop a program of studies for high school.

Titles of Subtests, Scales, Scores Provided: UNIACT Interest Inventory and Inventory of Work Related Abilities, each of which provides results for data, ideas, people and things work tasks. Reading and numerical abilities are tested as an option.

Forms and Levels Available, with Dates of Publication/Revision of Each: A single form is available, which was published in 1997.

Date of Most Recent Edition of Test Manual, User's Guide, Etc.: Counselor's Manual, 1998; Technical Manual, 1998; Directions for Administration, 1998; Assessment Booklet, 1997; Career Planning Guide (interpretation booklet for students), 2000; Technical Manual: Revised Unisex Edition of the ACT Interest Inventory (UNIACT), 1995.

Languages in Which Available: English only.

Time: Actual Test Time: an estimated 23 minutes for the two untimed inventories, plus an additional 30 minutes for timed ability tests.
Total Administration Time: 90 minutes.

Norm Group(s) on Which Scores Are Based: Nationally representative samples (1992) of 13,400 8th, 10th and 12th graders in 145 schools for UNIACT. Nationally representative samples (1997) of 16,300 8th and 10th graders in 146 schools for IWRA and ability tests.

Manner in Which Results Are Reported for Individuals:
   Types of Scores: World-of-Work Map regions for UNIACT and IWRA; lower 10%, lower 25%, middle 50%, upper 25%, and upper 10% for ability tests, plus a composite T score. Rank for career clusters (Holland types) based on both UNIACT and IWRA. Percentile bands for IWRA and ability composite.
   Report Format/Content:
      Basic Service: Two copies of a two-page Student Score Report including color highlighting of UNIACT and IWRA results on World-of Work map graphic and career cluster, career area, and example job lists. The Student Score Report also includes percentile bands for IWRA and ability composite results.
      Options: Score Report Labels, additional copies of Student Score Reports, Student List Report

Report Format/Content for Group Summaries:
    Options: Each of the following is available for single schools or for multiple schools in combination; Group Summary Reports (8), Student List Report, Data Tape, Data Diskette.

Scoring
    Machine Scoring Service:
        Cost of basic service per counselee: Included in the cost of the Student Assessment Set, which is $3.70 per student for Option A (including the ability tests) and $3.15 per student for Option B (without ability tests).
        Cost of options: Group Summary Report, single school, $28; Group Summary Report, multiple schools, $38; Student Score Report reprints (2 copies), $0.22 per student; List Score Report (2 copies), $0.11 per student; Label Score Reports (2 copies), $0.28 per student; Data Tape, Single School, $48; Data Tape, Multiple Schools, $58; Data Diskette, Single School, $28; Data Diskette, Multiple Schools, $38.
        Time required for scoring and returning (maximum:) 2 weeks
    Local Machine Scoring: Not available.

Computer Software Options Available: Not available.

Cost of Materials:
    Specimen Set: $12.40
    Counselee Materials: Student Assessment Sets, include answer sheet, student guidebook, prepaid scoring, and two copies of the Student Report.
    Student Assessment Sets, Option A (including ability tests), $3.70; Student Assessment Sets, Option B (without ability tests), $3.15; Test Booklets (reusable), $0.65.
Published Reviews: None cited.

Reviewed by

Robert C. Reardon
Professor and Program Director

Stacie H. Vernick
Career Advisor

Career Center
Florida State University

Description

The Career Planning Survey (CPS), available since 1998, is designed to prepare students to make informed educational and career decisions early in high school (grades 8-10). It includes a 16-page test booklet with a separate answer sheet that is computer scored. The CPS is based on assessed interests (UNIACT), self-rated abilities (IWRA), two optional academic ability tests, and current occupational preference ("trial job choice"), and it includes an interpretive guidebook. The CPS replaced two earlier ACT programs, the Career Planning Program (Level 1) and the Career Survey.

The publisher, American College Testing (ACT, 1998) indicates that the Career Planning Survey provides reliable information that reflects current career development theory, helps meet today's career guidance needs, and offers users a variety of benefits. The CPS can also help students develop personal plans, set career goals, and plan a program of studies to achieve those goals.

The Career Planning Survey is actually a new combination package of assessment and guidance materials developed over the years at ACT. The CPS includes the Unisex Edition of the ACT Interest Inventory (UNIACT) that assesses student likes and dislikes for 90 common activities on the basis of national norms. The UNIACT provides scores on scales for six career clusters – Business Contact, Business Operations, Technical, Science, Arts, and Social Service – that are familiar to some counselors as Holland Codes or RIASEC Types. ACT suggests that the UNIACT is especially helpful for younger persons who have not made the connection between the work world and the activities they would like to pursue in the future.

The CPS includes the Inventory of Work-Relevant Abilities (IWRA) to help students rate themselves in 15 work-relevant ability areas, many of which are not assessed by tests. These include abilities in the areas of Meeting People, Helping Others, Sales, Leadership (Management), Organization, Clerical, Mechanical, Manual Dexterity, Numerical, Scientific, Creative/Artistic, Creative/Literary, Reading, Language Usage, and Spatial Perception. Scores from the UNIACT and the IWRA are linked to the ACT World-of-Work Map, which locates career fields according to their involvement with data, ideas, people, and things. The World-of-Work Map is designed to help students bridge the gap between test scores and the work world. Testing time for the UNIACT and IWRA is about 45 minutes.

The Career Planning Survey also includes two optional academic ability tests covering reading (32 questions, 16 minutes) and numerical skills (24 questions, 14 minutes) to help students understand the importance of these two abilities in all occupations. The results are nationally normed by grade level.

Finally, the completed and scored CPS answer sheet produces a two-page, color-coded Career Planning Survey Report that is used in conjunction with the *Career Planning Guide* (ACT, 1997), a 24-page booklet of interpretive materials. The CPS Report includes two tables for the counselor showing test results related to academic abilities and work-relevant interests and abilities. The *Career Planning Guide* includes six units with topics, e.g., finding and exploring job possibilities, job characteristics, coursework planner, career area chart, and educational pathways to careers. Information about this program is available from ACT at http://www.act.org/cps/index.html.

Use in Counseling

ACT (1998) specified five assumptions undergirding the use of assessment in career counseling: (1) it should stimulate career exploration and examination of self in relation to careers; (2) it should provide information about a wide range of personal characteristics; (3) it should help counselors bridge the gap between test results and the use of planning information, especially in groups; (4) it should provide self-estimates as an alternative to ability tests; and (5) it should provide help for students in translating assessment results into personally relevant experiences. The CPS was developed with these principles in mind.

The CPS uses combined student information to suggest occupations and fields of study for further exploration. Every effort is made in the CPS program to encourage students to explore a wide range of occupations, e.g., those related to the "trial job choice." As a comprehensive career guidance program, CPS includes detailed instructions for administration of the program (ACT, 1998). For example, a scripted orientation session to the CPS is provided to the counselor, and other scripted sessions are provided for the group presentation of results. Detailed suggestions for group-based career exploration activities and follow-up are also provided in the 38-page *Counselor's Manual* (ACT, 1998), along with 8 pages of graphics for use in group interpretation sessions. Finally, a 16-page booklet with detailed directions for administering the CPS is provided for the counselor.

Technical Considerations

The 128-page *Career Planning Survey Technical Manual* (ACT, 1999) is easy to read and provides a great deal of psychometric data. It includes sections on the purpose of the assessment, its development and norms, and the reliability and validity of the individual instruments. Much more attention is afforded to the UNIACT and IWRA instruments than the two academic ability tests. A nationally representative sample of students in grades 8, 10, and 12 made up the normative sample for the CPS. The reading skills and numerical skills ability tests were normed by interpolation on a sample of ninth grade students. A total of 13,443 students comprised the normative sample for the UNIACT Interest Inventory and the 12th-grade norms for the IWRA. A total of 16,309 students comprised the normative sample for the IWRA and the ability tests. ACT (1999) reported that the normative groups for both instruments were fairly representative of the US population; however, areas of the country over-represented and under-represented in each sample were noted.

ACT (1999) suggested that the reliability of the CPS as an individual instrument is compromised by an assessment approach that involves multiple instruments as sources of information. Two forms of reliability were reported for the UNIACT Interest Inventory. Internal consistency, as measured by Chronbach's alpha, ranged from .85 to .91 (median=.86) across the six career cluster areas for the 8th-grade sample. Reliability across the six scales ranged from .87 to .92 (median=.87) for the 10th grade sample. In both samples, the Science scale had the highest internal consistency. For males, test-retest reliability ranged from .68 to .78 (median=.75) and for females, coefficients ranged from .69 to .82 (median=.78) across the six scales. Only test-retest reliability was reported for the IWRA, as determined through comparing scores on a paper-based IWRA and a multimedia format of the instrument with one to two weeks between testing. Reliability coefficients for grade 9 ranged from .71 to .78 (median=.72) and for grade 11 the range was from .69 to .78 (median=.75). Once again, the highest coefficient found corresponded to the Science scale for 9th-grade students, but the Arts scale demonstrated the highest reliability coefficient for eleventh graders.

A variety of studies were reported supporting different types of validity for each of the instruments. Scale intercorrelations on the UNIACT, indicative of convergent/discriminant validity, ranged from .22 to .70 for 8th graders, and from .12 to .66 for 10th-grade students. Findings of a principal components analysis provided evidence of the structural validity of the scales, and supported the two dimensions of the theory (Data/Ideas and People/Things). Results demonstrated that response style accounted for 54% of the total variance for 8th graders and 49% of total variance for 10th grade students. Findings demonstrated that the Data/Ideas and People/Things dimensions accounted for enough variance to indicate that these dimensions are appropriate and generalizable. Further, the UNIACT was found to be correlated in the expected directions with other interest measures. Scores on the UNIACT were correlated with scores on the IWRA to further establish convergent validity. Correlations ranged from .31 to .48 for 8th-grades, and from .35 to .50 for 10th-grades. "These results suggest that, when organized the same way, measured interests and informed self-estimates of ability tend to be related" (ACT, 1999, p. 42). There have been more than 40 criterion-related validity studies conducted with the ACT Interest Inventory, and ACT (1999) suggested that findings may be generalized to the current UNIACT Inventory because of the similarities between the instruments.

A large number of validity studies reported for the IWRA compare this instrument to the UNIACT. Convergent/discriminant validity studies found correlations between corresponding scales on the two instruments to range from .31 to .57 when comparing students in four samples of 8th, 10th, and 12th graders. ACT (1999) suggested, however, that inter-individual findings are much less relevant and instructive than intra-individual correlations. Hit rates were determined by assessing the number of individuals in a particular occupational group whose high point score corresponded to that of their criterion group. Hit rates

were higher when ability was determined with self-estimates; hit rates for general ability tests ranged from 28% to 39%, whereas the range for self-estimated ability tests was from 34% to 43%. Hit rates were determined for the UNIACT and IWRA individually as well as when used in concert with each other. Independent hit rates support the validity of both instruments, but substantially higher hit rates were found when high point codes suggested by the two instruments matched. ACT (1999) suggested that correspondence between scores on these two instruments results in the identification of more reliable options, thereby supporting the combination of these instruments in the Career Planning Survey.

Overall Critique

There are many strengths associated with the Career Planning Survey. It is a theory-based program, drawing heavily upon Holland's typology (1997) in providing interpretive materials for the assessment results. The World-of-Work Map provides an organized, clear pictorial depiction of a range of interests and skills to encourage student exploration of educational and career options. Vocational interests and self-estimates of ability are examined across the same six career clusters. The components of the CPS have been carefully researched and evaluated for almost a decade, and detailed information is provided to assist counselors in the use of the CPS program with groups and individuals. This includes answers to common questions or problems raised by counselors when interpreting the CPS results. Indeed, the documentation provided in the manuals to support the CPS program is outstanding. Professionals should be confident that the CPS fully meets the assumptions noted earlier that undergirded its development and guide its use.

Because it is a new product, there is limited research information available from the field regarding the use of the Career Planning Survey. As experience accumulates from practitioners, ACT will be able to continue to make improvements in this program and its effectiveness. The ACT career clusters and Holland types use slightly different terminology, which can be confusing to counselors using materials from different publishers. Although the use of ability self-estimates in the IWRA is commendable and ACT has researched this topic extensively, we have some slight reservations about the kinds of life experiences that beginning high school students have had that would enable them to respond meaningfully to the 15 ability areas included in the instrument. Happily, the Career Planning Guide (ACT, 1997) and other interpretive materials in the CPS program provide ways for counselors to address this issue by encouraging involvement in experiences that might provide means of exploring and developing abilities in areas of interest. Although the CPS examines interests and skills, there is less attention to the area of values, except as it is incorporated into the Career Planning Guide (ACT, 1997) section on Job Characteristics.

References

American College Testing Program. (ACT, 1997). *Career planning guide.* Iowa City, IA: Author.

American College Testing Program. (ACT, 1998). *Career Planning Survey: Counselor's manual.* Iowa City, IA: Author.

American College Testing Program. (ACT, 1999). *Career Planning Survey: Technical manual.* Iowa City, IA: Author.

Holland, J. L. (1997). *Making vocational choices: A theory of vocational personalities and work environments* (3rd ed.). Odessa, FL: Psychological Assessment Resources, Inc.

CareerScope Assessment & Reporting System (CareerScope®)

Jeffrey A. Harris, PhD
Vocational Research Institute—JEVS
1528 Walnut Street, Suite 1502
Philadelphia, PA 19102
info@vri.org.
www.vri.org

Target Population: Adolescents and adults reading at or above the 4th grade level and able to use a computer mouse.

Statement of the Purpose of the Instrument: Establish career interest and aptitude score profiles and occupational clusters in which the consumer can experience work activity satisfaction and probable success in occupational training.

Titles of Subtests, Scales, Scores Provided: CareerScope Interest Inventory: CareerScope Aptitude Battery: General Learning Ability, Verbal Aptitude, Numerical Aptitude, Spatial Aptitudes, Form Perception, Clerical Perception.

Forms and Levels Available, with Dates of Publication/Revision of Each: Copyright 2000.

Date of Most Recent Edition of Test Manual, User's Guide, Etc.: CareerScope User Guide v.4.0-2000.

Languages in Which Available: English only.

Time: Actual Test Time: Interest Inventory: Untimed (typically 15 minutes); Aptitude Battery—
25 minutes.
Total Administration Time: 45-60 minutes.

Norm Group(s) on Which Scores Are Based: Interest Inventory—18 years of age or older v. younger than 18 years of age (separate norms also reported by gender). Aptitudes—9th grade v. 10th grade v. adult.

Manner in Which Results Are Reported for Individuals
    Types of Scores: Interest Inventory—Scale percentile ranks as compared to total age appropriate norm group and as graphically displayed and statistically analyzed as standardized idiographic 12-scale profile. Aptitude Battery-Reported as standardized scores (mean=100, sd=20), as numerical percentile ranks and as a composite profile histogram display.

Report Format/Content:
    Basic Service: The consumer's Assessment Profile includes interest and aptitude score tables and graphic displays, with supporting narrative text, and career cluster recommendations (with descriptions of general work activities). The Counselor Report gives raw scores, corresponding percentile and standardized scores and viable career clusters in a concise tabular format.

Options: Assessment Profile career recommendations can be based aptitude scores or can be founded upon the synthesis of interest and aptitude profiles. Illustrative high-growth/high-replacement-rate occupations can be included/excluded from the respective career cluster recommendations.

Report Format/Content for Group Summaries:

Basic Service: The CareerScope Management System supports local configuration and generation of summary reports that identify examinees with specific score profiles and/or career cluster recommendations.

Scoring

Machine Scoring Service: Not available. All PC-based scoring and report generation is executed locally by software license owner.
Hand Scoring: Not available.
Local Machine Scoring: Not available.

Computer Software Options Available: CareerScope is computer based.

Ways in Which Computer Version Differs: CareerScope is a licensed software program that allows the purchaser to conduct an unlimited number of administrations, to create and assign "administration templates" that control the delivery of assessment tasks and then to generate reports locally for use by guidance personnel or the consumer.

Cost of Materials:

CareerScope is available on a metered (by the administration) and licensed (by the workstation) basis. Metered systems start at $500, plus a $5-10 per examinee fee based on the number of assessments purchased. A single workstation license of CareerScope is $3,000. This entitles the user to administer the assessment to an unlimited number of evaluees, but only on a single computer. Multiple workstation and network licenses are available, with volume purchase discounts starting with the second license. A 30-day, 5-administration "demo" copy of CareerScope is available (as a specimen set) to qualified, interested professionals looking to evaluate CareerScope in order to make a purchase decision. The demo system is available through local VRI representatives.

Additional Comments of Interest to Users: CareerScope operates on Windows and Macintosh networks and workstations. Program updates and upgrades, with enhanced feature sets and revised scoring algorithms, are scheduled for annual release.

Published Reviews:

Lustig, D., Brown, C., & Lott, A. (1998). Reliability of the CareerScope Career Assessment and Reporting System. *Vocational Evaluation and Work Adjustment Journal, 31*, 19-21.
Lustig, D., Brown, C., & Lott, A. & Larkin, V. (1998). Concurrent Validity of the CareerScope Career Assessment and Reporting System. *Vocational Evaluation and Work Adjustment Journal, 31*, 28-31.

Reviewed by

Clarence D. Brown
Associate Professor
Rehabilitation and Special Education
Auburn University

Description

CareerScope is a computer-based aptitude assessment, interest inventory, and reporting system developed by Vocational Research Institute (VRI). Aptitudes assessed are referenced to the U.S. Department of Labor (DOL) and include General Learning Ability (G), Verbal Aptitude (V), Numerical Aptitude (N), Spatial Aptitude (S), Form Perception (P), and Clerical Perception (Q). CareerScope does not measure other DOL aptitudes of Motor Coordination, Finger Dexterity, and Manual Dexterity, but has a feature that allows the user to input scores for these aptitudes when generated from other sources. The user also has the option of excluding these aptitudes when making recommendations or, in the absence of data, assuming the subject's performance to be average and including them in the analysis. The 12 interest areas, also referenced to the DOL's *Guide for Occupational Exploration* (GOE) include Artistic, Scientific, Plants and Animals, Protective, Mechanical, Industrial, Business Detail, Selling, Accommodating, Humanitarian, Leading/Influencing, and Physical Performing.

The CareerScope is a self-administered assessment system taking approximately one hour to complete; it requires a 4th-grade reading level. The system is designed with the novice computer user in mind. Requiring only minimal proficiency in the use of a mouse, the system guides the user through orientation and instructional phases prior to administering interest and aptitude items to ensure user understanding. In addition, each section is preceded by a practice session enabling the user to become familiar with the format of the subsequent subtests. The user can select either a standard (default) or customized administration. Standard administration includes presentation of all seven subtests in the same sequence for every assessment conducted. A customized assessment allows the user to select any combination of the seven subtests to be administered thus creating an assessment unique to the individual and their specific needs and the needs of the counselor. Completion of the CareerScope results in the production of two reports: the Assessment Profile and the Counselor Report. Both reports are designed to provide the evaluee and the counselor with easily understandable career information based on the relationship between aptitude scores and interest areas measured by CareerScope. Interest report results identify each of the DOL-GOE's 12 interest areas, subject response frequencies to the items on each of these scales (Like, ?, Dislike), and percentile scores (Total, Male, Female) for each interest area. An individual profile analysis of the interest assessment results in a rank ordering of the subject's highest interest areas.

Examinee performance on the aptitude assessment is also reported on both the Assessment Profile and the Counselor Report, but again in slightly different formats. Included in both reports are subtest raw scores (number correct and number attempted), standard scores, and percentile ranks for the six aptitudes measured. An adjusted score for each of the aptitudes using the standard error of measurement is provided in the Counselor Report only. The final section of both reports contains career recommendations based on the aptitude and interest assessment results. Examinees access GOE Work Groups by virtue of meeting or exceeding predetermined aptitude cutoff scores. The reports identify work groups accessed using both measured aptitude scores and adjusted (with Standard Error of Measure) aptitude scores.

The two software systems (Assessment Tasks and Management System) can be installed on a network or a personal computer. Network installation allows for data generated by multiple test stations to be stored to a central results file. Recommended system requirements include Windows® 95, 98, 2000, or NT 4.X, IBM-compatible CPU (minimum 486/66Mhz or better recommended), 17 MB free hard-drive space for Assessment Tasks, 16MB RAM to operate Assessment Program, 7MB free hard-drive space for Management System, and 16MB RAM to operate Management System (VRI, 2000).

Use in Counseling

Often counselors are faced with the challenge of interpreting the results of a client's interest and aptitude assessment in terms of career options or vocational training programs. The standard approach is to administer separate interest and aptitude measures that have little relationship to one another and then rely on the counselor's ability to mesh the two in relation to career options. The counselor must then attempt to explain to the client not only the results of the interest and aptitude assessments, but also how the two were used to select possible vocational options. The two CareerScope reports simplify this task, but a word of caution is in order. Counselors should have a working knowledge of the DOL-GOE's 12 occupational interest classification system, the aptitudes measured and their corresponding operational definitions, the 66 work groups for which an individual may qualify based on their performance, and a knowledge of how to use cutoff scores to access these work groups. This knowledge is essential if the counselor is expected to analyze and synthesize the assessment results and to discuss them with the examinee.

As a self-administered instrument, CareerScope frees the counselor from the typical test administration tasks, i.e., reading instructions and items, monitoring practice tests, timing. The individual conducting the examination must simply be available in the event there are unanticipated problems involving the hardware/software or in the event personal difficulties are encountered by the examinee.

Technical Considerations

CareerScope uses two sets of age-based norm groups. Youth norms are based on a national sample with an average age of 16.6 years and a mean educational level of 10.4 years. Adult norms are based on a national sample with an average age of 28.1 years and a mean of 11.9 years of education. Results of the interest assessment are reported as percentiles in both the Counselor's Report and the Evaluee Assessment Profile. The Counselor's Report presents raw scores, standard scores, percentile scores, and adjusted scores for each of the aptitude tasks. The Evaluee Assessment Profile reports the number correct of the number attempted (as does the Counselor's Report), and the standard score with percentile equivalent for each of the aptitude tasks.

Two reliability (Lustig, Brown, & Lott, 1998a; VRI, 1999a) and two validity (Lustig, Brown, Lott, & Larkin, 1998b; VRI, 1999b) studies of the CareerScope apttitude battery have been completed. Lustig et al. (1998a) administered the CareerScope to a group of college students (N=46). Using a test-retest procedure with a two-week interval between administrations, reliability coefficients for the aptitudes ranged from .52 to .83, with two above .80 and four below .80. The VRI (1999a) conducted a reliability study using 307 students in grades 7-12, which resulted in reliability coefficients ranging from .70 to .80. These studies suggest that the CareerScope can yield reliable aptitude scores, although additional studies are encouraged, especially with user groups that may differ from those included in the studies described.

College students (N=47) were the participants in a validity study conducted by Lustig et al. (1998b). Pearson product-moment correlation coefficients were computed between the aptitude standard scores of the CareerScope and theoretically similar aptitude standard scores of the General Aptitude Test Battery (GATB). Validity coefficients ranged from .36 to .86, with four correlations above .67. Using the same procedure, VRI (1999b) tested employees (N=115) of the Philadelphia Jewish Employment and Vocational Service (JEVS) and found validity coefficients ranging from .52 to .82. In both studies, the lowest validity coefficients were identified for the aptitudes of Form Perception and Clerical Perception. The VRI Research Brief (1999b) noted that the more highly speeded tests such as Form and Clerical Perception are likely to have lower validity coefficients than power tests.

Reliability of the CareerScope interest assessment was measured by the congruency of the ranks of the interest areas on the first administration compared to the second administration with 46 undergraduate and graduate students in a college of education. There was full or partial agreement for 98% of the participants (Lustig et al., 1998b). The VRI (1999c) also investigated the test-retest reliability of the interest assessment using 307 students in grades 7-12. Reliability coefficients ranged from .73 to .87 suggesting that the 12 interest areas of CareerScope are reliably measured for this population.

An easy-to-read user's manual (VRI, 1998) provides detailed information on the development of the system, system installation, scoring procedures for interest and aptitude assessment, and the establishment of cutoff scores.

Overall Critique

CareerScope offers a number of attractive features: (1) The entire assessment can be completed in approximately one hour and the low reading level (4th grade) makes the assessment accessible to an overwhelming majority of persons; (2) the system cross-references aptitudes and interests based on Department of Labor work groups providing information to both counselor and client useful in expanding job searches using additional occupational resources (i.e., Guide for Occupational Exploration, O*NET, etc.); and (3) the final product, separate reports for client and counselor, are readable and informative. Comments from study participants (Lustig et al., 1998b) indicated an ease in using computer technology as an assessment delivery mechanism, clear and concise instructions, and appropriate length.

Although participants in this study were comfortable using computers, individuals administering the CareerScope should be sensitive to any test anxiety that might be compounded as a result of persons having limited experience and familiarity with computers and/or computer assessments. Also, the absence of extensive reliability and validity studies conducted with diverse populations such as those served in the vocational rehabilitation system needs to be addressed.

References

Lustig, D. C., Brown, C. D., & Lott, A. C. (1998a). Reliability of the CareerScope Career Assessment and Reporting System. *Vocational Evaluation and Work Adjustment Journal, 31,* 19-21.

Lustig, D. C., Brown, C .D., Lott, A. C., & Larkin, V. M. (1998b). Concurrent validity of the CareerScope Career Assessment and Reporting System. *Vocational Evaluation and Work Adjustment Journal, 31,* 28-31.

Vocational Research Institute. (1998). User's guide: CareerScope. Philadelphia: Author.

Vocational Research Institute. (1999a). *Retest reliability of the CareerScope aptitude battery* (Research Brief #2). Philadelphia: Vocational Research Institute.

Vocational Research Institute. (1999b). *Concurrent validity of the CareerScope aptitude battery* (Research Brief #1). Philadelphia: Vocational Research Institute.

Vocational Research Institute. (1999c). *Retest reliability of the CareerScope interest inventory scales* (Research Brief #3). Philadelphia: Vocational Research Institute.

Differential Aptitude Tests (DAT) & Career Interest Inventory (CII)

G. K. Bennett, H. G. Seashore, and A. G. Wesman (DAT only)
The Psychological Corporation
555 Academic Court
San Antonio, TX 78204-2498
www.hemweb.com

Target Population: Students in grades 7-12 and adults.

Statement of the Purpose of the Instrument: The DAT is a battery of eight tests designed to measure students' ability to learn or to succeed in a number of different areas. The DAT is designed to be used alone or in conjunction with the *Career Interest Inventory,* a career guidance instrument designed to provide information about students' educational goals, interest in a variety of school subjects and activities, and interest in fields of work. When the DAT is used in conjunction with the *Career Interest Inventory*, a complete profile of students' interests and aptitudes can be developed.

Titles of Subtests, Scales, Scores Provided: DAT: Verbal Reasoning, Numerical Reasoning, Abstract Reasoning, Perceptual Speed and Accuracy, Mechanical Reasoning, Space Relations, Spelling, and Language Usage; additional score: Scholastic Aptitude (VR + NR). *Career Interest Inventory* Occupational Groups: Social Science, Clerical Services, Health Services, Agriculture, Customer Services, Fine Arts, Mathematics and Science, Building Trades, Educational Services, Legal Services, Transportation, Sales, Management, Benchwork, and Machine Operation.

Forms and Levels Available, with Dates of Publication/Revision of Each: Two levels of the DAT and *Career Interest Inventory* are available. Level 1 is designed to be used with students in Grades 7-9, Level 2 is designed to be used with students in Grades 10-12. Both levels of the DAT can be used with adults. However, it is recommended that only the Level 2 of the *Career Interest Inventory* be used with adults. The publication date of both the DAT and *Career Interest Inventory* is 1990. Only one of the two forms of the DAT is currently available, Form C. Only one form of the *Career Interest Inventory* is available. A *Partial Battery* is also available for both Levels 1 and 2 of the DAT. It consists of two tests, Verbal Reasoning and Numerical Reasoning. The *Partial Battery* may also be used with or without either level of the *Career Interest Inventory*.

Date of Most Recent Edition of Test Manual, User's Guide, Etc.: Technical Manual 1992.

Languages in Which Available: English and Spanish language edition with norms for students in Mexico only; available only from IEGE in Mexico DF, Mexico.

Time: Actual Test Time: 156 minutes for complete DAT battery; CII is untimed.
        Total Administration Time: Approx. 196 minutes for complete DAT battery; including untimed CII.

Norm Group(s) on Which Scores Are Based: DAT norms for each grade 7-12, males, females, and combined gender; DAT norms for 4 groups of adults. See norms booklets.

Manner in Which Results Are Reported for Individuals See Counselor's Manuals
   Types of Scores (e.g., standard scores, percentile ranks, verbal labels): raw scores, percentile ranks, stanines, national percentile bands for DAT; raw scores for CII.
   Report Format/Content
      Basic Service: DAT/CII: Individual Report; CII only; Individual Report.

Report Format/Content for Group Summaries:
   Basic Service: Group summary available upon request (listing of students and scores and/or total group scores)
   Options: See Counselor's Manuals. DAT/CII List Report by teacher/counselor or school, Student Profile, Counselor's Report (by teacher/counselor or school/district), Occupational Interest Report (by school), Career Planning Summary (by teacher/counselor, school, or district).

Scoring
   Machine Scoring Service: Prices valid through October 31, 2001.
      Cost of basic service per counselee: Basic scanning/scoring (complete battery with CII) $3.99; first copy of DAT with CII Individual Report $1.75, additional copies $0.38 each.
      Time required for scoring and returning (maximum): 21 calendar days
   Hand Scoring:
      Scored by: Counselee (CII only); Counselor (DAT)
      Time required for scoring: Approx. 10 minutes; see Scoring Assistant information.
   Local Machine Scoring:
      Provisions/conditions/equipment required: NCS SENTRY Scanners.

Computer Software Options Available: DAT/CII Scoring Assistant helps produce computer reports for results from hand-scored instruments.

Ways in Which Computer Version Differs: Reports are formatted differently from those obtained from TPC scoring services. Less interpretive text is provided. User sites can add special text to CII report, as an option.

Cost of materials:
   Specimen Set: DAT with CII is $32.50; CII only is $17; prices valid through 10/31/01.
   Counselee Materials: DAT/CII Practice Tests $26.50 for pkg of 25; Exploring Aptitudes; An Introduction to the Differential Aptitude Tests $18 for pkg of 25; Exploring Interests; An Introduction to the Career Interest Inventory $17 for pkg of 25; Using Test Results for Decision-making $18 for pkg of 25; Guide to Careers Student Workbook $111 (reusable blackline masters); Guide to a Career Portfolio Student Workbook $102.50 (reusable blackline masters).

Additional Comments of Interest to Users: The new edition of the Career Interest Inventory will be linked to the U.S. Department of Labor's O*Net.

Published Reviews:
Hattrup, K. (1995). Review of the Differential Aptitude Tests, Fifth Edition. In J. C. Conoley and J.C. Impara (Eds.), *The twelfth mental measurements yearbook.* Lincoln: Buros Institute, University of Nebraska-Lincoln.
Schmitt, N. (1995). Review of the Differential Aptitude Tests, Fifth Edition. In J. C. Conoley and J.C. Impara (Eds.), *The twelfth mental measurements yearbook.* Lincoln: Buros Institute, University of Nebraska-Lincoln.

Wang, L. (1995). Review of the Differential Aptitude Tests (DAT). *Measurement and Evaluation in Counseling and Development, 28,* 168-170.

Wilson, V. L. & Stone, E. (1994). Review of the Differential Aptitude Tests. Fifth Edition with Career Interest Inventory. In J. T. Kapes, M. M. Mastie, & E. A. Whitfield (Eds.), *A counselor's guide to career assessment instruments* (3rd ed.), Alexandria, VA: National Career Development Association.

Reviewed by

Lin Wang
Research Associate
ACT, Inc.

Differential Aptitude Test

Description

Published in 1990, the fifth edition of the Differential Aptitude Tests (DAT) can be used with the Career Interest Inventory (CII). The DAT is a multiple-aptitude battery used primarily in educational and vocational counseling, but it may also be used by employers for training or selection. Forms C and D, which constitute the fifth edition, are based on and replace Forms V and W of the 1980 edition. The tests still use a paper-and-pencil format. A computerized adaptive version of the DAT (DAT Adaptive) was introduced in 1987, but is now discontinued. Another derivative of the DAT is the Differential Aptitude Tests for Personnel and Career Assessment (DAT for PCA). Since the DAT Adaptive and the DAT for PCA have been reviewed elsewhere (Willson, 1995; Willson & Stone, 1994; Wing, 1995; Wise, 1995), they are not included in this review, which covers only the paper-and-pencil version of the DAT.

The DAT authors perceived aptitudes as abilities that are developed through education and training rather than simply inherited. The fifth edition measures the same eight aptitudes tested in previous editions. However, it features completely new items, reduced administration time (about three hours), and two levels (Level 1 for grades 7-9, and Level 2 for grades 10-12 and adults in postsecondary vocational programs). Although Forms C and D are alternate forms, only Form C is now in print. The readability of the tests at both levels is said to be at Grade 5. Multiple-choice items are used in all the tests. Users may choose to score the tests themselves or have them scored by the publisher. The

---

Note: Portions of this review were adapted from the author's original review in *Measurement and Evaluation in Counseling and Development* with permission of the Association for Assessment in Counseling.

scores of the Verbal Reasoning and Numerical Reasoning tests are combined for an additional Scholastic Aptitude score. An *Individual Report* provides raw scores, national percentile ranks, and stanines for separate and combined gender groups. Scores are accompanied with narratives for interpretation.

Use in Counseling

A DAT package contains a variety of information helpful to counselors. Three reports are available: individual reports, list reports, and counselor reports. When the CII is taken with the DAT, an individual's interest profile is also included in all the reports. Counselors are advised to attend closely to the DAT *Individual Report,* especially the one containing a career interest profile, because appropriate interpretation of this report has the greatest impact on an individual. The numerical and graphic information is presented and explained. The narratives in the report are clear and easy to understand.

The counselor's manual for the DAT with the CII is a practical guide to counselors for interpreting test results. The publisher offers some guidelines and illustrates the guidelines with eight cases of different combinations of the aptitude and interest profiles. In practice, however, counselors may encounter more different and complicated profiles than the eight cases present. Only knowledge, experience, and the will to help an individual can lead to the most appropriate and effective counseling session. Additional information in the DAT technical manual and the DAT norms book is also valuable to counselors.

Technical Considerations

Efforts were made to ensure the quality and the representativeness of the item tryout and norming studies in test development. However, the nonresponse issue was again not addressed, although the achieved normative sample was large and reflected the demographic characteristics of the 1980 census.

Scores derived from raw scores include percentile ranks, stanines, scaled scores, and normal curve equivalents (NCES). A new feature of the fifth edition, the scaled score (not available for the *Perceptual Speed and Accuracy* test) was developed for both comparing scores across levels and forms and for making a sample-free conversion of raw scores. Scaled scores are presented in the norms tables, but not reported to individuals. In order to compare scores from different editions and maintain longitudinal data, Form C is equated to Form V of the fourth edition.

Norms are provided for female, male, and combined-sex groups. No norms are given for ethnic minorities, although this issue was raised in a review of the fourth edition (Pennock-Roman, 1984). Because the non-white participants made up 27.7% of the norm sample, norming information about the ethnic groups would help counselors better interpret the DAT and the CII results for individuals from these subpopulations.

Internal consistency (KR-20) was assessed for all the tests except Perceptual and Speed Accuracy (PSA), a speed test for which internal consistency reliability is not appropriate. The KR-20 reliability coefficients, which range from .82 to .95 for all grade levels by gender groups, reflect the highly homogeneous domains sampled by the tests (Anastasi, 1988). The Mechanical Reasoning (MR) scores show the lowest reliability across levels, forms, and gender groups and are consistently lower for the females than for the males. Alternate-form reliability coefficients for all tests are also respectable, ranging from .73 to .90, with a median of .83. The alternate-form reliability coefficients for the PSA test range from .79 to .87.

Correlations among the DAT tests themselves and with other popular aptitude tests are provided as construct validity evidence. The within-battery correlation coefficients are typically in the .50s and .60, except those between the PSA and others, suggesting that the tests do measure somewhat different aptitudes. The correlations of the DAT with other aptitude tests are in the moderate to high range (.40 to .80). No factor analysis information is presented, although such information is usually used as construct validity evidence for an instrument of this nature.

Lack of criterion-related validity evidence has been noted in previous reviews. Predictive validity evidence is important because the DAT claims to measure a person's potential to learn and can be used for selection. To employers and college admission officers, predictive validity evidence might be the most important and relevant for practical reasons. Although data collection for predictive validity evidence can be very difficult, such evidence is nevertheless needed and can be established using various methodologies, such as a validity generalization method.

Overall Critique

The lasting popularity of the DAT among counselors is a tribute to the quality, credibility, and utility of the battery. The efforts that went into the development of this fifth edition of the DAT have significantly improved the quality of the battery.   The utility of the DAT can be further enhanced with improvement in several areas.

First, empirical data need to be collected and analyzed for construct validity evidence. This may also help to explain the high correlations among some DAT tests. Second, norms for ethnic minorities and examples of appropriate use of the norms will help counselors work better with students from these subpopulations. Third, criterion-related validity evidence must be established to support the intended use claimed by the DAT publisher.

It is worth noting that the fifth edition has been in use for almost a decade now, with the next revision likely to appear early in the new millenium.

During the 1990s, enormous developments in the technological world and widespread use of computers and the internet have had significant implications for how counselors work. The next edition of the DAT should be planned with these technical developments in mind.

Career Interest Inventory

Description
The Career Interest Inventory (CII) was designed to "assist students in making decisions concerning their educational and vocational plans" (The Psychological Corporation, 1991, p. 9). This first edition of the CII adopted a paper-and-pencil, self-report format, available in both a machine-scorable and a hand-scorable form. The Inventory can be given in group administrations. The Inventory is not timed, but the publisher recommends a 40-minute session. The CII can be used alone or with the Differential Aptitude Tests (DAT).

The CII measures students' interest in 15 occupational groups representing the world of work in the United States. The 15 occupational groups in the CII are derived from the U.S. Department of Labor's *Dictionary of Occupational Titles* (DOT); the work-activity statements in the Inventory were developed from the descriptions of the DOT occupations. The CII also yields information that assists an individual in exploring careers described in other sources from the U.S. Department of Labor, such as the *Guide for Occupational Exploration* (GOE), and the *Occupational Outlook Handbook* (OOH). Both the GOE and the OOH are directly linked to the DOT.

The CII is available in Level 1 and Level 2 for different age groups. Level 1, intended for grades 7-9, contains 120 work-activity statements and 32 high school course and activity statements. The 32 school-related items elicit information about a student's interest in high school subjects and activities. Level 2, for students in grades 10-12 and adults, contains 150 work-activity statements and 20 post-high school course statements. These course statements are used to determine a student's interest in postsecondary educational/vocational programs or alternatives.

Employing a five-point scale, ranging from "Like very much" to "Dislike a great deal," the CII yields a score for each of the 15 occupational groups. A Consistency Index is also recommended for distinguishing different response patterns that may yield the same scores for an occupational group. The CII scores are reported in the *Individual Report* as a profile showing an examinee's order of preference for the 15 occupational groups, the subject areas, and the school activities (Level 1 only). Other CII reports to individuals include the *Counselor's Report* and the *Hand-Scorable Booklet Report*. Two group reports are the *Occupational Interest Report* and the *Planning Summary*.

Use in Counseling

The CII package contains sufficient information for preparing, administering, scoring, reporting, and interpreting the CII scores. All the materials look attractive. The booklet *Exploring Interests* is particularly helpful in preparing individuals for the Inventory. Many individuals, especially younger students with few work experiences, are not familiar with an interest inventory. As a result, they may not know what vocational interests are. This lack of knowledge may affect the quality of the data collected and may yield unhelpful information about an individual's interest areas. With a variety of explanations, questions, and exercises, the short booklet provides a good orientation for users before they take the CII.

The information in the counselor's manual is clear, straightforward, and easy to use. What this reviewer finds most valuable is the interpretation of a variety of profiles of individuals' interests. Sample reports are printed and marked for illustration. For those problematic cases, such as various flat or invalid profiles, counselors are advised about how to identify clues to help counselees explore their interest areas.

Another feature worth mentioning is using the CII with special-needs populations, which include individuals with disadvantages and disabilities as well as individuals from other cultures. These individuals who tend to have greater difficulty than others in career development have the greatest needs for career counseling. In the counselor's manual, the characteristics of those special-needs populations are described and analyzed, with advice on using the Inventory effectively in career counseling with them.

Technical Considerations

The CII was developed using a nationally representative sample of about 100,000 students from grades 7-12. The publisher examined various aspects of the CII before finalizing the instrument. These aspects included content-appropriateness of the work-activity statements, administration time, users' feedback, and the reliability and validity indices.

Female, male, and combined means and standard deviations for the 15 occupational groups are given for each of the six grades in the counselor's manual. The manual also provides the percentages, by grade levels, of the females, males, and the combined samples having low, medium, and high interest scores for the 15 occupational groups. Data on the percentage of individuals expressing different attitudes toward subject areas and school activities are also presented.

A unidimensional scale was developed for each occupational group. Internal consistency reliability was estimated for each scale for both Level 1 and Level 2. The estimated reliabilities (Cronbach's coefficient alpha) are respectable, ranging from .82 to .94 at Level 1, and from .87 to .94 at Level 2. Standard errors of measurements are also provided, making it easier for counselors to locate the lower and upper boundaries for an individual's true interest score.

Content validity is evidenced by the fact that the CII items reflect the work-activities described in the DOT. Most correlations among the 15 occupational group interest scores are low to moderate, supporting the relative independence of the 15 groups. However, the correlations between the Machine Operation and the Building Trades groups are as high as .84 and .86 for Level 1 and Level 2, respectively. The publisher's explanation is that these occupational groups tend to be closely related in the real world of work. Even so, the work activity statements in these two groups need close examination to see whether the independence between the two groups, as measured by the correlations, can be increased. A factor analysis study was conducted, yielding eight factors for Level 1 and 10 factors for Level 2. The 15 occupational groups were mapped to the factors. It would help to know how the factors are related to the nine DOT categories underlying the 15 occupational groups.

This reviewer concurs with other reviewers that criterion-related validity evidence is sparse (Schafer, 1998; Zedeck, 1998). The only evidence of this nature was obtained through judgmentally matched scales of the Ohio Vocational Interest Survey Second Edition (OVIS II). It is certainly desirable and necessary for the publisher to accumulate evidence that relates the CII results to external criteria such as job performance, job satisfaction, and other established interest inventories. This reviewer hopes that more criterion-related validity evidence will be available for the next edition.

Overall Critique

The *Career Interest Inventory* is conceptually well formulated and soundly grounded in the world of work described by the DOT. The careful design in the development of the instrument is commendable. The addition of the CII to the family of interest inventories has provided counselors with another useful instrument. Moreover, when the CII is used together with the DAT, as recommended by the publisher, an individual's interest profile can be integrated with his or her aptitude profile to yield valuable information that counselors should find very useful. The instrument is user friendly, and interpretation of the assessment results can be done in a simple and informative manner.

Lack of validity evidence, especially criterion-related validity from the world of work, presents a problem in application because users are not sure to what extent the CII results can be generalized. Also, the CII national research program collected data only from students in grades 7-12. Therefore, counselors should be very careful when using the CII to help adults explore their career paths.

References

Anastasi, A. (1988). *Psychological testing* (6th ed.). New York: Macmillan.

Pennock-Roman, M. (1984). Differential Aptitude Tests. In D. J. Keyser & R. C. Sweetland (Eds.), *Test critiques* (pp. 226-245). Kansas City, MO: Test Corporation of America.

The Psychological Corporation (1991). *Counselor's manual for interpreting the Career Interest Inventory.* San Antonio, TX: Author.

Schafer, W. D. (1998). *Review of the Career Interest Inventory.* In J. C. Impara and B. S. Plake (Eds.), *The thirteenth mental measurements yearbook* (pp. 194-196). Lincoln, NE: University of Nebraska Press.

Willson, V. L. (1995). Review of the Differential Aptitude Tests for Personnel and Career Assessment. In J. C. Conoley & J. C. Impara (Eds.), *The twelfth mental measurements yearbook* (pp. 306-307). Lincoln, NE: University of Nebraska Press.

Willson, V. L., & Stone, E. (1994). Review of the Differential Aptitude Tests (DAT) with Career Interest Inventory (CII). In J. T. Kapes, M. M. Mastie, & E. A. Whitfield (Eds.), *A counselor's guide to career assessment instruments* (3rd ed., pp. 93-98). Alexandria, VA: National Career Development Association.

Wing, H. (1995). Review of the *Differential Aptitude Tests for Personnel and Career Assessment.* In J. C. Conoley and J. C. Impara (Eds.), *The twelfth mental measurements yearbook* (pp. 307-309). Lincoln, NE: Buros Institute, University of Nebraska-Lincoln.

Wise, S. L. (1995). Review of *Differential Aptitude Tests--Computerized Adaptive Edition.* In J. C. Conoley and J. C. Impara (Eds.), *The twelfth mental measurements yearbook* (pp. 300-301). Lincoln, NE: Buros Institute, University of Nebraska-Lincoln.

Zedeck, S. (1998). Review of the *Career Interest Inventory.* In J. C. Impara and B. S. Plake (Eds.), *Thirteenth mental measurements yearbook* (pp. 196-197). Lincoln, NE: Buros Institute, University of Nebraska-Lincoln.

Employability Competency System (ECS)

CASAS, Foundation for Educational Achievement
CASAS
5151 Murphy Canyon Road, Suite 220
San Diego, CA 92123
(800) 255-1036
www.casas.org
casas@casas.org

Target Population: Youth ages 16 through adults.

Statement of the Purpose of the Instrument: This system helps programs identify the skills needed by adults and youth to succeed in today's workforce and to determine whether participants should be placed into educational services such as English as a Second Language (ESL), Adult Basic Education (ABE), General Educational Development (GED) preparation classes, or vocational training programs. It is used by Workforce Investment Act (WIA) (Title 1, 2 & 3), Temporary Assistance for Needy Families (TANF), and School-to-Work programs across the nation as well as in workplace-based educational programs to meet accountability requirements for both native and non-native speakers of English.

Titles of Subtests, Scales, Scores Provided: Reading, Math, Listening, Critical Thinking, Oral Communication, Writing, pre-employment Work Maturity tests are all reported out as scaled scores.

Forms and Levels Available, with Dates of Publication/Revision of Each:
- ECS Appraisal Forms 120 & 130 Reading and Math
- ECS Appraisal – Computer Version of Form 130, 2000
- ECS Reading Forms 11-18 (Levels A-D) 1988, 1996, 1997, 2000
- ECS Math Forms 11-18 (Levels A-D) 1988, 1996, 1997, 2000
- ECS Listening Form 51, 52, 63-66 (Levels A-C) 1987, 1988
- Beginning Literacy Reading Forms 27 & 28, 1994
- ESL Appraisal Form 20 Reading & Listening, Levels A-C, 1997
- Pre-Employment / Work Maturity Checklists (for performance assessment of career awareness, resume prep, application forms, interviewing and work maturity) Forms A-G, 1990
- Writing Forms 400, 410, 411, 420, 421 (Levels A-D), 1994
- Critical Thinking for Employability, 1990
- Certification for Employability, Reading and Math Forms 501-504, Levels B and C, 1988
- Oral Communication Applied Performance Appraisal (OCAPA), Levels C & D, 1991
- Occupation Specific Tests:
- Auto Mechanics (Revised 1996 and available in English and Spanish) Forms 150 & 150S, 1988, 1997
- Clerical, Form 155, 1989
- Food Service, Form 160, 1989
- Health Occupations, Form 161, Level B, 1989

- Health Occupations, Form 162, Level C, 1989
- Workforce Skills Certification – Available January 2001
- Reading/Math Form 551, Level D, 2000
- Banking – Critical Thinking, Problem Solving, Applied Performance Form 562, 2000
- Health – Critical Thinking, Problem Solving, Applied Performance Form 572, 2000
- Hi-Tech – Critical Thinking, Problem Solving, Applied Performance Form 582, 2000
- Telecommunications – Critical Thinking, Problem Solving, Applied Performance Form 583, 2000
- Portfolio Assessment System – Standardized rubrics for scoring contained in teacher's manual. Student manual includes project guidelines & SCANS competencies assessed, 2000.

Date of Most Recent Edition of Test Manual, User's Guide, Etc.: 2000

Languages in Which Available: English (Some are available in Spanish).

Time: Actual Test Time: 30-60 minutes each form.
     Total Administration Time: Depends on how many skill areas tested–from 1-3 hours.

Norm Group(s) on Which Scores Are Based: Included both youth and adult students in basic education, ESL, high school completion, JTPA, and correctional education programs.

Manner in Which Results Are Reported for Individuals:
     Types of Scores: Tests are scored on a common numerical scale. The CASAS scale is divided into 5 levels: A - beginning literacy through E – advanced adult secondary. Each encompasses a range of scores which correspond to competency descriptors of performance in employment and life skills.

   Report Format/Content:
     Basic Service: "Student Profile by Competency" can be filled out by hand or computer generated using TOPSpro software at the assessment site.

Report Format/Content for Group Summaries:
     Basic Service: Both the "Class Profile by Competency Report" and the "Class Performance by Competency Report" can be filled out manually or computer generated using TOPSpro.

Scoring
     Machine Scoring Service:
     Cost of basic service per counselee: *$250 processing fee plus $0.25 per answer sheet plus $50 per report.*
       Hand Scoring:
       Scored by: Clerk; Counselor.
       Time required for scoring: A minute per form.
     Local Machine Scoring:
       Provisions/conditions/equipment required: TOPSpro software available for on site computers. Over 30 different reports may be generated for administrators, teachers and students. Unlimited scoring is permitted. Cost is $1999 for TOPSpro software plus $1.20 per set of test record forms/student. Windows 95 or NT 4.0 or higher, 16 mb ram, 40 mb space, CD-ROM, monitor with 800 x 600 resolution, SCANTRON 2000, 8000 or NCS OpScan 3, 4, 5, 7.

Computer Software Options Available: ECS Appraisal Form 130 currently available. More forms will be available in the future.
Specimen Set: $3 per sample test booklet.
Counselee Materials: Most forms are reusable. $2.40 per test booklet if ordered in sets.

Published Reviews:
Mueller, R. O. & Freitag, P.K. (1998). Review of the Comprehensive Adult Student Assessment System (CASAS). In J.C. Impara & B. S. Plake (Eds.) *Thirteenth mental measurements yearbook*. Licoln. NE: Buros Institute, University of Nebraska-Lincoln.

Reviewed by

Patricia K. Freitag
Assistant Professor of Educational Research

Ralph O. Mueller
Professor of Educational Research

Department of Educational Leadership
The George Washington University

Description

The Employability Competency System (ECS), previously known as the Comprehensive Adult Student Assessment System (CASAS), is more than just a test, which is both its greatest asset and a potential liability. It is an integrated competency-based curriculum management, instruction, and assessment system. The impressive array of materials for adult basic and alternative secondary education programs provides a coherent program, linking diagnostic assessment to instruction and subsequently to outcomes in terms of score gains on CASAS tests. Designed for use with persons whose functional skills are at or below the high school level, these materials have been effectively used in programs of school-to-work transition, correctional institutions, social service welfare programs, with second language learners, and in comprehensive high school programs for students with special needs. The extensive item bank allows these assessments to be easily adapted and customized for use in a variety of contexts and for a variety of purposes. The potential liability lies in assessing skills in functional contexts that are more appropriate and relevant to some settings (and curricula) over others. The primary purpose of the instruments is to provide for

Note: Portions of this review were adapted from the authors' original review in the *Thirteenth Mental Measurements Yearbook* with permission of the Buros Institute.

"learner-centered curriculum management, assessment, and evaluation" (CASAS, p. 2).

The assessments are an integrated hierarchical array of more than 80 instruments that measure adult "basic skills in a functional context" (CASAS, p. 4). The careful development of items and established item difficulties allow parallel assessment forms to be readily constructed from the extensive item bank in each skill area. This makes this system potentially useful for programs that do not use CASAS curriculum or instructional materials. Each assessment instrument requires about 60 minutes to be administered.

Customized instruments may be closely aligned with life skills, employability, high school completion, or English-as-a-Second-Language (ESL) curricula for adult learners. Support materials provide clear links between CASAS outcomes, the Secretary's Commission on Achieving Necessary Skills (SCANS) competencies, and research on those skills desired by employers. Intended applications of the instruments include (1) diagnostic placement of adult learners in appropriate program levels; (2) progress and monitoring assessment of learners; (3) outcome measures and competency certification of adult learners in life skills, employability, or ESL training programs; and (4) reporting mechanisms for data at the local, state, and federal levels. The major strengths of the CASAS system are the breadth of competency areas and assessment functions covered as well as the explicit links between pretest score, program placement, instruction, and the assessment of learner outcomes for CASAS-based adult learning programs.

The items include appropriate diagrams, charts, graphs, tables, reading passages, and oral components. The machine-scored answer sheets and selected response formats make these assessments easy to use, score, and interpret but limit the performance and authentic functional aspect of the tests. Some contextual cues in the items seem contrived whereas other tasks are quite realistic. In some areas the skills assessed seem most appropriate for the transition of secondary school students rather than adult learners in various home or employment contexts.

Supporting documentation consists of a technical manual, test administration guidelines, and scoring packets. These are clearly written and easy to follow. Instruments in each area are constructed at sequential levels with some overlapping items that link to the previous as well as next level. This enhances the diagnostic and placement uses for CASAS.

Uses in Counseling

It seems that CASAS has not yet been used extensively in the counseling field. Several states use CASAS as both an adult basic instructional program and program evaluation tool. Two studies emerge as key to the validation and reliable use of CASAS. Tadros (1997) reported significant gains for learners in the Even Start Family Literacy Program using the CASAS assessments for functional reading. In addition, adult learner participation was sustained beyond 49 hours in this project. Extensive data for CASAS norms are provided by the Iowa State Department study of Iowa's adult basic education using the CASAS Employment Competency System Appraisal Form 130 in the areas of reading and mathematics. Norm data for various target populations of interest are reported. This study demonstrated the broad use of CASAS with adult learners of different ages, ethnic origin, and years of education. In a report from the Iowa Department of Education (1997), CASAS scores compared favorably with those on the American College Testing's (ACT) Work Keys assessments, suggesting the appropriate use of CASAS materials in tandem with other diagnostic tools and in developing workplace learning programs. From our perspective, the CASAS might be most useful for counselors serving adult learners with special needs in transition from secondary school to work, in continuing or postsecondary education and training programs, or for placement within a level of a CASAS adult basic education program. Counselors should be trained in the use of the CASAS materials to become familiar with the assessments' administration and   scoring protocols. Training, through CASAS, will also allow the counselor to become more familiar with the wide variety of materials available and facilitate the selection of those most appropriate to their needs.

Technical Considerations

"The CASAS Item Bank provides statistically reliable and externally validated test items for the construction of instruments that measure basic skills in a functional context for youth and adults" (CASAS, p. 7). To justify this claim, two sections of the technical manual are devoted to evidence of the validity and reliability of CASAS tests. From the manual it is not clear whether or not the data in these sections were obtained from the calibration sample that is characterized broadly by the following statistics (p. 23); age range: 16-85 with 40% in the 21-30 group; ethnicity: 54% Hispanic, 18% Asian, 12% Chinese, 9% White, 4% Black; and gender: 50% female. Information on the sampling procedures used and the socioeconomic status, learning abilities, and residency of participants that might be relevant to assess the "appropriate use of test instruments for specific populations" (CASAS, p. 1) is not provided in the supplied manuals. Although this is promised in upcoming manuals, there are no norms provided for currently used disability categories or for second language learners. Internal consistency coefficients and IRT-based standard errors of estimate for tests are reported in the reliability subsection of the manual. The KR-20 reliabilities for the CASAS Forms are acceptable and for the most part above .80. The internal consistency data are presented separately for subgroups of students speaking various native languages (N=31, Form 77 to N=1,000, Form 71). Further, IRT-based standard errors of estimate are reported for CASAS Reading Forms 74 through 77. Given the careful development of items and use of overlapping items between forms, parallel forms show good reliability. One should be cautious in interpreting gain scores as students progress through levels of the CASAS program. Gain scores do not have the same underlying distribution as raw or scaled scores.

It seems that great care was taken during item-bank development to ensure the content validity of CASAS tests. With regard to the construct-related validity, the manual authors claim that "adult life skills problem-solving is the unobservable trait or ability assumed to underlie performance" (CASAS, p. 37). Similarly, specific evidence of the criterion-related validity is not provided to substantiate that, indeed, "[t]he instructional level indicated by a CASAS test depicts the learner's probability of success in accomplishing a given learning activity and related competency" (technical manual, p. 38). This is significant for adult learners in non-CASAS adult basic education. Gain scores estimated by CASAS instruments for adult learners in other education programs will likely have lower reliability than those reported in the test manuals.

Other validity evidence consists of data on three key CASAS claims that in 1993 were evaluated and supported by the Program Effectiveness Panel of the U.S. Department of Education. The claims are that "learners within educational programs that have adopted the key elements of CASAS (both the curriculum and corresponding assessment components) (1) demonstrate significant learning gains, (2) demonstrate increased hours of participation, and (3) achieve increased goal attainment compared to programs that have not adopted the key elements" (CASAS, p. 32). This is an expected result given the close alignment of instructional materials to the assessment instruments used. It would be interesting and important to see the results from CASAS assessments used with a variety of adult learners in other programs as well as how CASAS scores compare to other tests for adult basic education and employability skills when used with the same learners. The manual contains statistical analyses from various state and national studies, based on samples ranging in size from N=32 to N=1,326. Additional evaluation and research studies have added support to the validity of these assessments for use with other special populations. Although the reported data seem supportive of the above claims, note again that conclusions are based on analyses of gain scores that are known to have lower reliabilities than their raw score counterparts.

Overall Critique

The Comprehensive Adult Student Assessment System (CASAS) offers diagnostic, achievement, and competency tests in many content areas related to adult basic skills and employability. The use of CASAS might be limited to counselors who serve adult clients in basic education, literacy, and supportive employment contexts. However, counseling practitioners will benefit by becoming familiar with these instruments and materials to assess employability skills and program outcomes. The instruments available are reliable indicators of learner achievement in CASAS-based adult learning programs for a broad array of skill areas. It is possible for these instruments to be customized to meet the assessment needs in other adult education programs as well. Empirical evidence to support construct and criterion-related validity claims would strengthen the interpretation of score data as well as promote the general use of these instruments across adult basic education programs. Similarly, a more complete description of the calibration and validation samples would improve the assessment documentation. In our opinion, more thorough descriptions of study samples, clear specifications for instrument construction, and analysis of data from field-tested "performance measures" are needed. These additions would facilitate the general use of this extensive system for adult learner assessment and strengthen the program links among placement, instruction, and assessment.

References

CASAS Foundation for Educational Achievement (1993). *Comprehensive Adult Student Assessment System. Technical manual.* San Diego: Author

Iowa Department of Education (1997). *Extending the ladder: From CASAS to Work Keys assessments.* Des Moines, IA.

Tadros, L.C. (1997). Parents go back to school to help their children. *Early Child Development and Care,* 127-128, 167-178.

EXPLORE

ACT Staff Members
ACT, Inc.
2201 N. Dodge Street
Iowa City, IA 52243
www.act.org
epas @act.org

Target Population: Grade 8 and early in grade 9.

Statement of the Purpose of the Instrument: EXPLORE is the point of entry into ACT's Educational Planning and Assessment System (EPAS), which supports, documents, and assesses students' academic and career development through secondary school. EPAS is an articulated system including PLAN (grade 10), the ACT Assessment, and Work Keys, in addition to EXPLORE.

Titles of Subtests, Scales, Scores Provided: UNIACT Interest Inventory, English, Mathematics, Reading and Science Reasoning. Subscores are reported in the English test for usage/mechanics and rhetorical skills.

Forms and Levels Available, with Dates of Publication/Revision of Each: Form 01B which was released in 1996, and Form 02A which was released in 2000.

Date of Most Recent Edition of Test Manual, User's Guide, Etc.: Technical Manual, 1997; Program Guide 2000; Administrator's Manual, 2000; It's Your Future, Student Guide to EXPLORE, 2000; Maintaining the Content Validity of ACT's Educational Achievement Tests, 1998; Technical Manual: Revised Unisex Edition of the ACT Interest Inventory (UNIACT), 1995.

Languages in Which Available: English only.

Time: Actual Test Time: 120 minutes.
Total Administration Time: 135 minutes for test section plus 50 minutes for nontest sections.

Norm Group(s) on Which Scores Are Based: Nationally representative samples (1992) of 13,400 8th, 10th and 12th graders in 145 schools for UNIACT. Nationally representative sample (1995) of over 1,400 8th and 9th grade students in public and private schools for the academic tests.

Manner in Which Results Are Reported for Individuals
   Types of Scores: World-of-Work Map career areas, regions, for UNIACT. Scale Score (1-25) for each knowledge and skill area, plus a percentile band. Composite score, which is the average of the four ability test scores. Estimated PLAN composite score range.
   Report Format/Content :
      Basic Service: Two copies of a two-page Student Report, including color highlighting of UNIACT results on World-of-Work map graphic and career areas. The Student Roster includes self-reported career plans, self-reported educational plans for high school and beyond, scale scores, and both national and local percentile scores. Early Intervention Rosters help identify students needing extra attention.

Options: Alternative Student Roster (provides information in alternative sort order), student labels.

Report Format/Content for Group Summaries:

Basic Service: School Summary Reports provide aggregated data for each academic test.

Options: Item-Response Summary Report ; Standards for Transition Information Services (links to curriculum); Customized Scoring Reports (provides scoring information for selected subgroups); District Summary Report and Presentation Packet (like school summary report, but includes graphics and three-year trends; Data Tape, Data Diskette.

Scoring

Machine Scoring Service:

Cost of basic service per counselee: Included in cost of the Student Assessment Sets, which is $132 per package of 30.

Cost of options: Alternative Student Roster, $0.08 per student; Student Score Labels, $0.14 per student; Student Report Reprints, $0.11 per student; ; School Summary Report Reprint, $28; Customized Summary Report, $38; District Summary Report and Presentation Packet, $38.; Data Tape, Single School, $48; Data Tape, Multiple Schools, $58; Data Diskette, Single School, $28. Data Diskette Multiple Schools, $38; Standards for Transition Reports, $75 per set; Customized standards for transition reports, $50 per group.

Time required for scoring and returning (maximum): 15 working days.

Hand Scoring: Not available.

Local Machine Scoring: Not available.

Computer Software Options Available: Not available.

Cost of Materials:

Specimen Set: $6.

Counselee Materials: Student Assessment Sets, $132 per package of 30; Test booklets (reusable), $50 per package of 30.

Additional Comments of Interest to Users: New norms and score scale will be available in Fall 2001. Form 02B is projected for release in Fall 2003.

Published Reviews: None Cited

PLAN

ACT Staff Members
ACT, Inc.

Target Population: Recommended for Grade 10 in fall testing window from late September through December.

Statement of the Purpose of the Instrument: PLAN assesses students' progress at the midpoint of ACT's Educational Planning and Assessment System (EPAS), which supports, documents and assesses students' academic and career development through secondary school. EPAS is an articulated system including EXPLORE (Grade 9), the ACT Assessment, and Work Keys, in addition to PLAN.

Titles of Subtests, Scales, Scores Provided: UNIACT Interest Inventory, English, Mathematics, Reading and Science Reasoning. Subscores are reported in the English test for usage/mechanics and rhetorical skill, and in the Mathematics test for Pre-Algebra/Algebra and Geometry.

Forms and Levels Available, with Dates of Publication/Revision of Each: A new PLAN test form is released each fall, and use is limited to that academic year.

Date of Most Recent Edition of Test Manual, User's Guide, Etc.: Technical Manual, 2000; Program Handbook 2000; Administrator's Manual, 2000; Planning Guide for Students and Parents, 2000; PLAN Action Guide: A Handbook for PLAN Administrators, 2000: Maintaining the Content Validity of ACT's Educational Achievement Tests, 1998; Technical Manual: Revised Unisex Edition of the ACT Interest Inventory (UNIACT), 1995.

Languages in Which Available: English only

Time: Actual Test Time: 115 minutes.
   Total Administration Time: 135 minutes for test section plus 50 minutes for nontest
   sections.

Norm Group(s) on Which Scores Are Based: Nationally representative samples (1992) of 13,400 8th, 10th, and 12th graders in 145 schools for UNIACT. Nationally representative sample (1999) of over 7,400 10th grade students in public and private schools for the academic tests.

Manner in Which Results Are Reported for Individuals
   Types of Scores: World-of-Work Map career areas, regions, and cluster (Holland type) stanines for UNIACT. Scale Score (1-32) for each knowledge and skill area, plus a percentile band. Composite score, which is the average of the four ability test scores. Estimated ACT Assessment composite score range. Individual responses to each ability test items are reported and compared with the correct answer.
   Report Format/Content:
   Basic Service: Two copies of a two-page Student Report, including color highlighting of UNIACT results on World-of-Work map graphic and career areas. The High School list Report includes self-reported career plans, self-reported educational plans for high school and beyond, scale scores, and both national and local percentile score. Student Score Label

includes standard and percentile scores and subscores for ability tests. Early Intervention Roosters help identify students needing extra attention.

Report Format/Content for Group Summaries:
  Basic Service: School and District Profile Summary Reports provide aggregated data for each academic test, educational plans, career preferences, and post-graduation educational aspirations.
  Options: Item-Response Summary Report ; Standards for Transition Information Services (links to curriculum); Customized Profile Summary Reports (provides scoring information for selected subgroups); School and District Presentation Packets (like school summary report, but includes graphics and three-year trends; Data Tape, Data Diskette.

Scoring
  Machine Scoring Service:
    Cost of basic service per counselee: $8.25.
    Cost of options: Item Response Summary Report, $80 plus $5.25/school if more than one; Customized Profile Summary Report, $38 per subgroup; District Summary Report and Presentation Packet, $80 plus $5.25/school; Data Tape, $58; Data Diskette, $38; Standards for Transition Reports, $75 per set plus $5.25 if more than one; Customized Standards for Transition Reports, $50 per group.
    Time required for scoring and returning (maximum): 20 working days.
  Hand Scoring: Not available.
  Local Machine Scoring: Not available.

Computer Software Options Available: Not available.

Cost of Materials:
  Specimen Set: Selected items available at no cost.
  Counselee Materials: No cost for counselee materials when shipped. Their cost is included in the fee for scoring. None of the counselee materials are reusable.

Published Reviews:

Blackwell, M. (1995). Review of the PLAN. In J.C. Conoley and J.C. Impara (Eds.), *Twelfth mental measurements yearbook* (pp. 778-780). Lincoln, NE: Buros Institute, University of Nebraska-Lincoln.

Henning-Stout, M. (1995). Review of the PLAN. In J.C. Conoley and J.C. Impara (Eds.), *Twelfth mental measurements yearbook* (pp. 780-782). Lincoln, NE: Buros Institute, University of Nebraska-Lincoln.

Reviewed by

Patricia Henderson
Director of Guidance
Northside Independent School District
San Antonio, Texas

Description

EXPLORE and PLAN are two educational programs in American College Testing's (ACT) sequential Educational Planning Assessment System (EPAS). EXPLORE is developed for use in the 8th grade, PLAN for the 10th grade. The other programs in the system are the ACT Assessment and Work Keys, both developed for use in the 12th grade. The assessment-based programs provide information to students about their educational development in combination with information about their career interests. Support materials also are provided that help counselors, teachers and school administrators help students and their parents relate that information not only to each other but also to support decisions for the "next steps" in their lives.

The standardized, multiple-choice tests assess developmentally appropriate learned knowledge and thinking skills, such as problem-solving, grasping implied meanings, drawing inferences, evaluating ideas, and making judgments. In combination with UNIACT-R, ACT's career interest inventory, they provide students with links to the World-of-Work Map and to DISCOVER, ACT's computer-based career information and guidance system. The tests are designed to assess the educational development levels of all students in the context of their self-reported educational experiences and plans. They also report students' assessment of their needs for more/other assistance.

EXPLORE was introduced in the early 1990s. The PLAN is based on the P-ACT+, first introduced in the 1980s. Both are revised and updated continuously. The UNIACT was first published in 1971 and was most recently revised in 1989.

EXPLORE and PLAN were developed after a 1992 analysis of national curricula in four content areas: English, Math, Reading, and Science Reasoning. The studies were accomplished through review of state-published objectives for instruction and approved textbooks, consultation with practicing educators, and staff research. The tests are curriculum based, but are not course specific and were developed following standard practices for test development. The UNIACT-R measures students' career interests and those results, along with students' current career choice information are reported to lead students to career exploration via the World-of-Work Map. This map groups occupations in 23 career families grouped into six career clusters.

The standardized assessment component of both the EXPLORE and PLAN programs include four tests: English, Math, Reading, and Science Reasoning. Each is briefly described next.

The English tests consist of four prose passages. EXPLORE has 40 items related to the passages, PLAN has 50. Students' understanding of the Usage/Mechanics conventions of standard written English (punctuation, grammar and usage, and sentence structure), and of Rhetorical Skills (strategy, organization, and style) are measured. The items call for passage analysis rather than rote recall of rules of grammar. Items reference underlined portions of the passages and offer several change options, including "No Change."

The Math tests consist of problems, EXPLORE has 30; PLAN, 40. The tests measure students' math achievement levels, emphasizing solution of practical quantitative problems and quantitative reasoning rather than memorization of formulas, techniques, or computational skills. EXPLORE includes problems from pre-algebra, elementary algebra, geometry, and statistics/probability. PLAN presents problems drawn from pre-algebra, elementary algebra, coordinate geometry, and plane geometry. Calculators are permitted as appropriate in taking the PLAN.

The Reading tests present three prose passages. On the EXPLORE, 10 items relate to the content and meaning of the passages; on the PLAN, 25. The subject matter is drawn from fiction, the humanities, and social sciences. All the information needed by examinees is provided, and is not reliant on prior learning. The assessments measure students' levels of reading comprehension by referring to what's explicitly stated, and reasoning to determine implications, make comparisons and generalizations, and draw conclusions.

The EXPLORE Science Reasoning Test presents 6 passages and 28 items; the PLAN, 5 passages and 30 items. Students respond to multiple-choice items regarding their recognition and understanding of information provided in different formats: data representation (graphs, tables, other schematic figures), research summaries (experiment descriptions), and conflicting viewpoints. Examinees are asked to examine relationships between the information provided and the conclusions drawn or hypotheses developed, to generalize from the information to gain new information, or to draw conclusions or make predictions. Some items are drawn from materials from the content areas of biology, earth/space sciences, chemistry or physics, but students are not required to recall specific content.

Level 1 of the UNIACT-R is a 90-item inventory, useful for 8th through 12th grades. Ninth through 12th grade students initially wrote the items. Some examples are "Present information before a group," "Show children how to play a game or sport," "Write a movie script," "Draw cartoons." Inventory takers respond whether they "dislike," are "indifferent," or "like" such work-related activities. The activities are related to the six career cluster areas represented on the

World-of-Work Map: science, arts, social services, business operations, business contact, technical.

Use in Counseling

Since its inception in 1959, the guiding principles of ACT state that testing should inform "educational planning, career counseling, course planning and placement, instructional planning, program evaluation, and institutional planning" (ACT, 1998, p. 3). By including measures of educational development in combination with an inventory of career interests, EXPLORE and PLAN provide psychometrically sound means for helping students relate two dimensions of their development (educational and career) to the demands of a highly complex work world, and for facilitating their goal-setting and planning of educational routes to their future in that work world.

Students' reports detail their scores on the knowledge and skills assessments as national percentile ranks, and separately as percentiles of college-bound 10th graders. A composite PLAN score is estimated for EXPLORE takers, and a composite ACT Assessment score is estimated for PLAN takers. Students' PLAN reports also provide their Item Responses, so that specific goals may be targeted for their educational development.

In addition to the testing materials and reports, both programs provide support materials that assist school counselors, teachers, and administrators to implement an appropriate assessment process. Booklets are provided for students and parents to acquaint them with the tests and to help them make good use of the results: "It's Your Future! Student Guide to EXPLORE;" and for PLAN, "Planning Guide for Students and Parents." The latter includes a sample test and answer key. Both programs provide handbooks detailing information about the tests and the testing process. They also provide suggestions for pre- and post-testing activities, including ideas for interpreting students' test results.

Summary reports are provided, and an array of others is available for additional fees. These aggregated data are "potentially valuable information for curricular planning" (Blackwell, 1995, p. 778) if the test contents align with the school's curricula. It can provide externally developed measures for assessing schools' achievement of standards established by states and districts. ACT's "Standards for Transition," providing "Descriptions of the Skills and Knowledge Associated with EXPLORE/PLAN/ACT Assessment Scores," also make explicit the objectives of the assessment for assisting student preparation and for informing curriculum development and evaluation.

Because the UNIACT is a component of other ACT assessment-based programs counselors are enabled to assist students in tracking the development of their career interests over time. The inventory results stimulate students' career exploration and prime them for career guidance and research activities. With the

World-of-Work Map as a connector, guiding students from the assessments to use DISCOVER or some other source of career information is facilitated.

Technical Considerations

As a testing company ACT continuously strives for improvement of its products. Each assessment is grounded in strong initial and continuing research. Because EXPLORE, PLAN, and the UNIACT are standardized assessments used with large groups of students, the norms, reliability, and validity of the tests are well documented. In alignment with their endorsement of the "Code of Fair Testing Practices in Education" (Joint Committee on Testing Practices, 1988). ACT strives to ensure that each of its testing programs upholds the Code's standards for appropriate test development practice and use. They present the technical data for each program thoroughly.

To support their claims that EXPLORE and PLAN are tests for "every student," conscious efforts were made to use a nationally representative norming sample. The samples used to support the norming and scaling of the assessments were much larger than that required for statistical legitimacy. Possible underrepresentation of Blacks and Hispanics is noted, as is some discrepancy in the geographical regions of test-takers when compared to national demographics. These were compensated for by use of a statistically supported weighting procedure. PLAN is normed not only for all students, but also for "college-bound" students. Much work has been undertaken to ensure the gender fairness of the UNIACT. Although permission is granted to make modifications for students identified as having special educational needs, there were no disabled students in the norming populations.

Data are presented in the Technical Manuals that suggest reliability of EXPLORE's and PLAN's four academic area tests and for the composite scores, and across the test forms. The scaled scores were developed to have approximately constant standard errors of measurement– plus or minus 2 points for each test and 1 point for subtest scores at a 68% confidence level. There is evidence of a relationship between PLAN scores and ACT Assessment scores. Research has been done to support the estimated scores from EXPLORE to PLAN, and PLAN to the ACT Assessment. Evidence is provided of UNIACT's internal consistency, test-retest stability, and that supports the relationship between inventory results and score placements on the World-of-Work Map regions. Data are also presented that suggest UNIACT results are as reliable for minority group inventory takers as they are for Caucasian.

Research is presented to substantiate the content validity of EXPLORE and PLAN. Evidence is offered of the relationships between the test scores and the curricula of the four core subjects, between the test scores and students' grades in related courses, and between the test scores and students' overall grade point averages. Data support that there are distinctions between the contents of each of the tests. Content validity among the EPAS assessments is supported by evidence of the relationships between students' scores on more than one of the tests (e.g., between a student's EXPLORE and PLAN scores).

The validity of the placements of UNIACT scores on the World-of-Work Map has been established through analysis of thousands of jobs. There is substantial evidence of the criterion-related validity of the interest scales. Research also supports the value of the unisex scores, and that the constructs assessed for minorities are the same as those for nonminorities. Data also are provided of the lack of correlation between interest and ability measures, indicating that for meaningful career guidance both the interest and educational development measures should be used. The well-researched ACT/Holland hexagon provides the basis for the World-of-Work Map in establishing the relationship between individuals' work-related talents and temperaments and the requirements of specific occupations.

Computer-Based Version

The UNIACT can be taken online in DISCOVER. The EXPLORE and PLAN scores can be input into DISCOVER as ability measures. EXPLORE/PLAN, UNIACT, and DISCOVER all use the World-of-Work Map as the organizing construct of the work world. This provides a focus for supporting meaningful educational and career guidance of secondary school students.

Overall Critique

Strengths of EXPLORE and PLAN lie in the soundness of their development, in their links to curriculum and to each other, in their combining educational and career measures, and in the wealth of materials provided to support meaningful use of the test results.

The tests have been developed in accordance with solid practice. They are based on thorough initial research that led to relevant test content and statistical specifications. Formative evaluation and examination of anomalies result "in continuous creation of new items, item tryouts, item analysis, and new test booklets" (Blackwell, 1995, p. 778). Ongoing research regarding the meaning and relationships of scores augment the uses of the test results and provide for additional reports. The technical materials are written in user-friendly language and support responsible use of the tests by counselors.

The links to current secondary school curricula make the educational guidance and personal planning valid for students in most school systems in the United States. The best preparation for the tests by students is participation in academic course work. The educational assessments measure higher-order thinking skills, providing a different perspective on students' development than the assessments of rote memory. Information on students' educational development is useful not only to individual students, but also to the school system itself. In states with statewide curricula requirements and related test measures, correlation can be made between assessments. In some states, this provides opportunities for students to target learning goals that will enhance their performance on state tests.

The links between EXPLORE and PLAN provide longitudinal information for students, their counselors, and parents regarding their educational progress. Also longitudinal information provides feedback to teachers and administrators about individual students' development as well as about the school curricula. The link to the ACT Assessment allows for college-related goal-setting and educational planning.

With the emphasis on academics and the pursuit of further education and training after high school, the combination of educational and career information for students is a strength. Students' participation and persistence in schooling correlates with the relevance and seriousness of their career goals. In addition to providing a lynchpin for the educational-plus-career guidance approach, the World-of-Work Map provides logic for identification of career pathways.

The support materials encourage and make it easier for counselors to be responsible users of standardized tests. Activity sequences and plans are offered. Samples of written communications about the testing are provided.

EXPLORE and PLAN measure students' educational achievement and abilities. Given the history of PLAN's development, the best-supported application of its results is with college-bound students (Henning-Stout, 1995). The usefulness of EXPLORE/PLAN in career guidance is in the connection with the career interest inventory, the UNIACT. They do contribute information to student's anticipation of future levels of schooling. The career-related assessment measures students' interests, not their work-related aptitudes, values, temperament, or other factors important for individuals to consider in making career decisions. UNIACT does not predict success in a career pathway or placement.

Some cautions are offered about the application of the EXPLORE/PLAN scores. Because each of the four academic tests is scaled independently, the scores from one test (i.e., English, Reading, Math, or Science Reasoning) cannot be compared with the scores on the other tests. Although the score scales make the test results look similar, the scores from EXPLORE to PLAN cannot be directly compared. Rather, the estimated PLAN score is the means for relating the two.

Other weaknesses of the assessments relate to logistics. Although there is some support for the validity of self-reported data, the data provided about students' educational background and plans are self-reported. Counselors are encouraged to verify and/or update the information in working with students. The test administration is lengthy–over 3 hours. Suggestions are offered for breaking up the testing session. The cost of the assessments is more expensive than some other tests. Finally, the organizational structure of ACT makes large-system, cross-level ordering and servicing a bit awkward. For example, EXPLORE and PLAN are separated in the ACT, Inc. organizational structure, resulting in some differences in their ordering procedures and provision of services. The ACT staff members are accommodating.

EXPLORE and PLAN plus UNIACT facilitate implementation of a combined approach to career and educational guidance. Their links through the World-of-Work Map to DISCOVER support a series of activities necessary to provide systematic, developmentally appropriate assistance to students as they strive to set individualized goals and implement plans for achieving them.

References
American College Testing. (1995). *Technical manual: Revised unisex edition of the ACT interest inventory (UNIACT)*. Iowa City, IA: Author.

American College Testing. (1997). *EXPLORE technical manual.* Iowa City, IA: Author.

American College Testing. (1998). EPAS: ACT's educational planning and assessment system. Maintaining the content validity of ACT's educational achievement tests. Iowa City, IA: Author.

American College Testing. (1999). *PLAN technical manual.* Iowa City, IA: Author.

Blackwell, M. C. (1995). Review of *the PLAN.* In J. C. Conoley & J. C. Impara (Eds.). *The twelfth mental measurements yearbook.* Lincoln, NE: Buros Institute, University of Nebraska-Lincoln.

Henning-Stout, M. (1995). Review of the PLAN. J. C. Conoley & J. C. Impara (Eds.). *The twelfth mental measurements yearbook.* Lincoln, NE: The Buros Institute, University of Nebraska-Lincoln.

Joint Committee on Testing Practices (1988). *Code of fair testing practices in education.* Washington, DC:. American Psychological Association.

Occupational Aptitude Survey and Interest Schedule Second Edition (OASIS-2)

Randall M. Parker
PRO-ED, Inc.
8700 Creek Boulevard
Austin, TX 78757-6897
www.proedinc.com

Target Population: Grades 8-12 who have disabilities, do not have disabilities, or are disadvantaged.

Statement of the Purpose of the Instrument: The OASIS-2 Aptitude Survey was developed to assist students in their career search by providing them with information regarding their relative strengths in several aptitude areas related to the world of work. The OASIS-2 Interest schedule was developed to assist students in self-exploration, and career development.

Titles of Subtests, Scales, Scores Provided: The Aptitude Survey consists of five subtests: Vocabulary, Computation, Spatial Relations, Word Comparison, and Making Marks. A sixth score, obtained by summing the raw scores of Vocabulary and Computation subtests, measures General Ability. The Interest Schedule is composed of 240 items scored on a three-point scale anchored by the terms *like, neutral, and dislike.* Each item is assigned to one of 12 scales. Of the 20 items for each scale 10 are occupational titles (e.g., "Chemist"), and 10 are job activities (e.g., "develop new chemical products"). The 12 scores are Artistic, Scientific, Nature, Protective, Mechanical, Industrial, Business Detail, Selling, Accommodating, Humanitarian, Leading-Influencing, and Physical Performing.

Forms and Levels Available, with Dates of Publication/Revision of Each: There is only one form of both instruments available. The second edition was published in 1991.

Date of Most Recent Edition of Test Manual, User's Guide, Etc.: 1991

Languages in Which Available: English only

Time: Actual Test Time: The following time limits are applied to subtest administration of the Aptitude Survey: Vocabulary-9 minutes, Computation-12 minutes, Spatial Relations-8 minutes, Word Comparison-5 minutes, and Making Marks-30 seconds. No time limits are imposed in administration of the Interest Schedule.

Norm Group(s) on Which Scores Are Based: The present norm group consists of 1,505 students in 8th-12th grades residing in 13 states. The norm group is representative of the nation based on U.S. census data.

Manner in Which Results Are Reported for Individuals : The Aptitude Survey and Interest Schedule employ three kinds of scores: raw scores, percentiles, and stanines.

Report Format/Content: The Aptitude Survey and Interest Schedules can be hand or machine scored. The Student Profile details the raw scores, percentiles, and stanines in table and profile formats. An interpretation workbook is available to help students understand their scores and help them find specific job titles to be considered in career planning.

Report Format/Content for Group Summaries: Not available.

Scoring
Machine Scoring Service:
Cost of basic service per counselee: Cost included in purchase price. A printed report is returned.
Time required for scoring and returning: examiner must check answer sheets for completeness; returned approximately two weeks after receipt by PRO-ED, Inc.
Hand Scoring:
Scored by: Examiner.
Time required for scoring: Aptitude Survey—3-5 minutes per student; Interest Schedule—3-5 minutes per student.
Local Machine Scoring: Not available.

Computer Software Options Available: Not available.

Cost of Materials:
Specimen Set: $49 for Aptitude Survey or Interest Schedule (Examiner's manual, Student Test Booklet and protocols).
Counselee Materials:
OASIS-2 Aptitude Survey Complete Kit $144 (Examiner's manual, 10 Student Test Booklets 50 hand-scorable Answer Sheets, one sample Interpretation Workbook, and 50 Profile Sheets, all in a sturdy storage box).
OASIS-2 Interest Schedule Complete Kit $144 (Examiner's manual, 25 Student Test Booklets, 50 hand-scorable Answer Sheets, one sample Interpretation Workbook, and 50 Scoring Forms, all in a sturdy storage box).
Machine-scorable Answer Sheets $44 for 10.
Student Test booklets are reusable.

Additional Comments of Interest to Users: Data are being gathered to extend the norms to age 25; available in 2000.

Published Reviews:
Barnes, L. B. (1995). Review of the Occupational Aptitude Survey and Interest Schedule-Second Edition: Aptitude Survey. In J. C. Conoley & J. C. Impara (Eds.), *Twelfth mental measurements yearbook*. (pp. 698-699). Lincoln, NE: Buros Institute, University of Nebraska-Lincoln.
Dinero, T. E. (1995). Review of the Occupational Aptitude Survey and Interest Schedule-Second Edition: Aptitude Survey. In J. C. Conoley & J. C. Impara (Eds.), *Twelfth mental measurements yearbook* (pp. 698-699). Lincoln, NE: Buros Institute, University of Nebraska-Lincoln.

Reviewed by

Robert J. Miller
Professor of Special Education

Candice Hollingsead
Assistant Professor of Special Education
Minnesota State University, Mankato

Description

The Occupational Aptitude Survey and Interest Schedule: Second Edition (OASIS-2) is made of two separate components designed to assist students in grades 8-12 engaging in career research including self-exploration, vocational exploration, and career development. The components of the OASIS-2 are the Aptitude Survey (AS) and the Interest Schedule (IS).

The OASIS-2 Aptitude Survey, provides "a purposeful search and inventory of one's capacities, interests, and experiences" and provides the subject with "information regarding their relative strengths in several aptitude areas related to the world of work" (Parker, 1991a, pp. 1-2). The OASIS-2 AS, contains six subtest and yields six different scores. The total completion time limit is 35 minutes. The six subtests include–

- *Vocabulary* consists of 40 items. Each item in multiple-choice format contains a list of four words, two of which are synonyms or antonyms. Subjects are to find the "two words that have the same or opposite meanings." This subtest is timed at nine minutes.

- *Computation* consists of 30 items in multiple-choice format with five alternatives each. Subjects are to "work in their head or on scratch paper" the answer to numerical arithmetic and algebra problems. This subtest is timed at 12 minutes.

- *Spatial Relations* holds 20 multiple-choice items requiring visualization and comparison skills of two dimensional figures. The subject is asked to inspect and determine which one of the four figures presented can be constructed from the two-dimensional object. This subtest is timed at eight minutes.

- *Word Comparison*, the largest of the subtests, contains 100 items. Presentation per item is two sets of symbols. The response format is multiple-choice. The subject must determine if the presented two sets (words, numbers, or nonsense syllables) are different or the same. The subtest is timed at five minutes.

- *Making Marks* is divided into 2 sections of 30 seconds each. Subjects have an opportunity to draw a three-line asterisk in a series of 160 boxes as quickly as possible. This subtest measures how quickly the subject can make marks in a square. The subtest is timed at 60 seconds (one minute).
- *General Ability* is a summation of vocabulary and computation raw scores.

The individual administering the OASIS-2 AS should be trained and experienced in managing a standardized testing process efficiently. The Examiner's Manual states the instrument can be administered to groups or individuals. If administration is in a group, the ratio of one staff person for every 30 students is recommended. Each subject should be given sharpened pencils, scratch paper, student test book, and student answer sheet. The administrator will need a stop watch. Directions for administration specifically state "students are not allowed to use dictionaries, calculators, or other aids" during testing. The OASIS-2 AS may be hand or machine scored. Hand scoring requires 3-5 minutes per student answer sheet.

The Interest Schedule (OASIS-2 IS) is a vocational interest inventory. The information generated by completing the inventory is intended to be the basis on which students can explore realistic, systematic, and meaningful decisions about themselves and their futures. The OASIS-2 IS is not designed to predict the occupations that students should or will select in adult life.

This instrument consists of 240 items with each item assigned to one of 12 scales and each scale made up of 20 items. The 12 scales are Artistic, Scientific, Nature, Protective, Mechanical, Industrial, Business Detail, Selling, Accommodating, Humanitarian, Leading-Influencing, and Physical Performing. Subjects answer the 240 items regarding their likes and dislikes including 120 occupational titles and 120 short statements describing job activities. Three-choice response options for the individual include like (L), neutral (N), and dislike (D). Subjects are to read the occupational title or job description from the student booklet and fill in their corresponding answer on a student answer sheet.

The OASIS-2 IS is untimed and simple to administer, and most students can finish it in approximately 30 minutes. The manual suggests a ratio of 1 proctor to 30 student as desirable for administration and also suggests that the proctor should feel free to define words and explain terminology. The IS can be machine or hand scored. It will take between 3 and 5 minutes per student for the examiner to hand score and record the IS results.

Use in Counseling

With both the OASIS-2 AS and IS, the test manuals provide norm tables to convert raw scores to percentile and stanine scores. In addition, both test manuals provide the test administrator with steps for interpretation of test results.

These steps for interpretation provide a solid and structured format for presenting results to students.

The OASIS-2 is a career awareness and exploration instrument. As such, it "does not predict the occupations students will or should select for their life's work" (Parker, 1991b, p. 1). The OASIS-2 is well designed to assist 8th- through 12th-grade students in exploring their aptitudes and career interests as well as providing them with the opportunity to examine the relationship between personal aptitude and career choice. Use of OASIS-2 is enhanced through the *Interpretation Workbook,* which provides subjects the opportunity to match their interests and abilities to profiles of specific careers within varying occupational clusters.

The authors of this review believe the OASIS AS and IS to be particularly valuable tools in early career exploration for both general education students and students with special education needs at the middle school, junior high school, or early senior high school levels. These tests could easily be included as a portion of a career exploration unit in either English or social studies classes. The results of the OASIS-2 AS and IS could be enhanced with the use of community-based career exploration as a follow-up to completion of the OASIS-2. For example, a half day community-based career exploration activity could be based on the results of the OASIS-2 testing. Subjects could visit a job of interest and write a report exploring what they learned about the career option as well as what they learned about themselves during the career shadowing event.

The OASIS-2 is well suited to help special education personnel to develop Individual Educational Program (IEP) goals in the area of transition planning to specifically address the requirement for assessment of each student in the area of jobs and job training. The *Individuals with Disabilities Education Act* (IDEA) amendments of 1997 require assessment of the transition needs of each student with a disability to begin no later than age 14. Certainly, OASIS-2 is a valuable tool in addressing the transition assessment requirements as outlined in federal law. Finally, when administering these tests, special consideration should be provided students with low reading ability, visual limitations, learning disabilities, or limited English proficiency.

Technical Considerations
The norm group for the second edition of the OASIS- 2 has been expanded to 1,505 students in 8th through 12th grade. This norm group resides in 13 states and is representative of US census data for region of the country in which the sample resides, as well as gender, race, domicile, and grade level. The first edition of the OASIS AS (1983) included norms separated by gender and grade levels. However, since no statistically significant difference between gender and grade groups was evidenced, the second edition of the AS provides only total norm groups of males/females in 8th through 12th grades.

Norm tables are presented differently in the OASIS-2 IS. Item-by-sex cross tabulations were computed for all 12 interest scales. Differences were identified between males and females on five scales. Males were found to have significantly higher mean scores on two scales, Mechanical and Physical Performing. Females obtained significantly higher scores on three scales: Business Detail, Accommodating, and Humanitarian. As a result of these sex differences, separate male-female norms were prepared for these five scales. The remaining seven scales are represented by total group norms only.

The OASIS-2 AS employed four types of reliability measures during development: alpha, split-half, alternate forms, and test-retest. The alpha reliabilities for the *Vocabulary* and *Computation* subtests, ranged from .87 to .92 with a .88 median and .82 to .88 with a median of .84, respectively. Split-half reliabilities on the *Spatial Relations* subtest ranged from .70 to .92 with a median coefficient of .78. Alternate-forms reliability was computed for the *Word Comparison* and *Making Marks* subtests. *Word Comparison* reliabilities ranged from .85 to .94 with a median of .90. *Making Marks* reliabilities ranged from .86 to .90 with a median coefficient of .89. Test-retest reliabilities were assessed for all AS subtests over a 2-week interval and found to have stability over time. These coefficients ranged from .76 to .94. All reliability coefficients ranged from .70 to .94, with a median coefficient of .86.

The Standard Error of Measurement (SEM) for use in interpreting the reliability of stanine scores is provided by subtest in the Examiner's Manual. Each subtest in the OASIS-2 AS has an individually calculated SEM. Subtest SEMs range from a low of .62 plus or minus one stanine to an high of .92 plus or minus one stanine. The OASIS-2 AS demonstrates adequate reliability for student self-exploration and career development activities.

For the OASIS - IS, alpha and test-retest reliability were employed. Alpha reliability was based on a sample of 260 students in grades 8, 9, and 12 as well as a sample of 177 males and females in grades 8-12. Alpha coefficients ranged from .78 to .94 for the 260 students and from .85 to .95 for the 177 students when grouped by sex. The test-retest reliability was based on a 2-week interval with a sample of 54 junior and senior high students for the 12 subscales, and ranged from .66 to .91. Alpha coefficients indicate that the IS has adequate internal reliability, and test-retest studies suggest the IS scales to be relatively stable over time.

The OASIS-2 AS directly addresses construct validity in terms of four types of evidence: (1) factor analysis, (2) internal consistency, (3) relationships with other tests, and (4) convergent/discriminant validation. Pearson correlations between the OASIS-2 AS five subtest scores demonstrated high relationship with the 12 General Aptitude Test Battery subtests scores (US Department of Labor, 1970). These correlations were mostly in the .80's range; the lowest being .61.

In examining OASIS-2 AS convergent validity evidence, the ITED (Feldt, Forsyth & Lindquist, 1979) and the GATB were used. All coefficients for the ITED, except the *Making Marks* subtest were statistically significant at the .001 level. Convergent validity was also examined between the OASIS-2 AS and the GATB, with coefficients ranging from .53 to .87. Overall, the information provided regarding validity appears adequate.

For the OASIS-2 IS, the discussion of test validity provided by the test manual focused on the construct-related validity of the instrument. Factor analysis was completed on the 12 interest factors of OASIS-2 IS from data on 1,221 junior and senior high students of both sexes as well as separate groups of males (N = 551), and females (N = 558). This principal component analysis indicated that the 12 components extracted could be identified as corresponding to one of the IS scales. Evidence of content validity was based upon the fact that the 120 items related to occupational titles and to job activities in the *Guide for Occupational Exploration* (Harrington & O'Shea, 1984). In addition, internal consistency coefficients were computed for each of the 12 scales with the preponderance (108 or 45%) failing in the .60s. This degree of internal consistency information generally supports the validity of the instrument. No attempt was made to provide evidence of predictive validity. Adding this information would seem to be appropriate as the scale is to be used as a vehicle for "vocational exploration and career development."

Overall Critique

The OASIS-2 contains several improvements over its initial version of 1983. Changes were instituted in order to implement reviewer recommendations and reflect new materials/research information (Hammill, Brown & Bryan, 1989). The goals of the Second Edition were as follows: (1) improve psychometric characteristics, (2) improve usability, and (3) clarify/emphasize purpose. These goals have been specifically addressed through the following modifications: reformatted test items in *Student Booklet* which are more readable, increased examples within the instructions, clarified item drawings in the *Spatial Relations* subtest of AS, improved items for readability, amended scoring options (machine scoring, newly formatted hand-score sheet), and strengthened interpretive information regarding scales and including new norm tables. In conclusion, OASIS-2 is a well-designed and well- researched aptitude survey and interest inventory. It is easy to administer, score, and interpret, and should be a valuable tool for vocational exploration and career development activities for students of junior and senior school age. These reviewers recommend the use of the instrument for these purposes.

References

Feldt, L., Forsyth, R., & Lindquist, E. (1979). *Iowa Tests of Educational Development: Manual for teachers, counselors, and examiners.* Chicago: Science Research Associates.

Hammill, D. D., Brown, L., & Bryant, B. R. (1989). *A consumer's guide to tests in print.* Austin, TX: PRO-ED.

Harrington, T. F., & O'Shea, A. S. (1984). *Guide for occupational exploration* (2nd ed.). Circle Pines, MN: National Forum Foundation.

Parker, R. M. (1991a). *OASIS-2: Aptitude Survey: Examiner's manual.* Austin, TX: PRO-ED.

Parker, R. M. (1991b). *OASIS-2 Interest Schedule: Examiner's manual.* Austin, TX: PRO-ED.

U.S. Department of Labor. (1970). *Manual for the USES General Aptitude Test Battery, Section III: Development.* Washington, DC: US Government Printing Office.

PESCO 2001

Chuck Loch, Charles Kass, and Joseph Kass
PESCO International
21 Paulding Street
Pleasantville, NY 10570
pesco@pesco.org
www.pesco.org

Target Population: 8th grade to college; all populations except TMRs

Statement of the Purpose of the Instrument: To screen applicants for employers, training programs, program placement, and counseling.

Titles of Subtests, Scales, Scores Provided: Reasoning, Math, Language-GED Levels, General, Verbal, Numerical, Spatial, Form, Clerical, Manual, Finger, Eye-Hand Foot, Color Discrimination, Motor Coordination, Vocational Interest, Learning Styles, Job Temperament, Work Ethics, Work Attitude.

Languages in Which Available: English, Spanish, Greek, and others under development.

Time: Actual Test Time: Vary from 2 minutes to 22 minutes.
Total Administration Time: Time is based on the groups of tests administered.

Norm Group(s) on Which Scores are Based: Junior high school, high school, employed worker, welfare, and vocational technical.

Manner in Which Results are Reported for Individuals: Automatic printouts.
  Types of Scores: Reports are produced by percentile—aptitude level, verbal labels.
  Report Format/Content:
    Basic Service: System provides more than 25 preformatted reports and allows for the creation of unlimited reports.

Scoring
  Machine Scoring Service: Self-scoring online.
    Time requested for scoring: Instant online.

Computer Software Options Available: Computerized adaptive administration; Standard administration online. Voice for test administration.
Ways in Which Computer Version Differs: All manipulative tests are linked to the computer. Local Area Network and Wide Area Network available Windows 95, 98, and NT.

Additional Comments of Interest to Users: Testing available via the Internet.

Published Reviews: None cited.

Reviewed by

Jay W. Rojewski
Professor of Occupational Studies
University of Georgia

Description

The PESCO 2001 ONLINE computer assessment system (http://www/pesco.org) is a comprehensive, integrated package that provides 13 timed and 4 untimed units for measuring reasoning, math, and language skills, 11 vocational aptitudes, learning styles, work attitudes, vocational interests, and work temperaments. The computer-based PESCO 2001 system incorporates many features of its predecessor, the System for Assessment and Group Evaluation (SAGE), but also provides new features that allow for greater flexibility, quicker and easier test administration, and results in more detailed client information.

Cognitive skills are measured with a revised version of the Cognitive and Conceptual Abilities Test (C-CAT). The revised C-CAT measures three content areas (Language, 13 passages, 3 questions per passage, 45 minutes; Math, 36 problems, 45 minutes; and Reasoning, 18 sets of steps, 2 questions each, 45 minutes) with three alternate and parallel forms available in each area. Examinees use a five-option multiple-choice format. Results provide three types of information: General Educational Development (GED) levels, U.S. Department of Labor Secretary's Commission on Achieving Necessary Skills (SCANS) levels and index skills, and grade-level equivalency bands. For each test, material from specific worker-related tasks is presented.

The Vocational Aptitude Battery (VAB) measures 11 aptitude factors. Five units are paper-pencil tests that have a multiple-choice response format (General, combined scores of the Verbal, Numerical, and Spatial units; Verbal, 30 problems, 20 minutes; Numerical, 30 problems, 20 minutes; Form Perception, 60 problems, 6 minutes; and Color Discrimination, 36 problems, 4 minutes). Five assessments are performance tests that require manipulative responses and use an external unit connected to the computer (Spatial Relations, 20 problems, 15 minutes; Motor Coordination, unlimited matches, 3 minutes; Finger Dexterity, unlimited assemblies, 3 minutes; Manual Dexterity, unlimited assemblies, 3 minutes; and Eye-Hand-Foot Coordination, unlimited matches, 3 minutes). One test, Clerical, has both paper-pencil and performance/manipulative components; four sections, 50 problems each (Number and Name Matching, Alphabetical and Numerical Sorting). The VAB results correspond to measures available in the *General Aptitude Test Battery* (GATB). Each aptitude is defined according to publications produced by the U.S. Department of Labor including the *Dictionary of Occupational Titles* and *Handbook for Analyzing Jobs*.

The CITE Learning Styles Inventory (45 items, untimed) measures preferred learning styles (visual, auditory, or kinesthetic), modes of expression (oral or written), and ways of learning and working (alone or in groups). Examples of items include "I would rather do schoolwork in the afternoon than in the morning" and "I can learn and remember more when I have hands-on experiences." Respondents indicate whether each statement is *most like me, somewhat like me, not much like me,* or *least like me.*

The Work Attitudes Assessment provides an indication of attitudes and beliefs about the world of work and knowledge of employer expectations. This assessment contains 30 full-color pictures with written narrative that portrays various work situations. An example scenario begins, "At lunch, a worker was very upset about something." A picture accompanies this narrative on the computer screen depicting the situation. Beneath the picture a statement declares, "When workers don't get what they want they should act upset." Level of agreement with this situation is recorded using a four-point Likert-type response format ranging from strongly disagree to strongly agree.

The Vocational Interest Inventory (VII) identifies vocational interests and experience. Interests are structured around the 12 interest areas described in the *Guide for Occupational Exploration* and published by the U.S. Department of Labor. The VII contains 144 full-color pictures that depict activities (e.g., writing a story), rather than specific jobs, to have broad appeal to those with and without work experience. Interests are based on activities that reflect current occupations and occupations projected to grow dramatically over the next decade. A four-point scale ranging from no interest to great interest indicates level of interest for each activity. Examples of VII items include "Repair cars or trucks" which reflects work in Interest Area 5—Mechanical, Work Group 5—Craft technology, Job Title—Automotive mechanic; and "Give people first aid" which is found in Interest Area 10—Humanitarian, Work Group 3—Child and adult care, Job Title—Paramedic. Twelve statements are used to indicate respondents' experience with the major interest areas, e.g., artistic, scientific, or selling. Levels of experience are indicated on a four-point scale ranging from never to often. The VII is an untimed test, although the publisher estimates that 30-40 minutes are generally required.

The Temperament Factor Assessment (TFA) inventories personality traits with the same 11 temperament factors used by the U.S. Department of Labor to describe the adaptability requirements for workers in specific work situations, i.e., Worker Trait Groups. The TFA is untimed and contains 99 different picture scenarios displayed on the computer screen that depict various aspects of work, e.g., "When I work, I like to have instructions in front of me or firmly in my mind." A true/false response format is used.

The PESCO 2001 system is compatible with DOS, Windows 95™, and Windows NT™ operating systems. Assessment can be administered individually or with multiple users in both local-area and wide-area networks. The entire assessment battery can be taken in a single administration or in sections. Bookmarking allows open entry and open exit to any assessment. The system will automatically close a test on request and record the time expended on the test, the number and nature of each response, as well as the last question answered. When the test is resumed, the bookmarking feature allows users to continue where they left off. Use of the computer allows results to be immediately available. The PESCO system is currently available in both English and Spanish, but can be programmed for any language. A version of the assessment package that reads text is available for individuals with visual impairment or learning disability. Braille and large print versions of the assessment battery are also available. Noncomputerized versions of most PESCO assessments are available from its predecessor, the SAGE system.

Use in Counseling

The PESCO 2001 package includes several data management tools that users in high school or postsecondary education, vocational rehabilitation settings, and job training programs will find extremely helpful. A case management tool, Case Manager, allows users to maintain detailed profiles of their clients online, including intake information, eligibility determination, termination data, case notations, and other records. The Case Manager can track individual or group data and has the capacity of generating 40 predeveloped such as Individualized Education Plans (IEPs) and Individualized Written Rehabilitation Plans (IWRPs), or can generate customized reports.

Assessment results also interface with the JOBS (Job Opportunity-Based Search) Version V Matching and Placement Software system. The JOBS allows evaluators to compile an occupational profile for each test taker based on assessment results, e.g., work history, education, aptitudes, and interests. Work profiles can be compared to employment criteria compiled by the U.S. Department of Labor and matched with local education and employment opportunities. Customized reports can be developed that identify occupations that match the user's unique vocational profile.

Technical Considerations

Extensive information is available for each assessment unit that detail initial instrument development or revision, administration, and interpretation. Nationally representative norms are presented for comparison with locally developed norms. An impressive number of norm groups, including men and women with learning, physical, or mental disabilities, low IQ adolescents, high school students in vocational-technical programs, industrial workers, and normally functioning adults, are available.

The validity of the C-CAT appears adequate but users would benefit from additional information. Evidence of construct validity is lacking; specifically, information on how C-CAT results compare with independent measures of language, mathematics, and reasoning abilities would be especially helpful to define the constructs measured by the instrument. Internal reliability coefficients for the three C-CAT subtests are acceptable: Language forms, $r = .79$ to $.86$; Math forms, $r = .81$ to $.85$; and Reasoning forms, $r = .75$ to $.83$ (Loch, 1993a).

Technical manuals describe the actions taken to establish content and construct validity for the cognitive substests. Three types of validation were reported for the VAB. Construct validity was demonstrated through correlations with descriptive variables and IQ tests, as well as using correlations between separate VAB tests. Criterion validity was investigated through correlations with several criterion instruments: Strong positive correlations were reported between VAB and GATB tests requiring reading ability, $r \geq .75$; other tests revealed moderate correlations, $r \geq .44$. Estimates of test-retest reliability, $r = .60$ to $.91$, and internal consistency, $r = .57$ to $.93$, were generally acceptable for nonmanipulative tests (Loch, 1999).

The technical manual (Loch, 1993b) indicates that work to support the validity and reliability of the VII is "developmental." Complete data are promised in subsequent versions of the manual. Validity of the VII primarily relies on aspects of instrument development known to enhance validity, e.g., use of unambiguous objectives and performance domains, careful item sampling, and demonstrated relationships between instruments that measure similar constructs. The Interest Checklist (ICL) was used as a comparison instrument. Mediocre validity coefficients between the VII and ICL were reported, $r = .56$. Reliability is generally adequate with r values ranging from .69 to .88. Gender differences were also reported.

Overall, the TFA produced close agreement between individuals' TFA scores and the temperaments of occupations they were interested in and identified as being ideal. This finding supports the validity of the TFA as a measure of work temperament. However, anecdotal reports from VR counselors and job placement specialists are described in the technical manual that suggest a higher than expected incidence of temperament profiles containing a need for expressing personal feelings and a need to direct, plan or control work events. Individuals with emotional problems tend to report a greater need for stress-free environments then other respondents. As a result, Loch (Pesco International, 1992), recommends cautious interpretation of results. Consistency analyses indicated a high degree of reliability for the TFA although recent reliability data were not reported.

Overall Critique

The PESCO 2001 system is an impressive computer-based assessment package that targets a diverse group of potential users, particularly adolescents and adults with disabilities or disadvantage. The system takes a sophisticated, high-end approach to assessing work-related aptitudes and skills. Clearly defined tasks associated with entry-level work situations at a variety of ability levels are used. In fact, the system offers a single solution for a variety of user requirements and situations. Despite some concerns with instrument validity, TFA and VII in particular, professionals in vocational rehabilitation facilities, career assessment centers, and job training/placement services should find PESCO 2001 a valuable assessment tool. The report generation and data collection and manipulation features are quite impressive and enhance the usefulness of this system. Use of available government data (e.g., *Dictionary of Occupational Titles, Worker Trait Groups, GED, SCANS, Handbook for Analyzing Jobs*, etc.) and direct ties to similar assessment batteries (e.g., GATB) are also positive features.

A CD-ROM demonstration disk is available from the publisher. The disk gives an overview of the entire assessment package and provides a very good idea of test presentation, report generation capabilities, and the overall potential of the system. An Internet-based version of the assessment is planned for release around the middle of 2000.

References

Loch, C. (1993a). *The new cognitive and conceptual abilities test (C-CAT): A preliminary development manual*. Pleasantville, NY: Pesco International.

Loch, C. (1993b). *The new vocational interest inventory (VII): A preliminary administrator's development manual*. Pleasantville, NY: Pesco International.

Loch, C. (1999). *A manual of research and norm studies*. Pleasantville, NY: Pesco International.

Pesco International. (1992). *The temperament factor assessment unit technical manual*. Pleasantville, NY: Author.

PSI Basic Skills Test (BST)

W. W. Ruch, A. N. Shub, S. M. Moinat, and D. A. Dye
Psychological Services, Inc.
100 W. Broadway, Suite 1100
Glendale, CA 91210
testinfo@psionline.com
www.psionline.com

Target Population: Prospective clerical, administrative, and customer service employees in business, industry and government.

Statement of the Purpose of the Instrument: To assess abilities and skills that are important for successful performance in clerical, administrative, and customer service jobs.

Titles of Subtests, Scales, Scores Provided: 15 separate tests that may be used in any combination, including:

> BST 1—Language Skills, BST 2—Reading Comprehension,
> BST 3—Vocabulary, BST 4—Computation, BST 5—Problem Solving,
> BST 6—Decision Making, BST 7—Following Oral Directions,
> BST 8—Following Written Directions, BST 9—Forms Checking,
> BST 10—Reasoning, BST 11—Classifying, BST 12-Coding,
> BST 13—Filing Names, BST 14—Filing Numbers,
> BST 15—Visual Speed & Accuracy.

Forms and Levels Available, with Dates of Publication/Revision of Each: Form A and Form B (1981); hand/template-scored and optically scanned versions available.

Date of Most Recent Edition of Test Manual, User's Guide, Etc.: Technical Manual (1985); Administrator's Guide (1982).

Languages in Which Available: English only.

Time: Actual Test Time: 1.5 to 10 minutes per test.

Norm Group(s) on Which Scores Are Based: Norms are available for 7 clerical/administrative job families and across clerical/administrative jobs.

Manner in Which Results Are Reported for Individuals:
    Types of Scores: Raw number correct and corrected-for-guessing scores; percentile scores may be derived from norm tables.

Report Format/Content for Group Summaries: Not available.

Scoring

Machine Scoring Service:

Cost of basic service per counselee: Machine scoring service available from publisher ($.50 per test per candidate plus $150 base charge).

Hand Scoring

Scored by: Clerk; Counselor.

Time required for scoring: One to two minutes per test, with template.

Local Machine Scoring: May be accomplished using an NCS scanner and ScanTools software (publisher provides scoring application written in ScanTools).

Computer Software Options Available: Computer-administered version of test is available; standard administration; 12 of 15 tests available in computer-based format (BST 2-Reading Comprehension, BST 6-Decision Making and BST 8-Following Oral Directions not presently available in computer-based format).

Cost of Materials:

Test booklets—per package of 25

1-19 Total Packages	$59.25	Scoring Keys	$12.50
20-199 Total Packages	$49.25	Administrator's Guide	$14.00
200-1,999 Total Packages	$40.50	Technical Manual	$21.25
2,000+ Total Packages	$36.25		

Specimen Set: $80.75 (includes 1 of each test, Technical Manual, and Administrator's Guide).

Additional Comments of Interest to Users: New scanning and scoring software is under development to provide custom battery scores and reports, along with other features.

Published Reviews:

Stahl, M.J. (1985). Review of PSI Basic Skills Tests for Business, Industry, and Government. In J. V. Mitchell, Jr. (Ed.) *Ninth mental measurements yearbook* (1238-1239). Lincoln, NE: Buros Institute, University of Nebraska Press.

Zedeck, S. (1985). Review of PSI Basic Skills Tests for Business, Industry, and Government. In J. V. Mitchell, Jr. (Ed.) *Ninth mental measurements yearbook* (1239-1240). Lincoln, NE: Buros Institute, University of Nebraska Press

Reviewed by

Bruce Thompson
Professor and Distinguished Research Scholar
Department of Educational Psychology
Texas A & M University

Description

The PSI Basic Skills Tests for Business, Industry, and Government (BST) battery consists of 20 brief and easily administered tests, including 16 paper-and-pencil tests measuring cognitive and perceptual abilities and 4 typing-performance tests. Most of the tests have five-minute time limits, whereas the longest time limit is 10 minutes.

The 20 tests in the battery are published separately and may be administered in essentially any combination, although test #17, the unscored practice typing test, would doubtless always and only be used in conjunction with one or more of the remaining three scored typing tests.

The 20 tests were designed to assess abilities and skills relevant to successful performance of 11 major categories of clerical work. These 11 task categories include skills in filing, communicating orally, making decisions, calculating and summarizing data, supervising, typing, bookkeeping, shipping, using shorthand, requisitioning, and operating machines. The test developers considered these skills relevant to seven clerical job families: general clerk, information clerk, administrative clerk, figure clerk, typist, bookkeeping clerk, and machine-operator clerk.

In addition to typing skills, the tests in the nontyping portion of the battery are purported to measure five skill areas: reasoning, perceptual speed, verbal comprehension, numerical ability, and memory. All the nontyping tests have a multiple-choice format with the numbers of choices varying across the tests. For example, some tests have a dichotomous response format (e.g., "same" vs "different", "correct" vs "incorrect"), some a trichotomous response format (e.g., "connect" vs "message", vs "hold"), and some have items with four or five choices. One typing test involves retyping text (i.e., straight copy). One test involves typing from handwritten corrections (i.e., revised copy). One typing test involves typing from handwritten copy.

These typing tests were developed two decades ago in an era predating modern microcomputers and word processing software. The typing tests might be conceptualized more generically as keyboarding tests. However, care would have to be taken in generalizing the application of these three tests even to a word processing environment evaluating only keyboarding skills, because the context of the application may itself directly affect score reliability and validity.

Use in Counseling

Many counseling clients who are seeking career guidance information are not destined for placement in jobs requiring college or even high school education. The 20 tests in this battery have considerable appeal for use in counseling, because they can be administered in so many different combinations, and because each of the 20 measures is easy to administer and administration times are so brief (i.e., 1.5 to 10 minutes).

The tests might be used as components in making any of three types of decisions: (1) selection, (2) placement, or (3 promotion. Test scores might also be useful in an arena now experiencing considerable emphasis: credentialing the specific skills of graduates from high schools or occupation-specific training programs.

Technical Considerations

The test norms are based on the third of three studies, involving a sample consisting of 2,013 clerical workers from 16 organizations across the nation. The norms provide percentile equivalents for raw scores on the various tests.

Unfortunately, the normative data were collected nearly two decades ago, in 1981. It is not clear that the norming data are sufficiently contemporary to be still useful. Of course, even if the norms were more recent, best practice would still be to develop local norms "so that comparisons are specifically related to the user's application" (Ruch, Weiner, McKillip & Dye, 1985, p. 65). However, local norms could be compared or used in conjunction with the published test norms, if the norms were more contemporary.

The technical manual for the test reports only reliability score estimates for a single sample of 1,932 respondents. The estimates are based on a single estimation theory: principal components communality coefficients as lower-bound estimates of score reliability (cf. Hetzel, 1996). This statistical approach provides a reliability estimate in the internal-consistency family; this family also includes more familiar coefficients such as KR-20 and coefficient alpha.

There is nothing intrinsically wrong with using this estimation theory for calculating score reliability. Of course, this is a somewhat rarely applied estimation theory, and the user might be more confident in results based on a variety of different approaches. Furthermore, it appears that an extra factor was extracted, which may have led to somewhat exaggerated reliability coefficients in the form of these communality coefficients.

Reliability is a property of scores, and *not* exclusively of tests (Thompson & Vacha-Haase, 2000). Score reliability varies across every variation of (1) sample composition and (2) sample variability (Crocker & Algina, 1986, p. 144). Thus, users of these tests should compute their own reliability estimates on an ongoing basis. Also, to be sure that the score characteristics described in the technical manual will generalize to their settings, users should carefully compare their own sample compositions and variabilities with those reported in the manual.

The test manual asserts that "an essential characteristic of all measuring instrument is validity" (Ruch, Weiner, McKillip & Dye, 1985, p. 17). However, validity focuses on the use of test scores, and *not* on the test *per se* (Joint Committee, 1994).

The technical manual reports 3 validity studies involving sample sizes ranging from 278 newly hired clerks from 7 participating organizations to 2,328 employees in clerical positions in 46 independent companies. All validity coefficients were adjusted for attenuation based on a generic premise that score reliabilities were all .60. This value was apparently selected based on an unrelated general personnel study.

The validity coefficients were all small (mean correlations ranging from .13 to .25), but tended to be in predicted directions. Statistical significance was used to evaluate the validity coefficients, even though the sample sizes tended to be large, thus rendering these statistical tests of limited utility (Thompson, 1994). Analyses of score fairness across gender and ethnic groups did not detect any noteworthy biases.

Overall Critique

The 20 elements of this basic skills battery have the appeal that they can be administered in myriad combinations, each appropriate for a given counselee. Each test also requires only a brief administration time.

The norms for the measure are somewhat outdated. As noted previously, these data were collected some two decades ago. Of course, total number of correct responses might be used as a score, and these still may be quite useful in characterizing the basic skills and potentials of counselees.

One analysis reported in the technical manual evaluated the utility of the battery. Based on this analysis, it was reported that a hiring "company would be expected to realize a gain in employee productivity of $31,080 in the first year from optimal use of the generic battery" (p. 56). However, the baseline for this comparison apparently was using no test or impressionistic information whatsoever.

In summary, the norms for the tests are somewhat dated, but responsible users would probably want to develop local norms anyway, so the practical impact of this limitation is mitigated. The primary appeal of the BST battery of 19 scored tests involves the flexibility with which they can be administered in so many various combinations, and the short administration times for the tests.

References

Crocker, L. M., & Algina, J. (1986). *Introduction to classical and modern test theory*. New York: Holt, Rinehart and Winston.

Hetzel, R. D. (1996). A primer on factor analysis with comments on analysis and interpretation patterns. In B. Thompson (Ed.). *Advances in social science methodology* (Vol. 4, pp. 175-206). Greenwich, CT: JAI Press.

Joint Committee on Standards for Educational Evaluation. (1994). *The program evaluation standards: How to assess evaluations of educational programs* (2nd ed.). Thousand Oaks, CA: Sage.

Ruch, W. W., Weiner, J. A., McKillip, R. H., & Dye, D. A. (1985). *Technical manual: PSI Basic Skills Tests for Business, Industry, and Government*. Glendale, CA: Psychological Services, Inc.

Thompson, B. (1994). Guidelines for authors. *Educational and Psychological Measurement, 54,* 837-847.

Thompson, B., & Vacha-Haase, T. (2000). Psychometrics is datametrics: The test is not reliable. *Educational and Psychological Measurement, 60,* 174-195.

Tests of Adult Basic Education (TABE)

CTB/McGraw-Hill
20 Ryan Ranch Road
Monterey, CA 93940-5703
800-538-9547
adult_assessment@ctb.com
www.ctb.com

Target Population: Adult students, including literacy and ABE instruction groups and GED, Workforce Development, Vocational/Technical Programs, and School-to-Work Programs. The test is suitable for ages 14.5 to adult and can be administered to individuals or groups.

Statement of the Purpose of the Instrument: The Tests of Adult Basic Education (TABE) is a series of norm-referenced tests designed to measure achievement of basic skills commonly found in adult basic education curricula and taught in instructional programs. TABE assesses adult functional literacy and basic skills. Over the years, the test series has been continually updated based on extensive research. TABE 7&8 is the most recent edition. In keeping with current thinking about instruction and assessment, TABE 7&8 is designed to assess skills in contexts that are of high interest to adults: life skills, work, and education.

Titles of Subtests, Scales, Scores Provided: *TABE 7&8 Complete Battery*: a battery of norm-referenced tests, yielding Total Reading, Total Math, Total Language, and Total Battery scores. Reading, Mathematics Computation, Applied Mathematics, Language, Spelling. *TABE 7&8 Survey*: a shortened version of the tests in the Complete Battery. Reading, Mathematics Computation, Applied Mathematics, Language, Spelling. *TABE Work-Related Foundation Skills:* Reading, Language, Math. *TABE Work-Related Problem Solving*: an assessment of problem-solving skills in work-related contexts Problem-solving Competencies: Define a problem; Examine a problem; Suggest solutions; Evaluate solutions.

TABE's objectives are fully integrated, providing a complete picture of adult performance. TABE provides both norm-referenced and competency-based information to help administrators evaluate individuals' abilities and plan for specific educational and training needs. Norm-referenced information is provided in the form of scale scores and various derived scores, including percentiles and grade equivalents. Criterion-referenced information is provided in the form of objectives mastery scores.

Forms and Levels Available, with Dates of Publication/Revision of Each: TABE 7&8: L (Literacy); E (Easy); M (Medium); D (Difficult); A (Advanced); 1994. TABE-WF: D (Difficult); Health; Trade/Technical; Business/Office; General; 1996.

Date of Most Recent Edition of Test Manual, User's Guide, Etc.: TABE 7&8 Examiner's Manuals 1994; TABE 7&8 User's Handbook, 1995; TABE 7&8 Technical Report, 1996; TABE 7&8 Norms Book, 1995; TABE-WF and TABE-PS Technical Report, 1996; TABE-WF Norms Book, 1995; TABE-PS Examiner's Manual/Scoring Guide, 1994.

Languages in Which Available: English: TABE 7&8, TABE-WF, and TABE-PS; Spanish: TABE Español (Levels E and M only).

Time: Actual Test Time: Locator Test: Reading, 18 min; Mathematics, 16 min; Language, 15 min. Complete Battery: Reading, 50 min; Mathematics Computation, 15 min; Applied Mathematics, 50 min; Language, 39 min; Spelling*, 10 min; Total: 2 hours, 44 min; Survey: Reading, 25 min; Math Comp, 9 min; Applied Mathematics, 25 min; Language, 18 min; Spelling, 10 min; total, 1 hour and 27 min.

The Spelling test is optional and does not contribute to the total Battery scores.

Total Administration Time: Administrators should allow 10 minutes for instruction, recording names on answer sheets, etc.

Norm Group(s) on Which Scores Are Based: The TABE norming sample includes four reference groups: (1) Students in ABE programs (3,724 participants); (2) Students in Vocational/Technical School programs (533 participants) (3) Correctional facility program participants (both adult and juvenile) (1542 participants); (4) College students (307 participants).

Manner in Which Results Are Reported for Individuals: TABE is not scored on a mainframe. Reports can be generated by CTB or locally using TestMate TABE (software developed and sold by CTB). Also, automatic scoring is available on TABE-PC.

Types of Scores: Norm-referenced information is provided in the form of scale scores and various derived scores, including percentiles and grade equivalents. Criterion-referenced information is provided in the form of objectives mastery scores.

Report Format/Content:

Basic Service: CTB's Basic Service Scoring for TABE includes a Class List Report. This report shows student names and the scores achieved on each area assessed. *Individual reports are available at the completion of TABE-PC, showing precisely how well the examinee did on each area taken during the testing session. Options:* CTB offers Comprehensive reporting Plans for TABE. These plans include Student

Multi-Referenced Reports and Student Prescriptive Reports in addition to the Class List Reports. Optional reports for TABE include a Class Group Report, Class Objectives Report, and Building/District Summary Report.

Report Format/Content for Group Summaries: Optional reports for groups who took TABE include a Class Group Report, Class Objectives Report, and Building/District Summary Report.

Scoring

Machine Scoring Service:

Cost of basic service per counselee: TABE 7&8 Locator Test, $3.24; TABE 7 & Complete Battery, $3.24; TABE 7&8 Survey, $3.24.

All scoring requires a minimum order of $125 plus transportation charges. Basic service scoring includes a Class List Report (CLR).

Cost of options: TABEScore—a cost-saving package to meet the needs of smaller trade and technical schools. This product allows users to pre-pay for scoring when they purchase answer sheets for TABE. Users can then submit answer documents to CTB for scoring one at a time, if necessary, instead of waiting to submit a $125 minimum scoring order. This service is available only in groupings of 50; $240/50 counselees.

Time required for scoring and returning: 21 days

Hand Scoring:

Scored by: Clerk; Counselor.

Time required for scoring: Scoring time varies depending on the method used. TestMate TABE automates scoring by combining TABE answer document with a scanner and local computer.

Local Machine Scoring:
When TABE is administered as TABE-PC, the software performs the scoring and provides immediate results. Provisions/conditions/equipment required: PC with MS -DOS version 6.0 or higher. TestMate TABE scanning, scoring and reporting. *TestMate TABE and TestMate TABE Prescriptions hardware recommendations*

Computer Software Options Available: Standard administration on stand alone or networked PCs.
Other: TestMate TABE: The TestMate TABE Prescriptions module saves administrators time and provides each student with the most appropriate individualized instruction possible. It automatically correlates student test answers with objectives and determines skills mastered, identifies appropriate materials that focus on the student's areas of need, and creates an individual study plan.

Ways in Which Computer Version Differs: TABE-PC yields objective-mastery data for competencies, as well as norm-referenced scores to help administrators diagnose, evaluate, and place adults in targeted education or employment programs.

TABE-PC can provide test results immediately following a test, eliminating errors that can come with handscoring or scanning. In addition, TABE-PC operates in stand alone or networked environments. TABE-PC allows answer choices to be scrambled, increasing test security.

Cost of Materials: All prices provided in this response are based on CTBs 2001 Assessment Products and Services Catalog.
   Specimen Set: TABE 7&8: $24.10; TABE-WF: $31.75; TABE-PS: $15.85
   Counselee Materials: TABE 7&8 Test Books (reusable) Each package of 25 Test Books includes an Examiner's Manual.

   Practice Activity/Locator Test ($44.15); L ($37.15);
   Complete Battery: ($79.00); Survey ($79.00)
   Handscorable SCOREZE Answer Sheets ($27.85 pkg/25).
   Scannable Answer Sheets for Use with TestMate Software package of 50.
   Locator ($22.65); Complete Battery ($43.55); Survey ($22.65).
   CompuScan 48-column Answer Sheet: (pkg/50)
   Practice Exercise/Locator Test ($22.65); Complete Battery ($43.55); Survey ($22.65)
   Scantron Standalone Answer Sheets (pkg/50) ($22.25).
   TABE 7&8 Scoring Stencils (reusable) ($15.35).
   Locator ($16.50); Complete Battery ($32.50/set); Survey ($16.50).
   TABE-WF Test Books (reusable) (pkg/25) includes an Examiner's Manual
   TABE-PS Test Materials
   Each package of Test Books contains 25 consumable test books and includes an Examiner's Manual/Scoring Guide ($47.80).

Published Reviews:

Beck, M.C. (1998). Review of the Tests of Basic Academic Skills. In J. C. Impara & B. S. Plake (Eds.), *Thirteenth mental measurements yearbook* (pp. 1080-1083). Lincoln, NE: Buros Institute, University of Nebraska-Lincoln.

Rogers, B.G. (1998). Review of the Tests of Basic Academic Skills. In J. C. Impara & B. S. Plake (Eds.), *Thirteenth mental measurements yearbook* (pp. 1083-1085). Lincoln, NE: Buros Institute, University of Nebraska-Lincoln.

Reviewed by

Bruce G. Rogers
Professor of Educational Research
University of Northern Iowa
Cedar Falls, IA

Description

The Tests of Adult Basic Education (TABE) were designed to measure achievement in the types of competencies that are likely to be encountered in basic education programs for adults. Those competencies are assessed in the content areas of Reading, Language, and Mathematics (Spelling is an optional area). These tests are indirect measures of the types of skills required to accomplish basic tasks commonly required in most occupations.

The TABE has been a widely used test battery in the field of adult assessment for several years. A significant characteristic of the battery is its division into two versions. The shorter Survey version is intended to provide global information, whereas the Complete Battery is designed to provide more specific diagnostic information. They can be used alone or together as a pretest and a posttest. Each version has the subtests mentioned above, with both norm-referenced interpretations and objective-based interpretations given to facilitate decision making. As stated in the Manual, the intent of the test is to evaluate "true skills in working with real-life test stimuli" by using examples such as written descriptions of job interviews and floor plans of houses.

Each subtest is available in four overlapping skill levels, namely, Easy, Medium, Difficult, and Advanced. Each skill level represents a range of two or three grade levels. (In addition, there is a Literacy level, which focuses on pre-reading and beginning reading skills.) A 50-item Locator test can be used as the initial instrument to obtain results that can be interpreted by the counselor, using a chart, to select the appropriate level of either the Survey version or the Complete Battery. The test can be administered with booklets and answer sheets (which can be hand scored or machine scored) or with a microcomputer (which can then score the responses). The booklets are easy to read. On each page, items are neatly arranged with adequate white space. The style and size of the print appear to be appropriate for the grade level.

Note: Portions of this review were adapted from the author's original review in *the Measurement and Evaluations in Counseling and Development with permission of the Association for Assessment in Counseling.*

Each subtest begins with one or two practice problems, which are followed by a series of multiple-choice questions. The Reading test emphasizes the construction of meaning by testing vocabulary, critical thinking skills, and the use of reference materials. Vocabulary is assessed by presenting words in the context of simple sentences and asking for the meaning. Other skills are tested with a sequence of interpretive exercises, each containing a reading passage followed by six or seven questions. Within each interpretive exercise, some of the questions are factual whereas others are inferential.

The Mathematics Computation test is designed to focus on the four basic operations applied to whole numbers and fractions. It is expected that the typical student will be able to do most of the problems with mental arithmetic; however, for some of the problems, students may want to use scratch paper. Of the five options given, one is "None of the above," a strategy designed to reduce guessing and encourage actual computation. Usually, the options are arranged in numerical order, but not always. Some test takers may find the exceptions to be distracting, hence, counselors might appreciate having a rationale in the Administrator's Manual or the Technical Manual. The Applied Mathematics test is focused upon concepts rather than computation.

The Language test presents several types of exercises; some require the identification of errors in grammar, punctuation, and capitalization, whereas others require comprehension in order to combine sentences properly. All of the exercises are intended to measure skills used in revising a piece of writing. The optional test, Spelling, presents a brief sentence with a missing word followed by four options showing variant spellings of the word. The ability to recognize irregular spelling is thus addressed.

Four types of manuals are available for uses of TABE: (1) *Examiner's Manual* (CTB\McGraw-Hill,1994) which provides basic information about TABE along with directions for administering the tests; (2) *Norm Booklet* (CTB/McGraw-Hill 1995a) which contains tables for converting raw scores to percentiles, grade equivalents, and stanines along with directions for using the tables; (3) *Technical Report* (CTB/McGraw-Hill 1996) which discusses the topics of validity, reliability, and norms along with other detailed information on the technical aspects of the test; and (4) *User's Handbook*, also called the *Coordinator's Manual*, (CTB/McGraw-Hill 1995b) which contains very detailed descriptions of the test materials and interpretive information. It provides sample items and information for preparing students to take the test.

Use in Counseling

The construction of the TABE reflects a professional approach toward the measurement of basic skills. Curriculum guides and textbooks were analyzed and educational experts were consulted. As is customary for tests of this type, content validity was the main consideration. Toward that goal, the test manual states that the items were designed to represent essential instructional objectives. The manual also states that the content was aligned toward the General Educational Development (GED) tests; but counselors could have more confidence in the alignment process if the technical manual contained data to substantiate the correspondence between the GED and the TABE.

The manuals for the tests show the level at which each objective is assessed. In addition, very detailed charts are given to show the correspondence between the items and the objectives. These will be found valuable to the counselor in evaluating the content validity. The use of the procedures appears to be consistent with professional test development. Since some of the steps in the test development process involved the analysis of data, it would be helpful to counselors to have a summary of the results of that data analysis.

For many educational tests, items are classified according to thinking skills. Users of TABE will see an example of this in the charts showing the items classified into six categories according to the Rankin-Hughes Framework of Thinking Skills. At all four levels of the tests, two patterns are evident. First, for both the Mathematics Computation and the Spelling subtests, the modal classification, Gather Information, is the lowest category. Second, for the Reading, Language subtests, and Applied Mathematics, the modal classification, Analyze Information, is the third category. These detailed classification charts provide useful evidence related to the content validity of the tests and show a professional approach by the publishers. This information can help the counselor interpret the scores.

Technical Considerations

The sample for the national norming study was drawn from institutions that offered some type of basic education program for adults. Although the sampling procedure could not technically be described as a random sampling procedure, it did seek for representativeness by involving over 400 institutions in 49 states. It would appear that users can be confident that the normative data reflect reasonable estimates of the abilities for the population of persons who enroll in basic education courses. Several types of derived scores are available to users, including national percentiles, stanines, and grade equivalents. For each of these, both proper uses and limitations are discussed. A scoring sheet is provided for criterion-referenced score interpretation. For each objective, the scores on the relevant items are added and the resulting sum is graded as Nonmastery, Partial Mastery, or Mastery. Information on how these gradations were determined was not found in the Technical Manual, but it would certainly be useful to counselors for the interpretation of the mastery scores.

Reliability data in the manuals consist of the internal consistency measures from a single administration of each test using Kuder-Richardson Formula 20 (KR20) values. Standard error of measurement values are generated as a function of the scale scores. The emphasis in the manual on the interpretation of score bands is commendable. However, the "Microcomputer-Produced Scoring Report" shows point estimates but not confidence intervals. Perhaps that option will become available in the future. It is generally considered desirable to also show evidence of reliability from parallel forms administered over a certain time period, but, as of yet, that information is not in the Technical Manual.

In addition to the discussion on content validity, counselors would appreciate evidence about criterion-related validity. For example, correlations with grades in basic education courses and correlations with GED scores would be useful information. Because previous reviewers have questioned whether TABE actually measures what adults need to know, finding relationships between TABE scores and job performance would also yield relevant information.

Recently, a series called the Work-Related Foundation Skills has been introduced, which uses examples and language appropriate to the workplace context, in four forms, namely, Health, Trade, Business, and General. The four forms were designed to be comparable in their content objectives, but there is no supporting evidence presented in the Manuals. The items are written at the level of grades 7 and 8, making them adaptable for a wide variety of adult education programs. Unfortunately, the Manual does not contain any empirical data to substantiate the differential validity of these tests. Counselors should carefully examine these tests before adopting them. This reviewer suggests being very cautious until the publisher produces evidence for the counselors to consider.

A Work-Related Problem-Solving form was developed in response to a perceived need for an "authentic performance assessment" using "constructed-responses." It requires written responses in the form of numbers, words, and simple sentences. It does not measure the basic skills contained in the other TABE tests, but rather measures steps in problem solving, including the skills of defining, examining, and evaluating solutions. Unfortunately, the counselor will be challenged to interpret the resulting scores, since the Manual does not contain any evidence for the validity of the scores. The reliability data have internal consistency, but since the constructed-responses must be evaluated by human scorers, there is a need for evidence of inter-rater reliability. The counselor will need to examine these items carefully and make a judgment about their validity. After examining the items, this reviewer suggests being very cautious and perhaps waiting until the publisher is able to produce appropriate evidence for perusal.

Overall Critique

The TABE series is a relatively new addition to the many existing achievement tests, because only recently have there been strong programs for teaching basic skills to adults. It therefore fills a definite need in our culture. The items are well written, the booklets have an attractive appearance and the manuals provide good explanations with directions for those who administer the tests. For scores on the subtests, the norm-referenced interpretations are supported by data from meaningful norm groups. The criterion-referenced scores might be useful for remedial work, but they would benefit from more empirical support. The evidence on reliability and validity is preliminary and should be expanded. Overall, this test is constructed in a professional manner. Those counselors who work with adults in basic skills courses should give careful consideration to adopting the Tests of Adult Basic Education (TABE) as part of their evaluation program, but this reviewer suggests that they be very cautious of the new forms of the test until supporting data are made available.

References

CTB/McGraw-Hill (1994). *Examiners manual.* Monterey, CA: Author.
CTB/McGraw-Hill (1995a). *Norm booklet.* Monterey, CA: Author.
CTB/McGraw-Hill (1995b). *User's handbook.* Monterey, CA: Author.
CTB/McGraw-Hill (1996). *Technical report.* Monterey, CA: Author.

Wonderlic Basic Skills Test (WBST)

Eliot R. Long, Victor S. Artese and Winifred L. Clonts
Wonderlic, Inc.
1795 North Butterfield Road
Libertyville, IL 60048-1380
Mike.callans@wonderlic.com
www.wonderlic.com

Target Population: High school students and adults.
Statement of the Purpose of the Instrument: Short form measure of adult language and math skills for job or school training readiness.

Titles of Subtests, Scales, Scores Provided: Subtests: Verbal Skills and Quantitative Skills; Scores: Test of Verbal Skills: (Word Knowledge, Sentence Construction, Information Retrieval, Total). Test of Quantitative Skills; (Explicit Problem Solving, Applied Problem Solving, Interpretive Problem Solving, Total), Composite score..

Forms and Levels Available, with Dates of Publication/Revision of Each: V1, V2, Q1, and Q2, 1994.

Date of Most Recent Edition of Test Manual, User's Guide, Etc.: 10/99

Languages in Which Available: English only.

Time: Actual Test Time: 20 minutes for each test.
      Total Administration Time: 5 minutes for each test.

Norm Group(s) on Which Scores Are Based: Students in high schools, junior colleges, vocational schools and adults in work settings (manufacturing, financial services, fast food services, oil drilling, truck assembly, highway/construction).

Manner in Which Results Are Reported for Individuals
   Types of Scores: Scale score, Percentile distribution, GED scale, grade level.
   Report Format/Content:
      Basic Service: Individual score report—Summary report.
      Options: Quarterly Reports.

Report Format/Content for Group Summaries:
   Basic Service: Alphabetical listing, date, test scores. Local vs. National norms

Scoring
   Machine Scoring Service:
      Cost of basic service per counselee: $55 per quarter
   Hand Scoring: Not available.

Computer Software Options Available: Paper-and-pencil administration—computer diskette scoring.

Cost of Materials:
    Specimen Set: Sample Tests: No charge.
    Counselee Materials:
    Verbal   pkg/25 $ 95
    Quantitative   pkg/25 $ 95
    Composite   pkg/25 $130

Published Reviews:
Donlon, T. F. (1988). Review of the Wonderlic Basic Skills Test. In J. C. Impara & B. S. Blake (Eds.), *Thirteenth mental measurements yearbook.* (pp.1137-1139). Lincoln, NE: Buros Institute, University of Nebraska-Lincoln.

Reviewed by

Gerald S. Hanna
Professor of Educational Psychology

Kenneth F. Hughey
Associate Professor of Counselor Education

Kansas State University

Description

    The Wonderlic Basic Skills Test (WBST) is a short, multiple-choice battery designed to measure job-related verbal and quantitative skills of teenagers and adults seeking entry-level employment or entering vocational training programs. It surveys those skills identified as necessary for jobs classified in the lower three levels of the six-level General Educational Development (GED) scales of the U.S. Department of Labor (DOL).

    Both forms of the WBST come in two booklets, the 50-item Test of Verbal Skills and the 45-item Test of Quantitative Skills. Both have 20-minute time limits. We agree with Donlon's (1998) assessment that each is attractively designed and presented in a clear layout. The questions are in ascending order of

---

Note: Portions of this review were adapted from the first author's original review in the *Thirteenth Mental Measurements Yearbook* with permission of the Buros Institute.

difficulty; examinees are informed of this and advised to attempt each question in order. Each test is composed of three subtests, called GED Levels 1, 2, and 3, presented in that order. Three subscores for each test, based on items across GED levels, are also reported.

As Donlon (1998) noted, the GED scores are referenced to a DOL system of describing job requirements in terms of levels on dimensions of Reasoning, Mathematics, and Language. The WBST Verbal and Quantitative scales parallel the DOL Language and Mathematics scales. As an example of their DOL use, Computer Operator is said to require Level 3 mastery in Verbal, and a Level 2 mastery in Quantitative (Donlon, 1998).

The computer-generated Individual Score Report compares the examinee's scores with the skill-level requirements in the specified job. In addition, it reports grade equivalent scores and GED skill levels achieved. Also reported, if scoring is performed by the Wonderlic Reporting Service, are percentile ranks comparing the examinee (a) with adults at work and (b) with those employed in the job in question. Although scoring is complex, owing to its reliance on Item Response Theory (IRT), it can be completed locally by means of a PC and the scoring software.

Use in Counseling

One major intended use of the WBST is to assist in career counseling. The instrument seems in general to be a practical route to a set of descriptions of work force personnel that are carefully based on a comprehensive and detailed content foundation that is logically related through expert judgment to GED levels (Donlon, 1998). These descriptions of clients, in terms of presumed requisites of success in a job being considered, seem high in potential for informing client career and educational decision making.

Another major use of the WBST concerns applicant selection. The comparisons of examinees with descriptions of work force personnel have obvious potential for selecting job applicants.

Donlon (1998) reported that he "took the test, but selected answers so that only every fourth item was answered correctly. This yielded a score, but the user was referred to a warning that the response pattern was 'significantly different than expected' and that 'Retesting this examinee may be appropriate.' This is an excellent feature" (p. 113). Along similar lines, we incorrectly answered a larger fraction of early items than later (more difficult) items. This, too, yielded a score with a warning concerning irregular patterning.

The test directions discourage wild guessing, but encourage intelligent guessing by indicating that, "In a test of this type, it is unlikely that pure guessing will help you. However, if you think you know the answer, but are not certain, mark that answer and move on." We tested the truth of the first statement with two simulations by omitting eight items in Form QS-1 and comparing the score with that obtained when all eight of these items were answered with chance-level likelihood of getting them correct (i.e, two right, six wrong). We repeated that latter by "missing" a different two of the eight. In each case, a higher score resulted from our simulation of disregarding the advice and guessing randomly with average luck than from following the advice and omitting such items. We are concerned about providing directions that, if followed, will have an adverse impact on scores.

Technical Considerations

The User's Manual (Long, Artese, & Cloud, 1996) provides age, gender, and race information for the developmental samples. However, the reference groups that were subsequently used to provide the various kinds of normative data are not described in enough detail to enable judging the extent to which they are representative of the respective national populations of students in school and adult workers.

Test-retest reliability coefficients are reported for same-form and for alternate-forms. Findings are reported for various time intervals. These coefficients range from .84 to .93 for the Test of Verbal Skills and from .83 to .91 for the Test of Quantitative Skills. Coefficient alphas ranging from .90 to .95 are also reported. The variety of kinds of reliability evidence is highly commendable; however, the samples in these reliability studies are not described in terms of means and standard deviations. Hence, these findings are difficult to interpret. On a positive note, the use of IRT enabled standard errors of measurement to vary with score level. This is a highly desirable, yet uncommon, feature of reporting.

The developmental history of the test, particularly, its linkage to the job and skill descriptions in the *Dictionary of Occupational Titles* (U.S. Department of Labor, 1991), seems appropriate and consistent with the test's purposes. In particular, the decision to focus test content on skills identified as job requirements (in contrast to curriculum taught) seems very sound. Test content appears to be appropriate for the instrument's purposes. Items are well written, varied, and balanced in both content and format. Moreover, they are clearly relevant to the world of work without being job specific, gender specific, or subculture specific. Content-related validity evidence is, therefore, judged very favorably.

The User's Manual (Long et al., 1996) commendably points out that the WBST does not assess all job-relevant attributes, only verbal and quantitative skills. Likewise, users are warned that it does not provide detailed diagnostic information.

Predictive validity studies are not reported in the manuals. Because this is the kind of validity evidence that would merit the most weight in judging the utility of the test, its continuing absence is unfortunate.

Confidence in the WBST would be enhanced by the presence of more construct-related validity evidence. Although grade-progression data support the instrument's validity, and a good, evidence-based discussion explains how item ordering minimized the impact of speededness, other kinds of construct-related evidence would be desirable. For example, reports of studies concerning test wiseness, sensitivity to coaching, context dependence, and discriminant validity of subscores would be appreciated.

Overall Critique

The WBST is a short instrument designed to assess selected areas of achievement as they apply to the workplace and to provide information to assist in career counseling. Although the User's Manual (Long et al., 1996) reports a sufficient amount and variety of reliability findings, information concerning variability of the reliability samples is needed for their informed interpretation. The WBST reflects a sophisticated developmental program that was based on a solid foundation of DOL research. Although other kinds of validity evidence would strengthen confidence in its utility, its content is judged very favorably.

References

Donlon, T. F. (1998). Review of the Wonderlic Basic Skills Test. In J. C. Impara & B. S. Plake (Eds.), *Thirteenth mental measurements yearbook* (pp. 1137-1139). Lincoln, NE: Buros Institute, University of Nebraska-Lincoln.

Long, E. R., Artese, V. S., & Cloud, W. L. (1996). *Wonderlic Basic Skills Test user's manual.* Libertyville, IL: Wonderlic, Inc.

U. S. Department of Labor. (1991). *Dictionary of occupational titles* (4th ed.). Washington, DC: U. S. Government Printing Office.

Work Keys®

ACT, Inc. Staff
ACT, INC.
P.O. Box 168
Iowa City, IA 52243
www.act.org

Target Population: Business and Education: Potential educational use may include identification of proficiency in the defined testing areas, identification of educational needs, program evaluation, certification, and guidance and counseling. Business uses may include identification of training needs, training program evaluation, certification, and screening of individuals to be hired, promoted or transferred. In short, the target population includes all persons in transition into or within the workforce. This includes those entering or reentering the workforce, and those changing jobs or functions within jobs.

Statement of the Purpose of the Instrument: Work Keys is a national system enabling education and business to work together to strengthen achievement of workplace skills. The system is designed to help:

- Businesses fulfill their needs for workplace skills in hiring and training
- Individuals document their workplace skills
- States and schools comply with assessment guidelines, particularly for school-to-work and Workforce development programs
- Institution meet Tech-Prep initiatives
- Assessment of generic workplace skills

Titles of Subtests, Scales, Scores Provided: Work Keys assessments are not a battery but a series of assessments of eight skills that may be used in various and mixed combinations as required for determining competency attainment of examinees:

- *Applied Mathematics* (uses calculator)–paper-and-pencil/multiple-choice response; 33 items
- *Applied Technology*–paper-and-pencil/multiple-choice response; 32 items.
- *Listening & Writing* (a single assessment with separate scoring)–audiotape presentation/ constructed response; 6 messages.
- *Locating Information*–paper-and-pencil/multiple-choice response; 38 items.
- *Observation*–videotape presentation/multiple-choice response; 2 parts, 36 items.
- *Reading for Information*–paper-and-pencil/multiple-choice response; 30 items.
- *Teamwork*–videotape presentation/multiple-choice response; 2 parts, 36 items.

Work Keys scoring and scaling are based upon the Item Response Theory (IRT), probabilistic version of the undimensional subject model. Each Work Keys skill assessment is organized into hierarchical levels of increasing complexity. In each assessment, the highest continuous level achieved is reported as the skill level attained by an examinee. The number of skill levels vary by the assessment: Reading for Information scores range from Level 3 to Level 7, whereas Writing scores range from Level 0 to Level 5.

Forms and Levels Available, with Dates of Publication/Revision of Each:
There are three forms for:

- *Applied Mathematics* (introduced 1992, new form introduced 2001)
- *Listening & Writing* (introduced 1992, new form introduced 1998)
- *Reading for Information* (introduced 1998, new form introduced 2001)
- *Locating Information* (introduced 1993, new form introduced 2001)

There are two forms for:

- *Applied Technology* (introduced 1993, new form planned for release early 2001)
- *Teamwork* (introduced 1993, new form released 2000)
- *Observation* (introduced 1995, new form planned for release in 2001)

The combined answer booklet (28 pages) will accommodate all multiple-choice assessments and two constructed response assessments.

Date of Most Recent Edition of Test Manual, User's Guide, Etc.: The Work Keys Score Interpretation Guides (updated in 2000) are produced for business and education users. Occupational Profiles Booklets and Job Skill Comparison Charts are also updated on a periodic basis. Related material for student preparation and curriculum, Targets for Instruction (which include a separate booklet for each of the eight skill areas) are updated annually. Guidance information resulting from national profiling of jobs was updated in 1999 and will be updated each year.

Languages in Which Available: English only*
Applied Mathematics, Applied Technology, Locating Information, and Reading for Information assessments should be available in Spanish in 2001.

Time: Actual Test Time: Each assessment requires different periods of time with the range being 40 to 60 minutes, with four of the tests requiring 45 minutes.

Norm Group(s) on Which Scores Are Based: The Work Keys assessments are criterion-referenced and provide a metric that describes the skill requirements for individual jobs in terms of levels of proficiency. Each individual's skills are measured with respect to the content being assessed and independent of the performance of other examinees.

Manner in Which Results Are Reported for Individuals: The Work Keys assessments are designed to measure individuals' proficiency with respect to the skills covered in each criterion-referenced assessment. Upon completion of the scoring process, a set of standard reports is generated and sent to the designated recipient. Optional reports are available for an additional fee.

Report Form/Content:
  Memo to Examinee: This report indicates the examinee's skill level for each assessment administered, along with descriptions of the tasks associated with each particular skill level achieved and some strategies the individual may use to improve performance in that skill. Two copies of this report are provided per examinee.

  Summary Report: This report includes the examinee's score along with a brief description of the achieved skill level for each assessment administered. The format of this report makes it suitable for the examinee to copy and attach to a job description. One copy of this report is provided per examinee.

Report Format/Content for Group Summaries:

> **Basic Service**: Standard Aggregate Reports: One copy of each report is provided per client order.
>
> *Examinee Roster Report:* Using one line per examinee, this report lists information for everyone included in that assessment administration. If reported by the examinee, gender and ethnic information are included, along with each examinee's name, identification number, and skill level scores for each assessment taken.
>
> *Chart Essay Reports:* Up to five separately titled subreports can be generated as summaries for each assessment administered. These subreports present scores by gender, ethnicity, program of study, and grade level. Subreports are only generated for categories that include five or more examinees. Each subreport is identified in its title and contains a table and a chart that displays the distribution of the scores across the groups of interest.
>
> *Vocational Information Reports:* At the test administration, examinees are asked to select from a given list one job they are most interested in and to indicate the job they currently have. This report presents the percentage of examinees indicating interest in particular jobs and employed in particular jobs. The number and percentage of examinees seeking employment or wanting help in obtaining a job are also included.

Scoring

> **Machine Scoring Service:**
>
> > *Time required for scoring and returning (maximum)*: Scoring is conducted at ACT headquarters with a 10-day turnaround. Rapid scoring services are available at extra cost.
>
> **Hand Scoring:**
>
> > The *Listening and Writing* assessments are read and scored at ACT headquarters in Iowa City, Iowa.
>
> **Local Machine Scoring:**
>
> > *Provisions/conditions/equipment required:* Local machine scoring and reporting is available through special arrangements with ACT.

Computer Software Options Available: Computer-based testing (CBT) is not available at the time of this review. Web-based and computer-administered versions of the objective assessments are under development. In late 2000, *Applied Mathematics, Applied Technology, Locating Information*, and *Reading for Information* will be available in CBT. *Teamwork* and Observation will be available in CBT in 2001.

Cost of Materials:

Although Work Keys assessment fees to educational institutions have changed only once to date (and that was a decrease in cost), the prices listed below are subject to change at any time. The fees listed below are the pries in effect from fall 2000 through summer 2001.

Educational institution fees charged at the time of scoring are: *Reading for Information* ($3.20 per examinee), *Applied Mathematics* ($3.20 per examinee), *Applied Technology* ($3.20 per examinee), *Observation* $6.00 per examinee), and *Listening & Writing* ($16 per set per examinee). One administrator manual is sent free per 25 examinees, with additional copies at $5 each.

> **Specimen set:** Please note that secure review of the Work keys assessments can be arranged based upon application. Please contact ACT at 800/WORKKEY (967-5539) and ask for extension 1083. Practice sample test items for each assessment are available on ACT's website www.act.org/workkey.

Additional Comments of Interest to Users: In addition to the Spanish versions of *Applied Mathematics, Applied Technology, Locating Information,* and *Reading for Information* assessments that should be available in 2001, three new Work Keys assessments are under development: *Basic Computer Skills, Work Habits,* and *Listening for Understanding. (Basic Computer Skills* and *Listening for Understanding* will be CBT only.) A projected availability date has not yet been determined.

Published Reviews:

Reimer, J. (January 26, 1996). *A review and critique of the Work Keys system.* Paper presented at the annual meeting of the Southwest Educational Research Association, New Orleans.
Scruggs, C. (1994). Work Keys Assessments. In J. Kapes, M. Mastie & E. A. Whitfield (Eds.). *A counselor's guide to career assessment instruments* (3rd ed.). Alexandria, VA: National Career Development Association.

Reviewed by

John Townsend
Research and Curriculum Unit
Mississippi State University
Starksville, Mississippi

Description

Work Keys is an integrated system, developed by American College Testing (ACT), Inc., that provides an interrelated structure to measure, document, and improve an individual's generic workplace skills. Generic skills are those skills that are not specific to a particular job, but rather provide a foundation for learning and performing well on most jobs. ACT consulted with employers, educators, and labor organizations to develop a list of generic workplace skills that are used in a wide range of jobs, are teachable in a reasonable period of time, and facilitate job analysis (McLarty and Vansickle, 1997). The list of foundational skill areas selected for development by ACT is related closely to those skills identified at about the same time by the Secretary's Commission on Achieving Necessary Skills (SCANS).

The Work Keys system consists of four components: assessments, job profiling, instructional support, and research and reporting. These interactive components are developed around the skill areas reflected in each of the eight current assessments: *Reading for Information, Applied Mathematics, Listening, Writing, Applied Technology, Locating Information, Teamwork,* and *Observation.* Each skill area is measured by an assessment that is criterion referenced and is constructed with a number of levels, with each successive level more complex than the previous one. The assessments present workplace situations, reading materials, problems, and messages for examinees to respond to and/or solve. Within an assessment, the situations and problems represent many different jobs, occupations, and workplaces. Examinees do not need prior job-specific knowledge to do well on an assessment (ACT, 1997a).

The assessments are presented in a variety of formats. *Applied Mathematics*, *Applied Technology*, *Locating Information*, and *Reading for Information* are each presented in a booklet format with multiple-choice questions or problems. *Observation* and *Teamwork* are each presented in a video-based format with multiple-choice questions or problems. Examinees write constructed responses to the *Listening* and *Writing* assessment, administered through the use of audiotape. The resulting responses to the *Listening* and *Writing* assessment are scored twice; once to indicate how well the individual captured, retained, and recorded the information presented, and once to indicate the writing skill level of the examinee (ACT, 1996, 1997a, 1997b).

The *Applied Mathematics* assessment measures skill in applying mathematical reasoning to work-related problems. The test questions require the individual to set up and solve the types of problems and do the types of calculations that occur in the workplace. The assessment encourages the use of a calculator, and a formula sheet that includes all formulas required for the assessment is provided. The assessment contains skill strands that traverse across five levels of complexity and build upon each other, incorporating the skills assessed at the preceding levels.

The *Applied Technology* assessment is designed to measure the examinee's skill in solving problems of a technological nature. The content covers the basic principles of mechanics, electricity, fluid dynamics, and thermodynamics as they apply to machines and equipment found in the workplace. The assessment is oriented toward reasoning rather than mathematics, and therefore, the emphasis is on identifying relevant aspects of problems, analyzing and ordering those aspects, and applying existing materials or methods to new situations.   The assessment contains questions at four levels of complexity.

The *Listening* and *Writing* assessments are commonly administered simultaneously but measure two distinct but related skills. The assessment is administered via an audiotape that contains all directions and messages, read by a variety of speakers. Each message is read twice, and time is given between readings to allow note taking. After a message is given the second time, examinees have a specific amount of time to write before the next message is given. The *Listening* score is based on the accuracy and completeness of the examinee's written response. It is not based on mechanics or writing style. The *Writing* score is based on the writing mechanics (such as sentence structure and grammar) and writing style used in the examinee's responses. It is not based on the accuracy and completeness of the information, though the responses must be related to the stimuli and convey the message clearly. Five levels of difficulty are defined in these assessments.

Locating Information measures the individual's skill in using information presented in workplace graphics such as diagrams, floor plans, tables, forms, graphs, charts, and instrument gauges. Examinees are asked to locate, insert, compare, and summarize information in one graphic or in a group of related graphics. There are four levels of difficulty in the assessment. At the highest level, examinees are asked to make decisions and draw conclusions based on information contained in one or more graphics.

The *Observation* assessment, utilizing scenarios on videotape as stimuli for response, measures the examinee's skill in paying attention to instructions and demonstrations, and in noticing details. When presented with increasingly complex situations, individuals are asked to pay careful attention to steps to be followed in a process, to safety procedures, and to quality control standards. As each of the four levels of complexity are presented, factors influencing the complexity of an observation task include how many variables the task involves, how strongly the examinee is directed to pay attention to certain details, and how many distractors (e.g., extraneous details) are present and how strong these distractors are.

Reading for Information measures an examinee's skill in reading and understanding work-related instructions and policies. Passages take the form of memos, bulletins, notices, letters, policy manuals, and governmental regulations. Because the assessment uses workplace texts, the assessment is more reflective of actual workplace conditions than expository and classical narrative texts. The reading materials and the related questions comprise five levels of complexity.

The *Teamwork* assessment was developed to measure the examinee's skill in choosing behaviors and/or actions that simultaneously support relationships with the team and lead toward the accomplishment of work tasks. The assessment uses videotape of 12 teamwork scenarios, each accompanied by three questions. Examinees must recognize the goals of the team and identify ways to accomplish those goals in increasingly complex situations. Examinees must identify the most appropriate teamwork responses to specific situations.

Use in Counseling

The Work Keys system is intended to integrate various components in order to link individuals, educators, and employers in a variety of mutually supportive arrangements. It is unique in that the skill scales relate all the components of the system to each other and provide a common language for employers and educators to use when talking about how to improve the American workforce. The components should ideally be used in conjunction with one another but they may be used individually. The components include job profiles, assessment, instructional support, and research and reporting.

Profiling uses job analysis to identify the skills and the levels of those skills needed for particular jobs or occupations. These profiles are classified and reported in ACT's *Work Keys Occupational Profiles* by job title, OES number, Holland type, and ACT job family. Utilization of the *Work Keys Occupational Profiles* book allows the individual to become informed about the generalizable workplace skills that they are likely to need in selected occupations.

The assessments provide information related to two sets of criteria: the independent skill scale and job profiles. First, the scores gained on the assessments provide timely feedback on the individual's progress in acquiring generic employability skills. The individual can readily identify strengths and weaknesses related to these external referents and work with the educational institution to improve his/her abilities within the skill area. Second, if related to the job profiles, the scores allow the possibility for the individual to compare assessment results with job requirements in a direct and intuitively comprehensible manner.

The Work Keys instructional support component provides guidance to instructors, curriculum developers, counselors, and others to assist them in helping learners improve their workplace skills. The basis of this component is a series of guides called *Targets for Instruction* (ACT, 1997c). Each guide presents detailed descriptions of a particular skill area and of the characteristics that distinguish that skill level, and adaptable materials, techniques, and activities.

Research and reports from ACT assist in the exchange of information between businesses and educational institutions. The information gathered from agencies, businesses, and individuals allows for information to be provided to the school and individual that help provide students with career guidance.

Technical Considerations

The Work Keys assessments are criterion-referenced measures of generic employability skills. Each Work Keys assessment has been built by first defining a hierarchical skill scale and then creating test items to be representative of both the skill area and each skill level within the skill area. Validity is ascertained for the assessments based upon the three-part model of validity: content validity, construct validity, and criterion-related validity (Guion, 1980).

Samples of 2,000 examinees were randomly drawn for each of the selected-response assessments with the exception of *Observation,* which had a total of 449 examinees available at the time of the study, so all were used. The selected-response assessments have the following numbers of items and coefficient alpha: *Applied Mathematics*, 30 items, 5 levels, alpha = .86; *Applied Technology*, 32 items, 4 levels, alpha = .80; *Locating Information*, 32 items, 4 levels, alpha = .77; *Observation*, 36 items, 4 levels, alpha = .72; *Reading for Information*, 30 items, 5 levels, alpha = .80; and *Teamwork*, 36 items, 4 levels, alpha = .74 (White, 1999).

For the constructed-response assessments, *Listening* and *Writing*, the reliability study was based in generalizability theory. ACT used operational data from 7,097 high school juniors and seniors in one state who all took the same test form. The two-step analysis (A and B) produced a correlation between the two tests at .52. For these studies, all dimensions were assumed to be random (White, 1999).

Computer-Based Version

At publication, no computer-based version was available. A systems-based and PC-based versions are scheduled for release in 2001.

Overall Critique

Work Keys system assessments were designed to meet the following criteria:

1. The way in which the generic skill is assessed is generally congruent with the way the skill is used in the workplace.
2. The lowest level assessed is at approximately the lowest level for which an employer would be interested in setting a standard.
3. The highest level assessed is at approximately the level beyond which specialized training would be required.
4. The steps between the lowest and highest levels are large enough to be distinguished and small enough to have practical value in documenting workplace skills.
5. The assessments are sufficiently reliable for high-stakes decision making.
6. The assessments can be validated against empirical criteria.

The assessments appear to meet these criteria. The greatest strength of Work Keys appears to be its direct linkage to generic work skills as identified by the business community. Because its profiling component and assessment component address the same skill scales, the system allows the possibility to aggregate skill profiles over both jobs and individuals. This allows guidance counselors to better evaluate individuals in relation to the workforce's needs and requirements for entrance. Because the assessment is criterion referenced, it provides an external referent that is consistent with the growing need for individuals to continue to learn on the job.

The major weakness of the Work Key system is just the reverse side of the same coin, because it is a system within which a lack of usage by any component weakens the overall effectiveness of the other components. For example, without utilization of the profiles, the assessment score often loses its impact on an individual as it refers to a referent (i.e., to a job or occupation). Because Work Keys uses such a different scale, many educational institutions and agencies do not understand how to utilize the scores. Many tests used by schools rate the examinee on a grade level. Work Keys does not, but simply and adequately states a particular skill level attained within a skill area. This requires the counselor to have a broader knowledge of the business community locally, and in general to better assist the client.

Overall, the Work Keys assessments are feasible with respect to administration time and complexity, as well as cost. The external referents, empirical job analysis, and assessment results can be used to guide individuals as they prepare for the workforce, educators and trainers as they assist in this preparation, and employers as they seek qualified applicants.

References

ACT, Inc. (1995). *Targets for instruction brochure.* Iowa City, IA: Author.

ACT, Inc. (1996). *Test descriptions.* Iowa City, IA: Author.

ACT, Inc. (1997a). *Welcome to the Work Keys system.* Iowa City, IA: Author.

ACT, Inc. (1997b). *Work Keys score interpretation guide.* Iowa City, IA: Author.

ACT, Inc. (1997c). *Work Keys targets for instruction.* Iowa City, IA: Author.

Guion, R. M. (1980). On trinitarian doctrines of validity. *Professional Psychology, 11,* 385-398.

McLarty, J. R. (April, 1993). *Developing large-scale Guttman-scaled assessments.* Paper presented at the annual meeting of the National Council on Measurement in Education, Atlanta, GA.

McLarty, J. R., & Vansickle, T. R. (1997). Assessing employability skills: The Work Keys system. In H. F. O'Neil, Jr. (Ed.), *Workforce readiness: Competencies and assessment.* Mahwah, N. J.: Lawrence Erlbaum Associates, Publishers.

Stouffer, S.A., Guttman, L., Suchman, E. A., Lazarsfeld, P.F., Star, S.A., & Clausen, J. A. (1950). *Measurement and prediction.* Princeton, NJ: Princeton University Press.

White, A. S. (1999, June 24). *Summary of Work Keys validation and reliability.* Unpublished manuscript prepared by ACT, Inc.

CHAPTER 8 _____

Interest and Work Values Inventories

- Campbell Interest and Skill Survey (CISS)

- Career Assessment Inventory (CAI)

- COPSystem (CAPS/COPS/COPES)

- Career Values Card Sort Kit (CVCS)

- Chronicle Career Quest (CCQ)

- Harrington-O'Shea Career Decision- Making System (CDM)

- Interest Explorer

- Interest Determination, Exploration and Assessment System (IDEAS)

- Jackson Vocational Interest Survey (JKIS)

- Kuder General Interest Survey, Form E (KGIS-E)

- Kuder Occupational Interest Survey, Form DD (KOIS-DD) and Kuder Career Search with Person Match (KCS)

- Self-Directed Search, Fourth Edition (SDS)

- Strong Interest Inventory (SII) and Skills Confidence Inventory (SCI)

- Values Scale (VS)

- Vocational Interest Inventory (VII-R)

Campbell Interest and Skill Survey (CISS)

David P. Campbell
National Computer Systems, Inc.
PO Box 1416
Minneapolis, MN 55440
www.ncs.com

Target Population: High schools, colleges and universities, human resource departments, adults seeking career guidance, and placement firms. Individuals pursuing occupations that require college degrees.

Statement of the Purpose of the Instrument: The CISS instrument helps professional counselors and individuals obtain more complete career assessment information by providing an integrated measure of self-assessed interests and skills, The interest scales reflect an individual's attraction for specific occupational areas. The skill scales provide an estimate of an individual confidence in his/her ability to perform various occupational activities. The CISS Career Planner, a comprehensive career planning guide to help individuals use their results from the CISS instrument to design a career or study plan, lists an additional 299 occupations and 159 fields of study.

Titles of Subtests, Scales, Scores Provided: Seven orientation scales (influencing, organizing, helping, creating, analyzing, producing, and advertising), 29 basic scales (e.g., leadership, supervision, counseling, and international activities), 58 occupational scales (e.g., financial planner, translator, interpreter, and landscape architect). Additional occupations and fields of study are included in the CISS Career Planner.

Forms and Levels Available with Dates of Publication/Revision of Each: One form published in 1992.

Date of Most Recent Edition of Test Manual, User's Guide, Etc.: CISS manual, 1992.

Languages in Which Available: Enhanced Version: English and Spanish.

Time: Actual Test Time: 35-45 minutes.
       Total Administration Time: 35-45 minutes.

Norm Group(s) on Which Scores Are Based: Scales are standardized using a reference sample of 5,225 employed men and women representing a wide array of occupations.

Manner in Which Results Are Reported for Individuals
       Types of Scores: Standard scores presented numerically and graphically. Verbal labels describing interest/skill patterns.

Report Format/Content for Group Summaries: Not available.

Scoring

Machine Scoring Service:

Cost of basic service per counselee: Mail-in Report: Average price based on quantities purchased is about $8.20. Includes answer sheet, scoring and report.

Hand Scoring: Not available.

Local Machine Scoring:

Provisions/conditions/equipment required: NCS License requirements for Microtest Q 5.0: IBM or IBM compatible computer, Pentium II or higher processor, 32 MB RAM memory, 80 MB hard disk space, Microsoft Windows 95, 98 or NT, CD-ROM drive. IBM is a registered trademark of International Business Machines, Microsoft is a registered trademark and Windows is a trademark of Microsoft Corporation.

Computer Software Options Available: Not available.

Cost of materials: Prices of reports vary based on quantities ordered. Average cost of MTQ 5.0 report is $6.50. Specimen sets containing a manual and three test administrations are available. Call 800-627-7271 ext. 5151 for current prices.

Published Reviews:

Boggs, K. R. (1999). Campbell Interest and Skill Survey: Review and critique. *Measurement & Evaluation in Counseling & Development. 32,* 168-182.

Campbell, D. P. (1995). The Campbell Interest and Skill Survey (CISS): A product of ninety years of psychometric evolution. *Journal of Career Assessment. 3,* 391-410.

Hansen, J-I. C. & Neuman, J. L. (1999). Evidence of concurrent prediction of the Campbell Interest and Skill Survey (CISS) for college major selection. *Journal of Career Assessment. 7,* 239-247.

Savickas, M. L. (1998). Interpreting interest inventories: A case example. *Career Development Quarterly. 46,* 307-310.

Reviewed by

Kathleen R. Boggs

Director, Counseling Center
Associate Professor
Department of Educational and Counseling Psychology
University of Missouri-Columbia

Description

The Campbell Interest and Skill Survey (CISS) measures self-reported interests and skills for career planning. It is one of six Campbell Development Surveys, an integrated psychological battery for education, mental health, and human resources. Other instruments include the Campbell Organization Survey,

---

Note: Portions of this review were adapted from the author's review in *Measurement and Evaluation in Counseling & Development, 32,* 168-182.

Team Development Survey, Campbell-Hallam Leader Profile, and Campbell Community Survey.

The CISS evolved from Campbell's extensive earlier work on the Strong Vocational Interest Blank and the Strong-Campbell Interest Inventory. It has the advantage of applying years of test development knowledge and modern technology to a new instrument (Campbell, 1995) and adds a parallel skill scale for each interest scale.

The CISS items and responses are integrated into a single answer booklet for ease of administration. Items are up to date and each occupation includes a brief description. Respondents assess their level of interest in 200 academic and occupational items arranged alphabetically in three sections: 85 occupations (e.g., engineer, designing large building projects; photographer, taking pictures for a news magazine), 43 school subjects (e.g., chemistry, public speaking), and 72 activities (e.g., manage the work of others, operate scientific equipment) and their level of skill in 120 occupational activities (e.g., analyzing data, using statistical concepts; debating issues in a public forum). All 320 items are in a Likert-type response format of six choices from very positive to very negative without a middle or neutral alternative. Response positions for skill items reflect estimated levels of skill from Expert to None. High scores suggest self-confidence or self-efficacy rather than actual ability.

Interest and skill scores are reported on four types of scales: 7 Orientation Scales, 29 Basic Interest and Skill Scales, 60 Occupational Scales, and three Special Scales. In addition, there are three types of Procedural Checks. Results are reported in standard scores, a T-score system with mean of 50 and standard deviation of 10. The CISS General Reference Sample has a mean of 50 and the Occupational Scales have a standard deviation of 10.

The seven Orientations correspond to Holland's six types (Campbell et al., 1992) with some differences: Influencing reflects leadership whereas Enterprising relates to sales; Organizing deals with management and financial services whereas Conventional focuses on office and clerical work; and Holland's Realistic type is divided into the two CISS Scales of Producing, mechanical, construction, and farming activities, and Adventuring, military, police, and athletic activities. The CISS Orientations provide the organizational structure for the Basic Interest and Skill Scales and the Occupational Scales.

Use in Counseling

The CISS is most appropriate for individuals who plan to pursue careers requiring college education. It is useful with adults making career transitions, including retirement, or in understanding their job dissatisfactions. It may also be used for team building. The survey has a 6th grade reading level and is generally appropriate for adults and adolescents, ages 15 and older.

Interpretation may be individual or in groups. For ease of interpretation, four different patterns of interest and skill scores are reported: *Pursue* – areas for serious consideration as interest and skill (self-confidence) scale scores are both high; *Develop* – seek additional training to increase self-confidence or accept as hobbies, because interest scores are high and skill scores lower; *Explore* – gain understanding of why area is not more appealing or consider applying skills to another field as interests are lower and skills are high; and *Avoid* – activities not to consider, as interests and skills are both low. If both interest and skill scores are midrange or one is midrange and the other lower, no pattern is reported. Using an *Interest/Skill Pattern Worksheet*, a counselor may guide a client in transferring Orientation and Basic Scales to appropriate quadrants for discussion of interest and skill patterns. The *CISS Career Planner* (NCS, 1997) assists respondents in evaluating career directions, college majors, or occupations.

The *CISS Manual* (Campbell et al., 1992) is well written, informative, and easy to use. Concepts, development procedures, and technical information (norms, reliability, validity) are clearly described with appropriate examples. Case studies, guidelines for individual and group interpretations, and an interactive team building exercise are presented. An added bonus is an appendix with transparency masters for group interpretations. The manual would be an appropriate adjunct on scale construction in a psychometric theory course.

Technical Considerations

Norms for the Orientation Scales and the Basic Scales were based on a General Reference Sample of 5,225 employed people who enjoyed their work, including 5% (248) representing ethnic minorities. The 3,435 men and 1,790 women from 65 occupations completed questionnaires about type of organization they worked in, how they spent work time, education level, and other appropriate questions (e.g., certified/licensed). Modal education levels for the occupational samples indicated 9% had doctorate or professional degrees, 29% master's degrees, 53% bachelor's degrees, and 9% less than bachelor's degrees with variation within and between groups.

The CISS has combined gender or unisex scales that are easier to interpret than separate gender norms. However, as on other inventories, women and men still responded differently to many items (e.g., artistic versus mechanical activities). To balance these differences, for each Orientation and Basic Scale, separate raw score means were established for the 1,790 female and 3,435 male respondents and then averaged to give each gender equal weighting in development of unisex norms. In constructing the Occupational Scales, General Reference Sample statistics were weighted to reflect the female to male ratio of each occupational sample. To test these design strategies, separate female, male, and unisex scales were developed and compared for eight occupations; resulting data supported use of unisex scales. For Occupational Scales on which either gender is underrepresented (e.g., five or fewer) in the criterion sample, the unisex occupational interest mean is closer to the mean of the gender that is more adequately represented. For each Occupational Scale, the unisex, female, and male means are presented in the manual, information clinically useful with some clients. Even with unisex norms, examination of Orientation Scale means of 5,399 students and adults, indicated women scored higher on interest and skill measures on *C*reating and *H*elping whereas men scored higher on *A*dventuring and *P*roducing. On the 29 Basic Scales, women scored higher on Child Development and Fashion whereas men scored higher on Financial Services, Mechanical Crafts, Woodworking, Military/Law Enforcement, and Risks/Adventure. Similar findings have been reported on other inventories suggesting underlying differences in the structure of interests of women and men.

All scales evidence adequate test-retest reliability. Median test-retest reliabilities were mid to high 80s for interests and high 70s to low 80s for skills. Reliabilities for the shorter skill scales were consistently lower than the interest scales. The test-retest sample of 324 (230 men, 94 women) from 54 occupations took the inventory twice over 90 days. The respective 90-day test-retest median correlations for the interest and skill scales were Orientation Scales .87, .81; Basic Scales .83, .79; and Occupational Scales .87, .79.

Internal consistency was also adequate. Based on 4,842 employed adults, median alpha coefficients for interest and skill scales were both .87 for the Orientation Scales and .86 and .79, respectively, for the Basic Scales. The alpha coefficient was lowest for the Creating Orientation Skill Scale and Performing Arts Basic Skill Scale, indicating less homogeneity than other scales. Because the Occupational Scales were empirically developed by contrasting responses of specified groups, measures of internal consistency are not appropriate.

The Basic Interest and Skill Scales were created as homogeneous scales by identifying clusters of items with high intercorrelations. Then, the Basic Scales were factor analyzed to identify the Orientation Scales. Low intercorrelations of the Orientation Scales and reasonable intercorrelation patterns of the Basic Scales support their validity. Mean interest and skill scores of 58 occupations on each Orientation and Basic Scale further support validity of the Orientation and Basic Scales.

For each Orientation and Basic Scale, the items seem relevant. The median corrected item-total score Pearson Correlation Coefficients for the Orientation and Basic Scales were .59 for interests and .58 for skills. The median Pearson Correlation Coefficients between Interest and Skill Scales was .70 for the Orientation Scales and .68 for the Basic Scales.

In contrast to the Basic Scales, the Occupational Scales are generally longer, have a heterogeneous item content, and were developed empirically by contrasting responses from occupational samples with those of a general reference group. The power of each item to discriminate between the occupation criterion sample and the General Reference Sample is about half a standard deviation.

A minimum of 50 workers was obtained for 51 occupations. Nine other samples of 35 to 49 were also used for scale construction as data looked reasonable. Thus, sample sizes for the 60 occupations ranged from 35 to 199, median of 76. Number of females in each occupational sample ranged from 1 to 156, median of 20; the males, from 2 to 189, median of 52.

Degree of separation between an occupational sample and the General Reference Sample, in standard deviation units for each Occupational Scale, is substantial and supports validity of the Occupational Scales. The Validity Index for interest scales ranged from 1.0 to 2.9 with median of 2.0 and for skill scales, from .9 to 3.5 with median of 1.8 indicating separation of about two standard deviations between people in an occupation and the General Reference Sample. For each Occupational Scale, means and standard deviations were presented for the three highest and three lowest scoring occupations. For the highest occupations, their relation to the criterion occupation appears obvious (e.g., statistician, bookkeeper, and financial planner scored highest on accountant), further supporting validity of the scales. Evidence of concurrent criterion validity of the CISS was reported with real estate sales (Mason, Sherry, & Otto, 1995) and of the Occupational Scales for college major selection (Hansen & Neuman, 1999).

The Academic Focus and Extraversion Scales evidence good construct validity and test-retest reliabilities for their defined purposes. Two types of evidence for validity were reported: correlations of each scale with the Orientation and Basic Scales and mean scores of the 58 occupational criterion samples on each Special Scale. Mean scores of individuals by education level were also reported for the Academic Focus Scales. The 90-day test-retest reliability correlations for the interest and skill scales, respectively were Academic Focus .87, .77; Extraversion .85, .82, and Variety .76, .69. Because reliability coefficients of the Variety Scales are lower and their interpretation is not clear, the scales should be treated with caution.

The three Procedural Checks were adequately designed to detect problems with answer sheet completion or scoring. Each has decision rules for labeling a profile "Doubtful" or "Invalid."

Overall Critique

The CISS is a useful instrument for career assessment as it was well constructed and technically tested. The 11-page individual profile was designed to be self-interpreting. It is comprehensive with results presented in a direct manner in clear language that avoids psychological jargon. Dynamic verbs, suggesting action, name the Orientations. Four defined patterns of interest/skill scores enhance interpretation. The *Interest/Skill Planning Worksheet* and the *CISS Career Planner* assist respondents to organize results, consider themes, and make greater use of their results. The extensive data, interpretation guides, case studies, and transparency masters make the *CISS Manual* valuable in learning the instrument and resolving interpretation of seemingly inconsistent scores.

Adding a parallel skill scale for every interest scale extends usefulness of the inventory. Exploring response sets with a client is important in interpreting CISS skill scores (Davis, 1994). If ability tests are employed with the CISS, a counselor may help a client compare perceived and measured levels of ability, a useful process in career decision making.

At the item level, an excellent feature is the six-point Likert-type response format that gives respondents greater variety than does a three-choice format (Davis, 1994; Fuqua & Newman, 1994). Addition of descriptive phrases to clarify occupations is especially helpful for younger test takers or persons whose first language is not English or Spanish.

The Orientation Scales are based on a theory similar to Holland's (1997) although the theory is not explained. Descriptions of the Orientations are adequate.

The psychometric properties of the instrument are generally impressive. Using a standard score of 50 to represent the mean of the General Reference Sample on all sets of scales increases clarity of interpretation. Whether the method used to develop the unisex scales effectively creates valid scales for both genders, especially if either gender is underrepresented in criterion samples, needs further study (Davis, 1994; Fuqua & Newman, 1994; Hood & Johnson, 1997). Representativeness of ethnic minority individuals is compromised in occupations where responses of five or fewer women or men were in the norm group (Davis, 1994). The CISS needs to be cross-validated with a gender-balanced sample (Davis, 1994).

Even though the authors prudently suggested occupational criterion sample means for males and females may be suspect for samples under 30, the scales still perform as intended (D. P. Campbell, personal communication, August 16, 1998). Available studies (e.g., Hansen & Neuman, 1999) indicate the scales work as designed, and the CISS will continue to generate research to address psychometric issues (e.g., construct, concurrent and predictive validity). Portions of this review were based on a previously published review (Boggs, 1999).

References

Boggs, K. R. (1999). Campbell Interest and Skill Survey: Review and critique. *Measurement and Evaluation in Counseling and Development, 32,* 168-182.

Campbell, D. P. (1995). The Campbell Interest and Skill Survey (CISS): A product of ninety years of psychometric evolution. *Journal of Career Assessment, 3,* 391-410.

Campbell, D. P., Hyne, S. A., & Nilsen, D. L. (1992). *Manual for the Campbell Interest and Skill Survey.* Minneapolis, MN: National Computer Systems.

Davis, K. L. (1994). Review of the inventory Campbell Interest and Skill Survey (CISS). *Journal of Psychoeducational Assessment, 12,* 424-428.

Fuqua, D. R., & Newman, J. L. (1994). Review of the Campbell Interest and Skill Survey. In J. T. Kapes, M. M. Mastie, & E. A. Whitfield (Eds.) *A counselor's guide to career assessment instruments* (3rd ed., pp 138-143). Alexandria, VA: National Career Development Association.

Hansen, J. C., & Neuman, J. L. (1999). Evidence of concurrent prediction of the Campbell Interest and Skill Survey (CISS) for college major selection. *Journal of Career Assessment, 7,* 239-247.

Holland, J. L. (1997). *Making vocational choices: A theory of vocational personalities and work environments* (3rd ed.). Odessa, FL: Psychological Assessment Resources.

Hood, A. B., & Johnson, R. W. (1997). *Assessment in counseling: A guide to the use of psychological assessment procedures* (2nd ed.). Alexandra, VA: American Counseling Association.

Mason, K., Sherry, P., & Otto, S. (1995, April). *Validity of the Campbell Interest and Skill Survey with sales occupations.* Paper presented at the annual meeting of the Rocky Mountain Psychological Association.

National Computer Systems. (1997). *CISS Career Planner.* Minneapolis, MN: Author.

Career Assessment Inventory (CAI)

Charles B. Johansson
National Computer Systems, Inc.
PO Box 1416
Minneapolis, MN 55440
www.ncs.com

Target Population: High schools, two- and four-year colleges, human resource departments, vocational rehabilitation programs, and job service agencies.

Statement of the Purpose of the Instrument: The Career Assessment Inventory instruments (both versions) are interest inventories designed to measure one's occupational interests for use in career exploration and career decision making. The Enhanced Version provides a mixture of occupations that require various amounts of postsecondary education. The Vocational Version focuses on occupations requiring 0-2 years of postsecondary education.

Titles of Subtests, Scales, Scores Provided: Enhanced Version: 6 General Occupational Themes, 25 Basic Interest Scales, 111 Occupational Scales, Administrative Indices and 4 nonoccupational scales. Vocational Version: 6 General Occupational Themes, 22 Basic Interest Scales, 91 Occupational Scales, Administrative indices and four nonoccupational scales.

Forms and Levels Available with Dates of Publication/Revision of Each: Enhanced Version: one form published 1985. Vocational Version: one form, published 1978, revised in 1980, 1982 and 1984.

Date of Most Recent Edition of Test Manual, User's Guide, Etc.: Enhanced Version Manual published 1986. Vocational Version Manual, 1984.

Languages in Which Available: Enhanced Version: English and Spanish. Vocational Version: English, Spanish, and French.

Time: Actual Test Time: 30-40 minutes.
         Total Administration Time: 30-40 minutes.

Norm Group(s) on Which Scores Are Based: Enhanced Version: General Theme Scales based on a normative sample of 900 employed adults. Norms for the occupational scales were developed by scoring occupational subgroup samples independently. Vocational Version: General Theme Scales based on a normative sample of 1,500 employed adults. Norms for the Occupational Scales were developed by scoring occupational subgroup samples independently.

Manner in Which Results Are Reported for Individuals
    Types of Scores: Both versions. Standard scores and percent response.
    Report Format/Content (including narrative text, if any):
        Basic Service: Both versions. Profile Report graphically presents the scores on each scale. Preprinted interpretive information is included at the end of the report. A counselor's copy is provided with each report.

Options: Both versions. Interpretive Report presents several pages of narrative statements that explain the individuals score on the scales. It also provides a page number reference to the Occupational Outlook Handbook for the highest occupational scores (OOH references updates every two years). Includes a three-page detachable counselors copy.

Scoring
Machine Scoring Service:
Cost of basic service per counselee: Both versions. Average cost of Profile Report is $5.90. Prices vary with quantity ordered. Includes answer sheet, scoring, and report.
Cost of options: Both versions. Average cost of mail-in Interpretive Report is $8.70. Includes answer sheet, scoring, and report.
Time required for scoring and returning (maximum): 24-hour turnaround.
Hand Scoring: Not available.
Local Machine Scoring:
Provisions/conditions/equipment required: NCS License Agreement. Minimum computer requirements for Microtest Q 5.0: IBM or IBM compatible computer, Pentium II or higher processor, 32 MB RAM memory, 80 MB hard disk space, Microsoft Windows 95, 98 or NT, CD-ROM drive. IBM is a registered trademark of International Business Machines, Microsoft is a registered trademark and Windows is a trademark of Microsoft Corporation.

Computer Software Options Available: Not available.

Cost of materials: Cost of reports for MTQ 5.0 scoring: Enhanced Version and Vocational Version. Profile Reports: average cost $4.40 includes scoring and report (answer sheets purchased separately). Prices vary with quantity purchased. Interpretive Report: average cost $7.20 includes scoring and report (answer sheet purchased separately). Prices vary with quantity purchased. Specimen Sets containing a manual and three administrations are available at a discounted price. Call 800-627-7271 ext. 5151 for current prices.

Additional Comments of Interest to Users The format of the mail-in profile reports of both versions of the Career Assessment Inventory were updated in 1999. This is the first stage of several changes being made to keep the inventory a valuable and contemporary career exploration tool.

Published Reviews:

Hinkle, J. S. (1992). Review of the Career Assessment Inventory. In J. J. Kramer & J. C. Conoley (Eds.), *Eleventh mental measurements yearbook*. Lincoln, NE: Buros Institute, University of Nebraska-Lincoln.

Kehoe, J. F. (1992). Review of the Career Assessment Inventory. In J.J. Kramer & J.C. Conoley (Eds.), *Eleventh mental measurements yearbook*. Lincoln, NE: Buros Institute, University of Nebraska-Lincoln.

McCabe, S. P. (1988). Review of the Career Assessment Inventory. In J.T. Kapes & M.M. Mastie (Eds.), *A counselor's guide to career assessment instruments*, (2th ed). Alexandria, VA: National career Development Association.

Rounds, J. B. (1989). Review of the Career Assessment Inventory. In J.C. Conoley & J.J. Kramer (Eds.), *Tenth mental measurements yearbook*. Lincoln, NE: Buros Institute, University of Nebraska-Lincoln.

Vacc, N. A. (1992). Review of the Career Assessment Inventory. In J.J. Kramer & J.C. Conoley (Eds.), *Eleventh mental measurements yearbook*. Lincoln, NE: Buros Institute, University of Nebraska-Lincoln.

Wegner, K.W. (1992). Review of the Career Assessment Inventory. In D. J. Keyser & R. C. Sweetland (Eds). *Test critiques,* Vol. IX. Austin, TX: PRO-ED.

Reviewed by

Claire Usher Miner
Licensed Professional Counselor
Assessment & Counseling Services
Austin, Texas

Stephen M. Sellers
School Counselor
Dobie Middle School
Austin, Texas

Description

The Career Assessment Inventory (CAI) is an interest inventory first published in 1975 by National Computer Systems (NCS), authored by Charles B. Johansson. Having worked on the Strong-Vocational Interest Blanks and the Strong-Campbell Interest Inventory (now entitled the Strong Interest Inventory), Johansson patterned the CAI after the Strong. The instruments are similar in that they both generate scores on Holland's RIASEC areas, provide scores on basic interest scales and occupational scales, and offer profile and narrative reports to respondents. The CAI differs from the Strong in that the occupations it includes are predominantly technical and nonprofessional, whereas the majority of occupations on the Strong are professional. Also, the CAI produces standard scores based on combined gender groups, whereas the Strong produces gender-specific scores.

The CAI has a Vocational Version (CAI-VV) and an Enhanced Version (CAI-EV). The original version, the CAI-VV, was designed for use with those individuals who aspire to technical or nonprofessional careers. The CAI-EV was developed to broaden the applicability of the instrument to those individuals who aspire to professional careers. It includes more items and occupational samples that measure professional interests, specifically in the investigative and enterprising areas. Both versions can be used with individuals aged 15 and older.

The inventory uses a combined question and response booklet format. The CAI-VV contains 305 items; the CAI-EV, 370 (to expand coverage to professional careers). Users respond to the items on a five-point scale ranging from "Like very much" to "Dislike very much." There are three sections of the instrument: Activities, School Subjects, and Occupations. The Activities items (e.g., "work with small hand tools") comprise the largest percentage of the inventory. The School Subjects items contain explanations in some areas (e.g., "geology (rocks and fossils)"). In the CAI-EV, the Occupations items contain activity descriptions (e.g., "actor/actress (entertains on stage)"), primarily designed to reduce gender stereotypic responses to them.

The inventory generates a Profile Report and an Interpretive Report. The Profile Report yields scores and graphs on six General Theme Scales (GTSs) representing the RIASEC areas, Basic Interest Area Scales (BIAs; 22 for the CAI-VV, 25 for the CAI-EV), Occupational Scales (OSs; 91 for the CAI-VV, 111 for the CAI-EV), and Administrative Indices and Special Scales (Response Percentages, Total Responses, Response Consistency, Fine Arts-Mechanical, Occupational Extroversion/Introversion, Educational Orientation, and Variability of Interests). Although scores are based on a combined gender norm group, gender-specific normative information is also provided. The report also includes all item responses, which can be helpful to the counselor in situations where no high interest areas are reported.

The Interpretive Report is a narrative explanation of the client's scores. It contains scores and graphs of the results, as well as cross-references to the *The Dictionary of Occupational Titles* and the *The Occupational Outlook Handbook*. A Counselor's Summary is also provided which contains the client's scores, graphs on all the scales, and item responses.

Both versions have Spanish translations. The CAI-VV has a Canadian French version. Both versions require about 30 to 40 minutes to complete. The reading level for the CAI-VV is reported to be 6th grade; for the CAI-EV, 8th grade. Vacc and Hinkle (1994) noted that, unfortunately, no standard readability index is reported for either the instrument or the narrative report. Some lower-level readers may find the narrative report difficult to read and comprehend (Vacc, 1992).

The User Qualification Level for the CAI is "B." Counselors can mail completed inventories to NCS for scoring or can administer the assessment online. Costs for mail-in scoring are $6.20 per Profile Report or $9.25 per Interpretive Report. Costs of all reports decrease with increasing quantities. Answer sheets are scored by NCS within 24 hours of receipt.

Use in Counseling

The CAI manual suggests that the following types of clients could benefit from the assessment: (1) high school students who may or may not plan to acquire postsecondary education; (2) students who plan to attend vocational, technical, or business schools; (3) community college entrants who may or may not be considering transferring to a university; (4) students who discontinue their university education; (5) vocational rehabilitation clients; and (6) adults considering career changes to technical or nonprofessional fields.

The CAI-VV is appropriate for clients who have nonprofessional and technical aspirations. However, since it contains a smaller subset of the occupations presented in the CAI-EV, counselors may choose to use the CAI-EV with these clients to encourage career exploration into professional areas.

The CAI-EV is recommended for samples of clients with diverse aspirations which include professional goals. The manual cautions, however, that in homogeneous settings where clients' interests are professional (for example, elite private high schools), the technical items may be distracting. In such settings, an instrument such as the Strong may be more appropriate.

The manual also suggests that the CAI can be used to help make employee screening, hiring, and placement decisions. However, there is a lack of predictive validity information in the manual for all CAI scales. Thus, users should not view CAI scores as predictors of employee retention and success nor client satisfaction in careers. Instead, the CAI should be used only as a tool to stimulate clients' exploration activities.

Some current users of the CAI report that clients find the CAI easy to complete and appreciate the user-friendly organizational format of the profile and narrative reports. It is also less expensive than the Strong. However, these users recognize that a revision of the instrument is necessary to update items and strengthen occupational coverage on the instrument. Furthermore, Vacc (1992) noted that large-group administration of the CAI is problematic due to the complexity of its interpretation.

Technical Considerations

The CAI-VV uses a reference sample of 750 males and 750 females to calculate standard scores for the GTSs and BIAs. The CAI-EV has a new reference sample of 450 females and 450 males, which covers a broader spectrum of occupational membership.

Occupational criterion samples were collected to calculate the OS scores for both versions. Sample sizes of some occupational groups are small; for example, machinist has 70 males and no females in both versions.

Only test-retest reliabilities using small samples are reported for the Special Scales. These correlations are generally moderate to high for both versions, with Variability of Interests showing less stability over time than the others.

Internal consistency of the GTSs and BIAs is generally high. For the CAI-VV, median item-scale correlations for the six GTSs range from .59 to .67. For the CAI-EV, internal consistencies range from .93 to .95. For the BIAs, the CAI-VV has median item-scale correlations which range from .59 to .88. The CAI-EV yields internal consistencies for these scales of .86 to .95.

Test-retest reliabilities for the CAI scales are also high. For the GTSs on the CAI-VV, median correlations for one week to 6- to 7-year intervals range from .80 to .94. For the CAI-EV, median correlations range from .82 to .93 for one week to 2- to 3-month time periods. For the BIAs, reliabilities range from

.77 to .93 for the CAI-VV; for the CAI-EV, .82 to .92. For the OSs, the CAI-VV yields median test-retest reliabilities from .82 to .95, whereas the CAI-EV's reliabilities are from .88 to .92. Studies of the CAI-EV with longer elapsed time periods would be informative.

Content validity for the GTSs was ensured by a rational-empirical method of item selection. Only those items that represented the six Holland areas conceptually and that correlated with similar scales on other instruments were included. For the BIAs, items that intercorrelated highly were used to create homogeneous scales that made conceptual sense. The OSs were developed by selecting items that differentiated females in an occupation from their female reference group *and* that differentiated males in the occupation from their male reference group. Thus, combined gender occupational scales were created that measure core interests common to both males and females in an occupation.

Construct validity for the GTSs was established by correlating the scales with the like-named scales from other instruments. For example, for both versions, correlations with Strong-Campbell scales are in the .70s and .80s. For the BIAs, correlations are in the .70s and .80s for the CAI-VV and in the .60s, .70s, and .80s for the CAI-EV. For the OSs, both versions yield moderate correlations with similar scales on the Strong-Campbell.

Concurrent validity has been established for the GTSs and BIAs by an examination of the mean scale scores for the occupational groups. For example, on both versions the aircraft mechanics score highest on the "Realistic" theme, whereas the secretaries score lowest. Likewise, aircraft mechanics score highest on "Mechanical/fixing," whereas secretaries score lowest. Concurrent validity for the OSs was established by the examination of the amount of overlap in the distribution of scores for the occupational groups and the reference sample. The median overlap percentages are in the low 30s, indicating good separation between the occupational and reference samples.

Rounds (1989) cautioned against using the GTSs as measures of the Holland types, and Wegner (1992) noted that the intercorrelations between the scales do not support the hexagonal model. For example, among females who had completed the CAI-VV, R and S (opposites on the hexagon) correlate more highly than do R and C (adjacent on the hexagon) (.20 and .05, respectively). The Strong and the Self-Directed Search yield scores that are more consistent with Holland's theory of the structure of vocational interests.

Computer-Based Version

The licensing fee for the MICROTEST Q Assessment System scoring software is $89 per year. Reports generated through the software cost about $2 less than the mail-in reports. There are no studies cited in the manual on the equivalency of the computer and paper-and-pencil versions.

Overall Critique

A strength of the CAI is the care that was taken in its development to ensure against gender bias, both in the selection of gender-neutral items and the use of combined gender-normed scales. However, the strategy of norming occupational scales on combined gender groups using only items to which males and females respond similarly is based on the assumption that gender differences in interests are not important in the prediction of occupational choice or satisfaction. Unfortunately, the CAI manual presents no predictive validity studies of the occupational scales that could support this assumption.

In addition to concern with gender issues, another strength of the CAI is that the average score ranges for workers *not* employed in an occupation are provided. This allows clients to explore occupations where they score above their own gender norms, especially in situations where there are no "similar" scores as compared to the combined gender norm group.

Although the CAI is self-administering with some basic instructions, it does require computer-scoring and sophisticated interpretation skills. A well-trained counselor is necessary to interpret the various scores appropriately, particularly in reference to the norm groups that are presented. The CAI manual is easy for counselors to understand; however, it should be revised to reflect recent graphic changes in the profile reports.

This inventory has applicability to a diversity of clients, but it has some serious weaknesses. The items should be updated (for example, "typing" changed to "keyboarding"); the occupational scales need to be updated and expanded to include more recently emerging careers; and predictive validity studies should be conducted to support the instrument's suggested uses. Without these studies, use of the CAI for individual decision-making purposes is not warranted.

References

Rounds, J. B. (1989). Review of the Career Assessment Inventory: The Enhanced Version. In J. C. Conoley & J. J. Kramer (Eds.), *Tenth mental measurements yearbook* (pp. 139-141). Lincoln, NE: Buros Institute, University of Nebraska-Lincoln.

Vacc, N. A. (1992). Review of the Career Assessment Inventory, Second Edition (Vocational Version). In J. J. Kramer & J. C. Conoley (Eds.), *Eleventh mental measurements yearbook* (pp. 150-151). Lincoln, NE: Buros Institute, University of Nebraska-Lincoln.

Vacc, N. A. & Hinkle, J. S. (1994). Review of the Career Assessment Inventory In J. T. Kapes, M. M. Mastie, & E. A. Whitfield (Eds.), *A counselor's guide to career assessment instruments* (3rd ed., pp. 146-150). Alexandria, VA: National Career Development Association.

Wegner, K. W. (1992). Career Assessment Inventory: The Enhanced Version. In D. J. Keyser & R. C. Sweetland (Eds.). *Test critiques*, Vol. IX (pp.36-47). Austin, TX: PRO-ED.

COPSystem (COPS, CAPS and COPES)

Robert Knapp, Lila Knapp, and Lisa Knapp-Lee
EdITS
PO Box 7234
San Diego, CA 92167
edits@k-online.com
www.edits.net

Target Population: Junior high, high school and adult (COPS II 4th grade and up)

Statement of the Purpose of the Instrument: The COPSystem instruments are designed to provide individuals with coordinated measures of interests, abilities and work values. Scores on any one, two, or all three of the assessments provide a starting point for career exploration.

Titles of Subtests, Scales, Scores Provided: All three assessments keyed to 14 COPSystem Career Clusters: Science Professional, Science Skilled, Technology Professional, Technology Skilled, Consumer Economics, Outdoor, Business Professional, Business Skilled, Clerical, Communication, Arts Professional, Arts Skilled, Service Professional and Service Skilled. CAPS subtests include: Mechanical Reasoning, Spatial Relations, Verbal Reasoning, Numerical Ability, Language Usage, Word Knowledge, Perceptual Speed and Accuracy and Manual Speed and Dexterity. The COPES scales are Investigate vs. Accepting, Practical vs. Carefree, Independence vs. Conformity, Leadership vs. Supportive, Orderliness vs. Flexibility, Recognition vs. Privacy, Aesthetic vs. Realistic and Social vs. Reserved.

Forms and Levels Available, with Dates of Publication/Revision of Each: COPS (1995), COPS Professional level (COPS-P, currently being revised), COPS Form R (COPS-R, 1992), COPS Intermediate Inventory (COPS II, 1997), COPS Picture Inventory (COPS-PIC, 1993), Spanish COPS (SPOC, 1995), Spanish CAPS (1976), Career Ability Placement Survey (CAPS, 1976) and Career Orientation Placement and Evaluation Survey (COPES, 1995).

Date of Most Recent Edition of Test Manual, User's Guide, Etc.: COPS Technical Manual (2001), CAPS Technical Manual (1992), COPES Manual (2001).

Languages in Which Available: English and Spanish

Time: Actual Test Time: COPS 20-30 minutes, CAPS 40 minutes, COPES 20-30 minutes.
Total Administration Time: COPS 25-35 minutes, CAPS 50 minutes, COPES 25-35 minutes.

Norm Group(s) on Which Scores Are Based: Junior high/high school and community college students.

Manner in Which Results Are Reported for Individuals

   Types of Scores: raw scores, percentiles, stanines, verbal labels

   Basic Service: COPSystem scores keyed to the 14 COPSystem Clusters as described in the interpretive booklet. The interpretive booklet provides information about each cluster including: a definition of each career cluster, related courses of study, sample occupations, related college majors, necessary skills and abilities, activities for experience, career planning worksheet, educational planning worksheet, and local job interview sheet. *Options*: Self-Scoring, Machine-Scoring through EdITS or local onsite machine-scoring. (Machine scoring provides individual printouts.)

Report Format/Content for Group Summaries:

Basic Service: Summary of Interest-shows the percent of times one of the 14 career clusters was chosen by examinees as one of their top three areas of interest; Needs Assessment Summary provides a summary of student responses to a career planning questionnaire; Examinees by Interest Area is a listing of students interested in one of three top Career Clusters. Basic List Report is a condensed summary of student responses to the COPS, CAPS and COPES. Record Labels have same information as basic list on self-adhering labels.

Scoring

Machine Scoring Service:

Cost of basic service per counselee: Depends on quantity; this price includes the cost of the booklets and scoring service combined and ranges from $5.32 to $5.88 for all three instruments.

Cost of options: File copy $0.50 for all three assessments ($0.40 per assessment). Basic List Report ($0.40 per examinee), Summary of Interests ($0.20 per examinee), Needs Assessment Summary $0.20 per examinee) and Examinees by Interest Area ($0.20 per examinee).

Time required for scoring and returning (maximum): 10 days.

Hand Scoring:

Scored by: Counselee; Clerk; Counselor.

Time required for scoring: 15-20 minutes per test.

Local Machine Scoring:

Provisions/conditions/equipment required: Onsite Scoring, software allows you to use an optical mark reading scanner and an IBM PC or compatible computer to scan, edit, and profile the COPS, CAPS and COPES career instruments. Hardware Requirements: NCS OpScan series or Scantron Scan Mark 2250 and 2500 scanner with two-sided read capability; laser printer; IBM PC/XT/AT/PS2 or compatible with 12 megabytes RAM.

Computer Software Options Available: A Windows-based program for taking thes test on computer is under development and should be available in 2002.

Ways in Which Computer Version Differs: Very similar, one test on the CAPS will be different.

Cost of Materials:

Specimen Set: $22.

Counselee Materials: All material is consumable. Each assessment may be used as a stand-alone instrument. Prices vary according to quantities. Self-Scoring of all three assessments combined, ranges from $3.66 to $5.02. Contact publisher for prices of individual assessments.

Additional Comments of Interest to Users: Technical manuals are currently being revised. A computerized version of COPSystem is in development. CAPS will be revised in 2001. Each assessment may be used as a stand-alone measurement. A computerized guidance system is in development.

Published Reviews:
Mueller, D. J. (1985) Career orientation placement and evaluation survey. *Measurement and Evaluation in Counseling and Development, 18,* 132-134.
Wickwire, P. N., & Faldet, B. (1994). Review of the Career Occupational Preference System Interest Inventory (COPS). In J. T. Kapes, M. M. Mastie, & E. A. Whitfield (Eds.), *A counselor's guide to career assessment instruments* (3rd ed., pp. 158-161). Alexandria, VA: National Career Development Association.

Reviewed by

Pat Nellor Wickwire
The Nellor Wickwire Group
Hermosa Beach, CA

Description

The Career Occupational Preference System (COPSystem) (Knapp, Knapp, & Knapp-Lee, 1990) is a systematic self-awareness-based approach to clustered career exploration. Three separate but coordinated assessment instruments, alternate assessment instruments adapted for selected populations, and interpretive and explicative support materials are available in the COPSystem. Results of assessment and numerous follow-through materials provide for access to most systems of occupational information.

The comprehensive system has a theoretical base and a research base. Extensive research and development for more than 20 years have tested and confirmed an inventory of interests, a battery of multiple aptitudes, a survey of work values, and resource materials to assist individuals in career exploration, decision making, and planning. Students, intermediate through college, as well as adults, have the opportunity to relate their coordinated interests, abilities, and values to homogeneous occupational clusters, and, thus, to specific, focused information about careers and occupations.

The three assessment instruments are the Career Occupational Preference Interest Inventory, Career Ability Placement Survey, and the Career Orientation Placement and Evaluation Survey. The instruments were renormed in 1997 in a national sampling of intermediate, high school, community college, and college students; data from this renorming are currently being incorporated into COPSystem documents. Information available in COPSystem print publications is utilized in this review.

The Career Occupational Preference System Interest Inventory (COPS) is designed to measure personal characteristics of interests in specific activities performed in jobs in terms of their relationship to occupational clusters. Interests, what people like to do, along with abilities and work values, are basic to career exploration and decision making.

COPS interests reflect area and level clusters established through factor analysis within the interest domain related to occupations. Area clusters include meaningfully related activity preferences, with wide ranges of occupations within each cluster; level clusters (e.g., professional, skilled) are characterized by differences in autonomy and responsibility. Interests measured are within the following clusters:

science, professional	science, skilled
business, professional	business, skilled
arts, professional	arts, skilled
service, professional	service, skilled
technology, professional	technology, skilled
technology, consumer economics	outdoor
communication	clerical

COPS forms include self-scoring and machine-scoring, each with 168 items. For each item, examinees determine their feelings about performing the listed activity, and record whether they like or dislike the activity very much or moderately. Examinees can complete the inventory in 20-30 minutes. Weighted responses are totaled and reported in a COPS profile with percentiles that represent a comparison of the individual's responses with those of the normative sample.

The Career Ability Placement Survey (CAPS), 1976 Edition, is designed to provide a profile of individual abilities in terms of their relationships to occupational clusters. Multiple aptitudes, what people can do, are considered important in relation to interests and work values in career exploration and decision making.

CAPS abilities are consistent with the results of prior and continuing research using factor analysis within the aptitude domain related to occupations. Abilities measured are the following:

mechanical reasoning	spatial relations
verbal reasoning	numerical ability
language usage	word knowledge
perceptual speed and accuracy	manual speed and dexterity

CAPS forms include self-scoring and machine scoring. Examinees are timed at 5 minutes for each of the eight tests; each test is one page long. With prerecorded instructions, examinees can complete the battery in 51 minutes. CAPS results are reported in a profile with percentiles, stanines, and stanine ranges that represent a comparison of the individuals responses with those of the normative sample.

The Career Orientation Placement and Evaluation Survey (COPES), 1995 Edition, is designed to measure primary personal values demonstrably connected to vocational motivation in a broad variety of occupations. Values, what people value doing, along with interests and abilities, are considered relevant in career exploration and decision making.

COPES nonhierarchical dimensions are based on prior and continuing research using factor analysis to identify preeminent work value constructs related to occupational clusters. Values measured are the following:

investigative versus accepting	practical versus carefree
independence versus conformity	leadership versus supportive
orderliness versus flexibility	recognition versus privacy
aesthetic versus realistic	social versus reserved

COPES forms include self-scoring, with 128 items, and machine-scoring, with 160 items. For each item, examinees select between two paired comparison statements in responding to "I value jobs or activities in which . . . ." Examinees can complete all items in 30-50 minutes. COPES results are reported in a profile with percentiles and ranges that represent a comparison of the individual's responses with those of the normative sample.

Use in Counseling

The COPSystem is designed to serve as a systematic approach to career exploration, decision making, and planning for youth and adults. Based on 14 occupational (career) clusters identified through factor analysis, COPSystem offers the opportunity for youth and adults to determine and to outline what they like to do (interests), what they can do (abilities), and what they value doing (work values). The three components of interests, abilities, and work values are instrumental in employment and career selection, maintenance, success, and satisfaction. Furthermore, these components have strong implications for exploration, decision making, and
planning for education and training, and for temporary and continuing life styles.

In the COPSystem (ERAS/Educational Research and Services, 1995), information from the assessment of interests, abilities, and work values is coordinated; intersections of the highest measures are identified and related to occupational clusters. Clusters are defined; sample occupations in each cluster are listed, and key resources for additional information about the occupations are identified. Clusters are related to school subjects, needed skills and abilities, activities for experience, and college majors. Planning worksheets to build on information derived from the COPS, CAPS, and COPES are provided.

COPSystem informational support materials include the *Career Briefs Kit, Career Cluster Booklets, Occupational Cluster Charts*, and *Occupational Briefs on CD-ROM*. Complementary assessment instruments include the Study Attitudes and Methods Survey, for students; Dimensions of Self-Concept, for students; and Dimensions of Self-Concept-W, for adult workers.

Adapted alternate forms of the assessment instruments include the Career Occupational Preference System-Professional Interest Inventory (COPS-P), for those involved in, directed toward, or reevaluating professional careers; COPS Intermediate Inventory (COPS-II), for those at grade 4 reading level and above; the COPS-R, for those at grade 6 reading level and above, with gender-balanced norms; the COPS Picture Inventory of Careers (COPS-PIC), for nonreaders and for those for whom English is a second language; Making a Terrific Career Happen (MATCH), for high school graduates, college students, and adults interested in reevaluating career goals, seeking outplacement, and entering or reentering the workforce; Sistema de Preferencia Ocupacional de Carreras, for Spanish-speaking and Spanish-reading individuals; and Spanish CAPS. Additionally, a computerized version of the COPSystem and a Spanish edition of COPES are in development.

The COPSystem offers these and other options for individual and group student and adult Use in Counseling in various settings, including education, training, employment, work, agency, and private practice. Awareness of personal likes and dislikes, capabilities, and values can be coupled with awareness of careers, occupations, and jobs through COPSystem assessment, counseling, curriculum, and instruction, and can lead to predictable, desired, and measurable outcomes. The COPSystem provides for content, process, and structure in personalized, sequential, focused, and directed career exploration, decision making, and planning.

With the COPSystem, counseling can result in increased self-, career and occupational, and educational awareness, understanding, and action. Specific outcomes can occur, such as awareness, understanding, and action related to the significance and meaningfulness of work; the complexities and the possibilities in the interrelatedness of careers, education, and work; the breadth of potential strategies for personalized approaches; the potential depth, definitiveness, and benefits attainable through career exploration, decision making, and planning; and search and research of source material.

The COPSystem can be used in direct and indirect services and programs offered to individuals and groups in counseling. In addition, systemic approaches can be considered. In one futures scenario, for example, the COPSystem has potential for use as a springboard and catalyst for a school-wide, department-wide, or district-wide education and career planning curriculum. The team approach, with administrative, instructional, student services, and classified staff, and with students, parents, and community, can be implemented to lead, develop, deliver, and evaluate an integrated, sequenced quality program. Given system-wide data, efforts can be focused on planned experiences directed toward interconnectedness and intraconnectedness of career exploration, decision making, and planning in education and the larger community. Specific results for students can be such as individualized career plans that can be consistently implemented and monitored for progress, and that can support ultimate career success and satisfaction. Counseling can be a major direct and indirect functionary, with roles in design, consultation, collaboration, coordination, and management, and in one-to-one and group counseling, group guidance and instruction, and assessment and evaluation.

Technical Considerations

Norms for the 1995 COPS are based on a national sample of 19,640 students in grades 7 through 12 and on a national sample of 3,040 college students (Knapp, Knapp, & Knapp-Lee, 1995). Gender norms are included, although activity items are seen as free of gender bias. Confirmation and reevaluation of content and factor structure are conducted every few years. Internal consistency of scale scores was determined through alternate form reliability with correlations from .84 through .93. Supportive data regarding construct and predictive validity for COPS have resulted from studies of relationships with similar inventories, college major choices, vocational group scores, occupations in the military, and postgraduation employment and education.

CAPS norms are based on a national sample of intermediate, high school, and community college students in five geographical regions (Knapp, Knapp, & Knapp-Lee, 1992). Annually, samplings from the regions are compared with original data. Alternate form reliability was identified with correlations from .70 through .89, and test-retest reliability was identified with correlations from .70 through .95; standard error of measurement data based on alternate form reliability showed consistency of stanine placement. Intercorrelations of test scores for numerous samples have been, in general, of low magnitude. Supportive data regarding construct and predictive validity for CAPS have resulted from studies of relationships with conceptually similar aptitude tests, with achievement tests, with course grades, and with postgraduation studies.

1995 COPES norms are based on a national sample of 3,211 students in grades 7 through 12 (Knapp & Knapp-Lee, 1996). Frequent reevaluation of COPES is conducted. Internal consistency of scale scores was determined through alpha reliability estimates for two different samples, with coefficients from .70 to .83 evaluated as reasonable when compared with reliabilities of other inventories of values. Intercorrelations of scales based on a sample were of low magnitude and demonstrated scale independence. Supportive data regarding construct and predictive validity for this and earlier editions of COPES have resulted from studies of relationships with similar values inventories, course marks, choices of vocational courses, and postgraduation jobs and courses of study.

Overall Critique

The COPSystem provides for a systematic experience in clustered career exploration, decision making, and planning for youth and adults. Coordinated and interrelated assessment of

personal interests, abilities, and work values forms the foundation of the experience, which includes directed and supported investigation of career clusters, occupations, and jobs.

The COPSystem has a studied, comprehensive theoretical and research base. Research and development have been consistently conducted since its inception; alternate assessment instruments with readability indices and other characteristics adapted for selected populations, recommended sequential processes for investigation and planning, and detailed resource materials have been among the results. Recent renorming and revision of materials are expected to perpetuate the uniqueness of the system.

The COPSystem is useful in education, employment, work, agency, and private practice settings. As recommended in earlier reviews (Bauernfeind, 1988; Wickwire & Faldet, 1994), counselors are strongly encouraged to become involved in active use of the COPSystem.

References

Bauernfeind, R. H. (1988). Review of the Career Occupational Preference System (COPS) Interest Inventory. In J. T. Kapes & M. M. Mastie (Eds.), *A counselor's guide to career assessment instruments* (2nd ed., pp. 81-85). Alexandria, VA: National Career Development Association.

ERAS/Educational Research and Services. (1995). *Career Occupational Preference System comprehensive career guide.* San Diego, CA: EdITS.

Knapp, L., & Knapp-Lee, L. (1996). *Manual: COPES: Career Orientation Placement & Evaluation Survey, 1995 ed.* San Diego, CA: EdITS.

Knapp, L., Knapp, R. R., & Knapp-Lee, L. (1992). *Career Ability Placement Survey (CAPS): CAPS technical manual.* San Diego, CA: EdITS.

Knapp, R. R., Knapp, L., & Knapp-Lee, L. (1990). *COPSystem technical manual.* San Diego, CA: EdITS.

Knapp, R. R., Knapp, L., & Knapp-Lee, L. (1995). *COPS examiner's manual.* San Diego, EdITS.

Wickwire, P. N., & Faldet, B. (1994). Review of the Career Occupational Preference System Interest Inventory (COPS). In J. T. Kapes, M. M. Mastie, & E. A. Whitfield (Eds.), *A counselor's guide to career assessment instruments* (3rd ed., pp. 158-161). Alexandria, VA: National Career Development Association.

Career Values Card Sort Kit (CVCS)

Richard L. Knowdell
Career Research and Testing, Inc.
P.O. Box 611930
San Jose, CA 95161
cards@career trainer.com

Target Population: Adults.

Statement of the Purpose of the Instrument: A tool to allow clients to prioritize their career values in as little as five minutes and then to use their knowledge of their values to improve career decision making.

Titles of Subtests, Scales, Scores Provided: Exercises in the leader's manual include (1) memory scan, (2) growing person/changing values, (3) new career/life landscapes, (4) mastery scale, (5) career values diary.

Forms and Levels Available, with Dates of Publication/Revision of Each: 1998 edition is the only form available.

Date of Most Recent Edition of Test Manual, User's Guide, Etc.: 1998.

Languages in Which Available: English, Russian, Spanish, German, Japanese, Swedish, Dutch and Islandic.

Time: Actual Test Time: 10-15 minutes.
    Total Administration Time: Can be self-administered.

Manner in Which Results Are Reported for Individuals: In discussion with client.

Report Format/Content for Group Summaries: Not available.

Scoring
    Machine Scoring Service: Not available.
    Hand Scoring: Not applicable.
    Local Machine Scoring: Not available.

Computer Software Options Available: Available on CD-ROM from UP-software.

Cost of Materials:
Specimen Set: $8 (manual and deck of cards)

Additional Comments of Interest to Users: Very user friendly.
Published Reviews:
Diamond, E. E. (1998) Review of the Career Values Card Sort. In J. C. Impara & B. S. Plake
    (Eds.), *The thirteenth mental measurements yearbook*. Lincoln, NE: Buros Institute, University of Nebraska-Lincoln.

Kinnier, R. T. (1998) Review of the Career Values Card Sort. In J. C. Impara & B. S. Plake (Eds.), *The thirteenth mental measurements yearbook*. Lincoln, NE: Buros Instirute, University of Nebraska-Lincoln.

Reviewed by

Richard T. Kinnier
Professor

Jerry L. Kernes
Doctoral Candidate

College of Education
Arizona State University

Description

The stated objectives of Career Values Card Sort (CVCS) activities are to (1) define factors affecting career satisfaction; (2) define one's intensity of feeling about these factors; (3) determine areas of value conflict and consequence and; (4) apply learnings from the card sort to career decisions. It is available in several languages including English, Russian, Spanish, German, Japanese, Swedish, Dutch, and Icelandic. The Sort consists of 41 cutout cards. Each card is approximately 3 inches by 2 inches. Value labels (e.g., "Independence," "Security," "Fast Pace") are printed on each card in bold, capitalized letters. Under each value label is a brief definition of the value. For example, under the label of "Security" are the words, "Be assured of keeping my job and a reasonable financial reward."

In addition to the 41 value-labeled cards, five same-sized cutout cards labeled "Always Valued," "Often Valued," "Sometimes Valued," "Seldom Valued," and "Never Valued" are included. These are to be used as column headings. We think that it would be preferable to have the category cards look different from the 41 value-label cards (perhaps be bigger and a different color for easier sorting).

Note: Portions of this review were adapted from the first author's original review in the *Thirteenth Mental Measurements Yearbook* with permission of the Buros Institute.

Individuals using the Card Sort are instructed to place the cards in the appropriate column. Individuals are further instructed to "lay your cards out so that you can see all your choices in one glance. Move quickly, following your feelings," and "your Always Valued column should have no more than eight cards in it" (Knowdell, 1998, p. 3).

After the cards are laid out, individuals are instructed to rank order the values and to transcribe them on a Summary Sheet in order to have a more permanent record of their rankings. A Summary Sheet sample and a blank Summary Sheet are included in the manual. The basic self-administration and the transcription of the sortings are fairly straightforward and clearly described procedures.

Use in Counseling

A manual accompanies the card sort list providing a rationale for the card sort and directions for the activities in the list. The overview poses the question of what one wants from a career and specifies such career values as where one lives and works, what is appealing about a job, what kind of people choose their job, working conditions, level of responsibility, and salary.

There is no scoring system other than the transcription of rank-ordered value labels onto a summary sheet. Beyond that the author provides several additional exercises or activities for the user. These activities are similar to the values clarification or self-assessment exercises found in numerous career-development workbooks or textbooks published during the past two decades. They include activities such as considering one's values in light of an imminent career decision. For another activity the author suggests that participants keep logs of their work activities for a week at a time and then consider how their highest values are accommodated. In another the author asks participants to complete the sentence, "As a result of my learnings on the Values Card I plan to…" (Knowdell, 1998, p. 4). Worksheet samples and blank worksheets for completing some of the exercises are found inside the manual.

Some individuals may find some of the activities helpful. However, we found a few of the activities to be less than inspiring or engaging. For example, we found some of the instructions for the Career Values Diary activity to be tedious and we thought that the Career Values Worksheet sample to be somewhat unclear. Unfortunately, in our opinion, the practice of overstocking career development manuals and assessments with superficially developed exercises is commonplace. In these kinds of manuals or assessments we would rather see a shorter list of critically and popularly acclaimed activities or at least some guidance form the author(s) about which activities are most highly recommended.

Technical Considerations

The author provides no information on how the CVCS was developed. A list of four "objectives" is found page 3 and a brief overview of career values is presented on page 1. The overview is basically a brief reference to the criteria of a clarified value (from the values clarification literature). There are no norms for this assessment device.

No reliability studies were reported in the manual. The most appropriate type of reliability probably would be test-retest. Evidence that individuals' sortings are fairly stable over a short period of time would be a good indication that the CVCS was reliable and would provide some support for the validity of that particular list of values.

No formal procedures were used (and/or reported in the manual) on how the list was constructed. In our opinion, the list does have good face validity but a more formal validation procedure is needed.

Overall Critique

The CVCS is a self-administered card sort designed to help individuals identify or clarify their career-related values. It consists of 41 values, each printed and defined on separate cards. The cards were nicely formatted and the directions for how to sort the cards and transcribe the values are clear.

We think that the exercise of sorting and thinking about the implication so the rankings can be an effective intervention for helping individuals with their career decision making. We were less impressed with the quality and clarity of some of the supplemental activities. We would encourage the author to be more selective in his recommendation of activities.

The CVCS has good face validity but more psychometric work is needed. Specifically, the list of values should be more formally validated. One way to do this would be to construct the list from established measures (e.g., Rokeach's Value Survey) and then to have expert judges refine the list. Additionally, a test-retest study could provide us with an indication of the Card Sort's temporal reliability.

Nevertheless the CVCS appears to be a useful device. The number of values (41) seems manageable, the list seems representative of the career values found in other career value assessments, and the definitions are clearly written. For most people the assessment would probably be an enjoyable and a helpful experience.

References
Knowdell, R. L. (1998). *Career Values Card Sort*. San Jose, CA: Career Research & Testing.

Chronicle Career Quest (CCQ)

Chronicle Guidance Staff
Chronicle Guidance Publications, Inc.
66 Aurora Street
Moravia, NY 13118-3576
bettilou@chronicleguidance.com

Target Population: Middle School through Adult (Form S for middle school)

Statement of the Purpose of the Instrument: (1) To provide an easily administered self-scoring interest inventory requiring a maximum of 40 minutes to complete and score; (2) To provide an interest inventory coordinated with a comprehensive program of career planning and information; (3) To provide two forms—one for middle schools and slower readers and one for high school all students and adults; (4) To provide an instrument with an accepted and comprehensive model for ordering the world of work.

Titles of Subtests, Scales, Scores Provided: Scales are the 12 Guide for Occupational Exploration (GOE) interest areas.

Forms and Levels Available, with Dates of Publication/Revision of Each: Form S and Form L.

Date of Most Recent Edition of Test Manual, User's Guide, Etc.: 1987, 1991; 2000-2001 revision in progress as of December 2000.

Languages in Which Available: English only.

Time: Actual Test Time: 20 minutes.
Total Administration Time: 45 minutes.

Manner in Which Results are Reported for Individuals: Interpretation Guide and World of Work Chart
Types of Scores: See Administration Guide and Technical Manual.

Report Format/Content for Group Summaries: Not available.

Scoring
Machine Scoring Service: Not available.
Hand Scoring: *Scored by:* Counselee; Clerk; Counselor.
Time required for scoring: Less than 10 minutes.
Local Machine Scoring: Not available.

Computer Software Options Available: Instruments serve as a checklist with Chronicle Perspectives Plus software.

Ways in Which Computer Version Differs: The items are in random order. They are not grouped under each GOE Interest heading as they are in the print version.

Cost of Materials: $40.50 to $60.50 for 25 copies of Form S; $49.50 to $69.50 for 25 copies of Form L

Specimen Set: Forms S & L Interest Inventory Interpretation Guide, Administrators Guide, Career Paths, Report to Parents ($3.50). All of the above plus Career Crosswalk ($13.50). Free sample specimen sets are available. Call 800-622-7284.

Counselee Materials: Form L instrument, Career Paths Form L; Form S Instrument, Interpretation Guide; Occupational Profiles; Report to Parents; Administrator's Guide; Technical Manual; Crosswalk

Additional Comments of Interest to Users: CGP is in the process of revising support materials. Instruments have been programmed for use in Chronicle Perspectives PLUS software. CGP initiated a new study of the computerized version of Chronicle Career Quest.

Published Reviews:

Daniel, L. G. (1995) Review of the Chronicle Career Quest. In J. C. Conoley & J. C. Impara (Eds.), *The twelfth mental measurements yearbook.* Lincoln, NE: Buros Institute, University of Nebraska-Lincoln.

Thompson, D. (1995). Review of the Chronicle Career Quest. In J. C. Conoley & J. C. Impara (Eds.), *The twelfth mental measurements yearbook.* Lincoln, NE: Buros Institute, University of Nebraska-Lincoln.

Reviewed by

Larry G. Daniel

Associate Dean, College of Education and Human Services
Professor, Division of Educational Services and Research
University of North Florida

Description

The Chronicle Career Quest (CCQ) is a group-administered career guidance instrument that includes three major components: an *Interest Inventory* (1991a, 1991b) , a self-scoring *Interpretation Guide* (1993a, 1993b), and a *Career Paths* (1989a, 1989b) occupational profile. Both short (Form S) and long (Form L) forms of the *Interest Inventory* are available. The inventory presents examinees with a number of occupational "activities" (i.e., items) to which examinees indicate their degree of interest. These activities are categorized across 12 broad interest areas. As documented in the CCQ publication *Career Crosswalk* (1993), this categorization is consistent with a structuring of occupations

---

Note: Portions of this review were adapted from the author's original review in *The Twelfth Mental Measurements Yearbook* with permission of the Buros Institute.

used by the United States Employment Service in its *Guide for Occupational Exploration* (1979).

Form S (short form) includes nine items across each of the 12 interest areas for a total of 108 items, and Form L (long form) includes 12 items across each of the 12 interest areas for a total of 144 items. Items are brief and specific, with each denoting a single work-related activity (e.g., "Examine slides under a microscope," "Care for sick or injured people"). The Form S items are identical to items included in Form L, with an occasional minor wording change. Form L simply includes three additional items for each interest area not included in Form S. The response format across the two forms varies slightly. Form S uses the dichotomous response options *like* (L) and *dislike* (D). Form L uses a three-option format of *uninteresting* (U), *interesting* (I), and *very interesting* (VI). According to the *Technical Manual* (1992b), items were subjected to rigorous content analysis and latent trait analysis during the inventory's early development. These analyses resulted in reduction of an original pool of 240 activities into the 108 and 144 activities included, respectively, in forms L and S, as well as modification of wording in a number of the retained items.

Use in Counseling

As noted in the *Technical Manual*, Form S is intended for use with students in grades 7-9. Form L is intended for use with students in grades 10-12. However, the accompanying *Administrator's Guide* (1992a) suggests that Form S may be used with students as late as grade 10 if occupational awareness, motivation, and/or reading level are somewhat low. Moreover, Form L may be used with students as early as grade 9 if they have at least some occupational awareness. Form L is also recommended for use with college students and other prevocational adults. Hence, counselors in middle school, high school, college, and adult education settings could find one or both forms of the inventory useful.

Once the *Interest Inventory* is completed, students are directed to complete the *Interpretation Guide*. The instrument may be easily scored by the examiner or by the average student. Students then use the 12 interest area scores to determine the several interest areas that represent their major occupational interests and are referred to a listing of job titles included in the *Interpretation Guide* that are consistent with their interest areas. Students now proceed to the third component of the instrument, the *Career Paths* occupational profile. In this phase, they select one or more of the jobs to research further. The completed *Career Paths* profile includes descriptive information about such things as duties associated with the job, training requirements, salary, hours, and opportunities for advancement. All this information may be useful in assisting the student in making a career choice.

Technical Considerations

The technical manual includes information about reliability and validity studies related to the *Interest Inventory* component of the CCQ. These data are based on responses of 1,554 examinees for Form S and 1,329 examinees for Form L. In general, the samples for these studies included a fair representation of males and females across several different geographic regions of the United States, as well as wide diversity in ethnicity generally reflective of percentages in the actual American population.

Internal consistency reliabilities for scores on the full scale of both forms were in the mid-.90s. Interest subscale reliabilities for scores on form L were in the .80 range, with a few coefficients as low as the mid-.70s, and a few as high as .90. Alphas for subscale scores for Form S average in the mid-.70s, and range from .58 to .87.

Content validity was addressed by comparing the occupational activities depicted in the inventory's items to occupational categories as delineated by the *Guide for Occupational Exploration*. Construct validity was addressed by examining inter-correlations among the 12 interest area subscale scores across several administrations of the instrument using different samples. In general, these correlations were consistent with models hypothesized by Holland, thus supporting the construct validity of the scores yielded by the interest inventory.

Overall Critique

On the whole, the CCQ is a defensible system for assisting students in determining career opportunities. The format of the interest inventory allows each occupational activity (item) to be rated in isolation of all others. Hence, unlike other similar instruments (e.g., Career Directions Inventory, Kuder Occupational Interest Survey), the CCQ yields scores that reflect *absolute* opinions about each occupational activity rather than *comparative* assessment of activities. The *Career Paths* occupational profile that ultimately results from the completion of the *Interest Inventory* is a logical process that allows the student to critically examine multiple facets of a given occupation. The various documents associated with the three components of the instrument are well organized and written generally at an appropriate level for middle and high school students. Another nice feature is the color-coding of the three component documents across each form of the instrument (white for Form S and blue for Form L). This helps the administrator or the examinee to avoid selecting the wrong accompanying documents when moving from one phase of the CCQ process to the next.

The CCQ is not without its shortcomings, however. One questionable feature in the presentation of the *Interest Inventory* is the intentional grouping together of all items relative to each interest area. This procedure for ordering of the items may encourage response set. On the other hand, this procedure facilitates ease of scoring. As a solution, the authors might consider randomly arranging the items to discourage response set along with designing a computer program to sort and regroup the items into meaningful categorizations for scoring purposes.

The number of response options is also problematic. Generally, by allowing for greater response variance, a test developer increases the reliability of scores on individual test items. This trend is demonstrated in the reliability data presented in the technical manual for Form S as compared to Form L. Subscale reliability coefficients for data from Form S, which allows for only two response options, were noticeably lower than those for data from Form L, which allows for three response options. The authors might even consider using additional scale steps with either of the forms to allow for even greater response variance.

An additional problem relative to reliability is the absence of studies of equivalence or stability of scores from the *Interest Inventory*. Considering that the age ranges for the two forms of the instrument overlap, investigation of the equivalence of the forms across a given sample would add to the knowledge of the instrument's psychometric properties. Moreover, stability of scores determined by two administrations of the instrument across a relatively short interval would indicate the degree to which factors relative to a given testing occasion affect scores on the instrument.

Finally, several typographical and other related proofreading errors were noted in the text of the *Technical Manual*. For example, n's of subsamples included in the reliability studies do not always add up to the N of the full sample. Although these are by no means major flaws, they do cause some confusion in interpreting the technical information presented in the text. The authors may wish to further review and edit the technical manual to correct these errors.

Despite the aforementioned problems, the CCQ is a promising tool for counselors desiring to direct their students toward occupational choices. When used in conjunction with other sources of information about students, the CCQ serves well both to direct students toward appropriate interest areas and to educate students on various careers.

References

Chronicle Guidance Publications, Inc. (1989a). *Career paths form L.* Moravia, NY: Author.

Chronicle Guidance Publications, Inc. (1989b). *Career paths form S.* Moravia, NY: Author.

Chronicle Guidance Publications, Inc. (1991a). *Chronicle Career Quest interest inventory form L.* Moravia, NY: Author.

Chronicle Guidance Publications, Inc. (1991b). *Chronicle Career Quest interest inventory form S.* Moravia, NY: Author.

Chronicle Guidance Publications, Inc. (1992a). *Chronicle Career Quest administrator's guide.* Moravia, NY: Author.

Chronicle Guidance Publications, Inc. (1992b). *Chronicle Career Quest technical manual.* Moravia, NY: Author.

Chronicle Guidance Publications, Inc. (1993a). *Chronicle Career Quest career crosswalk.* Moravia, NY: Author

Chronicle Guidance Publications, Inc. (1993b). *Chronicle Career Quest interpretation guide form L.* Moravia, NY: Author.

Chronicle Guidance Publications, Inc. (1993c). *Chronicle Career Quest interpretation guide form S.* Moravia, NY: Author

U.S. Department of Labor. (1979). *Guide for occupational exploration.* Washington, DC: U.S. Government Printing Office.

Harrington O'Shea CareerDecision-Making System®Revised (CDM)

Thomas F. Harrington and Arthur J. O'Shea
American Guidance Services, Inc.
4201 Woodland Road
Circle Pines, MN 55014-1796

Target Population: Middle school through adult

Statement of the Purpose of the Instrument: A multidimensional systems approach to career decision making that uses an individual's self-knowledge of interests, stated career choices, school subjects, work values, and future training plans to suggest career options for further exploration.

Titles of Subtests, Scales, Scores Provided:

Level 1 Booklet

Scales	Scores
Crafts Interest Area	Crafts Interest Area Score
Scientific Interest Area	Scientific Interest Area Score
The Arts Interest Area	The Arts Interest Score
Social Interest Area	Social Interest Area Score
Business Interest Area	Business Interest Area Score
Office Operations Interest Area	Office Operations Interest Area Score

Level 2 Survey Booklet

Scales	Scores
Crafts Interest Area	Crafts Interest Area Score
Scientific Interest Area	Scientific Interest Area Score
The Arts Interest Area	The Arts Interest Area Score
Social Interest Area	Social Interest Area Score
Business Interest Area	Business Interest Area Score
Office Operations Interest Area	Office Operations Interest Area Score

Forms and Levels Available, with Dates of Publication/Revision of Each: CDM Level 1 (Middle School and Low level Readers), 1982: CDM-R. 1993, 2000; CDM Level 2 (High School through Adult), 1982: CDM-R, 1993, 2000

Date of Most Recent Edition of Test Manual, User's Guide, Etc.: 2000

Languages in Which Available: Hand-Scored Editions (Level 1 Booklet, Level 2 Survey Booklet and Interpretive Folder) are available in English and Spanish. Computer-Scored Edition (Level 2) is available in English.

Time: Actual Test Time: 20-40 minutes
  Total Administration Time: 25-45 minutes

Norm Group(s) on Which Scores Are Based: No derived scores. Standardization samples 1991: Level 1-965; Level 2-996. Sample defined based on 1990 U.S. Census data.

Manner in Which Results Are Reported for Individuals: Hand scored (Levels 1 and 2) or computer generated (Level 2)
  Types of Scores: Interest Area Raw Score; percentile Rank Norms, by gender, for Interest Area Raw Scores.
  Report Format/Content: Level 1: Interest Area Results and Interpretive Information included in Survey Booklet (i.e., survey results and student self report of career choices, work values, preferred school subjects, abilities and future plans). Level 2: Summary Profile and Interpretive Folder which includes survey results and student self-report of career choices, work values, preferred school subjects, abilities and future plans.

Report Format/Content for Group Summaries: Available August 2000.
  Basic Service: Computerized version contains group summary reports for Level 2 only. Level 2 Group Summary Report is four pages: Page 1 reports students' selection of Career Choices and School Subjects. The tables list first and second choices from 18 Career Clusters for each gender and the total group as well as school subjects preferred by the group. Page 2 reports students' selection of Work Values and Abilities. The tables list choices from 15 Work Values and 14 Abilities for each gender and the total group. Page 3 reports students' selection of Future Plans and Local Frequency Distributions and percents. The tables list choices from 10 Future Plans and the number of students scoring within selected interest area score intervals. Page 4 reports students' selection of Suggested Career Clusters based on the survey results. This table lists first and second choices from 18 Career Clusters for each gender and the total group.

Scoring
  Machine Scoring Service: Not available.
  Hand Scoring:
    Scored by: Counselee
    Time required for scoring: About 5-10 minutes.
  Local Machine Scoring: CDM-Windows version available August 2000. Provisions/conditions/equipment required: System requirements are 32 megabytes of RAM and 7 megabytes of hard drive space. Scantron or NCS dual head scanner.

Computer Software Options Available: Available August 2000 Level 2 only. Standard administration online: Other: Scanning and key entry of raw scores.

Ways in Which Computer Version Differs: Survey items and content of Hand-scored Survey Booklet 2 are the same as the Computer-scored version. The computer report integrates the individual's survey results and self-reported preferences of stated career choices, preferred school subjects, work values, abilities and future training plans with related occupational information from the Level 2 Interpretive Folder. The CDM Computer-scored version has four methods of administration:
1. enter item answers
2. enter raw score totals
3. enter data by scanning
4. administer online

The online administration is flexible and very user friendly. Group reports can be produced form all methods of data entry.

Cost of Materials:
    Specimen Set: $9.95
    CDM Manual: $29.95
    Counselee Materials: Level 1 Booklet (25 per pkg) $52.95; Level 2 Survey Booklet and Interpretive Folders (25 per pkg) $52.95; Audiocassette $14.95.
    Computer Materials: Scannable Level 2 Survey Booklets and Interpretive Folders (25 per pkg) and Group Identification Sheet $52.95. Software and User Guide $150.

Additional Comments of Interest to Users: New computer-related and engineering job opportunities are included, as are rapidly growing non-technical positions. Career Clusters cover 90% - 95% of all current U.S. jobs. Color changes, new typography, and a contemporary design make CDM easier to use. The RIASEC equivalent for the six Career Interest Areas is provided. CDM's school subject listings match today's curricular offerings. There are new sources of career information and a direct link to the Internet. An Annotated Bibliography of recently published research is now included in the CDM Manual. (The CDM-R was not restandardized.)

Published reviews:
Neubert, D. (1995). Review of the Harrington-O'Shea Career Decision-making System Revised. In J.C. Conoley & J.C. Impara (Eds.). *Twelfth mental measurements yearbook.* Lincoln, NE: Buros Institute, University of Nebraska - Lincoln.
Shaffer, M.B. (1995). Review of the Harrington-O'Shea Career Decision-Making System Revised. In J.C. Conoley & J.C. Impara (Eds.). *Twelfth mental measurements yearbook* (p. 457). Lincoln, NE: Buros Institute, University of Nebraska-Lincoln.

Reviewed by

Vicki L. Campbell
Associate Professor

Gretchen W. Raiff
Graduate Student

Department of Psychology
University of North Texas

Description

The 2000 revision of the Career Decision-Making System (CDM-R) is well designed to present the components of career planning. The "system surveys not only interests, but also stated career choices, school subjects, work values, abilities, and future training plans" (Harrington & O'Shea, 2000, p. 1). The interest survey is based on Holland's theory of vocational types, renamed for occupational relevance (Crafts, Scientific, The Arts, Social, Business, Office Operations). Added to the basic hexagonal structure are 18 "career clusters" that erations). Added to the basic hexagonal structure are 18 "career clusters" that fall within the six career interest areas and provide a useful way to conceptualize job themes.

The 2000 CDM-R makes few changes from the 1991 version. Revisions center on adding emerging jobs and careers to the career clusters (e.g., in high technology), improving readability, and adding a link to the Internet. Broad changes were made to the CDM in the 1991 revision, which split the test into Level 1 for younger students (7th through 10th grade) and Level 2 for senior high school students and adults. A Spanish translation of Level 1 and Level 2 has been available since 1993.

Using the CDM-R encourages users to integrate their interests, abilities, and values and prepares them to "approach the career advisor as a professional resource person" (Harrington & O'Shea, 2000, p. 2). Level 1 is an introduction to career planning, and Level 2 helps advanced planners take steps to facilitate decisions about college majors, career training, or select an occupation. Although the order and means for collecting data vary between the two levels, both guide users to self-administer an interest survey and select their most preferred work values, abilities, school subjects, future educational plans, and possible career choices.

Interpretive materials help users examine career areas identified by the interest survey in relation to self-report information (values, abilities, etc.). Actual job titles grouped with corresponding values, school subjects, and abilities help users evaluate how well their career plans hold together. The Level 1 summary page, and the color-coded, user-friendly Level 2 Interpretive Folder offer a big-picture view of the user's top three career clusters, preferences, and corresponding career information. Job titles are labeled with abbreviations for growth outlook and education and training required. Administration time is 30 to 45 minutes but does not include time for interpretation, which will vary depending on how the materials are used. For example, the Interpretive Folder lists seven steps, and the manual describes a sample career workshop with five meetings.

Use in Counseling

The CDM-R is suitable for junior high school students through adults. Level 1 can introduce younger students to career planning, help them make appropriate school course choices, give them basic occupational information, and help them explore how their interests and values can apply to the world of work. For advanced students and adults, the Level 2 Interpretive Folder provides an opportunity to clarify job requirements and focus interests on specific careers.

The CDM-R manual offers several excellent tools to help school guidance counselors or career counselors plan a career development program. In addition to steps for individual administration, a Group Exploration Program offers a workshop format. Case examples nicely illustrate key career development concepts, such as ideas for working with individuals who demonstrate unrealistic career goals, and looking out for possible gender stereotyping.

Technical Considerations

The 2000 edition of the CDM-R relies primarily on psychometric information for the 1991 revision and the 1981 CDM that has been reviewed previously (Neubert, 1995; Shaffer, 1995; Vansickle, 1994). Most of the information addresses the interest scales, with some evaluation of the self-report sections.

The system uses interest scale raw scores that are described as domain referenced. The authors note the benefits of raw scores and make their case for the necessity of looking to "one's personal hierarchy of interests" (Harrington & O'Shea, 2000, p. 39). Nonetheless, percentile rank norms are reported for Level 1 and 2 interest scale raw scores for the 1991 standardization sample. Use of these norms will raise the issue of gender differences on the scales; however, this topic is clearly addressed in the manual.

The CDM-R interest scales are very internally consistent (median .90 Level 1; .93 Level 2). Test-retest reliability is slightly lower, and the only information for the CDM-R (Level 1) is for a group of 45 unemployed adults after one month (median .79). The stability of CDM codes and self-report information is reported, with percentages of agreement demonstrating "general consistency over the five-month interval" (Harrington & O'Shea, 2000, p. 68). The equivalence of interest scores for the CDM-R Level 1 and 2 and the CDM-R and the CDM is supported, which is important because of the reliance on CDM data. Hand-scoring errors have been reduced for the CDM-R (4% Level 1, 1% Level 2) in comparison to the CDM (6%). Other studies showed that the transparent scoring system and description of expressed interests prior to filling out the interest survey had little influence on scores.

All validity information discussed in the body of the manual uses the 1981 CDM. An annotated bibliography includes 19 additional articles, 4 of which use the CDM-R. Evidence for the construct, concurrent, and predictive validity of the interest scales, and to some extent, the self-report information, is provided. The intercorrelations of the interest scales (English and Spanish-language) in different samples are discussed as support for the construct validity and cross-cultural validity of the instrument. The authors conclude that there is support for the cross-cultural relevance of the CDM; however, others have questioned whether the hexagonal structure proposed by Holland holds up across cultures or even among ethnic groups within the U.S. (Rounds & Tracey, 1996).

"Exploration validity" is an important concept for the CDM-R, given that the primary objectives are to help users learn about themselves and progress in career decision-making. Tittle (1978) coined the term, pointing out that whether career instruments stimulate client exploration may be more important than traditional forms of validity. The CDM-R manual does little to address exploration validity with the exception of two studies included in the bibliography. These showed use of the CDM-R can result in increased vocational identity and decreased career indecision (Caligiuri, 1996, cited in Harrington & O'Shea, 2000), and increased knowledge of career decision-making (Luzzo & Taylor, 1995, cited in Harrington & O'Shea, 2000).

Computer-Based Version

Computer software is available for the CDM-R Level 2 English version. The survey items can be administered online, data can be entered directly into the program, or a scannable survey booklet can be used. A computer-based version is also available as a part of the Guidance Information System, from Riverside Publishing Company. Computer-scoring generates a report of the individual's interest scale scores, self-reports, and suggested career clusters, and for the career advisor a breakdown of interest survey responses. A Group Summary Report summarizes career goals, interests, and school subjects as a possible aid to curriculum planners and administrators. Research has found that the computer-based CDM was slightly more reliable than the paper-and-pencil version.

Overall Critique

As a career exploration and planning system, the CDM-R offers several benefits. It provides broad exposure to career information inexpensively, the system has been carefully developed, and its psychometric characteristics compare favorably to similar instruments. The strength of the CDM lies in the attractive way it encourages exploration and career planning. The Interpretive Folder (Level 2) and overall attention to ease of use appear extremely engaging.

Another strength is the extensive, well-written CDM-R manual. It is a solid instruction to the system, and a benchmark for career assessment systems seeking to educate a broad audience about career development concepts, theory and counseling. Past critiques about scoring errors, the transparency of a self-scoring system, and problems with assessing one's own abilities are readily addressed.

The primary criticism of the CDM-R is the limited psychometric evaluation of this version and the sparse research addressing the primary purpose of career exploration. Most information uses the 1981 CDM and has not been updated, although there is support for the equivalence of the CDM-R. The authors' use of the CDM in a variety of cultures is to be applauded, but the relevance and usefulness to different cultural and socioeconomic groups need further investigation. An examination of materials suggests the CDM-R's greatest strength is encouraging exploration. However, research supporting this view is just beginning. More studies of this type would be useful to those deciding whether to select the CDM-R for a career decision-making program.

References

Harrington, T. F., & O'Shea, A. J. (2000). *The Harrington-O'Shea Career Decision-Making System-Revised Manual.* Circle Pines, MN: American Guidance Service.

Neubert, D. (1995). Review of the Harrington-O'Shea Career Decision-Making System Revised. In J. C. Conoley & J. C. Impara (Eds.), *Twelfth mental measurements yearbook* (pp. 456-457). Lincoln, NE: Buros Institute of Mental Measurements, University of Nebraska – Lincoln.

Rounds, J., & Tracey, T. J. (1996). Cross-cultural structural equivalence of RIASEC models and measures. *Journal of Counseling Psychology, 43,* 310-329.

Shaffer, M. B. (1995). Review of the Harrington-O'Shea Career Decision-Making System Revised. In J. C. Conoley & J. C. Impara (Eds.), *Twelfth mental measurements yearbook* (pp. 457). Lincoln, NE: Buros Institute, University of Nebraska – Lincoln.

Tittle C. K. (1978). Implications of recent developments for future research in career interest measurement. In C. K. Tittle & D. G. Zytowski (Eds.), *Sexfair interest measurement: Research and implications* (pp. 123-128). Washington, DC: National Institute of Education.

Vansickle, T. R. (1994). Review of the Harrington-O'Shea Career Decision-Making System Revised. In J. T. Kapes, M. M. Mastie, & E. A. Whitfield (Eds.). *A Counselor's Guide to Career Assessment Instruments* (3rd ed., pp. 174-177). Alexandria, VA: National Career Development Association.

Interest Explorer

Riverside Publishing Staff
Riverside Publishing
425 Spring Lake Drive
Itasca, IL 60143
630-467-7000
www.riverpub.com
rpcwebmaster@hmco.com

Target Population: Level 1 is for middle school or junior high students, grades 6-8. Level 2 is for high school students, grades 9-12, as well as adults.

Statement of the Purpose of the Instrument: The *Interest Explorer* is a career guidance and counseling instrument designed to help middle school, junior high, and high school students, as well as adults, make wise educational and career-planning decisions about their futures. It provides information about students' interests in 14 career areas that are directly linked to publications of the Department of Labor, including the *Guide for Occupational Exploration* (GOE), the *Occupational Outlook Handbook* (OOH), and the *O*NET Dictionary of Occupational Titles*. Borrowing from the Department of Labor's classification scheme, the career areas defined by the *Interest Explorer* were formed on the basis of similarity of work activities and educational requirements.

Titles of Subtests, Scales, Scores Provided: Measures levels of interest in 14 career areas: Animals and Plants; Arts; Business Services; Computer Technology; Customer Services; Educational and Social Services; Engineering Technology; Legal Services; Management and Administration; Mechanical and Craft Technology; Medical Sciences; Physical and Life Sciences and Mathematics; Protective Services; Sales.

Forms and Levels Available, with Dates of Publication/Revision of Each: Level 1 (middle school/junior high) and Level 2 (high school and adult); published in 1998.

Date of Most Recent Edition of Test Manual, User's Guide, Etc.: Preliminary Technical Manual, 1999.

Languages in Which Available: English only.

Time: Actual Test Time: Approximately 30-35 minutes (Assessment is untimed.).
   Total Administration Time: Approximately 40-45 minutes.

Norm Group(s) on Which Scores Are Based: Not norm-referenced; however, instrument tryout data were gathered from students in grades 6-9 for Level 1 (N=1,718), and grades 8-12 for Level 2 (N=2,752).

Manner in Which Results Are Reported for Individuals:
   Types of Scores: The *Interest Explorer* report shows in graphical format a student's interest levels in the 14 career areas, form highest to lowest. These data are derived from a student's

responses to work activity statements that are linked to the career areas. The career area rankings are determined by raw score totals. The graph also documents the degree of interest (High, Medium, or Low) in each career area.

Report Format/Content:
Basic Service: Individual four-page report that includes graph depicting interest levels in 14 career areas and narrative text about the two highest areas of interest. The report also provides information on the student's interests in school courses and general opportunities (such as working with others), listing courses and opportunities the student likes and those he or she dislikes or is undecided about. In addition, the report shows the student's results form the *Iowa Tests of Educational Development® (ITED®)*. This combined report allows the student, teacher, and counselor to compare achievement test results from *ITED* with interests as evidenced through the *Interest Explorer*.

Report Format/Content for Group Summaries: Not available.

Scoring
    Machine Scoring Service:
        Cost of basic service per counselee: $2.30
        Cost of options: $0.25 for extra copy, per student
        Time required for scoring and returning (maximum): 15 working days
    Hand Scoring: Not available.
    Local Machine Scoring: Not available.

Computer Software Options Available: Not available.

Cost of Materials:
    Specimen Set: No specimen set, but samples available upon request
    Counselee Materials: Reusable Student Survey Booklets (Level 1 or Level 2), package of 25, including booklets and Directions for Administration, $41.50. Machine-Scorable Answer Documents (Level 1 or Level 2), package of 50, $30. Directions for Administration (single copy), $4.

Additional Comments of Interest to Users: Counselor's Manual for Interpreting the *Interest Explorer* published in Fall 1999. The manual provides sample score reports and case studies, with suggested interventions. Also includes all relevant technical information.

Published Reviews: None cited.

Reviewed by

Sharon A. Sackett
Senior Consultant
MDA Consulting Group, Inc.
Minneapolis, MN

Description

The Interest Explorer (Riverside Publishing, 1999) is a new vocational interest measure designed to help junior and senior high school students make educational and vocational decisions. Developed with the school-to-careers movement in mind, the Interest Explorer measures interest in 14 career areas that were derived in part from the organizational scheme of the *Guide for Occupational Exploration* (GOE). The results of the Interest Explorer can be linked to several other Department of Labor publications, including the *Dictionary of Occupational Titles* (DOT), the *Occupational Outlook Handbook* (OOH), and O*NET.

The Interest Explorer is intended for joint administration with an achievement battery, the Iowa Tests of Educational Development® (ITED; Feldt et al., 1996), to present an overall picture of a student's skills and interests.

The Interest Explorer items contain "activity-related" statements that reflect a variety of school subjects, opportunities (aspects of work), and career areas/occupations derived from both the GOE and DOT. Two forms or levels of the instrument are available. Level 1 contains 140 items and is intended for students in grades 6-8 (middle school and junior high), whereas Level 2 contains 180 items and is designed for high school students and adults. The publisher states that the items in both forms are written at a fifth grade, or lower, reading level. Responses are made on a five-point Likert-type scale: "Like a Great Deal," "Like," "Undecided," "Dislike," "Dislike a Great Deal." Individual item responses are summed to create raw score totals for each career area. Scores are not standardized but are interpreted in raw form. "High Interest" corresponds to an average item response of 3.5 or greater, "Medium Interest" is determined by an average item response greater than 2.5 but less than 3.5, while an average item response of less than 2.5 indicates "Low Interest."

Although the endpoints of the response scale clearly represent high and low interest, it can be argued that the middle response option of "Undecided" does not represent the true midpoint of the scale. "Undecided" may be a reasonable response, but the midpoint may be closer to "Indifferent" or "Neither Like nor Dislike." Although the "Undecided" midpoint can be found in other instruments, its use here is problematic given the method used to compute career area scores. An individual who responded "Undecided" to all items in a career area would be described as having "Medium Interest" in that area. This is a potential problem, and counselors need to be cautious when interpreting results that indicate "Medium Interest."

The front cover of the four-page combined report contains a letter to the student that presents the instruments as starting point for the career exploration process. The ITED® and Interest Explorer reports appear inside on facing pages, and the back cover contains definitions of the 14 career areas and ITED® scores. Although the combined report does not include an integrated interpretation of the results, the Interest Explorer section instructs the respondent to "consider the achievement test results on the opposite page and talk with your counselor or teachers about which skill areas can help in pursuing a career that interests you." The career area results are presented in a bar chart, the Career Areas Graph, that depicts the level of interest (High, Medium, Low) in each of the 14 career areas. Raw scale scores are not presented on the report, but the career areas are ordered from highest to lowest level of interest. The report also contains a narrative description of the top two career areas, including typical activities, occupational titles, and courses that might help one pursue a career in that field. According to the *Preliminary Technical Manual*, narrative information is also provided for special cases in which there is either low or high interest in all or almost all areas.

The second section of the report describes the student's interest in school courses and "opportunities" in various occupations (for example, "Working Outdoors"). The results are based on one item per scale and are reported in separate tables under two headings: "Like" and "Dislike or Undecided." Although the item responses are treated appropriately in this section, there is more room for improvement. Leona Tyler's (1955, 1964) early research on the development of vocational interests in children and adolescents showed that the ability to express dislikes was critical for the emergence of an individual pattern of interests. A high proportion of "like" responses tended to suppress the emergence of interest patterns. Thus, the extent to which a student has begun to identify *dislikes* is critical information and worth highlighting, and probably should not be combined with "undecided" results.

It is reasonable that Level 1 courses are fewer in number than Level 2 courses, which include advanced topics. However, the number of Level 1 opportunities exceeds Level 2 (14 versus 12), and the two forms show other differences that are not easily understood. For example, "Work with Animals" appears in Level 1 but not in Level 2; "Work Outside" appears in Level 2 but not in Level 1. "Influence Others" appears on both forms, but "Be Persuasive" appears on the Level 1 form alone.

Use in Counseling

Level 1 of the Interest Explorer was developed for use with students in grades 6-8 as an introduction to career exploration, to help them identify educational goals and select courses to pursue in high school. As one of the "Iowa Tests," the ITED® is a norm-referenced achievement test that is widely used in grades 9-12. However, because the ITED® is not administered to students below grade 8, the Interest Explorer is not currently available for students in grades 6 or 7. According to the publisher, a Level 1 report may eventually be developed for joint use with the Iowa Tests of Basic Skills® (ITBS), which is administered to students in grades 6-8.

Level 2 of the Interest Explorer was designed to help high school students and adults with advanced career exploration based on "a more specific understanding of themselves and the world of work" (p. 3). Because a standalone report is not currently available, the Interest Explorer cannot be administered to adults at the present time.

Although the items for both levels are written at a grade 5 reading level or lower, some of the phrasing and terminology in both forms appears rather sophisticated. Also, although not necessarily a problem, the items vary dramatically in terms of their specificity and complexity. The specific and complex items tend to comprise the career areas, whereas the shorter and more general items measure interest in courses and opportunities. One of the most specific and complex items is "Organize and assign work projects for converting computer software to hardware."

Both levels of the Interest Explorer are administered via reusable survey booklets and separate machine-scorable answer sheets. The *Directions for Administration* booklet can be used with either level. This booklet presents an overview of the 14 career areas, offers suggestions for preparing students for administration, and contains a reproduceable "question-and-answer" section that may be distributed to students prior to adminstration. According to the publisher, a *Counselor's Guide for Interpreting the Interest Explorer* is planned for release in 2001 that will include case studies, sample reports, and suggestions for interpreting the results. Given the association with the GOE classification structure, the results of both forms of the Interest Explorer can be further explored with the GOE, DOT, OOH, and O*NET.

Technical Considerations

At the time of this writing, technical information about the Interest Explorer is quite limited. All available information is presented in the *Preliminary Technical Manual*. According to the publisher, a final version of the *Technical Manual* is planned for release in 2001.

Descriptive summary statistics are presented separately for boys and girls in grades 8-12. The career area means and standard deviations cannot be used for comparison purposes when interpreting individual results because computed scores do not appear on the report.

Reliability evidence addresses the internal consistency of the 14 scales that comprise the career areas. The alpha coefficients for Level 1 range from .79 (Management & Administration) to .94 (Computer Technology). The internal consistency reliability coefficients for all but two of the career areas are in the .80s. The reliability coefficients for Level 2 are somewhat higher, with a low of .85 (Sales) and a maximum of .97 (Computer Technology). Fifty percent of the career areas show internal consistency reliability coefficients in the .90s. Standard errors of measurement are reported for both levels but are of little practical use in the absence of reported scores.

Validity evidence for the Interest Explorer comes from primarily from analyses of the internal structure of the instrument. Scale intercorrelations for Level 1 (N = 1,718) range from .12 (Animals & Plants, Computer Technology) to .84 (Engineering Technology, Mechanical & Craft Technology). Level 2 scale intercorrelations (N = 2,752) range from .11 (Medical Science, Computer Technology) to .81 (Engineering Technology, Mechanical & Craft Technology). The *Preliminary Technical Manual* contains a summary of the results of an exploratory factor analysis of the career area items, which yielded seven factors. The actual data are not presented, but the *Manual* states that the factors "are logically consistent with the scales to which they load, thus supporting scale homogeneity and relative independence of the scales" (p. 20). Given the derivation of the Interest Explorer items, the content of the instrument is assumed to adequately represent the intended content domain.

Overall Critique

The opportunity to view achievement and vocational interest results in a single document is an attractive feature of the Interest Explorer and ITED® combined report. The association between the Interest Explorer and Department of Labor publications also is appealing. However, it is premature to offer final conclusions or recommendations concerning the Interest Explorer. Given the instrument's intended purpose as a tool for educational and vocational decision making, validity evidence concerning how well the Interest Explorer predicts such decisions clearly is necessary. Test-retest reliability data also are needed. The test developers might consider modifying the report format to separate "dislike" from "undecided" courses and opportunities. The report might also encourage students to learn more about undecided areas. A special counselor's report that contained actual scores and information about the distribution or variability of item responses that yield midrange scores for the career areas also would be helpful. Alternatively, the response options or scoring format could be changed so that "undecided" responses are not interpreted as reflecting "medium interest."

References

Feldt, L. S., Forsyth, R. A., Ansley, T. N., & Alnot, S. D. (1996). *ITED® norms and score conversions with technical information, Form M Complete Battery*. Itasca, IL: Riverside Publishing.

Riverside Publishing. (1999). *Interest Explorer preliminary technical manual.* Itasca, IL: Author.

Tyler, L. E. (1955). The development of "vocational interests": I. The organization of likes and dislikes in ten-year-old children. *Journal of Genetic Psychology, 86*, 33-44.

Tyler, L. E. (1964). The antecedents of two varieties of vocational interests. *Genetic Psychology Monographs, 70*, 177-227.

Interest Determination, Exploration and Assessment System (IDEAS)

Charles B. Johansson
National Computer Systems, Inc.
PO Box 1416
Minneapolis, MN 55440
www.ncs.com

Target Population: Junior high, middle school and high school students, special education, "students at risk" and adults.

Statement of the Purpose of the Instrument: The IDEAS instrument is a self-contained, self-scorable, interest inventory that serves as an introduction to career planning. It provides scores on 16 basic interest scales that help students and adults identify and explore occupational areas of interest. The inventory workbook includes updated OOH and DOT references, follow-up activities, websites, and suggested school courses.

Titles of Subtests, Scales, Scores Provided: Sixteen broad interest categories covered mechanical/fixing, protective services, nature/outdoors, mathematics, science, medical, creative arts, writing, community service, educating, child care, public speaking, business, sales, office practices, food service.

Forms and Levels Available with Dates of Publication/Revision of Each: Two forms, School version published in 1977, revised 1990, and revised 1996. Adult version published in 2000 (same as school version but done without school age scoring graphs and with fewer animated graphics, looks less juvenile).

Date of Most Recent Edition of Test Manual, User's Guide, Etc.: Most recent users guide 1990.

Languages in Which Available: Enhanced Version: English and Spanish.

Time: Actual Test Time: 20-25 minutes.
Total Administration: Time 20-25 minutes.

Norm Group(s) on Which Scores Are Based: Students in grades 7-9, grades 10-12, and adults.

Manner in Which Results Are Reported for Individuals
 Types of Scores: Raw and standard scores.
 Report Format/Basic Service: Individuals score and graph their own results. Printed interpretive information and follow-up activities are included in the IDEAS test workbook.
 Options: Student version or Adult Version.

Report Format/Content for Group Summaries: Not available.

Scoring
  Machine Scoring Service:
  Hand Scoring:
  Scored by: Counselee.
  Time required for scoring: 40-50 minutes.
  Local Machine Scoring: Not available.

Computer Software Options Available: Not available.

Cost of Materials: Tests sold in packages of 50. Approximate price is $1.25 each.
  Specimen Set: Specimen sets are available (manual and 3 tests). Call NCS at
  800-627-7271 ext 5151 for current prices.

Additional Comments of Interest to Users: *Occupational Outlook Handbook* (OOH) references list in the IDEAS test workbook are updated every two years to correspond to the most recent edition of the OOH. In the last revision a separate test booklet and workbook were developed. The scoring graphs, interpretive data, and several follow-up activities are included in the workbook.

Published Reviews:
Miller, R. J. (1992). Review of IDAS: Interest Determination, Exploration and Assessment System. In J. J. Kramer & J. C. Conoley (Eds). *The eleventh mental measurements yearbook*. Lincoln, NE: Buros Institute, University of Nebraska - Lincoln.

Reviewed by

Tammi Vacha-Haase
Assistant Professor

Lydia P. Buki
Assistant Professor

Department of Psychology
Colorado State University

Description

The Interest Determination, Exploration and Assessment System (IDEAS) is a "relatively inexpensive, paper-and-pencil, self-scoring career exploration tool" (Johansson, 1996) for grades 7-12 and adults. The instrument is appropriate for a broad measurement of career interests and may be used to narrow interests to three possible career areas for continued exploration.

IDEAS was first introduced in 1977 as the offspring of the longer Career Assessment Inventory (CAI), also developed by Johansson. The original version consisted of 112 items with 14 scales. The inventory was described as being based on a "strong technical and empirical background" (Swanson, 1987, p. 258) with concerns regarding gender fairness, potential for scoring errors, representativeness of the scales and thoroughness of the manual being identified (Swanson, 1987).

Item response statistics were updated, normative information from a wider demographic base of respondents was collected, and scales were modified to reflect changes in the occupational world for the 1990 version. With these revisions, IDEAS now consists of 128 items, and it includes two additional scales in an attempt to represent a balance of the six Holland types (Realistic, Investigative, Artistic, Social, Enterprising, and Conventional). The 16 scales measured in IDEAS include Mechanical/Fixing, Protective Services, Nature/Outdoors, Mathematics, Science, Medical, Creative Arts, Writing, Community Service, Educating, Child Care, Public Speaking, Business, Sales, Office Practices, and Food Service.

The English language version of IDEAS was given a "cosmetic makeover" in 1996 to enhance its appeal and its usefulness. Graphics, layout, and colors were updated, although items and scoring remained the same. A workbook was developed to provide a useful and easily used interpretative guide to the instrument. A workbook for adults has recently been published, *Focusing on Your Future in the Changing World of Work.*

A Spanish translation of the IDEAS test items was developed in 1990. This translation was revised and updated to include a translation of the workbook in 2000, although a Spanish translation of the manual is not currently available. The Spanish version is a translation of the original English version of the test items and the workbook, rather than being psychometrically developed for the Spanish speaker. As Johansson (1996) indicated, "Although careful attention has been given to ensure an accurate translation, separate norms have not been developed for the Spanish version. Consequently, the translation should be used with caution and with consideration of the psychometric properties of the inventory" (p. 5). This statement continues to be true for the 2000 revision, as the revised translation has not yet been normed.

Use in Counseling

IDEAS, reportedly written at a sixth grade reading level, measures career interests in 7th-12th graders and adults. The 16 scales are said to be homogenous, with each scale being composed of 8 items. The scales are designed to be broad in nature, differentiating between general categories rather than direction toward a specific career.

IDEAS can be completed in approximately 40 minutes and is easily administered to a large group or individually. Items are answered by circling a letter on a five-point Likert scale ranging from L "like the activity very much" to D "dislike the activity very much." The instrument allows students and adults to rate their level of interest in various activities (e.g., "Make a rug from yarn." "Tell stories to children.") and occupations (e.g., "Be a banker." "Be an interior decorator.").

After rating the items, instrument takers may self-score IDEAS using the grids provided underneath the top page, which is carbonless paper. Scores are calculated by adding columns, with the sums being transferred to the profile in the workbook. Although directions are ample and clearly stated, given the potential for misscoring, administrators may want to supervise younger groups more closely.

Once scores have been plotted on the profile, interpretation is self-guided through the workbook, beginning with a basic explanation for self-interpretation of results using standard scores. The workbook provides brief descriptions and possible jobs for the 16 areas of interest correlated with the scales. In addition, test takers are presented with open spaces for responding to open ended questions that further explore thoughts about career interests, identify possible additional resources, and make a plan for further action. The workbook highlights recommendations for the process of learning more about jobs in an interest area, including internet addresses and listings from the Dictionary of Occupational Titles (DOT) and the Occupational Outlook Handbook (OOH). Users should be aware the OOH has been updated since the latest version of IDEAS has been published, and although test takers are referred to the 1990/91 version, there is a 2000/2001 version on the Internet [http://stats.bls.gov/ocohome.htm].

The layout of the test item booklet and workbook published in Spanish in 2000 is essentially the same as that of the 1996 English version. The most notable difference is that in the Spanish version, Spanish speakers are referred to the DOT and OOH, but samples of the kind of information available in these books are not provided. In addition, instrument takers are referred to four Internet sites, all of which provide information only in English.

Technical Considerations

The manual provides three norm tables, separating male and female norm averages for grades 7-9, grades 10-12, and adults. Norms are not separated for genders in the workbook as test takers plot their scores on a profile using a composite average of an equal representation of females and males. As noted by Miller and Hoffbauer (1994), the sample for standardization was quite adequate, including grades 7-9 (N=1,770; 950 females, 820 males), 10-12 (N=2,891; 1,683 females, 1,208 males), and adults (N=900; 450 females, 450 males).

Separate norms were not developed for the Spanish translation. This is problematic, as a constellation of factors may render norms based on English answers obsolete for those who take the Spanish translation of the instrument. For example, differences in level of acculturation, culture of origin, socioeconomic status, and ethnicity may result in different norms. Differences in status accorded to professionals in different countries could also bias the results. By ignoring these factors and processes, a great disservice may be done to a test taker whose level of interest in a given field is misrepresented. The potential for misuse of the results is greater in this case because this is a self-administered instrument. It may be wise to provide additional consultation and opportunity for debriefing to students and/or adults who have taken the Spanish translation.

The current manual (Johansson, 1996) introduces the procedure for the original development of IDEAS. Development of the instrument has been reviewed elsewhere (e.g., Swanson, 1987; Wegner, 1994). In summary, the manual provides basic information regarding the development of IDEAS, but as noted in previous critiques, additional resources (such as the manual describing techniques to develop the CAI) are required for adequate information of inventory development. In addition, although the manual provides several appendices with additional information regarding reliability and validity, necessary information (e.g., sample size, exact sample composition, methods and procedures for data collection) is consistently absent. This lack of information makes it difficult to truly assess the instrument's psychometric properties.

Although scores, not tests, are reliable or unreliable, previous findings of score reliability on IDEAS have been positive. Alpha coefficients reported in the manual for internal consistency on the 16 scales ranged from .80 to .90.

Test-retest coefficients were reported for three time periods (one week, two weeks, and 30 days), with each sample consisting of over 50 percent high school or college students, with the rest adults. Sample size was 54 for one week, 31 for two weeks, and 42 for 30 days. Scores were not analyzed separately for gender or ethnic background. As reported in the manual (Johansson, 1996), one week test-retest coefficients on scale scores ranged from .83 (Creative Arts) to .95 (Mechanical/Fixing) with a test-retest median coefficient of .91. Two week test-retest coefficients ranged from .79 (Food Service) to .96 (Writing) for a median coefficient of .89, with 30 day test-retest reliability coefficients ranging from .81 (Medical) to .92 (Child Care) for a median of .86.

Content validity was reported to be a guiding factor in the development of the IDEAS scales, as item intercorrelations, cluster analyses, and cross-validation analyses using various student and adult samples were heavily relied upon (Johansson, 1996). Item-scale correlations for the 16 IDEAS scales presented in the manual indicated high consistency for each item scale for both school-aged and adult samples.

Construct validity for IDEAS was assessed by correlating its scales with similar scales on the CAI and Strong Interest Inventory (SII). Given items for IDEAS come from the CAI, it is of no surprise that the correlations between scales for these two instruments were all above .92. When comparing scales on the SII and IDEAS, correlations were also high, .80 and above. Construct validity was also assessed through scale intercorrelations based on Holland types. Although the manual indicates expected correlations (both high and low) between the scales and the identified related (or unrelated) Holland codes, a closer review of the correlation matrix indicates that these results are not as clearly differentiated as might be expected.

Concurrent validity was assessed through exploration of data from students and adults employed in relevant occupations. Although the manual states, "Overall, good concurrent validity was exhibited for the IDEAS scales" (Johansson, 1996, p. 15), the accuracy of this statement is difficult to evaluate given the information provided in the manual.

Predictive validity of IDEAS does not appear to have been addressed at this point. This has been cited as a previous concern (Swanson, 1987). In addition, Wegner (1994) indicated having "qualms about the validity of eight-item scales, despite evidence of good reliability" (p. 316).

The manual includes very little information about the 1996 Spanish translation of the instrument; no published information is available describing the development of the 2000 revision and update. To create the 1996 version, "National Computer Systems commissioned a native speaker to translate the IDEAS test booklet instructions and items into Spanish. The resulting draft was reviewed by an editor who consulted Spanish native speakers from other ethnic backgrounds on phrasing issues. To further ensure its accuracy, the translation was proofread and appraised by an independent translator" (Johansson, 1996, p. 5). Although the resulting translation is of adequate quality, and Spanish speakers from many nationalities and ancestries would understand most words, there were several shortcomings with this translation.

First, the translation was not developed using the back translation method, which is the most accepted method for developing translations of psychological material. Second, information about the translators' background (e.g., the translators' ancestries, level of formal education attained in English and Spanish, and experience with vocational counseling and psychology) was not provided, making it difficult to assess the adequacy of the methodology employed. Third, there are inconsistencies in the way gendered nouns are used throughout this version. Some items include the male and female versions of a noun (e.g., "Ser vendedor/a de bienes raíces"), whereas others do not (e.g., "Ser médico/doctor"). Last, and perhaps most important, despite National Computer System's efforts to obtain the best possible translation, the lack of psychometric data for this version makes it impossible to evaluate its adequacy for use with Spanish-speaking populations.

The 2000 revision improved on the earlier version by making most items gender neutral. For example, the item previously mentioned now reads "Ser médico/a o doctor/a." The tone of the test items was changed by using the informal pronoun "tú" instead of the more formal "Usted." However, certain words were changed in the most recent version, which alter the meaning of several items. For example, the English item "Speak up for your viewpoints" read "Expresar sus puntos de vista" (express your points of view) in the 1996 Spanish translation and "Defender mis puntos de vista" (defend my points of view) in the 2000 revision. Despite the fact that the wording of many items has been changed, no effort has been made to establish the psychometric equivalence of the two Spanish translations, or of the Spanish and English versions.

An additional factor that the test user should bear in mind is that IDEAS appears to be built on several assumptions: (1) there is equal opportunity across occupations, (2) there is equal opportunity across levels of occupational responsibility for all test takers, and (3) Spanish- and English-speaking populations differ only in terms of language preference. For instance, the English and Spanish versions include the following statement in the instructions: "Don't worry about salary, status, or training. Keep in mind that all occupations and careers are open to everyone." Although it appears that the intent of this instruction is to encourage the instrument taker to examine current interests without taking certain external factors into account, it may be misrepresenting the effects of discrimination and developmental and other differences among populations.

Overall Critique

Overall, the English version of IDEAS is a well-constructed interest inventory that provides a vehicle for continued exploration of measured interests and potential careers. Past criticisms have been somewhat negated in the current version of IDEAS and the updated manual.

The manual, however, remains somewhat inadequate, with the absence of crucial information to truly evaluate psychometric properties. This criticism is similar to that provided by Wegner (1994), and Swanson (1987) who described the manual as lacking "the detail necessary to fully understand and evaluate the inventory" (p. 257). In addition, limitations of the instrument expressed by Swanson (1987) continue, including identified concerns regarding the comprehensiveness of the scales, potential for errors in scoring, and gender fairness. Although Wegner (1994) indicated "issues of gender and racial bias" have been addressed appropriately, concerns remain, and caution should be exercised when using the instruments with populations for which norms are not available. In particular, extreme caution should be exercised when using the Spanish translation, given that its psychometric properties are not known. Preference would be for separate norms not only for the English and Spanish versions of the instrument, but also for African American, Asian and Pacific Islander, Hispanic, and Native American Indian populations. In contrast to Wegner (1994) who stated, "There are both combined and separated-gender norms, and it appears that minorities are adequately represented in both" (p. 316), we are a bit more cautious regarding the appropriateness of the norms.

Withstanding the above criticisms, the strengths of this interest measurement inventory are plentiful. The English version of IDEAS is an easily administered, time- sensitive, self-scoring career exploration inventory. The instrument appears to be successful in balancing psychometric concerns with having an easily self-administered, self-scored, and self-interpreted instrument. The recent cosmetic changes have brought about attractive graphics, colors, and layout. The workbook is an excellent complement to the questionnaire and provides an easily understood comprehensive self-guided exploration of career interests. In line with the intended purpose of the instrument, IDEAS is appropriate for integration in a school curriculum and the general workplace for broad exploration of career interests.

References

Johansson, C. B. (1996). *Manual for IDEAS: Interest Determination, Exploration and Assessment System.* Minneapolis, MN: National Computer Systems.

Miller, R. J., & Hoffbauer, D. (1994). Review of the Interest Determination, Exploration and Assessment System. In J. T. Kapes, M. M. Mastie, & E. A. Whitfield (Eds.), *A counselor's guide to career assessment instruments* (3rd ed., 99. 179-182). Alexandria, VA: National Career Development Association.

Swanson, J. L. (1987). Interest Determination, Exploration and Assessment System. In D. J. Keyser & R. C. Sweetland (Eds.), *Test critiques* (Vol. VI, pp. 253-259). Austin, TX: PRO-ED.

Wegner, K. W. (1994). Interest Determination, Exploration and Assessment System—Enhanced Version. In D. J. Keyser & R. C. Sweetland (Eds.), *Test critiques* (Vol. X, pp. 309-317). Austin, TX: PRO-ED.

Jackson Vocational Interest Survey (JVIS)

Douglas N. Jackson
SIGMA Assessment Systems, Inc.
P.O. Box 610984
Port Huron, MI 48061-0984
sigma@sigmaassessmentsystems.com
www.sigmaassessmentsystems.com

Target Population: Adolescent and adult

Statement of the Purpose of the Instrument: The Jackson Vocational Interest Survey (JVIS) was developed to assist high school and college students and adults with educational and career planning. It is composed of 34 basic interest scales that encompass work role dimensions relevant to a variety of occupations and workstyles indicative of work environment preferences.

Titles of Subtests, Scales, Scores Provided: The JVIS measures 34 vocational interest areas using 17-item scales. Creative Arts, Performing Arts; Mathematics, Physical Science, Engineering, Life Science, Social Science, Adventure, Nature-Agriculture, Skilled Trades; Personal Services, Family Activity, Medical Service, Dominant Leadership, Job Security, Stamina, Accountability, Teaching, Social Service, Elementary Education, Finance, Business, Office Work, Sales; Supervision, Human Resources Management, Law, Professional Advising; Author-Journalism, Academic Achievement, Technical Writing; Independence, Planfulness, Interpersonal Confidence.

Forms and Levels Available, with Dates of Publication/Revision of Each: There is one form of the JVIS available. The manual was first published in 1977 and a send edition appeared in 2000. The JVIS test booklet was updated in 1991 and 1999. The JVIS Profile Sheets and Reports have been revised to include 1999 norms.

Date of Most Recent Edition of Test Manual, User's Guide, Etc.: JVIS manual, 1977, JVIS Applications Handbook, 2000, JVIS Occupations Guide, 2000.

Languages in Which Available: English, French and Spanish.

Time: Actual Test Time: Approximately 45 minutes.
    Total Administration Time: Hand scoring done in 10 minutes or less.

Norm Group(s) on Which Scores Are Based: 3,300 individuals with a split of 1,750 males and 1,750 females.

Manner in Which Results Are Reported for Individuals
    Types of Scores: Percentile ranks and raw scores.
    Report Format/Content
        Basic Service: The JVIS Basic Report includes a basic interest profile of scores on the 34 JVIS scales, a profile of 10 general occupational themes, administrative indices, academic orientation, similarity to 17 educational clusters and a ranking of 32 occupational groups. JVIS Extended Report adds personalized narrative interpretation summaries and resources for career exploration.

Report Format/Content for Group Summaries: Not available.

Scoring

> **Machine Scoring Service:**
> *Cost of basic service per counselee*: Basic Report approximately $4.50-7.50 per report (depending on quantity ordered). Extended Report approximately $7.30-10.50 per report (depending on quantity ordered).
> *Time required for scoring and returning (maximum)*: Reports are scored and returned within 48 hours of receipt.
> **Hand Scoring:**
> *Scored by*: Counselor.
> *Time required for scoring*: Ten minutes or less.
> **Local Machine Scoring:**
> *Provisions/conditions/equipment required*: SIGMASOFT Scanning Utility—NCS Sentry 3000 or compatible optical mark scanner required. Please call or check web page for prices.

Computer Software Options Available: Computerized administration.

Cost of Materials:

> **Specimen Set:** JVIS Examination Kit $76 Prices subject to change. Kit includes one of each of the following: JVIS Test manual; JVIS Applications Handbook; JVIS Occupations Guide; machine scorable answer sheet for Extended Report; reusable test booklet; handscorable answer sheet and profile sheet.

Additional Comments of Interest to Users: JVIS.com.

Published Reviews:

Brown, D. T. (1989). Review of the Jackson Vocational Interest Survey. In J. C. Conoley & J. J. Kramer, (Eds.). *The tenth mental measurements yearbook* (pp. 401-403). Lincoln, NE: The University of Nebraska Press.

Jepsen, D. A. (1992). Jackson Vocational Interest Survey. In D. J. & R. C. Sweetland (Eds.), *Test Critiques Vol. IX* (pp. 308-318) Austin, TX: Pro-ed.

Shepard, J. W. (1989). Review of the Jackson Vocational Interest Survey. In J. C. Conoley & J. J. Kramer, (Eds.). *The tenth mental measurements yearbook* (pp. 403-404). Lincoln, NE: The University of Nebraska Press.

Verhoeve, M. (1988). Jackson Vocational Interest Survey: Ten years after. *Guidance and Counselling, 4*, 45-50.

Reviewed by

Robert E. Shute
Associate Professor Emeritus of Education
Pennsylvania State University

Description

The Jackson Vocational Interest Survey (JVIS) is a forced-choice instrument consisting of 289 pairs of statements representing work-related activities (e.g., "setting the interest rates on bank deposits") or general work styles (e.g., "doing jobs requiring perseverance"). The test taker is asked to select one item from each pair of statements as being more interesting (preferred) than the other item or, if neither item in the pair is especially attractive, to select the item that is "least disliked." The selection of preferred work activities or work styles is to be done without regard for the respondent's level of training or experience. A seventh-grade reading level is reported for the instrument. The test booklet was revised in 1991 to reflect current career vocabulary. The JVIS Manual was published in 1977 and is still in use. A new manual was scheduled to be released in late 1999.

The test takes from 45 minutes to 1 hour to complete (although there is no specified time limit) and about 10-15 minutes are needed for administrative activities (giving directions, answering questions, etc.). Instructions are clear, but additional instruction may be needed to reinforce the method for choosing between two paired statements in terms of preference without regard for necessary training or experience. Some test takers may need additional help with the vocabulary of the test statements.

The test booklet is available in English, French, or Spanish editions. The Web version and the personal computer version (SigmaSoft JVIS for Windows) are in English only. The procedures for scoring and for obtaining individual reports will vary depending upon whether the test is taken using the printed test booklet, the World Wide Web, or the personal computer. Two answer sheets are available for the printed version–one for hand scoring and one for the mail-in scoring service. With practice, hand scoring and drawing the profile should take about 10-15 minutes and will yield scores and a profile of the 34 Basic Interest Scales only. With mail-in scoring, the user may select to receive either the Basic Report or the Extended Report. The personal computer software will produce the Basic Report, the Extended Report, or a Data Report that contains scores for use by other programs. The World Wide Web JVIS may be taken online, and the Extended Report will be mailed to the user.

Whether produced by mail-in scoring, scoring by the personal computer software version, or scoring available via the World Wide Web version of the

JVIS, the Basic Report contains detailed profiles and comparisons of 34 Basic Interest Scales, 10 General Occupational Themes, 17 College and University Academic Clusters, a measure of Academic Satisfaction, 32 Job Groupings, and Administrative Indices. The Extended Report has all of the material in the Basic Report, but adds narrative summaries of the user's three highest-ranked educational and occupational clusters as well as a list of career-related books and activities. The Basic Report is more colorful and attractive than the Extended Report.

Use in Counseling

The JVIS is promoted as a career interest measure that focuses primarily on professional occupations and jobs that require some training. It is intended to be used for career and educational counseling, exploration and planning for high school-aged individuals, college and university students, and adults. Also, it could be used to help adults redirect their careers, or businesses could use this survey to restructure their workforce according to employee preferences for work activities and work behaviors.

In addition to the *JVIS Manual* (Jackson, 1977), other materials to aid interpretation and promote client exploratory activities include the *JVIS Applications Handbook* (Verhoeve, 1993) and the *JVIS Occupations Guide* (Sigma Assessment Systems, 1995). These materials would be especially helpful to the counselor working directly with a client.

As with all interest measures, the primary benefit to clients and to the counselor is to provide a framework for discussion about careers, personal work-related preferences, self-exploration, and enhanced career knowledge. This survey could be used with other instruments, such as personality and achievement tests, to provide feedback for a realistic discussion of plans and alternatives.

Technical Considerations

The JVIS was developed in 1977 using the concept that "interest dimensions (scales) could be defined that would transcend individual occupational groups and permit the user to measure broader interest areas that cut across a number of occupations" (Davidshofer, 1988, p. 97). Thus, a person's preferences for work activities and work styles (environments) would yield a relatively small number of "basic interest" scales that would represent broad, but discreet, areas of occupational interest rather than specific jobs. The resultant 34 Basic Interest Scales include 26 Work Role preferences (e.g., law, engineering, performing arts, and social science) and 8 scales for Work Style (e.g., independence, stamina, and accountability). The Work Style scales reflect the individual's desire to work in an environment that supports or requires certain modes of behavior.

The original JVIS (Jackson, 1977) was developed using multivariate statistical procedures that were quite sophisticated at the time. All of the previously mentioned scales are derived from the answers to the 289 forced-choice item pairs. The JVIS purports to be a gender-fair test in terms of the applicability of the test statements to males and females. Scale scores are obtained by counting the frequency of selected items that comprise a particular scale. Each scale among the Basic Interest Scales, for example, is comprised of 17 statements. However, by indicating a preference for one statement in an forced-choice item pair, the other statement cannot be counted toward the score for another scale– even though the examinee may like that choice too.

Separate scores are provided for each gender as applicable to each scale on the reports. Since the original 1977 norms are no longer used to produce the reports, test users will have to wait for the new JVIS Manual to make a judgment about the utility of the new norms. A representative of the publisher indicated that current reports are now based upon normative data from a representative sample (obtained in 1995) of about 2,500 male and female high school students from the United States and Canada (P. Tremblay, personal communication, July 14 & 16, 1999). An additional set of 2,500 high school students is to be added to the normative pool in late 1999.

Data on reliability and validity, based on the new normative groups, is not available at this writing. The publisher has not provided new reliability and validity data since the original publication date of 1997, although those data did indicate respectable test-retest and internal consistency reliabilities for the Basic Interest Scales as well as the General Occupational Themes. Predictive validity has not been established, and construct validity claims are equivocal. Since the JVIS was revised somewhat in 1991, and new norm groups are being used for the reports, the soon-to-be-published updated JVIS Manual should be quite helpful for potential users.

Computer-Based Versions

In 1999, the JVIS was made available in a personal computer version (SigmaSoft JVIS for Windows) as well as in an online World Wide Web version at www.JVIS.com. Both versions provide clear instructions and the survey is simple (and entertaining) to take in these formats. The personal computer version will allow the user to score and print either the Basic or the Extended Report on site, whereas the user of the online version must wait for the Extended Report (only) to be mailed. Complete information on all JVIS versions, including costs of materials and scoring, may be found at www.sigmaassessmentsystems.com.

Overall Critique

The major strengths of the JVIS include: (1) a relatively inexpensive means of taking the survey, including via personal computer or the World Wide Web, (2) ease of interpretation by counselors or by many counselees due to the clear graphical output and well-written descriptions of the various scales, (3) the attempts to create a means for discussing work-related preferences and work styles that are not bound to particular occupations, and (4) the efforts to create a psychometrically and theoretically sound instrument.

Other reviewers such as Jepson (1994), Juni & Koenig (1982), and Murphy & Davidshofer (1991) expressed concerns about certain aspects of the JVIS including the following: (1) the limited theoretical background for the Work Style scales, (2) the arrangement of some items that could cause response bias, (3) the possible confusion caused by the forced-choice format, (4) the limitations of the 1977 norm groups, (5) the somewhat lengthy administration and testing time, and (6) the lack of demonstrated predictive validity.

Additional concerns of this reviewer are as follows: (1) the current *JVIS Manual* and available reliability and validity data are outdated; (2) there are no reliability or validity data or norms supporting the use of the instrument with an adult working population or for adults returning to the workforce, especially for such promoted applications as restructuring the workforce in a business setting; (3) outdated resource materials (many over 20 years old) are provided to users of the Extended Report or to those who purchase the *JVIS Occupations Guide* (Sigma Assessment Systems, 1995); and (4) the lack of guidelines and/or data supporting the use of the JVIS with individuals with limited education, physical and mental limitations, or for diverse racial and ethnic groups.

Many of the professional organizations listed in the Extended Report and the JVIS Occupations Guide now have World Wide Web addresses. These should be listed, as applicable, in all new revisions of JVIS support materials.

References

Davidshofer, C. O. (1988). Jackson Vocational Interest Survey (JVIS). In Kapes, J. T. & Mastie, M. M. (Ed.) *A counselor's guide to career assessment instruments.* (2nd ed., pp. 95-99). Alexandria, VA: National Career Development Association.

Jackson, D. N. (1977). *Jackson Vocational Interest Survey manual.* Port Huron, MI: Sigma Assessment Systems, Inc.

Jepson, D. A. (1994) Jackson Vocational Interest Survey. In Kapes, J .T., Mastie, M. M. & Whitfield, E. A. (Ed.). *A counselor's guide to career assessment instruments.* (3rd ed., pp. 183-188). Alexandria, VA: National Career Development Association.

Juni, S. & Koenig, E. J. (1982). Contingency validity as a requirement in forced-choice item construction: A critique of the Jackson Vocational Interest Survey. *Measurement and Evaluation in Guidance, 14,* 202-207.

Murphy, K. R. & Davidshofer, C. O. (1991). *Psychological testing: Principles and Applications (2nd ed.).* Englewood Cliffs, NJ: Prentice Hall.

Sigma Assessment Systems, Inc.(1995). *JVIS Occupations Guide*. Port Huron, MI:

Verhoeve, M. A. (1993). *JVIS applications handbook*. Port Huron, MI: Sigma Assessment Systems, Inc.

Kuder™ General Interest Survey Form E (KGIS–Form E)

Frederic Kuder

National Career Assessment Services, Inc.
601 Visions Parkway
PO Box 277
Adel, IA 50003
www.kuder.com
ncasi@ncasi.com

Target Population: 6th-12th grade students, adults reentering school or the work force.

Statement of the Purpose of the Instrument: Assesses interests in order to help students select educational courses and begin exploring potential careers.

Titles of Subtests, Scales, Scores Provided: (1) Verification (V) score; (2) Vocational Interest; Outdoor, Mechanical, Computational, Scientific, Persuasive, Artistic, Literary, Musical, Social Service and Clerical; also provides three-letter RIASEC code.

Forms and Levels Available, with Dates of Publication/Revision of Each: Form E, 1988

Date of Most Recent Edition of Test Manual, User's Guide, Etc.: 1988

Languages in Which Available: English only.

Time: Actual Test Time Unlimited.
     Total Administration Time: 45-60 minutes.

Norm Group(s) on Which Scores Are Based: Males and females, grades 6-8 and grades 9-12.

Manner in Which Results Are Reported for Individuals
     Types of Scores: Percentile scores grouped in high, average and low ranges, for own and other gender. V-scale is a raw score.
     Report Format/Content :
          Basic Service: Narrative for machine scored; profile for hand scored. All accompanied by interpretive leaflet.

Report Format/Content for Group Summaries: Not available.

Scoring
     Machine Scoring Service:
     Cost of basic service per counselee: Cost included in purchase price.
     Time required for scoring and returning (maximum): Minimum 24-hour turnaround at NCASI plus shipping time.

Hand Scoring:
    Scored by: Counselee; Clerk; Counselor.
    Time required for scoring: Variable, approximately 10 minutes.
Local Machine Scoring: Not available.

Computer Software Options Available: Not available.

Cost of Materials:1999 prices.
    Specimen Set: $8 for self-scored; $9 for machine scored.
    Counselee Materials: Self-scored edition includes package of 25 consumable booklets/answer sheets, interpretive leaflets and memorandum of instruction: $70 with discounts for 100 or more assessments.

Additional Comments of Interest to Users: The KGIS self-scored edition was recently converted from its former pin-punch format to a pencil/paper version. The KGIS is also compatible to the new Kuder Career Search Person Match database, allowing participants to input their activity preference scales to receive their top 25 matches based upon interest ranking.

Published Reviews:
Mehrens, W. A. (1994). Review of the Kuder General Interest Survey, Form E. In J. T. Kapes, M. M. Mastie & E. A. Whitfield (Eds.), *A counselor's guide to career assessment instruments* (3rd ed.). Alexandria, VA: National Career Development Association.
Williams, J. A. & Williams, J. D. (1984). Review of the Kuder General Interest Survey, Form E. In D. J. Keyser & R. C. Sweetland (Eds.), *Test critiques*, Vol. I, (pp. 395-401). Kansas City, MO: Test Corporation of America.
Williams, J. A. & Williams, J. D. (1988). Review of the Kuder General Interest Survey, Form E. In J. T. Kapes & M. M. Mastie (Eds.), *A counselor's guide to career assessment instruments* (2nd ed.). Alexandria, VA: National Career Development Association.

Reviewed by

Mark Pope
Associate Professor
Division of Counseling
College of Education
University of Missouri - St. Louis

Description

    The Kuder General Interest Survey, Form E (KGIS-E), is the lower extension of Frederic Kuder's measures of vocational interests, which evolved from the need to measure vocational interests at the junior high or middle school level.

Note: Portions of this review were adapted from the author's original review in the *Twelfth Mental Measurements Yearbook* with permission of the Buros Institute.

In order to accomplish this task, the KGIS-E attempts to avoid the use of concepts about which the individual's knowledge may change considerably such as specific occupational titles; to restrict the vocabulary used in the survey to a sixth-grade reading level; to use a larger number of items on each scale to enhance reliability since the responses of younger people tend to be slightly less reliable; and to report scores on broad interest areas not on specific occupations. The broad interest areas for which scores are reported include Outdoor, Mechanical, Computational, Scientific, Persuasive, Artistic, Literary, Musical, Social Service, and Clerical.

The version reviewed here is the 168-item self-scorable version that Pope (1993) previously reviewed in the Mental Measurements Yearbook. A machine-scored mail-in version that generates a profile report is also available; however, no onsite machine-scored version is now offered that was available previously. The materials for the self-scorable version of the KGIS-E include a "preliminary edition" (1988) of a general manual; a 42-page consumable booklet that includes a one-page test taker instructions, 12 pages of survey items, a self-scorable answer "pad" that consists of an original answer sheet for all 168 items and eight pages of alternating carbon paper and scoring sheets, one sheet of instructions for converting your KGIS-E scores to RIASEC codes and for filling out the "interpretive leaflet" (final page), two profile sheets (one for 6-8 grade norms and one for 9-12 and adult norms), and an interpretive report form (labeled an "interpretive leaflet"); along with a memorandum of instructions for the test administration. No other materials are supplied with the KGIS-E. In previous editions, an 8 1/2 by 11 inches sheet of white corrugated cardboard and a stainless steel, T-shaped pointed punch pin were included; however, the new format used for the first time in the 1999 printing uses carbon paper forms to transfer the responses to the scoring sheets.

The "preliminary edition" of the general manual is a 45-page booklet that contains three sections (general, interpretive, and technical) along with two substantial appendices and a references list concerning the KGIS-E. The "preliminary edition" was published in 1988 directly after the 1987 restandardization was completed and has not been updated since then. The general section begins with a subsection on why vocational interests are measured at all followed by an overview to the KGIS-E, a list and description of the scales, a narrative on the development of the KGIS-E, and ends with a "how-to" subsection on it's use in guidance and counseling. The interpretive section contains specific detailed information on the use of the KGIS-E; it's administration, scoring, and interpretation. The technical section consists of information on the history and construction of Kuder's inventories in general and the KGIS-E in particular along with the development of the 1988 norms, the raw to percentile score conversion tables, scale intercorrelations, and reliability and validity data.

The response format used in the KGIS-E is the forced-choice triad which consists of three activities that the test taker is instructed to mark the one they like most along with the one they like least. This format is contrasted with the fixed response format, which consists of a single item with a three to seven option Likert-type response (like-indifferent-dislike and its variations). Although the forced-choice triad may be relative free from response bias, it also forces a differentiation between three items which might be similarly valued, that is, for which the individual might have responded all like or all dislike using the fixed response format.

Use in Counseling

The purpose of the KGIS-E is to "stimulate career exploration and suggest career possibilities" (Kuder, 1988, p. 4) rather than suggest specific occupational options. KGIS-E measures broad interest areas rather than focusing on specific occupational exploration and should, therefore, be used where the reporting of these broad interest areas is more appropriate. Because career interest patterns do not become more concrete until age 15 or so (Strong, 1943), the KGIS-E is recommended for use with "younger people, those with limited experiential backgrounds, and, in general, those who are not yet ready to focus on specific occupational exploration" (Kuder, 1988, p. 4).

An important issue for a junior high school or high school student and their parents might be the stability of vocational interests over time because, if interests change substantially, it would limit the application of the scores received on any career interest measure. The publishers of the KGIS-E responded to this immediately on the first page of the manual with a discussion on stability of interests in younger people citing specific research using both the KGIS-E and the Kuder Preference Record.

In the 1987 redevelopment of the KGIS-E, the profile sheet was redesigned to allow the test taker to calculate their RIASEC code. This enables comparison with most of the other career interest inventories, which generate this same code (Strong Interest Inventory, Self-Directed Search, Vocational Preference Inventory, etc.). Pope (1993) stated that, "although the data used to justify this procedure and the mathematic calculation used to arrive at the scores are somewhat suspect, the resultant code when used cautiously as an estimate of the RIASEC model can be useful in career exploration for the individual student/client" (p. 544). The method and justification for this conversion are included in the interpretive and technical sections of the manual.

Two substantial appendices are also included that contain Kuder interest inventories' background (Appendix A) and a sample interpretive counseling session (Appendix B). Appendix A is very useful to put the KGIS-E into an historical perspective regarding the development of the other Kuder inventories and

Appendix B also very useful to the counselor who is preparing for an interpretive session with a student/client.

One special issue has arisen with the new publisher. In the "product information" brochure announcing the new Kuder line of products, the publisher has included this sentence in bold letters: "(All products shown meet Qualification Level A–no special qualifications require.)" This means that the publisher has determined that they will sell *all* Kuder inventories and other materials to anyone who orders them. This is a bold step for the publisher and one, which is not supported by other commercial publishers. No other career assessment inventory is sold so casually. Qualification Level B requires that the purchaser have taken and passed a course in psychological testing at an accredited university or college which is the qualification level for the Strong Interest Inventory and Myers-Briggs Type Indicator and almost all other career assessment inventories.

Technical Considerations

The current version of the KGIS-E represents a restandardization, which occurred in 1987. In a subsection in the technical section, the publisher noted the changes from the 1963 to 1987 standardizations. The publisher concluded that the changes seen in these scores reflect the changes in sex role stereotypes, which occurred over that period of time.

Mehrens (1994) reported that the validity data from the 1987 standardization and other studies is quite limited, but compelling nonetheless. The relationships between the six RIASEC scales on the Vocational Preference Inventory and the 10 KGIS-E scales were presented in a correlation matrix. "The correlation patterns are generally what one would expect" (p. 192).

In the popular press as well as in the professional literature in recent years, interest inventories have received scrutiny for their use of separate gender norms instead of a combined, universal norm. The publisher has responded to this in the manual, which has a separate section on the use of separate gender normative data and includes a disclaimer regarding innate biological gender differences versus environmentally provoked gender differences.

An issue, which was addressed only marginally in the manual, was the use of the KGIS-E with cultural groups different from the dominant American culture. In the preliminary manual, which was reviewed here, no summary demographic data were included from the 1987 restandardization other than general geographic, gender, and educational data. Pope (1993) asked the publisher for ethnicity, race, and economic status data when completing his review for Buros' MMY. He was told by the publishers at that time that there were data for 11,550 students of the 13,007 students in the restandardization sample, but that data could not be located prior to publication. Since no updated manual has been published since then, such data are still not available to the professional user. Pope stated then that such a situation "is intolerable for a major psychological inventory. Data should be available and saved as historical reference if for no other reason" (p. 544). Obviously, there are many more reasons for the publication of this type of data, such as basic utility with a variety of cultural populations.

Only one study that reported results from a culture different from the dominant American culture was included in the general manual. Epperson and Hammond (1981) looked at the scores on the KGIS-E for a sample of 66 male and 68 female ninth-grade Native Americans and found substantial differences. This important study makes the case for developing local normative data especially if the KGIS-E is to be used with persons who are not represented by the dominant American culture.

The KGIS-E along with the other Kuder interest inventories and materials were purchased in July, 1999 from CTB McGraw-Hill by National Career Assessment Services, Inc (NCASI). Since then, NCASI has reprinted much of the Kuder materials.

The NCASI marketing department, in updating their marketing materials declared that "(t)his edition has been revised to reflect current usage" when the only change has been a physical change in the response/scoring process. Instead of using a push-pin and corrugated board in marking the answers on the answer sheet, the new edition uses pencil and carbon paper forms. This is a substantial physical revision. The new procedure is much better, although not perfect. When readying the inventory for scoring, the four sheets of carbon paper are simply messy to deal with.

Also, the "product information" brochure on the Kuder product line, when describing the KGIS-E, states that it is "(b)est used for 6-8 grade. Effective for 6-12 grade, post-secondary, adult." This is bit of a stretch since no post-secondary or adult norms have ever been included in any technical manual ever issued in the history of the KGIS-E. An argument could be made that, since career interest patterns are stable over time from about age 16, no normative data other than high school is ever needed for any measure of such broad patterns. It is at best a questionable assertion without reporting any data.

The 42-page consumable, combined administration/questions/ answer/profile/interpretive form contains very detailed and user-friendly instructions that enables the test taker to easily complete the administration and scoring process almost unaided by a counselor/test administrator. In this self-scorable format (as with any self-scorable format with large numbers of items) there is substantial room for error, but, because of the peculiar format of this inventory, there is even more room for error to occur especially in the scoring procedure.

First, the instructions in the consumable booklet are not very explicit concerning how to open the answer sheet section to enable the scoring to be done. Then the scoring is very tedious. The scorer must find the starting place for each scale and then follow the circles and lines, counting the punched holes, until they reach the end place. Four of the six pages have two different scales on the page, which contributes, to confusion. Then the beginning place for scoring scales 5 and 6 is the same item and toward the end of the scoring for these two scales it is not easy to differentiate between the two scales. It is quite awkward and tedious to accurately score this type of answer sheet. The publisher has included research that verifies the increased error rate for the self-scored version. In response to these previously published criticisms (Pope, 1993), the new publisher has used two different ink colors (one black, one red) to better differentiate the items that are scored on each page where two scales are being scored. It is a better technique that should help to reduce the error rate.

Overall Critique

The KGIS-E has substantial reasons to recommend its use with junior high and high school students and with adults who need a measure with a lower reading level. The Kuder interest inventories have a long and respected place in the history of career interest measurement. Pope (1993) recommended that, as a result of the cost and being able to get results without having to be computer scored, this is a good instrument to be used in school districts where cost is a major concern.

Further, of the major self-scorable career interest inventories (Self-Directed Search, Vocational Preference Inventory, Career Occupational Preference System), the KGIS-E should be chosen for use with junior high school students who want to get a RIASEC code for use in career exploration and especially for use with computerized career information systems, many of which use the RIASEC codes to generate occupational choice options and/or narrative reports.

Unfortunately, the KGIS-E normative data are out of date and limited in applicability due to lack of reporting of other culture-specific data. It continues to rely on the 1987 restandardization sample for its validity and reliability with no reported plans for a new standardization study. The new publishers of the KGIS-E have already made some important changes in the scoring procedures. It is hoped that they will update this important and useful instrument having a special market niche.

References

Epperson, D. L., & Hammond, D. (1981). Use of interest inventories with Native Americans: A case for local norms. *Journal of Counseling Psychology, 28,* 213-220.

Kuder, F. (1988). *Kuder General Interest Survey-Form E: General manual* (preliminary edition). Adel, IA: National Career Assessment Services.

Mehrens, W. A. (1994). Review of the Kuder General Interest Survey (Form E). In J. T. Kapes, M. M. Mastie, & E. A. Whitfield (Eds.), *A counselor's guide to career assessment instruments* (3rd ed., pp. 189-193). Alexandria, VA: National Career Development Association.

Pope, M. (1995). Review of the Kuder General Interest Survey (Form E). In J. C. Conoley & J. Impara (Eds.), *The twelfth mental measurements yearbook* (pp. 543-545). Lincoln, NE: Buros Institute, University of Nebraska-Lincoln.

Kuder Occupational Interest Survey
Form DD (KOIS-DD)

Frederic Kuder
National Career Assessment Services, Inc.
601 Visions Parkway
PO Box 277
Adel, IA 50003
www.kuder.com
ncasi@ncasi.com

Target Population: Grades 10-12, college students, adults making career changes or reentering school or the work force.

Statement of the Purpose of the Instrument: Assesses interests to assist in selecting college majors and identifying potential careers.

Titles of Subtests, Scales, Scores Provided: (1) Verification (V) score; (2) *Vocational Interest Estimates*: Outdoor, Mechanical, Computational, Scientific, Persuasive, Artistic, Literary, Musical, Social Service, and Clerical; (3) *Occupational Scales;* 109, of which 33 are normed on both male and female criterion groups, 32 on male groups only and 11 on female groups; (4) *College Majors Scales*: 40, of which 14 are normed on both male and female groups, 8 on male groups only and 4 on female groups; (5) *Experimental Scales*: 8.

Forms and Levels Available, with Dates of Publication/Revision of Each: Form DD, 1985.

Date of Most Recent Edition of Test Manual, User's Guide, Etc.: 1991

Languages in Which Available: English only.

Time: Actual Test Time: Unlimited.
            Total Administration Time: 30-40 minutes.

Norm Group(s) on Which Scores Are Based: *Vocational Interest Estimates*: 1,583 males, 1,631 females selected from high school, college and private agency users. *Occupational Scales*: Groups of 200 or more males or females, age 25 or over, self-identified as employed at least three years in their occupation and satisfied with their occupational choice. *College Major Scales*: Groups of 200 or more males or females, in their junior or senior years of a nationally distributed sample of colleges and universities.

Manner in Which Results Are Reported for Individuals
    Types of Scores: Vocational Interest estimates are reported in percentiles, grouped in high, average, and low ranges, for own and other gender. Occupational and College Major Scales are scored by lambda coefficients, which are similar to correlation.

Report Format/Content:

Basic Service: V-Score and other data are combined into an individual "Dependability Statement." Individualized report incorporates computer-printed rank-ordered scales on a pre-printed narrative form. Two copies are given; one for inventory-taker shows no numerical data; counselor copy includes all scores.

Report Format/Content for Group Summaries: Not available.

Scoring

Machine Scoring Service:

Cost of basic service per counselee: Cost included in purchase price.

Time required for scoring and returning (maximum): Minimum 24-hour turnaround at NCASI plus shipping time.

Hand Scoring: Not available.

Local Machine Scoring:

Provisions/conditions/equipment required: See computer software options available.

Computer Software Options Available: Standard administration online.

Ways in which computer version differs: The KOIS DD/PC is computer administered; that is, items are presented on-screen and responses made on the keyboard, obviating the need to fill in bubbles and saving approximately 20 minutes of administration time. The inventory is scored within a few seconds of the final response and results are presented on-screen or in print copy, as requested. A unique feature tracks the development of the V-score and, if it falls below expected levels, asks the survey-taker if they wish to reconsider any of their previous responses. In addition, the PC version asks the survey-takers what they wish to discover from their inventory (identify possible occupations or college majors, confirm a tentative choice or other), and at the end of the profile asks the degree to which the survey was responsive to their expressed wish. This latter item is intended to generate an appropriate user set and to provide information that may be useful to the counseling process.

Cost of materials: 1999 prices

Specimen Set: $9.

Counselee Materials: Packages of 25 consumable test booklets/answer sheet, scoring, individualized narrative reports and memorandum of instruction: $175 with discounts for 100 or more assessments. PC-based package includes 3-1/2" disk with 10 pre-paid assessment credits, binder with inserts, user guide and online reporting: $85 with discounts for 100 or more assessments.

Published Reviews:

Herr, E. L. (1989). Review of the Kuder Occupational interest Survey. Form DD. In J. C. Conoley & J. J. Kramer (Eds.), *Tenth mental measurements yearbook* (pp. 425-427). Lincoln, NE: Buros Institute, University of Nebraska-Lincoln.

Herr, E. L. and Ashby, J. S. (1994). Review of the Kuder Occupational Interest Survey, Form DD. In J. T. Kapes, M. M. Mastie & E. A. Whitfield (Eds.). *A counselor's guide to career assessment instruments*. (3rd ed.). Alexandria, VA: National Career Development Association.

Jepsen, D. A. (1988). Review of the Kuder Occupational Interest Survey, Form DD. In J.T. Kapes & M. M. Mastie (Eds.), *A counselor's guide to career assessment instruments*, (2nd ed.). Alexandria, VA: National Career Development Association.

Jepsen, D. A. (1988). Review of the Kuder Occupational Interest Survey, Form DD. *Measurement and Evaluation in Guidance, 17*, 217-219.

Tenopyr, M. L. (1989). Review of the Kuder Occupational Interest Survey, Form DD. In J. C. Conoley & J. J. Kramer (Eds.), *Tenth mental measurements yearbook* (pp. 427-429). Lincoln,
NE: Buros Institute, University of Nebraska-Lincoln.

Kuder Career Search with Person Match™ (KCS)

Frederic Kuder and Donald G. Zytowski
National Career Assessment Services, Inc.

Target Population: Like the Form E, the KCS is designed for grades 6-12, college students, adults.

Statement of the Purpose of the Instrument: The KCS offers 21st century career exploration matching survey-taker interests to real persons happy and satisfied in a variety of careers, rather than matching to occupational groups.

Titles of Subtests, Scales, Scores Provided: Unlike the Form E, the KCS provides (1) **Activity Preference Scales**; Nature, Mechanical, Science/Technical, Art, Music, Communications, Human Services, Sales/Management, Computations, Office Detail; (2) **Kuder Career Clusters**: Outdoor/Mechanical, Science/Technical, Arts/Communications, Social/Personal Service, Sales/Management, Business Detail; (3) 25 top matches in the Person Match database.

Forms and Levels Available with Dates of Publication/Revision of Each: Kuder Career Search, 1999

Date of Most Recent Edition of Test Manual, User's Guide, Etc.: 1999

Languages in Which Available: English and Spanish, with additional translations to follow.

Time: Actual Test Time: Unlimited.
      Total Administration Time: 30-40 minutes.

Norm Group(s) on Which Scores are Based: The norm group used for the Kuder Career Search consists of the original 1,500 males and females who comprise the Person Match reference pool.

Manner in Which Results are Reported for Individuals: For the Kuder Career Search a report is presented in paper form for self-scored and mail-back versions and on-screen for the Internet-based version.
   Types of Scores: Scoring for the Kuder Career Search includes the activity preference scales, reported in rank order by percentiles with the percentiles shown, the Kuder Career Clusters reported in rank order by percentiles with the percentiles not shown, the Person Matches reported in rank order.
Report Format/Content:
   Basic Service: For the Kuder Career Search the activity preference scales, Kuder Career Clusters, detail of careers by educational level and steps for continuing career exploration are presented in a report on either paper or on-screen depending upon format selected.
   Options: The KCS Person Match features is available as on option on the mail-back and Inteformat.

Report Format/Content for Group Summaries:
 Basic Service: Group summaries are available with the Kuder Career Search. Those using the Internet-based format may access a secure database of group results to monitor, sort, or create group summary reports.

Scoring
 Machine Scoring Service:
  Cost of basic service per counselee: Cost included in purchase price
  Time required for scoring and returning (maximum): Minimum 24-hour turnaround at
   NCASI plus shipping time
 Hand Scoring:
  Scored by: Counselee, Clerk, Counselor.
  Time required for scoring: Approximately 20 minutes.
 Local Machine Scoring: Not available.

Computer Software Options Available: Standard administration online.

Ways in Which Computer Version Differs: The KCS electronic format havs items presented on-screen and responses made on the keyboard, obviating the need to fill in bubbles and saving approximately 20 minutes of administration time. The inventory is scored within a few seconds of the final response and results are presented on-screen or in print copy, as requested. The unique Person Match feature allows survey-takers to simply click the cursor to view the Person Match job sketches, search the Person Match database or link to the *Occupational Outlook Handbook* for additional career exploration. Results may be saved to a computer hard drive for future access or printed as mentioned above.

Cost of Materials: 1999 prices.
 Specimen Set: $9.
 Counselee Materials: For the KCS, packages of 25 or 100 assessments may be purchased for all formats, which include consumable surveys, memorandum of instruction and individual narrative reports. Depending upon the format selected prices range from $2.50-$8.25 per assessment with group discounts and multiyear pricing available.

Additional Comments of Interest to Users: Additional comments regarding the Kuder Career Search include mention of Kuder's one-of-a-kind Person Match, offering a continually updated database to represent the new and emerging careers of the 21st century. The feature allows greater involvement by survey-takers through the review of their job sketches and the interactive format available on the Internet. The KCS report also provides survey takers with a detail of occupations by education level and steps for continuing career exploration. Instructional materials and administration/interpretation overheads are provided by the publisher free of charge with assessment purchases.

Published Reviews: None cited.

Reviewed by

Kevin R. Kelly
Professor, Department of Educational Studies
Purdue University

Description

The Kuder Occupational Interest Survey Form DD (KOIS-DD) was originally published in 1966 and most recently in 1985. The KOIS-DD is unique in that it does not include occupational titles to measure interests. It consists of 100 triad items representing 300 different activities. Test takers respond to each triad (e.g., Build birdhouses– write articles about birds–Draw sketches of birds) by indicating their most and least preferred activities. Written at the sixth-grade reading level with a 30-40 minute administration time, it is appropriate for administration for high school students in grade 10 through adults at all stages of career development (Kuder & Zytowski, 1991). The KOIS-DD is a mail-back, machine-scored instrument; a hand-scored version is not available.

The KOIS-DD yields a Report Form with five types of scores: Dependability Statement, Vocational Interest Estimates, and Occupational, College Major and Experimental scales. The Dependability Statement reflects item completion, sincerity and accuracy of responses, and interest level. The Dependability Statements indicate that (1) the results are dependable, (2) caution is warranted because of unusual interest patterns, or (3) the report cannot be printed because of incomplete responding.

Vocational Interest Estimates (VIEs) are reported for 10 areas: Outdoor, Mechanical, Computational, Scientific, Persuasive, Artistic, Literary, Musical, Social Service, and Clerical. The VIEs are reported in rank order with percentile ranks. Two separate sets of VIEs are reported, one in comparison to the same sex and the second in comparison to the other sex. The VIEs are categorized as High (above 75th percentile), Average (25th –75th percentiles), and Low (below 25th percentile). The VIEs are more specific than the six Holland interest types. Zytowski (1976) provided a formula for converting VIEs to Holland type equivalents.

There are 109 Occupational Scales, with 33 normed with both female and male occupational groups, 32 normed for males only, and 11 normed for females only. The Occupational Scales are reported in rank order of similarity and placed in one of three categories: "Most Similar," "Next Most Similar," and "The Rest Listed in Order of Similarity." The occupations listed in the "Most Similar" category fall within three standard errors of the top score. The "Next Most Similar" category is composed of occupations that fall between three and four standard errors of the top score. "The Rest" category consists of the remaining occupations listed in order of descending similarity. The test takers receive rank-ordered lists in comparison to the 65 male and the 44 female occupational criterion groups.

There are 40 College Major Scales, with 14 normed with both male and female students, 8 normed with male students only, and 4 normed with female students only. Similar to the Occupational Scales, the College Major scales are presented in rank order in categories of Most Similar, Next Most similar, and The Rest in comparison to both male and female criterion groups.

Finally, the KOIS-DD Report Form includes eight experimental scales. The M and W scales reflect differences between the general interests of men and women and the test taker's profile of interests. The MBI and WBI scales reflect need for social approval. The S (son), D (daughter), F (father), and Mo (mother) scales were designed to measure maturity of interests. There is little interpretive information regarding the experimental scales in the KOIS-DD manual.

The next generation of the Kuder Preference Records, the Kuder Career Search (KCS) with Person Match, was introduced in 1999. The KCS consists of 60 activity triad items (e.g., Write advertising – Be in charge of a public library – Publish a newspaper); 48 items are taken directly from the KOIS-DD and the remainder are new. The KCS is also written at the sixth-grade reading level and can be administered in 30 minutes. The KCS is available in machine- and hand-scored versions. However, the Person Match cannot be accessed with the hand-scored version.

The KCS has five significant innovations in comparison to the KOIS-DD. First, its use extends downward to students as young as eighth grade. Second, the VIEs have been renamed Activity Preferences and have been given updated scale names: Nature, Mechanical, Science/Technical, Art, Music, Communications, Human Services, Sales/Management, Computations, and Office Detail. Third, the Activity Preferences are now combined into six Career Cluster scores corresponding closely to the Holland interest types: Outdoor/Mechanical (Realistic), Science/Technical (Investigative), Arts/Communication (Artistic), Social/Personal Service (Social), Sales Management (Enterprising), and Business Detail (Conventional). The Career Clusters are presented in rank order without percentile ranks. Fourth, career information is integrated directly into the KCS report. A listing of three levels of occupational titles is provided for each of the Career Cluster areas; the first level includes occupations requiring a high school diploma or GED, the second lists occupations requiring 1-2 years of postsecondary training, and the third lists occupations requiring four or more years of college. Approximately 20 job titles are presented in each of the three levels for each Career Cluster. The fifth and most significant innovation is the integration of Person Match into the KCS, the realization of Kuder's (1980) aspiration to move from person-to-job matching to person-to-person matching. Each test taker is provided with five Person Matches, which are job titles (e.g., Accounting Clerk, Physical Education Teacher) and descriptive job sketches written by job incumbents. These five Person Matches represent the top 1% of matches between the test taker's interests and those of a database of workers representing 90% of the job titles in the Occupational Outlook Handbook table of contents (Zytowski, 1999).

Use in Counseling

The basic purpose of the KOIS-DD is to enable individuals to compare their interests to those typical of workers in a wide variety of occupations and college majors. It is assumed that congruence of interests will promote job satisfaction, continuance, and achievement. Similar to other interest inventories, the KOIS-DD was designed to enhance self-understanding, increase the number and types of career options considered by the test taker, promote exploration on nontraditional occupations, stimulate information seeking, and confirm the appropriateness of aspirations (Kuder & Zytowski, 1991; Zytowski & Kuder, 1986).

Similar to the KOIS-DD, the KCS Activity Preference and Career Cluster components share the basic goals of enhancing self-knowledge, widening occupational aspirations, and stimulating career exploration. The Person Match was designed with the additional goal of exploring possible selves and stimulating consideration of different life paths (Zytowski, 1999). The revolutionary idea of matching people with people instead of jobs shifts the emphasis from a convergent process of matching person and job characteristics to a more divergent process of considering the different career paths taken by persons with similar interest profiles.

Zytowski and Kuder (1986) reported that college students preferred the KOIS-DD to the Person Match at an approximate ratio of 2 to 1. Zytowski and Kuder (1986) speculated that the KOIS-DD may be preferred by students who desire concrete, unambiguous direction from an interest test; whereas the Person Match may be preferable for students at a higher level of cognitive development. It appears that the KOIS-DD and Person Match meet distinct client needs in counseling.

Technical Considerations

Although KOIS-DD Verification Score norms are not reported, the manual includes Verification Score distributions of groups that were instructed to respond to the KOIS-DD with "sincere" and "best impression" response sets. Male and female norms are provided for the Vocational Interest Estimates. Mean lambda scores for 23 occupational and seven college major groups are also provided. No normative data are reported for the remaining 86 occupations and 33 college majors.

There is evidence regarding the internal consistency and stability of the KOIS-DD VIEs. The KR-20 coefficients for the VIEs were in the range of .47 for Persuasive to .85 for Social Service. The homogeneity of these scales is less than desirable, which accounts for the term Vocational Interest Estimates. There were stronger findings regarding the stability of VIE rank orders. The retest reliability coefficients for a two-week period were in the range of .70 for Literary to .84 for Artistic with a median of .80. These findings are comparable to those found for other interest inventories (Kuder & Zytowski, 1991).

Because internal consistency estimates are not reported for the KOIS-DD Occupational and College Major scales in the manual, it is not possible to evaluate the homogeneity of these scales. Two types of stability data were reported. When the order of complete sets of Occupational and College Major scale scores was considered, the median reliability coefficient was .90. When the retest reliabilities were calculated for scale scores without regard for order, the median reliability was .93 for high school boys and .96 for college women (Kuder & Zytowski, 1991).

The Verification Scale has been demonstrated to be effective in differentiating sincere responders from test takers instructed to create a "best impression" response profile (Kuder & Zytowski, 1991). There is no evidence in the manual regarding the validity of the Vocational Interest Estimates. Concurrent validity evidence for 30 core occupational scales is provided in the manual. In general, there is a high rate of "hits" between occupational group and highest occupational scale score for validity study participants. Zytowski (1976) found strong evidence of the predictive validity of the Occupational Scales for occupational selection 12-19 years following KOIS-DD administration. The specific findings were as follows: (1) approximately half of the participants were in occupations consistent with adolescent and young adult KOIS-DD results, (2) the college major scales had slightly higher predictive value than the occupational scales, and (3) these results are similar to those attained for the Strong Interest Inventory (SII). This study remains the strongest evidence of the predictive value of the occupational and college major scales.

Although a manual preview has been released, no normative, reliability, or validity information is provided for the Kuder Career Search Activity Preferences, Career Clusters, or Person Matches.

Computer-Based Versions

The KOIS-DD is available in a PC-based format that provides immediate feedback to the test taker. The KCS is available in PC-based and Internet formats, both of which provide immediate feedback. [Both versions provide access to the Person Match database, which enables the test taker to search for interesting job titles and sketches beyond those provided in the KCS report.] The PC-based version incorporates the complete *Occupational Outlook Handbook* (OOH). The Internet version provides access to the *OOH* website. An important auxiliary resource is the Kuder Person Match database on CD-ROM that includes job sketches for approximately 1,500 persons representing 90% of the occupations in the United States. The database has a search engine that facilitates access to the job sketches, each of which includes an *OOH* reference.

Overall Critique

The KOIS-DD was derived from a long line of ingenious and methodologically sophisticated interest measurement research by Frederic Kuder. It has four clear strengths. First, the KOIS-DD is based on responses to familiar activities so that the influence of occupational stereotypes is reduced. Second, the KOIS-DD includes a validity index. Third, it provides feedback regarding both basic interests and similarity to occupations and college majors. The inclusion of the college major scales is a real asset in working with college students to find an appropriate major. Fourth, existing evidence suggests that the KOIS-DD is equal to its peers in predicting long-term occupational membership.

The KOIS-DD has five weaknesses. First, the homogeneity of some of the Vocational Interest Estimates is unacceptably low. This is a genuine concern when working with clients who are highly indecisive or lacking in career maturity. Second, and most troubling, is that fact that most of the criterion groups were sampled more than 30 years ago. No criterion groups have been added or updated in the past 11 years. As a result, the occupational and college major scale feedback is based on the interest characteristics from job incumbents in the 1950s, 1960s, and 1970s. It seems likely that there have been changes in the characteristics of these occupational and college major groups over the past four decades that are not represented in this form of the KOIS-DD. Third, the existing criterion groups are not representative of the racial and ethnic composition of the United States (Fouad, 1999). The KOIS-DD may be of limited utility for members of racial and ethnic minority groups. Fourth, the KOIS-DD does not include new and emerging occupations, such as information management. Clients who are looking to enter new disciplines may be frustrated because their occupational interests are not reflected by the KOIS-DD. The final weakness is the lack of information regarding the experimental scales. These scores cannot be interpreted to clients because of the near complete lack of concurrent validity evidence to guide interpretation.

The KOIS-DD is a beautifully constructed measurement device that needs to be updated. Counselors should be cautious in interpreting the occupational and college major scales because of the age of the criterion group research.

The KCS is truly innovative. The test developers showed good judgment in substituting the label Activity Preferences for Vocational Interest Estimates and reporting the Career Clusters in six areas that correspond to the Holland interest types. The Person Match, one of the most exciting recent innovations in interest assessment, is the realization of Kuder's dream of replacing static person-job matching with person-to-person matching. The Person Match job sketches breathe life into the assessment process by explicitly acknowledging that a given interest profile can be pursued in a number of different career paths and by providing a description of how people in different jobs live their lives. The best feature of the Person Match may be that it contextualizes career information.

The KCS also has some glaring weaknesses. First, there is not yet any supporting reliability of validity information. This is serious concern for the Activity Preference scales because they are based on fewer items than the KOIS-DD VIEs. Thus, the internal consistency of the Activity Preferences is likely to be lower than that of the VIEs, which are unacceptably low. Reliability appears to be a serious problem, especially considering the KCS has been designed for use with a younger population that tends to have a less crystallized interest pattern. Second, the method for selecting Person Matches is not specified in the preview manual. It is not possible to evaluate their validity in the absence of supporting information. At this point, it is recommended that the KCS with Person Match be considered a career- and self-exploration tool rather than an instrument to confirm client aspirations. All interpretations of KCS findings should be given with the statement that the findings are tentative and subject to error. This caution may be lifted once sufficient reliability and validity evidence is supplied. Finally, counselors should understand that the Person Match is a very different type of interest feedback. The fact that college students had rather strong preferences for the KOIS-DD over Person Match suggests that some clients are upset or troubled by the possibility that there are several distinct and viable career paths to pursue. The effects of this type of feedback on middle and high school students remains to be determined. Counselors should be prepared for adverse reactions to the Person Match. Although mature clients may find this information to be rich and meaningful, it may be upsetting to students seeking to narrow and focus their choices.

References

Fouad, N. A. (1999). Validity evidence for interest inventories. In M. L. Savickas & A. R. Spokane (Eds.), *Vocational interest: Meaning, measurement, and counseling* (pp. 193-209).

Kuder, F. (1980). Person-matching. *Educational and Psychological Measurement, 40,* 1-8.

Kuder, F, & Zytowski, D. G. (1991). *Kuder Occupational Interest Survey Form DD general manual* (3rd ed.). Adel, IA: National Career Assessment Services.

Zytowski, D. G. (1976). Predictive validity of the Kuder Occupational Interest Survey: A 12- to 19-year follow-up. *Journal of Counseling Psy*Self Directed Search-R: 4th Edition (SDS-R)

Self Directed Search-R: 4th Edition (SDS-R)

John L. Holland
Psychological Assessment Resources, Inc.
16204 N. Florida Avenue
Lutz, FL 33549
www.parinc.com
custserv@parinc.com

Target Population: High school students, college students, and adults.

Statement of the Purpose of the Instrument: The SDS-R is an easy-to-use, self-administered test that helps individuals find the occupations that best suit their interests and skills.

Titles of Subtests, Scales, Scores Provided: Holland Code, numerical scores in 6 Holland (RIA-SEC) categories (Realistic, Investigative, Artistic, Social, Enterprising, Conventional), Aspirations code.

Forms and Levels Available, with Dates of Publication/Revision of Each:
Professional User's Guide; Technical Manual; Form R Assessment Booklet; Form R Occupations Finder; Form R Alphabetized Occupations Finder; Dictionary of Holland Occupational Codes (DHOC), 3rd Edition; The Self-Directed Search and Related Holland Career Materials: A Practitioner's Guide. All Qualification Level A. Publication date for all: 8/24/94, except DHOC (12/17/96) and Practitioner's Guide (2/27/98).

Date of Most Recent Edition of Test Manual, User's Guide, Etc.: 8/24/94 (except DHOC 12/17/96 and Practitioner's Guide, 2/27/98).

Languages in Which Available: English, English-Canadian, French-Canadian, Spanish (also translated into over 20 other languages).

Time: Total Administration Time: 30-45 minutes.

Norm Group(s) on Which Scores Are Based: 2,602 students and working adults: 1,600 females and 1,002 males, ranging in age from 17-65 years, with 75% Caucasians, 8% African Americans, 7% Hispanics, 4% Asian Americans, 1% Native Americans, and 5% from other ethnic backgrounds; data were collected in 10 high schools, nine community colleges, 19 colleges or universities, and a variety of other sources throughout the U.S.

Manner in Which Results Are Reported for Individuals: Holland Code.
    Types of Scores: Percentile ranks for high school students, college students, and adults.
    Report Format/Content: Form R Windows Computer Version or Interpretive Report (10-15 page report): includes careers and educational programs that match the person's Holland Code. Report also describes the RIASEC system and provides concrete suggestions for further exploration.

Report Format/Content for Group Summaries: Not available.

Scoring
      Machine Scoring Service: SDS-R Professional Report Service
        Cost of basic service per counselee: $7.60 in quantities of 25
        Time required for scoring and returning (maximum): Within 24 hours of receipt, on next
        business day.
    Hand Scoring:
        Scored by: Counselee; Clerk.
        Time required for scoring: 5-10 minutes.
    Local Machine Scoring: Not available.

Computer Software Options Available: Standard administration online. Other: SDS-R on the Internet (www.self-directed-search.com).
SDS-R: CV (computer version) on-screen administration and report.
SDS-R: IR (interpretive report).

Ways in Which Computer Version Differs: A report is generated automatically based on the individual's responses to the test.

Cost of Materials:
    Professional User's Guide $23; Technical Manual $23; Form R Assessment Booklets (pkg/25)
    $29; Form R Alphabetized Occupations Finder (pkg/25) $33; Form R You and Your Career
    Booklet (pkg/25) $24; Educational Opportunities Finder (pkg/25) $45. Also available:
    Dictionary of Holland Occupational Codes (DHOC) $49.
    The Self-Directed Search and Related Holland Career Materials: A Practitioner's Guide $31.
    Specimen Set: One of each: Form R Assessment Booklet, Form R Occupation Finder, Form R
    You and Your Career Booklet, Educational Opportunities Finder, Leisure Activities Finder
    —cost $10 plus shipping.
    Counselee Materials: Form R Assessment Booklet (not reusable); Occupations Finder
    (reusable); Form R Alphabetized Occupations Finder (reusable); Form R You and Your
    Career Booklet (reusable); Educational Opportunities Finder (reusable); Leisure Activities
    Finder (reusable).
Additional Comments of Interest to Users: The SDS Family of Career products provides a set of self-assessment tools for a variety of populations, available in paper-and-pencil, computer, and professional report service versions. An audiotape version is also available for individuals with reading limitations.

Published Reviews:
Conneran, J. M. & Hartman, B. W. (1993). The concurrent validity of the Self Directed Search in
    identifying chronic career indecision among vocational education students. *Journal of Ca-*
    reer Development, 19, 197-208.
Dumenci, L. (1995). Construct validity of the Self-Directed Search using hierarchically nested
    structural models. *Journal of Vocational Behavior, 47,* 21-34.
Spokane, A. R. & Holland, J. L. (1995). The Self-Directed Search: A family of self-guided career
    interventions. *Journal of Career Assessment, 3,* 373-390.

Self-Directed Search-E: 4th Edition (SDS-E)

John L. Holland
Psychological Assessment Resources, Inc.
16204 N. Florida Avenue
Lutz, FL 33549
custserv@parinc.com
www.parinc.com

Target Population: Adults and older adolescents with lower educational levels.

Statement of the Purpose of the Instrument: Assess career interests among individuals with limited reading skills.

Titles of Subtests, Scales, Scores Provided: Holland Code, RIASEC scores, Aspirations Code.

Forms and Levels Available, with Dates of Publication/Revision of Each: Professional User's Guide; Technical Manual; Form E Assessment Booklet; Form E Jobs Finder; Form E You and Your Job Booklet. All Qualification Level A. Publication date for all 7/23/96.

Date of Most Recent Edition of Test Manual, User's Guide, Etc.: 7/23/96.

Languages in Which Available: English, English-Canadian, Spanish.

Time: Total Administration Time: 35-45 minutes.

Norm Group(s) on Which Scores Are Based: 719 individuals 15-72 years of age from a variety of ethnic and educational backgrounds.

Manner in Which Results Are Reported for Individuals: Two-letter Holland Code.

Report Format/Content for Group Summaries: Not available.

Scoring
    Machine Scoring Service: Not available.
    Hand Scoring:
        Scored by: Counselee.
        Time required for scoring: 10 minutes.
      Local Machine Scoring: Not available.
      Computer Software Options Available: Not available.

Cost of Materials:
Professional User's Guide $23
Technical Manual $23
Form E Assessment Booklets $29 (pkg/25)
Form E Jobs Finder $29 (pkg/25)
Form E You and Your Job Booklet $23 (pkg/25)

Specimen Set: One of each: Form E Assessment Booklet, Form E Jobs Finder, Form E You and Your Jobs Booklet, Educational Opportunities Finder, Leisure Activities Finder—cost $10 plus shipping.
Counselee Materials:
Form E Assessment Booklets (not reusable).
Form E Jobs Finder (reusable).
Form E You and Your Job Booklet (reusable).

Additional Comments of Interest to Users: Audiotape is available—individual still has to fill in answers on the paper-and-pencil booklet. Print size in booklet is larger size to help people who have reading difficulties.

Published Reviews:
Conneran, J. M. & Hartman, B. W. (1993). The concurrent validity of the Self Directed Search in identifying chronic career indecision among vocational education students. *Journal of Career Development, 19,* 197-208.
Dumenci, L. (1995). Construct validity of the Self-Directed Search using hierarchically nested structural models. *Journal of Vocational Behavior, 47,* 21-34.
Spokane, A. R. & Holland, J. L. (1995). The Self-Directed Search: A family of self-guided career interventions. *Journal of Career Assessment, 3,* 373-390.

Self Directed Search-CP: Career Planning (SDS-CP)

John L. Holland
Psychological Assessment Resources, Inc.
16204 N. Florida Avenue
Lutz, FL 33549
custserv@parinc.com
www.parinc.com

Target Population: Individuals on the career development track.

Statement of the Purpose of the Instrument: Developed to answer the demands of the many SDS organizational users, the SDS-CP focuses exclusively on occupations at upper levels of career responsibility and their corresponding educational requirements. Also helps employees plan for future professional advancement; helps individuals affected by organizational changes make career transitions; and helps employees reentering the workforce to establish new career foundations.

Titles of Subtests, Scales, Scores Provided: Holland Code, RIASEC Scores.

Forms and Levels Available, with Dates of Publication/Revision of Each:
Professional User's Guide; Technical Manual; Form CP Assessment Booklet; Form CP Career Options Finder; Exploring Career Options booklet.
All Qualification Level A.   Publication date for all 1/15/91.

Date of Most Recent Edition of Test Manual, User's Guide, Etc.: 1/15/91

Languages in Which Available: English only.

Time: Total Administration Time: 15-25 minutes.

Norm Group(s) on Which Scores Are Based: Regular Form R sample. Pairwise correlations of section and summary code scores for Form R and Form CP.

Manner in Which Results Are Reported for Individuals: Three-letter Holland Code
    Types of Scores: SDS Manual provides percentile ranks for adults.
    Report Format/Content
        Basic Service: 15-24 page report generated by either the Form CP IR (Interpretive Report) or Professional Report Service lists careers that match the individual's Holland Code.

Report Format/Content for Group Summaries: Not Available

Scoring
    Machine Scoring Service: SDS-CP Professional Report Service.
        Cost of basic service per counselee: $8.50 in quantities of 100.
        Time required for scoring and returning: Within 24 hours, on the next business day.
    Hand Scoring:
        Scored by: Counselee
        Time required for scoring: 5-10 minutes.
    Local Machine Scoring: Not available.

Computer Software Options Available: SDS-CP Interpretive Report

Ways in Which Computer Version Differs: Counselor enters scores from a paper-and-pencil administration and the IR software automatically generates a report.

Cost of Materials:
    Professional User's Guide $23.
        Technical Manual $23.
        Form CP Assessment Booklets (pkg/25) $39.
        Form CP Career Options Finder (pkg/25) $39.
        Form CP Exploring Career Options Booklet (pkg/125) $37.
    Specimen Set: One of each: Form CP Assessment Booklet, Form CP Career Options Finder, Form CP Exploring Career Options Booklet, Educational Opportunities Finder, Leisure Activities Finder—cost $10 plus shipping.
    Counselee Materials: Form CP Assessment Booklets (not reusable).
    Form CP Career Options Finder (reusable).
    Form CP Exploring Career Options Booklet (reusable).

Published Reviews:
Conneran, J.M. & Hartman, B.W. (1993). The concurrent validity of the Self Directed Search in identifying chronic career indecision among vocational education students. *Journal of Career Development*, 19, 197-208.
Dumenci, L. (1995). Construct validity of the Self-Directed Search using hierarchically nested structural models. *Journal of Vocational Behavior*, 47, 21-34.
Spokane, A.R. & Holland, J.R. (1995). The Self-Directed Search: A family of self-guided career interventions. *Journal of Career Assessment*, 3, 373-390.

Self-Directed Search-Career Explorer (SDS-CE)

John L. Holland
Psychological Assessment Resources, Inc.
16204 N. Florida Avenue
Lutz, FL 33549
custserv@parinc.com
www.parinc.com

Target Population: Middle or junior high school students.

Statement of the Purpose of the Instrument: Helps students assess and explore interests for future education and career planning.

Titles of Subtests, Scales, Scores Provided: Holland Code, RIASEC Scores, Aspirations Code

Forms and Levels Available, with Dates of Publication/Revision of Each: Professional User's Guide; Technical Manual; Career Explorer Self Assessment Booklet; Career Explorer Careers Booklet; Career Explorer Exploring Your Future with the SDS Booklet.
All qualification Level A. Publication date for all 1/31/94.

Date of Most Recent Edition of Test Manual, User's Guide, Etc.: 1/31/94

Languages in Which Available: English only.

Time: Total Administration Time: 35-45 minutes.

Norm Group(s) on Which Scores Are Based: 102 students in grades 6-8.

Manner in Which Results Are Reported for Individuals: Two-letter Holland Code
    Report Format/Content:
        Basic Service: 8-12 page report generated by either the IR (Interpretive Report) software or the mail-in Professional Report Service provides general educational and vocational information to junior high and middle school students who are beginning to think about potential careers.

Report Format/Content for Group Summaries: Not available

Scoring
    Machine Scoring Service: Not available.

Hand Scoring: Not available.
  Scored by: Counselee.
  Time required for scoring: 5-10 minutes.
Local Machine Scoring: Not available.

Computer Software Options Available: SDS Career Explorer: Interpretive Report.

Ways in Which Computer Version Differs: Counselor enters the individual's 2-letter code from a paper-and-pencil administration and the software generates the 8-12 page report to help the individual begin his or her educational and vocational exploration.

Cost of Materials:
Professional User's Guide $23
Technical Manual $23
Career Explorer Self Assessment Booklet, $42 (pkg/35).
Career Explorer Careers Booklet, $42 (pkg/35).
Career Explorer Exploring Your Future with the SDS Booklet, $35 (pkg/35).
  Specimen Set: One of each: Career Explorer Self Assessment Booklet, Career Explorer Careers Booklet, Career Explorer Exploring Your Future with the SDS Booklet, Teachers Guide—cost $10 plus shipping.
  Counselee Materials:
  Career Explorer Assessment Booklets (not reusable).
  Career Explorer Careers Booklet (reusable).
  Career Explorer Exploring Your Future with the SDS Booklet (reusable).

Published Reviews: None cited.

Reviewed by

Joseph C. Ciechalski
Professor
Department of Counselor & Adult Education
East Carolina University

Description

The Self-Directed Search (SDS) is an easy-to-use self-administered, self-scored, and self-interpreted interest inventory that assists individuals in finding occupations that are similar to their interests. It is based on John Holland's theory of vocational choice, which assumes that most people can be categorized into one of six personality and environmental types. The six personality and environ-

---

Note: Portions of this review were adapted from the author's original review in the *Thirteenth Mental Measurements Yearbook* with permission of the Buros Institute.

mental types are: Realistic (R), Investigative (I), Artistic (A), Social (S), Enterprising (E), and Conventional (C). Currently, there are four forms of the SDS: Form R, Form E, Form CP, and the Career Explorer. Each of these forms is designed for use with specific and distinct populations.

The Self-Directed Search (SDS) Form R: 4th Edition was revised in 1994. Form R is the original or regular form of the SDS and is designed for use with high school students, college students, and adults. This form of the SDS consists of the *Assessment Booklet, The Educational Opportunities Finder, You and Your Career, The Occupations Finder,* and the *Leisure Activities Finder.*

Like the 1985 edition, Form R of the *Assessment Booklet* is divided into five scales: Occupational Daydreams, Activities, Competencies, Occupations, and Self-Estimates. Only 67 of the 228 items contained in the *Assessment Booklet* were revised in the current version. The *Assessment Booklet* is used by the examinees to determine their three-letter Summary Code. Except for the Occupational Daydream scale, all of the remaining scales are used to calculate the examinee's three-letter Summary Code.

The examinee's three-letter Summary Code is used with *The Occupations Finder* to identify occupations that match this code. Revised in 1996, *The Occupations Finder* lists over 1,300 occupations arranged according to Holland's "RIASEC" system. *The Occupations Finder* also lists the nine-digit DOT number as well as the educational level of the occupation.

The *You and Your Career Booklet* was revised in 1994 and helps the examinees to better understand their three-letter Summary Code using six easy-to-follow steps. This booklet concludes with a most informative section on Making Career Decisions. In addition to the above booklets, *The Educational Opportunities Finder* and the *Leisure Activities Finder* were included with Form R.

Formerly called the *College Majors Finder, The Educational Opportunities Finder* (EOF) was revised in 1997. The EOF contains over 750 programs to assist individuals in locating educational opportunities consistent with an individual's Summary Code. Also revised in 1997, *The Leisure Activities Finder* lists over 750 leisure activities (hobbies, sports, and avocations) according to the first two letters of the Summary Code.

The Self-Directed Search (SDS) Form E: 4th Edition contains 198 items written at the sixth grade reading level whereas the directions are written at the fourth grade level. Form E of the SDS consists of the *Assessment Booklet, The Jobs Finder, and You and Your Job.*

Like Form R, the *Assessment Booklet* consists of five scales, but these are divided as follows: Jobs You Have Thought About, Activities, Skills, Jobs, and Rating Your Abilities. Instead of calculating a three-letter Summary Code, Form E requires one to find a two-letter Summary Code. *The Jobs Finder,* like *The Occupations Finder* of Form R, is used to classify over 800 job titles using the two-letter Summary Code.

The revised *You and Your Job* booklet, like the *You and Your Career* booklet of Form R, is used to help individuals better understand their scores and to use *The Job Finder*. In an earlier review of Form E, Ciechalski (1998) stated that, "The 1990 Revision of Form E reflects the author's dedication to improving on an already popular and well established instrument" (p. 892). The same statement applies to this revision of Form E.

The Self-Directed Search (SDS) Form CP: Career Planning focuses on long term career planning and occupations that require high levels of education and training. Form CP of the SDS was specifically designed for professionals and adults in career transition. It differs from Form R in three ways: (1) it contains new items focusing only on adult workers; (2) there are no Daydreams or Self-Estimates scales in the *Assessment Booklet*; and (3) *The Career Options Finder* contains over 1,300 occupational titles exclusively at the upper levels of career responsibility. This form also consists of the *Assessment Booklet*, *The Career Options Finder* (COF) and the interpretive booklet, *Exploring Career Options*.

The Self-Directed Search (SDS) Career Explorer was designed for middle and junior high school students. It consists of the *Self-Assessment Booklet*, *The Careers Booklet*, and the interpretive booklet *Exploring Your Future*. *The Assessment Booklet* contains 204 items. Of the 204 items, 30 items are new and 174 items came from other forms of the SDS.

The SDS Career Explorer is written at the third grade reading level. It was designed to introduce middle and junior high school students to vocational planning and to suggest ways of obtaining additional information about careers. Like Form E, the Career Explorer form yields a two-letter Summary Code. *The Careers Booklet,* a shorter version of the *Occupations Finder*, lists over 400 job titles according to Holland's code. Unlike the other forms of the SDS, this form focuses more on vocational exploration rather than on choosing a career.

The SDS has been adapted in over 25 countries. In addition, there are English Canadian (Form R & Form E), French Canadian (Form R), Spanish (Form R & Form E), and Vietnamese (Form E) versions of the SDS. For those who are visually impaired, there is a Braille edition of the SDS available.

Use in Counseling

The *SDS Professional User's Guide* (Holland, Powell, & Fritzsche, 1997) combines information on all four forms of the SDS into one comprehensive volume. This guide is a most valuable resource for both veteran and new users of the SDS.

According to the *SDS Professional User's Guide* (1997), the SDS has a number of uses. The SDS may help those individuals who are not certain about which career to pursue or those individuals who are considering a second career. It may be used for diverse populations. For example, the SDS has been used in middle schools, high schools, adult centers, employment offices, and correctional institutions and has met with satisfaction. It may also be used in placement and staff development in both business and industry. The SDS is a useful research tool as evidenced by the numerous studies cited in the *SDS Professional User's Guide* (1997).

In addition to the suggested uses and applications of the SDS mentioned above, the *SDS Professional User's Guide* (1997) contains well-written chapters on administering and scoring the SDS. To address the concerns of some former reviewers dealing with the errors encountered in scoring the SDS, the authors of the *SDS Professional User's Guide* state that, "The scoring of the SDS should be supervised and checked because test takers do make scoring errors"(p.15).

Information to assist counselors in the interpretation of the SDS is included in chapter 5, Interpretive Ideas, of the *SDS Professional User's Guide.* Chapter 5 not only describes the content and structure of the SDS, but also includes a number of SDS profiles which provide counselors with illustrative examples for using and interpreting the SDS with individuals.

Technical Considerations

The *SDS Technical Manual* (Holland, Fritzsche, & Powell, 1997) is completely revised and contains valuable information about the history, development, research, and technical aspects of the SDS. Like the *SDS Professional User's Guide* (1997), the *SDS Technical Manual* combines information about all four forms of the SDS. The Manual contains a total of 105 tables (66 in the text and 39 in the appendices).

Normative data were developed by administering the 1994 edition of Form R to a sample of 2,602 students and adults. There were 1,600 females and 1,002 males ranging in age from 17 to 65 years of age. This sample consisted of 47% white, 8% African-American, 7% Hispanics, 4% Asian Americans, 1% Native Americans, and 5% from other groups. Demographic variables by gender, age, and ethnic background and education are contained in separate tables in the technical manual.

Internal consistency coefficients (KR-20) for the Activities, Competencies, and Occupations scales ranged from .72 to .92 and the summary scale coefficients ranged from .90 to .94. Correlation coefficients between the two Self-Estimates ratings per scale ranged from .37 to .84. According to the authors of the *SDS Technical Manual,* these coefficients indicate that the ratings contain shared variance and that each contributes some variance.

Test-retest reliability was tested over 4-12 week time intervals. The resulting coefficients ranged from .76 to .89 indicating stability.

The concurrent validity of the 1994 SDS, like earlier editions of the SDS, was found by assessing the "percentage of hits." According to the authors of the technical manual, "The percentage of hits equals the percentage of a sample whose high point code and one-letter aspiration or occupational code agree" (p. 23). The range of hit rates for most interest inventories is 40% to 55%. For the 1994 SDS sample, the overall hit rate was 54.7% (the high end of the range).

Technical information on the alternate forms (Forms E, CP, and Career Planning) are included in Chapter 4 of the technical manual. Chapter 4 describes the development of the alternate forms as well as validity and reliability information. The results cited in the technical manual indicate that all four forms are equivalent.

Computer-Based Versions

Computer-based versions of the SDS are available for Forms R and CP. The computer versions administer, score, and interpret the SDS. A narrative report based on an individual's score is generated by the computer. In addition, the computer-based version includes, *My Vocational Situation,* a 2-page questionnaire that provides an indication of the level of career assistance a client may need.

Interpretive Reports (IRs) are available for Forms R, CP, and the Career Explorer. These software reports are unlimited use programs that interpret the client's SDS scores and produce a narrative report. To use this service, counselors must key the scores into the computer and the software program generates a 10-15 page Interpretive Report based on the information keyed in from the *Assessment Booklet.*

Professional report services are available for Form R, Form CP, and the Career Explorer. Prepaid mail-in answer sheets are sent to the publisher. A 15-24 page report, which includes an explanation of Holland's theory, individual's scores, Summary Code, and a list of matching careers are returned by the publisher to the counselor.

Form R of the SDS is available on the Internet (www.self-directed-search.com). Regardless of which computer-based form one uses, this reviewer believes that examinees should see a counselor for assistance in interpreting their results.

Overall Critique

In summary, the Self-Directed Search (SDS) Form R: 4th Edition and all of the alternate forms reflects the authors' continuing work and dedication to improving on an already outstanding instrument. It is a well-developed instrument with numerous studies to support its use. As Daniels (1994) stated in an earlier review of the SDS, "Its popularity among practitioners and researchers alike is testimony to its perceived utility and effectiveness" (p. 211). The SDS is and continues to be an excellent interest inventory.

References

Ciechalski, J.C. (1998). Review of the Self-Directed Search, Form E - 1990 Revision. In J.C. Impara & B.S. Plake (Eds.), *The thirteenth mental measurements yearbook* (pp. 893-894). Lincoln, NE: Buros Institute, University of Nebraska-Lincoln.

Daniels, M.H. (1994). Review of the Self-Directed Search, In J.T. Kapes, M.M. Mastie, & E.A. Whitfield (Eds.), *A counselor's guide to career assessment instruments* (3rd ed. p. 208-212). Alexandria, VA: National Career Development Association.

Holland, J.L., Fritzsche, B.A., & Powell, A.B. (1997). *The Self-Directed Search technical manual.* Odessa, FL: Psychological Assessment Resources, Inc.

Holland, J.L., Powell, A.B., & Fritzsche, B.A. (1997). *The Self-Directed Search professional user's guide.* Odessa, FL: Psychological Assessment Resources, Inc.

Strong Interest Inventory®

E.K. Strong
Consulting Psychologists Press, Inc.
3803 E. Bayshore Road
Palo Alto, California 94303
www.cpp-db.com

Target Population: 14 years and up.

Statement of the Purpose of the Instrument: The Strong Interest Inventory assessment tool measures a client's interests in a broad range of occupations, work activities, leisure activities, and school subjects.

Titles of Subtests, Scales, Scores Provided: General Occupational Themes: Realistic, Investigative, Artistic, Social, Enterprising, Conventional; Basic Interest Scales (25); Occupational Scales (211); and Personal Style Scales (4).

Forms and Levels Available with Dates of Publication/Revision of Each: Profile (1994. Interpretive Report (1994); Professional Report (1994); Entrepreneur Report with the MBTI Instrument (1997), Career Report with the MBTI instrument, Strong and Skills Confidence Inventory Profile.

Date of Most Recent Edition of Test Manual, User's Guide, Etc.: 1994.

Languages in Which Available: English, French, French Canadian, Italian, Anglicized adaptation.

Time: Actual Test Time 35-40 minutes.
    Total Administration Time 35-40 minutes

Norm Group(s) on Which Scores Are Based Over 55,000 people from across the United States representing age, gender, and ethnic percentage based on U.S. census data

Manner in Which Results are Reported for Individuals: Profile, interpretive
    Types of Scores: standard scores and verbal labels
    Report Format/Content:
        Basic Service: Strong Profile, Standard Edition, Strong Profile, High School Edition
        Options: Strong interpretive Report, Strong Professional Report, Strong and MBTI Entrepreneur Report, Strong and MBTI Career Report Strong and Skills Confidence Inventory Profile.

Report Format/Content for Group Summaries: Not Available.

Scoring
   Machine Scoring Service: Mail-in Software, Web Administration Site.
      Cost of basic service per counselee: $6.90
      Cost of options: Interpretive $11.29; Professional $13.57; Entrepreneur $15.85; Career, $15.85; Skills Confidence $8.79
      Time required for scoring and returning (maximum):
   Hand Scoring: Not Available
   Local Machine Scoring:
      Provisions/conditions/equipment required: Mail-in Scoring

Computer Software Options Available: Standard administration on-line and CPP Web Administration Site.

Ways in which computer version differs: Ability to keep client date electronically; ability to keep client notes electronically. Option: ability to administer over the Internet

Cost of materials:
   Specimen Set: $14.20 (Profile Item Booklet/Answer Sheet and Where Do I Go Next Booklet)
   Counselee Materials: Where Do I Go Next? ($4.00), Career Exploration: A Journey of Discovery ($18.00 pkg/25), Making It in Today's Organizations Using Strong and MBTI ($4.50 each), Exploring Career Options with the Strong video ($99.00)

Additional Comments of Interest to Users: New material for 2000 includes the Strong Business Report; the Strong Profile, College Edition: Finding Passion in Your Career-Integrating Skills Confidence with the Strong

Published Reviews:
Borgen, F. H. (1988). Review of the Strong-Campbell Interest Inventory. In J. T. Kapes & M. M. Mastie (Eds.), *A counselor's guide to career assessment instruments* (2nd ed.), Alexandria, VA: National Career Development Association.
Westbrook, B.W.,& Norton,J.J. (1994). Strong Interest Inventory (SII). In J.T. Kapes, M.M. Mastie, & E.A. Whitfield (Eds.). *A counselor's guide to career assessment instruments*, (3rd ed. Pp.215-218). Alexandria, VA: National Career Development Association.

Skills Confidence Inventory (SCI)

Nancy E. Betz, Fred H. Borgen, and Lenore W. Harmon
Consulting Psychologists Press, Inc.
3803 East Bayshore Road
Palo Alto, CA 94303
www.cpp-db.com

Target Population: People 15 years old and above. Use the inventory with college students and adults entering the workforce or exploring new careers.

Statement of the Purpose of the Instrument: The instrument measures your clients' perceived level of confidence in performing skills related to the six General Occupational Themes (GOTs).

The report shows whether a client has very little, little, moderate, high or very high confidence in skills related to the six GOTs. It opens your discussion of your client's confidence level in his or her skills, a factor that could be preventing the client from considering high-interest careers.

Titles of Subtests, Scales, Scores Provided: Results are prioritized into: High Priority; High Confidence, High Interest; Possible Options If Interest Develops; High Confidence, Little Interest, Good Option If Confidence Increases; Little Confidence, High Interest, Low Priority; Little Confidence, Little Interest.

Forms and levels Available, with Dates of Publication/revision of Each: Level B, published since 1996.

Date of Most Recent Edition of Test Manual, User's Guide, Etc.: 1996.

Languages in Which Available: English and Canadian French.

Time:　Actual Test Time: Less than 30 minutes.
　　　　Total Administration Time: 40-50 minutes.

Norm Group(s) on Which Scores Are Based: Percentiles are based on 1,147 working adult participants. The normative sample of college students consisted of 706 enrolled in introductory psychology courses at Ohio State University and Iowa State University.

Manner in Which Results Are Reported for Individuals:
　　Types of Scores: Approximate percentile equivalents based from 1.0 to 5.0.
　　Report Format/Content:
　　　　Basic Service: Includes Holland's Hexagon and the General Occupations. Included as a one-page report at the end of the six-page *Strong Profile*. The report shows whether a client has very little, moderate, high or very high confidence in skills related to the six GOTs.
　　　　Options: The *Skills Confidence Inventory* is available only in combination with materials for the *Strong Interest Inventory*. Also feature: Strong, Skills Confidence and MBTI® Entrepreneur Report Combined Item Booklet/Answer Sheets; Strong and Skills Confidence Preview Kit; Strong, Skills, and Confidence and MBTI® Career Report Combined item Booklet/Answer Sheets.

Report Format/Content for Group Summaries: Not available.

Scoring
　　Machine Scoring Service:
　　　　Cost of basic service per counselee: We offer mail in scoring that has a five-day turnaround period. It is a one-page report that follows the six-page *Strong Profile*. The price of scoring is included in the original ordering price.
　　Hand Scoring: Not available.
　　Local Machine Scoring: Not available.

Computer Software Options Available: Computerized adaptive administration.

Ways in which computer version differs: It does not differ. It allows the user to administer and score both inventories onsite and to print the combined profile.

Cost of Materials:

Strong and Skills Confidence Preview Kit		$49
(Prepaid Strong and Skills Confidence combined Item Booklet/Answer Sheet, Skills Confidence Inventory Applications and Technical Guide).		
Prepaid Strong Interest Inventory® and Skills Confidence Inventory Combined		$97.30 pkg/10
Item Booklet/Answer Sheets for mail-in scoring		
Strong, Skills Confidence, and MBTI® Entrepreneur Report		$199 pkg/10
Combined Item Booklet/Answer Sheets* for mail-in scoring (includes Skills Confidence Profile)		
Strong and Skills Confidence CPP Software System		$14.50 pkg/25
Combined Item Booklet/Answer Sheets		
Skills Confidence Inventory Applications and Technical Guide		$37.80 each
Strong Interest Inventory® and Skills Confidence Inventory Profile Administration	10-99	$9.20 each
	100-499	$8.55 each
	500+	$7.80 each
Strong Interest Inventory® and Skills Confidence Inventory Profile Plus strong Interpretive Report Administration.	10-99	$14.70 each
	100-499	$13.70 each
	500+	$12.50 each
Strong Interest Inventory® and Skills Confidence Inventory Profile Plus Strong Professional Report Administration.	10-99	$14.70 each
	100-499	$13.70 each
	500+	$12.50 each
Strong, Skills Confidence, and MBTI® each	10-99	$13.30
Entrepreneur Report Administration	100-499	$12.40 each
must also purchase Strong and Skills Profile Administration	500+	$11.30 each
Skills Confidence Report Forms	(100 sets)	$76.50 box

*These two reports utilize the same answer sheet. Each report is charged separately.

Additional Comments of interest to Users: Lack of experience may lead to lower skills confidence scores, rendering the scores somewhat less meaningful. Lower levels of confidence should be considered to indicate areas where new learning might be attempted.

Published Reviews: None Cited

Reviewed by

Nicholas A. Vacc
Joe Rosenthal Excellence Professor
Department of Counseling and Educational Development
University of North Carolina at Greensboro

Deborah W. Newsome
Assistant Professor
Department of Education
Wake Forest University

Description

The Strong Interest Inventory, which was most recently revised in 1994, is also known as the Strong or the SII. It is a vocational interest questionnaire designed for use by high school students, college students, and adults. The SII is composed of four sets of scales: General Occupational Themes, which are based on the six vocational interest types proposed by John Holland; Basic Interest Scales, which report consistency of interests or aversions in 25 specific areas; Occupational Scales, which indicate similarities between a respondent's interests and the interests of individuals working in specific occupations; and Personal Style Scales, which are used to explore preferences concerning working style, learning environment, leadership style, and propensity toward risk taking and adventure (Harmon, Hansen, Borgen, & Hammer, 1994).

The 1994 revision is composed of 317 items: 282 from the 1985 version and 35 new items. Some items were deleted from the 1985 version because they were dated (e.g., "Pursuing bandits in a sheriff's posse"). Others were changed to make the language more contemporary. The new items are listed in the *Applications and Technical Guide*, which replaced the manual and the user's guide of the 1985 version. Some items on the six General Occupational Themes were revised to improve internal reliability. Four new scales (i.e., Applied Arts, Culinary Arts, Computer Activities, and Data Management) were added to the Basic Interest Scales, the Domestic Arts Scale was deleted, and the Adventure Scale was moved to the new Personal Style Scales, which resemble the deleted Academic Comfort and Introversion/Extroversion Scales of the 1985 version. For the Occupational Scales, three scales were changed in relation to their Holland codes, and new data were collected, resulting in the representation of 211 vocations, including 14 new occupations. Of these, 102 are paired with separate scales for men and women, and 7 are represented by a single gender.

The Administrative Indexes, which show response percentages for each section of the Strong, were modified slightly for the 1994 version. Fewer responses (300 rather than 305) are required for a valid profile, new infrequency scales were developed, and procedures for calculating total percentages of Like/Indifferent/Dislike responses were changed. Also, the Strong Profile has been extensively redesigned to facilitate interpretation and understanding for the client (Harmon et al., 1994).

For the first time in its history, the Strong includes the option of a Skills Confidence Inventory (SCI; Betz, Borgen, & Harmon, 1996), which is designed to be administered with the Strong Interest Inventory. The 60-item SCI measures a respondent's self-perceived ability to successfully complete a variety of tasks, activities, and coursework. Items correspond with the SII's General Occupational Themes, with 10 items constituting each theme scale. Scores on each scale range from 1 to 5 with scores of 3.5 or higher representing areas of high skill confidence. The SCI is recommended for use with college students and adults who have some amount of work experience. Results of the SCI are reported on a single-page profile that compares the respondent's perceived capabilities with his/her expressed interests in each of the six General Occupational Themes.

Use in Counseling

The main reasons for using the Strong are to identify the test taker's interests, provide a framework for organizing interests into categories within the world of work, and help the test taker identify potential occupations that may not have been considered previously. The Inventory can be used to help people select majors or training programs, choose occupations, determine midcareer changes, plan for retirement, or understand reasons for job dissatisfaction.

Scores on the Strong Profile are presented so that interpretation moves from general to more specific information. Steps for interpretation are outlined in the *Application and Technical Guide*, which also provides assistance in interpreting unusual profiles and using the Strong with different age groups, cultures, genders, and special populations.

Career professionals using the Skills Confidence Inventory can help clients simultaneously examine their interests and perceived abilities, to interpret vocational interest patterns. The combined use of the SII and SCI provides information that neither inventory alone provides. The integrated profile categorizes each theme area by priority for exploration. High confidence and interest in a theme signal a need for further exploration. When confidence is higher than interest or vice-versa, the counselor can help the client explore reasons for the discrepancy. It is important to emphasize that confidence in a particular area does not reflect actual ability or the potential to develop ability (Betz et al., 1996).

Technical Considerations

Data for the normative group (i.e., General Reference Sample) of the 1994 version were collected in 1992 and 1993 from more than 55,000 adults. Approximately 38,000 of these were employed adults between the ages of 25 and 60 who reported job satisfaction and success. General Reference Samples were created by randomly selecting 200 men and 200 women from each occupation for which new data were collected. When fewer than 200 males or females were available in a particular occupation, all eligible respondents were included. The combined General Reference Sample consisted of 18,951 adults (i.e., 9,467 women and 9,484 men). Of the individuals who identified their race/ethnicity, 378 were African American, 363 were Asian American, 349 were Hispanic American/Latino, 77 were Native American/American Indian, and 17,365 were Caucasian American. More than 99% had completed high school, and a majority had completed four or more years of college, indicating that the generalizability of the data is skewed toward a more highly educated subset of the population (Lattimore & Borgen, 1999).

All scales of the Strong yield standard scores with a mean of 50 and a standard deviation of 10 (Harmon et al., 1994). Scores are based on the combined male and female General Reference Sample, with the exception of the Occupational Scales, which provide two sets of standard scales derived from gender-based samples.

Item selection for the 1994 version was based on the premise that people who have found satisfying work in an occupation tend to respond to items in a way that is characteristic of others in their occupation (Harmon et al., 1994). The General Occupational Themes and Basic Interest Scales are reported to be highly reliable in terms of internal consistency and test-retest consistency over extended time periods (Hood & Johnson, 1997). Cronbach's alpha coefficients for the General Occupational Themes were .90 or higher for each of the six scales. Test-retest reliabilities calculated for adults at three- and six- month intervals ranged from .84 for the Enterprising Scale to .92 for the Realistic Scale. The same test-retest coefficients for the Basic Interest Scales ranged from .80 to .94. Harmon et al. (1994) stated that, because the 1994 Basic Interest Scales correlated highly with earlier versions, results of earlier studies of the scales may be generalized to the 1994 scales. For the Occupational Scales, test-retest coefficients ranged from .80 to .99. Test-retest coefficients for the new Personal Scales ranged from .81 to .92, with alpha coefficients ranging from .78 to .91 (Harmon et al., 1994).

The General Occupational Themes and Basic Interest scales are reported to possess a high degree of content validity because of the way they were constructed (Hood & Johnson, 1997). Empirical studies have shown that both sets of scales discriminate among people employed in different types of occupations (Harmon et al., 1994). Lattimore and Borgen (1999) reported evidence of concurrent validity for the six General Occupational Themes across college-educated racial-ethnic groups. Concurrent validation studies indicated that the Occupational Scales differentiate between people in a given occupation and people in general. Concerning predictive validity, between 55% and 70% of people who have taken the Strong have entered occupations congruent with their Occupational Scale scores (Hood & Johnson, 1997). Some evidence of concurrent validity for the Personal Style Scales was demonstrated by examining how known groups differed on the scales. For example, differences on the Learning Environment Scale were examined in relation to the educational levels of the respondents. However, Hood and Johnson (1997) cautioned that the Personal Style Scales lack the established validity of the other scales.

The normative group for the Skills Confidence Inventory was composed of 1,147 adults and 706 college students (1,853 respondents) who participated in data collection for the 1994 edition of the Strong (Betz et al., 1996). Raw scores were transformed to percentile equivalents, which are presented in the *Applications and Technical Guide*.

Internal consistency of the 10-item scales was reported to range from .84 to .88. Three-week test-retest reliability coefficients for college students ranged from .83 to .87 for the Social Scale. Betz et al. (1996) reported evidence of concurrent validity based on the inventory's ability to separate college students and adults, men and women, and groups of people working in different occupations according to theoretically expected differences in skills confidence. Significant correlations between interest and skills confidence within the same General Occupational Theme (GOT) and low correlations between interest and skills levels in different GOTs provided evidence of construct validity, as did close correspondence between the GOT interest classification of each occupation and the highest skills confidence scores of sampled members of the given occupation.

Computer-Based Version

The 1994 computer-based version runs on Microsoft Windows, provides immediate access to scoring and interpretation, and can be obtained through the Consulting Psychologists Press (http://www.cpp-db.com). Four administration options are provided: *interactive* – the Inventory is completed on the computer, *scanning* – the paper-and-pencil version is completed and the data are scanned into the computer, *manual "key-in"* – the paper-and-pencil version is completed and the test user keys in the responses manually, and *Internet*—the Inventory is completed online. The software provides a password security system, technical support, free system upgrades, user's guide, and extensive online support.

Westbrook and Norton (1994) cited studies by Vansickle, Kimmel, and Kapes and Vansickle and Kapes indicating that the computer-based version of the SII can be completed more quickly than the paper-and-pencil version and does not differ significantly in scale means and standard deviations from the non-computer-based version. Hansen, Neuman, Haverkamp, and Lubinski (1997) reported that user reactions to the two administration modes were reasonably similar in most areas, with the computer-based version being easier to follow, easier on the eyes, and more interesting. To date, the literature contains no studies of users' responses to the Internet-based version of the SII.

Overall Critique

Whiston (2000) and the authors consider the Strong a model for other interest inventories based on its psychometric properties. The Inventory provides a valuable measure of vocational interests and presents information to clients in a clear and understandable form. The 1994 version reflects contemporary issues and changes in the world of work and is considerably more comprehensive than other career or interest inventories. However, the samples selected for norming purposes were volunteers and may not adequately represent the broad spectrum of individuals in a given occupation.

To address the sampling procedures weakness of the 1985 version, demographic data are provided in the 1994 *Applications and Technical Guide*. However, the data are based on the full research sample rather than the final General Reference Sample. Further, specific information about the response rates on the Occupational Scales is not included for the 1994 version, although a detailed discussion of the steps used to create the Occupational Scales is provided. Although the *Applications and Technical Guide* does not depict the exact items used to construct each scale, the descriptions of differences that exist among scales seem to provide sufficient information to help the test administrator understand how to interpret the scales to clients.

A nagging concern continues to be the high level of education reflected in the sample, particularly as it concerns racial-ethnic groups. Yet, despite this and the other limitations, the Strong continues to be a robust career-assessment instrument that provides a valuable measure of vocational interests for the test taker, and the authors recommend its use by counselors. The optional addition of the Skills Confidence Inventory provides a useful measure of perceived ability that supplements the career professional's efforts to assist clients in making decisions about academic majors, occupations, and changes in career direction.

References

Betz, N. E., Borgen, F. H., & Harmon, L. W. (1996). *Skills Confidence Inventory Applications and Technical Guide*. Palo Alto, CA: Consulting Psychologists Press.

Hansen, J. C., Neuman, J. L., Haverjamp, B. E., & Lubinski, B. R. (1997). Comparison of user reaction to two methods of *Strong Interest Inventory* administration and report feedback. *Measurement and Evaluation in Counseling and Development, 30,* 115-137.

Harmon, L. W., Hansen, J. C., Borgen, F. H., & Hammer, A. L. (1994). *Strong Interest Inventory Application and Technical Guide.* Palo Alto, CA: Consulting Psychologists Press.

Hood, A. B., & Johnson, R. W. (1997). *Assessment in counseling: A guide to the use of psychological assessment procedures* (2nd ed.). Alexandria, VA: American Counseling Association.

Lattimore, R. R., & Borgen, F. H. (1999). Validity of the 1994 *Strong Interest Inventory* with racial and ethnic groups in the United States. *Journal of Counseling Psychology, 46,* 185-195.

Westbrook, B. W., & Norton, J. J. (1994). Strong Interest Inventory (SII). In J. T. Kapes, M. M. Mastie, & E. A. Whitfield (Eds.). *A counselor's guide to career assessment instruments,* (3rd ed, pp. 215-218). Alexandria, VA: National Career Development Association.

Whiston, S. C. (2000). *Principles and applications of assessment in counseling.* Belmont, CA: Brooks/Cole - Wadsworth.

Values Scale (VS)

Donald E. Super and Dorothy D. Nevil
Consulting Psychologists Press, Inc.
3803 East Bayshore Road
Palo Alto, CA 94303
www.cpp-db.com

Target Population: People 16 years and older who can read at an eighth-grade level.

Statement of the Purpose of the Instrument: It helps people achieve career goals by identifying important extrinsic and intrinsic values by discussing and identifying values; a client can focus career development on the most personally satisfying career. The distinctive contribution of a values measure in career counseling is the light it sheds on what a person wants from life, and thus from the work and other roles, as distinct from how he or she thinks it might be found.

Titles of Subtests, Scales, Scores Provided: 21 values scored: Ability Utilization, Achievement, Advancement, Aesthetics, Altuism, Authority, Autonomy, Creativity, Economic Rewards, Life Style, Personal Development, Physical Activity, Prestige, Risk, Social Interaction, Social Relations, Variety, Working Conditions, Cultural Identity, Physical Prowess, Economic Security.

Forms and Levels Available, with Dates of Publication/Revision of Each: Level B.

Date of Most Recent Edition of Test Manual, User's Guide, Etc.: 1986.

Languages in Which Available: English.

Time: Actual Test Time: Less than 30 minutes.
        Total Administration Time: 40-50 minutes.

Norm Group(s) on Which Scores Are Based: Samples were taken from 6,000 high school students, university students and adults.

Manner in Which Results Are Reported for Individuals:
   Types of Scores: Standard Scores in 21 scales with each scale consists of five items, at least two of which relate to values in general.
   Report Format/Content:
      Basic Service: There is a report form and score sheet. Information is grouped into Inner-Oriented, Material, Physical Prowess, and Physical Activity.
      Options:

Report Format/Content for Group Summaries: Not available.

Scoring
   Machine Scoring Service: Mail-in scoring with five-day turn-around.
   Hand Scoring: Scored by counselor.
   Local Machine Scoring: Not available.

Computer Software Options Available: Not available.

Cost of Materials:
   Specimen Set: Values Scale Preview Kit $62 (Values Scale Item Booklet: Values Scale Non-Prepaid Answer Sheet, Values Scale Report Form; Values Scale Manual). $62.

Values Scale Item Booklets reusable	$53.25
Non-Prepaid Values Scale Answer Sheets for hand scoring	$32.70 pkg/25
Values Scale Report Forms for hand scoring	$32.70 pkg/25
Values Scale manual	$56.00 each

Published Reviews:
Schoenrade, P. (1998). Review of the Values Scale. In J. C. Impara & B. S. Plake (Eds.). *Thirteenth mental measurements yearbook.* Lincoln, NE: Buros Institute, University of Nebraska-Lincoln.

Reviewed by

Patricia Schoenrade
Professor of Psychology
William Jewell College

Description

The Values Scale (VS) is an easy-to-administer inventory useful for identifying the importance of some 21 individual values particularly relevant to career choice and the workplace. The 106-item scale requires ratings of importance on a 1-4 scale. For each item, the respondent considers the stem "Right now or in the future, it is important for me to ….". It is suitable for high school, university, and adult populations. The developers indicate that it is also suitable for elementary or middle school respondents, though this reviewer is not convinced that reliability will be adequate for these groups. The scale requires about 30-45 minutes to administer, and it can be administered to individuals or groups.

The authors explain that the scale was prepared to "provide an instrument to measure intrinsic and extrinsic values not assessed by existing measures" (Nevill & Super, 1989, p. 1). Subsets of items assess each of 21 different values: Ability Utilization, Achievement, Advancement, Aesthetics, Altruism, Development, Physical Activity, Prestige, Risk, Social Interaction, Social Relations, Variety, Working Conditions, Cultural Identity, Physical Prowess, and Economic Security, with each scale composed of five items. The items cover a

Note: Portions of this review were adapted from the author's original review in the *Thirteenth Mental Measurements Yearbook* with permission of the Buros Institute.

wide range of topics, including abstract values (e.g. "reach a high standard in my work;" "use new ideas and methods"), social considerations (e.g. "live where people of my religion and race are accepted"; "be with other people while I work"), pragmatic concerns, (e.g. "have a good income"; "set my own working hours"); and specific activities (e.g. "use powerful machines"; "take part in sports and other physical activities").

The prior edition of the VS was published in 1986, though the initial version was prepared in 1980. It was developed by representatives of the Work Importance Study, a multinational consortium drawing members from some 12 countries. Development was an intensive process including definitions of values by multinational teams, drafting of initial items, testing, and refinement. The multinational cooperation allowed the developers to take into account differences in government, religious emphasis, and socioeconomic variables.

The response sheet is well designed for hand scoring if samples are small and, for larger samples, computer scoring is available. The inventory includes a 20-category occupational group response; these responses may be converted to Holland Codes (Holland, 1985), which then facilitate comparisons with tables of norms for the several career groups provided in the accompanying manual. Raw scores are easily converted to standard scores using another table in the manual. The profile form permits ipsative as well as normative interpretation.

The VS is accompanied by a comprehensive 55-page manual (Nevill & Super, 1989). It describes the scale's use and applications, traces the history of development, reviews relevant literature, and provides extensive cross-cultural normative tables for comparison. In addition, norms are provided for high school, college, and adult samples and for Holland Code Types. The manual is prepared in a readable style and format.

Use in Counseling

The VS will be of considerable help to career counselors attempting to assist those who are uncertain of appropriate career directions. The developers observe that "both the counselor and the counselee need to understand the latter's degree of preparation for making career decisions" (Nevill & Super, 1989, p. 5). They thus indicate that, useful as the score is, it must still be understood in the context of the respondent's life situation and stage of development. The authors provide a model of career development assessment based on earlier work by Super (1983), describing the way in which the VS fits into the process.

The VS will help the first-time or experienced job-seeker to identify values and priorities with which to narrow the field or rule out undesirable job possibilities. It will encourage the respondent to take an in-depth look at what he or she seeks from a job..

The scale may also provide a helpful starting point for the client who has just begun to contemplate possibility of changing jobs. The simply worded, straightforward items will help that client reconsider what is important to him or her in the next career decision. In work settings involving large numbers of respondents, the VS might conceivably be viewed as an aid to deciding whether and individual is well placed in her or his current situations.

Technical Considerations

Extensive normative data are available in the manual. Tables allow comparison of scores to those of international populations including several in Belgium, Italy, Canada, Portugal, Yugoslavia, and the United States. For some of these, data for more than one age group (e.g. high school, university, or adults) are provided. Although some of the samples are more than a decade old, their size is sufficient to suggest that they probably remain quite applicable.

Alpha reliability coefficients for the 21 value scales for both university students and adults reveal that internal consistency is adequate (.67) to very good (.87), with most scales tending toward the latter.

The instructions preceding the items—"Right now or in the future, it is important for me to…"—might lead one to anticipate low reliability, as the two (right now and in the future) could be quite different. In fact, this does not seem to be as significant a problem as this reviewer might have expected. Test-retest correlations on university samples range from .50 to .82, with most scales in the .65-.80 range. Test-retest data on adult populations are not available, and the authors explain that these data are harder to obtain for adult populations. The university student data, however, are encouraging since this group might reasonably be expected to exhibit less test-retest consistency than would older adults.

The argument for validity of the VS is, first, based upon its development; that is, cross-cultural involvement, the process of construction and refinement, and the item selection process. In addition, a number of validity studies are reported indicating expected differences between the genders, differentiation among career codes, and factor analytic studies. The manual invites further validation research and is written in part to encourage such research. Insofar as it is possible to tap values through a face-valid self-report measure, the VS appears to do so adequately. Although the number of values would make it impossible to present all of the relevant comparisons in a limited space, the scale makes a number of the discriminations that would be expected of an inventory useful for career development counseling. The information provided is quite adequate to encourage more researchers to do field research of this type.

Overall Critique

The VS (which might have been more accurately named the Work-Related Values Scale) appears to be a sound instrument for career counseling purposes. The values assessed are applicable to a wide spectrum of work situations. The ease of scoring for ipsative and normative interpretations permits application to both individual and group situations, and to long-term planning as well as immediate placement. Validity and reliability data reflect the scale's careful development, and, though test-retest data are not presented for adult samples, the data for younger samples suggest good reliability. The manual is extremely thorough and user friendly. The extensive normative tables drawn from various countries permit comparison among ethnically diverse samples as well as among career groups. Although individual counselors may have a slightly different understanding of some of the values assessed, the overall picture the scale provides should prove a helpful basis from which to proceed for both client and counselor.

References
Holland, J. L. (1985). *Making vocational choices: A theory of vocational personalities and work environments* (2nd ed.). Englewood Cliffs, NJ.: Prentice-Hall.
Nevill, D. D. & Super, D. E. (1989). *The values scale: Theory, application, and research manual* (2nd ed.). Palo Alto, CA.: Consulting Psychologists Press.
Super, D. E. (1983). Assessment in career guidance: Toward truly developmental counseling. *The Personnel and Guidance Journal, 61,* 555-562.

Vocational Interest Inventory, Revised (VII-R)

Patricia W. Lunneborg
Western Psychological Services
12031 Wilshire Blvd.
Los Angeles, CA 90025
www.wpspublish.com

Target Population: High school students, young adults.

Statement of the Purpose of the Instrument: The *Vocational Interest Inventory Revised (VII-R)* measures students' relative interest in Roe's eight occupational areas (Service, Business Contact, Organization, Technical, Outdoor, Science, General Culture, and Arts and Entertainment), which essentially classify all jobs. Its unique longitudinal research provides excellent long-term predictive validity for college majors. Students compare their interests with the scores of graduating college students who took the instrument as high school juniors. Unlike most other tests, which compare high school students with adults in middle, the VII-R compares high school students with other high school students who have gone on to complete specific college majors.

Titles of Subtests, Scales, Scores Provided: Service, Business, Contact, Organization, Technical, Outdoor, Science, General Culture, and Arts and Entertainment.

Date of Most Recent Edition of Test Manual, User's Guide, Etc.: 1993

Languages in Which Available English only.

Time: Actual Test Time: 20 minutes or less.
Total Administration Time: 20 minutes or less.

Norm Group(s) on Which Scores Are Based: 27,000 high school juniors.

Manner in Which Results Are Reported for Individuals Computer report with narrative and graphic elements—samples in manual.
Types of Scores: Percentiles.
Report Format/Content:
Basic Service: The VII-R is computer scored, using WPS TEST REPORT prepaid Mail-In Answer Sheets. It provides a personalized, narrative report, in duplicate, that is easy to understand. The report includes a profile of occupational interests, an analysis and discussion of all scores at or above the 75th percentile, and a profile of college majors that shows how similar the examinee's scores are to the average scores of people who have graduated in 25 popular college majors. Also included is a list, in rank order, of college majors that are compatible with the examinee's interests.

Report Format/Content for Group Summaries: Not available.

Scoring
    Machine Scoring Service:
        Time required for scoring and returning (maximum): 24-hour turnaround and mailing time.
    Hand Scoring: Not available .
    Local Machine Scoring:
        Provisions/conditions/equipment required: On-site scoring for original VII, not VII-R. Use computer disk (IBM).

Computer Software Options Available: Standard on-line for original VII.

Cost of Materials: Kit $69.50 Includes 4 SPS TEST REPORT prepaid VII-R Mail-in Answer Sheets for computer scoring and interpretation, 1 Manual
MANUAL $40
VII-R MAIL-IN ANSWER SHEET
Includes test items
1-9 Answer Sheets, each $9.80
10+ Answer Sheets, each $8.75
VII DISK (3.5")
Provides 25 administration of the original VII (not the VII-R).
PC with DOS Operating System
1 Disk $155
2+ Disks $140
VII PC ANSWER SHEET (Pads of 100)
1 Pad $15
For use with the VII Disk. Includes test items.
Free shipping.

Published Reviews:
Law, J. G., Jr. (1998) Review of the vocational Interest Inventory-Revised. In J. C. Impara & B. S. Plake (Eds) *Thirteenth mental measurements yearbook.* Lincoln, NE: Buros Institute, University of Nebraska-Lincoln.

Reviewed by

William D. Schafer
Associate Professor of Measurement, Statistics, and Evaluation
College of Education
University of Maryland

Description
    The purpose of the Vocational Interest Inventory – Revised (VII-R) is to assess the comparable strengths of high school students' interests in eight occupational areas developed from Roe's (1956) work. The eight occupational interest areas, organized into a two-dimensional circular array somewhat like Holland's (1973) structure, are, in a natural order around the circle, Service, Business

Contact, Organization, Technical, Outdoor, Science, General Culture, and Arts and Entertainment.

The student responds in under a half-hour to 112 two-choice items on a two-sided, machine-scorable answer sheet. The first 56 consist of pairs of occupations (e.g., Police Chief; Draftsperson) and the second 56 are pairs of activities (e.g., Baby-sit; Talk people into voting for our schools). In each case, the student is to choose the one that interests him or her more. The instructions strongly indicate that virtually all items are to be answered and that even a small percentage of omits compromises scorability.

Scoring is done by the publisher using proprietary algorithms. An extensive test report is produced that includes a percentile profile and descriptions of the scales. Interpretations of the profiles emphasize the combinations of scales above the 75th percentile. Possible occupations are grouped into those that do and those that do not generally require at least a bachelor's degree. Possible college majors are organized by a rating of similarity of the student's scores with the average scores of examinees who were graduates in those majors. The sample report in the manual seems fairly satisfying and gives reasonable advice to the student about how to use the information it contains.

The present manual, which first appeared in 1993, describes norms that are based on samples collected in 1987. The original Vocational Interest Inventory, which was normed in 1979, remained the same.

Use in Counseling

Although the VII-R was designed to be self-interpreting for the student, its stated intent is for use in a career-counseling program under the direction of a trained vocational counselor. The items and interpretive reports are intended to be accessible to a 10th-grade audience. Although the activities seem straightforward, many of the occupations might be unfamiliar to high-school students (e.g., Library Page). Overall, the VII-R seems best suited to a college-bound or early college population.

Technical Considerations

Norms are based on a 1987 sample of over 27,000 juniors and seniors, who were high school students in Washington State. Although adequate in size, geographic homogeneity may affect the usefulness of the norms. For example, 86% of the norm group were White, whereas Blacks, Hispanics, and Native Americans, at 2% each, together were equivalent to the number of Asians, at 6%. Over 90% of the norm group intended to go on to postsecondary education. Finally, the nature of the jobs that were common at the time in Washington State may differentiate the norm group from the experiences of students in other regions.

Gender bias was investigated at the item level and items that correlated with sex were edited. It was felt that this procedure makes separate sex-norms unnecessary. Nevertheless, differences of up to about a full standard deviation are reported between men and women on some scales.

Internal consistency and test-retest reliabilities are marginally adequate, with the weakest results generally for the Technical scale. Law (1998) compared the reliability data of the VII-R with that of the 1990 Strong Interest Inventory and found the latter to have the stronger results. Almost all the reliability data for the VII-R are reported for samples collected prior to the 1987 renorming.

Alpha coefficients for the occupations subscales ranged from .16 (Technical) to .72 (Science). The alpha coefficients for the activities subscales were from .33 (Technical) to .61 (Science). For the full scales, the alpha coefficients ranged from .41 (Technical) to .80 (Science). Odd-even split-half reliabilities ranged from .54 (Cultural) to .80 (Science) and occupations-activities split-half reliabilities went from .40 (Technical) to .80 (Science). Six-month test-retest coefficients ranged from .66 (Technical) to .85 (Science). Subscale standard errors of measurement based on the test-retest coefficients ranged from 3.96 (Outdoor) to 5.80 (Technical). These standard errors were developed for transformed scores with a mean of 50 and a standard deviation of 10. Thus, if confidence intervals of plus-and-minus one standard error are placed around two scores for interpretive purposes, they will need to differ by almost the standard deviation of a typical subscale for the pair of subscale scores to be judged reliably different.

Validity data show that the VII-R results correlate with intended majors and with educational programs actually chosen by students. Relationships with other scales are generally as theoretically expected. The factor structure of the VII-R is approximately consistent with Roe's organization of these occupational interest dimensions. The data show four underlying dimensions, which are Service (e.g., attending to the tastes, needs, and welfare of others) vs. Technical (e.g., production, maintenance, and transportation); Business Contact (e.g., face-to-face personal persuasion) vs. Science (e.g., research and service in the natural and life sciences); Organization (e.g., managing, controlling, and structuring) vs. Outdoor (e.g., agriculture, fishing, hunting, forestry, and mining); and Arts & Entertainment (e.g., creative arts, and sports) with no opposite polar referent. General Culture (e.g., humanities and social sciences) does not appear to be associated with any replicable underlying dimension. The consistency between the validity evidence for the latter two scales and the theoretical perspective of the VII is not as strong as it is for the other six scales.

Computer-Based Version

Microcomputer administration and scoring is available. The user purchases a programmed disk that allows up to 25 single-student administrations.

The disk contains a user's guide with instructions for the program. A new disk must be purchased after the 25 administrations. Either the student or the administrator enters student responses. Should the administrator enter the data, a microcomputer answer sheet is available for the student to fill out and for the administrator to use.

The microcomputer administration is not adaptive; the student responds to the same items that are in the paper-and-pencil version. However, scoring and interpretations are available far more quickly than for the paper-and-pencil version, which must be mailed to Los Angeles for processing and printing of interpretive reports.

Overall Critique

The VII-R has been developed carefully and the material available for interpretation is useful. It seems best suited for use with college-bound high school students or college freshmen than with other populations.

Its primary weaknesses are its limited norm group and concerns that the items, particularly the occupations, may not have the same meaning across both geography and time. The students who were in the norm group came exclusively from Washington State, consequently underrepresenting both Black and Hispanic students, and within that population, college-bound students were overrepresented. Several of the occupations in the items seem dated and may not be as common elsewhere as they are in Washington State.

References

Holland, J. L. (1973). *Making vocational choices*. Englewood Cliffs, NJ: Prentice-Hall.

Law, J. G., Jr. (1998). [Review of the Vocational Interest Inventory – Revised. In J. C. Impara & B. S. Plake (Eds.), *The thirteenth mental measurements yearbook* (pp. 1120-1121). Lincoln, NE: Buros Institute, University of Nebraska-Lincoln.

Roe, A. (1956). *The psychology of occupations*. New York: Wiley.

Career Development/Career Maturity Measures

- Career Attitudes and Strategies Inventory (CASI)
- Career Beliefs Inventory (CBI)
- Career Development Inventory (CDI)
- Career Factors Inventory (CFI)
- Career Maturity Inventory (CMI)
- Career Thoughts Inventory (CTI)

Career Attitudes and Strategies Inventory (CASI)

John L. Holland and Gary D. Gottfredson
Psychological Assessment Resources
16204 N. Florida Avenue
Lutz, FL 33549
custserv@parinc.com
www.parinc.com

Target Population: Adults

Statement of the Purpose of the Instrument: This instrument helps to identify and clarify career problems and stimulates constructive discussion of these areas.

Titles of Subtests, Scales, Scores Provided: (1) Job Satisfaction; (2) Work Involvement; (3) Skill Development; (4) Interpersonal Abuse; (5) Family Commitment; (6) Risk-Taking Style; (7) Dominant Style; (8) Career Worries; (9) Geographical Barriers; Interpretive Summary Booklet provides three score ranges with easy-to-understand interpretation for each scale.

Forms and Levels Available, with Dates of Publication/Revision of Each: Manual; Inventory Booklet; Hand-Scorable Answer Sheet; Your CASI Interpretive Summary Booklet. All Qualification Level A. Publication date for all: 7/22/94.

Date of Most Recent Edition of Test Manual, User's Guide, Etc.: 7/22/94

Languages in Which Available: English only.

Time: Actual Test Time: Self-administered.
Total Administration Time: 35 minutes.

Norm Group(s) on Which Scores Are Based: 747 (36% men, 64% women), 17-77 years old, mixed educational background, 6 ethnic groups.

Manner in Which Results Are Reported for Individuals Raw scale scores are transferred to interpretive summary booklet, which provides three score ranges with easy-to-understand interpretation for each scale.
    Types of Scores (e.g., standard scores, percentile ranks, verbal labels): 9 scale scores: (Job Satisfaction, Work Involvement, Skill Development, Dominant Style, Career Worries, Interpersonal Abuse, Family Commitment, Risk-Taking Style, Geographical Barriers plus a Career Obstacles checklist).

Report Format/Content (including narrative text, if any): None.

Report Format/Content for Group Summaries: None.

Scoring
   Machine Scoring Service: Not available.
   Time required for scoring and returning (maximum): 5 minutes to score and profile.
   Hand Scoring:
       Scored by: Clerk; Counselor.
       Time required for scoring: 5 minutes to score and profile.
   Local Machine Scoring: Not available.

Computer Software Options Available: Not available.

Cost of Materials: Manual $23; Inventory Booklet (pkg/25), $22; Hand-Scorable Answer Sheets (pkg/25), $22; Your CASI Interpretive Summary Booklet (pkg/25) $22.
       Specimen Set: One each: Inventory Booklet, Hand-Scorable Answer Sheet, Your CASI Interpretive Summary Booklet. No Charge.
       Counselee Materials: Inventory Booklet, reusable; Hand-Scorable Answer Sheet, not reusable; Your CASI Interpretive Summary Booklet, not reusable.

Published Reviews:
Brown, M. B. (1998). Review of Career Attitudes and Strategies Inventory. In J. C. Impara & B. S. Plake (Eds.). *The thirteenth mental measurements yearbook*. Lincoln, NE: Buros Institute, University of Nebraska-Lincoln.
Kinnier, R. T. (1998). Review of Career Attitudes and Strategies Inventory. In J. C. Impara & B. S. Plake (Eds.). *The thirteenth mental measurements yearbook*. Lincoln, NE: Buros Institute, University of Nebraska-Lincoln.

Reviewed by

Michael B. Brown
Associate Professor of Psychology
East Carolina University

Description

The Career Attitudes and Strategies Inventory (CASI) is a self-scored, self-profiled, and self-interpreted inventory developed to identify the attitudes, feelings, and obstacles that affect the careers of adults. The nine scales of the CASI survey areas related to career adaptation, and taken together are intended to provide an assessment of the client's job stability. The scales include Job Satisfaction, Work Involvement, Skill Development, Dominant Style, Career Worries,

Note: Portions of this review are adapted from the author's original review in the *Thirteenth Mental Measurements Yearbook* with permission of the Buros Institute

Interpersonal Abuse, Family Commitment, Risk-Taking Style, and Geographical Barriers. The resulting score profile provides an overview of the positive and negative aspects of a client's career adjustment.

Following in the tradition of the *Self-Directed Search* (Holland, 1994), the inventory is intended to be completed and scored by the client. The CASI consists of three parts: The 130-item questionnaire, a self-scoring answer sheet, and an Interpretive Summary. The materials are attractively done. The four-page test booklet is well designed and easy to read. The assessment procedure is relatively straightforward. For each item on the inventory the client chooses whether a statement is True, Mostly True, Mostly False, or False. Examples of statements include "I don't like change in my life" and "I listen to advice about how I should do my job." Responses are indicated by circling the appropriate response on the answer sheet. The two true responses are each designated by an upper case letter "T"; the lighter colored T is circled for Mostly True and the darker T for mostly true. A similar system using upper case letters "F" indicates Mostly False or False. The answer sheet also includes a separate checklist of 21 potential career obstacles.

The carbonless answer sheet automatically transfers the answers to a scoring grid. The client adds up his or her raw scores and transfers them to a profile sheet on the Interpretive Summary, which provides a visual representation of the relative strength of each of the aspects of the client's career. Each scale has three potential interpretations, each corresponding to one of three raw score ranges. The interpretive summaries are succinct and clearly written.

The 46-page manual, although brief, is clearly written and organized. Practical applications of the CASI and scoring procedures are concisely described. Interpretive information includes a brief description of each scale along with 14 case profiles. The illustrative profiles are helpful and include persons with a range of ages and occupations, although occupations that require more education and training predominate. The major limitation of the illustrative profiles is the brevity of case material and corresponding interpretations.

Although the CASI is not an overly complex instrument, the authors suggest that the user should read and become familiar with literature on vocational identity (such as Holland, Johnston, & Asama, 1993). An article by Gottfredson (1996) provides an additional discussion of the CASI. The manual has a very useful section on becoming a competent user of the inventory. There is a even short "test" to help the user assess understanding of the basic concepts of the CASI.

Use in Counseling

The authors believe that the CASI is most useful for evaluating job dissatisfaction, job changing, work adjustment, or work dysfunction. They view it as an effective way to identify and gather information about career problems, promote discussion, and recommend its use as a way for professionals to broaden their assessments to include relevant aspects of career adjustment.

The CASI is also recommended for use on an organizational level. It may be used as a needs assessment tool, providing information about sources of worker dissatisfaction or identifying potential areas of need to be addressed by training and development programs. The authors suggest the use of the CASI as a program evaluation tool, comparing pre- and post-intervention scores to identify changes resulting from organizational interventions. They also view the inventory as a helpful tool in assessing the outcomes of individual counseling.

The CASI may be most useful to the career counselor when used as a checklist to obtain a client's self-rating in a number of areas that are relevant to career adjustment. As such it can be used to rapidly "screen" for client opinions and attitudes and generate information for discussion between client and counselor. I would certainly find it useful as a pre-interview survey, a device to generate discussion or to identify potentially problematic areas that would benefit from further exploration. The suggestion that the CASI be used by counselors providing personal counseling as a broad assessment device to gather information about the client's career issues is appealing, although counselors reading this book are not likely to overlook the career domain in counseling.

The CASI was developed as a supplement to other measures of aptitudes, interests, and specific career-relevant characteristics, and additional instruments must be administered if the counselor is interested in these domains.

Technical Considerations

The current inventory is the third version in the development of the CASI. The first version was developed by the authors based on theoretical concepts, clinical experience, and the use of a 135-person exploratory analysis group. The second version was created from item analyses using both data derived from the first version and new data collected from an additional 266 individuals. Many new items were added to improve the scale. The third version is derived from further refinement of the second version.

The normative sample consists of persons who participated in the research on the second and third versions. The resulting group of 747 persons range in age from 17-77. Women are overrepresented in the norm group (64% women, 26% men, 11% unreported), although the manual points out that there appear to be only small differences in the scores of men and women. The majority of the group is composed of persons with some education beyond high school (only 10% of the sample had 12 or fewer years of education). It is difficult to ascertain the actual ethnic composition of the norm group, as over one-third of the group were not asked to provide an ethnic identification. There is no indication of the geographic representation or socioeconomic status of the sample. Normative data provided for career obstacles are considered "approximate" as identical instructions were not given to each of the two groups used in the norming process.

Internal consistency reliability coefficients for the CASI scales ranged from .76 to .92, which is adequate for this type of inventory. Test-retest reliability was assessed using a small sample ("N=38-40") of working adults between the ages of 25 and 54. The average interval was 13 days, and test-retest reliabilities of the scales ranged from .66-.94. This sample is too small to adequately determine test-retest reliabilities.

Validity is inferred through a number of methods. One of the difficulties in assessing the validity of the CASI is that different versions were used at different points during its development to determine validity. For instance, data on some aspects of concurrent validity were obtained by using 112-134 persons who completed Version 2 of the CASI. Note that this is a rather small group, and that Version 3 is likely to be somewhat different from Version 2. Caution is suggested when interpreting the validity data, since both the norm group and the CASI itself appear to have undergone substantial changes from the first to the third version.

Concurrent validity is addressed through correlation of the CASI and the Hoppock Job Satisfaction Blank, a two-item indicator of general happiness, career search activities, and measures of vocational identity and personality type. Correlation coefficients are provided for the correlations between various scales and the measures of concurrent validity. Correlations for each of these comparisons are said to be in the expected direction. For example, persons with low scores on Job Satisfaction and high scores on Career Worries, Interpersonal Abuse, and Family commitment report being involved in a number of job search activities. The CASI and the Hoppock Job Satisfaction Blank have a correlation of .86, while the CASI and the measure of general happiness have a correlation of .71, which is consistent with a positive relationship between the two measures of job satisfaction and positive disposition.

Construct validity is inferred through an examination of the intercorrelations between various CASI scales. As an example, the Job Satisfaction Scale is negatively correlated with the Career Worries and Interpersonal Abuse Scales. Correlations range between -.60 for Job Satisfaction and Career Worries to .53 for Career Worries and Interpersonal Abuse Scales. Correlations are all said to "appear predictable from the scale titles."

Overall Critique

The lack of adequate norms and limitations in the determination of its validity presents serious drawbacks for the CASI. In addition, there are no data that illuminate the extent, if any, of ethnic differences on the CASI. The structure and appearance of the materials give it a look of psychometric sophistication that exceeds its present technical state. This is of particular importance when clients self-score and interpret their results, as there is a danger that the client would consider the results to be more exact than warranted by its technical characteristics. I recommend that the use of the CASI be preceded by a discussion of the limitations of the instrument and the meaning of its scale scores.

The answer system, combined with the compact layout of the answer sheet, may prove confusing for some clients. Counselors who use the CASI will need to ensure that clients understand the directions for answering and are able to maintain their place as they complete the survey. Some clients may need more guidance to follow the directions for self-scoring, or the counselor may decide to do the scoring for the client. The interpretations may require more detailed explanation and integration by the counselor, particularly for clients who are less sophisticated or have lower verbal ability.

Given these substantial limitations, is there a use for the CASI? I think that there is, provided the counselor use the results as one broad source of career information about the client. It may be a useful tool to stimulate client self-exploration and further discussion in the counseling session. It should be used in an ipsative rather than normative fashion until better psychometric data is produced that would allow the user to make normative comparisons with confidence.

References

Gottfredson, G. D. (1996). The assessment of career status with the Career Attitudes and Strategies Inventory. *Journal of Career Assessment, 4*(4), 363-381.

Holland, J. L. (1994). *The Self-Directed Search*. Odessa, FL: Psychological Assessment Resources.

Holland, J. L., Johnston, J. A., & Asama, N. F. (1993). The Vocational Identity Scale: A diagnostic and treatment tool. *Journal of Career Assessment, 1*, 1-12.

Career Beliefs Inventory (CBI)

John D. Krumboltz
Consulting Psychologists Press, Inc.
3803 East Bayshore Road
Palo Alto, CA 94303
www.cpp-db.com

Target Population: People 13 years and older who can read at an 8th-grade level.

Statement of the Purpose of the Instrument: It is a counseling tool designed to help people identify career beliefs that may be preventing them from achieving their career goals. The fundamental premise upon which the CBI is based is that people make a number of assumptions and generalizations about themselves and the work world based on their limited experiences. The CBI can help counselors initiate explorations of the career assumptions on which their clients operate.

Titles of Subtests, Scales, Scores Provided: 25 scales are placed under the following five categories: My Current Career Situation, What Seems Necessary for My Happiness, Factors That Influence My Decisions, Changes I Am Willing to Make, and Effort I Am Willing to Initiate.

Forms and Levels Available, with Dates of Publication/revision of Each: Level A.

Date of Most Recent Edition of Test Manual, User's Guide, Etc.: 1991.

Languages in Which Available: English, Australian and Canadian French.

Time: Actual Test Time: Less than 30 minutes.
Total Administration Time: 40-50 minutes.

Norm Group(s) on Which Scores are Based: Samples were taken from California, Maine, Texas, Ohio, Indiana, Virginia, Nebraska, Pennsylvania, Missouri, Maryland, Michigan, and New York. It wasn't a random sample since data collection depends on the interest and cooperation of colleagues who had access to individuals and groups willing to take the CBI.

Manner in Which Results Are Reported for Individuals:
   Types of Scores: Standard scores from 10 to 50. The scale scores are 10 times the average item weight in each scale.
   Report Format/Content:
      Basic Service: There is an inventory and profile available to customers with the Profile offering more detailed information. This 10-page all-inclusive booklet provides four pages of new interpretive information that helps client understand their score for each of the 25 scales.
      Options: It comes in either a self-scorable booklet, a Career Beliefs Inventory Preview Kit and the option to purchase CBI Applications and Technical Guide as well as a prepaid CBI Profile Answer Sheet.
Report Format/Content for Group Summaries: Not available.

Scoring
   Machine Scoring Service: Not available.
   Hand Scoring:
      Scored by: Counselor.
   Local Machine Scoring:
      Provisions/conditions/equipment required: We offer mail-in scoring that has a five-day turnaround period.

Computer Software Options Available: Computerized adaptive administration.

Ways in Which Computer Version Differs: None.

Cost of Materials:
   Specimen Set: Career Beliefs Inventory Client Kit (CBI Self-Scorable Booklet, Exploring Your Career Beliefs Workbook) $12.80.
   CBI Self-Scorable Booklets $44.90 pkg/10
   CBI Applications and Technical Guide $47.80 each
   Career Beliefs Inventory Profile Preview Kit: (CBI Item Booklet Prepaid, CBI Profile Answer Sheet; Exploring Your Career Beliefs, CBI Applications and Technical Guide) $60
   CBI Item Booklets $55.10 pkg/25
   Prepaid CBI Profile Answer Sheet $71.10 pkg/10

Career Beliefs Inventory (CBI) Hand-Scoring Option
   CBI Item Booklets $55.80 pkg/25
   CBI Non-prepaid Answer Sheets for hand scoring $57.80 pkg/25
   CBI Scoring Keys for hand scoring $53.50 set

Additional Comments of interest to Users: There is a new *Exploring Your Beliefs* workbook ($7.00) that shows clients how beliefs, interests and personality relate to career development. There is also a "Career Beliefs Inventory" application that provides a summary of administration, scoring, and interpretation.

Published Reviews:
Bolton, D. L. (1995) Review of the Career Beliefs Inventory. In J. C. Conoley & J. C. Impara
      (Eds.). *The twelfth mental measurements yearbook.* Lincoln, NE: Buros Institute, University of Nebraska-Lincoln.
Guion, R. M. (1995) Review of the Career Beliefs Inventory. In J. C. Conoley & J. C. Impara
      (Eds.). *The twelfth mental measurements yearbook.* Lincoln, NE: Buros Institute, University of Nebraska-Lincoln.
Wall, J. E. (1994). Review of the Career Beliefs Inventory. In J. T. Kapes, M. M. Mastie, &
      E. A. Whitfield (Eds.). *A counselor's guide to career assessment instruments (3rd ed.).* Alexandria, VA: National Career Development Association.

Reviewed by

Michael E. Hall
Director, Career Management Services
Charlotte, NC

Jack R. Rayman
Director, Career Services
Pennsylvania State University

Description

The Career Beliefs Inventory (CBI) is a self-report instrument designed to facilitate career decision making that is "based on a more accurate view of [oneself] and the world of work" (Krumboltz, 1991, p. 2). The CBI presents individuals with an opportunity to examine and "then test whether their assumptions are accurate and alter their view if they find contradictory evidence" (p. 2). The inventory results, reported as scaled scores, are of two types: (1) a score corresponding to the instruments 25 scales, and (2) an estimate of response accuracy, called an Administrative Index. An individual's results may be interpreted, using percentile ranks, by referencing similarity to any of eight norm groups.

Currently, there are two administration options for the CBI. The item booklet/prepaid answer sheet option requires that the answer sheet be mailed to the publisher's scoring center, where a CBI Profile is produced and returned to the counselor for interpretation. The advantage of this option is accuracy in scoring and the provision of the Administrative Index. The second option, the self-scorable booklet and results, has the advantage of allowing same-day results, but hand-scoring increases the potential for error and the Administrative Index requires additional calculation. The Self-Scorable option includes "Understanding Your Results," a four-page interpretation section. A workbook, *Exploring Your Career Beliefs* (Levin, Krumboltz & Krumboltz, 1995), has been published to aid counselors and clients in the use of the CBI and to integrate it with Strong Interest Inventory and Myers-Briggs Type Indicator results. To aid career professionals with administration, scoring, and interpretation, there are the *Manual for the Career Beliefs Inventory* (Krumboltz, 1991) and the *Career Beliefs Inventory Applications and Technical Guide* (Krumboltz, 1999).

A survey of published articles about the CBI suggests that the instrument has enjoyed at least a modest amount of professional interest. Due to the CBI's dubious technical adequacy, the majority of the articles recommended cautious use of the scale scores. In contrast, Heppner and Johnston (1993), in their clarion call for campus career counseling to be enhanced by the development of a sophisticated diagnostic system, recommended the CBI as one of four diagnostic instruments that could be used to assess the internal dynamic variables which frequently block individuals in their career planning and change. Wall (1994) advocated that the CBI be used to generate counselor-client discussions, but suggested caution until more research established the scales' psychometric properties and their relationship to career progress.

Use in Counseling

The *Manual* implies that "best practice" with respect to use of the CBI would be its use "at the beginning of the counseling process" as "a springboard for counselors and clients to discuss…attitudes and assumptions that need to be examined when making and implementing choices" (p. 2). Therefore, skilled career professionals will analyze the multiple levels of results–low scores on the 25 Scales, the Scales' five superordinate categories, the Administrative Index, and the actual items themselves–in order to extract those beliefs that may be blocking clients' career choice implementation.

However, there are three uses of the CBI that are typically overlooked. First, is the appropriateness of the CBI for use in small groups and career education classes. Making use of group dynamics and social learning, clients can be receptive to peer feedback in ways different than that received from career professionals. The *Applications and Technical Guide* (Kromboltz, 1999) contains 14 reproducible masters that can be used to orient client groups to the CBI, as well as to aid in the interpretation of the results. A second overlooked use of the CBI is the interpretation of high scores. Although low scale scores indicate potential blocks to career action, high scores may be indicators of strengths that can aid clients in challenging and overcoming career barriers. Third, since acknowledging that identifying career beliefs that block career aspirations is not tantamount to their removal, the CBI's author includes in the *Manual* a six-step model that could be used by counselors to facilitate clients exploration of appropriate actions.

Technical Considerations

The technical information available in the *CBI Applications and Technical Guide* (Krumboltz, 1999) appears to be based on the same sample of 7,500 that was used to norm the instrument in 1991. In her review of the CBI, Wall (1994) questioned whether the norms were nationally representative and whether various minority subgroups are proportionally represented. It appears that no attempt has been made to address this issue; thus the concern remains. On a positive note, an effort has been made to explain the psychometric characteristics (both positive and negative) of the CBI and their practical importance to the counseling practitioner. These technical explanations are thoughtfully articulated and insightfully presented in practitioner-friendly language.

Presumably in response to criticisms about the modest levels of reliability of the instrument, Krumboltz (1999) has developed a fairly elaborate and convincing rationale for why high reliability is not important in the case of the CBI. First, he states that high reliability is unimportant because of the purpose of the CBI, which he suggests is not for selection or classification but rather for purposes of exploration. He therefore concludes that too much precision would be wasteful. Second, he points out that a more reliable instrument would have been impractical, requiring considerably more items per scale with attendant increased time of administration and cost. He suggests that a tradeoff between precision and cost was necessary. Third, he points out that the consequences of lower reliability for the CBI would not be serious. Put another way, it is assumed that clients will be cautious about making life decisions based on the results of the CBI. Finally, Krumboltz holds that higher reliability could have been gained only at the cost of reducing the instrument's conceptual breadth and complexity. These well-articulated explanations of the CBI's modest reliability are all good points; however, they suggest that the CBI should be thought of more as a treatment or exercise and less as a measurement device.

Krumboltz has elaborated the section of the *CBI Applications and Technical Guide* addressing validity using distinctly more counselor-friendly language; however, there is little new technical information or data here beyond that from the 1991 *Manual*. Face validity, concurrent validity, and construct validity are addressed in turn. Most interesting is a new section addressing what Krumboltz calls "Consequential Validity." This appears to be a further attempt to address previously expressed concerns about the psychometric characteristics of the instrument. "Consequential Validity" is defined as "the social consequences of measuring what an instrument purports to measure." Since the intended social consequence of the CBI according to Krumboltz (1999) is –

> a dialogue between the client and career professional in which the client clarifies his or her beliefs, examines the usefulness of those beliefs in achieving his or her goals, and lays the groundwork for constructive action. Therefore, the CBI's consequential validity rests, at least in part, on how well it performs this function. (p. 30)

Put simply, this discussion of consequential validity appears to provide further justification for the rather modest psychometric characteristics of the CBI.

In summary, the current version of the *CBI Applications and Technical Guide* provides the user with CBI norms, refined practitioner-friendly information about both reliability and validity, brief discussions of gender differences, group and ethnic comparisons, and a brief analysis of the factor structure of the scales. The actual data supporting the psychometric properties of the CBI appear to be no more extensive than that appearing in the first *Manual* (1991), but the technical explanations are considerably more user friendly and insightful.

Overall Critique

The premise that an individual's career beliefs can measurably affect career behavior both positively and negatively seems intuitively obvious. Clear empirical evidence in support of this premise, however, is difficult to find, and the CBI offers little to assist the practitioner in validly and reliably measuring career beliefs. Given the uncertain nature of identifying, measuring, and evaluating the impact of career beliefs on career behavior, the CBI remains most useful as a stimulus to individual and group introspection and discussion. This does not in any way depreciate its value as an instrument that has significant utility in the hands of career practitioners and their clients.   Indeed, the CBI shows great promise as a career-counseling tool, and practitioners and researchers alike should be encouraged to continue to use it, experiment with it, and conduct research with it.

Finally, Krumboltz is to be commended for his effort to create user-friendly materials to enhance the utility of the CBI for counselors and clients alike. Most notable here are the workbook (Levin, Krumboltz & Krumboltz, 1995) *Exploring Your Career Beliefs*, and the revised and user-friendly *Applications and Technical Guide* (Krumboltz, 1999), which includes a set of 14 reproducible masters designed to help career professionals orient clients to the CBI and enhance understanding of career beliefs and their impact on career decision making.

References

Heppner, M. J. & Johnston, J. A. (1993). Career counseling: A call to action. In J. R. Rayman (Ed.), *The changing role of career services* (pp. 57-78). San Francisco: Jossey-Bass.

Levin, A. S., Krumboltz, J. D., & Krumboltz, B. L. (1995). *Exploring your career beliefs: A workbook for the Career Beliefs Inventory with techniques for integrating your Strong and MBTI results.* Palo Alto, CA: Consulting Psychologists Press.

Krumboltz, J. D. (1991). *Manual for the Career Beliefs Inventory.* Palo Alto, CA: Consulting Psychologists Press.

Krumboltz, J. D. (1999). *Career Beliefs Inventory applications and technical guide.* Palo Alto, CA: Consulting Psychologists Press.

Wall, J. E. (1994). Review of the Career Beliefs Inventory. In J. T. Kapes, M. M. Mastie, & E. A. Whitfield (Eds.), *A counselor's guide to career assessment instruments* (3rd ed., pp. 253-257). Alexandria, VA: National Career Development Association.

Career Development Inventory (CDI)

Donald E. Super, Albert S. Thompson, Richard H. Lindeman,
Jean P. Jordaan and Roger A. Myers
Consulting Psychologists Press
3803 East Bayshore Road
Palo Alto, CA 94303
www.cpp-db.com

Target Population: High School and College; Grades 8-12 (School Form), Freshmen, Sophomores, Juniors, and Seniors (University Form).

Statement of the Purpose of the Instrument: Used to help students make educational and career plans. For general use as a sound instrument for assessing career development and vocational maturity. It is also useful in evaluating programs and services.

Titles of Subtests, Scales, Scores Provided: 8 scales: Career Planning, Career Exploration, Decision-Making, World of Work, Knowledge of Preferred Occupational Group, Career Development Attitudes, CD Knowledge and Skills, Career Orientation. Scores are reported in Standard Score Form.

Forms and Levels Available, with Dates of Publication/revision of Each: School Form 1979; College and University Form 1981.

Date of Most Recent Edition of Test Manual, User's Guide, Etc.: 1981 Manual; 1982 Supplement for College and University Form; 1984 Technical Manual.

Languages in Which Available: English.

Time: Actual Test Time: 25 minutes.
        Total Administration Time: 30 minutes (instruction).

Norm Group(s) on Which Scores Are Based: 9-12 High School Form; Freshmen, Sophomores, Juniors, and Seniors, College and University Form.

Manner in Which Results Are Reported for Individuals:
    Types of Scores: Standard Scores reported with scale descriptions and percentiles.
    Report Format/Content:
    Basic Service: Computer-scored profile.

Report Format/Content for Group Summaries:
    Basic Service: Group Summaries available by request. Contact information and Research Services Department.

Scoring
   Machine Scoring Service:
      Cost of basic service per counselee: $4.80 prepaid Answer Sheet.
      Time required for scoring and returning (maximum): 24-hour turnaround + mail time.
      Palo Alto, Minneapolis, Washington, DC.
   Hand Scoring: Not available.
   Local Machine Scoring: Not available.

Computer Software Options Available: Not available.

   Cost of Materials:
   Specimen Set: Manual, Test Booklet, Answer Sheet (High School and College) $30.
   Counselee Materials: Reusable Test Booklet; Prepaid Answer Sheet.

Published Reviews:
Hansen, J. C. (1985). Review of the Career Development Inventory. *Measurement and Evaluation in Counseling and Development 17(4)*, 220-224.
Harmon, L. W. (1994). Review of the Career Development Inventory. In J. T. Kapes, M. M. Mastie and E.A. Whitfield (Eds.), *A counselor's guide to career assessment instruments* (3rd ed.) Alexandria, VA: National Career Development Association.
Johnson, S. D. (1985). Review of the Career Development Inventory. In D. J. Keyser & R. C. Sweetland (Eds.), *Test critiques IV,* Kansas City, MO: Test Corporation of America.
Locke, D.C. (1988). Review of the Career Development Inventory. In J. T. Kapes & M.M. Mastie (Eds.), *A counselor's guide to career assessment instruments* (2nd ed.). Alexandria, VA: National Career Development Association.
Pinkney, J. W. (1985). Review of Career Development Inventory. In J. V. Mitchell (Ed.), *Ninth mental measurements yearbook: Vol. 1* (p. 271). Lincoln, NE: University of Nebraska-Lincoln.
Sundre, D. L. (1998). Review of Career Development Inventory. In J. C. Impara & B. S. Blake (Eds.), *Thirteenth mental measurements yearbook.* Lincoln, NE: Buros Institute, University of Nebraska-Lincon.

Reviewed by

Donna L. Sundre
Associate Professor of Psychology &
Associate Assessment Specialist
Center for Assessment & Research Studies
James Madison University

Description
   The Career Development Inventory (CDI) is designed to measure "career development and vocational or career maturity" (Thompson & Lindeman, 1981,

Note: Portions of this review were adapted from the author's original review in the *Thirteenth Mental Measurement Yearbook* with permission of the Buros Institute.

p. 1). The instrument is the product of over 40 years of adolescent career decision-making readiness, development, and maturity research, and it represents the
operational definition of Donald Super's model. Two forms (S and CU) are
available. Form S is intended for students in grades 8-12; Form CU is designed
for college and university students. The latter form was produced through minor
word and occupational group modifications to achieve greater congruence with
college-level context and occupational choices.

Both CDI forms are composed of 120 items that produce eight scales:
Career Planning (CP); Career Exploration (CE); Decision Making (DM); World
of Work Information (WW); Knowledge of Preferred Occupation (PO); Career
Development Attitudes (CDA); Career Development Knowledge (CDK); and
Career Orientation Total (COT). The instrument is divided into two parts. Part I,
Career Orientation, consists of four 20-item scales (CP, CE, DM, and WW). The
Career Development Attitudes (CDA) scale is considered a conative scale, and is
formed through the combination of the CP and CE scales. The Career Development Knowledge scale, which is considered a cognitive scale, is similarly formed
through combination of the DM and WW scales. The four basic scales of Part I
are combined to form the Career Orientation Total (COT) scale, which represents
Super's career maturity construct. Part II consists of the 40 items comprising the
Knowledge of Preferred Occupation (PO) scale, which is selected by the student
after responding to occupations of interest across 20 groups of 5 representative
occupations each.

Consistent with Super's developmental model, the manual suggests that
when using Form S, the PO scale should be used only with students in grades 11-
12 given the advanced terms, ideas, and maturity requisite for occupational development and choice. The User's Manual Volume I (Thompson & Lindeman,
1981) provides clear directions for administration. Due to scoring complexities,
the publisher's scoring service is recommended.

Use in Counseling
The authors contend the instrument can be used for three major purposes:
"individual counseling, group assessment, and program evaluation and planning." (Thompson & Lindeman, 1981, p. 3). The manual is exceptionally well
written and organized, and counselors will find it of great assistance, particularly
Part III, Uses of CDI Results, which features a section dedicated to each of the
recommended purposes of the instrument. Counselors will find helpful information concerning the nature of career development and individual readiness to
make realistic choices. The manual provides sound guidance concerning interpretations of the various scales for determining readiness for choice, diagnostics,

understanding profiles, planning individual and group guidance programs, and uses for program evaluation and research.

An exemplary case study is included that counselors will find quite helpful in illuminating the possibilities for working with individuals in career guidance. Levinson, Ohler, Caswell, & Kiewra (1998) have also suggested that the CDI is useful for stimulating students' interest in career planning, and this approach may provide a fine impetus for a group guidance program. A recent book (Osborne, Brown, Niles, & Miner, 1997) has been published that explicates Super's Career Development, Assessment, and Counseling (C-DAC) model and its applications for counseling. Within this model, the CDI is one of several instruments selected to measure several dimensions of career development that form a framework for counseling intervention.

Regardless of whether counselors choose to use the CDI alone or as part of a battery, this book provides a concise, balanced description of the instrument with integration of much more recent literature than the publisher's test manual and technical bulletin. It also provides a fine case study using the CDI and offers separate chapters on counseling adolescents, college students, and adults in accordance with Super's life-span career development model. Given the age of the CDI's supporting manuals, these more recent publications will be valuable resources for potential users.

Technical Considerations

In an earlier review, this author highlighted two 1986 revisions to the computer-generated score reports: graphic percentile rank profiles and the addition of a local norms column alongside the national norms. Although users are cautioned against overreliance on normative information displayed in this way, the modification was, and is, very useful. The provision of local norms is an important improvement, particularly since the earlier norms are now at least 20 years old. Further, the manual authors deemed the norms for both the S and CU forms unrepresentative of the target populations. A particular concern for the norms is the underrepresentation of minorities. This flaw has become magnified over the years, given the dramatic changes in the workforce and the demographics of the nation. The local norms option represents an important means for test users to address this problem at both the school and college settings.

The School Form User Manual (Thompson & Lindeman, 1981) provided internal consistency and standard error of measurement (SEM) estimates for grades 9-12 total groups and by gender. In general, these reliabilities have been found to be sufficient with the exception of the two cognitive scales, Decision Making (DM) and Preferred Occupation (PO) scales. These two scales are both problematic, particularly for females. The manual points out this problem, but it has not been addressed. The authors reported that the Cronbach alphas for the PO scale improved for the 11th and 12th grades over those observed for the 9th and 10th grades. The reliabilities also appeared to improve a bit for boys from 9th to 12th grades with estimates of .61, .55, .64, and .71 respectively. However, the Cronbach alphas reported for females across the same grades were .53, .53, .67, and .57 respectively. The SEMs of course follow a similar pattern and were larger for the DM and PO scales than the other scales. The uneven scale reliabilities have been noted many times by many reviewers. The manual provided excellent guidance for interpretation and application of the SEMs, and cautioned users about use of particular scale scores with individuals.

Test-retest reliability findings reported in the Technical Manual (Thompson & Lindeman, 1984) appeared fairly unstable for the Decision Making (DM), World of Work (WW), and the Preferred Occupation (PO) scales even over a relatively brief three-week period. All other scales produced adequate test-retest reliabilities over the same time period. Parallel findings were observed with the CU form; however, the Supplement to the User Manual (Thompson & Lindeman, 1982) in which these results were reported provided considerably lower alpha coefficients for the DM, WW, and PO scales for the total group and by gender. In fact, though normative differences were reported by class level, the alphas were omitted for these three scales. The SEMs for these three scales are in double digits, another indication of low reliability. The manual authors contend that the alphas were not appropriate due to lack of variance in the sample, but variability over grade levels would be consistent with a developmental theory of career maturity. Therefore, the lack of variability observed may be indicative of a flaw in the scales or perhaps the norming sample. However, the fact that many researchers have observed low reliabilities for these scales suggests the problem resides with the scales. Many users will want to use these scales with individuals, but these scale reliabilities do not provide evidence of sufficient internal homogeneity to merit individual use. Test-retest reliabilities conducted over a short two-week delay were also fairly low for the cognitive scales: Decision Making (.65), World of Work (.43), and Preferred Occupation (.62). If counselors want to use these scales, particularly for work with individuals, caution is clearly advised. The general consensus among reviewers and researchers seems to be caution with use of the individual scales and a recommendation for use of the composite scales CDA, CDK, and TOT for sufficient reliability.

Validity evidence is the primary consideration for selection of any instrument. The CDI user manuals report content and construct validity estimates. The content validity for both forms S and CU relies on past research and continued explication of Super's model of career maturity. The current forms of the instrument have been refined and revised from earlier preliminary forms.

Construct validity was explored via factor analysis and investigation of subgroup differences (gender, grade, and academic program) thought to be consistent with theoretical expectations. Evidence for the School form consisted of the observation of a general absence of gender differences, which was considered theoretically consistent. In the 11th and 12th grades, females begin to outperform males on the cognitive scales, and the authors assert this result is also expected. An observed general pattern of increasing total and scale scores over grades was also considered positive validity evidence, though the increases were slight. However, it should be noted that the data show almost as large career development differences within each grade as between grades. Curricular program differences were also tested and, though they were generally small, they were in the expected directions.

Results for the College and University form followed the same general design; however score increases by years in college were certainly not large. It should be noted that most college classes are much more heterogeneous than high school classes, and changes over class years might be legitimately muted. However, the difference observed over the four-year period amounted to about a half of a standard deviation. Females scoring higher on the cognitive scales was considered as positive construct validity evidence; however those differences were quite small, less than one SEM. Differences expressed by major fields were quite large for some scales, and these results were consistent with theoretical expectations.

The report of correlation coefficients of the CDI scales with other assessment instruments are of much greater interest to potential users. These results demonstrated consistently positive correlations between measures of academic abilities such as the Iowa Tests of Educational Development (ITED) and the Differential Aptitude Battery with the cognitive scales of the CDI. Moderate correlations were reported for the conative scales with career maturity scales such as the Salience Inventory (SI) from the Work Importance Study. These results would be expected given their lower reliability estimates. The report of nonsignificant impact for socioeconomic status on CDI scales was a positive finding as well.

The manuals also reported factor analysis results supporting the two-factor model upon which the instrument was developed. The results consistently show a two-factor structure with the cognitive scales (DM, WW, and PO) loading on the first factor, and the conative, attitudinal scales (CE and CP) loading on the second factor. Given the recurrent findings of low reliability of the scales, particularly the cognitive scales, use of these factors, rather than the individual scales would improve the reliability while maintaining fidelity to Super's model. However, Super preferred increasing the number of items per scale to enhance reliability and was preparing to do so when he encountered his final illness (Savickas and Hartung, 1996).

Overall Critique

A great deal of research has been conducted on the CDI subsequent to publication of the manual and technical bulletin. This work provides continued support for the CDI as an operational definition of Super's model, its predictive and concurrent validity, and the growing number of successful international adaptations (Dupont, 1992; Punch and Sheridan, 1985; Savickas and Hartung, 1996; Seifert, 1991). Savickas and Hartung (1996) offer by far the most thorough, yet concise, review of psychometric studies and applied research pertaining to the CDI, and counselors considering use of the CDI would be well served to read this informative article.

The widespread continued use of the CDI is likely. Despite the flawed reliabilities of the cognitive scales, the measure has much to recommend it. Given the rapid changes in the workforce, the demographics of the nation, and the major role the infusion of technology will continue to play in the economy, a major revision in many career choice, development, and maturity scales is needed. It is hoped that the CDI will receive the psychometric attention it deserves to preserve its important role in career development assessment well into the 21st century.

References

Dupont, P. (1992). Concurrent and predictive validity of Career Development Inventory. *International Journal for the Advancement of Counseling, 15,* 163-173.

Levinson, E. M., Ohler, D. L., Caswell, S. & Kiewra, K. (1998). Six approaches to the assessment of career maturity. *Journal of Counseling and Development, 76,* 475-482.

Luzzo, D. A. (1993). A multi-trait, multi-method analysis of three career development measures. *The Career Development Quarterly, 41,* 367- 374.

Osborne, W. L., Brown, S., Niles, S. & Miner, C. U. (1997). *Career development, assessment, and counseling: Applications of the Donald E. Super C-DAC approach.* Alexandria, VA: American Counseling Association. (ERIC Document Reproduction Service No. ED 408 530).

Punch, K. F. & Sheridan, B. E. (1985). Some measurement characteristics of the Career Development Inventory. *Measurement and Evaluation in Counseling and Development, 17,* 196-202.

Savickas, M. L. & Hartung, P. (1996). The Career Development Inventory in review: Psychometric and research findings. *Journal of Career Assessment, 4,* 171-188.

Seifert, K. H. (1991). Measures of career development and career choice behaviour. *Applied Psychology: An International Review, 40,* 245-267.

Thompson, A. S. & Lindeman, R. H. (1981). *Career Development Inventory, Vol. 1, User's manual.* Palo Alto, CA: Consulting Psychologists Press, Inc.

Thompson, A. S. & Lindeman, R. H. (1984). *Career Development Inventory, Vol. 2, Technical Manual.* Palo Alto, CA: Consulting Psychologists Press, Inc.

Career Factors Inventory (CFI)

Judy M. Chartrand, Steven B. Robbins and Weston H. Morrill
Consulting Psychologists Press
3803 E. Bayshore Road
Palo Alto, CA 94303
cpp-db.com

Target Population: 13 years and up.

Statement of the Purpose of the Instrument: The CFI is designed to help people identify their own difficulties in the career-planning and decision-making process.

Forms and Levels Available with Dates of Publication/Revision of Each: Self-Scorable Booklet and Interpretation Internet accessible via www.skillsone.com.

Languages in Which Available: English only.

Time: Actual Test Time: 10 minutes.
            Total Administration Time: 10 minutes.

Manner in Which Results Are Reported for Individuals Self-scoring booklet
   Basic Service: Self-scoring covering results or each of the scales
   Options: Internet accessible via www.skillsone.com Narrative text is provided.

Report Format/Content for Group Summaries: Not available.

Scoring
   Machine Scoring Service: Via website
      Cost of basic service per counselee: Self-Scorable $1.91; Internet career package including five other assessments $24.95.
      Time required for scoring and returning (maximum): Internet results are immediate.
   Hand Scoring:
      Scored by: Counselee.
      Time required for scoring: 5 minutes.
   Local Machine Scoring: Not available.

Computer Software Options Available: Internet accessible via www.skillsone.com

Cost of Materials:
   Specimen Set: CFI Self-Scorable Booklet and Interpretation; CFI Applications and Technical Guide $133.30.
   Counselee Materials: CFI Self-Scorable Booklets $19.10 pkg/10 and $2.70 single.

Additional Comments of Interest to Users: CFI Applications and Technical Guide $34.50 each.

Published Reviews: None cited.

Reviewed by

Darrell Anthony Luzzo
Dean of Career Development Services
Mt. Hood Community College
Gresham, Oregon

Description

Over the past several years, results of several research projects have demonstrated that career indecision and career undecidedness stem from several different factors. It would be a mistake, therefore, to assume that all types of career indecision and undecidedness require the same career intervention strategy. In the 1980s, Dr. Steven B. Robbins and his colleagues (Robbins, Morrill, & Boggs, 1987) began the process of developing a measure to assess the various antecedents of career decision making in hopes of providing career counselors with important information with which to determine appropriate treatments for clients. Several years later, Consulting Psychologists Press published a commercially available version of the Career Factors Inventory (CFI; Chartrand, Robbins, & Morrill, 1997).

Robbins and his colleagues began developing early versions of the CFI in the 1980s, first at the University of Utah and later at Virginia Commonwealth University (VCU). It was at VCU that Robbins and his colleagues teamed with Judy Chartrand to further develop and validate the CFI. In 1990, Chartrand, Robbins, Morrill, and Boggs published a research version of the CFI in the *Journal of Counseling Psychology*. Since that time, the CFI has been validated among multiple user groups, including high school and college students, employed adults, and midlife career professionals.

The CFI includes 21 items, all of which are responded to with options on a 5-point scale. Some of the items are followed by traditional *strongly disagree* (1) to *strongly agree* (5) options (e.g., Before choosing or entering a particular career area, I need to answer, who am I?), whereas others require responses to semantically opposing terms [e.g., "When I think about actually deciding for sure what I want my career to be, my hands feel: *dry* (1) to *wet* (5)]. The CFI's 21 items are divided into four scales: Need for Information (6 items), Need for Self-Knowledge (4 items), Career Choice Anxiety (6 items), and Generalized Indecisiveness (5 items). Most individuals are able to complete the CFI within 5 or 10 minutes.

Use in Counseling

As Chartrand and Robbins (1997) claim, "Currently the CFI is the only published instrument designed to measure multiple antecedents of career indecision" (p. v). As such, it represents an important addition to the cadre of vocational assessments available for use in career counseling contexts.

The CFI is a career choice *process* measure. Consequently, it can be useful in ascertaining the degree to which a client or groups of clients are ready to engage in the career decision-making process. "The CFI can also help undecided individuals uncover the source of their indecision" (Chartrand & Robbins, 1997, p. 1). Results of the CFI can help counselors develop intervention strategies specifically designed to help clients cope with and overcome particular factors contributing to their career indecision.

Because the CFI was designed with a broad range of career counseling clients in mind, it can be effectively used with individual clients or in small or large group settings. Furthermore, its use is not limited to high school or college students. Employed adults, unemployed individuals seeking work, and persons exploring new career opportunities are also likely to benefit from completing the CFI and receiving interpretive feedback from a professional career counselor.

Technical Considerations

The *CFI Applications and Technical Guide* (Chartrand & Robbins, 1997) reports means and standard deviations across all four CFI scales for one high school general sample (N = 683), two college general samples (total N = 782), a college ethnic minority sample (N = 154), a college counseling sample (N = 331), and two adult samples (total N = 312). Chartrand and Robbins acknowledge that the norms represented in the *Guide* are not equivalent to a representative national sample. However, they explain that during the development and validation of the CFI, the inventory was administered to several diverse samples, including groups of inner-city youth and ethnic minority students seeking assistance at the Chicano/Latino Learning Resource Center of a major university in the Midwest.

The *CFI Applications and Technical Guide* presents internal consistency reliability data across five different samples, including ninth graders (N = 501), two groups of college students (total N = 545), female offenders (N = 132), and adults in a career course (N = 60). Internal consistency reliabilities across the four CFI scales ranged from .68 to .91 (median = .80), and for total CFI scores ranged from .83 to .92 (median = .85). Two-week test-retest reliabilities across the four CFI scales among two college student samples (total N = 100) ranged from .68 to .84 (median = .76), whereas three-month test-retest reliabilities among a high school sample (N = 88) ranged from .57 to .66 (median = .63).

As summarized by Chartrand and Robbins (1997), evidence of the CFI's validity includes the absence of gender and ethnic differences across the four CFI scales, a decrease in CFI scores following participation in career decision-making classes and workshops, and expected relationships between CFI scale scores and various other career development and personality measures (e.g., Career Choice Status Inventory, Career Development Inventory, Career Decision Scale). The *Applications and Technical Guide* also reports evidence supporting the CFI's construct validity, including results of research supporting a factor structure and pattern of scale intercorrelations consistent with the theoretical underpinnings of the CFI.

Overall Critique

Although the internal consistency and test-retest reliabilities for the CFI are somewhat lower than ideal, the CFI appears to be a valuable career counseling tool. Its primary strength is the manner in which it fills the void that previously existed among the family of assessments available to counselors. In a nutshell, the CFI provides counselors with an effective vehicle for evaluating the various antecedents of career indecision.

One of the CFI's greatest strengths is the *Applications and Technical Guide* (Chartrand & Robbins, 1997). In addition to chapters on the development of the CFI (including norms, reliability, and validity information) and procedures for inventory administration and scoring, the authors provide counselors with a useful model for CFI interpretation. In their discussion of CFI interpretation strategies, Chartrand and Robbins present several individual counseling case studies and group application ideas that can help counselors develop a plan for small and large group interpretation of CFI results.

Although the CFI was only recently published commercially by Consulting Psychologists Press (Chartrand, Robbins, & Morrill, 1997), Robbins and his colleagues have devoted nearly two decades to its development and validation. Their use of the CFI among multiple user groups (e.g., high school students, traditional-age college students, nontraditional-age and returning adult college students, employed adults, unemployed individuals seeking work) and in a variety of contexts (e.g., businesses, institutions, government agencies, schools, individual counselors' offices) has helped to establish the CFI as an effective career counseling assessment that is sure to increase in popularity in the years to come.

References

Chartrand, J. M., & Robbins, S. B. (1997). *Career Factors Inventory: Applications and technical guide.* Palo Alto, CA: Consulting Psychologists Press.

Chartrand, J. M., Robbins, S. B., & Morrill, W. H. (1997). *Career Factors Inventory.* Palo Alto, CA: Consulting Psychologists Press.

Chartrand, J. M., Robbins, S. B., Morrill, W. H., & Boggs, K. (1990). Development and validation of the Career Factors Inventory. *Journal of Counseling Psychology, 37*, 491-501.

Robbins, S. B., Morrill, W. H., & Boggs, K. (1987). *The construction and validation of the Career Factors Inventory.* Unpublished manuscript, Virginia Commonwealth University, Richmond, VA.

Career Maturity Inventory (CMI)

John D. Crites and Mark L. Savickas
Distributed by Careerware
A Division of Bridges
808 Commerce Park Drive
Ogdensburg, NY 13669
www.careerware.com

Target Population: Middle School-Adult

Statement of the Purpose of the Instrument: Career readiness assessment that measures attitudes and competencies necessary for youth and adults to make effective career decisions.

Titles of Subtests, Scales, Scores Provided: Attitude Test identifies attitudes and feelings toward making a career choice (25 questions). Competence test: measures knowledge about occupations and decisions involved in choosing a career (25 questions).

Forms and Levels Available, with Dates of Publication/Revision of Each: Published and copyrighted, 1995.

Date of Most Recent Edition of Test Manual, User's Guide, Etc.: 1995.

Languages in Which Available: English only.

Time: Actual Test Time: No time limit.
        Total Administration Time: Approximately 45 minutes.

Norm Group(s) on Which Scores Are Based: Grades 5-12.

Manner in Which Results Are Reported for Individuals: Raw scores.
    Report Format/Content: None.
        Options: None

Report Format/Content for Group Summaries: Not available.

Scoring
    Machine Scoring Service: Not available.
    Hand Scoring:
        Scored by: Counselee.
        Time required for scoring: 5 minutes.
    Local Machine Scoring: Not available.

Computer Software Options Available: Not available.

Cost of Materials: 25/$50

Counselee Materials: Questionnaire

Published Reviews: None cited.

Reviewed by

Patricia Jo McDivitt
Vice-President,, Educational Measurement
And Test Development, ETS-12 Works, Inc.
San Antonio, TX

Description

The current form of the Career Maturity Inventory (CMI) is a 1995 revision of an instrument that was first known as the Vocational Development Inventory (VDI). Administered in 1961, the VDI was the first instrument to measure the process of career decision making. Conceptually, the VDI has its philosophical origins formulated on the works of Donald Super's Career Pattern Study, which theorizes that an individual's career maturity can be defined by his or her standing along several dimensions of career maturity (Super, Crites, Hummel, Moser, Overstreet and Warnath, 1957). The original version of the VDI consisted of an Attitude Scale with 50 statements relating to an individual's attitude and feelings toward making a career choice.

The VDI was revised in 1973 to include not only an assessment of a student's attitudes and feelings toward career decision-making but also to include an assessment of a student's knowledge of occupational information. With this revision, the instrument included the Competence Test. The Competence Test consisted of five subtests: Self-appraisal, Occupational Information, Goal Selection, Planning, and Problem-Solving. The Competence Test was published in 1973; and with its addition, the instrument became known as the Career Maturity Inventory (CMI). Studies were conducted to support the CMI's internal consistency, reliability, and construct and criterion-related validity. Research was also conducted to document the usefulness of the CMI for program evaluation.

The CMI was again revised in 1978 to include 25 new items added to the original 50-item Attitude Scale. The additional items allowed for the construction of Attitude Scale subscales, including orientation to career choice, involvement in career choice, independence in career choice, compromise in career choice, and decisiveness in career choice. The 1978 edition of the CMI took approximately 2½ hours to administer, including 30 minutes for the Attitude Scale and 2 hours for the Competence Test (Crites, 1978).

The most recent edition of the CMI was published in 1995. The CMI Revised (CMI-R) includes content appropriate for use with high school students, as well as for use with postsecondary individuals. This edition was also revised to include items that are free of ethnic, racial, and gender bias. The CMI-R provides for three scores: Attitude Scale, Competence Test, and overall Career Maturity. Although the CMI-R adheres as closely as possible to the Model of Career Maturity, as outlined by Crites (1961, 1976), the Attitude Scale subscales were eliminated. Instead, the authors selected five items from each of the 1978 subscales to comprise the CMI-R Attitude Scale. As a result, the Attitude Scale component of the CMI now consists of 25 diverse statements, ranging from those dealing with one's attitude about work, "Work is dull and unpleasant," to those dealing with one's attitude about finding satisfying work, "There may not be any opening in the job I want most." In selecting the items, the authors retained those items eliciting higher percentages of "mature" responses with each advance in grade level (Crites, *Theory and Research Handbook*, 1995, 47-50.).

The CMI-R also includes a substantial revision to the Competence Test. Despite the fact that the 1978 Competence Test had acceptable psychometric characteristics, the test administration time proved to be too long, and many of the items were considered to be inappropriate for use with postsecondary individuals. As a result, the CMI-R Competence Test consists of only 25 revised and new items. Each item consists of a short narrative. The items are divided into five sections, with five items per section. In the first section, the individual is asked to read the item which consists of a short appraisal of someone's abilities, interests, and values. The individual is asked to agree or disagree with the appraisal. For example, "Cheryl operates an IBM Personal Computer on her job and also does typing at home on her Macintosh. Her interests are in working with data rather than things." In the second section, the individual is asked to read the descriptions of five occupations. The individual is asked to agree or disagree with the description. For example, "All these occupations require, at least, a college education for entry: social worker, stockbroker, and forester." The third section of the Competence Test asks the individual to read five narratives. Each narrative describes a career choice for a person. The individual is asked to determine whether or not the career choice is appropriate. For example, "Jody likes to work with ideas, and in college her best grades were in anthropology, political science, and philosophy. Possible occupations for her are journalist, lawyer, and urban planner." Section four asks the individual to read five narratives, each describing someone's career plan. The individual is asked to determine whether or not the career plan is ordered correctly. The last section of the Competence Test, section five, also consists of five narratives, each describing a solution to a career problem. The individual is asked to determine whether or not the solution to the hypothetical career problem is a good one or not.

An additional enhancement to the CMI-R is the introduction of the Career Developer (CDR) supplement. The purpose of the CDR is to allow for an individual's interpretation of each item in the CMI-R. For example, once the individual has completed the CMI-R, he/she is given the CDR. The CDR asks the individual to look again at the answers to the CMI-R and fill in the circle for each answer in the CDR. The individual is then asked to look carefully at each item and read the explanation as to what the more mature response to a particular item would be. By providing this information, the CDR can be used as a tool for discussion between the counselor and the individual, allowing for an individual's enhanced opportunities for gaining career maturity. It also provides for the counselor to have the opportunity to teach the process of career decision-making (Crites and Savickas, *Career Developer*, 1995).

Additional changes to the CMI-R include changes to the response format, including changing from True (T) and False (F) in the previous edition to Agree (A) and Disagree (D) in the Revised edition. Individuals are asked to read the statements or narratives in the assessment booklet. If they agree or mostly agree with the statement, they are to fill in the circle for A. If they disagree or mostly disagree with a statement, they are to fill in the circle for D. The CMI-R also includes several scoring options: hand-scoring, machine-scoring, and a combination of hand- and machine-scoring. By providing these scoring options, results can be retained for future reference and review.

Use in Counseling

Many individuals lack the knowledge, experiences, and self-awareness of abilities and interests to make appropriate career decisions. As a result, counselors often use career-development instruments to measure career maturity or the degree to which an individual is ready to make wise, realistic career decisions. The CMI-R is appropriate for use in assessing career maturity because it consists of items that survey important attitudes about career decision making. The CMI was first developed to be used with high school students for the purpose of surveying students' attitudes and competencies that are important in helping students plan and choose a career. The CMI-R was revised to include item content also appropriate for use with postsecondary individuals.

The CMI-R, when combined with the CDR, can be used successfully with a individual to teach the process of career maturity and career decision-making. The CDR allows the counselor to "teach the test" by providing the counselor the opportunity to discuss with the individual why a given response to an item was or was not a mature response. This "teaching the test" feature of the CDR is important as it provides for each individual the opportunity to discuss his/her attitudes toward career decision-making and his/her ideas about career choices. Through the discussion, the individual may also begin to incorporate new ideas into his/her thinking, which may well lead to a more realistic attitude toward making a career decision. To assist the counselor in the process of teaching the test, instructional materials are available. These materials developed by Crites (1973) explain each response and provide for what would be the rationale for a mature response. In addition, the CMI Sourcebook (CMI 1995 Sourcebook, pp. 58-70) provides valuable information concerning how to use the CMI-R item rationales to enhance an individual's career maturity.

The CMI-R, with item rationales, may also be used effectively in process-oriented career counseling groups. The groups do not discuss which occupational choice might be best for an individual, rather the group discusses which career decision-making process might best be used for everyone in the group. In this case the "teach the test" model works well because those members of the group who already have a well-developed attitude toward career decision-making may serve as role models. The role models can also serve to help the counselor confirm or contradict the thinking of a particular group member. The group member can also be encouraged to think about or experiment with new attitudes and behaviors, designed to enhance the process of career decision-making (Savickas, 1990).

Technical Considerations

Technical data concerning the CMI-R are provided in the 1995 CMI Sourcebook. The Sourcebook provides information concerning item selection. All items selected for use in the CMI-R of the Attitude Scale were taken from the 1978 version of the CMI. Despite the fact that the 1995 Sourcebook states that they have the same reliability as the items in the previous edition (CMI 1995 Sourcebook, p. 49), additional research is needed. Items were selected to represent the former subscales of the previous edition. Twenty-five items were deemed sufficient to achieve high reliability for total scores. Items were selected based upon the following criteria: (1) maximum item variances, ideally 50/50 splits between the agree and disagree options; (2) high item/scale correlations from the previous edition; (3) longitudinal item data analyzes to identify those items with no significant differences at the .01 level; and (4) items deemed to be highly differentiating across grades.

For the CMI-R Competence Test, new items were written to be parallel to the 1978 items. They were written to cover the same competency areas and were distributed equally across the former subscales, with five items per scale. Although the items were written to have content validity, empirical evidence is needed and validity studies need to be conducted.

The CMI-R was not normed on a given population. Rather hypothetical norms for grades 5 through 12 were derived using a computer-generated model that specifies all possible combinations of scores. The computer-generated norms were based upon a finite population of over 4 million students in grades 5 through 12 across the United States. Large samples were drawn to construct the hypothetical norms for both the Attitude Scale and the Competency Test (1995 CMI Sourcebook, p. 91).

Most of the research on the CMI is based upon research conducted on earlier versions of the instrument. For example, during a 10-year period (1961-1971) many research projects included the use of the VDI. As a result of the early research, the reliability and validity of the original instrument has been well documented. With the addition of the Competence Test, published in 1973, a substantial number of additional studies were conducted to support the CMI's internal consistency, reliability, and construct and criterion-related validity. These studies tend to support the validity of the previous edition of the CMI (Healy, 1994, 271). To be considered a valid and reliable instrument, similar studies are needed with the CMI-R.

Overall Critique

The CMI has a long-standing reputation and is considered one of the leading instruments in the assessment of career maturity. The current edition of the CMI has corrected some of the earlier concerns related to test administration time and content of the items. The improvements have made the instrument more user friendly and also appropriate for use with high school students, as well as adults. With the introduction of the Career Developer (CDR), the usefulness of the instrument for teaching individuals the process career decision-making and for helping individuals gain career maturity has been greatly enhanced. However, further research is needed to confirm reliability and construct and criterion-related validity of the items.

References

Crites. J. O. (1961). A model for the measurement of vocational maturity. *Journal of Counseling Psychology, 8*, 255-259.

Crites, J. O. (1978). *Administration and use manual* (2nd ed.). Monterey, CA: CTB/McGraw-Hill.

Crites J. O. (1976). Career counseling: A comprehensive approach. *The Counseling Psychologist, 6*, 2-12.

Crites. J. O. (1973). Rationales for the career maturity inventory attitude scale (form A-1) items. Unpublished manuscript. University of Maryland, College Park, MD.

Crites J. O. (1995). *Theory and research handbook 1995 revised edition.* Published by John O. Crites. Distributed by ISM Information Systems Management, Inc., Careerware.

Crites J. O. & Savickas M. L. (1995). Career developer. Published by John O. Crites. Distributed by ISM Information Systems Management, Inc., Careerware.

Crites J. O. & Savickas M. L. (1995). *Revised form attitude scale and competence test CMI sourcebook*. Published by John O. Crites. Distributed by ISM Information Systems Management, Inc., Careerware.

Healy, C. C. (1994). Career maturity inventory. In Kapes, J. T., and Mastie, M. M., and Whitfield, E. A. (Eds.) *A counselor's guide to career assessment instruments*. (3rd Ed.), Alexandria, VA: National Career Development Association.

Savickas, M. L. (1990). Developing career choice readiness. Paper presented at the Annual Convention of the American Association for Counseling and Development, Cincinnati, Ohio.

Super, D. E., Crites, J. O., Hummel R. C., Moser, H. P., Overstreet, P. L., & Warnath, C. F. (1957). *Vocational development: A framework for research*. New York: Teachers College Bureau of Publications.

Career Thoughts Inventory (CTI)

James P. Sampson, Gary W. Peterson,
Janet G. Lenz, Robert C. Reardon, and Denise E. Saunders
Psychological Assessment Resources, Inc.
16204 North Florida Avenue
Lutz, FL 33549
custserv@parinc.com
www.parinc.com

Target Population: Adults, college students, and high school students

Statement of the Purpose of the Instrument: The CTI is a self-administered and objectively scored measure of negative career thinking designed to improve the quality of career decisions and the quality of career service delivery.

Titles of Subtests, Scales, Scores Provided: (1) Decision-making Confusion; (2) Commitment Anxiety; (3) External Conflict; CTI Total Score as well as scores on the three construct scales.

Forms and Levels Available, with Dates of Publication/Revision of Each: Professional Manual; Workbook; Test Booklet. All qualification Level B. Publication date for all: 7/24/96.

Date of Most Recent Edition of Test Manual, User's Guide, Etc.: 7/24/96.

Languages in Which Available: English only.

Time: Actual Test Time: Self-administered.
            Total Administration Time: 7-15 minutes.

Norm Group(s) on Which Scores are Based: National sample of over 1,500 adults, college students, and high school students.

Manner in Which Results are Reported for Individuals: The CTI yields a CTI Total Score as well as scores on three construct scales.
    Types of Scores: Raw scores to T score conversions for adults, college students, and high school students.
    Report Format/Content: Exercises in the CTI Workbook help individual improve career thinking and develop an Individual Action Plan.

Report Format/Content for Group Summaries: Not available.

Scoring
    Machine Scoring Service: Not available.
    Hand Scoring:
        Scored by: Counselee; Clerk; Counselor.
        Time required for scoring: About five minutes.

Local Machine Scoring: Not available.

Computer Software Options Available: Not available.

Cost of Materials:
CTI Introductory Kit (includes Manual, five Workbooks, and 25 Test Booklets) $109
CTI Professional Manual $30
CTI Workbook $8
CTI Workbooks (pkg/10) $69
CTI Test Booklets (pkg/25) $43
Specimen Set: None; Option; purchase manual; one free copy of each component; manual may be returned.
Counselee Materials: Workbook (not reusable) Test Booklet (not reusable).

Additional Comments of Interest to Users: CTI is a self-help instrument that is ideal for use in career counseling centers and career development programs.

Published reviews: None cited.

Reviewed by

Rich Feller
Professor

Joe Daly
Professor

School of Education
Colorado State University

Description
The Career Thoughts Inventory (CTI) is a 48-item inventory designed to provide a measure of dysfunctional thinking related to career decision making. It is used, in conjunction with a 36-page workbook, with adults considering a career change, and college and high school students choosing a field of study, an occupation, or employment. The goal of the CTI is to improve the quality of career decisions and the quality of career counseling. Part of a new genre of assessment tools that move beyond basic assessment to provide an instructional stimulus within the delivery of career services, the CTI offers value-added features to counselors, evaluators, and researchers. By integrating the assessment function with a comprehensive theory-based model (Peterson, Sampson & Reardon, 1991) on intervention, clients can immediately do something with the results. It uniquely purports to engage the clients and make more efficient use of their time

and the time of their human service practitioner, while more effectively incorporating the assessment concepts into intervention strategies for change (Sampson, Peterson, Lenz, Reardon, & Saunders, 1996, p.1).

The primary use of the CTI within direct client service is to serve as (1) a screening device identifying those most likely to express problems in making career choices because of dysfunctional thinking, (2) a needs assessment identifying the nature of dysfunctional thinking and needs related to decision making confusion, commitment anxiety and external conflict, (3) a readiness assessment (Sampson, Peterson, Reardon, & Lenz, in press) used to make preliminary decisions about the level of practitioner support required in relation to individual needs, and (4) a learning resource to be used with various counseling interventions.

The CTI's goals for utility can be seen as a client takes 7-15 minutes to indicate a level of agreement with 48 statements describing thoughts that some people have when considering career choices. Many of these thoughts are negative. A two-layer answer sheet can be hand scored in 5 to 8 minutes and provides raw scores in four areas: CTI Total (a single global indicator of dysfunctional career thinking), Decision Making Confusion (14 items such as "I'll never understand myself well enough to make a good career choice"), Commitment Anxiety (10 items such as "My interests are always changing"), and External Conflict (5 items such as "I know what job I want, but someone's always putting obstacles in my way"). Profiles for adults, college students, and high school students appear on the back of the test booklet where raw scores can be converted to standard scores and to percentiles.

The CTI also has demonstrated its value in research, evaluation, and theory development. It can be used to measure learning outcomes of interventions that involve identifying, challenging, and altering cognition. It has been used as the dependent variable in at least eight dissertations (Dipeolu, 1997; Kilk. 1997; Osborn, 1998; Railey, 1997; Saunders, 1997; Slatten, 1999; Strausberger, 1998; Voight, 1999) related to career problem solving and decision making. It should also prove to be useful as a tool "to further validate theory and to create new theoretical constructs associated with career problem solving and decisionmaking" (Sampson et. al., 1996, p. 2).

Although the CTI is self-administering and self-scoring (Gilbert, 1997), we observed that students can have difficulty with the scoring because of limited test-taking support information on the test booklet. Some discussion of what to expect and how to score the inventory proved to be very helpful. Our sample also reacted to the negative phrasing of the statements, which the authors explain is necessary to make use of the *CTI Workbook*. A discussion prior to taking the CTI of what to expect and how to score the inventory proved to be very helpful.

Thus the CTI's intended use with a side-by-side practitioner relationship or group supervision as advised by the authors is necessary.

Use in Counseling

Tools that help clients learn what to do next offer positive advantages to the counseling process. The CTI stands out by addressing the relationship between specific dysfunctional career thinking and exploratory behavior. The substance and level of specific interaction between client and counselor can be very rich and specific as a result of the inventory items. The three construct scales also bring a needed language to almost any decision-making challenge.

The CTI offers a sound model to drive counselor action and practitioner instruction. By offering a client-counselor collaborative model and a comprehensive system, it can get clients "talking back" to specific dysfunctional thoughts which will lead to new actions. Although this may require new thinking about how to conduct their work, a counselor's study of the comprehensive and easy-to-learn model from the *Professional Manual* adds a new dimension to practice.

Technical Considerations

The Professional Manual is clear and thorough in presenting the information related to the technical qualities of the CTI. Norms are provided for "adults" (N=571), "college students" (N= 595), and "high school students" (N= 396). The normative samples were geographical well distributed and generally representative in terms of gender and ethnicity. The authors recommend the development of local norms to further enhance the usefulness of the Inventory.

Both internal consistency (alpha coefficients) and stability (test-retest) measures of reliability are reported. Internal consistency coefficients are shown for each scale for all three groups. Alpha coefficients for the CTI total (.93 - .97) and DMC (.90 - .94) were high across all groups. Alpha coefficients for CA (.79 - .91) and EC (.74 - .81) were lower. As one would expect the shorter the scale the lower the reliability.

Test-retest correlations over a four-week period are shown for college and high school students. Stability data for the adult population were not reported. Total score test-retest reliability was .89 for college students, but dropped to .69 for high school students. Reliabilities for the subscales ranged from .82 to .74 for college students and from .72 to .52 for the high school students. Given the nature of the constructs being measured by the CTI, one would not expect the test-retest correlation to be as high as the measures of internal consistency. The high school coefficients are low, especially for the EC scale. Increasing the number of EC items would help address the low reliability of this scale.

Item and construct development for the CTI is based on the cognitive information processing theory of career development. Factor analysis of CTI items resulted in the three constructs scales (DMC, CA and EC) of the inventory. Intercorrelations of the CTI scales with the content dimensions of CPI range from .62 to .92.

Convergent validity data for the CTI shows good relationships between the CTI total score, DMC, CA, and EC scale scores and scores on My Vocational Situation, Career Decision Scale, Career Decision Profile, and the NEO Personality Inventory. Analysis of Variance studies showing significant differences in CTI scores of client and nonclient populations at Florida State University and Ohio State University provided good evidence of the criterion-related validity of the instrument.

Technically, the CTI is a well-developed inventory with good reliability and validity that does a good job of doing what it says it does. The exception to this statement is the EC scale of the inventory. The low reliability of this subscale raises questions as to its usefulness, especially with high school students.

Overall Critique

The CTI reflects the daily action research being conducted at the Career Center at Florida State University where the authors test their ideas with clients as they build theory and transform traditional career services. This gives credibility to the CTI and its continued development. This model may find some resistance from those who might question a cognitive approach yet its clarity can be easily appreciated.

The CTI should not be considered a self-help inventory. The authors state in the *Professional Manual* (Sampson et. al., 1996, p. 22) that practitioners and professionals using the CTI should have experience and training in career development, career service delivery, and cognitive-behavioral theory. They should also be very familiar with the *Professional Manual* and all components of the CPI. As Gilbert (1997) suggests this is not a typical assessment found in employment agencies or college and high school career centers. Counselors in these settings would need to have the background and training mentioned and be willing to meet the demands of the CTI on both the counselor and the client. The client needs to understand the purpose of the CTI and to have some understanding of the four content domains that are being measured. The counselor needs to understand the inventory and the workbook and how to facilitate the clients use of both. The CTI covers a lot of ground in a short time. Although it demands much from users, its returns are great for the client, the quality of the process, and structure of delivering career services.

References

Dipeolu, A. O. (1997). A study of the relationship between learning disabilities, dysfunctional career thoughts, and adjustment to disability (Decision-making confusion, commitment, conflict, anxiety, career thoughts inventory). (Doctoral dissertation, Florida State University, 1997). *Dissertation Abstracts International*, 58 (07), 3938B.

Gilbert, H. B. (1997, January). *Career Thoughts Inventory: A review and critique.* Paper presented at the annual meeting of the Southwest Educational Research Association, Austin, TX. (ERIC Document Reproduction Service No. ED 408 526).

Kilk, K. L. (1997). The relationship between dysfunctional career thoughts and choosing an academic major. (Doctoral dissertation, University of Northern Colorado, 1997). *Dissertation Abstracts International*, 58(08), 3038A.

Osborn, D. S. (1998). The relationships among perfectionism, dysfunctional career thoughts, and career indecision. (Doctoral dissertation, Florida State University, 1998). *Dissertation Abstracts International*, 58(08), 3746A.

Peterson, G. W., Sampson, J.P., Jr., & Reardon, R. C. (1991). *Career development and services: A cognitive approach.* Pacific Grove, CA: Brooks/Cole.

Railey, M. G. (1997). The relationship between dysfunctional career thoughts and career interests with respect to offender status of female inmates and probationers. (Doctoral dissertation, Florida State University, 1997). *Dissertation Abstracts International*, 58 (06), 3325B.

Sampson, J. P., Jr., Peterson, G. W., Lenz, J. G., Reardon, R. C., & Saunders, D.E. (1996). *Career Thoughts Inventory: Professional manual.* Odessa, FL: Psychological Assessment Resources.

Sampson, J.P., Jr., Peterson, G.W., Reardon, R.C., & Lenz, J.G. (in press). Using readiness assessment to improve career services: A Cognitive Information Processing approach. *The Career Development Quarterly.*

Saunders, D. E. (1997). The contribution of depression and dysfunctional career thinking to career indecision. (Doctoral dissertation, Florida State University, 1997). *Dissertation Abstracts International*, 58(07), 3953B.

Slatten, M. L. (1999). *Dysfunctional career thoughts and self-appraised problem-solving ability among substance abusers.* Unpublished doctoral dissertation, Florida State University.

Strausberger, S. J. (1998). The relationship of state-trait anger to dysfunctional career thinking and vocational identity. (Doctoral dissertation, Florida State University, 1998). *Dissertation Abstracts International*, 59(10), 3747A.

Voight, L. (1999). *Parental attachment and ego identity as antecedents of career identity.* Unpublished doctoral dissertation, Florida State University.

CHAPTER 10

Personality Assessments

- Comprehensive Personality Profile (CPP)
- Jackson Personality Inventory-Revised (JPI-R)
- Myers-Briggs Type Indicator (MBTI)
- Sixteen Personality Factor (16PF) Questionnaire
- Student Styles Questionnaire (SSQ)

Comprehensive Personality Profile (CPP)

Larry L. Craft
Wonderlic, Inc.
1795 North Butterfield Road
Libertyville, IL 60048-1380
mike.callans@wonderlic.com
www.wonderlic.com

Target Population: Employers and human resource personnel.

Statement of the Purpose of the Instrument: The purpose of the CPP is to help organizations effectively match candidates whose personality characteristics are most compatible with the demands of the job.

Titles of Subtests, Scales, Scores Provided: Primary Traits: emotional intensity, intuition, recognition, motivation sensitivity, assertiveness, trust, exaggeration. Secondary Traits: ego drive, interpersonal warmth, stability, empathy, objectivity, independence, aggressiveness, decisiveness, tolerance, efficiency.

Forms and Levels Available, with Dates of Publication/Revision of Each: 1996

Date of Most Recent Edition of Test Manual, User's Guide, Etc.: 1998

Languages in Which Available: English, French, and Spanish

Time: Actual Test Time: 20 minutes.
   Total Administration Time: 10 minutes.

Norm Group(s) on Which Scores Are Based: Over 42,000 individuals in over 500 different occupations in over 500 organizations.

Manner in Which Results Are Reported for Individuals
   Types of Scores: Verbal labels, percentiles, narration
   Report Format/Content:
      Basic Service: Summary data page, selection report, percentile scores, job factor compatibility, supervisory report personality profile narrative, individual self-report

Report Format/Content for Group Summaries: Not available.

Scoring
   Machine Scoring Service: Not available.
   Hand Scoring: Not available.
   Local Machine Scoring: CD ROM and scoring software.

Computer Software Options Available: Standard administration and scoring online.

Cost of Materials:
Specimen Set: No charge for sample questionnaire
Counselee Materials: CPP sold in package of 25 for $500 or five for $125. Components: (1) questionnaire, (2) user's manual, (3) CD-ROM, (4) scoring software

Published Reviews: None cited.

Reviewed by

Gary W. Peterson
Director of Training

Stephen R. Hill
Doctoral Candidate

Psychological Services in Education
Florida State University

Description

The Comprehensive Personality Profile (CPP), created by Larry Craft, is a profiling system designed to match personality traits of applicants or job incumbents to essential characteristics of jobs (Wonderlic, 1999). The ultimate aim of the 88-item CPP is to foster employee satisfaction and job performance while reducing high costs of organizational turnover. Although originally designed to be a predictor of success in sales occupations (Craft Systems' Mission, 2000), the present CPP profiling system is designed for use in employee selection, improvement of management effectiveness, human resource development, and work team building and communication.

The CPP Questionnaire consists of 88 True/False statements such as, "I always look forward to situations which reward me with prestige or peer approval." The questionnaire may be administered either using paper-and-pencil or directly on a PC, and can be completed in 20-30 minutes. However, if paper and pencil format is used, the test proctor must transpose the examinee's responses into the computer. Upon completion of the Questionnaire, five reports may be selected from the computer report menu: (1) the *Selection Report* compares an applicant's personality traits *vis-a-vis* a wide variety of administrative, sales, and management job functions; (2) the *Manager's Supervisory Report* makes specific recommendations regarding how to motivate and develop new employees; (3) the *Sales Managers Report* relates personality traits to critical sales duties; (4) the *Sales Training Report* provides suggestions pertaining to supervision and training of new hires; and (5) the *Individual's Self Report* provides an interpretive report for the applicant or employee.

The results of the CPP questionnaire yield percentile scores on 7 Primary traits, 10 Secondary traits, 10 Management Performance traits, 10 Sales Performance traits, and 7 Administrative Performance traits based on norms established on 1,350 employees, applicants, and business technology students. An individual is also classified in terms of four personality types: Driver, Motivator, Thinker, or Supporter. Percentile scores on the Primary traits are contrasted with the norms of a designated occupation. Descriptive information is also presented on the high and low characteristics of each Primary trait. The 7 Primary traits, identified through exploratory factor analysis, include Emotional Intensity, Intuition, Recognition Motivation, Sensitivity, Assertiveness, Trust, and Exaggeration, whereas the 10 Secondary "content" traits, derived from the author's experience, observations, and literature review, include Ego Drive, Interpersonal Warmth, Stability, Empathy, Objectivity, Independence, Aggressiveness, Decisiveness, Tolerance, and Efficiency.

Scores on the Primary traits are also combined to yield three interpersonal interaction styles: Temperament, Ego Style, and Social Style. Each interaction score is derived by plotting two Primary trait scale percentile scores in a quadrant of a 2 X 2 (high – low) matrix. The Temperament profile is based on a combination of Emotional Intensity and Intuition, the Ego Style profile on Recognition Motivation and Sensitivity, and the Social Style profile on Assertiveness and Trust. Both the User's Manual and the respective reports provide graphical representations and general descriptions of personality dimensions along with summaries of their strengths, weaknesses, and plausible career directions. Each of the reports provides descriptors that offer useful, yet general, guidance and direction for an individual, a supervisor, and/or a trainer. Unfortunately, the substance of these personality descriptors may be so broad that they lack distinctive individual characteristics.

An Accuracy Index was designed to take into account several response sets. The Accuracy Index is composed of three components, each contributing to a single score: (1) the tendency toward exaggeration, (2) the specific faking of items and item contradictions, and (3) the percentage of Ideal vs. Real discrepancies. This last validity indicator, the Ideal/Real discrepancy, provides useful feedback to applicants regarding the extent of their own self-appraised person-job fit with respect to the job or position for which they may be applying.

Use in Counseling

Although the CPP was not specifically designed for use in career counseling, there may well be some potential applications to be explored in practice and research. In contrast to other common measures of personality structure, such as the NEO or 16PF, the CPP was designed explicitly to relate personality traits to job characteristics. With this in mind, one could surmise that the CPP could facilitate career exploration by drawing linkages between self-knowledge and occupational knowledge (i.e., the degree of match between trait scores and the demands of selected occupations). Thus, the CPP could be used in career counseling in the same way that interest inventories and values inventories are now used. In fact, the CPP could complement the use of such instruments in career counseling. For example, the results of the CPP yield a seven-point personality code that is matched to occupations. Second, the Ideal vs. Real discrepancy index may serve as an indication of the extent to which individuals believe they possess the personality characteristics associated with occupations under consideration. Used in this way, it could assist career clients in critically evaluating their own beliefs and perceptions regarding the extent to which they perceive a match between themselves and an occupation or job.

The purposes for which the CPP was expressly designed are personnel selection and human resource development. However, the use of the CPP in selection with any degree of utility requires a thorough job analysis and concurrent validation to ascertain whether certain personality traits or interactions of those traits are actually predictive of essential duties and tasks of a particular job within an organization. Even with job-relevant information, the most appropriate use of the CPP in personnel selection would be in the latter stages of the selection process as a confirmatory device to identify potentially problematic person-job discrepancies both from the employer's perspective and from the client's perspective.

If the CPP is found to be associated with job performance in a given organizational context, it may facilitate human resource development by helping incumbents become aware of their job-related strengths and weakness. For example, an employee may become cognizant of a gap between a measured level of Sensitivity and a desired level for the job. Training could then be designed to help the employee acquire sensitivity skills and apply them to appropriate situations, thereby potentially increasing job performance and satisfaction. Further, for employees seeking advancement or job transfer within an organization, the CPP may be helpful in assessing their potential for a new job as well as areas of further growth and development.

Finally, the CPP is recommended for use in promoting effective team building and communication. In team building, certain dominant personality types could be balanced with individuals who are comfortable as followers to make the composition of work or problem-solving teams more complementary. To guide a supervisor, the Manual lists traits, provides definitions, and states how they may be applied to team building. For example, High A's (i.e., Assertiveness) "will clearly express where they stand and what they want" (Wonderlic,

1999, p. 69). Although effective communication is a goal in any organization, whether the use of CPP scores is effective or useful for such purposes remains an open question.

Technical Considerations

Normative data on the 7 Primary traits are presented for 350 occupations based on samples from over 42,000 in over 500 different positions in over 500 organizations. The normative sample was 63% male and 37% female. A minimum of 25 incumbents was used to establish norms for an occupation. For each occupation listed in the appendix, mean scores and standard deviations are presented for each Primary trait as well as the proportion of individuals in the norm group belonging to each of the four personality types: Driver, Motivator, Thinker, and Supporter.

Information regarding the reliability of the Primary trait scales is provided in the User's Manual, but not for the Secondary trait scales. Coefficient alpha internal consistency coefficients range from .73 (Assertiveness) to .85 (Trust), with a median of .81. The length of scales varies between 11 and 13 items. Six-week stability coefficients range from .65 to .85 with medians of .77 and .78 for two student samples.

During the course of development, the CPP item pool was reduced from 400 original items (Craft Systems' Mission, 2000) to the present 88 items. An exploratory factor analysis with varimax rotation was used to create the seven factors. However, important data are omitted in the User's Manual regarding the factor structure of the instrument such as the eigenvalues of factors, a scree plot, the percentage of variation accounted for in the matrix by the seven factors, the complete matrix of factor loadings, and the intercorrelations among the scales comprising the Primary traits. The User's Manual reports the loading of only the single item with the highest loading for each factor.

Evidence of convergent and discriminant validity is based on correlation coefficients between scales of the CPP and scales of the 16PF, the Myers-Briggs Type Indicator (MBTI), the California Psychological Inventory (CPI), and the Millon Clinical Multiaxial Inventory (MCMI). These studies employed clinical patients with the exception of the MBTI, which was conducted with college students. Convergent validity coefficients ranged as high as $r = .59$ between the CPP Trust scale and the CPI Tolerance scale, and as low as $r = -.17$ between the CPP Emotional Intensity scale and the CPI Self-Control scale. Some scales failed to demonstrate convergent validity when expected. For example, the CPP Assertiveness scale failed to achieve a significant correlation with the CPI Dominance scale, and the CPP Intuition scale did not significantly correlate with the MBTI Intuition scale.

With respect to criterion-related validity, in one regression study reported in the appendix of the manual and found in an online journal, the seven Primary traits collectively accounted for nearly 10% of the adjusted variance in sales performance (Predicting sales performance, 1998; Wonderlic, 1999). The scales Recognition, Motivation, and Exaggeration captured a significant amount of variation in the model. A second regression study indicated that a composite CPP score was significantly ($p < .05$) correlated with sales commissions, $r = .115$. Although the User's Manual states, "Numerous research studies have been conducted which demonstrate the value of the CPP is predicting sales, productivity, work quality, and many other aspects of job performance" (Wonderlic, 1999, p. 59), no studies are cited, nor did a search of the research literature by the present authors of the CPP render any such studies that were clearly independent of the developer (e.g., Parks & Waldo, 1999).

Overall Critique

The intent and hope of the CPP are indeed admirable. From only 88 items and 7 empirically derived personality scales, one can estimate reliable matches between 7 personality dimensions and characteristics of 350 occupations that are free of racial or sex bias. The outcome of the match could be used for personnel selection, human resource development, and possibly career counseling. However, in order to accomplish such goals, a psychometrically sound instrument, dependable norms, and a track record of methodologically sound validation studies across a variety of occupations and organizations are required.

Regarding psychometric qualities of the CPP, most of the reported internal consistency coefficients of the respective Primary scales appear to be adequate, especially given only 11-13 dichotomously scored items per scale. Nevertheless, much technical information about the nature of the scales was omitted from the User's Manual. The internal consistency coefficients of the Secondary scales are not reported. The extent to which the Primary scales or Secondary scales are independent was not reported. The standard errors of measurement of the percentile scores of the Primary and Secondary scales were also omitted. According to User's Manual, the factor structure has not been replicated, nor subjected to a confirmatory factor analysis.

The establishing of occupational norms was an ambitious undertaking involving over 42,000 test takers. Nevertheless, the samples for many occupations were less than 50. One wonders about the dependability of such small samples in terms of accurately representing an occupational classification.

With respect to validity, convergent validity coefficients were ascertained for only one instrument assessing personality in which the factors were derived through factor analysis (i.e., the 16PF). We would recommend a convergent validity study also be conducted using a measure of the "Big Five" such as the NEO. Documentation of more criterion-related studies demonstrating the connection between CPP scores and job performance, job tenure, and job satisfaction would also make the publisher's claims more compelling. Finally, the ability of the CPP to discriminate successfully between members of different occupational classes would also lend to establishing confidence in the measure as a selection or counseling instrument.

In conclusion, although we applaud the intent of the CPP and the work that has already been invested in its development, we believe there is still more work to be done before the claims of the developers can be confidently affirmed.

References

Craft Systems' Mission: Research Portfolio. (2000). *[online]*. Available: www.craftsystems.com/libraryarticles/portfolio/portfolio.html

Parks, C.A., & Waldo, D. (1999). Assessing voluntary turnover likelihood using personality traits measured during pre-employment selection. *Current Research in Social Psychology [online], 4*(4). Available: www.uiowa.edu/~grpproc/crisp/crisp.4.4.htm

Predicting sales performance: Accuracy and compatibility in personality measurement. (1998). *Journal of Modern Business [online].* Available: www.dcpress.com/jmb/page11.html.

Wonderlic Personnel Test, Inc. (1999*). Comprehensive Personality Profile user's manual.* Libertyville, IL: Author.

Jackson Personality Inventory-Revised (JPI-R)

Douglas N. Jackson
SIGMA Assessment Systems, Inc.
P.O. Box 610984
Port Huron, MI 48061-0984
sigma@sigmaassessmentsystems.com
www.sigmassessmentsystems.com

Target Population: Adolescent and adult

Statement of the Purpose of the Instrument: The JPI-R was developed to provide a set of measures of personality that reflect a variety of interpersonal, cognitive, and value orientations. These variables are relevant in a wide range of settings such as those involving work, educational/organizational behavior, or interpersonal situations.

Titles of Subtests, Scales, Scores Provided: The JPI-R measures 15 distinct personality traits using 20-item scales. Analytical: complexity, breadth of interest, innovation, tolerance; Extroverted; sociability, social confidence, energy level; Emotional: empathy, anxiety, cooperativeness; Opportunistic: social astuteness, risk taking; Dependable: organization, traditional values, responsibility.

Forms and Levels Available, with Dates of Publication/Revision of Each: The JPI-R is a revision of the original JPI, and was published in 1994.

Date of Most Recent Edition of Test Manual, User's Guide, Etc.: 1994

Languages in Which Available: English and French.

Time: Actual Test Time: Approximately 45 minutes.

Norm Group(s) on Which Scores Are Based: 1,107 college students, 893 blue-collar workers, 555 senior executives

Manner in Which Results Are Reported for Individuals
  Types of Scores: Standard scores, percentile ranks, raw scores
  Report Format/Content:
    Basic Service: The JPI-R Basic Report consists of a profile of the 15 JPI-R scale scores, descriptions of high and low scorers for each scale, a profile of the five JPI-R cluster scores, administrative indices, and a table of raw responses.

Report Format/Content for Group Summaries: Not available.

Scoring
  Machine Scoring Service:
    Cost of basic service per counselee: Basic Report approximately $4.50 -$7.50 per report (based on quantity ordered).
    Time required for scoring and returning (maximum): Reports are scored and returned within 48 hours of receipt.
  Hand Scoring:
    Scored by: Counselor
    Time required for scoring: Three minutes approximately.
  Local Machine Scoring:
  Provisions/conditions/equipment required: SIGMASOFT Scanning Utility—NCS Sentry 3000 or compatible optical mark scanner required. Please call or check web page for prices.

Computer Software Options Available: Computerized adaptive administration.

Cost of Materials:
  Specimen Set: JPI-R Examination Kit $59. (prices subject to change). Kit includes one of each of the following: JPI-R Test manual; five reusable test booklets; ten quick score answer sheets; ten profile sheets, and one machine-scorable answer sheet for a Basic Report.

Additional Comments of Interest to Users: Original JPI materials are available while quantities last. Please call for availability and prices.

Published Reviews:

Goldsmith, R.E. (1986). Convergent validity of four innovativeness scales. *Educational and Psychological Measurement, 46,* 81-87.

Pettinger, D. J. (1998). Review of the Jackson Personality Inventory-Revised. In J. C. Impara & B. S. Blake (Eds.). The Thirteenth Mental Measurements Yearbook (pp. 556-557). Lincoln, NE: The University of Nebraska Press.

Reddon, J.R. & Jackson, D.N. (1989). Readability of three adult personality tests: Basic Personality Inventory, Jackson Personality Inventory, and Personality Research Form-E. *Journal of Personality Assessment, 53,* 180-183.

Zachar, P. (1998). Review of the Jackson Personality Inventory-Revised. In J. C. Impara & B. S. Blake (Eds.). The Thirteenth Mental Measurements Yearbook (pp. 557-560). Lincoln, NE: The University of Nebraska Press.

Reviewed by

David A. Jepsen

Professor
Division of Counseling, Rehabilitation and Student Development
University of Iowa

Description

The Jackson Personality Inventory-Revised (JPI-R) assesses an array of personality qualities important for a person's current functioning. It is one of several self-report psychological instruments developed by Douglas R. Jackson, including the well-known Personality Research Form and Jackson Vocational Interest Scale, that demonstrate "state-of-the-art" scale development methods and user-friendly manuals. The JPI-R is a 1994 revision of a previously published inventory (Jackson, 1977) retaining the scale structure and scoring, but incorporating contemporary scale development procedures, new scale names, new and broader-based norms, new items for one scale, and the addition of complete item lists in the manual.

The JPI-R contains 300 true-false statements printed in a reusable booklet requiring 35-45 minutes to complete. The author claims that items are written for the high school level. Answer sheets may be scored by machine or by hand. Each scale contains 20 items–10 keyed true and 10 keyed false–and is designed to permit definition of each pole of a bipolar personality dimension with positively worded content. Raw scores are transferred to a male or female profile sheet that allows translation to gender-normed standard scores. Percentile ranks for appropriate norm groups can be obtained from tabled data in the manual.

Use in Counseling

The author specifies that the JPI-R is designed to provide comprehensive personality descriptions for use with normal populations (rather than for diagnoses of pathology), and it may also serve as an aid in career counseling and person-job matches. The JPI-R scores are reported for 15 content scales that have common names such as Breadth of Interest, Cooperativeness, Social Confidence, Risk Taking and Traditional Values. Scale content can be explained easily with the aid of two tables contained in the manual (Jackson, 1994): a table of Trait Descriptions and a table listing all keyed items for each scale. For example, personality traits of high scorers on the Social Confidence scale are described as "Confident in dealing with others, self-assured, composed" and traits for a low scorer are portrayed as one who "Feels awkward among people, self-depreciating, timid." The closer a score is to either end of the scale, the greater the probability the person will demonstrate behavior reflecting the personality trait measured by the scale. The author encourages scale score interpretations that faithfully represent the definitions provided, thus avoiding misunderstandings or guesses about the score meanings.

The 15 scales are organized into five clusters labeled Analytical, Emotional, Extroverted, Opportunistic and Dependable. The Extroverted Cluster, for example, contains three scales: Sociability, Social Confidence, and Energy Level. The Profile Sheet contains scores for the content scales grouped into the five clusters. Jackson argues that the five clusters have content comparable to, if not exactly identical with, the popular Big Five trait cluster (Digman, 1990). Indeed, JPI-R concurrent validity claims are supported by data showing correlations with familiar measures of these five traits, e.g., Personality Research Form (Jackson, 1989); Minnesota Multiphasic Personality Inventory (Hathaway, McKinley & Butcher, 1989), and Jackson Vocational Interest Survey (Jackson, 1977).

Available norms suggest that the JPI-R is best suited for undergraduate college students and selected adult populations. Extrapolation to other groups, such as adults seeking career counseling, seems plausible. High school normative tables (date unspecified) based on an earlier version of the JPI are also reported in the Manual. Comparisons of college norms groups from the 1970s and 1990s suggests considerable norms stability across historical periods. A laudable inclusion not often found in such inventories is the extensive norms tables for an adult "blue-collar" population (629 males and 264 females), primarily people engaged in physical labor such as auto assembly workers, roofers, welders, and machine operators.

The JPI-R will seem like an unfinished instrument for counselors accustomed to translating inventory scores in terms of similarities to occupational groups or personality types. The modal profile analysis studies described in the manual's research section is a start. Jackson provides 10 profiles for each gender based on a sophisticated clustering procedure. If these findings are replicated and extended, users will be able to make broad interpretations about probabilities for behaviors across a wide variety of situations. The advantage of the JPI-R in its present form is that it offers counselors wide-ranging and user-friendly personality descriptions that should provide an easy avenue to rich personal material.

Technical Considerations

The scales were constructed and purified through two empirical item analysis procedures designed to maximize internal consistency reliabilities and interscale independence, and minimize desirability response bias. Data reported in the manual suggest these efforts have been largely successful. The scale scores are approximately normally distributed, having a mean at the center of the scale, i.e., about 10.0. Items selected for the scales had acceptably high item-scale bise-rial correlations, low interscale redundancy, and low correlations with a Desir-ability scale. Two scales were employed to detect unusual or "nonpurposeful responding" among JPI-R takers during inventory development: an Infrequency scale composed of 20 items from across all 15 scales that a general population endorses relatively infrequently (30% or less) and a Response Consistency Index, the within-person correlation between paired half-scores.

Standard scores on the profile sheets are based on 1990s separate gender norms groups equally weighted for college students, blue collar workers, and ex-ecutives. Norms tables are available for gender, life stage (or age surrogate) and occupational groupings, but not for ethnic or cultural groups. The norms group descriptions do not mention either racial or ethnic or cultural composition, thus making score interpretations difficult for JPI-R takers who identify with cultures distinctly different than the presumed majority group.

Most reliability evidence rests on internal consistency estimates from four college student samples (total N=1,691). Both Cronbach's alpha and Bent-ler's theta statistics were used, the latter being more appropriate for some scales, such as Risk Taking, which the author argues are dimensionally complex. Alphas were above .70 for all scales except Tolerance, Social Astuteness, and Responsibility, and thetas were all above .80. Across all scales, the alpha medi-ans ranged from .78 to .82 and the theta medians were .90 and .93, suggesting adequate scale internal consistency. Mean item-total biserial correlations ranged from .47 (Tolerance) to .71 (Innovation), suggesting adequate scale homogeneity. Although these general conclusions give confidence that scale scores are repro-ducible, there are exceptions that merit caution in a scale-by-scale interpretation. For example, Tolerance and Social Astuteness consistently produce the lowest internal consistency and homogeneity estimates.

Concurrent validity data demonstrate that JPI-R scores correlate with scales assessing similar content. Intercorrelations among the 15 scales are gener-ally low and are highest with scales from the same cluster. Principal components factor analysis yielded five solutions (accounting for 65% of the total variance), which were rotated to yield psychologically meaningful factors while including all the scales. The resulting factors match the five clusters described earlier with factor loadings ranging from .48 (Risk Taking on Factor 4, the Opportunistic cluster) to .80 (Sociability on the Extroverted cluster).

Multitrait/multimethod studies established that the JPI-R scales discrimi-nate among the same characteristics as self-rating scales, adjective checklists, and peer ratings by friends and roommates. Nearly all convergent validities showed higher positive values than did the correlations with irrelevant traits. The evi-dence for convergence across methods is convincing, and apparently JPI-R inter-preters can be confident that scores can be related to everyday behavior and personality descriptions. Some scales are less convergent than others across methods. For example, Social Astuteness consistently showed the lowest, and often not statistically significant, correlations across methods, thus raising some questions about how easily content interpretations can be performed. The author discusses difficulties in identifying appropriate Social Astuteness adjectives that would yield high correlations for self and peer ratings; the same difficulty may arise during scale score interpretations.

The scales were constructed to suppress socially desirable response biases and the results from two faking studies support the conclusion that people instructed to make a particular impression score about the same as those not so instructed.

Overall Critique

The Jackson Personality Inventory-Revised is one of the best standardized inventories available for providing well-defined, multidimensional personality descriptions. By using the personality trait descriptions, the comparable adjectives and the items themselves, a user can construct elaborate personality descriptions and thus stimulate discussions about typical everyday events and behaviors, such as career decisions and adaptation to work settings.

Users are cautioned about interpretations with nonmajority students or clients because there are no appropriate norms groups. Further caution should be exercised with a few scales because evidence of reliability and validity is less convincing than for other scales. Despite these few limitations, the JPI-R offers a useful tool for describing everyday functioning in varied and stimulating terms.

Contemporary work world complexity and the everyday problems it presents may best be addressed by helping people consider changing work tasks, groups and settings rather than occupational titles and their relatively fixed implications. The JPI-R can be used in career assessment to identify general personality qualities that are important across settings, groups and tasks.

References

Digman, J. M. (1990). Personality structure: Emergence of the five-factor model *Annual Review of Psychology, 41*, 417-440.

Hathaway, S. R., McKinley, J. C., & Butcher, J. N. (1989). *Minnesota Multiphasic Personality Inventory II, user's guide.*

Jackson, D. N. (1977). *Jackson Vocational Interest Survey manual.* Port Huron, MI: Sigma Assessment Systems.

Jackson, D. N. (1994). *Jackson Personality Inventory – Revised manual.* Port Huron, MI: Sigma Assessment Systems.

Jackson, D. N. (1989). *Personality Research Form manual* (3rd ed.). Port Huron, MI: Sigma Assessment Systems.

Myers-Briggs Type Indicator® (MBTI®)

Isabel Briggs Myers and Katherine C. Briggs
Consulting Psychologists Press, Inc.
3803 E. Bayshore Road
Palo Alto, CA 94303
www.cpp-db.com

Target Population: 14 years and up.

Statement of the Purpose of the Instrument: The MBTI® instrument helps counselor/career professionals/ consultants improve work and professional relationships, increase productivity, and identify leadership and interpersonal communication preferences for clients.

Titles of Subtests, Scales, Scores Provided: Extraversion-Introversion, Sensing-Intuition, Thinking-Feeling, Judging-Perceiving.

Forms and Levels Available, with Dates of Publication/Revision of Each: Self-Scorable (1998), Prepaid Profile and Interpretive answer sheets (1998), Interpretive Report for Organizations answer sheet (1998), Team Report Answer Sheet (1998), Career Report Answer Sheet (1998), MBTI® Step II Profile and Expanded Interpretive answer sheets, Strong and MBTI® Career Report answer sheets, Leadership Report Using FIRO-B™ and MBTI® answer sheet (1998).

Date of Most Recent Edition of Test Manual, User's Guide, Etc.: 1998 MBTI® Manual, Third Edition.

Languages in Which Available: English, Spanish, German, French, Dutch, French Canadian, Italian, Korean, Portuguese, Danish, Norwegian, Chinese, Swedish, Anglicized adaptation.

Time: Actual Test Time: 15-25 minutes.
          Total Administration Time: 15-25 minutes.

Norm Group(s) on Which Scores Are Based: 3,200 adults 18 years and older from across the US. Percentages of age, gender, and ethnic group matched 1990 US census percentage.

Manner in Which Results Are Reported for Individuals:
   Types of Scores: Verbal labels, standard scores.
   Report Format/Content:
      Basic Service: Self-Scorable booklet or mail-in Profile and/or Interpretive report.
      Options: Interpretive Report for organizations, Team Report, Career Report, Expanded Interpretive (Step II), Leadership Report with FIRO-B™, Career Report with Strong, Entrepreneur Report with Strong.

Report Format/Content for Group Summaries:
   Basic Service: MBTI Team Report.

Scoring
Machine Scoring Service: Mail-in, Scoring Software, Network Software, Web Accessible via CPP software.
   Cost of basic service per counselee: $5.60
   Cost of options: $7.50-$14 depending on report
   Time required for scoring and returning (maximum): Mail-in: 48 hours plus mail; Software: immediate.
Hand Scoring:
   Scored by: Counselee; Clerk; Counselor.
   Time required for scoring: 10 minutes.
Local Machine Scoring
   Provisions/conditions/equipment required: CPP software system, Web administration on-site—PC only, Windows 95, 98, or Windows NT 4.0, 20 MB free hard disk space.

Computer Software Options Available: Computerized adaptive administration; standard administration online; Internet service via career professionals website.

Ways in Which Computer Version Differs: None.

Cost of Materials:
   Specimen Set: $12.75.
   Counselee Materials: Form Self-Scorable $5; Introduction to Type and College $4.80; Introduction to Type $4.50; Introduction to Type and Careers $5.90; Introduction to Type in Organizations $6.50; Introduction to Type and Teams $7.20.

Additional Comments of Interest to Users: The MBTI assessment tool was revised in 1998. The new Form M is the most current form of the instrument.

Published Reviews:
Thompson, B. & Ackerman, C. M. (1994). Review of the Myers-Briggs Type Indicator.
   In J. T. Kapes, M. M. Mastie & E. A. Whitfield (Eds.). *A counselor's guide to career assessment instruments* (3rd ed.). Alexandria, VA: National Career Development Association.
Wiggins, J. S. (1989). Review of the Myers-Briggs Type Indicator. In J. C. Conoleyr &
   J. J. Kramer (Eds.), *The tenth mental measurements yearbook* (pp. 537-539). Lincoln, NE: Buros Institute, University of Nebraska-Lincoln.

Reviewed by

Charles C. Healy
Professor of Education
University of California, Los Angeles

Description

A revised, improved version of the Myers-Briggs Type Indicator (MBTI) and its manual were released in 1998. The MBTI continues to focus on selected

Jungian (1971) concepts as modified by its authors to gauge people's preferred ways of perceiving, judging, and directing their energies both outwardly and inwardly. Responses to the 93 forced-choice items in the new Form M are all scored to categorize a person as one or the other pole of four, relatively independent bipolar scales: Extraverted-Introverted (E-I), Sensing-iNtuition (S-N), Thinking-Feeling (T-F), and Judging-Perceiving (J-P). Each pole is termed a preference. In Form M, male and female responses to the T-F items are not weighted differently as they are in earlier forms, but still many more women than men score in the Feeling direction.

Unlike scores from most other inventories, the scores from the four MBTI scales are grouped into sets of four, termed types. Each preference on a scale is combined with every preference of the other three scales, yielding 16 types. A respondent is assigned the type that has his or her four preferences. Respondents receive their four scale scores and their type score. The manual and accompanying interpretive materials emphasize the type interpretations, but provide considerable information about the meanings of individual preference scores.

Type descriptions are summaries of key, positively worded elements from the scales comprising them. Theoretically, scales in a type interact and that interaction modifies their meaning. In addition, the interpretation of the S-N and T-F scales depend in part on whether they are favored by the person in dealing with the external world, that is, whether they are or are not dominant. As a consequence, the key descriptors of a scale vary somewhat over the four types of which it is an element. For example, thinking (T) is described as "practical and analytical, focused on facts" when paired with sensing (S) and as "logical and analytical, focused on possibilities" when paired with iNtuition (N).

Use in Counseling

Designed for use in training and counseling, the MBTI is one of the most frequently used personality inventories, selling more than two million copies a year. Counselors report that its positive, everyday scale and type descriptions help them to engage clients in affirming self-understanding, exploring educational and career choices, and improving communication at work and in relationships. The manual provides many suggestions from practice of how knowledge of preferences might aid clients in such areas.

The authors repeatedly remind users that the MBTI results are descriptions, not prescriptions. Preference scores are intended to suggest factors to consider in decision making and interactions with others. Despite substantial improvements in the MBTI, users need to remember that many of the suggested uses, although more explicit and better illustrated, have not been tested experimentally. As such those suggestions need to be recognized as hypotheses to be tested. This is especially the case if the MBTI is to be substituted for other measures for purposes such as selecting college majors or occupations or improving communication. For example, in a comparison of the ability of interest inventory and MBTI scores to distinguish the subfield preferences of MBA students, Martin and Bartol (1986) found the interest inventory, but not the MBTI scores, to be effective. Relatedly, in a comparison of the ability of the S-N scores and relationship resource scores to account for differences in the quality of couples' communication, Kobes and Lichtenberg (1997) found that relationship resource scores, but not S-N preferences, accounted for differences.

The manual emphasizes the importance of clients' agreement about their MBTI scores in its interpretation. It provides guides to use in verifying client agreement and suggests that most respondents agree with their four preferences and a majority with their type. One can expect clients to give more credence to suggestions emanating from preferences with which they agree. As a consequence, counselors will want to secure independent judgments from clients. Also, new Preference Clarity Categories of "slight," "moderate," "clear," and "very clear" for each preference based on the proximity of a score to its scale's midpoint indicate the portion of a preference's items chosen by the respondent. "Slight" and "moderate" preferences are more likely than the "clear" and "very clear" preferences to change upon retest. When either preference agreement or clarity is low, the authors appropriately advise caution in interpretation.

Although positive aspects of each preference are emphasized, the authors allow that there may be deficits associated with each preference and list typical work stressors for each. Findings by Healy and Woodward (1998) that particular MBTI preferences and their interactions relate to some career development obstacles support a preference-deficit linkage and suggest exploring the typical stressors of a client's preferences to identify possible counseling needs.

Technical Considerations

The MBTI has stirred substantial controversy. Researchers question such features as interpreting individual scales as bipolar categories rather than as a continuous dimension, modifying scale interpretations based upon the type of which they are a member, and also modifying interpretation depending upon whether S, N, T, or F is deemed to be a dominant function. And, although research indicates that the MBTI samples the domains of four of the Big Five Personality Factors, McCrae and Costa (1989) contend that MBTI scale descriptions need to be changed to be consistent with the relationships which MBTI scales have shown with scales of other personality measures.

The revised MBTI Form M and the third edition of its manual are likely to encourage continued use of the MBTI and lessen, but not eliminate, criticisms. The manual provides a clear description of the rationale guiding item selection and summarizes findings from a confirmatory factor analysis that support a four-factor solution corresponding to the four MBTI scales. The manual reports that Form M scores correlate very highly with corresponding scale scores of the earlier Form G. For a sample of 101 adults who completed Forms M and G at the same time, scale correlations ranged from .87 to .90, percentage of agreement on preferences ranged from 79% to 90%, and there was 60% agreement on type classification.

The Item Response Theory (IRT) that guided item selection increased scale reliability and maximized discrimination near the midpoints of the four scales. Internal consistency estimates for the national sample of men and women combined were high, ranging from .90 to .92. The manual also reported high test-retest coefficients for the scale scores from three samples, ranging from .83 to .95, and 55% to 80% of the people in these samples were categorized the same type on retest. Comparisons of scores from Form M and G, moreover, indicate that Form M is less likely to yield a preference or type score with which a respondent disagrees. Nevertheless, the controversy over whether the scales are measuring bipolar or continuous variables is likely to persist. In part, this is because the validity of the preferences is based upon their relation to other personality traits that have normal distributions instead of bimodal distributions, and the evidence for those relationships comes from studies that almost always employ continuous MBTI scores.

Especially pertinent because of past criticisms are summaries in the manual of results of multiple tests of the claim that types are more than the sums of their parts. Essentially, these studies show that in many instances considering some hypothesized scale interactions increases predicted variance in particular criteria beyond what would be accounted for if one considered only the effects of the scales. Also in some, but not all instances, considering whether the S, N, T, or F functions are dominant increases variance accounted for in particular criteria. Although these findings do not always support type interpretations, they strengthen the argument for using type interpretations. The willingness of the authors to undertake such tests on their standardization sample and to share their findings is certainly commendable.

Computer-Based Version

Form M can be taken and scored on the computer using software licensed by the publisher. Booklets can be either computer or hand scored. Computer scoring of Form M yields IRT-weighted scores; hand scoring yields scores that closely approximate them. The authors report very high degrees of agreement between computer and hand scoring for the eight preference scores, ranging from 94% to 99%. Agreement on type classification is not reported. Continuous MBTI scores are now available, however, only through computer scoring.

Overall Critique

In summary, the 1998 MBTI provides clear, reliable information about a person's preferences that many counselors and clients feel has been helpful. Improvements in the 1998 edition increase the likelihood that it will yield meaningful information. With proper interpretation it can provide useful hypotheses for counselors and their clients to evaluate. As long as counselors are aware of the criticisms cited in the literature, the MBTI is likely to be a useful career counseling tool.

References

Healy, C. C. & Woodward, G. A. (1998). The Myers-Briggs Type Indicator and career obstacles. *Measurement and Evaluation in Counseling and Development, 31*, 74-85.

Jung, C. G. (1971). *Psychological types* (H.G. Baynes, Trans., revised by R. F. C. Hall), Princeton: Princeton University Press. (Original work published 1923.)

Kobes, K. J. & Lichtenberg, J. W. (1997). *Personality similarity, interpersonal perception, and relationship satisfaction.* Paper presented at the annual meeting of the American Educational Research Association, Chicago, IL. (ERIC Document Reproduction Service No. ED 423 453).

Martin, D. C. & Bartol, K. M. (1986). Holland's Vocational Preference Inventory and the Myers-Briggs Type Indicator as predictors of vocational choice among Master's of Business Administration. *Journal of Vocational Behavior, 29*, 51-65.

McCrae, R. R. & Costa, P. T. (1989). Reinterpreting the Myers-Briggs Type Indicator from the perspective of the five-factor model of personality. *Journal of Personality, 57*, 17-40.

Sixteen Personality Factor (16PF®)[1] Questionnaire

Raymond B. Cattell, A. Karen S. Cattell,
and Heather E.P. Cattell
Institute for Personality and Ability Testing, Inc.
P.O. Box 1188
Champaign, IL 61824-1188
www.ipat.com
jes@ipat.com

Target Population: Sixteen-year-olds and older adults.

Statement of the Purpose of the Instrument: Measures the entire domain of normal range personality.

Titles of Subtests, Scales, Scores Provided: 5 Global Factors: Extraversion, Anxiety, Tough-Mindedness, Independence, Self-Control. 16 Primary Factors: Warmth, Reasoning, Emotional Stability, Dominance. Liveliness, Rule-Consciousness, Social Boldness, Sensitivity, Vigilance, Abstractedness, Privateness, Apprehension, Openness to Change, Self-Reliance, Perfectionism, Tension. Composite scores for Creativity, Adjustment, and numerous other criterion-related scales are also available.

Forms and Levels Available, with Dates of Publication/Revision of Each: 16PF® Fifth Edition© 1993 – One Form; 16PF® Fourth Edition© 1967-1969 – Forms A, B, C, D, and E.

Date of Most Recent Edition of Test Manual, User's Guide, Etc.: 1994.

Languages in Which Available: About 35 languages in addition to English.

Time: Actual Test Time: Untimed.
      Total Administration Time: 35-40 minutes.

Norm Group(s) on Which Scores Are Based: General population adult norms, sexes separate and combined, representative of 1990 census.

Manner in Which Results Are Reported for Individuals
    Types of Scores: Sten scores – mean of 5.5, standard deviation of 2, Range 1-10.
    Report Format/Content: 1. *Basic Score Report (BSR)*: 5 global factors, 16 primary scales, and criterion scores and validity indices. Graphs included. 2. *Basic Interpretive Report*: same as BSR and includes narrative interpretation. 3. *Personal Career Development Profile Plus*: Same as BSR plus career interest scores and 125 occupational interest scores and self-

---

[1] "16PF" is a registered trademark of the Institute for Personality and Ability Testing Inc.

review and planning exercises. This report also includes a section that can be handed back to the test-taker, which could be useful in a counseling situation.

Report Format/Content for Group Summaries: 1. Average sten scores with means and standard deviations for 5 global factors and 16 primary scales; 2. Group frequency data graphed; 3. Profiles of each counselee; 4. Data disk.

Scoring

    Machine Scoring Service: Cost of service may vary with the number purchased at one time. Costs below assume that 10 or more report certificates are ordered at the same time.
    Cost of basic service per counselee: Basic Score Report price - $7.50 each; Basic Interpretive Report price - $12 each; Personal Career Development Profile Plus price - $20 each.
    Cost of options: Data Summary Report – Average price - $4.60 each
    Hand Scoring:
    Scored by: Clerk.
    Time required for scoring: Minutes.
    Local Machine Scoring:
    Provisions/conditions/equipment required: (1) IBM compatible plus leased hardware key (dongle). Unit use metered (OnSite system). (2) OnFax system gives automated scoring and reporting via fax.

Computer Software Options Available: Standard administration online.
Other: Global Factor Pattern Interpretation-Unlimited use for interpretation only, no scoring.

Ways in Which Computer Version Differs: Print format and stationary only. Content identical. Prices for OnSite are the same as listed above. Price for Global Factor Pattern Interpretation Program-$195.

Cost of Materials: 16PF® Fifth Edition Complete Set-$107 Includes: Manual, test, scoring keys and profile sheets for 25 counselees plus one BIR score report.
    Specimen Set: 16PF® Fifth Edition Trial Packet - $46 Includes: Manual, test, answer sheet, and BIR score report.
    Counselee Materials: single use free trial packets (without manual) available at no charge. One to a customer, please. Reusable questionnaires-$15/10; Answer Sheets-$12.50/25; Individual Record Forms-$8/25.

Published Reviews:
Cattell, H. E. P., & IPAT Staff, (in press). The Sixteen Personality Factor Questionnaire. In W. Dorfman and M. Herson (Eds.), *Understanding psychological assessment: A manual for counselors and clinicians.* New York, NY: Plenum Publishing Corp.
Cattell, H. E. P., Mead, A. D. & Cattell, R. B. (in press). The Sixteen Factor Personality Questionnaire. In S.R. Briggs, J. M. Cheek & E. M. Donahue (Eds.), *Handbook of adult personality inventories.* New York, NY: Plenum Publishing Corp.
McLellan, J. J. (1995). Review of the Sixteen Personality Factor Questionnaire, Fifth Edition. In J. C. Conoley and J. C. Impara (Eds.), *The twelfth mental measurements yearbook.* Lincoln, NE: The Buros Institute, University of Nebraska-Lincoln.
Rotto, P. C. (1995). Review of the Sixteen Personality Factor Questionnaire, Fifth Edition. In J. C. Conoley and J. C. Impara (Eds.), *The twelfth mental measurements yearbook.* Lincoln, NE: The Buros Institute, University of Nebraska-Lincoln.

Schuerger, J. M. (1995). Career assessment and the Sixteen Personality Factor Questionnaire. *Journal of Career Assessment, 3,* 157-175.

Reviewed by

Timothy R. Vansickle
Vice President
Riverside Publishing

Description

The 16PF Personal Career Development Profile (PCDP) and 16PF Personal Career Development Profile *Plus* (PCDP *Plus*) are expert reports based on more than 30 years of consulting experience by Dr. Verne Walter. His experience in consulting, using the various forms of the Sixteen Personality Factor Questionnaire has been translated into a report that is generated from an individual's responses to the 185-item 16PF Fifth Edition questionnaire. This interpretive report must be generated via computer. The PCDP may be generated in its original 1995 format (continuous revision of this format has occurred since 1978) or the user may select the 1997 "option plus" report. Both reports provide similar information and when the reports differ, these will be noted.

The 16PF Fifth Edition is the latest version of the venerable Sixteen Personality Factor Questionnaire (16PF). Originally developed by Raymond B. Cattell almost half a century ago, the test was revised and updated in 1994 (Conn & Rieke, 1994; Walter, 1995).

The new edition, like previous editions, is designed to measure normal personality traits (Conn & Rieke, 1994; Russell & Karol, 1994). The 16PF Fifth Edition reports 16 primary personality factors, five global personality factors (i.e., second-order factors), and three response indices (i.e., validity scales). The 21 factor scores are reported as sten scores or standard tens (Conn & Rieke, 1994). The 16 primary factors include Warmth (A), Reasoning (B), Emotional Stability (C), Dominance (E), Liveliness (F), Rule-Consciousness (G), Social Boldness (H), Sensitivity (I), Vigilance (L), Abstractedness (M), Privateness (N), Apprehension (O), Openness to Change (Q1), Self-Reliance (Q2), Perfectionism (Q3), and Tension (Q4). The five global factors include Extraversion (EX), Anxiety (AX), Tough-Mindedness (TM), Independence (IN), and Self-Control (SC) (Conn & Rieke, 1994; Russell & Karol, 1994; Walter, 1995). The global factors are closely aligned to the big five personality factors that have emerged in the personality literature. Most of the items in the 16PF Fifth Edition have the following format: endorse, do not endorse, or cannot decide. Fifteen items have best answers and are located at the end of the instrument. These 15 items make up the Reasoning (B) factor. It is important to note that these scales are bipolar and that there is not a "best" score to be obtained except possibly for the Reasoning (B) factor.

In the previous editions of the PCDP, the 16 primary factors were used to estimate Holland's (1985) six types (Realistic, Investigative, Artistic, Social, Enterprising, and Conventional). With the release of the current PCDP, the 16 primary factors are used to estimate the seven personality orientations from the Campbell Interest and Skill Survey (CISS) (Campbell, Hyne, & Nilsen, 1992). The seven personality orientations include Influencing, Organizing, Helping, Creating, Analyzing, Producing, and Adventuring. The last personality orientation (adventuring) is called Venturing in the PCDP reports. It is apparent that there is a strong relationship between the six Holland types and the seven personality orientations. Producing and Adventuring are both highly related to the Realistic type in Holland's theory (Walter, 1995).

The PCDP uses empirical and rational weights applied to combinations of the primary factors to produce an estimated score for the CISS personality orientations. For example, the significant factors related to the CISS Influencing orientation include Warmth (A), Reasoning (B), Dominance (E), Social Boldness (H), Vigilance (L), Apprehension (O), and Openness to Change (Q1). All except Apprehension are positively weighted. The various combinations of factors for the estimated scales were determined by regression analysis. In addition to the seven personality orientations, the PCDP estimates 20 of the 29 CISS Career Field Interests and 58 of the Occupational Scales.

The PCDP also estimates the Response-to-Power-Measure role patterns (Sweaney, 1977). These patterns include Leadership Role (Authoritarian, Participate, and Permissive), Subordinate Role (Ingratiator, Cooperator, and Free-Thinker), Interaction Role (Confrontive, Controlling, Objective, and Supportive), and Effective Leadership. Several other estimated scales are produced including three adjustment scales, a creativity index, elected leadership, and interest for formal educational pursuits.

The PCDP *Plus* adds to the already long list of estimated scales by including scores for 69 female occupation scales and 66 male occupational scales from the Strong Interest Inventory (SII) (Harmon, Hansen, Borgen, & Hammer, 1994). The author made assignments of those occupational scales found under the Realistic type of the SII to either the Producing or Venturing scales based on expert knowledge of careers. Hence, the PCDP *Plus* provides additional exploratory career information to the client and the counselor. At the time of this review, both the PCDP and the PCDP *Plus* versions were available; however, the PCDP *Plus* version will become the standard report option.

Use in Counseling

The PCDP and PCDP *Plus* are designed to help individuals integrate their strengths into their career planning process. The basic premise of the PCDP is that, although people know their strengths, they are seldom integrated in a way to help them function well in the world of work. An outgrowth of more then 30 years of personnel consulting, the PCDP provides insights into a person's strength patterns, career interests, and need for personal growth. Additionally, the PCDP is intended for use by professional management consultants, career counselors, human resource managers, and other decision makers by providing ready-made interpretive reports. These reports ease the often difficult and time-consuming aspects of interpreting such a large number of scales and estimated scores.

Ideally, the PCDP and PCDP *Plus* are intended to aid in the selection and placement of individuals. Hence, hiring authorities have a standardized method of making decisions about how individuals will function given various aspects of the job such as leadership, occupational interests, and general problem-solving ability. It is also intended to help employees discover hidden talents and to direct these employees to training and development experiences that will lead to greater career satisfaction and progress.

The PCDP and PCDP *Plus* have also been used to help students choose a course of study. It provides a lengthy list of occupational choices to aid in the career exploration of young adults.

Technical Considerations

The 16PF Fifth Edition is designed to be administered to individuals 16 and over (McLellan, 1995). It is a measure of normal personality development and status. The scales are homogenous groups of 11 to 15 items for each of the 16 primary factors. These scales were developed by combining those items from the item pool that had the highest factor loadings with its own item group, or bundle (Conn & Rieke, 1994) into a scale for a specific factor. The global factors were developed by factor analyzing the 16 primary factor scores. Hence, the global factors have many more items associated with those scores. However, the global factor scores are not computed from the item responses, but rather from factor loadings applied to the 16 primary factor scores.

The 16PF Fifth Edition consists of one form that was developed using a stratified sample for gender, race, age, and educational background (Carrington-Rotto, 1995). With respect to the normative sample, education level is somewhat higher than that of the 1990 U.S. Census. In addition, adults older that 54 were underrepresented in the norm sample, which included 2,500 individuals randomly sampled from over 4,400 individuals who took the final experimental form of the 16PF Fifth Edition.

Reliability estimates for the global factors are somewhat higher than those for the 16 primary factors. Two-week test-retest reliabilities for the global factors range from .84 to .91 (McLellan, 1995). The primary factor reliabilities for the same two-week interval ranged from .68 to .87. As one would expect, the reliabilities decrease slightly as the test-retest interval increases. The internal consistency for all factors using Cronbach's alpha range from .64 to .85 (Conn & Rieke, 1994). No reliability estimates are given for the estimated scores produced in the PCDP reports.

Validity of the PCDP report has been established primarily through clinical and expert judgment of the author and other practitioners. The only evidence of validity found in the various PCDP manuals is the regression analysis conducted for producing the estimated scale scores. Reported Multiple Rs, for the estimated scales, range from .33 to .75 and cross-validated Multiple Rs range from .28 to .73. Squaring the Multiple R provides an estimate of the variance accounted for in the estimated scale score. For example, $.33^2 = .109$ or about 11 percent of the variance is accounted for in the model. Validity of the underlying assessment, the 16PF Fifth Edition, has been established at the construct level by comparing the current edition with the 16PF Fourth (Form A). In this approach, the factor structure was replicated for the global factors. Correlations range from .65 to .81 for these factors. The results generally supported the factor structure of the 16PF Fifth Edition. The construct validity of the 16PF Fifth Edition was also investigated by looking at other instruments, including the Personality Research Form E (PRF), Myers-Briggs Type Indicator (MBTI), California Psychological Inventory (CPI), and NEO Personality Inventory-Revised. Lastly, the validity of the 16PF and the PCDP reports have been established through empirical studies using various occupational groups (e.g., sales persons) and through the expert judgments of various clinicians and consultants. Ultimately, the validity of this or any assessment involves the use of the scores by the practitioner.

Computer-Based Version

The 16PF Fifth Edition is available via the Onsite System Software. Onsite provides a local option for administration, scoring, and reporting of the 16PF as well as other assessments published by IPAT. The software runs on any IBM-compatible personal computer and includes a Windows version. No comparability information between the computer-based and paper-pencil administration was found in the literature.

As this review was being finalized, the 16PF Fifth Edition also became available via the Internet. Called NetAssess, the service offered by the publisher provides a scoring and report generation option available 24 hours a day, 365 days a year, that delivers the requested interpretive report via e-mail. A number of 16PF reports are available through this service. No evidence as to the equivalency of this mode of assessment to either the paper-pencil mode or to the stand-alone computer-based 16PF was available at the time of this review.

Overall Critique

The PCDP reports produce a large number of scales that must be understood and integrated to use effectively. This is true for both the client and the counselor. The literature on the various versions of the Sixteen Personality Questionnaire (16PF) is quite extensive and the reader is urged to review this literature to understand the nature and the controversy of reporting such a large number of personality factors. Interpreting the large number of scale scores can be daunting, thus making computer-generated reports indispensable.

The 16PF Fifth Edition and the resulting PCDP reports can be one more tool in the counselor's tool chest. However, as others have pointed out (Olson & Matlock, 1994) the assumption that personality traits are most powerful in career choice has not yet been proven. Instruments that measure vocational interest (e.g., Self-Directed Search, Campbell Interest and Skills Survey, Strong Interest Inventory, Unisex Edition of the ACT Interest Inventory, and many others) should remain a staple used by practitioners when helping individuals explore career options. There are a limited number of career or occupational profiles available for the 16PF Fifth Edition and hence there is not an easy-to-use process for matching a person's personality profile with an occupation. Additionally, all reports rely on the 16 primary factors for creating all of the estimated scores, which in turn, produce the interpretive paragraphs the client and counselor receive. The reliabilities of these factors are somewhat lower than that of the global factors. This fact should be taken into account when working through the report with clients. Predictive statements about future behavior or job success should be avoided or at least made in terms of the standard error of measurement.

Finally, it appears to be most appropriate to assess a person's abilities, interests, values, and personality to get a complete picture of the individual. This information should be integrated by the both the client and the counselor as part of the career exploration and career choice process. Some practitioners recommend an order for administration of these different assessments (e.g., interests, abilities, values, and personality). However, it may be that obtaining and working through all of the information as part of the career exploration process is of most value to the client. The 16PF Fifth Edition and the associated PCDP reports can provide a substantial amount of information to aid the career exploration process.

References

Campbell, D., Hyne, S. A., & Nilsen, D. L. (1992). *Campbell Interest and Skills Survey*, Minneapolis, MN: National Computer Systems.

Carrington-Rotto, P. (1995). Review of the Sixteen Personality Factor Question-naire, Fifth Edition. In J. Conoley & J. C. Impara (Eds.), *Twelfth mental measurements yearbook* (pp. 948-949). Lincoln, NE: Buros Institute, University of Nebraska-Lincoln.

Conn, S. R. & Rieke, M. L. (1994). *16PF Fifth Edition technical manual.* Champaign, IL: Institute for Personality and Ability Testing.

Harmon, L. W., Hansen, J. C., Borgen, F. H., & Hammer, A. L. (1994). *Strong Interest Inventory applications and technical manual.* Palo Alto, CA: Consulting Psychologists Press, Inc.

Holland, J. L. (1985). *Making vocational choices: A theory of careers.* Englewood Cliffs, NJ: Prentice-Hall.

McLellan, M. J. (1995). Review of the Sixteen Personality Factor Questionnaire, Fifth Edition. In J. C. Conoley & J. C. Impara (Ed.), *Twelfth mental measurements yearbook* (pp. 947-948). Lincoln, NE: Buros Institute, University of Nebraska-Lincoln.

Olson, G. T. & Matlock, S. G. (1994). Review of the Sixteen PF Personal Career Development Profile. In J. T. Kapes, M. M. Mastie, & E. A. Whitfield (Eds.), *A Counselor's Guide to Career Assessment Instruments*, (3rd ed., pp. 302-305). Alexandria, VA: National Career Development Association.

Russell, M. T. & Karol, D. (1994). *16PF Fifth Edition administrator's manual.* Champaign, IL: Institute for Personality and Ability Testing.

Sweaney, A. B. (1977). *Handbook: Response to power measure.* Witchita, KS: Test Systems, Inc.

Walter, V. (1995). *16PF Personal Career Development Profile: Technical and interpretive manual.* Champaign, IL: Institute for Personality and Ability Testing.

Student Styles Questionnaire (SSQ)

Thomas Oakland, Joseph Glutting, and Connie Horton
The Psychological Corporation
A Harcourt Assessment Company
555 Academic Court
San Antonio, TX 78204-2498
www.psychcorp.com

Target Population: Grades 3-12, ages 8-17.

Statement of the Purpose of the Instrument: Measures learning, relating, and working styles of students.

Titles of Subtests, Scales, Scores Provided: Extroverted/Introverted, Thinking/Feeling, Practical/Imaginative, Organized/Flexible.

Forms and Levels Available, with Dates of Publication/Revision of Each: 1 form (1996).

Date of Most Recent Edition of Test Manual, User's Guide, Etc.: Manual (1996); Classroom Applications Booklet (1996).

Languages in Which Available: English only.

Time: Actual Test Time: Untimed.
        Total Administration Time: Can be completed in less than 30 minutes.

Norm Group(s) on Which Scores Are Based: Approximately 8,000 students in standardization sample; stratified by age, sex, race/ethnicity, geographic region, and school type.

Manner in Which Results Are Reported for Individuals:
    Types of Scores: Prevalence-based T scores.
    Report Format/Content: The professional report sections include General Description; Personal Styles—Important Beliefs, Social Factors, Family Factors, Educational Styles—Attitudes Toward School, Relationships with Teachers, Relationships with Classmates, Learning Styles, Instructional Styles, Curriculum Content; Occupational Styles; Room for Growth; Summary.

Report Format/Content for Group Summaries: Not available.

Scoring
    Machine Scoring Service: Not available.
    Hand Scoring:
        Scored by: Clerk; Counselor.
    Local Machine Scoring:
        Provisions/conditions/equipment required: Record Forms, Windows® Kit.

Computer Software Options Available: Not available.

Cost of materials: Prices valid through 2001.
    Specimen Set: Complete kit $91.
    Counselee Materials:
    Question Booklets, pkg/25– $62. (reusable).
    Ready Score Answer Documents, pkg/25–$33.
    Manual $70.
    Windows Kit for local machine scoring $104.
    Classroom Applications Booklet $21 (reusable).

Published Reviews: None cited.

Reviewed by

James Rounds
Professor of Educational Psychology and Psychology

Molly C. McKenna
Doctoral Candidate

Department of Educational Psychology
University of Illinois at Urbana-Champaign

Description

The Student Styles Questionnaire (SSQ) is a relatively new measure constructed in the spirit of the Myers-Briggs Type Indicator (MBTI). Where the MBTI is targeted toward older adolescents and adults, the SSQ was designed specifically for children aged 8-17. In development, rather than simply modifying the MBTI for a younger audience, the authors undertook a rigorous standardization of a new instrument, using data from more than 14,000 students in construction and validation. Nevertheless, the SSQ retains, with relatively few modifications, many of the qualities of the MBTI, seeking primarily to expand its use into the classroom for a younger population.

The SSQ was designed, like the MBTI, to reflect normal temperament and individual differences. As stated in the manual, the measure is intended to "identify the ways students prefer to gain energy and direction, gather and integrate information, make decisions, and generally orient their lives" (Oakland, Gutting, & Horton, 1996, p. 1). The SSQ was developed to reflect the same set of Jungian temperaments represented by the MBTI, but the manual devotes little time to linking the measure directly to Jungian theory. The test is designed to assess temperament, learning, and personal styles by measuring preferences for what are termed eight well-established styles. These eight styles are arranged into four bipolar scales; Extroverted-Introverted (E-I), Practical-Imaginative (P-M), Thinking-Feeling (T-F), and Organized-Flexible (O-L). Scores are computed by summing total points for each pole of the dimension, and then selecting the pole with highest total as the preferred style. Interpretation and classification can either be based on preferences for individual styles, four combinations of style preferences (based on scores for P-M and O-L), or the 16 combinations resulting from linking all four preferred styles.

The SSQ consists of 69 items. On each item, respondents are forced to choose one of two statements; the two statements represent opposite preferences on the scale to which the item belongs. The instrument is written at a third-grade reading level, and can be administered individually or in groups. The SSQ is untimed, and most individuals complete the measure in approximately 30 minutes. Scoring is completed by a teacher or other adult, and detailed instructions are on each answer form. Computerized scoring and interpretive software is available, though written responses must be keyed in.

Use in Counseling

The SSQ is predominantly aimed at teachers or other school personnel seeking an additional source of information about a particular student's preferences. The authors recommend that the results of the SSQ be integrated with other sources of information about a particular child. They do not seem to advocate discussing test results directly with children or labeling or categorizing children by their types; rather, they imply that the instrument is best used as a tool for understanding a child's behavior as a reflection of his or her preferences.

Specifically, the authors of the SSQ suggest that the measure can be used to identify aptitudes, compensate for weak areas, promote personal and interpersonal development, enhance understanding of others, provide information about learning styles, promote educational development through customizing instruction and explaining problem behaviors, and explore vocational aspirations. Indeed, the technical portion of the manual provides several tables that identify correlational patterns between preferred styles and vocations, class subjects, activities, and involvement in special programs.

All of these uses proceed from the identification of a child's style preferences. Armed with an understanding of the situations in which a child is most comfortable, the environments which are easiest for him or her to navigate, and the ways a child prefers to gain and process information, instructors and administrators can more appropriately design educational plans for individual children. The authors of the test also suggest that the SSQ is suitable for research and evaluation, including longitudinal study.

Technical Considerations

As mentioned previously, the SSQ has been administered to over 14,000 children and adolescents in development and validation. The standardization sample has clearly been modeled after the WISC-III, using a stratified design to assemble a normative base of 8-17 year olds. Therefore, the normative sample has been carefully organized to be representative of age, gender, race/ethnicity, geographic region, and school type. The manual contains extensive information on the SSQ's psychometric properties based on this sizable sample.

Test-retest reliability of scale scores over seven months was computed using a sample of 137 participants representing the full age range for which the SSQ is intended. The reliability coefficients range from .67 to .80, averaging .74, indicating satisfactory stability of SSQ scale scores. The authors also include information on confidence limits for SSQ standard scale scores; the 90% confidence interval for most scales ranges from ± 7.38 to ± 9.48.

Evidence of internal validity of scale scores is offered in the form of factor analyses, including parcel analysis (clustering of items for factoring), which the authors argue is necessary due to the dichotomous format of the items. Tables show factor loadings using both item scores and parcel scores, and indicate that a four-factor structure (E-I, P-M, T-F, O-L) results in appreciably high loadings for all items on their intended factors. The parcel analyses were repeated across three age groups, with similar results. Correlations between the four scales revealed the highest correlation was between the Practical-Imaginative scale and the Organized-Flexible scale ($r = .24$), demonstrating that a score on one scale is relatively independent of scores on the other scales.

In establishing external validity, the authors of the SSQ focused heavily on contrasting groups to examine relationships between preferred styles and vocational preferences, subject preferences, activity preferences, special program involvement, and self-evaluation. This is, at best, a preliminary method for establishing validity. In general, these analyses revealed that individuals scoring high on particular styles tended to like activities congruent with that style, confirming the theoretical basis of the SSQ. Convergent and discriminate validity were also examined, comparing SSQ style scores with inventories assessing children's values, temperament as measured by the MBTI, achievement scores, and intellectual ability. Results from these analyses showed that style scores were not highly correlated with children's academic achievement or intelligence. SSQ style scores were related in theorized ways to children's values; however, while three of the four style scales were appropriately related to the corresponding scales on the MBTI, the fourth scale (Practical-Imaginative) was correlated not only with the corresponding MBTI scale (Sensing-Feeling), but also with the MBTI Judging and Perceiving scales. This suggests that the SSQ Practical-Imaginative scale represents a broader construct than the MBTI scale to which it was designed to be analogous.

Overall Critique

The SSQ is a carefully developed and standardized instrument, with a comprehensive manual to suggest interpretations and uses. Although there is little research using the SSQ outside of its development, the manual provides adequate information for beginning users to start working with the measure. Instructions for the administration of the test are clearly written and explained. One immediate concern is in scoring the measure; the irregular weighting of items makes it seem likely that even trained individuals may make computational errors in summing scores and transferring these sums to the appropriate places on the scoring sheet. It would seem the obligation of the test developers to evaluate the accuracy of scoring before releasing the SSQ.

Being based on the MBTI, the SSQ is vulnerable to many of the critiques commonly leveled at that measure. Most prominent is the fact that the MBTI is quite popular with practitioners, but the target of much deserved critical scrutiny from academics. This criticism is often leveled at the structural assumptions behind type-based measures. For example, as mentioned in prior reviews of the MBTI, the bipolar preference model is still without much empirical support (Wiggins, 1989). Prior research has failed to find the bipolarity necessary to justify using discontinuous types on each scale (e.g., Girelli & Stake, 1993). The authors of the SSQ have attempted to address this in deemphasizing the dichotomous nature of the style scales, but the manual (Oakland, Glutting, & Horton, 1996) fails to provide evidence of a bipolar distribution of styles in support of this preference model. This lack of bipolar score distribution indicates that type-based scales can result in misclassification of individuals whose scores fall in the middle of each scale. Moreover, validity of classification into distinct types is weak (Wiggins, 1989). Although some individual SSQ style preferences do seem to be associated with congruent activity preferences, the manual fails to provide evidence, such as cluster analysis (e.g., Lorr, 1991), that the types generated by the SSQ are truly distinct.

In general the SSQ looks to be a reliable measure; however, the sample for which test-retest data is reported (137 participants) is disappointingly small given the number of students included in the normative sample. Additionally, the influence of confidence intervals around individual scores is downplayed. The table for converting difference scores into prevalence-based T-scores for use by practitioners in the manual (p. 229) makes no mention of measurement error; however, the 90% confidence intervals are so large for some scales that they span nearly 20 points, which is over half of the range of possible T-scores. Since the T-scores used for type assignment are generated from difference scores that have already discriminated between the ends of each scale, this affects only the interpretation of strength of preference. No information is provided about measurement error or confidence intervals at the difference score level. Such information would be useful in understanding how to interpret scores for individuals whose preferences lie in the midrange of each scale.

However, the largest unanswered question with regard to the SSQ involves its eventual use in the classroom. First, type assignment for children of the age for which the SSQ is intended is of concern. It must be remembered that these are kids, and the limitations of category assignment, even simple personality types, can be enormous at times when children are still discovering who they are, what they like, and how they relate to the world. It is unclear how these categorizations will be maximally useful for educators. For example, an instructor might discover via the SSQ that a particular child has an Introverted style; this information could be used to tailor the learning environment, but the debate still remains over whether to place the child in the situation that they prefer or to encourage the child to adapt to different situations by exposing her to nonpreferred circumstances.

Of even greater concern, however, is the number of unsupported inferences that the manual makes from SSQ scores and types. Each section on interpreting style preferences or style combinations contains an enormous number of inferences about such areas as general characteristics, social relationships, family relationships, classroom applications, classroom environment, positive reinforcement, tests, possible occupations, and potential pitfalls. For example, the section describing the Flexible style contains 70 inferences of qualities related to this style, including that students who prefer this style may "upset others with their surprises" or "drop out of school as soon as they legally can." Although the authors caution the reader about applying these interpretations to individuals, the manual offers virtually no empirical evidence to support the recommended interpretations.

The SSQ may serve as a useful tool for practitioners who seek information about student preferences in a format consistent with the MBTI, one of the more popular personality measures available. However, considerable additional evidence is needed in support of its underlying structure, use of types, and inferences made from style preferences. Generally, its usefulness and contribution to student assessment should be more carefully and empirically evaluated.

References

Girelli, S. A., & Stake, J. E. (1993). Bipolarity in Jungian type theory and the Myers-Briggs Type Indicator. *Journal of Personality Assessment, 60,* 290-301.

Lorr, M. (1991). An empirical evaluation of the MBTI typology. *Personality and Individual Differences, 12,* 1141-1145.

Oakland, T., Glutting, J. J., & Horton, C. B. (1996). *Student Styles Questionnaire: Manual.* San Antonio: Psychological Corporation.

Wiggins, J. S. (1989). Review of the Myers-Briggs Type Indicator. In J. C. Conoley & J. J. Kramer (Eds.), *The tenth mental measurements yearbook* (pp. 537-539). Lincoln, NE: Buros Institute, University of Nebraska-Lincoln.

CHAPTER 11

Instruments for Special Populations

- Arc's Self-Determination Scale (Arc-SDS)
- Brigance Life Skills/Employability Skills Inventories (LSI/ESI)
- Learning/Working Styles Inventory (LWSI)
- Life-Centered Career Education Competency Assessment: Knowledge and Performance Batteries (LCCE)
- Reading-Free Vocational Interest Inventory:2 (R-FVII:2)
- Street Survival Skills Questionnaire (SSSQ)
- Transition Planning Inventory (TPI)

The Arc's Self-Determination Scale (Arc-SDS)

Michael L. Wehmeyer and Kathy Kelchner
The Arc of the United States
1010 Wayne Avenue, S-650
Silver Spring, MD 20910
http://thearc.org

Target Population: Adolescents ages 13-20, with cognitive (mental retardation, learning disabilities), developmental, and other disabilities.

Statement of the Purpose of the Instrument: The primary purpose of *The Arc's Self-Determination Scale* is to enable students to self-assess instructional needs related to self-determination and to serve as a vehicle for students and teachers (or others, including counselors) to discuss educational goals and objectives to promote student self-determination. A secondary use of the scale is as a research instrument to provide a self-report measure of self-determination.

Titles of Subtests, Scales, Scores Provided: Completion of the scale yields a total self-determination score and subscale scores in each of the four essential characteristics of self-determination (Autonomy, Self-Regulation; Psychological Empowerment; Self-Realization). Scale construction was based on a model developed by researchers at The Arc, and subscales reflect the four "essential characteristics" of self-determined behavior.

Forms and Levels Available, with Dates of Publication/Revision of Each: Adolescent Version, finalized and published in September 1995.

Date of Most Recent Edition of Test Manual, User's Guide, Etc.: Procedural Guidelines to the Use of the Arc's Self-Determination Scale, published September 1995. Includes guidelines for use, scoring instructions, and norm information.

Languages in Which Available: English, although there is a French translation available that is currently being validated at the University of Quebec.

Time: Actual Test Time: Depends upon level of students' ability. The assessment was normed with multiple administrative accommodations available, including reading questions to student, reading to class, students completing individually, and so forth. Many students can complete the scale in 30 minutes or less, but students with mental retardation may require more time.
Total Administration Time: As above, 30 minutes and up.

Norm Group(s) on Which Scores Are Based: The scale was normed with 500 adolescents (13-20 years) receiving special education services under the category of learning disability, mental retardation, emotional disability, and other health impairment. The primary audience for the scale is students with mild cognitive disabilities (mild mental retardation, learning disabilities) or emotional or developmental disorders.

Manner in Which Results are Reported for Individuals: Scale administrators can select three levels for "scoring" the results and using the scale. At the basic level, particularly with students with more significant mental retardation, the scale can be completed, but not scored and used simply as a means of generating discussion about self-determination. Scoring the assessment yields raw scores, which can be converted to percent correct scores and also to norm-referenced scores. Thus they can be reported as a percent of total questions "correct" or "positive" or they can be reported as a normed score ranging from 0 to 100.

> **Report Format/Content**: The last page of the protocol includes a way to record raw scores for each Domain and Subdomain, to calculate a total raw score, and to convert raw total and subscale scores into percent correct and a standard score. This page also includes a bar graph for teachers/students to illustrate both standard and percent-correct scores.

Report Format/Content for Group Summaries: Not available.

Scoring
> **Machine Scoring Service:** Not available.
> **Hand Scoring:**
>> *Scored by*:   Counselee; Counselor.
>> *Time required for scoring*:   15 minutes.
> **Local Machine Scoring:**   Not available.

Computer Software Options Available: Not available.

Cost of Materials:
> **Specimen Set:** Not available but copy of protocol available free from The Arc with self-addressed stamped envelope.
> **Counselee Materials:** Copy of Procedural Guidelines and 25 protocols-$68.33. Set of 25 protocols only-$29.17. The scale is distributed by the Council for Exceptional Children (888-CED-SPEC) or is available from The Arc's Publications department (800-433-5255).

Additional Comments of Interest to Users: The scale is a self-report measure and, as such, users are cautioned against viewing scores as representing "true" or "absolute" self-determination, but instead a student's perceptions of his or her relative self-determination. In addition, there are numerous threats to validity and reliability associated with the use of self-report measures with individuals with cognitive disabilities, and users should not use the scale score for diagnostic or placement decisions.

Published Reviews: None cited.

Reviewed by

Pamela J. Leconte
Assistant Research Professor
Department of Teacher Preparation and Special Education
George Washington University

Description

The *Arc's Self-Determination Scale* (Arc-SDS) is a self-reporting, paper-and-pencil instrument designed with support from a federal grant (Self-determination Assessment Project funded by the U.S. Department of Education) by Wehmeyer and Kelchner (1995) for The Arc of the United States. To date, only the original 1995 versions are available for adolescents and adults (Wehmeyer and Schwartz, 1998). Adolescent and adult versions are "identical with selected wording changes in questions...(e.g., replace 'school' with 'work')" (Wehmeyer and Schwartz, 1998, p. 7). Because the Arc-SDS was normed using mostly adolescents and the *Procedural Guidelines* discuss only adolescents, this review refers to the use of the Scale with adolescents. The Arc-SDS provides students with cognitive disabilities and educators "a tool that assists them in identifying student strengths and limitations in the area of self-determination" (Wehmeyer & Kelchner, 1995, p. 1). Second, it furnishes researchers with a tool that will allow them to examine relationships between self-determination and factors that either promote or inhibit "this important outcome" (Wehmeyer and Kelchner, 1995, p. 1).

The Arc-SDS contains 72 items divided into four sections. The four sections equate the "essential characteristics of self-determination" (Wehmeyer, Kelchner, and Richards, 1996; Wehmeyer and Kelchner, 1995): autonomy, self-regulation, psychological empowerment, and self-realization. Reportedly, these essential characteristics are manifested by "component elements of self-determination, including choice and decision-making" (Section One), problem solving, goal setting, and attainment skills (Section Two); internal locus of control orientations; positive self-efficacy and outcome expectancies (Section Three); and self-knowledge and understanding (Section Four) (Wehmeyer, Kelchner, and Richards, 1996). The protocol is presented on 8½ x 11" paper, horizontally positioned in a booklet of four pages printed on both sides (to total eight). Black ink is printed on varying lines with gray, light blue, or white backgrounds. The administration manual suggests that items are written on a fourth-grade reading level or "lower when possible" (Wehmeyer, 1995, p. 6).

The *Procedural Guidelines* serve as the administrator's manual. Chapter One contains descriptions of the scale and potential problems with self-report measures. Other chapters address theoretical issues, scale construction, administration procedures, scoring and interpretation, norms, reliability, and validity.

Of the 72 items, 32 comprise the first section, Autonomy. The respondent is to select one of four options for each item and to check the answer that "BEST tells how you act in that situation" (Wehmeyer and Kelchner, 1995, p. 2). An example item states "I deal with salespeople at stores and restaurants." The respondent then selects one of the four options: "I do not even if I have the chance," or "I do sometimes when I have the chance," or "I do most of the time I have the chance," or "I do every time I have the chance." The Autonomy section has items categorized into subdomains. For example, Independence: routine personal care, family-oriented functions and Independence: Interaction with the environment. The other four subdomains are based on "preferences, beliefs, interests, and abilities" in recreational and leisure time, community involvement and interaction, post-school directions, and personal expression. These items were adapted from the *Autonomous Functioning Checklist* (Sigafoos, Feinstein, Damond, & Reiss, 1988), developed to measure parent observations of behavioral autonomy in adolescence.

Section Two, Self-regulation, is divided into two subdomains: Interpersonal cognitive problem-solving and Goal setting and task performance. In the first subsection, respondents are to fill in or connect the beginning and end of six stories with the "BEST answer for the middle of the story." For example, "Beginning: Your friends are acting like they are mad at you. You are upset about this." The middle section includes six blank lines, followed by the "Ending: the story ends with you and your friends getting along just fine."

The second subdomain of Section Two provides three items, for which the respondent checks one of two options, followed by a self-generated list. For example, item #39 asks "Where do you want to live after you graduate?" Option one states "I have not planned for that yet." Option two states "I want to live" (fill in the blank). This is followed by the instruction "List four things you should do to meet this goal."

Section Three, Psychological Empowerment, includes 16 forced choice items for which respondents select one option each. For example, item #42 states "I usually do what my friends want" or "I tell my friends if they are dong something I don't want to do." The final section addresses self-realization. It includes 15 items with directions to "Tell whether you think each of these statements describes how you feel about yourself or not." Item #54 provides a typical example, "I do not feel ashamed of any of my emotions." Respondents must check either "agree" or "disagree." Items from this section were adapted from the *Short Index of Self-Actualization* (Jones & Crandall, 1986).

Use in Counseling

The Arc-SDS was designed to measure self-determination perceptions of adolescents and adults with disabilities, especially those with mild mental retardation and learning disabilities. Underscoring that the Arc-SDS not be used as a diagnostic or prescriptive tool, due to "difficulties with reliability and validity from self-report measures," (Wehmeyer, 1995, p. 5) the authors recommend that the administration be repeated over time to determine any individual improvements. The Arc-SDS was constructed to fill a void in specifying measurable characteristics of self-determination (Wehmeyer et al., 1996) and evaluating outcomes of educational efforts to increase self-determination. The developers explain that typically people with mental retardation or other cognitive disabilities have not had opportunities to voice their opinions, be self-determined, or demonstrate self-determination. They intend that the Arc-SDS be used to help change these realities.

The Arc-SDS can be group or individually administered and educators and counselors can use Arc-SDS results to "generate discussion" (Wehmeyer, 1995, p. 6) about self-determined behaviors and to isolate items that the student "finds interesting, problematic, or wants to discuss more broadly" (Wehmeyer, 1995, p. 6). Educators and counselors can also score and compare Total, domain (section) and subdomain scores with Arc-SDS norms and analyze the individual's strengths and needs within and across the domains. Developers caution that the norms should be used only as points of comparison, because "it is not students' performance...that is important, but the opportunity to set them in control of their learning experience" (Wehmeyer, 1995, p. 7). Scoring produces a total self-determination score and section scores in each of the four essential characteristics categories of self-determination to provide more specific information for instructional and counseling purposes.

Technical Considerations

It is possible to achieve 148 points on the Arc-SDS; higher scores indicate higher self-determination. The Arc-SDS was developed and normed with 500 adolescents with and without disabilities from five states (Wehmeyer, 1995; Wehmeyer and Schwartz, 1998). This process was preceded by a research sample of 408 adolescents and adults with a mean age of 36.34, of whom 55% were female, 81% were Caucasian, and 9% were African-American (Wehmeyer, 1995, p. 52). This was followed by a pilot test of 261 secondary-age students with cognitive disabilities from three states (Wehmeyer, 1995, p. 66). Norms are based on responses from 500 students (223 males, 210 females, 67 gender unknown) with (e.g., mental retardation, learning disabled, emotional disorders) and without disabilities from urban, suburban, and rural schools in Texas, Virginia, Alabama, Connecticut, and Colorado.

Internal consistency, reliability (Cronbach alpha =.90), for the total Scale is adequate (Wehmeyer, 1995). The Self-Regulation subscale is excluded since it requires open-ended questions. Since this is the only evidence of reliability reported, developers may want to conduct test-retest studies to determine if the Arc-SDS scores are stable over time. This type of reliability information would be especially important when the Arc-SDS is used to assess change.

Developers demonstrated concurrent criterion-related validity by relating the Arc-SDS with other "conceptually related measures" (Wehmeyer and Schwartz, 1998, p. 7) such as self-efficacy and locus of control. For example, most relationships with other standardized instruments ranged from moderate to strong (.25 to .50), and yielded the highest relationships with the Psychological Empowerment domain (Wehmeyer, 1995). The Scale has adequate construct validity (though the explanation is brief), including factorial validity as determined by several factor analyses and discriminative validity studies. Factor analyses demonstrated that factors "reflect the constructs" they are intended to measure (Wehmeyer, 1995).

Overall Critique

The Arc-SDS is discussed in professional literature, but does not seem to be well known by practitioners at this point. Accommodations are advised (e.g., reading items and marking responses for students with reading problems), and instructions should be read to respondents. The guidelines indicate that 30 minutes to 1 hour is sufficient time to administer the Arc-SDS, not accounting for accommodations.

Scoring can be completed "collaboratively" with administrators, but developers warn that students should direct this process as much as possible in order to prevent bias from the administrators. They advise collaboration as it "is most likely too complex for self-scoring" (Wehmeyer, 1995, p. 7). Scoring is explained in the Procedural Guidelines, not on the protocol. Scoring can become cumbersome since the protocol does not include the weights given to responses—the administrator must refer to the weights in the Guidelines, then return to the protocol for scoring. Scoring Section Two is challenging. The Guidelines give examples of "story" answers, but administrators' latitude in judgment could compromise objectivity. Section Two's sub-scale on "goal setting and task performance" can be misleading in that it asks for task *planning* rather than task *performance*. The Scale was designed for adolescents with mental retardation and learning disabilities, but the items often reflect limited options. For example, goal items include postgraduation plans, work plans, and transportation plans with no mention of postsecondary educational options.

Scale layout appears "busy" and can confuse respondents with visual perception or tracking problems. The Arc-SDS contains sufficient variety to thwart boredom, and though it is recommended to administer in one sitting, respondents should be monitored continuously, especially in group settings. Although the print size is adequate, persons with attention problems may be frustrated or confused by the closely organized items in Section One. The differently shaded bands, particularly those in light blue on gray backgrounds, also may make reading challenging for people with poor visual acuity or tracking problems. Administrators can provide their own definitions for vocabulary that respondents may not understand, which could influence outcomes.

The Arc-SDS is the first assessment of its kind designed for students with severe cognitive disabilities. Dual reasons for developing the Arc-SDS include self-assessment and research, which cause some of the design problems. Construction for self-assessment as the sole purpose would enhance the instrument, making it more useful for students. Research could then be conducted on results of these self-reports. Regardless, the Scale can be a useful tool for initiating the topic of self-determination.

References

Jones, A.P., & Crandall, R.   (1986). Validation of a short index of self-actualization. *Personality and Social Psychology Bulletin, 12,* 63-73.

Sigafoos, A.D., Feinstein, C.B., Damond, M., & Reiss, D. (1988). The measurement of behavioral autonomy in adolescence: The Autonomous Functioning Checklist. In C.B. Feinstein, A. Esman, J. Looney, G. Orvin, J. Schimel, A. Schwartzberg, A. Sorsky & M. Sugar (Eds.), *Adolescent Psychiatry* (Vol. 15, pp. 432-462). Chicago: University of Chicago Press.

Wehmeyer, M.L. (1995). *The Arc's Self-determination Scale: Procedural guidelines.* Arlington, TX: The Arc of the United States.

Wehmeyer, M.L., & Kelchner, K. (1995). *The Arc's Self-determination Scale: Adolescent Version.* Arlington, TX: The Arc of the United States.

Wehmeyer, M.L., Kelchner, K., & Richards, S. (1996). Essential characteristics of self-determined behavior of individuals with mental retardation. *American Journal on Mental Retardation, 100*(6), 632-642.

Wehmeyer, M.L., & Schwartz, M. (1998). The relationship between self-determination and quality of life for adults with mental retardation. *Education and Training in Mental Retardation and Developmental Disabilities, 33*(1), 3-12.

Brigance Life Skills/Employability Skills Inventories (LSI/ESI)

Albert H. Brigance
Curriculum Associates, Inc.
P.O. Box 2001
N. Billerica, MA 01862
www.curriculumassociates.com
cainfo@curriculumassociates.com

Target Population: Secondary/Adult Education.

Statement of the Purpose of the Instrument: Life Skills Inventory (LSI) evaluates basic skills and functional life skills in context of real world situations. Employability Skills Inventory (ESI) assesses basic and employability skills necessary for job seeking and on the job.

Forms and Levels Available, with Dates of Publication/Revision of Each: LSI: 1994, ESI: 1995.

Date of Most Recent Edition of Test Manual, User's Guide, Etc.: LSI: 1994, ESI: 1995.

Languages in Which Available: English only.

Time: Actual Test Time: Untimed testing. Total Administration Time: At tester discretion.

Norm Group(s) on Which Scores Are Based: Tests are not normed.

Manner in Which Results Are Reported for Individuals
    Types of Scores: Rating scales/learner knowledge.

Report Format/Content for Group Summaries: Not available.

Scoring
    Machine Scoring Service: Not available.
    Hand Scoring: Not available.
    Local Machine Scoring: Not available.

Computer Software Options Available: Not available.

Cost of Materials:
    Specimen Set: Submitted for review at no charge.

    Counselee Materials: LSI/ESI Manuals $89.95 each (reusable). Learner Record Books $24.95 each, 10 pack $229 each, 100 pack (sold separately for each). Program Record Books $12.95 each (sold separately for each)

Published Reviews: None cited.

Reviewed by

Linda H. Parrish
Regents Professor

Ellen Blair
Visiting Assistant Professor

Department of Educational Psychology
Texas A & M University

Description

The Brigance Employability Skills Inventory (ESI) and the Brigance Life Skills Inventory (LSI) are two of the nine instruments that comprise the Brigance System that spans the developmental ages from early childhood to adulthood. Because of the similarity in design and purpose, it is understandable why schools employ the entire system throughout their districts. The titles within the system are Inventory of Early Development (1978, 1991), Comprehensive Inventory of Basic Skills (1976), Inventory of Essential Skills (1981), Assessment of Basic Skills-Spanish Edition (1983), Employability Skills Inventory (1995), and Life Skills Inventory (1994). In addition to these inventories, Brigance has three instruments that are referred to as the Brigance Screens. These include Early Preschool Screen (1990), Preschool Screen (1985), and K & 1 Screen.

The inventories are popular with teachers for many reasons. One reason is that the format is easy to follow. All inventories are packaged in large seven-ring binders that easily open between the examiner and the student. The student's page is printed in large letters and pictures, and the examiner's page displays comprehensive information needed to administer the inventory. Moreover, additional copies of the student's materials may to reproduced for group administration.

Other reasons for the Brigance's popularity is the ease of administration that requires no special training. Assessment can be completed by a paraprofessional under professional supervision. In addition, the inventories do not require any specialized materials. The inventory binder and student and class record-keeping documents are inclusive of all necessary items for administration.

Perhaps the most important reasons for the inventories' popularity with teachers are their flexible use and their relationship to instruction. Teachers can administer all or parts of the inventories to determine the important question, "Has the student adequately mastered this specific skill?" Depending upon the answer to that question the teacher can then make curricular decisions that closely mirror the information learned from the inventory results. Supplemental and related materials are supplied to assist with this effort, as well as goals and objectives software for the development of Individual Education Plans (IEPs).

The ESI and the LSI are particularly noteworthy for their use in secondary throughout adult education situations. Both inventories consist of a comprehensive binder that includes all components of the assessment plus the introduction section, which is the equivalent to a user's guide, and a reference and appendix section. They each include two booklets that allow for individual student or class reporting.

The ESI contains eight sections. Each of these and an example of subtests are as follows:

1. Reading Grade-Placement (word recognition and vocabulary comprehension).
2. Career Awareness and Self-Understanding (job interests, choosing a career).
3. Job-Seeking Skills and Knowledge (interview questions, pay and benefits).
4. Rating Scales (self-concept, attitudes and self-discipline rating scales).
5. Reading Skills (employment forms, directions for performing manual skills).
6. Speaking and Listening Skills (listening observations checklist).
7. Pre-employment Writing (applications, resume writing).
8. Math Skills and Concepts (number facts, measures, estimating, calendar/time).

The LSI has 10 skill components. Each of these and an example of subtests are as follows:

1. Speaking and Listening (personal data response, checklists similar to ESI).
2. Functional writing (form completion, personal data, finance information).
3. Common signs and Warning Labels (directional, warning/safety, public/private).
4. Telephone (basic, vocabulary, costs).
5. Money and Finance (values, making change, charts & tables).
6. Food (groups, preparation, diet, restaurant vocabulary).
7. Clothing (sizes, labels).
8. Health (medical vocabulary, infections, drugs, birth control).
9. Travel and Transportation (traffic symbols, gasoline mileage, maps, driver's license).
10. Rating Scales (self-concept, multiple scales designed to rate 1-9 skills).

Although these instruments do not have alternative forms, each offers a "Quick-Screen" in addition to the complete administration of the entire inventory. This is a shorter version of the inventories that consists of similar items from the selected assessment areas. It is designed to give an overview of the level at which the learner is functioning. The results from the Quick-Screen can be used to help one: (1) determine the appropriateness of using the complete assessments in the Inventories, (2) provide information about a learner's competency in major life-skills areas, and, (3) help one determine an area in the inventory in which to begin assessing.

The recordkeeping system of the ESI and LSI is contained in *The Learner Record Book*, which allows initial performance and progress data to be maintained using a simple format and color coded-system corresponding to the first, second, and third evaluations. Futhermore, skills that are mastered are simply circled, whereas those that require more attention are underlined, readily communicating results to both teacher and learner. Observations from the testing situation are also recorded. Again, the author demonstrates familiarity with the school setting by providing a method for calculating a "score" if one is necessary for school program requirements. This is done by assigning a numerical value to the checks that the rater has marked. For example: Much Improvement Needed = 0; Could be Improved = 3; Acceptable = 4; and Very Good = 5. This system assumes a perfect score of 100 and is very compatible with traditional school scoring methods (Brigance, 1994, p. 209).

The administration time varies, but individual assessments are reported to take from 10 to 20 minutes each depending upon the learner. Because the evaluator chooses which assessment components to give to yield the information that is needed, the total time spent assessing students is controlled by the administrator. Certain assessment areas also provide the option for group-administered tests, decreasing the amount of time needed to obtain results for several individual learners.

Use in Counseling

The author wisely cautions against using the results obtained from the Emploability Skills Inventory and the Life Skills Inventory exclusively to determine educational placements for students; however, the information gleaned from these inventories can, in fact, aid in that process. Teachers and counselors can refer to this assessment data when determining which academic and/or occupational training setting best matches the skills that a student has mastered, or alternatively, needs to acquire.

In addition, data from these two assessment instruments can provide specific goals and objectives for a student's Individual Education Plan (IEP) or the important, Individualized Transition Plan (ITP), which is required by the Individual with Disabilities Education Act of 1997. Because of the integrated nature of the skills included in the ESI and LSI (i.e., academic, life, and employment-related skills) these instruments have the potential to greatly assist in transition from school to work planning and programming. Parents and students will recognize the value of mastery or acquisition of these important transition skills.

The author presents information confirming the relationship of the ESI to the Comprehensive Adult Student Assessment System (CASAS) and the Secretary's Commission on Achieving Necessary Skills (SCANS).

Technical Considerations

The publishers of the Brigance do not apologize for not providing a technical manual for the ESI or LSI with data that is typically representative of a published assessment instrument. They maintain that their instruments are criterion referenced and as such measure the learner's knowledge against relevant standards. They tell precisely what the learner has mastered and what still needs to be learned. According to the Introduction section of the ESI:

> The criterion-referenced test is designed to help determine the curriculum needs of the individual. Post-testing will indicate more than just growth; it will show what the learner has learned and what remains to be mastered. Then teaching can start with the assurance that no time will be wasted presenting what the learner already knows. The learner also can participate in the learning process by helping to set learning goals and by observing the progress made. (Brigance, 1995, p. vi.)

In point of fact, the author continues by asserting that a norm-referenced test, standardized tests that measure the learner's score against those of other learners who have taken the same test, has a potential limitation. "The drawback is that the test gives a numerical score, not specific information about what the learner actually learned and still needs to learn" (p. vi.).

Even so, the publisher of the Brigance instruments has begun the process of standardization and validation with the Comprehensive Inventory of Basic Skills-Revised (CIBS-R). Standardization of the CIBS-R has employed traditional reliability and validity studies and culminated in the publication of the CIBS-R Standardization and Validation Manual (Glascoe, 1999). Glascoe reports that the CIBS-R was standardized on a large population from across the United States under conditions that characterize the classrooms setting where the Inventory is used. The sample was representative of the nation's ethnicity, income, level of education and other routinely used demographic datapoints (Glascoe, 1999, p. 31).

As part of this research, test-retest, interrater or interexaminer, alternate forms, and internal consistency reliability were determined (p. 32). In addition, validation efforts consisting of content, concurrent, predictive, construct, and discriminant validity studies were conducted. For example, correlations were obtained with individually administered diagnostic achievement tests such as the Woodcock-Johnson Psychoeducational Battery, the Wide Range Achievement Test, the Peabody Individual Achievement Test, and the Wechsler Intelligence Scale for Children-3rd edition (p. 58).

The reviewers present this information on this one Brigance instrument within the series (the CIBS-R) to demonstrate that the author and publisher understand the importance of such technical qualities. Given the comprehensive nature of this analysis of the CIBS-R, it is reasonable to expect that other instruments within the Brigance System will also undergo this process. In particular, it is recommended that the ESI and LSI undergo a process similar to the CIBS-R, particularly for the purpose of establishing reliability and validity for populations with which it is likely to be used. Also, group norms can be established to confirm the type of skills presented in the LSI and ESI that would be useful to students, teachers, counselors, and researchers.

Overall Critique

The ESI and LSI are important entities in the ever-growing area of secondary and adult assessment, training, and employment. Their comprehensive, yet compact presentation make their use more accessible to the many teachers who employ them in their classes. Their user-friendly directions and no-frills recording devices are familiar to teachers, and therefore more likely to be used. The price of this Brigance duo is affordable for wide distribution and the invitation to photocopy individual assessment pages for group purposes is appealing.

Often teachers are heard to say that the report from an individual student's psychological evaluation is interesting, but not immediately relevant for their instructional purposes. This is not the case for the ESI and LSI. Teachers can easily tie the assessment with instruction and they are given additional resources to do just that. The wide use of this system is evidence that it is a valuable tool for students, teachers, and counselors.

It would be even more valuable if the author or publisher would conduct the technical studies of the type recently completed on the CIBS-R by Glascoe and associates at Vanderbilt University.

References

Brigance, A. H. (1994). *Brigance Life Skills Inventory*. North Billerica, MA: Curriculum Associates, Inc.

Brigance, A. H. (1995). *Brigance Employability Skills Inventory*. North Billerica, MA: Curriculum Associates, Inc.

Glascoe, F. P. (1999). *Brigance Comprehensive Inventory of Basic Skills-Revised (CIBS-R) Standardization and Validation Manual*. North Billerica, MA: Curriculum Associates, Inc.

Learning/Working Styles Inventory (LWSI)

Helena Hendrix-Frye
Piney Mountain Press, Inc.
PO Box 333
Cleveland, GA 30528
www.pineymountain.com
cyberguy@stc.net

Target Population: Grades 8-Adult, Special Needs, At Risk, Tech Prep, School-to-Work, JTPA, Welfare-to-Work and Corrections

Statement of the Purpose of the Instrument: For teachers and students to better understand the physical, social, environmental and working conditions under which an individual prefers to learn and work. The presentations are available in video and multimedia formats in order to meet the needs of special learners.

Titles of Subtests, Scales, Scores Provided: Scales provided are Physical Domain—Kinesthetic; Visual, Tactile; Auditory. Social Domain—Individual; Group. Environmental Domain—Design; Light; Sound; Temperature. Mode of Expression—Oral Expressive; Written Expressive. Work Characteristics Domain—Outdoors/Indoors; Sedentary/Nonsedentary; Lifting/Nonlifting; People/Data/Things.

Forms and Levels Available, with Dates of Publication/Revision of Each: Paper/Pencil Form: 1991-Video Form; 1994—Software Form; 1991, 1994, 1997—Multimedia CD Form; 1999—Optical Scan Form; 1994

Date of Most Recent Edition of Test Manual, User's Guide, Etc.: 1999

Languages in Which Available: English and Spanish

Time: Actual Test Time: Untimed.
Total Administration Time: 20 minutes.

Norm Group(s) on Which Scores Are Based: The Learning Working Styles is a criterion-referenced inventory based on a continuum of scores on the construct. Each item relates to the total construct and total score. (1) 585 females/615 males, in grades 9-12; (2) 150 At-Risk Vocational, At-Risk and Gifted High School Students; (3) 50 male/50 female high school students enrolled in vocational training.

Manner in Which Results Are Reported for Individuals
Types of Scores: Full scale results, preference scores, descriptions of students styles, verbal labels.
Report Format/Content:
Basic Service: Data are presented in graphs and narrative text. Group reports may be generated by customer on software program or by publisher.
Options: Database storage of your scoring data.

Report Format/Content for Group Summaries:
  Basic Service: Data presented in tables and graphs.
  Options: Database storage of your scoring data.

Scoring
  Machine Scoring Service:
    Cost of basic service per counselee: $1.50 per individual
    Time required for scoring and returning (maximum): 100: 48 hours/101-500-one week/501-2000 two weeks.
  Hand Scoring:
    Scored by: Counselee; Clerk; Counselor.
    Time required for scoring: 10 minutes.
  Local Machine Scoring:
    Provisions/conditions/equipment required: Chatsworth Card Reader; NCS Sentry 3000, Optscan 3, Optscan 5; Scantron, DOS and Windows with minimal memory requirements.

Computer Software Options Available: Computerized adaptive administration. Standard administration online; Other: Scanner entry, interactive computer administration, key-in manual entry.

Ways in Which Computer Version Differs: Standard online administration for Apple, Mac, DOS, and Windows. The new multimedia Windows CD version has real voice narration, video clips, real-life visuals, and on-screen tutorials. Multisite testing and network versions are available for all computer versions.

Cost of Materials:
  Specimen Set: No charge.
  Counselee Materials: Media Kit: one guide, one video, software 100 reproducible response forms, one site license $495 (reusable). Multimedia CD: $395 (reusable). Computer Disk Version: $349 (reusable). Video Version: one guide, one reproducible test, one video, one scoring disk. Internet Version: $49.94 (reusable).

Additional Comments of Interest to Users: New Multimedia CD Version that allows online administration with live voice, visuals and video clips now available.

Published Reviews: None cited.

Reviewed by

Patricia L. Sitlington
Professor of Special Education

Jennifer McGlashing
Graduate Assistant in Special Education

University of Northern Iowa

Description

The Learning/Working Styles Inventory (LWSI) is designed to be used with all individuals, including individuals with special needs, in grades 7-12 and in postsecondary facilities that train or retrain individuals in marketable skills. According to the Technical Report (n.d.), the intent of the LWSI is to provide teachers and counselors with a "quick, inclusive, nontechnical, inexpensive method of assessing an individual's opinion about how he/she prefers to learn and work" (p. 1).

The LWSI consists of 75 one-sentence statements to which the individual is asked to respond on a 4-point scale, with 4 being "most like me" and 1 being "least like me." The responses in between are "somewhat like me" and "not much like me." A sample item is: "I remember what I learn by closing my eyes to recall it."

The content of the LSWI is divided into five major domains, with each domain having specific elements or areas that are measured (a total of 25 elements or areas). The *Physical Domain* relates to how individuals absorb and retain new and difficult information. Elements that are measured in this domain are kinesthetic, visual, tactile, and auditory. The *Social Domain* measures whether individuals prefer to study or learn alone or in a group. The *Environmental Domain* relates to whether individuals prefer to study or learn under different types of environmental conditions, including the aspects of formal or informal design, bright or dim light, warm or cool temperature, and with or without sound. The *Mode of Expression Domain* measures whether individuals prefer to express ideas and thoughts in oral or written form. The *Work Characteristics Domain* relates to whether individuals prefer to work outdoors or indoors, engage in sedentary or nonsedentary tasks, work in jobs requiring lifting or no lifting, and work with people, data, or things.

The individual's style usage is then defined as *major, minor,* or *negligible*, based upon the scores in the respective elements within each domain. Major usage indicates that he/she feels comfortable with this style and finds it necessary for learning. Minor usage indicates that the individual uses or desires this condition, but normally as a second choice or in conjunction with other styles and conditions. Negligible usage indicates that the individual does not prefer or feel comfortable with this style if other choices are available.

The LWSI may be administered individually or in small or large groups. The administration format may be written, audiovisual, and/or on the computer. The written administration consists of the individual reading the items to him/herself or the administrator reading the items to the individual. The participant responds by marking the number that best describes how he/she feels about each statement. The audiovisual administration consists of the administrator or the individual inserting a videotape on which each statement is read and a brief video image designed to illustrate the statement is provided. Again, the participant responds by marking the number that best describes how he/she feels about each statement. Participants may be provided with a script of the inventory if they wish to read along with the audiovisual presentation. A worksheet is provided for computing scores in each of the 25 areas. Individuals can then enter their scores on a grid to show graphically which areas are major and minor learning styles. The computer versions are described in a later section. The publisher also indicated that a multimedia Learning/Working Styles Inventory was scheduled for release soon. This option was not available for review at this time.

Use in Counseling

As stated in the Technical Report, the LWSI was developed as a quick, nontechnical method of assessing an individual's opinion of how he/she prefers to learn and work. The inventory is not a test with right or wrong answers, but a way to help the individual find out how he/she prefers to learn. The handscored and computer versions yield a profile that visually presents (through a line graph) how the student scored in each of the 25 areas. In addition, the computer versions provide a printout of teaching techniques based on the individual's scores, such as "a learning environment with noise is preferred by this individual."

Group profiles are also available from the computer versions that provide a grid with each student's major or minor learning and working styles indicated. This could be one possible beginning tool in assisting the individual in examining his/her own learning styles and approaching the best ways to learn in any type of environment. It may also be helpful in developing the Individualized Education Program (IEP) for students receiving special education services.

Technical Considerations

The publisher indicates that the LWSI is a criterion-referenced inventory. The field test group reported in the *LWSI Technical Report* (n.d.) appeared to be for the version that did not include the Work Characteristics Domain. The group consisted of 1,200 individuals, 585 females and 615 males, in grades 9-12. The individuals were general education students as well as special education students who were participating in general education courses. Only mean scores and standard deviations for each style within the four domains are provided in the Technical Report.

The test-retest method was used for the purpose of assessing reliability of the LWSI, with 5-10 days between the test and retest. The inventory was given to 100 high school students in grades 9-12, 50 males and 50 females. Students with special needs were included in the sample if they were participating in general education classes. The coefficients for each element ranged from .91 for sound/noise to .56 for auditory, with coefficients for all but two of the 25 areas at .70 or above. The median coefficient was .82.

Content and construct validity are discussed briefly in the Technical Report. Evidence of these validities is based on the author's experience using similar instruments with students with and without special needs. Concurrent validity was explored by administering the Dunn and Dunn Learning Styles Inventory to a group of 150 at-risk, vocational, and gifted high school students six days after the LWSI. Correlations between the two inventories on each of 16 learning styles factors ranged from .66 to 1.00, with a median of .92

Computer-Based Version

The publisher of the LWSI offers several computer-based options. These include IBM Windows and MS-DOS computer administration and scoring, as well as computer administration and scoring using Macintosh and Apple computers. Administration of the LWSI using the computer-based approach takes approximately 20 minutes. A mouse is required to select the responses. Students are provided the opportunity to go back and change their answers if they choose. The respondent also has the option to exit at anytime, and may save his/her answers on the Windows version; however, this option is not available on the Macintosh version until the individual has completed the entire inventory.

The results are available to be printed out immediately following the completion of the inventory. The printout provides descriptions of the domains and learning styles for the individual. Instructions are provided at the beginning of the program, and are clear and easy to read. Scoring via Chatsworth Card Reader, NCS Scanner, and Scantron Card Reader is available for some computer versions.

Overall Critique

The strengths of this instrument lie in its ease of administration and variety of methods of administration. The results are also presented clearly and can be easily understood and applied by the respondent or person working with the respondent. This will facilitate the participation of the learner in his/her own career assessment process. The computer versions allow the respondent to go back and change an answer, and the instructor component allows the administrator to keep track of each individual's learning styles and to save them. The videotape version contains pictures of a wide variety of jobs with good ethnic and gender balance.

The weaknesses of the LWSI lie in the apparent lack of a field test group that included the Work Characteristics Domain and in the lack of consistency among the administration options included. Within the computer version the same responses to the items yielded different learner profiles on the Windows and Macintosh versions. In addition, the Macintosh version ran more slowly than the Windows version and the respondent cannot exit the program at any time and save responses as he/she can on the Windows version. Of most concern, however, was the fact that a number of the frames in the videotape presentation did not clearly illustrate the learning style area being explored, so they would be of little help to an individual in determining his or her preferred style – and may actually be misleading. An additional concern is the length of the instrument: 75 statements. It would appear to be better to provide a break to respondents as they are going through the items, or that the LWSI be given in two separate sessions (apparently not possible with the Macintosh version). A final concern is the minimal technical data provided. Data from different field test samples, as well as additional reliability and validity studies, could make the LWSI more useful.

Reference

Piney Mountain Press. (n.d.) *Learning/Working Styles Inventory technical report.* Cleveland, GA: Author.

Life Centered Career Education Competency Assessment: Knowledge and Performance Batteries (LCCE)

Donn E. Brolin
The Council for Exceptional Children
1920 Association Drive
Reston, VA 20191-1589
cecpubs@cec.sped.org

Target Population: The tests are developed for students who have mild disabilities and who can read at the third grade level or above. The tests can be used successfully with students who have learning disabilities, mild mental retardation, and emotional or behavioral disorders. It is also useful for students with sensory impairments, students at-risk, adults, students with emotional/behavior disorders, and low-achieving students.

Statement of the Purpose of the Instrument: The primary purpose of these criterion-referenced batteries is to identify areas of strengths and weaknesses in 20 of the 22 competencies comprising the Life Centered Career Education curriculum, and to gauge effectiveness of the instructional program.

The LCCE Knowledge Battery is available in parallel forms, A and B, and is designed to pinpoint specific competency deficiencies. The LCCE Performance Battery offers two alternative forms provided for all skills tested. The items are primarily performance-based and should be administered to students before and after the instructional units. Together, the LCCE Knowledge Batteries and the LCCE Performance Batteries can be used to provide a comprehensive career/life skills assessment.

Titles of Subtests, Scales, Scores Provided:
Subtests: "Daily Living Skills Questions"
          "Personal Social Skills Questions"
          "Occupational and Guidance Questions"
Scores: are recorded by administrator on form called the Student Competency Assessment Record (SCAR) and should be used to record each student's KB and PB results.

Forms and Levels Available, with Dates of Publication/Revision of Each: The Knowledge Battery is available in two forms, A and B. Includes an Administration Manual and a Technical Report. It is presented in a multiple-choice format.

The Performance Battery is available in two alternative forms for each of the 21 competency units. The KB and PB are written for those students who can read at the third grade reading level or above.

The original publication date of LCCE Knowledge Batteries and LCCE Performance Batteries is 1992. Minor revisions occurred in 1997.

Date of Most Recent Edition of Test Manual, User's Guide, Etc.: 1995.

Languages in Which Available: English only.

Time: Actual Test Time: 2-4 hours depending on abilities of students taking test.

Norm Group(s) on Which Scores Are Based: The test is not norm referenced. Standardized on students in grades 9-12 who have mild mental retardation or specific learning disabilities

Manner in Which Results Are Reported for Individuals
　　Types of Scores: KB: The scores are reported as a total number correct out of a total of ten questions. There are 10 questions for each of the first 20 competencies. A score of 8 is considered "competent," i.e., passing.
　　PB: Items are primarily performance-based. Scores below 8 on each PB test would suggest the need for further instruction.
　　Report Format/Content:
　　　　Basic Service: None available. Test administrator records scores on SCAR

Report Format/Content for Group Summaries: Not Available.

Scoring
Machine Scoring Service: Not available.
　　Hand Scoring:
　　　　Scored by: Clerk; Counselor.
　　　　Time required for scoring: 5-10 minutes.
　　Local Machine Scoring:
　　　　Provisions/conditions/equipment required: If a scoring machine is available and students are able to successfully use Scantron-type answer sheets, a 200-item sheet can be used. The test administrator will need to create an answer sheet for the machine available.

Computer Software Options Available: Not available.

Cost of Materials:
　　　　Specimen Set: The Knowledge Battery sells for $125
　　　　　　The Performance Battery sells for $225.
　　Counselee Materials: KB: Test booklets sell for $20 per pack of 10. If separate answer sheets are used, the booklets are reusable. It is illegal to photocopy the test booklets. PB: Test forms are legally reproducible.

Additional Comments of Interest to Users: The Council for Exceptional Children does plan to present the test on CD-ROM in the future.

Published Reviews: None cited.

Reviewed by

Patricia S. Lynch
Senior Lecturer
Department of Educational Psychology
Texas A&M University

Description

The Competency Assessment Knowledge and Performance Batteries are instruments designed to be used with the Life Centered Career Education (LCCE) Curriculum, an outcome-based curriculum of functional competencies in three domains: daily living skills, personal-social skills, and occupational guidance and preparation. The Knowledge Battery is a standardized, criterion-referenced instrument consisting of 200 multiple-choice items that measure the three LCCE domains. The LCCE contains 22 competencies within the 3 domains and the Knowledge Battery includes 10 items for each of the first 20 competencies. The Performance Battery is a nonstandardized, criterion-referenced instrument containing 105 performance items that assess the first 21 LCCE competencies. The 22nd competency, *Obtaining Specific Occupational Skills,* is dependent on individual student training and cannot be assessed by one set of items, so it is not measured by either battery. The test manual for both Knowledge and Performance Batteries includes a rationale for, and an overview of, the LCCE curriculum; a comprehensive guide to administration and scoring; and two forms (A and B) of the test. The Knowledge Battery also includes an extensive technical report. Data from the Knowledge Battery, when combined with LCCE Performance Battery measures, can be used to provide a comprehensive career assessment.

The LCCE Knowledge Battery is written at a fourth-grade reading level, and the standardization allows for either a written or an oral administration of the test, to accommodate for reading difficulties. Directions for administering the Knowledge Battery are very detailed and clear. It is designed to be administered to groups of six to eight students at a time, but may be administered to as many as 15. Students may either mark the appropriate response to each multiple-choice item directly on the test protocol or responses may be marked on National Computer Systems (NCS) answer sheets. Because the entire battery contains 200 items, it is recommended that students be assessed over one domain at a time. The Daily Living domain is the longest, with 90 items, and may take up to 2 hours to administer. The Personal Social domain contains 70 items and the Occupational Guidance and Preparation domain contains 40 items. Tests may only be hand scored, using either an answer key for protocols with answers circled, or

NCS templates for responses marked on NCS answer sheets. Items 1 through 10 assess the first LCCE competency, items 11 through 20, the second, etc. Competency scores for each of the 20 competencies are calculated, with 80% or more correct (8 out of 10) indicating a mastery score for that competency.

The Performance Battery consists of a variety of assessment activities, including open-ended questions, role-plays, card sorts, and hands-on activities. Students' daily living, personal-social, and occupational functioning skills are determined based on their actual performance of those skills. In some instances, due to limitations associated with assessing certain subcompetencies in the classroom setting, advanced knowledge or cognitive questions are used. Thus, the performance batteries contain three types of items: performance, simulated performance, and performance-related knowledge. Of the total 105 items, 57% are performance-related knowledge, 33% are performance, and 10% are simulated performance. The manual includes a list of materials that are needed for each performance test.

Each test within the Performance Battery contains five questions, some of which may be administered in small groups and some of which must be administered individually. It is estimated that each competency will take one to two class periods to complete and completion of the entire Performance Battery would take 22 to 24 class periods (the length of time for a class period is not defined). The individual competency tests include scoring sheets with scoring guidelines; the manual cautions that examiners should consider local characteristics of the school and community in judging students' responses. A competency is mastered when a student scores 80% (four out of five items correct) on the corresponding test.

Use in Counseling

The LCCE Curriculum was designed for high school students with mild mental retardation or specific learning disabilities who need a functional curriculum to prepare them for the transition from school to work. For students for whom the LCCE curriculum is their high school curriculum, the following measures are recommended. The Performance Battery should be used as a pretest to determine where instruction should begin. Subsequently, after each unit of instruction, the appropriate Performance Battery should be administered to determine both student performance and effectiveness of instruction in the particular competencies being measured. The Knowledge Battery is designed to be administered annually to assess student growth in each competency.

Competencies are not considered mastered unless students achieve mastery (80% correct) on both the Knowledge and Performance Batteries. Scores for each competency (from both Knowledge and Performance Batteries) are transferred to a Student Competency Assessment Record (SCAR), which is included in the test manual. This provides a comprehensive summary of a student's performance on the 22 LCCE competencies. This information is very useful in the development of Individual Education Plans and for planning the transition from school to work. Competencies are written in terms of measurable behaviors and are appropriate for student goals and objectives.

Technical Considerations

The development of the LCCE Knowledge Battery occurred over a seven-year period and included five field tests, which resulted in a 400-item test. Based on feedback from field site users, who recommended a shorter battery, this test was converted to two 200-item tests, Form A and Form B. The final battery, including both forms, was then field tested to establish reliability, validity, and equivalency of forms; to determine major psychometric dimensions of the instrument; to develop normative data; and to facilitate the use of the test for teachers.

The norm group consisted of 177 students served by special education at 10 different sites across the country. The median age of the group was 15 years and 73% of the students were in grades 9, 10, and 11. Seventy-five percent of the students were classified as "educable mentally handicapped" and 75% of the group was Anglo. Although the LCCE Knowledge Battery has not been standardized with middle/junior high age students, the author states that it would be useful in assessing this group as well.

To determine parallel form reliability, all students in the norm group completed Form A in one session and then completed Form B in a second session two weeks later. Equivalency correlations for the different domains between Form A and Form B ranged from .68 to .88; the equivalency correlation for the total test was .90. Test-retest reliability coefficients for the different domains range from .68 to .85; Form A's test-retest reliability was .85 and Form B's was .82. Given the probable wide range of individual differences among the sample group, the Knowledge Battery seems to yield reliable scores.

Validity of the LCCE Knowledge Battery was addressed during the field testing process in the areas of construct, content, and criterion-related validity. The technical manual indicates that validity was addressed through input from special educators across the country, who compared LCCE skills to those in other existing curricula. Validity of the Knowledge Battery was assessed through calculation of item analyses and item difficulties, in combination with evaluation by experts as well as test consultants and administrators. In terms of criterion-related validity, correlations between student mastery and teacher judgment of mastery ranged from .04 to .48 and were found to be statistically significant for 17 of the 20 competencies. The validity of the entire 200-item test has not yet been established; however, since the curriculum is divided into domains, each domain is assessed and taught separately, and educational planning is made according to domains. However, with the wide range of individual differences among students for whom this assessment is appropriate, the Knowledge Battery appears to have adequate validity for many, if not all, uses.

There are no reliability or validity data available for the Performance Battery. The test manual indicates that versions of the battery were field-tested in, and evaluated by, 20 different school districts. In addition, the Performance Battery was reviewed by several experts in the field, who made recommendations and suggestions for revision. However, this is all the information provided.

Overall Critique

The LCCE Knowledge Battery, combined with the Performance Battery and the LCCE Curriculum, provides a complete instructional program for secondary students needing a functional curriculum. Although the Knowledge Battery may be used separately from the complete program, because it is based on the LCCE Curriculum it is most effectively used as a part of the complete package (Susan Bergert, personal communication, December 15, 1999). There are a variety of support materials available for this program, including comprehensive lesson plans and a demonstration video. Also, the Council for Exceptional Children provides both regional and onsite training to teachers who plan to use the LCCE Curriculum. There is also a companion third instrument available, *Competency Rating Scale* (CRS), which is a checklist on which persons knowledgeable about individual students can rate them on each of the 97 LCCE subcompetencies.

Primary concerns are related to the norm group on which the Knowledge Battery was standardized; with 73% Anglo students and the use of the term "educable mentally handicapped," which is very vague. This does not seem to be a typical group of high school students in a functional high school program. It would be advisable for school districts to develop local norms and to conduct reliability and validity studies on their own populations. The author does address the issue of cultural diversity; 15 items on Form A and 17 items on Form B of the Knowledge Battery have been flagged as being potentially culturally biased. The administration manual states that these items may need to be modified before administering the test.

Another concern is the lack of technical information related to the Performance Battery. Although a field test was conducted and the Performance Battery was evaluated by experts, it is still necessary to obtain and provide evidence of reliability and validity.

Worthy of note is the attention to individual differences in the manuals of the LCCE Knowledge and Performance Batteries. There are four checklists in the manuals (Communication Styles, Curriculum Content, Instructional Strategies, and Evaluation Techniques), which are designed to assess the appropriateness of each area in relation to cultural and ethnic diversities. These are useful tools for evaluating all instruction and are an indication of the student-centeredness of the LCCE curriculum, which discourages the assumption that poor student performance is always indicative of poor student ability. In addition, the manual includes suggestions for incorporating multicultural education into the LCCE curriculum. Finally, the publisher appears open to suggestions from persons using both the LCCE curriculum and the Knowledge and Performance Batteries.

Bibliography

Brolin, D. E. (1992). *Competency assessment knowledge batteries.* Reston, VA: Council for Exceptional Children.

Brolin, D. E. (1992). *Competency assessment performance batteries.* Reston, VA: Council for Exceptional Children.

Brolin, D. E. (1997). *Life centered career education. A competency based approach* (5th ed.). Reston, VA: Council for Exceptional Children.

Reading-Free Vocational Interest Inventory:2 (RFVII:2)

Ralph L. Becker
Elbern Publications
P.O. Box 09497
Columbus, OH 43209

Target Population: Ages 12 to 62; mental retardation, learning disabled, disadvantaged, and regular classroom students.

Statement of the Purpose of the Instrument: To measure the vocational interests of the special needs student/adult and regular classroom students.

Titles of Subtests, Scales, Scores Provided: Scales: Automotive, Building Trades, Clerical, Animal Care, Food Service, Patient Care, Horticulture, Housekeeping, Personal Service, Laundry Service and Materials Handling. Scores: Standard scores and percentiles, descriptive ratings. There are five cluster scores composed of the 11 scales.

Forms and Levels Available, with Dates of Publication/Revision of Each: R-FVII:2 Published in 2000.

Date of Most Recent Edition of Test Manual, User's Guide, Etc.: January 2000.

Languages in Which Available: English only.

Time: Actual Test Time: 20 minutes or less.
     Total Administration Time: 30 minutes.

Norm Group(s) on Which Scores Are Based: Mental Retardation, Learning Disabled, Disadvantaged, Regular Classroom Students. Males/females in each group.

Manner in Which Results Are Reported for Individuals Profile/Score Form.
    Types of Scores: Standard scores, percentiles, descriptive ratings.
    Report Format/Content:
       Basic Service: A four-page report of performance completed by the examiner for each examinee.

Report Format/Content for Group Summaries: Not available.

Scoring
    Machine Scoring Service: Not available.
    Hand Scoring:
       Scored by: Clerk; Counselor.
       Time required for scoring: 10 minutes.
    Local Machine Scoring: Not available.

Computer Software Options Available: Not available.

Cost of Materials:
   Specimen Set: $47.75 (10 test booklets + one manual). Exam. Set (one test booklet + one manual) $34.50
   Counselee Materials:
   Manual $33 (for examiner only–reusable)
   Pkg. of 20 test booklets (examinee, non-reusable) $36.50
   Pkg. of 40 test booklets or more $34.50 per set of 20

Additional Comments of Interest to Users: We are considering the possibility of computer programming the test in the future.

Published Reviews: This is a new test and no reviews have been prepared.

Reviewed by

Stephen W. Thomas
Chair and Professor
Department of Rehabilitation Studies
East Carolina University

Description

The *Reading-Free Vocational Interest Inventory: 2* (R-FVII: 2) was released in 2000, and "like its predecessor (R-FVII, Revised), is a non-reading vocational preference inventory for use with individuals with mental retardation, learning disabilities, the disadvantaged, and regular classroom students" (Becker, 2000, p. 3). The current inventory has been in existence since 1967 and is a revision of the 1975 and 1981 R-FVII. The second edition manual has been extensively rewritten and the inventory nationally re-normed on over 15,000 individuals in five different school/training, rehabilitation, and work settings. It appears that the developer has attempted to rectify many of the problems with the manual, test booklet, norms, and standardization identified by past reviewers of the R-FVII (Cantwell, 1994; Domino, 1988).

The test booklet contains 165 line drawn pictures of men and women performing jobs and work activities presented in 55 triads, two rows of triads per page. Many pictures have been redrawn to update work settings, several have been moved into different triads, and all 165 pictures were enhanced by including dark hair or a hat on each target worker. Both written instructions in the booklet and oral directions ask the student/client to draw a large circle around one of the three pictures that "you like best," incorporating a forced-choice technique. The consumable inventory booklet can be used for untimed individual or group administration (with separate instructions for both), and takes approximately 20 minutes or less for participants to complete. It is then hand scored and results entered on the *Record of Interest and Cluster Scores* form attached to the back of the booklet, which takes 15-20 minutes. Examples include pictures of a person operating a drill press, delivering office supplies, using a copier, driving a taxi cab, working in a restroom, ironing shirts, painting a wall, carrying a patient's bedpan, and working at a computer. The first triad in the inventory booklet contains the three activities of servicing a car with gas, building a wall, and delivering mail. The manual indicates that the pictures represent "a wide range of occupations and job tasks" found at the unskilled, semiskilled, and skilled levels of work.

Raw scores for "like" responses are totaled and converted to T-scores, percentile scores, and descriptive ratings (i.e., High, Above Average, Average, Below Average, Low) for the 11 Interest scales (Automotive, Building Trades, Clerical, Animal Care, Food Service, Patient Care, Horticulture, Housekeeping, Personal Service, Laundry Service, and Materials Handling). A new feature of the R-FVII: 2 is the Cluster Scores section on the record form that combines two or more of the 11 Interest scores to form five broad occupational groups. The five Cluster Scores are Mechanical (Automotive plus Building Trades), Outdoor (Animal Care plus Horticulture), Mechanical-Outdoor (Automotive, Building Trades, Animal Care, Horticulture, plus Housekeeping), Food Service-Handling Operations (Food Service plus Materials Handling), and Clerical-Social Service (Clerical, Patient Care, Personal Service, plus Laundry Service). Percentile scores and Cluster Quotients, with a mean of 100 and a standard deviation of 15, are used for converting and interpreting summed raw scores. Narrative space is provided for writing interpretations (incorporating additional historical and test information) and recommendations.

Use in Counseling

The R-FVII: 2 manual provides four examples of completed *Record of Interest and Cluster Scores* forms to assist in entering and interpreting the results. Although no case studies accompany the four example forms, the *Interpretation/Recommendation* section at the end of each completed sample form provides useful narrative information for better understanding the case.

As with past versions of the instrument, the R-FVII: 2 manual and inventory booklet are accompanied by the revised *Occupational Titles List*. This 38-page publication contains an alphabetical listing of 816 unskilled, semiskilled, and skilled occupations (with *Fourth Edition Dictionary of Occupational Titles* nine-digit codes), the same jobs classified by the R-FVII: 2 Interest Areas, definitions of master terms and titles, and seven "Steps for Selecting Occupations for Workers and Trainees." One of the seven "Steps" requires the review and use of supplemental information with the R-FVII: 2 (e.g., education/training, work experience, other test scores, attitudes, individual's needs), which is an appropriate activity when interpreting any test results. In the hands of skilled users, the *Occupational Titles List* can provide examples of related jobs to be used in further assessment, counseling, planning, education, training, and placement.

The *R-FVII: 2 Manual* indicates that the value of the inventory is dependent on its use with individuals who can understand and make decisions about the pictures presented. Additionally, the inventory may not provide meaningful information for counseling with individuals whose career aspirations and abilities are at the "high-tech", technical, and professional levels. Use with mentally retarded, learning disabled, disadvantaged, and regular classroom students/clients whose job goals and abilities are consistent with the range of unskilled, semi-skilled, and skilled jobs represented in the inventory would be appropriate.

Technical Considerations
New and additional technical information has been added to the R-FVII: 2, including new and expanded norm groups, reliability, and validity studies. During 1997-1998, the R-FVII:2 was administered to 15,564 individuals (6,505 with mental retardation) in 26 states and Puerto Rico. There are separate norm tables for males and females, youth and adults in the five categories of Mental Retardation, Learning Disabled, Regular Classroom, Adult Disadvantaged, and Adult Sheltered Work, for all 11 Interest Areas and five Clusters, ranging in sample size from 765 to 1,140.

Internal consistency reliability coefficients were determined using the Kuder-Richardson #20 formula, on four groups (younger and older MR males and females) for all 11 Interest and five Cluster scales. Reliability coefficients ranged from .72 to .95 with most falling in the .80s and 90s (sample sizes ranged from 402 to 426). Materials Handling had the lowest reliability with coefficients ranging from .72 to .78. The interest areas of Patient Care (all in the .90s) and Automotive (half .90s, half 80s), and the Mechanical Cluster (half .90s and half in high .80s) demonstrated the highest internal consistency reliability. The manual points out that reliability coefficients were "modestly higher" for older mentally retarded males and females (ages 16-21) than for the younger group (ages 12-15).

Test-retest reliability with a two-week interval between administrations was reported on 16 different groups. Sample sizes were relatively small ranging from 41 to 76 individuals for all five norm categories. Results yielded coefficients primarily in the .80s and .90s. Materials Handling was the least reliable with coefficients reported mostly in the .70s for both males and females. Interest scales most reliable for males were Automotive and Building Trades; and for females, the highest reliabilities were found in Clerical, Patient Care, Personal Service, and Housekeeping. All Cluster raw score reliabilities were in the .80s and .90s, but as the author states, "The higher reliability coefficients for clusters (none were in the .70s) may be a function of test length..." (Becker, 2000, p. 31). Overall, reliability as obtained on the standardization sample "are of sufficient magnitude to suggest that the items of the R-FVII: 2 yield stable results over a two-week interval" (Becker, 2000, p. 31). The Standard Error of Measurement (SEM) is extensively reported with a discussion of how it can be used in interpretation.

The manual presents evidence on all three currently acceptable forms of validity: content, criterion related, and construct. Two forms of content validity are presented. The first was based on the use of job activities as the rationale for developing and standardizing the pictures/items and scales, but no statistical data are presented. The second used two approaches to item analysis. The first used the method of extreme groups item analysis where the R-FVII: 2 results from a group of 1,988 males and females from eight norm group classifications were analyzed to see how well each item related to the scale score. The second approach used the internal consistency evidence previously reported, which yielded coefficients in the .80s or above.

In the area of criterion-related validity, the R-FVII: 2 was compared to the *Geist Picture Interest Inventory* (GPII, 1988 version). Pearson *r* correlations are reported in two tables for females and males from four norm groups. Significant correlations at the .05 and .01 levels are reported for nearly all female and most male groups, supporting criterion-related validity.

Construct validity was established by testing three hypotheses. The first hypothesis, "The items and subtest scores correlate highly," refers to the discrimination indexes presented under content validity item analysis discussed earlier in this review. The second hypothesis, "The incumbent workers engaged in an occupation represented on the R-FVII: 2 should score higher on the scale that defines their occupation," was supported through a comparison of R-FVII: 2 interest scores to the employment setting for 477 mentally retarded workers. The third hypothesis, "Scales with similar characteristics but different titles and item content will show large, positive correlations; however, negligible to negative intercorrelations should be obtained for scales with dissimilar characteristics," was supported through a variety of intercorrelation tables for interests and clusters by norm group. The developer states that "In general, the results of this study offer support for the construct validity of the R-FVII: 2 scales and clusters' (Becker, 2000, p. 58).

Overall Critique

The R-FVII was one of the first picture interest inventories that specifically addressed the needs of individuals with mental retardation. The most recent edition, R-FVII: 2, has made some revisions to the pictures to update job activities and better clarify the target worker in the line drawn picture. The *R-FVII: 2*

Manual has been extensively revised with expanded norm tables and standardization. The inventory, and in particular the manual, are much improved over the earlier versions.

There continues to be a concern about the ambiguity of drawings in picture interest inventories in general that may make it difficult to ascertain the nature of some activities. Also, immigrants from other countries may not be able to relate to the settings, tools, or activities presented. Individuals who have ability and interest in "high tech," technical, and professional careers would be better served with a more broad-based interest inventory. Although some dated pictures have been eliminated and replaced with new ones reflecting more current work activities, there is only one picture each of an individual operating a computer, a FAX machine, and a copier. Additional pictures in these and related areas would be helpful. Some disability advocates argue that the R-FVII interest areas represented by the inventory stereotype and limit employment opportunities for individuals with disabilities. However, the new *R-FVII: 2 Occupational Titles List* does provide a larger and more current listing of jobs by interest area than the previous edition, but not by cluster.

The five new cluster areas are a welcome addition to the inventory; however, information on how to interpret and use these cluster scores is limited. Four examples of the completed record forms are contained at the end of the manual, but lack case study information or interpretive descriptions of the findings.

The R-FVII: 2 fills a void for an interest inventory that offers a pictorial format and a range of unskilled, semiskilled, and skilled jobs that would be appropriate for students and adults who are mentally retarded, learning disabled, and disadvantaged. The interest and cluster results provide meaningful information for vocational assessment, counseling, planning, education, training, and job placement when used in conjunction with additional, relevant information.

References

Becker, R. L. (2000). *Reading-free vocational interest inventory: 2 manual* (2nd ed.). Columbus, OH: Elbern Publications.

Cantwell, Z. C. (1994). Reading-free vocational interest inventory (R-FVII). In J. T. Kapes, M. M. Mastie & E. A. Whitfield (Eds.). *A Counselor's Guide to Career Assessment Instruments* (3rd ed. pp. 325-330). Alexandria, VA: National Career Development Association.

Domino, G. (1988). Reading-free vocational interest inventory–revised (R-FVII Revised). In J. T. Kapes & M. M. Mastie (Eds.). *A Counselor's Guide to Career Assessment Instruments* (2nd ed. pp. 270-274). Alexandria, VA: National Career Development Association.

Street Survival Skills Questionnaire (SSSQ)

Lawrence T. McCarron and Dan Linkenhoker
McCarron-Dial Systems, Inc.
P.O. Box 45628
Dallas, TX 75245
214-634-2863
214-634-9970 (fax)
www.mccarrondial.com
mds@mccarrondial.com

Target Population: The SSSQ may be used with individuals 9 1/2 years of age through adults who are being served by special education, prevocational or vocational rehabilitation programs. Although applicable to a wide range of handicapping conditions, the SSSQ is particularly appropriate for persons with developmental disabilities.

Statement of the Purpose of the Instrument: The SSSQ was constructed to assess community relevant adaptive skills in a comprehensive fashion. Specifically, it provides an objective and reliable method of assessing various aspects of adaptive behavior, a baseline behavioral measure to gauge the effects of training, and a prediction of the individual's potential for success in adapting to community living conditions and vocational placement.

Titles of Subtests, Scales, Scores Provided: The SSSQ consists of nine volumes (subtests), each relating to a specific area of adaptive behavior: Basic Concepts; Functional Signs; Tool Identification and Use; Domestic Management; Health, First Aid and Safety; Public Services; Time; Money; and Measurement. Within each volume, there are 24 pages of four pictures each with relevant questions on the facing page. the examiner asks the question, and the subject indicates (orally or by pointing) the correct answer. Using the age-appropriate norm table, the raw score for each subtest is converted to a scaled score (mean of 10; standard deviation of 3). In addition, the total test raw score may be converted to a "Survival Skills Quotient" (SSQ), with a mean of 100 and standard deviation of 15.

Forms and Levels Available, with Dates of Publication/Revision of Each: Only one form/level of the instrument is available; originally published in 1979; last revision was 1993.

Date of Most Recent Edition of Test Manual, User's Guide, Etc.: 1993

Languages in Which Available: English only.

Time: Actual Test Time: 30-45 minutes.
        Total Administration Time: 30-45 minutes.

Norm Group(s) on Which Scores Are Based: Normative data for adolescents and adults were obtained from two groups. The developmentally disabled group consisted of 400 individuals from sheltered workshops and community employment programs in five states. The average age of this group was 25 years with a range from 15 to 55; the mean IQ was 58 (range 28 to 80). To provide a standard of comparison for normal young adults about to enter competitive employment, a second group was assessed. This group consisted of 200 adolescents in secondary school prevocational programs who were considered to have a high probability of successful competitive employment in the community as well as the capacity to live autonomously in an apartment. The average age was 17 (range 14 to 18) with a mean IQ of 97 (range 80 to 121).

Younger age norms are also provided. The normative sample for children ages 9 1/2 up to 12 years of age consisted of 120 normal children with a mean age of 10 years, 11 months. the mean grade level was 4.8 (range 4 to 6); the mean IQ on the Otis was 99 (range 55 to 150 with a standard deviation of 16.3). Norms for ages 12-15 were obtained form 197 normal children with a mean age of 14 years., 0 months. The mean grade level was 8.0 range 6 to 10), and the mean IQ on the Otis was 98.6 (range 55 to 150; standard deviation of 16).

The salient characteristics for each of the normative samples are presented in the manual as well as detailed information regarding reliability and validity (content, construct, concurrent and predictive.)

Manner in Which Results are Reported for Individuals:

Types of Scores: The raw score (number of correct responses) for each subtest is converted to a scaled score (mean of 10; sd=3). A scaled score of 10 (range 7-13) indicates typical performance, whereas a discrepancy of three or more scaled score points (range 4-7) indicates moderate deficits. A scaled score discrepancy of six or more (range from 0-4) indicates severe problems in knowledge of adaptive behavior. Conversion tables based on a mean of 100 and a standard deviation of 15 are also provided so that the individual's total test score may be converted to a Survival Skills Quotient (SSQ). This allows a direct comparison between SSQs and IQ scores.

Report Format/Content:

Basic Service: The SSSQ is easy to score and interpret. In addition to comparing an individual's score with a normative group as described above, a "profile of adaptive behavior" may be depicted by plotting the scaled scores on the front of the score form. Information for individual program planning is provided as relative strengths and needs across the nine subtests are readily identified. Also included with the SSSQ is a "Master Planning Chart" (MPC), which provides a means of describing the individual's level of achievement in each of the nine content areas. Each of the 24 items that comprise a subtest is identified on the chart by a word that corresponds to the content of the item. By shading or marking those items with correct answers, an incorrect answer can be easily recognized as it appears as a blank area on the MCP. This provides an item-by-item analysis of performance, which may be used as a guide for structuring programming/training.

Report Format/Content for Group Summaries: Not available.

Scoring
  Machine Scoring Service: Not available.
  Hand Scoring:
    Scored by: Clerk; Counselor.
    Time required for scoring: 5 minutes.
  Local Machine Scoring:
    Provisions/conditions/equipment required: A computer program, SSSQ Computer Report, is available for $225. The software is licensed for use on one computer, but there is no additional "per use" charge. In addition to the automatic scoring and plotting of the

scores according to age-appropriate norms, the SSSQ Report provides narrative interpretations of the evaluee's performance in the nine content areas of functioning. Each of these areas is then broken down into content "subareas" which are analyzed with respect to the individual's own average level of performance. A list of relative strengths and needs is printed as well as specific page references to the Curriculum Guides for the SSSQ. In this way, the report may serve the needs of the assessor with statistical analysis to be later incorporated into a general assessment report and assist the program planner in the specification of training goals. The software is available for Macintosh and IBM or compatibles.

Computer Software Options Available: Not available.

Cost of Materials:
Specimen Set: $350; this price includes the nine-volume set of SSSQ subtests, Manual Curriculum Guides, and one package each of the Score Forms and Master Planning Charts. The materials are all packaged in a sturdy carrying case.
Counselee Materials: The only expendable items are the Score Forms ($23 per pkg. of 50) and the master Planning Charts ($15 for 50).

Published Reviews:
Haring, T. G. (1992). Review of the Adaptive Behavior: Street Survival Skills Questionnaire. In J. J. Kramer & J. C. Conoley (Eds.), *Eleventh mental measurements yearbook* (pp. 11-14). Lincoln, NE: Buros Institute, University of Nebraska-Lincoln.
Musgrave, J. R., Marso, K. Shelton, D., & Plumlee, S. (1997). A comparison of the McCarron-Dial System's predicted residential levels, Haptic Visual Discrimination Test and Street Survival Skills Questionnaire with a criterion-referenced independent living skills assessment. *Vocational Evaluation and Work Adjustment Bulletin, 30*(1), 4-8.

Reviewed by

Gary M. Clark
Professor of Special Education
University of Kansas

Description

The Street Survival Skills Questionnaire (SSSQ) was originally published in 1980 in response to the need for an objective measure of adaptive behavior for persons with developmental disabilities. The assessment was designed to provide particular emphasis on prevocational competencies as well as social adaptation and independent living in the community. It was designed also to provide an objective alternative to observational rating scales and to avoid some of the disadvantages of subjective ratings by parents or other caregivers. The focus on assessing specific adaptive behaviors of adolescents and adults with mental retardation or other types of developmental disabilities restricts its use to this population, but provides professionals in the field of developmental disabilities an objective measure that yields an alternative to current observational or rating scales.

The 1993 version of the instrument presents items in a pictorial, multiple-choice format. It is individually administered and is a nonreading assessment except for a few competencies where reading is essential to the skills being measured. The SSSQ is not timed and the pictorial response options make responses easier for individuals with poor verbal skills or with fine motor problems. There are nine subtests, each of which relates to a separate domain of adaptive behavior. The subtests include Basic Concepts; Functional Signs; Tool Identification and Use; Domestic Management; Health, First Aid, and Safety; Public Services; Time; Money; and Measurement.

The SSSQ kit contains the pictorial test items, an examiner's manual, answer booklets, a curriculum guide, and a master planning chart. The examiner's manual includes information on the purpose and development of the instrument, validity and reliability data, administration and scoring procedures, norms, interpretation guidelines, and a discussion of implications for training. The answer booklet is a four-page form that presents space for the examiner to score each item as pass or fail and a profile form for recording raw scores, scaled scores, and the Survival Skills Quotient. (SSQ). There is an SSSQ computer-generated report that provides automatic scoring and plotting of the scores according to age-appropriate norms and narrative interpretations of the individual's performance in nine content areas.

The test format of the SSSQ is based on the nine subtests of adaptive behavior, each with 24 pages of four pictures per page. Each page is an item eliciting a response showing knowledge or understanding. The administrator tells the evaluee, "I will show you a page with four pictures. I will ask you a question, and you are to point to the picture that is the best answer to the question" (McCarron & Linkenhoker, 1993, p. 29). An example item from the section on identification and use of tools is a page with four drawings of tools (axe, miter saw, hack saw, and crowbar). The examiner asks, "Which tool is used for chopping firewood?"

Use in Counseling

The test authors make a broad claim for four major applications of the SSSQ: (1) classification with respect to mental retardation, (2) vocational program placement, (3) residential program placement, and (4) training strategies (McCarron & Linkenhoker, 1993). Predicting success or determining a type or level of vocational placement for older adolescents or adults with developmental disabilities are highly questionable, particularly with students between the ages of 14 and 16. Therefore, in career counseling, extreme caution should be used when making decisions based upon the results from the SSSQ. However, results may provide direction for determining goals and objectives that should be included in the transition planning of students' Individualized Educational Programs (IEPs) at school.

The authors of the SSSQ take the view that assessed abilities on the SSSQ should be a basis for vocational placement in one of several levels of vocational placement: community employment, transitional, extended workshop, work activities, and day care. This is contrary to the national view of advocates for persons with mental retardation and developmental disabilities who believe that a more person-centered approach involves matching an individual's specific abilities, preferences, and interests with the demands and expectations of a specific job in the competitive marketplace. In other words, current recommended practice suggests that unless an individual or his/her family prefers a day care situation, work activities, or an extended workshop placement, there is no reason to predict that most persons could not be in competitive employment (with or without supports) or transitional supported employment with a goal of competitive employment.

The SSSQ uses items for assessment that are highly related to communication skills and are only inferentially related to general employment success. Most of the items are much more related to community living skills and independent living than to employment. For this reason, the usefulness of the SSSQ for career counseling or recommendations for vocational placement is limited.

Technical Considerations

The normative data for the SSSQ were based on two reported groups. One group consisted of 400 adolescents and adults with developmental disabilities (ages 15-55) and the other was 200 adolescents from prevocational secondary programs. The latter was intended to be the "normal" comparison group. No ages are provided, but it is assumed that they must have comprised a typical high school age group ranging from 14-18. For some reason, this norm population, reflected in Table 22 of the manual (McCarron & Linkenhoker, 1993, p. 34) is described by the authors as "*normal* [authors' emphasis) adults who had predominantly high scores [on the SSSQ]" Not only is there some question about high school students being an adequate adult sample, but the predominantly high-scoring sample resulted in a negatively skewed distribution. The authors did acknowledge the skewed distribution and raised cautions for interpreting the SSQ (Survival Skills Quotient) with individuals of above average intelligence.

The norm table for the target population of the SSSQ, adolescents and adults with mental retardation and developmental disabilities, is labeled in the manual as Table of Norms for Adult Neuropsychologically Disabled (Table 20, p. 33). This term was not used in the initial description of the sample, or previously defined, and is puzzling given the difficulty in differentiating environmental and neurological etiologies in mental retardation.

Test-retest reliability was calculated over a one-month interval of time. The test-retest coefficients for subtests ranged from .87 to .95, with the total scores showing an exceptional reliability coefficient of .99. Internal consistency coefficients, using the Kuder-Richardson 20 formula was .97, with subtests indicating a range from .68 to .96. The standard errors of measurement were low and added to the impressive reliability indices.

The SSSQ manual presents validity data using procedures that relate to content, construct, concurrent, and predictive validity. Content validity data were derived using a thorough and sophisticated item selection process. Overall construct validity data based on a factor analysis appears acceptable, but four of the nine subtests had low indicators of communality with other subtests. That is, the proportion of variance within each of those subtests was not shared with the other subtests suggesting that they retained a sufficient variance specific to themselves. The concurrent validity approach was traditional and used the San Francisco Vocational Competency Scale (SFVCS, Levine & Elzey, 1968) as the criterion of vocational competency and the Progress Assessment Chart (PAC, Gunzburg, 1963) as the criterion for adaptive behavior, both of which are not the most currently or frequently used measures of adaptive behavior and employability. The predictive validity evidence was confounded by using data that combined the SSSQ with the Behavior Rating Scale (BRS). Although there were statistically significant correlations between the SSSQ and the various concurrent and predictive criterion measures, the evidence does not support using the SSSQ for classification of individuals as having mental retardation nor its utility for vocational placement.

Overall Critique

By itself, the SSSQ does not provide the kind of information that counselors need for informing themselves or their clients about the clients' employability or their ability to maintain employment. It could be used, though, in conjunction with situational assessment or other observational assessments to identify areas of emphasis in adaptive behavior training. The SSSQ profile may provide some direction to relative strengths, and the linkage of the profile to the *Curriculum Guides for SSSQ* (McCarron, Cobb, Smith, & Barron, 1982) could provide counselors or teachers with specific instructional procedures and strategies for a training program that is targeted to individual needs. Beyond this, the generally outdated view of extremely restricted vocational placement options put the SSSQ in direct philosophical conflict with The Association for Persons with Severe Handicaps (Meyer, Peck, & Brown, 1991), the Division on Career Development and Transition of the Council for Exceptional Children (Sitlington, Neubert, Begun, Lombard, & Leconte, 1996), and professionals in education and rehabilitation (Murphy & Rogan, 1995; Parker & Schaller, 1996).

References

Gunzburg, H. (1963). *Progress Assessment Chart of Social and Personal Development manual.* Bristol, IN: Aux Chandelles.

Levine, S., & Elzey, F. (1968). *San Francisco Competency Scale manual.* New York: Psychological Corporation.

McCarron, L., & Linkenhoker, D. (1993). *Adaptive behavior: Street Survival Skills Questionnaire.* Dallas, TX: McCarron-Dial Systems.

McCarron, L., Cobb, G., Smith, C., & Barron, P. (1982). *A curriculum guide for the SSSQ.* Lubbock, TX: Research and Training Center in Mental Retardation, Texas Tech University.

Meyer, L. H., Peck, C. A., & Brown, L. (Eds.). (1991). *Critical issues in the lives of people with severe disabilities.* Baltimore: Paul H. Brookes.

Murphy, S. T., & Rogan, P. M. (1995). *Closing the shop: Conversion from sheltered to integrated work.* Baltimore: Paul H. Brookes.

Parker, R. M., & Schaller, J. L. (1996). Issues in vocational assessment and disability. In E. M. Szymanski & R. M. Parker (Eds.), *Work and disability: Issues and strategies in career development and job placement* (pp. 127-164). Austin, TX: PRO-ED.

Sitlington, P. L., Neubert, D. A., Begun, W., Lombard, R. C., & Leconte, P. J. (1996). *Assess for success: Handbook on transition assessment.* Reston, VA: Council for Exceptional Children.

Transition Planning Inventory (TPI)

Gary M. Clark and James R. Patton
PRO-ED, Inc.
8700 Shoal Creek Boulevard
Austin, TX 78757-6897
www.proedine.com

Target Population: All identified students with disabilities who are 16 and over and are identified for some type of special education or related service to meet the mandate of IDEA that require planning for transition services.

Statement of the Purpose of the Instrument: The TPI is an instrument for identifying and planning for the comprehensive transitional needs of students. It is designed to provide school personnel a systematic way to address critical transition planning areas.

Titles of Subtests, Scales, Scores Provided: The TPI is composed of four forms: Student Form, Home Form (in English and Spanish), School Form, and Profile and Further Assessment Recommendations Form. The TPI consists of 46 transition planning statements, organized according to planning areas: Employment, Further Education/Training, Daily Living, Leisure Activities, Community Participation, Health, Self-Determination, Communication, and Interpersonal Relationships that are rated of a six-point Likert scale. These planning areas relate closely to the domains used by various states. Each planning area has three or more items related to knowledge, skills, or behaviors associated with successful adjustment in that area. Results are profiled so that comparisons across the three sources of information can be made.

Forms and Levels Available, with Dates of Publication/Revision of Each: There is only one form and level for each scale. The instrument was published in 1997.

Date of Most Recent Edition of Test Manual, User's Guide, Etc.: 1997

Languages in Which Available: English for Student and School; Spanish and English for home.

Time: Total Administration Time: Will vary; typically 10-20 minutes; can be group administered to students and parents.

Norm Group(s) on Which Scores Are Based: This is a standardized criterion-referenced instrument that does not provide norm-referenced scores.

Manner in Which Results Are Reported for Individuals : The goal of the TPI is to generate information that leads to the development of comprehensive transition plans for students by identification of areas in which more in-depth assessment is needed, identification of knowledge and skills needs that should be addressed through the development of instructional goals and objectives, and identification of services and supports needs that should be addressed through the development of linkage goals and related activities.

    Report Format/Content: The Profile and Further Assessment Recommendations Form summarizes the information from school, home, and student. All 46 transition planning statements are listed for each reference. All statements with scores of 0, 1, or 2 need to be examined and explained.

Report Format/Content for Group Summaries: Not available.

Scoring
  Machine Scoring Service: Not available.
  Hand Scoring:
    Scored by: Examiner.
    Time required for scoring: 15-20 minutes.
  Local Machine Scoring: Not available.

Computer Software Options Available: Not available.

Cost of Materials: Complete Kit $126 (Administration and Resource Guide, 25 Profile and Further Assessment Recommendation Forms, 25 School Forms, 25 Home Forms, and 25 Student Forms, all in a sturdy storage box.)
Spanish Home Forms $24
    Specimen Set: $35 (Administration and Resource Guide, 1 of each form).

Additional Comments of Interest to Users: The Administration and Resource Guide includes an extensive list of over 600 transition goals that are correlated to each planning statement and a comprehensive resource list.

Published Reviews
Career Development for Exceptional Individuals, Volume 20, pp. 201-202, Fall 1997.

Reviewed by

Karl F. Botterbusch
Professor

Jeffery C. Lund
Research Assistant

Research and Training Center
Stout Vocational Rehabilitation Institute
University of Wisconsin-Stout

Description

According to its manual (Clark & Patton, 1997, p. 9), the Transition Planning inventory (TPI) was designed "as a formal assessment and planning tool for use with students with disabilities in individualized education planning . . to provide school personnel with a systematic way to comply with the Federal mandate for addressing transition services planning and to use recommended practices in IEP planning." The purpose of transitional assessment is to generate information leading to the development of comprehensive school-to-work transition plans for students. This instrument is designed for all disability groups. In practice, planning is accomplished by identifying (1) where more in-depth assessment is needed, (2) the knowledge and skills to be learned through the development of instructional goals and objectives, and (3) the services and supports needs that should be addressed through the development of linkage goals and related activities.

Developed by Gary M. Clark and James R. Patton, the TPI uses the following three data collection forms to assess the student: *Student Form, Home Form*, and *School Form*. The fourth form, *Profile and Further Assessment Recommendations Form,* combines and analyzes data from the other three forms to make recommendations. Each form consists of 46 items separated into nine categories: *Employment, Further Education/Training, Daily Living, Leisure Activities, Community Participation, Health, Self-Determination, Communication*, and *Interpersonal Relationships*. Each item in the Student, Home, School, and Profile and Further Assessment Recommendations Forms measures the same traits or behaviors across all forms. However, each form words the item differently. For example, Employment Question 2 states, "I can choose a job that fits my interest and abilities" in the Student Form; "Can choose a job that fits his/her interests and abilities" in the Home Form; "Makes informed choices among occupational alternatives, based on his/her own interests, preferences, and abilities" in the School Form; and "Makes informed choices" in the Profile and Further Assessment Recommendations Form. Example items of each of the eight remaining categories (as taken from the Profile and Further Assessment Recommendations Form) are as follows: "Knows how to gain entry into vocational/technical school" from Further Education/Training, "Performs everyday household tasks" from Daily Living, "Uses settings that offer entertainment" from Leisure Activities, "Participates as an active citizen" from Community participation, "Maintains good mental health" from Health, "Recognizes and accepts own strengths" from Self-determination, "Has needed writing skills" from Communication, and "Displays appropriate social behavior in variety of settings" from Interpersonal Relationships.

The ratings from the three data collection forms are compiled in columns on the Profile and Further Assessment Recommendations Form. Each item is compared across the three forms. This final form is designed to identify the areas in which more comprehensive assessment may be needed, identify the skills and knowledge needed by the student, and identify services and support needs.

School personnel providing ratings need to know that the ratings they give are not comparisons of the student's competency with same-age peers. The ratings are individual determinations of achievement or performance levels using knowledge of the student and of the kinds and levels of performance required for successful demonstration of each competency.

Although the TPI has no time limits, self-administration time is typically 15-20 minutes, with special needs administration ranging from 20-30 minutes. The manual indicates that specific adaptations to administer the instrument (e.g., translators or interpreters for non-English speaking or hearing impaired individuals; large-print, Braille, or audiotape versions for persons with visual deficits) may be needed. The instrument is provided in English-language text only. This change in format should not invalidate the content of the items. The School Form is self-administered and completed by school personnel with a direct working knowledge of the student. A school representative should explain the forms to the parent(s) and student before they complete the instrument. According to the manual (Clark & Patton, 1997) both the Parent and Student Forms can be administered using three different methods:

1. Independent self-administration is for parents and/or students the school representative knows are able to "read with comprehension and respond independently in writing"
2. Guided self-administration is for parents and/or students the school representative knows are able to "read with some level of comprehension and respond independently but still request or indicate a need for some assistance"
3. Oral administration is recommended for parents and/or students who do not read or write well enough to complete the TPI form independently. A school representative should administer the instrument. A translator or interpreter should be used for individuals who are deaf or with limited English speaking skills.

Guidelines and scripts provided for the administration of each section describe in more specific detail the skill or ability about which the question is asked. For example, Question 3 in the employment area states, "Knows how to get a job." If the student or parent does not understand the meaning, the script could be referred to. For that item it states, "Students know the basic steps of looking for a job, applying for a job, and making a good impression, in a job interview." The manual further states that since the instrument is not norm referenced, it is not crucial that the administration procedures in the manual be strictly followed.

The ratings for each of the individual items in the three forms are then transferred to the Profile and Further Assessment Recommendations Form so comparisons can be made across the three forms. If a difference in ratings is found (more than one rating higher or lower than others), then it is recommended that that item be discussed among the three participants.

Use in Counseling

By discussing the rating on the three forms, service areas of need can be identified. These identified needs should then be considered and used by school officials to develop the students Individualized Education Program (IEP).

> The TPI was designed as a formal assessment and planning tool for use with students with disabilities in individualized education planning. It focuses on the major areas of transition services planning that have emerged in the literature and from legislation in recent years. It was designed to provide school personnel with a systematic way to comply with the federal mandate for addressing transition services planning and to use recommended practices in IEP planning. (Clark & Patton, 1997, p. 9)

This instrument is designed to take a student's Individualized Education Plan (IEP) from assessment to the creation of a transition plan for the student. Although not intended specifically for counseling, it can assess possible future needs of the student that may require counseling.

Technical Considerations

All three forms of the instrument use the same item format:

	Not Appropriate	Strongly Disagree						Strongly Agree	Don't Know
Knows how to get a job	NA	0	1	2	3	4	5		DK

This format provides the student, parent, or teacher both a method of first deciding if the item is relevant or if the rater has no knowledge of the student's performance on this item. If the rater has knowledge of the item, then it is rated between 0 and 5. As indicated above, these ratings are combined on the Recommendation Form.

Reliability for the TPI was determined using test-retest and internal consistency methods. Internal consistency reliability across the nine categories ranged from .84 to .92 on the School Form, .76 to .94 on the Parent Form, and .70 to .87 on the Student Form. Test-retest reliability across the nine categories ranged from .87 to .98 on the School Form, .70 to .91 on the Parent Form, and .70 to .84 on the Student Form

Validity was assessed using content and criterion-related methods, according to the manual (Clark & Patton, 1997). Beginning with 250 items, 49 items were selected and then rated for relevance by direct service staff, school administrators, and higher educators. A high degree of agreement was reported.

As reported in the manual, a test of concurrent validity was conducted by correlating the TPI with the *Wechsler Intelligence Scale for Children-Third Edition* and the *Vineland Adaptive Behavior Scales* on a sample of 48 students. "Due to the small number of cases, many correlations were not significant. However, a number of coefficients are significant and of considerable magnitude" (p. 76). No statistical data regarding validity are included in the TPI manual. The manual states the predictive validity of this instrument is yet to be examined.

Overall Critique

The TPI was designed to provide an assessment of the multiple transition needs of students with disabilities–

> as a formal assessment and planning tool for use with students with disabilities in individualized educational planning. . . . It was designed to provide school personnel with a systematic way to comply with the federal mandate for addressing transition services planning and to use recommended practices in IEP planning. (Clark & Patton, 1997, p. 9)

The lack of any predictive validity information on this instrument concerns the reviewers. This instrument, by its own definition, is designed to assist students with disabilities with the creation of an individual plan for possible future needs. The predictive validity needs to be addressed before users can assume that the ratings foresee future behavior.

The parent and student forms can be administered in three ways, depending on the respondent's level of literacy and understanding. Although the manual states that responses should not differ due to different administration methods, the presence of a teacher or other school official during the administration of an instrument could have a major influence on the parent or the student.

The omission of a Spanish-language format for the TPI is also of concern, especially considering the large number of people whose primary language is Spanish. Although the manual states translators may be required for non-English speaking individuals, the presence of a translator, which may or may not be a teacher or other school official, could also have a major influence on the parent or student.

This instrument does show potential for use in screening for planning of transition services and IEPs. Through the inclusion of the student, parents, and school personnel in a joint venture to accomplish a common goal, the TPI addresses the major planning areas as perceived by the primary participants in the planning process.

The TPI may also be useful for group discussions with the student, parents, and school personnel concerning possible inconsistencies between the three groups in perceived abilities and skills of the student. Discussions on these inconsistencies may identify behavior differences between home and school on the part of the student. It may also identify unrealistic perceptions of the students abilities by any of the parties involved. This group discussion could be especially beneficial in the development of the Individualized Education Program for the student.

Reference
Clark, G. M., & Patton, J. R. (1997). *Transitional Planning Inventory.* Austin, TX: PRO-ED.

CHAPTER 12

Additional Career Assessment Instruments

Jerome T. Kapes
Professor Emeritus of Educational Psychology
Texas A & M University

Linda Martinez
Doctoral Student in Educational Psychology
Texas A & M University

Tammi Vacha-Haase
Assistant Professor of Psychology
Colorado State University

In previous chapters of this book, 56 major career assessment instruments are described and reviewed. In this chapter, an additional 270 instruments are briefly described and essential information such as publisher, date of publication, intended populations, and published reviews is provided. The entries for each instrument are grouped into logical categories that are parallel, but are not identical to, those used to organize the major instrument reviews. Although this chapter includes 23 more instruments than were covered in the previous edition of *A Counselor's Guide,* this number was achieved by dropping 100 instruments and adding 123 not previously included. However, even with these additions there are instruments not included that may be useful for some career assessment applications. For example, types of instruments usually not included are those which primarily assess educational achievement, general intelligence, specific aptitude measures without broad applications, and abnormal personality and adjustment. Also, although each instrument is included under only one category, in many cases it can be argued that it could also fit into one or more other categories. The User's Matrix, provided in Appendix D, attempts to reflect this overlap of categories.

To facilitate the use of this chapter, the following key to the categories of information presented is provided:

- **Type of Instrument**. The categories used to organize the instruments in the order presented are –
  A. Multiple Aptitude, Achievement, and Comprehensive Measures

    B. Specific Aptitude and Achievement Measures
    C. Interest Inventories
    D. Measures of Work Values, Satisfaction, and Environments
    E. Card Sorts
    F. Career Development/Maturity Measures
    G. Personality Assessments
    H. Instruments for Special Populations

- **Name**. The name of the instrument is listed first in boldface print. Common acronyms, when used, are provided in parenthesis immediately following the name.

- **Publisher**. Only the name of the publisher is provided. The addresses and, when available, phone numbers, e-mail addresses, and Web page of the publishers are listed in Appendix B. Additional information about the instruments can be obtained by contacting the publisher.

- **Date**. The date given refers to the initial date the instrument was published and/or when it was last revised. A range of dates, (e.g., 1960-1993) signifies ongoing development and revision of the instrument during that time span. "No Date" indicates that the date of publication was unavailable.

- **Population**. The population refers to the group or groups of individuals for whom the publisher indicates the instrument is appropriate.

- **References**. Several of the major sources of instrument reviews are cited in an abbreviated form. An annotated bibliography of each source is presented in Appendix A. The key to the abbreviations is as follows.
    CG refers to *A Counselor's Guide to Vocational Guidance Instruments*-First Edition (1), *A Counselor's Guide to Career Assessment Instruments*-Second Edition, (2) or *A Counselor's Guide to Career Assessment Instruments*-Third Edition, (3).
    MY refers to the *Mental Measurements Yearbooks*. The number immediately following denotes the volume number (Volumes 6-13). The number following the colon refers to the test number.
    TC is the abbreviation for *Test Critiques*. The number following the colon is the page number.
    TP5 is the abbreviation for *Tests in Print V*. The number following the colon is the test number.

T3 or **T4** is the abbreviation for *Tests*-Third or Fourth Edition.   The number following the colon is the page number.

AT:98 refers to *Assessment for Transitions Planning: A Guide for Special Education Teachers and Related Service Personnel* (Clark, 1998).

MG and **MD** refer to *Measurement and Evaluation in Guidance* and *Measurement* and *Evaluation in Counseling and Development*, respectively.   The number following the colon refers to the month and year of the issue in which the review is found (e.g., 10/92 denotes October, 1992).

B:93 refers to *Vocational Evaluation Systems and Software: A consumer's Guide* (Brown et al., 1993).

- **Brief Description**. This section provides an overview of what is measured and includes the titles of some of the scales associated with each instrument. Additional comments are included for some instruments (e.g., to indicate a major use, special reports or support materials available, or training required for administration).

A. MULTIPLE APTITUDE, ACHIEVEMENT AND COMPREHENSIVE MEASURES

Name of test/Publisher/Date/Population	Reference(s)	Brief Description
ACCU Vision – Workplace Success Skills Learning Resources 1990 – 1999 High School to Adults		Designed to identify & measure workplace skills. Consists of 5 video modules divided into the following sections: Interpersonal Skills, Listening, Structuring Work Activities, Trainability, & Graphs & Charts. "Keyed to the SCANS foundational skills for entry-level positions." Individual or group administration.
Activity Vector Analysis (AVA) Walter V. Clarke Associates 1948 – 1994 Prospective Employees		Designed to determine if an individual is a match for the job. Consists of 5 separate parts: Activity Vector Analysis, Job Rating Scale, Job Expectations, Behaviorally Based Interview Questions, & Job Model. Paper/pencil or computer administered; must be interpreted by a certified person.
Apticom Vocational Research Institute 1985 Adolescents to Adults	CG2,3 T4:308	Uses a dedicated microcomputer to administer 3 types of assessment batteries: Aptitude, Interest, & Educational Skills Development. Computer scores assessment batteries & synthesizes aptitude and interest scores. Results identify job families consistent with DOL's job matching constructs.
Aptitude Interest Inventory Educational Technologies/Invest Learning 1993 – 1996 High School to Adults	MY13:14 TP5:168	A computer-based measure of aptitude & interest. Aptitude yields scores in 7 areas: clerical perception, vocabulary, numerical computation, numerical reasoning, spatial visualization, inductive reasoning, & analytical reasoning. Interest yields scores in 3 areas: data, people, things. Revised version of the ABCD/IBCD. Administered via computer. Restricted to licensed sites.
Basic Skills Locator Test (BSLT) Piney Mountain Press 1998 Age 15 to Adults	TP5:259	Designed to assess math & language skill levels of individuals functioning at the 12th-grade level or below. Results provided in terms of GED & grade levels. Results correlated to DOL job classifications, OOH, DOT, & GOE. Computer scored, machine scored, or publisher scored. Computer version available.
Career and Vocational Form of the SOI-LA Basic Test SOI Systems 1975 Adolescents to Adults	T3:787	Measures 24 cognitive abilities that predict career & vocational options. Consists of subtests taken from the SOI-LA Basic Test. Paper/pencil tests. Suitable for groups. Instructions for self-administration. Computer analysis available.
Career IQ and Interest Test (CIQIT) Pro-Ed, Inc. 1997 Age 13 to Adults		Assists individuals in identifying possible job choices. Consists of a CD-ROM that includes vocational aptitude test, interest measure, & recent OOH information. Aptitude survey measures 6 factors such as general ability & manual dexterity. Interest schedule measures 12 factors such as artistic & nature

Name of test/Publisher/Date/Population	Reference(s)	Brief Description
Career Profile Assessment New Concepts Career Development Corporation 1998 Junior and Senior High School		Assesses 10 aptitudes & 12 interests using a computer-based system. Aptitudes include reasoning, mathematics, language, learning, numerical, spatial, & color discrimination. Interest assessment covers the 12 GOE categories. Output tied to DOT Worker Qualification Profile & New Concepts career information.
Career Programs Assessment Test (CPAT) ACT, Inc. 1981 – 1994 Adults	T4:189	Measures both the entry-level & academic skills important to success in educational programs offered by career schools, colleges & other postsecondary institutions. Basic skills test include Language, Reading, & Numerical.
Career SnapShot 2001 New Concepts Career Development Corporation 1997 Middle School to Adults		Evaluates multiple aptitudes used with DOL Worker Trait Profiles. The KFME version has 24 exercises to assess Motor Coordination, Finger and Manual Dexterity and Eye-Hand-Foot Coordination using 8 hand tools & an electronic counter. Can be converted to TABE and DAT scores and to Worker Traits.
Career Technical Assistance Program (C-Tap) WestEd 1998 Grade 9 to Adults		Designed to assist students in learning/refining career-technical skills & to assess readiness for entry-level jobs and/or postsecondary training. Consists of 3 parts: portfolio, project, & written scenario. Referenced to standards in career areas, such as agriculture, business, & health careers.
COIN Basic Skills and Career Interest Survey COIN Educational Products 1996 High School to Adults		Provides aptitude and interest information for career planning. Basic skills component uses Wonderlic Basic Skills Test to assess math & language skills used in the workplace. Survey assesses activities in 7 areas of interest. Scores are combined & linked to matching occupations & reported in GED levels.
Comprehensive Ability Battery (CAB) Institute for Personality and Ability Testing 1975 – 1982 Grade 10 to Adults	MY9:255 MY8:484 TP5:644 T4:486	Consists of 4 test booklets containing 20 subtests, each designed to measure a primary ability factor related to performance in industrial settings. Examples of scores reported are verbal & numerical ability, clerical speed & accuracy, memory span, etc.
Employee Aptitude Survey (EAS) Psychological Services 1952 – 1995 Adults	CG3 MY5:607 TP5:937 T4:488	Designed as a diagnostic tool for employee selection & vocational guidance. Consists of 10 ability tests such as Verbal Comprehension, Numerical Ability, Space Visualization, Visual Speed & Accuracy, Manual Speed & Accuracy, & Symbolic Reasoning. Machine or hand scored.

Name of test/Publisher/Date/Population	Reference(s)	Brief Description
ETSA Tests Employers' Tests & Services Associates 1957 – 1990 Grade 10 to Adults	MY11:139 TC9:219 TP5:973 T4:491	Measures general & specific job aptitudes through 8 different tests: general mental ability, office arithmetic, general clerical ability, stenographic skills, mechanical familiarity, mechanical knowledge, sales aptitude, & personal adjustment index. Available on the Internet.
Flanagan Aptitude Classification Test (FACT) SRA/London House 1951 – 1994 High School to Adults, Prospective Employees	MY7:675 TP5:1042 T4:506	Designed to predict success in various occupational fields via composite occupational scores. Consists of 16 subtests such as inspection, coding, memory, precision, assembly, scales, coordination, judgment & comprehension, arithmetic, patterns, components, tables, etc.
Flanagan Industrial Tests (FIT) SRA/London House 1960 – 1996 Adults	MY8:981 TC2:282 TP5:1043 T4:506	Measures 18 aptitudes or job tasks involved in supervisory, technical, office, skilled, & entry-level job demands. Designed for selection, placement, reassignment, or reclassification of employees.
Hay Aptitude Test Battery Wonderlic, Inc. 1947 – 1997 Adults	MY12:179 MY9:470 TP5:1180 T4:600	Assesses clerical & numerical aptitude through 4 paper/pencil tests. Tests include warm-up (which is not scored), number perception, name finding, & number series completion. Designed to aid in the selection of clerical workers. Hand scored.
Industrial Reading Test (IRT) Psychological Corporation 1976 – 1978 Grade 10 to Adults	MY9:504 TP5:1256 T4:507	Contains 9 readings passages & 38 test items on work-relevant topics to assess reading comprehension. Some passages depict sections of technical manual; others are written in the form of company memoranda. All passages are at the secondary reading level.
IPI Aptitude-Intelligence Test Series Industrial Psychology International 1982 – 1986 Adults	TC2:363 TP5:1323 T4:579	Consists of various aptitude & personality tests such as: dexterity, blocks, parts, numbers, tools, judgment, fluency, sales, etc. Aids in employee selection in 28 job fields such as computer programmer, dental technician, sales, clerk, etc.
Job Effectiveness Prediction System (JEPS) Life Office Management Association 1986 Adults	T4:627	Paper/pencil test which measures a variety of skills required for a wide range of clerical & technical/professional positions. Examples of subtests include Numerical Ability, Mathematical Skill, Spelling, etc. Used for selection/placement of employees in insurance companies.

Name of test/Publisher/Date/Population	Reference(s)	Brief Description
Job Skills Testss Ramsay Corporation 1981 – 1991 Job Applicants and Industrial Workers	MY9:551 TP5:1353	Designed to measure abilities of industrial workers. Assesses individuals in 4 areas: Reading - read a passage & answer questions, Oral Directions – following directions, Measurement - to measure, & Arithmetic - simple arithmetic skills.
Missouri Aptitude and Career Information Inventory (MACII) Missouri Testing and Evaluation Service 1979 Grade 9 to 12	T3:829	Assesses verbal & quantitative aptitudes, & career interests. Combines a test that measures understanding of words & ability to perform fundamental number operations with a career interest measure. Users are asked to indicate occupational likes & dislikes through a list of over 250 titles.
Motivational Approach of Personal Potential International Assessment Network 1995 Age 13 to Adults		Designed to assist individuals in career decision making. Consists of 71 triads, yielding scores in areas such as: interest in job contents, temperament for the job, aptitude for the job, & mathematical capacity. Administered online with a variety of scoring profiles. Available in 6 languages.
Multidimensional Aptitude Battery (MAB) Sigma Assessment Systems 1982 – 1999 Grade 10 to Adults	MY10:202 TC2:501 TP5:1731 T4:45	Assesses aptitudes & intelligence through 5 verbal & 5 performance subtests. Yields a profile of scores. Can be individually or group administered using paper/pencil or IBM compatible disk. Mail-in scoring generates narrative report.
NOCTI Occupational Competency Tests National Occupational Competency Testing Institute 1986 Students in Vocational and Technical Programs	TP5:1792	Multitude of competency tests in 3 categories: Experienced Workers, Industrial Assessments, Job Ready Assessments. Occupations include: Accounting, Appliance Repair, Carpentry, Commercial Art, Die Making, Electronics Technology, Mechanical, Medical Assistant, Pipefitter, Retail Trades, & many more.
Phoenix Ability Survey System Lafayette Instrument 1979 – 1983 Age 15 to Adults	MY11:290	Designed to measure vocationally related abilities., then match the results using a computer to specific occupations from the DOT. Scores yielded on 30 ability factors, such as manual dexterity, two-hand coordination, perceptual speed, verbal reasoning, hand strength, & following directions.
Professional Employment Test Psychological Services 1986 – 1988 Potential Employees	MY12:312 TP5:2072 T4:497	Assesses reading comprehension, reasoning, quantitative problem solving, & data interpretation. Consists of 40 items and yields one total score. Provides a sample item for each area with an explanation of the correct response. Individual or group administration.

Name of test/Publisher/Date/Population	Reference(s)	Brief Description
Revised Beta Examination-Third Edition (BETA-III) The Psychological Corporation 1931 – 1999 Adults	MY9:1044 TP5:2212 T4:498	Assesses mental abilities in individuals having limited or no reading skills. Consists of 6 tests: mazes, coding, paper form boards, picture completion, clerical checking, & picture absurdities. Can be group administered. Available in Spanish.
Scholastic Level Exam (SLE) Wonderlic, Inc. 1937 – 1988 Age 15 to Adults		A 50-question, 12-minute timed test of cognitive ability or aptitude for learning. Measures students' ability to understand instructions, keep up with classroom pace, solve problems & use occupational training on the job.
Schubert General Ability Battery (GAB) Slosson Publishing 1986 Grade 10 to Adults	MY7:386 TC3:579 TP5:2324 T4:47	Assesses intellectual abilities including verbal, arithmetic, & syllogistic measures of reasoning ability. The 4 subtests are designed to indicate individuals' levels of success and/or placement in school, college, & business.
Success Skills 2000 Employment Technologies 1991 – 1997 High School to Adults		A video-based, computer-scored test for corporate recruiting & development of entry-level professionals in 4 major categories: engineering, professional & finance, supervision, sales & marketing. Measures critical skills in 3 broad categories: applied problem solving, interpersonal effectiveness, & accountability.
System for Assessment and Group Evaluation (SAGE)/ **Compute-A-Match** PESCO International 1980 – 1986 Age 15 to Adults - Special Populations	CG2 T3:806 B:93	Matches aptitudes, educational level, attitudes, & temperament of individuals to jobs & training. Composed of 5 separate components: vocational aptitude battery, vocational interest inventory, measurement of general educational development, assessment of attitudes toward others in working environment, & assessment of temperament.
Technical Test Battery (TTB) Saville and Holdsworth, Ltd. 1992 Adults	T4:638	Consists of 4 separate instruments: Mechanical Comprehension designed to assess understanding of basic mechanical principles, Numerical Computation designed to assess numerical ability in a technical setting, Spatial Recognition to measure spatial ability, & Visual Estimation of spatial perception.
Training House Assessment Kit Training House 2000		Designed to offer smaller organizations a wide range of reproducible assessments for managers to use to identify & target development needs. Consists of 25 instruments such as Proficiency Assessment Report, Self-Awareness Profile,

Name of test/Publisher/Date/Population	Reference(s)	Brief Description
USES General Aptitude Test Battery (GATB) U.S. DOL/North Carolina O*Net Center 1947 – 1982 Ages 16 to Retirement	CG1,2,3 MY9:1304 TC5:150 T5:1015	Consists of 12 subtests measuring 9 aptitudes that can be related to USES Occupational Aptitude Patterns. Aptitudes include verbal, numeral, spatial form perception, clerical, motor coordination, & finger & manual dexterity. Currently under revision & will be renamed the Ability Profiler.
Valpar Aviator Valpar International 1998 Age 15 to Adults		Computerized instrument that measures GED Reasoning, Math, & Language. Tests 7 aptitude factors such as general learning ability, verbal, numerical, & spatial perception. Includes 2 pictorial interest surveys. Matches the interest & aptitude results with its internal occupational database. Computer administered.
Valpar Pro 3000 Valpar International 1999 Age 15 to Adults		Windows based version of Valpar's System 2000 modular software package. Consists of a required system manager & optional modules, such as Career Planner, Compass (computerized assessment), Compass Lite (without work samples), DOT, OOH, & Spatial/Nonverbal assessment.
Valpar System 2000 Valpar International Corporation 1991 – 1994 High School to Adults		Computerized modular system consisting of a required system manager & 16 modules such as: Computerized Assessment, Compass Lite, DOT Database, GOE, Work History, Career Planner, DOT Job Description, OOH, Census Database, PET Survey, & Spatial/Non-Verbal. Predecessor of the Pro 3000 system.
Valpar Test of Essential Skills (VTES) Valpar International 1998 Ages 15 to Adults		Designed to combine basic skills testing with job related criteria. Yields academic grade-level scores & DOL work-related GED language & math scores. Math & English tests are available in 2 parallel forms. Computer generated reports can be customized.
Vocational Evaluation System New Concepts Career Development Corporation 1971 – 1997 Middle School to Adults		Audiovisual programs that assess individual's interest & ability for performing routine tasks. Activities encompass a number of job titles such as Air Conditioning & Refrigeration, Cook & Baker, Diesel Engine Repair, Machine Trades, Drafting, & Masonry. Formerly known as the Singer Evaluation System.
VOC-TECH Quick Screener (VTQS) CFKR Career Materials 1984 – 1990 Grade 10 to Adults	MY12:411 TP5:2822	A screening tool that assesses career aptitudes, interest, & training plans. Aids in matching career goals with jobs, & identifies job options & training. Designed for noncollege-bound persons. Computer version available.

Name of test/Publisher/Date/Population	Reference(s)	Brief Description
V-TECS Assessments Vocational-Technical Education Consortium of States 1986 – 1999 High School to Adults		V-TECS is a consortium of agencies that provide occupational skills training in business/industry, education, & the military. Criterion-referenced item banks for 31 occupations are available, consisting of 3 types of items: written, performance & scenario. Tests tied to curriculum materials.
Watson-Glaser Critical Thinking Appraisal (WGCTA) The Psychological Corporation 1942 - 1994 Adults	MY13:358 T4:227 TC3:682 TP5:2857	Measures 5 aspects of critical thinking: drawing sound inferences, recognizing assumptions, deductive reasoning, drawing conclusions, & evaluating arguments. The 80 items contain content that may be controversial, thereby providing a measure of the extent of bias effect on the ability to think critically.
Wesman Personnel Classification Test (PCT) The Psychological Corporation 1946 – 1965 Adults	MY7:400 TC3:711 TP5:2871 T4:500	Measures 2 major aspects of mental ability: verbal reasoning & numerical ability. Verbal items are analogies & numerical items include basic math skills & understanding of quantitative relationships. Aids in the selection of sales people & middle management personnel.
Wonderlic Personnel Test Wonderlic, Inc 1939 – 1998 Adults	MY11:475 TC1:769 TP5:2899 T4:500	Yields a single score that predicts job applicants' ability to learn on the job, understand directions, innovations, & routine tolerance. Available in 6 equivalent forms & 13 languages. Individually or group administered by a trained clerk. Includes recommended cut-off scores for various occupations.
World of Work Inventory (WOWI) World of Work 1970 – 1995 High School to Adults	CG3 MY13:368 T4:545	Designed to assess temperaments, interests, & aptitudes as they relate to the DOT career families. Consists of 516 items that yield 17 interest, 4 ability, and 12 temperament scores, provided in a profile format with a narrative summary report. Paper/pencil or computer-based version available.

B.   SPECIFIC APTITUDE AND ACHIEVEMENT MEASURES

Name of Test/Publisher/Date/Population	Reference(s)	Brief Description
Bennett Hand Tool Dexterity Test (BHTDT) The Psychological Corporation 1981 High School to Adults		Designed to measure manual dexterity & gross motor coordination. Subject removes 12 bolts from one vertical board & places them on another. Task requires the use of four tools: two open end wrenches, one adjustable wrench, & one screwdriver.
Bennett Mechanical Comprehension Test (BMCT) The Psychological Corporation 1940 – 1994 Adults	MY11:41 TC8:4 TP5:302 T4:484	Assesses ability to understand physical & mechanical principles. The 68 test items can be group administered by company personnel or by optional tape recordings. Two equivalent forms available. Correlates score with DOT job categories.
Candidate Profile Record (CPR) Richardson, Bellows, Henry & Co. 1982 – 1989 Applicants for Clerical Positions	MY12:62 TP5:390 T4:596	Designed to predict job success in clerical positions. Consists of a 105-item autobiographical inventory, yielding one score pertaining to underlying abilities related to job success, primarily in banking industries. A companion job analysis instrument is available to help determine its usefulness in other settings.
Clerical Abilities Battery (CAB) The Psychological Corporation 1985 – 1987 Adults	MY11:71 TP5:532 T4:596	Measures filing, proofreading, & mathematical skills. Tests ability to copy & compare information, use tables, & reason with numbers. The 7 tests can be administered separately or as a total battery. Available in 2 forms: A-industry, B-schools.
Clerical Skills Test Series Walden Personnel Testing and Training 1990 Adults	T4:597	Designed to measure clerical skills. A series of tests that measures proficiency in 20 areas such as attention to detail, problem solving, spelling, alphabetizing & filing, PC graphics, bookkeeping, electronic knowledge, & mechanical comprehension. Hand scored.
Computer Operator Aptitude Battery (COAB) SRA/London House 1973 – 1974 Computer Operator Applicants and Trainees	TP5:669 T4:614	Consists of 3 subtests: sequence recognition, format checking, & logical thinking. Scores from subtests combine to predict job performance of computer operators & to identify those applicants with the potential to succeed as a computer operator.
Computer Programmer Aptitude Battery (CPAB) SRA/London House 1964 – 1993 Computer Programmer Trainees	MY11:85 TP5:670 T4:614	Designed to assess an individual's potential to succeed as a computer programmer. Consists of 5 aptitude subtests: verbal meaning, reasoning, letter series, number ability, & diagramming. Oriented for both computer-experienced & inexperienced students.

Name of Test/Publisher/Date/Population	Reference(s)	Brief Description
Crawford Small Parts Dexterity Test (CSPDT) The Psychological Corporation 1946 - 1981 High School to Adults	MY5:871 TP5:722 T4:632	Measures eye-hand coordination & fine finger dexterity in two parts. Part I-Subject uses tweezers to insert pins in close-fitting holes, & then places collars on the pins. Part II-Subject places small screws in holes by hand, & then uses a screwdriver to screw them down.
Customer Service Skills Assessment Program Employment Technologies 1989 – 1997 High School to Adults		A video-based, computer scored diagnostic system that focuses on the key functions of the customer service job. Includes a series of multiple-choice questions that are job relevant & that provide a standardized assessment of a candidate's ability to do the job.
Dvorine Color Vision Test The Psychological Corporation 1944 – 1958 General Population	TP5:862 MY6:955 T4:476	Designed to identify defective color vision. Consists of 2 parts that determine type & degree of vision defect. Each plate features a design of colored dots against a background of contrasting dots that appear shapeless to the colorblind.
General Clerical Test (GCT) The Psychological Corporation 1944 – 1988 Adults	MY12:158 TC3:296 TP5:1078 T4:599	Assesses abilities needed for many higher-level administrative & paraprofessional positions. Consists of 9 tests that yield 3 ability scores: clerical speed & accuracy, numerical ability, & verbal ability.
Group Test of Musical Ability NFER-Nelson Publishing Co., Ltd (England) 1988 Ages 7 – 14	MY12:173	Designed to measure musical ability. Consists of 2 tests: a 24-item Pitch Test requiring the respondent to identify the higher of 2 notes & a 10-item Pulse Test requiring the respondent to compute number of pulses in a series of tempos. All test items & directions are on a cassette tape.
Intuitive Mechanics SRA/London House 1956 – 1984 Adults	T4:633 TP5:1299	Paper/pencil test that measures the ability to understand mechanical relationships or to visualize internal movement in a mechanical system. Used in vocational counseling or personnel selection to identify individuals with high mechanical interest & ability.
Job Skills PESCO, Inc. 1998 Prospective Employees		Designed to measure individual's proficiency with various software applications. Consists of 50 tests such as Word, Access, Medical Secretary, Excel, Word Perfect, & Internet Basics. Three levels of testing in every standard test: basic, intermediate, & advanced skills. Companion to PESCO 2001 System.

Name of Test/Publisher/Date/Population	Reference(s)	Brief Description
Mechanical Movements SRA/London House 1984 Adults	T3:1067 TP5:1636	Measures finger dexterity, eye-hand coordination, & visualization abilities required in office & factory tasks. May also be used by special educators to evaluate motor skills. Contains 7 subtests that can be used separately or in combination.
Minnesota Clerical Test (MCT) The Psychological Corporation 1933 – 1979 Clerical Applicants	MY9:713 MY6:1040 TP5:1693 T4:603	Designed to measure clerical aptitude. Focus is on perceptual speed & accuracy in 2 tasks: name comparison & number comparison. Each part consists of 100 pairs that the subject must identify as identical or dissimilar. Screens entry-level positions such as typists, clerks, etc.
Minnesota Paper Form Board-Revised The Psychological Corporation 1970 – 1995 Adults	MY9:1045 TP5:2217 T4:637	Consists of 64 two-dimensional diagrams that assess spatial perception & mechanical-spatial ability as they relate to artistic & mechanical aptitudes. Aids in employee selection for occupations such as drafting, engineering, & electrical work.
Minnesota Rate of Manipulation Test (MRMT) American Guidance Service 1931 – 1969 Grade 7 to Adults	MY7:1046 MY6:1077 TP5:1700 T4:635	Measures arm-hand dexterity using a form board with 60 round holes & 60 cylinders that fit into the holes. Consists of 5 different manipulative activities: placing, turning, displacing, one-hand turning, & two-hand turning. Also provides norms & instructions for the blind.
Minnesota Spatial Relations Test (MSRT) American Guidance Service 1930 – 1979 Grade 10 to Adults	MY9:723 TP5:1703 T4:478	Assesses spatial visualization ability & the ability to manipulate three-dimensional objects. This timed test consists of the transfer of blocks from one board to their proper place in the connected board as quickly as possible.
Musical Aptitude Profile The Riverside Publishing Co. 1965 – 1995 Grades 4 – 12	MY12:251 TP5:1752	Designed to measure an individual's musical aptitude. Assesses 3 basic factors: tonal, rhythmic, & expressive/aesthetic. Yields 11 scores such as melody, harmony, tempo, meter, balance, & style. Directions & testing items are administered via an audiocassette tape.
O'Conner Finger Dexterity Test Lafayette Instrument Company 1920 – 1926 Age 14 to Adults	MY6:1078 T3:1069	Designed to measure motor coordination, & finger & manual dexterity. Consists of plate containing 100 holes arranged in 10 rows. Subject's task is to insert small metal pins, in groups of three, as rapidly as possible.

Name of Test/Publisher/Date/Population	Reference(s)	Brief Description
O'Conner Tweezer Dexterity Test Lafayette Instrument Company 1920 – 1928 Age 14 to Adults	MY6:1079 T3:1069	Designed to measure motor coordination, & finger & manual dexterity. Consists of plate containing 100 holes arranged in 10 rows. Subject's task is to insert small metal pins, one by one, into each of the holes, using metal tweezers.
Office Skills Test SRA/London House 1977 – 1984 Entry Level Applicants in the Business Field	MY9:857 TP5:1836 T4:603	Designed to measure clerical ability of entry-level job applicants via 12 subtests: checking, coding, filing, form completion, grammar, numerical, oral directional, punctuation, reading comprehension, spelling, typing, & vocabulary.
Pennsylvania Bi-Manual Worksample American Guidance Service 1943 – 1945 Age 16 to 39	T4:635	Measures manual dexterity & eye-hand coordination in two parts: Assembly-requires manually assembling bolts & nuts, & then placing them in a hole in the board, & Disassembly-requires removing the assemblies from the hole, taking them apart, & returning the parts to their bins.
Perceptual Speed SRA/London House 1987 Adults	T4:604	Measures the ability to quickly identify similarities & differences in visual configuration. This 5-minute timed test can be used to aid in selecting personnel for occupations requiring rapid perception of inaccuracies in written material, numbers, or diagrams.
Purdue Pegboard SRA/London House 1941 – 1992 Grade 9 to Adults	TP5:2125 T4:514	Measures gross movement of hands, fingers, & arms, & tip of finger dexterity. Consists of pegboard containing 2 rows of 25 holes into which pins are inserted individually with the right hand, left hand, & both hands.
Short Employment Tests (SET) The Psychological Corporation 1972 – 1993 Adults	MY13:287 T4:611 TP5:2406	Designed to measure verbal, numerical, & clerical aptitudes via 3 tasks: recognize synonyms, perform arithmetic computations, & locate proper names in an alphabetical list & assign codes to the amount associated with each name.
Short Tests of Clerical Ability (STCA) SRA/London House 1959 – 1997 Applicants for Office Positions	MY13:287 MY8:1039 TP5:2408 T4:611	Measures 7 clerical aptitudes & abilities: arithmetic, business vocabulary, checking, coding, directions-oral & written, filing, & language. Useful for selection & placement in various office jobs such as secretary, stenographer, office clerk, etc.

Name of Test/Publisher/Date/Population	Reference(s)	Brief Description
Space Relations (Paper Puzzles) SRA/London House 1984 Adults	T4:498	Used in vocational counseling or personnel selection to identify individuals with mechanical ability & experience. Consists of 30 items that measure an individual's ability to visually select a combination of flat pieces that fit together to cover a given two-dimensional space.
Space Thinking (Flags) SRA/London House 1959 – 1984 Adults	TP5:2460 T4:498	Measures the ability to visualize a rigid configuration when it is moved into different positions. This 5-minute timed test may be used to aid in identifying individuals with mechanical interest & ability.
SRA Clerical Aptitudes SRA/London House 1947 – 1996 Grade 9 to Adults	T4:611	Measures 3 aptitudes necessary for job performance in office positions: vocabulary, arithmetic, & detail checking. Designed for assistance in selection of office personnel.
SRA Mechanical Aptitudes SRA/London House 1947 – 1996 Grade 12 to Adults	T4:637	Measures ability to learn mechanical skills in 3 areas: mechanical knowledge, space relations, & shop arithmetic. Designed for assistance in selection of entry-level applicants & trainees.
SRA Pictorial Reasoning Test (PRT) SRA/London House 1967 – 1973 Age 14 to Adults	T4:498	Provides a general measure of the learning potential of individuals from diverse backgrounds with reading difficulties. Helpful in identifying an individual's potential for training & employment.
SRA Test of Mechanical Concepts SRA/London House 1976 – 1986 Grade 8 to Adults	MY8:1045 T4:637	Measures an individual's ability to visualize & comprehend basic mechanical & spatial interrelationships. Reports 4 scores: mechanical interrelationships, mechanical tools & devices, spatial relations, & total.
Stromberg Dexterity Test (SDT) The Psychological Corporation 1945 – 1981 Trade School & Adults	MY4:755 TP5:2515 T4:638	Designed to aid in choosing workers for jobs requiring speed & accuracy of arm & hand movement. Test consists of 54 red, blue, & yellow discs & a durable board containing 54 holes on one side. Subject is timed sorting discs by color & placing them in the holes.

Name of Test/Publisher/Date/Population	Reference(s)	Brief Description
Technology and Internet Assessment H & H Publishing Company 1999 Middle School to Adult		Designed to assess an individual's strengths & weaknesses in basic computer knowledge, the Internet, & information technology skills. Scores yielded in 8 areas such as use of computer, specific computer skills, basic Internet knowledge, & ethics of technology. Administered & scored via the Internet.
USES Clerical Skills Test U.S. DOL/North Carolina O*Net Center 1990 Applicants for Clerical Positions	TP5:2796	Assesses individual's clerical skills. Consists of 7 subtests: Plain Copy Typing, Transcribing Machine Operation, Dictation, Spelling, Statistical Typing, Medical Spelling, & Legal Spelling. Yields 4 scores: typing, transcribing machine operator, spelling, & dictation. Norms are based on experienced workers.
Valpar 300 Series Dexterity Modules (VDM) Valpar International 1995 Age 15 to Adults		Designed to measure motor coordination, & manual & finger dexterity. Five modules are currently available: Small Parts Assembly, Asymmetric Pin Placement, Tool Manipulation, Bi-Manual Coordination, & Angled Pin Placement. Modules are criterion referenced to DOL standards.
Wiesen Test of Mechanical Aptitude (WTMA) Psychological Assessment Resources 1999 Age 18 to Adult		Designed to assess mechanical aptitude. Consists of simple drawings that cover broad mechanical/physical concepts such as basic machines, movement, gravity/center of gravity, basic electricity/electronics, transfer of heat, & basic physical properties. Individual or group administration.

C. INTEREST INVENTORIES

Name of Test/Publisher/Date/Population	Reference(s)	Brief Description
Armed Services-Civilian Vocational Interest Survey (ASCVIS) CFKR Career Materials 1983 – 1985 Middle School to Adults	MY10:13 TP5:179	Measures interests in jobs available in the armed services and/or related civilian jobs. Consists of a 6-page survey yielding ratings in 8 areas such as service & transportation, administrative/clerical/personnel, computer & data processing, & scientific/technical/electronic. Primary focus is careers that do not require a traditional college degree. Self-administered, self-assessed, & self-scored.
Business Careers Interest Inventory Peregrine Publications 1997 – 1999		A computer & Internet based-assessment designed to assist business oriented students & employees to further define their interests. Yields scores in 8 areas similar to Holland types. Can be used with Discovering Your Career in Busi-

Name of Test/Publisher/Date/Population	Reference(s)	Brief Description
Career Assessment Battery Piney Mountain Press 1991 Grade 8 to Adults, Non-readers	T4:330	A survey measure that assesses an individual's self-perception of interests, abilities & needs. Addresses 112 major worker trait clusters utilizing a video/CD presentation. Users make occupational choices in areas such as School Subjects, Work Load, Work Area, Work Situations, etc.
Career Compass Meridian Education Corporation 1988 – 1996 Junior High to High School		Covers general career clusters, major work groups, & specific occupations based on student responses to 70 work activity questions. Program printouts provide a career interest profile, additional information & a listing of related sample occupations for top 3 interest clusters.
Career Directions Inventory (CDI) Sigma Assessment Systems 1982 – 1996 High School to Adults	CG2.3 MY10:44 TP5:406 T4:313	Developed to assist individuals in planning their career & educational futures. Consists of 100 forced-choice triads yielding scores on 15 interest scales, such as administration, art, clerical, food service, & industrial arts. Focus on careers not requiring a college education. Available in French.
Career Exploration Inventory (CEI) Jist Works, Inc. 1992 Adolescents to Adults	MY13:49 TP5:407 T4:330	A self-scoring & self-interpreting measure that identifies the user's major interest clusters, explores a variety of work, leisure & educational options, & develops a career action plan.
Career Exploration Series (CES) CFKR Career Materials, Inc. 1979 – 1992 Grade 9 to Adults	MY13:50 MY11:60 TP5:408 T3:814	Designed to help students identify specific jobs that match their educational goals & interest areas. Focuses on 6 occupational areas such as agriculture-conservation-forestry, business-sales-management-clerical, consumer/home economics-related fields, etc.
Career Finder Wintergreen/Orchard House 1984 – 1993 Grade 5 to Adults		A computer assessment of 18 items. Printout provides the 20 best matches from over 450 occupations. Gives current information on job duties, salary ranges, educational requirements, availability, & easy reference to the DOT.
Career Guidance Inventory Wintergreen/Orchard House 1972 – 1989 Grade 7 to College	MY11:61 MY9:197 T4:313 TP5:410	Measures comparative strength of students' interests in trades, services, & technologies. Scores reported for 14 engineering-related occupations (e.g., carpentry, masonry, technology), & 11 nonengineering-related occupations (e.g., communications, medical technology).

Name of Test/Publisher/Date/Population	Reference(s)	Brief Description
Career Key (CK) Lawrence Jones 1993 High School to Adults	MD:7/90	Self-administered instrument that assesses Holland codes & directs the user to occupations related to his/her type. Provides explanation of Holland's theory & gives volume/page number of identified occupations in Encyclopedia of Careers & Vocational Guidance. Available only online: www.ncsu.edu/careerkey
Career Orientation and Planning Profile (COPP) Center on Education and Training for Employment 1982 – 1991 Grade 7 to Adult		Designed to be both "a career guidance assessment & a career/life planning process." Consists of a series of self-assessment instruments that yield a profile containing interests, abilities, skills, & career opportunities. Also includes data summaries sorted by categories such as grade, sex, age, subject, & state level.
Career Planning System (CPS) The Conover Company, Ltd. 1985 Grade 9 to Adults		Software designed for individuals with limited experience in planning careers. Consists of 50 questions to identify interests. Provides printout of results & priorities for exploration. Includes a tracking system to assist with interest area changes & options. Requires Apple II System.
COIN Career Targets COIN 1990 – 1993 Middle School to High School		Provides assessment, career exploration & individual career plans. Includes a self-scored, self-administered inventory linking students' interests to 14 career clusters, an exploration of the world of work, & activities that emphasize the importance of education & the development of a high school plan.
COIN Educational Inventory COIN Educational Products 1994 Grades 11 and 12		Designed to provide an interest assessment to be used in postsecondary educational planning. Consists of 4 parts: Assessing Interests, Exploring Personal Interests & Postsecondary Education & Training, Selecting Postsecondary Training, and Choosing a Postsecondary School.
College Major and Vocational Program Selector COIN 1990 Grade 11 to College Sophomores		Part 1 is a self-assessment that helps students to identify characteristics about themselves & relate personal characteristics to over 600 college majors & vocational programs. In Part II, students match themselves with a Personal Orientation & select the matching college majors or vocational programs.
College Major Interest Inventory (CMII) Consulting Psychologists Press 1990 High School to Adults	CG3 MY12:84 TP5:618	Designed to assist students in the educational decision-making process. Consists of 399 items arranged into 6 sections. Yields percentile scores on 70 scales, including 33 educational clusters, 13 school & college, & 6 general educational area scales. Must be machine scored.

Name of Test/Publisher/Date/Population	Reference(s)	Brief Description
Curtis Interest Scale Psychometric Affiliates 1959 Grade 9 to Adults	MY6:1052 TP5:752 T4:544	Assesses interest in 10 areas: business, mechanics, applied arts, direct sales, production, science, entertainment, interpersonal, computation, & farming. Also yields a rating for the desire for responsibility.
Dole Vocational Sentence Completion Blank (VSCB) Stoelting Company 1979 – 1983 Junior High to Adults	TC9:193	Designed to assist students in planning & implementing educational & career goals. Consists of 21 items using a sentence completion format. Intended to be used to complement other interest inventories such as the Kuder or Strong. Individual or group administration.
Educational Interest Inventory (EII) Wintergreen/Orchard House 1962 – 1989 Grade 10 to Adults	MY11:123 MY9:377 TP5:905 T4:315	Measures interest in formal, postsecondary educational programs. Includes 235 forced-choice items. Consists of 47 scales: agriculture sciences, engineering, foreign language, health sciences, psychology, law, home economics, etc.
Emerging Occupations Interest Inventory CFKR Career Materials, Inc. 1986 Junior High School to Adults		Computer program that matches an individual's interests against the characteristics of nearly 100 occupations. A specific occupation for which the individual is best suited is indicated at the conclusion. User is referred to accompanying guide book that provides in-depth information regarding various occupations.
Explore the World of Work (E-WOW) CFKR Career Materials, Inc. 1989 – 1991 Adults	TP5:993 T3:821	Designed as a quick assessment using 36 graphics: 24 work activities & 12 work values. Developed for adult retraining & reentry programs. This instrument is a pictorial form of JOB-O to accommodate low reading levels. Available in Spanish.
Gordon Occupational Checklist II The Psychological Corporation 1961 – 1981 Grade 8 to Adults	MY9:443 MY7:1019 TP5:1100 T4:316	Designed to measure areas of job interests for individuals seeking education & job training below the college level. Includes 6 broad vocational interest categories: business, arts, outdoors, technical-mechanical, technical-industrial & service.
Group Interest Sort The Conover Company, Ltd. 1987 Elementary Grades, Non-readers		Consists of 50 questions presented in a multimedia format: audiovisual, print, & computer-based. Utilizes activities rather than job titles. Intended for use with individuals who know little about the world of work.

Name of Test/Publisher/Date/Population	Reference(s)	Brief Description
Guide for Occupational Exploration Inventory (GOE) JIST Works, Inc. 1996 Grade 6 to Adults	T4:316	Explores career, education, & lifestyle options. Yields a graphic interest profile with 7 factors such as leisure, home, & education/school. Eighth-grade reading level. Cross-referenced to standard occupational information sources. Map with GOE information provided. Group or individually administered.
Guilford-Zimmerman Interest Inventory Consulting Psychologists Press, Inc. 1963 – 1989 Adults	MY12:174 TPS:1157	Assesses career interests & personal values. A 150-item inventory that aids in job searches by determination of areas compatible with interests & values. This self-scoring instrument yields scores on 10 scales: mechanical, service, aesthetic, clerical, mercantile, leadership, literary, scientific, creative, & natural.
High School Career-Course Planner CFKR Career Materials, Inc. 1983 – 1990 Adolescents	MY12:181 TPS:1200 T3:824	Used to evaluate career interest & develop a course plan that is consistent with self-assessed career goals. Measures interests in 6 occupational areas working with people, working with tools, creating new things, solving problems, & doing physical work.
How Well Do You Know Your Interests? Psychologists and Educators Inc. 1957 – 1975 Grade 10 to Adults	MY11:165 TPS:1222 T4:335	Designed to measure attitudes toward jobs, activities, things, & people in 10 vocational areas: business, mechanical, outdoor, service, research, amusement, visual art, literacy, music & general work attitudes.
Individual Career Exploration (ICE) Scholastic Testing Service 1976 – 1986 Grade 3 to 12	MY8:1581 T3:825	Assesses interests, experience, abilities, & ambitions of students & relates them to future occupations in 8 areas: service, business contact, organization, technology, outdoor, general science, culture, & arts & entertainment. Picture & verbal forms.
Job Search Inventory (JSA) U.S. DOL/North Carolina O*Net Center 1985 Job Applicants	MY13:163 TPS:1351	Designed to assist students in selecting realistic occupations. Consists of 81 items yielding 5 scores: interest, leisure, training, work, & a total. Two forms are available: one uses the 4th edition of The Guide for Occupational Exploration & the other uses an information sheet describing the 66 work groups.
Judgement of Occupational Behavior-Orientation 2000 (JOB-O 2000) CFKR Career Materials 1978 – 1999 Grade 4 to Adults	CG1 MY12:200 MY10:16 MY9:560 TPS:1350	Uses a 9-item questionnaire to yield 9 scores: education, interest, inclusion, control, affection, physical activity, hands/tool/machinery, problem solving, and creating ideas. Scores are compared to 120 job titles. Designed to emphasize job awareness and promote job exploration. Three versions: grades 4-6, 7-10, and 10-adult.

Name of Test/Publisher/Date/Population	Reference(s)	Brief Description
Leisure to Occupations Connection Search (LOCS) Jist Works, Inc. 1999 Grade 7 to Adults		Designed to measure interests through a nontraditional approach. Consists of a list of 100 leisure activities such as learning a new language, gardening, & building things. Test takers rate their activity & skill in each. Occupations are directly cross-referenced to the OOH & GOE. Self-administered & interpreted.
Leisure/Work Search Inventory Jist Works, Inc. 1994 – 1999 High School to Adults	MY13:181 TP5:1483 T4:337	Designed to assess interests by measuring leisure activities. Consists of a list of 96 leisure related activity statements the test taker responds to by circling the degree he/she likes or dislikes the activity. Provides a graphical profile of 12 interest areas. Group administered & self-scored.
Occupational Clues Jist Works, Inc. 1993 Adolescents to Adults	T4:318	Used to clarify skills, experiences, values, and other traits necessary for informed career decisions. Based on 6 checklists: occupational interests, work-related values, leisure activities, home activities, school and training subjects, and work experience. Long and short forms available.
Ohio Vocational Interest Survey II (OVIS II) The Psychological Corporation 1969 – 1983 Grade 7 to Adults	CG3 MY9:1090 TP5:1841 T4:338	Designed to measure an individual's interests using a data, people, things model. Consists of 253 items scored on 23 scales such as manual work, music, visual arts, health services, clerical, performing arts, communications, management, & quality control. Scale clarity index also provided.
School-to-Work Career Survey Piney Mountain Press 1998 Grade 7 to Adults		Designed to assist students in identifying career options in 5 career pathways: Art & Humanities, Agricultural & Environmental, Business & Marketing, Health & Human Services, & Engineering & Industrial. Consists of a 75-item survey delivered via a video, worksheets, or on a computer.
UNIACT IV American College Testing 1973 – 1984 High School to Young Adults	MY9:43 TC:1	A unisex interest inventory designed to eliminate sex-role stereotyping. A component of the ACT Career Planning Program & the Discover computer-based guidance system. Students respond to 90 activities grouped into 6 areas: science, creative arts, social service, business contact, business detail, & technical.
USES Interest Checklist U.S. DOL/North Carolina O*Net Center 1979 Adults	MY11:453	Users check "like," "dislike," or "uncertain" for 210 work activity statements. Designed for individuals with no stated work interest or who are unaware of the variety of available jobs/occupations. Used as a counseling tool; does not yield scaled scores.

Name of Test/Publisher/Date/Population	Reference(s)	Brief Description
USES Interest Inventory (USES II) U.S. DOL/North Carolina O*Net Center 1981 Age 16 to Retirement	CG3	Designed to measure an individual's strengths of interests in 12 occupational areas such as artistic, scientific, accommodating, humanitarian, selling, protective, business detail, & physical performing. Consists of 162 items divided into 3 parts: job activity statements, occupational titles, & life experiences.
Vocational Interest Assessment System (VIAS) New Concepts Career Development Corporation 1995 Middle School to Adults		Designed to assist individuals in exploring interests related to occupations. Consists of 126 career clips in a variety of occupations, both traditional & nontraditional. Reading skills are not required due to the video format. Responses can be entered into a computer or a standard answer sheet.
Vocational Interest Exploration System (VIE) McCarron-Dial Systems 1991 Age 14 to Adults	T4:340	Computer-assisted interest assessment program designed to assess an individual's preferences for type of work & working conditions. Yields scores in 3 areas: selection of jobs based on work preferences, occupational exploration, & job review comparison. Individual administration.
Vocational Interest Inventory and Exploration Survey (VOC-TIES) Piney Mountain Press 1994 Age 13 to Adults	MY12:408 T5:2832	Designed for 3 major purposes: "to enable students to discover what vocational training entails; to determine student's vocational preferences; and to promote the concept of career equity by showing students in nontraditional roles." A Nonreading test that presents 15 training programs by video. A selection of short-term career objectives is provided.
Vocational Research Interest Inventory (VRII) Vocational Research Institute 1985 – 1992 High School to Adults	MY11:458 TP5:2836 T4:325	Measures 12 interest areas tied to the GOE & DOT. Provides individuals with a profile analysis. Contains separate pre-vocational & vocational norms. Two versions: paper/pencil & software compatible with Apple/IBM personal computers. Available in Spanish.
Work Exploration Checklist Finney Company 1993 – 2000 Grade 7 to Adult		Designed to assess an individual's interests in past, present, & future activities. Consists of a 4-page checklist yielding results in GOE codes & RIASEC themes. An electronic version is also available as part of the Occupational Guidance CD-ROM.
Work Preference Questionnaire PAQ Services 1982	TP5:2925	Designed to assess preferences in job activities. Scores are provided by weighted combinations of 150 items divided into 16 dimensions of work such as making decisions/communicating, operating vehicles, performing physical

D. MEASURES OF WORK VALUES, SATISFACTION AND ENVIRONMENTS

Name of Test/Publisher/Date/Population	Reference(s)	Brief Description
California Life Goals Evaluation Schedules Western Psychological Services 1966 – 1969 Grade 10 to Adults	MY7:47 TC6:60 TP5:371 T4: 103	Aids in differentiation of life goals from interests. Measures 10 life goals through 150 statements answered on a 5-point scale. Used in career planning, college counseling, & retirement adjustments. Takes about 30 minutes to administer; is easily scored & interpreted.
Campbell Organizational Survey (COS) NCS Assessments 1988 – 1994 Working Adults	MY12:60 TP5:382 T4:525	Designed to assess individual's attitudes about aspects of work. Provides scores on 17 scales such as supervision, benefits, job security, and an index of overall satisfaction within the organization. Scores provided in individual profile report with charts and graphs. May be taken online via the Internet.
Career Anchors: Discovering Your Real Values Jossey-Bass Pfeiffer and Company, International 1990 Adults	MY13:46 TP5:396 T4:572	Identifies career anchors, uncovers real values to help make better career choices. Yields 8 scores, such as technical/functional competence, general managerial competence, service/dedication to a cause, pure challenge, & lifestyle. Includes orientation & career anchor interviews. Group administered.
Career Values Scale Talico 1987 – 1991 Adults		Aids in evaluation of career interests, goals, needs, & aspirations. The questionnaire consists of 80 items of preference alternatives in 4 categories: work environment, employment position, ambition, & career introspection.
Fleishman Job Analysis Survey (F-JAS) Management Resouce 1992 – 1996 Adults	TP5:1044	A 74-item questionnaire used to determine ability requirements of jobs. Users respond to statements on a 7 point Likert-scale. Covers the full range of human abilities such as cognitive, psychomotor, etc. Self-scored.
Hall Occupational Orientation Inventory (Hall) Scholastic Testing Service 1968 – 1989 Grade 3 to Adults	CG1 MY12:175 TC1:300 TP5:1163	Measures psychological needs that are correlated to personality traits & job characteristics identified by the U.S. Dept. of Labor. Provides 22 scores such as self-actualization, creativity, location concern, etc. Useful in broadening the individual's perceptions of potential & priorities. Four levels available.
Individual Style Survey (ISS) Psychometrics Canada Ltd. 1989 – 1990 Grade 9 to Adults	MY13:144 TP5:1253	Provides a structured activity for self & interpersonal development, with an emphasis on the unique way in which individuals respond to events & people in the environment. Includes a self-perception form & 3 forms to give to others to assess the user's style.

Name of Test/Publisher/Date/Population	Reference(s)	Brief Description
Job Descriptive Index (JDI) Bowling Green State University 1969 – 1997 Adults	MY12:199 TC9:319 TP5:1348 T4:531	Provides an assessment of job satisfaction in any occupational field. Measures the following 5 components of satisfaction: work on present job, present pay, opportunities for promotion, supervision on present job, & people on present job.
Job Style Indicator (JSI) Career Research & Testing 1988 – 1993 Adults	MY13:164 TP5:1355 T4:509	Contains 16 items that compare perceptions of a particular job with an individual's personal style. Reveals the preferred work style of a specific job & is useful in exploring the person-job match. Designed to complement the Personal Style Indicator.
Minnesota Importance Questionnaire (MIQ) Vocational Psychology Research 1967 – 1981 Age 16 to Adults	CG1,2,3 MY11:243 TC2:481 TP5:1694	"Designed to measure 20 (21) psychological needs (and their underlying values) found relevant to work satisfaction." Scores yielded include: ability utilization, achievement, recognition, supervision-technical, variety, altruism, & autonomy. Can be used with the MSQ. Part of Minnesota Work Adjustment Project.
Minnesota Job Description Questionnaire (MJDQ) Vocational Psychology Research 1967 – 1968 Adults	MY8:1050 TC6:350 TP5:1695 T3:1012	Measures the working environment in terms of a profile of need-satisfaction characteristics. Aids in the person-job match of jobs along 21 reinforcer dimensions such as variety, creativity, security, recognition, authority, independence, etc.
Minnesota Satisfaction Questionnaire (MSQ) Vocational Psychology Research 1963 – 1977 Age 16 to Adults	CG3 MY9:721 TC5:1701	Designed to measure an employee's satisfaction with his/her job. Long form consists of 100 items; short form consists of 20 items. Scores yielded on 20 scales such as authority, company policy, social service, & human relations. Can be used with the MIQ. Part of Minnesota Work Adjustment Project.
Personal Style Indicator (PSI) Career Research & Testing 1988 – 1989 Adults	MY13:228 TP5:1952	A 16-item questionnaire that reveals personality & work style. Yields scores on behavioral, cognitive, affective & interpersonal dimensions. Contains detailed descriptions of 21 behavioral patterns. Self-administered & self-scored.
Position Analysis Questionnaire (PAQ) PAQ Services 1969 – 1992 Adults	MY12:299 TC5:326 TP5:2016 T4:513	Contains 189 job elements sampling what employees do to get their jobs done. Focus is on 6 behavioral areas: information input, mediation processes, work output, interpersonal activities, work situation & job context, & miscellaneous aspects.

Name of Test/Publisher/Date/Population	Reference(s)	Brief Description
Position Classification Inventory (PCI) Psychological Assessment Resource 1991 Adults	T4:513	Uses Holland Codes to classify positions/occupations to assess person-job fit. Employees & supervisors complete an inventory that describes demands & skills required in a job by rating items on a 3-point scale. Both scores are compared to aid in determination of job fit.
Rokeach Value Survey Consulting Psychologists Press 1967 – 1983 Age 11 to Adults	MY12:334 TP5:2246 TC1:549 T3:250	A self-scoring survey that contains items related to life-style & behavioral values. Utilizes a list of 18 terminal values & 18 instrumental values to aid in the determination of value priorities & assist in making life choices. A value's score is its rank.
Salience Inventory (SI) Consulting Psychologists Press 1985 – 1987 Grade 6 to Adults	CG3 MY11:339 TP5:2282	Designed "to assess the relative importance of the work role in the context of other life roles." Consists of 170 items divided into 3 scales: commitment, participation, & value expectation. Five major life roles are assessed under each of the 3 scales: homemaker, worker, student, citizen, & leisurite.
Satisfaction Research Questionnaire (SRQ) Sigma Assessment Systems 1992 Adults		Measures job satisfaction using 6 scales that reflect work & work environments: challenge, comfort, co-workers, pay, resource adequacy, & total score. Respondents either agree or disagree with 80 statements. Machine-scored by publisher.
Survey of Interpersonal Values (SIV) SRA/London House 1960 – 1993 Adolescents to Adults	TC2:759 TP5:2581 T4:152	Measures 6 values involving relationships between people: support, conformity, recognition, independence, benevolence, & leadership. The 90 items are arranged in sets of 3 with each item ranked from "most" to "least" important.
Survey of Personal Values (SPV) SRA/London House 1964 – 1997 Grade 10 to Adults	MY10:354 TC2:773 TP5:2588 T4:586	Measures 6 values: practical mindedness, achievement, variety, decisiveness, orderliness, & goal orientation. This self-report consists of 90 items. Each item contains 3 of the 6 values that are ranked by selecting "most" or "least" important.
Survey of Work Values Bowling Green State University 1975 – 1976 Employees	MY12:383 TP5:2593 T4:541	Designed to identify individual's attitudes toward work. Consists of 54 items yielding scores in 6 areas: social status, activity preference, upward striving, attitude toward earnings, pride in work, & job involvement. Individual or group administration.

Name of Test/Publisher/Date/Population	Reference(s)	Brief Description
Values Preference Indicator (VPI) Consulting Resource Group International 1990 Adults	TP5:2804 T4:542	Designed to assess personal value preferences. Consists of 3 parts: Identifying Key Values, Prioritizing Your Values, & Time Test. Yields 21 scores in areas, such as accomplishment, acknowledgement, challenge, friendship, organization, expertise, & tranquility. Individual or group administration.
Work Environment Scale (WES) Consulting Psychologist Press 1974 – 1989 Employees and Supervisors	MY12:417 TP5:2917 T4:594	Designed to assess the social climate of various work settings. Consists of 90 items yielding scores on 10 scales including involvement, supervisor support, peer cohesion, autonomy, task orientation, work pressure, clarity, control, physical comfort, & innovation. Individual or group administration.
Workmate Piney Mountain Press 1998 6th Grade to Adults		Designed to identify & examine work-related values, attitudes, and temperaments. Graphical printouts generated for 15 job related areas such as risking, competing, helping, persuading, receiving recognition, working with others, physical, & routine. Group or individual administration.
Work Motivation Inventory (WMI) Teleometrics International 1967 – 1973 Adults	MY8:1189 TP5:2921 T4:554	Yields 5 work maturation scores: basic creature comfort, safety & order, belonging & affiliation, ego-status, actualization, & self-expression. Separate measures are designed for managers & employees. Self or group administered.

E.   CARD SORTS

Name of Test/Publisher/Date/Population	Reference(s)	Brief Description
Deal-Me-In Career Systems 1985 – 1992 High School to Adults	CG3	A deck of 52 color-coded playing cards divided into suits that correspond to 4 interest categories: people, data, things, ideas. Can be used with a companion guide (It's in the Cards) that covers 22 job situations in 4 work areas: job search, job orientation, performance & reputation, & enrichment & enhancement.
Learning Skills Profile Hay/McBer 1993	MY13:179 TP5:1467	Designed to measure skills critical to job performance. Assesses the following skill groups: interpersonal, information, analytical, & behavioral. The partici-pant uses one or both decks of cards to rate his/her skills or the skill demands of

Name of Test/Publisher/Date/Population	Reference(s)	Brief Description
Missouri Occupational Card Sort (MOCS) University of Missouri Career Center 1982 Grade 11 & 12. College, & Adults	CG3 MG:10/81	An interest card sort designed to broaden knowledge of self & of specific occupations. Encourages further self & career exploration by increasing the number of occupations under consideration. Contains 90 occupations divided equally into the six Holland types.
Motivated Skills Card Sort (MSCS) Career Research and Testing 1981 – 1994 Grade 7 to Adults	CG3 MY13:204 TP5:1719	Provides assessment of proficiency in & motivation to use 48 skills. Primarily used to identify skills important to an individual's career satisfaction & success. Contains 48 skill cards & 8 category cards.
Occupational Interests Card Sort (OICS) Career Research and Testing 1981 – 1994 Grade 7 to Adults	CG3 MY13:213 TP5:1819	Designed to assist individuals in identifying & clarifying preferred occupations. Contains 113 occupation cards, 5 category cards, & 9 supplementary activities designed to stimulate career exploration. Occupation cards are sorted into 5 levels of interest.
Retirement Activities Card Sort Career Research & Testing 1992 – 1994 Retired Adults or Adults Planning to Retire	MY13:262 TP5:2207	Designed to assess adults in planning retirement & understanding the process of change. Consists of 48 common pastimes such as meditation, cultural events, group leadership, & entertaining. Cards are organized & classified to help individuals determine personal criteria related to retirement.s
Slaney Vocational Card Sort R. B. Slaney 1978 – 1981 High School to Adults	CG3	Provides insight into the relationship between interests, abilities, & personality traits & occupational selection. Contains 80 occupational titles selected from the Strong-Campbell Interest Inventory. Holland code is determined from client ranking of Holland types.
Vocational Insight and Exploration Kit (VIEK) Psychological Assessment Resources 1970 – 1992 High School to Adults	CG3 MY9:1337 MG:10/81	Focuses on eliminating career indecision by broadening self-awareness & self-exploration, increasing the range of vocational options, & clarifying pros & cons of vocational alternatives. Uses job titles & is based upon Holland's 6 types.

F. CAREER DEVELOPMENT/MATURITY MEASURES

Name of Test/Publisher/Date/Population	Reference(s)	Brief Description
Assessing Specific Competencies (ASC) Education Associates 1984 – 1996 Individuals Seeking Employment	MY12:33 TP5:183 T4:309	Assesses employability skills and work maturity/job retention. Consists of true/false and multiple-choice items. Yields scores in 11 skill areas such as making career decisions, developing a resume, completing an application, & interviewing for a job. Group or individual administration; computer version available.
Assessment of Career Decision Making (ACDM) Western Psychological Services 1988 High School and College Students	CG2,3 MY10:16 TP5:200 T4:310	Designed to measure a student's willingness to accept responsibility for making a career decision. Consists of a 94-item true/false inventory yielding scores on 6 scales such as rational, intuitive, & school adjustment. Designed to be used with the Career Planning Program. Machine scored. Sixth-grade reading level.
Barriers to Employment Success Inventory (BESI) Jist Works, Inc. 1997 Individuals with Restricted Abilities	T4:310	Identifies barriers inhibiting individuals in their job searches. Consists of multiple choice, short answer, & true/false statements in areas such as personal/financial, emotional/physical, training & education, career decision-making/planning, & job seeking knowledge. Eighth-grade reading level.
Career Action Inventory Career Systems 1988 Adults		A 75-question self-assessment inventory to determine what an individual is doing now about career planning & professional development. Includes a comprehensive discussion of inventory results & offers specific ideas for taking action to improve chances for success.
Career Awareness Inventory (CAI) Scholastic Testing Service 1974 – 1980 Grade 3 to 12	CGI MY11:59 MY8:994 MG:7/80	Assesses students' occupational awareness in 7 areas: related occupations, contact with occupations, job characteristics, functions of occupations, grouping of occupations, work locations of occupations, & self-assessment of career awareness. Can be used to evaluate the effectiveness of career education programs.
Career Decision Profile Lawrence Jones 1989 High School to Adults		A 16-item paper/pencil measure of career decision status. Includes 6 subscales: decidedness, comfort, self-clarity, knowledge about occupations & training, decisiveness, & career choice importance. Covers 3 dimensions: how decided one is, comfort with decision, & reasons for indecision.
Career Decision Scale (CDS) Psychological Assessment Resources 1976 – 1987 High School to Adults	CG2,3 MY9:194 TP5:404 T4:526	Provides estimates about students status in the career decision-making process; also used to judge the effectiveness of career development interventions. Consists of 19 items, yielding percentile scores on certainty & indecision scales. Hand scored.

Name of Test/Publisher/Date/Population	Reference(s)	Brief Description
Career Development Profile Talico 1987 Adults	MD:1/86	Assesses interests, ambitions, motivations, & goals among management & supervisory-level employees. Aids in identifying developmental needs & strategies for accomplishment of career goals.
Career Leverage Inventory Career Systems 1983 – 1994 Adults		A 35-question survey designed to help employees identify & assess their realistic career options. Provides new ways to think about career growth, how to prioritize & set career goals, & how to build back-up plans so individuals always have options.
Career Mastery Inventory (CMAS) Crites Career Consultants 1975 – 1992 High School to Adults		Part 1 includes 90 behavioral & attitudinal statements rated on a 7-point Likert scale. Involves 6 scales: organizational adaptability, position performance, work habits & attitudes, co-worker relationships, advancement, & career choice & plans. Part 2 consists of 20 statements of problem situations on the job.
Career Profile System Life Insurance Marketing and Research Association, Inc. 1983 – 1992 Insurance Candidates and Sales Representatives	MY13:52 TP5:421	Predicts success in insurance sales. Consists of 3 instruments: Student Career Profile, Initial Career Profile, & Advanced Career Profile. Yields scores in many areas such as motivating goals, financial situation, career expectations, work history, & income needs & expectations.
COIN Clue COIN Educational Products 1996 Grades 5 and 6		Provides activities in career exploration, assessment and planning. Content includes activities to answer questions, such as What is work?, Why is work important?, and How do I get the work I want? Jobs are grouped into 7 categories, including Designers & Builders, Helpers & Healers, and Transportation.
Employability Inventory Education Associates 1987 Prospective Employees	MY12:135 TP5:935	Assesses skills related to job seeking & job keeping. Sixty-eight job-related situations are presented for the examinee to react to by choosing from a multiple choice selection. Yields 68 item scores. Topics include job opening, developing resumes, interviewing, and keeping a job. Computer version available.
Employability Maturity Interview (EMI) The National Center on Employment & Disability 1987 Rehabilitation Clients	MY11:132 TP5:936	Designed to "assess readiness for vocational rehabilitation planning." Based on the individually administered Adult Vocational Maturity Assessment Interview, consisting of 10 open-ended questions presented orally in a specific sequence. Scored by administrator using guidelines on the back of the response booklet.

Name of Test/Publisher/Date/Population	Reference(s)	Brief Description
Evaluating the Participant's Employability Skills Education Associates 1984 – 1989 Individuals Seeking Employment	MY12:145 TP5:978	Designed to measure a person's "understanding of the employment process." Includes both pretest & posttest. Each consist of 50 questions in three parts: 20 true/false, 15 multiple-choice, & 15 open-ended. Available in paper/pencil format or on computer disk.
Gains I &II Wintergreen/Orchard House 1995 Grades 4 to 11	TP5:1069	Diagnostic tool for determining students career development needs. Uses a pre-test format to assess student's needs & a posttest to show students progress. GAINS I (Gr 4-7) consists of 26 items. GAINS II (Gr 8-11) consists of 34 items. Correlates with NOICC "National Career Development Guidelines."
Job Search Attitude Inventory JIST Works, Inc. 1994 Adolescents to Adults	T4:532	Identifies positive & negative attitudes about job possibilities. Consists of 32 items on 4-point scale. Scoring uses a graphic profile based upon 4 dimensions: luck vs. planning, involved vs. uninvolved, self-directed vs. other-directed, & active vs. passive. Individual or group administration.
Job Seeking Skills Assessment (JSSA) The National Center on Employment & Disability 1988 – 1994 Vocational Rehabilitation Clients	MY12:201 TP5:1352	Assesses individual's job-seeking skills, yielding 2 scores: job application & employment interview. Job application scored on 5 criteria such as neatness/legibility, spelling, & completeness. Employment interview scored using 33 factor weighted checklist in a mock interview setting. Video camera is recommended.
Minnesota Satisfactoriness Scales (MSS) Vocational Psychology Research 1965 – 1982 Employees	MY8:1050 TP5:1702	Designed to measure an employee's job satisfactoriness. Yields scores in 5 areas: performance, conformance, dependability, personal adjustment, & general satisfactoriness. Usually completed by supervisor judging employee's behavior. Part of Minnesota Work Adjustment Project.
My Vocational Situation (MVS) Consulting Psychologists Press 1980 – 1987 Grade 9 to Adults	CG2 MY9:738 TC2:509 TP5:1754	Designed to identify 3 possible difficulties in making career decisions: lack of vocational identity, need for information or training, & environmental or personal barriers. Self-administered & hand scored.
What - Where - How? Jist Works, Inc. 1998		Designed to assist individuals in the job hunting process. Consists of 45 true-false statements, showing scores on 3 pie charts including What (self-assessment), Where (job target), & How (job hunting technique). Based on

Name of Test/Publisher/Date/Population	Reference(s)	Brief Description
Work Adjustment Scale (WAS) Hawthorne Educational Services 1991 Age 16 to Adults	MY13:366 TP5:2913 T4:326 AT:98	Designed to measure an individual's readiness for work. Consists of 54 items, yielding scores in 4 areas including work-related behavior, interpersonal relations, social/community expectations, & a total. Useful for planning a student's transition from school to work. Individual administration.

G.   PERSONALITY ASSESSMENTS

Name of Test/Publisher/Date/Population	Reference(s)	Brief Description
Adult Personality Inventory (API) Institute for Personality and Ability Testing 1982 – 1996 Age 16 to Adults	MY12:20 TC6:21 TP5:86 T4:98	Assesses individual differences in personality, interpersonal style, & career/ life-style preferences. Consists of 324 items that measures 21 scales. The self- report inventory is computer scored. Designed for employee selection, coun- seling, & personal development programs.
Applicant Review CHC Forecast 1983 – 1996 Job Applicants		Designed to measure honesty & emotional stability. Consists of 102 items with 7 subscales, such as personal honesty, honesty of others, punishment, past behavior, & moral reasoning. Scores are combined to form an honesty score. There are built-in controls for faking & social desirability response bias.
California Psychological Inventory (CPI) Consulting Psychologists Press 1957 – 1995 Age 14 to Adults	CG3 MY11:54 TP5:372 T4:103	Designed to assess psychological functioning. Consists of 462 items yielding scores on 25 scales such as dominance, self-control, empathy, independence, work orientation, & managerial potential. Uses culturally universal & easy to understand folk concepts. Available in 10 languages. Hand or machine scored.
Career/Personality Compatibility Inventory Associated Consultants in Education 1989 Adults	T4:573	Designed to determine personality type as it relates to careers. Consists of 48 items yielding a profile to show compatibility between personality and career choice. Profile also suggests job selection criteria and possible career choices. Self- administered and self-scored.
Career Suitability Profile Management Strategies 1984 – 1993 Adults	T4:573	Based on 10 personality factors that measure fundamental personality character- istics that control career interests, abilities, & the capacity to perform. Com- puter scored; provides a personalized 30-page description of results.

Name of Test/Publisher/Date/Population	Reference(s)	Brief Description
Edwards Personal Preference Schedule (EPPS) The Psychological Corporation 1953 – 1959 Age 18 to Adults	MY9:378 TC1:252 TP5:908 T4:111	A forced-choice inventory based on Murry's Needs. Contains 225 pairs of comparison statements. Assesses 15 areas of needs & motives: abasement, achievement, affiliation, aggression, autonomy, change, deference, dominance, endurance, exhibition, heterosexuality, etc.
Employee Effectiveness Profile Jossey-Bass Pfeiffer & Company International Publishers 1986 Managers	MY12:136 TP5:939	Designed to determine employee effectiveness. Consists of a 20-item question-naire using a Likert-type scale. Yields a type score in a matrix that has 6 categories: deadwood, trainee, problem child, marginal, workhorse, & star. Individual administration.
Employee Reliability Inventory (ERI) Bay State Psychological Associates, Inc. 1986 – 1998 Adults and Job Applicants	MY12:137 TP5:944 T4:575	Assesses various dimensions of preemployment reliability and work behavior. Consists of 81 true-false items assessing behavior in 7 areas such as freedom from disruptive alcohol & substance abuse, emotional maturity, long term job commitment, & safe job performance. Available in Braille and 5 languages.
Forer Vocational Survey: Men-Women Western Psychological Services 1957 Adolescents to Adults	MY5:135 TP5:1050 T4:315	Designed to evaluate interpersonal behavior, attitudes toward people, work, & supervision & work dynamics. User completes sentence stems that measure reactions to specified situations, causes of feelings & actions, & vocational goals.
Fundamental Interpersonal Relations Orientation-Behavior (Firo-B) Consulting Psychologists Press 1967 – 1996 High School to Adults	MY9:416 T4:114	Measures interpersonal dynamics for building productive professional relation-ships & enhancing productivity & career potential. Based on a model that identifies 3 interpersonal expressed & wanted needs: inclusion, control & affection.
Gordon Personal Profile-Inventory (GPP-I) The Psychological Corporation 1951 – 1998 Grade 10 to Adults	MY13:133 TC2:326 TP5:1101 T4:115	Combines 2 measures to assess 8 aspects of personality. The profile examines ascendancy, responsibility, emotional stability, & sociability to yield a measure of self-esteem. Assesses cautiousness, original thinking, personal relations, & vigor.
Guilford-Zimmerman Temperament Survey (GZTS) Sheridan Psychological Services 1949 – 1978 Age 16 to Adults	MY9:460 TC8:251 TP5:1158 T4:115	Identifies strengths & weaknesses associated with personality & temperament. The 10 traits measured are activity, restraint, ascendancy, sociability, emotional stability, objectivity, friendliness, thoughtfulness, personal relations, & masculinity/femininity. A computer-generated report is also available.
Insight Inventory Human Resource Development Press	MY13:149 TP5:1273	Designed to measure the ways a person uses his/her individual personality. Measures 4 personality styles: getting one's way (direct or indirect), responding to people

Name of Test/Publisher/Date/Population	Reference(s)	Brief Description
Job Choice Decision-Making Exercise (JCE) Assessment Enterprises 1981 - 1988 High School to Adults	MY11:187 TP5:1347	Designed to measure an individual's need for achievement, power, & affiliation. Decision-making behavior is the basis for the scoring. The JCE-B is available for lower reading levels (6th to 7th grade). Self-administered. Software is avail-able for scoring on PC or compatibles.
Keirsey Character Sorter Prometheus Nemesis Book Company 1978 - 1997 Adults		Designed to assess temperaments. Consists of 36 items yielding scores as 2 letter MBTI type codes: Guardian (SJ), Artisan (SP), Idealist (NF) & Rational (NT). Each code is described & examples are given. Used with the book, "Please Understand Me". Available only online at http://www.keirsey.com/.
Meyer-Kendall Assessment Survey (MKAS) Western Psychological Services 1986 - 1991 Adults	MY12:234 TP5:1660 T4:580	Consists of 105 dichotomous items assessing personal functions relevant to work performance. Yields 12 scales. Intended for use by management consultants as part of a comprehensive assessment; not for general personnel screening. Must be computer scored.
Neo Personality Inventory-Resived Measurement for Human Resources 1993 Individuals Seeking Vocational Counseling	MMY11:258 MMY10:214 TC10:443 TC8:527 T3:201	Provides a systematic assessment of emotional, interpersonal, experiential, attitudinal, & motivational styles based on the 5 factor model of personality. Factors include: Neuroticism, Extraversion, Openness, Agreeableness, & Conscientious. Also provides 30 facet scale scores. Available in both software and mail-in machine scoring versions
Occupational Personality Assessment (OPA) Measurement for Human Resources 1993 Individuals Seeking Vocational Counseling	MY13:214 TP5:1821	Designed to be a fully computerized occupational test battery. Consists of tests assessing the following: interest, experience, commercial orientation, work & personal motivation, & management & entrepreneurial attitudes. Available in English, German, & French.
Occupational Personality Questionnaire (OPQ) Saville & Holdsworth, Ltd 1984 - 1990 Adults	MY11:267 TP5:1822	Designed to measure personality & motivational characteristics relevant to the world of work. Yields 31 scores in the following 4 areas: relationships with people, thinking style, feelings & emotions, & social desirability. Available in 10 languages, such as Dutch, German, Spanish, & Japanese.
Occupational Preference Inventory (OPI) PAQ Services 1999 Grade 11 to Adults		Computer-based assessment designed to assist individuals in making career de-cisions. Consists of 150 work characteristics yielding 5 profile reports con-taining the following: Preference, predicted MBTI & Aptitude scores, Personal Interest Profile, Report Descriptions & Administrator Job-Match Report.
Occupational Stress Inventory (OSI) Psychological Assessment Resources, Inc. 1981 - 1998 Adult Workers	CG3 MY11:279 TP5:1825 T4:536	Designed to measure occupational adjustment. Consists of 3 questionnaires: Oc-cupational Roles, Personal Strain, & Personal Resources. Raw scores & standard scores are provided for 14 scales. Machine or hand scored; computerized software available.

Name of Test/Publisher/Date/Population	Reference(s)	Brief Description
Personal Audit SRA/London House 1941 - 1992 Grade 9 to Adults	TP5:1928 T4:581	Measures personality traits objectively to assess personal adjustment essential to job satisfaction & success. Traits measured include seriousness-impulsive-ness, firmness-indecisiveness, frankness-evasion, contentment-worry, etc. For education, clinical, & industrial use.
Personal Skills Map (PSM) Emotional Learning Systems 1981 - 1993 Elementary to Adults	CG2 TC5:318 TP5:1948 T4:249	Designed to measure major components of emotional intelligence. Consists of 213 items that are self-descriptions & reactions to situations. Provides research-based assessment of intrapersonal, interpersonal, & life management skills directly related to achievement, performance, adjustment, & healthy living.
Personality Research Form (PRF) Sigma Assessment Systems 1965 - 1996 Age 11 to Adults	CG3 MY10:282 TP5:1965 T4:134	Designed to measure personality within a normal rang. Forms AA & BB consist of 440 items yielding scores on 22 scales; Forms A & B consist of 300 items yielding scores on 15 scales.Scores reported as standard (T) score. Also available in French & Spanish. Hand or machine scored.
Sales Attitude Checklist SRA/London House 1960 - 1992 Individuals Interested in Sales Positions	CG3 MY10:282 TP5:1965 T4:134	Designed to assess sales attitudes & habits via 31 self-descriptive, forced-choice items. Specifically intended for use in identifying potentially successful salespeople.
Sales Personality Questionnaire (SPQ) Saville & Holdsworth Ltd. USA 1987 - 1990 Sales Applicants	MY9:1066 TP5:2267 T4:647	Designed to assess personality characteristics designated as necessary for a successful career in sales. Consists of 108 items yielding scores in 12 areas such as relationships with people, persuasive, confident, empathetic, conscientious, resilient, & social desirability. Group or individual administration.
Self-Motivated Career Planning Guide Institute for Personality and Ability Testing 1978 - 1984 High School to Adults	MY12:337 TP5:2774	Designed to help individuals identify & develop vocational goals. Consists of 7 paper/pencil assessments such as Personal Orientation Survey, Education Sum-mary, Personal Career Life Summary, & Personal Development Survey, plus a 16PF personality assessment & interpretive report.
Singer-Loomis Inventory of Personality (SLIP) Moving Boundaries 1984 - 1996 Grade 9 to Adults	MY11:355 MY9:1099 TP5:2364	Contains 15 situations, each followed by 8 items to which the individual responds to using a 5-point Likert scale. Describes the user's personality from a Jungian perspective by providing the individual with a description of thought patterns & how situations or problems are approached.
Strategic Assessment of Readiness for Training (START) H & H Publishing Co. 1994	MY10:334 MY9:1131 TP5:2411	Diagnoses learning strengths & weaknesses in work settings. Consists of 56 multiple-choice items measuring anxiety, attitude, motivation, concentration, identifying important information, knowledge acquisition strategies, monitoring

Name of Test/Publisher/Date/Population	Reference(s)	Brief Description
Strength Deployment Inventory Personal Strengths Publishing 1973 - 1996 Adults	T4:499	Designed to assess individual's ability to relate to others under two conditions: when things are going well & when there is a conflict. Scores are yielded on 7 motivational value systems such as altruistic-nurturing, assertive-directing, & flexible-cohering. Also yields 13 scores relating to stages of conflict.
Styles of Teamwork Inventory (STI) Teleometrics International 1963 - 1995 Adults in Work Teams	TP5:2507	Assesses individual's attitudes & behaviors concerning work-team situations. Consists of 80 items, yielding scores in 5 areas: synergistic, compromise, win-lose, yield-lose, & lose-leave. Inventory results in an overall preferred style. Individual or group administration.
SureHire Psychological Services 1998 Job Applicants	MY11:392 MY8:1048 TP5:2549 T4:590	Designed to assess the competencies necessary for individuals seeking employ-ment in convenience stores. Yields a graphical representation of percentile scores in 4 areas, including problem solving, work orientation, customer service orientation, & a composite total. Individual or group administration.
Survey of Work Styles (SWS) Sigma Assessment Systems 1987 - 1993 Adults		A computerized personality assessment that gathers information on 4 factors, (self-awareness, centeredness, perceptions, & decision making). Identifies individuals as having 1 of 8 work styles such as forecaster, enthusiast, or-ganizer, precisionist, caretaker, purist, etc.
Temperament Comparator (TC) SRA/London House 1957 - 1996 Adults	MY13:311 TP5:2592	A paper & pencil inventory that assesses 18 relatively permanent temperament traits that contribute to basic behavior. Determines potential for successful performance in sales & higher-level professional & managerial positions.
Thurstone Temperament Schedule SRA/London House 1949 - 1991 Grade 9 to Adults	MY9:1234 TP5:2648 T4:586	Consists of 120 short questions that yield temperament profile scores for 6 personality traits: active, impulsive, dominant, stable, sociable, & reflective. Hand-scored carbon insert (answers transfer to scoring key on inside of test booklet). Appraisal/selection of applicants.
Viewpoint Psychological Services 1997 Job Applicants	MY6:192 TC2:815 TP5:2757 T4:586	Available in 5 different instruments or combinations of instruments: Workview-4 measures conscientiousness, trustworthiness, managing work pressure & get-ting along with others; Workview-6, measures the above plus drug & alcohol avoidance & safety orientation; Serviceview measures people-related attitudes.
Vocational Implications of Personality (VIP) Talent Assessment 1986 Grade 7 to Adults		A computerized personality assessment that gathers information on four factors (self-awareness, centeredness, perceptions, & decision making) & then identifies individuals as having 1 of 8 work styles such as forecaster, enthusiast, organizer, precisionist, designer, etc.

Name of Test/Publisher/Date/Population	Reference(s)	Brief Description
Vocational Preference Inventory (VPI) Psychological Assessment Resources 1953 – 1985 Grade 10 thru Adults	TP5:2835 T4:325	Designed to assess an individual's personality in areas, such as interpersonal relations, values, self-concepts, & coping behaviors. Consists of 160 occupational titles yielding scores on 11 scales including 6 Holland types & additional scales such as acquiescence, masculinity-femininity, status, & self-control

H. INSTRUMENTS FOR SPECIAL POPULATIONS

Name of Test/Publisher/Date/Population	Reference(s)	Brief Description
Adaptability Test SRA/London House 1943 - 1994 Applicants or Employees Limited in Adaptability	MY7:333 TP5:58 T4:483	Contains 35 items including word definitions, analogies, arithmetic computation, & series designed to differentiate between those who would perform better in routine jobs & those who could be placed in jobs that demanded more learning ability.
Ashland Interest Assessment (AIA) Sigma Assessment Systems 1997 Individuals with Restricted Abilities		Identifies work preferences by presenting 144 pairs of work-related activities. Yields scores on 12 scales such as arts & crafts, personal service, food service, clerical, sales, and protective service. Printed in large type and written at a 3rd grade reading level. Hand or machine scored. Computer version available.
Barsch Learning Styles Inventory – Revised Academic Therapy Publications 1980 - 1996 Grade 9 to Adults	MY9:11 TP5:244	Designed to measure learning through sensory channels. Self-report instrument consisting of 24 items yielding raw scores in 4 areas: auditory, visual, tactile, & kinesthetic. Completed in 5-10 minutes. Study tips component is provided to maximize individual's learning style.
Becker Work Adjustment Profile (BWAP) CTB Macmillan/McGraw-Hill 1989 Grade 10 to Adults	MY11:33 TP5:275 T4:447	Assesses work habits, attitudes, & skills important to work readiness, job adjustment, & employability. The questionnaire consists of a rating scale completed by an evaluator on job behavior items such as appearance, judgement, punctuality, productivity, & work safety.
Career Inventories for the Learning Disabled (CILD) Academic Therapies Publication 1983 High School to Adults, Learning Disabled	MY9:193 TP5:398 T4:459	Uses 3 inventories to aid in career choices: Attributes to assess dominant personality characteristics, Abilities to profile strengths in auditory, visual, & motor areas, & an Interest inventory to assist in determining if an individual's interest matches his/her abilities. Inventories administered orally by examiner.
C.I.T.E. Learning Styles Inventory Piney Mountain Press 1988-1998 Age 7 to Adults	MY12:218 TP5:1476 T3:780	Assesses 9 areas: auditory language, visual language, auditory numerical, visual numerical, auditory-visual-kinesthetic, group learner, social learner, oral expressive, & written expressive. Vocational version considers environmental & working conditions. Audiovisual presentation available.

Name of Test/Publisher/Date/Population	Reference(s)	Brief Description
Employment Barrier Identification Scale (EBIS) Behavior Science Press 1982 - 1999 Age 15 to Adults	MY9:384 T3:880	Evaluates an individual's employability. Includes job skills, education, environmental support & personal survival skills. Identifies areas where the individual may need training. Can be presented orally to examinees with low literary skills.
Endorele Seversen Transition Rating Scales (ESTRS) Practical Press 1991 Ages 14 to 21 with a Disability	AT:98	Designed to provide information concerning transition for individuals with disabilities. Form J for students with mild disabilities consists of 84 items. Form R for students with moderate to severe disabilities consists of 136 items. Both forms have 5 subscales such as jobs & job training, & home living.
Functional Assessment Inventory Stout Vocational Rehabilitation Institute 1984 - 1989 Adults - Special Populations		Designed to assess vocationally relevant strengths & weaknesses regarding an individual's capacity for work & other productive activities. Consists of 40 items yielding ratings ranging from normal to severe impairment. A companion client form, the Personal Capacities Questionnaire, is also available.
Geist Picture Interest Inventory Western Psychological Services 1959 - 1971 Grade 8 to Adults, Non-readers	MY6:1054 TP5:1074 T4:333	Provides scores for 11 or 12 interest areas such as persuasive, clerical, mechanical, scientific, outdoor, artistic, social service, etc. Also provides scores for 7 motivational areas such as family, prestige, financial, environmental, etc. Male & female versions.
Key Educational Vocational Assessment System (KEVAS) Key Education 1985 High School to Adults, Disabled & Non-Disabled	T4:317 B:93	Includes 20 apparatus, achievement, interest, & personality tests that must be administered by two trained examiners. Measures such variables as hearing, visual & color acuity, auditory & visual reaction time, abstract reasoning ability, response to stress, vocational interest, etc.
Learning Style Profile National Association of Secondary School Principals 1986 - 1990 Grades 6 to 12 - Special Populations	MY12:217 TP5:1472	Designed to measure how students learn and prefer to learn. Yields 23 scores in areas such as cognitive skills, perceptual responses, persistence orientation, verbal risk orientation, & study & instructional preferences. Also available in Spanish.
Learning Styles Inventory Price Systems 1976-1996 Grades 3 to 12 – Special Populations	T4:243	Designed to assess individual learning preferences in the following areas: sociological needs, immediate environment, emotionality, & physical needs. Computerized summary of results is provided with suggested strategies for instructional and environmental alternatives to individual learning situations.

Name of Test/Publisher/Date/Population	Reference(s)	Brief Description
McCarron-Dial System McCarron Dial System 1973 - 1986 Special Populations	CG2,3 MY11:231 TP5:1610 T4:327	Designed to provide a comprehensive assessment to be used in educational & vocational planning. Assesses 5 factors: verbal-spatial-cognitive, sensory, motor, emotional, & integration coping. Includes 7 tests such as Peabody Picture Vocational Test-R, Behavior Rating Scale, & Emotional Behavior Checklist.
Microcomputer Evaluation of Career Areas (MECA) The Conover Company, Ltd. 1986 - 1992 Grade 7 to 12, Disadvantaged & Disabled	B:93	Designed for vocational exploration via 15 work samples containing 3 tasks each, such as automotive, building maintenance, cosmetology, graphic design, custodial housekeeping, electronics, small engines, food service, health care, business & office, manufacturing, distribution, & computers.
Personnel Tests for Industry--Oral Directions Test (PTI-ODT) The Psychological Corporation 1946 - 1974 Bilingual Persons with English as a Second Language	TP5:1974 T4:497	A wide-range assessment of general mental abilities & an individual's comprehension of verbal, numerical, & oral directions. English test requires 15 minutes & is hand scored. Used as a screening device for vocational trainees & industrial personnel. May be used with persons of limited English proficiency.
Pictorial Inventory of Careers (PIC) Talent Assessment 1992 Middle School to Adults - Special Populations	CG2,3	Reading free instrument designed to measure vocational interests. Consists of 119 real-life pictorials depicting vocational technical careers from 17 vocational clusters, & 11 career cluster definitions. Each cluster is represented by 7 scenes emphasizing the work environment, not the individual. Hand or machine scored.
Practical Assessment Exploration System (PAES) Talent Assessment 1991 Special Populations		A Curriculum Based Vocational Assessment Program that provides hands-on evaluation. Evaluation & transition data includes job skill, quality of performance, work rate, interests, & behavioral barriers to employment & training.
Preliminary Diagnostic Questionnaire (PDQ) West Virginia Research and Training Center 1981 - 1994 Rehabilitation Clients	MY11:297 TP5:2030	Assesses functional capacities regarding employment of individuals with disabilities. Scores are yielded on 8 subscales: work information, preliminary estimate of learning, psycho-motor skills, reading retention, work importance, personal independence, internality, & emotional functioning. Orally administered.
Prevocational Assessment Screen (PAS) Piney Mountain Press 1985 - 1994 Grades 9 to 12 - Special Populations	CG3 MY12:305 TP5:2054	Assesses motor & perceptual abilities for requirements of local vocational training programs. Yields 16 time & error scores in 8 areas: alphabetizing, etch a sketch maze, calculating, small parts, pipe assembly, o rings, block design, & color sort. Individual administration.

Name of Test/Publisher/Date/Population	Reference(s)	Brief Description
Program for Assessing Youth Employment Skills (PAYES) Educational Testing Service 1966 - 1979 School Drop Outs, Disadvantaged Adolescents	CG2 MY9:1001 TC9:411 TP5:2081 T4:319	A nonsexist measure of attitudes, cognitive skills, & vocational preference for disadvantaged youth. Provides a structured approach to identify an individual's comprehension of attitudes, interests, knowledge, & skills needed to find, obtain, & maintain a job.
Responsibility and Independence Scale for Adolescents (RISA) Riverside Publishing 1990 - 1992 Ages 12 to 20 - Special Populations	MY12:325 TP5:2204 T4:238 AT:98	Norm-referenced instrument designed to measure adolescents' adaptive behavior in the areas of responsibility and independence. Consists of 9 subscales in functional areas such as self-management, social maturity, social communication, domestic skills, money management, citizenship, personal organization, transportation skills, & career skills.
Skills Assessment Module (SAM) Piney Mountain Press 1981 - 1994 Age 13 to 18 - Special Populations	MY11:364 TP5:2421 T4:328 B:93	Assesses general aptitude, specific work behavior, & learning styles via 3 paper/pencil tests & 12 work samples such as mail sort, payroll, computation, patient information memo, pipe assembly, block design, small parts, color sort, circuit board, etc.
Social & Prevocational Information Battery (SPIB) CTB/McGraw-Hill 1975 - 1986 Grade 7 to 12 - Special Populations	CG3 MY11:367 TP5:2443 AT:98	Designed to assess competencies & skills of mildly retarded students, necessary for everyday living in the community. Yields scores in 10 areas: purchasing habits, budgeting, banking, job-related behavior, job search skills, home management, health care, hygiene & grooming, functional signs, & a total.
Talent Assessment Program (TAP) Talent Assessment, Inc. 1988 Middle School to Adult - Vocationally Disabled	CG3	Reading-free assessment of functional aptitudes. Consists of 10 hands-on tests, such as Form Perception, Ability to Follow Patterns, Color Discrimination, & Tactile Discrimination. Results are compiled into a profile that can be compared with job requirements in the DOT and OOH.
Tests for Everyday Living (TEL) CTB Macmillan/McGraw-Hill 1975 Grade 7 to 12 - Special Populations	MY9:1281 TP5:2734 T3:674 AT:98	Measures knowledge of skills necessary to perform everyday life tasks. Consists of 7 tests: purchasing, habits, budgeting, banking, job-search skills, job-related behavior, home management, & health care. Designed for poor readers.
Transition Behavior Scale, 2nd edition (TBS-2) Hawthorne 1991 - 1999 High School - Special Populations	TP5:2779 T4:323	Designed to assess the readiness of an individual to enter the world of employment & independent living. Consists of 62 items, yielding scores in 3 areas: work-related behavior, interpersonal relations, & social/community expectations. Manual includes IEP goals, objectives, & interventions.

Name of Test/Publisher/Date/Population	Reference(s)	Brief Description
USES Basic Occupational Literacy Test (BOLT) United States Employment Service 1971 - 1983 High School Dropouts	MY11:453 MY8:491 TP5:2795	Designed to measure basic reading & arithmetic skills of school dropouts who are referred for occupational training or remedial education. Provides scores for reading vocabulary, reading comprehension, arithmetic computation, & arithmetic reasoning.
USES Non-Reading Aptitude Test Battery (NATB) United States Employment Service 1965 - 1982 Grade 9 to Adults, Disadvantaged	CG1 MY9:1305 TP5:2799	Nonreading adaptation of the GATB that includes 7 or 8 pencil/paper tests & 4 performance tests. Provides 9 scores: intelligence, verbal, numerical, spatial, form perception, clerical perception, motor coordination, finger dexterity, & manual dexterity.
Valpar Component Work Sample Series Valpar Corporation 1974 - 1993 General Population & Industrially Injured Persons	CG1	Consists of 22 work samples designed to measure broad worker traits, such as use of small tools, vocational readiness, upper extremity range of motion, simulated assembly, etc. Yields scores & clinical observations that can be used for job training & placement & for constructing programs.
Vocational Adaptation Rating Scales (VARS) Western Psychological Services 1980 Mentally Retarded Persons Age 13 to Adults	MY9:1334 TP5:2824 T4:467	Uses parents', teachers', & professionals' ratings to measure maladaptive behaviors likely to hinder vocational adjustment. Provides frequency & severity scores in 17 areas such as verbal manners, communication skill, respect for property, rules & regulations, etc.
Vocational Assessment & Curriculum Guide (VACG) Exceptional Education 1993 Mentally Retarded Employees	MY13:356 T4:467	Designed to identify & assess skill deficits in employment expectations; prescribe training goals, & evaluate training effectiveness. Consists of 49 items, yielding 10 scores, such as attendance/endurance, independence, production, behavior, communication skills, & grooming/eating.
Vocational Behavior Checklist (VBC) West Virginia Rehabilitation Research and Training Center 1978 Adults	MY9:1335 TP5:2827 T3:851	Designed for use with rehabilitation clients. Assess 7 skills: prevocational, job-seeking, interview, job-related, work-performance, on-the-job/social, & union-financial-security.
Vocational Decision Making Interview Jist Works, Inc. 1993 Special Populations	TP5:2828	Assesses the vocational decision-making capacities of individuals with disabilities. Consists of 54 items, yielding scores in 4 areas: decision-making, readiness, employment readiness, self-appraisal, & a total. Uses an interview format that is orally administered to individuals.

Name of Test/Publisher/Date/Population	Reference(s)	Brief Description
Vocational Evaluation Systems (Singer) New Concepts Corporation 1971 Grades 7 to 12 - Special Populations	B:93	Provides a wide variety of occupational information via 28 independent & versatile work samples such as bench assembly, electrical wiring, plumbing & pipe fitting, needle trades, cook & baker, cosmetology, office services, information processing, machine trades, etc.
Vocational Interest Temperament and Aptitude System (VITAS) Vocational Research Institute 1979 Educationally and/or Culturally Disadvantaged	CG1 T3:658 B:93	Contains 21 independent work samples based on 16 Work Groups. Samples include laboratory, engineering & craft technology, production work, quality control, financial detail, oral communications, etc. Requires training to administer.
Vocational Learning Styles Piney Mountain Press 1991 Age 14 to Adults		A multisensory learning styles assessment designed for school & work. Considers traditional style factors, as well as environmental & working styles critical to training & job success. Scoring formats include self, computer, & machine.
Vocational Training Inventory and Exploration Survey (VOC-TIES) Piney Mountain 1986 - 1991 Disadvantaged & Mildly Handicapped Youth	T3:840	A multimedia kit used to identify vocational interests, enhance vocational awareness, & promote sex equity by showing persons in nontraditional roles. Includes a video for 15 commonly available vocational programs. Apple/IBM program provides printout of interests.
Vocational Transit Vocational Research Institute 1989 MR, LD, Brain Injured	T4:329 B:93	Designed to allow individuals to demonstrate their true aptitudes by accommodating alternative learning styles, short-term memory deficits & attention span difficulties. Subtests include motor coordination, manual dexterity, finger dexterity & form perception.
Wide Range Achievement Test (WRAT3) Wide Range, Inc. 1940 - 1993 Age 5 to Adult - Special Populations	MY12:414 TP5:2879 T4:210	Designed to assess the skills necessary to learn how to read, spell, & perform basic arithmetic operations. Provides absolute, standard, & grade scores on each of the 3 subtests: Reading, Spelling, & Arithmetic. Individual administration. Two equivalent forms are available.
Wide Range Interest-Opinion Test (WRIOT) Wide Range, Inc. 1972 - 1979 Special Populations	CG3 MY9:1366 TC4:673	Designed to "measure the strength of 18 interest & 8 attitude clusters." Consists of 150 sets of 3 pictures each yielding scores arranged into 7 categories such as liberal arts, business, & sports. Also yields scores on 8 opinion & attitude scales such as ambition, risk, & sex stereotype. Currently under revision.

Name of Test/Publisher/Date/Population	Reference(s)	Brief Description
Work Adjustment Inventory (WAI) PRO-ED, Inc. 1994 Adolescents and Young Adults - Special Populations	MY13:365 TP5:2912 T4:326	A norm-referenced assessment of 6 work-related temperaments: activity, empathy, sociability, assertiveness, adaptability, & emotionality. Provides age- & gender based scores that can be displayed graphically. Third-grade reading level. Useful for transition planning for students with disabilities & at-risk youth.
Work Performance Assessment (WPA) The National Center on Employment & Disability 1987 - 1988 Job Trainees - Special Populations	MY13:367 TP5:2923	Designed to assess work-related social/interpersonal skills. Consists of 19 assessment situations involving supervisors, workers, & co-workers. Yields scores on 19 supervisory demands, such as greet each trainee, explain supervisory error, provide detailed instructions, & socialize with each trainee.
Work Skills Development Package (WSD) Attainment Company 1982 - 1999 Mentally Retarded, Mentally Ill, Physically, Disabled		A prevocational training program containing 20 work samples, grouped into 4 difficulty levels, that assess 3 prevocational skills: discrimination between objects, manipulation of small objects, & application of basic concepts. Examples of work samples are box packaging, tactile discrimination, etc.
Work Personality Profile (WPP) The National Center on Employment & Disability 1986 Vocational Rehabilitation Clients	MY11:476 TP5:2924	Designed to assess fundamental work role requirements that are essential to achievement and maintenance of suitable employment. Consists of ratings on 58 items, yielding 16 scores such as acceptance of work role, ability to profit from instruction or correction, & ability to socialize with co-workers.
Work Skills Development Package (WSD) Attainment Company 1982 - 1999 Mentally Retarded, Mentally Ill, Physically, Disabled		A prevocational training program containing 20 work samples, grouped into 4 difficulty levels, that assess 3 prevocational skills: discrimination between objects, manipulation of small objects, & application of basic concepts. Examples of work samples are box packaging, tactile discrimination, etc.
Work Temperament Inventory (WTI) The National Center on Employment & Disability 1993 Workers – Special Populations	MY13:368 TP5:2928	Designed to identify an individual's traits & match those traits to occupations. Yields scores on 12 scales including directive, repetitive, influencing, variety, expressing, judgments, alone, stress, tolerances, people, & measurable. Individual or group administration.

APPENDIX A

Sources of Information About Testing and Career Assessment

David A. Jepsen
Professor of Counseling, Rehabilitation and Student Development
University of Iowa

Jerome T. Kapes
Professor Emeritus of Educational Psychology
Texas A & M University

Introduction

This section contains a list of information sources about assessment instruments and their use in enhancing career development. Included are textbooks, reference books, and monographs selected because their content has application to career assessment issues and career guidance problems faced by counselors, teachers, and administrators. The list of psychometric texts contains many that have undergone several revisions, indicating their continued value. Recent textbooks about career development have been included when they address general issues of test selection and usage or refer to innovative approaches in career assessment. In addition, materials for special populations, the familiar volumes of test bibliographies and reviews, and a list of periodicals are included here. A brief list of Internet sources has been added.

The list is not intended to be exhaustive, rather it is representative of the best resources available. Readers should find sufficient information in these sources to answer most questions about career assessment instruments and their application to the career development process.

Standards for Publishers and Users of Tests

American Counseling Association. (1989). *Responsibilities of users of standardized tests.* Alexandria, VA: Author.

This is a revision of the original *Responsibilities* statement first published in 1978 by the American Personnel and Guidance Association (APGA), now the American Counseling Association (ACA). This version, developed by the Association for Assessment in Counseling (AAC) on behalf of ACA contains the following sections: Introduction, Test Decisions, Qualification of Test Users, Test Selection, Test Administration, Test Scoring, Test Interpretation, Communicating Test Results, and Extension of These Principles. The target audience is members of ACA and its divisions. The statement should also be of interest to test developers, teachers, administrators, parents, and the general public.

American Psychological Association. (1999). *Standards for educational and psychological testing.* Washington, DC: Author.

Co-sponsored by the American Psychological Association, American Educational Research Association, and the National Council on Measurement in Education, these standards address technical problems, ethics, and applicability of tests in both research and clinical settings. The contents are divided into an introduction and 15 chapters organized into three parts: Part I. Test Construction, Evaluation, and Documentation; Part II. Fairness in Testing; and Part III. Testing Applications.

Eyde, L. D., Robertson, G. J., Krug, S. E., & Associates. (1993). *Responsible test use: Case studies for assessing human behavior. Washington, DC: American Psychological Association.*

This publication from the American Psychological Association is a guide to competent test use through proper selection, administration, and interpretation. Authored by the Test User Training Work Group of APA, it is intended as a training resource. Included are 78 real-life case studies based on empirically devised testing problems with analysis of proper test use and misuse. The cases are arranged in a sequence covering training, selection, administration, scoring, feedback to clients, and policy issues.

Joint Committee on Testing Practices (1988). *Code of fair testing practices in education.* Washington, DC: American Psychological Association.

The code was developed by a Joint Committee on Testing Practices, which involved six professional associations. A total of 21 standards for educational test developers and users are presented in four areas: Developing/Selecting Tests, Interpreting Scores, Striving for Fairness, and Informing Test Takers.

Joint Committee on Testing Practices (2000). *The rights and responsibilities of test takers: Guidelines and expectations.* Washington, DC: American Psychological Association.

These guidelines were developed by the Joint Committee, which is composed of six professional associations involved with the practice of educational measurement. The intent of the document is to describe clearly reasonable expectations and responsibilities for test takers, developers, and administrators of psychological and educational tests. Separate listings of rights and responsibilities for both test takers and testing professionals are provided.

Prediger, D. J. (1993). *Multicultural assessment standards: A compilation for counselors*. Alexandria, VA: Association for Assessment in Counseling/American Counseling Association.

The purpose of these standards is to further the realization of diversity, development, and dignity in respect to the use of psychological assessments with multicultural populations. The 34 standards contained in this report were identified from five source documents that address testing and/or multicultural standards for education, counseling, or psychological testing.

Psychometric Texts and Monographs

Aiken, L. R. (2000). *Psychological testing and assessment* (10th ed.). Boston: Allyn & Bacon.

This textbook covers the usual historical and psychometric background information and also has a chapter on testing special abilities (e.g., mechanical) and another on assessment of interests, attitudes, and values. The latter chapter is devoted primarily to discussions of the Strong and Kuder inventories.

Anastasi, A., & Urbina, S. (1997). *Psychological testing* (7th ed.). Upper Saddle River, NJ: Prentice-Hall.

The seventh edition of this popular textbook was revised to cover advances in psychological testing in the 1990s. Chapters on technical and methodological principles provide a comprehensive treatment or norms, reliability, validity, and item analysis. Chapters or sections of chapters on multiple aptitude measures, occupational testing, self-report personality inventories, and measuring interests and attitudes have direct application to career development.

Drummond, R. J. (1999). *Appraisal procedures for counselors and helping professionals* (4th ed.). Upper Saddle River, NJ: Prentice-Hall.

The author uses a systems approach to organize assessment knowledge, skills, and competencies. Includes chapters on assessing ability and intelligence, aptitude, achievement, career and employment, and personality, all of which are relevant to career assessment. Also includes chapters on many other topics useful to professionals who conduct assessments.

Hood, A. B., & Johnson R. W. (2001). *Assessment in counseling: A guide to the use of psychological assessment procedures* (3rd ed.). Alexandria, VA: American Counseling Association.

This textbook about psychological assessment procedures discusses the use of over 100 instruments as applied to counseling. Case examples help illustrate use of tests. A four-chapter section covers career and life planning assessment.

Lichtenberg, J. W., & Goodyear, R. K. (Eds.) (1999). *Scientist-practitioner perspectives on test interpretation.* Boston: Allyn & Bacon.

This book focuses on the practices of test interpretation grounded in psychological theory and research. Each of eight chapters incorporates a different theoretical perspective and reviews relevant research.

Lowman, R. L. (1991). *The clinical practice of career assessment: Interests, abilities, and personality.* Washington, DC: American Psychological Association.

The author presents an interdomain career assessment model based on Holland's hexagon that is designed to integrate test and nontest data about interests, abilities, and personality. Career assessment is conceptualized as a clinical activity and Lowman addresses issues about what and how to assess and how to integrate findings.

Lyman, H. B. (1997). *Test scores and what they mean* (6th ed.). Englewood Cliffs, NJ: Prentice-Hall.

This handy text, first published in 1963, is written for users of test information who have very little formal training in measurement. It covers general features of tests and testing, as well as how to understand test scores and convey their meaning to students and clients.

Osborne, W. L., Brown, S., Niles, S., & Miner, C.U. (1997). *Career development, assessment, and counseling: Applications of the Donald E. Super C-DAC approach.* Alexandria, VA: American Counseling Association.

This book expands on the C-DAC model developed by Super in the early 90s. It provides an overview of both theory and research that stimulated the model, as well as a description of the instruments used to implement the model. Chapters on practical applications of the model with high school, university, and adult students/clients are also provided.

Walsh, W. B., & Betz, N. E. (1994). *Tests and assessment* (3rd ed.). Englewood Cliffs, NJ: Prentice-Hall.

One of six parts in the text covers the assessment of interests and career development. Five interest inventories, two work values inventories, four measures of career development and career maturity, and three measures of career indecision are described and illustrated. The book is written specifically for a counselor audience.

Watkins, C. E., Jr., & Campbell, V. L. (Eds.). (2000). *Testing and assessment in counseling practice.* (2nd ed.) Mahwah, NJ: Lawrence Erlbaum.

This volume includes several chapters written by advocates for, or authors of, specific personality inventories, interest inventories, card sorts, and career choice process scales. Additional chapters cover models and issues in using tests in counseling and with computer applications.

Whiston, S. C. (2000). *Principles and applications of assessment in counseling.* Belmont, CA: Brooks/Cole–Wadsworth.

This book is intended as a comprehensive introduction to appraisal and assessment for counseling students. It includes examples and applications, and focuses on the importance of using assessment results to evaluate the efficacy of counseling. Major areas of assessment covered include intelligence and general ability, achievement and aptitude measures, assessment in career counseling, appraisal of personality, and marriage and family assessment. Also discussed are issues and applications of assessment including diagnosis, assessment with special populations, ethical and legal issues, and technological applications.

Zunker, V. G., & Norris, D. S. (1998). *Using assessment results for career development* (5th ed.). Pacific Grove, CA: Brooks/Cole.

After three introductory chapters on assessment concepts and the rationale behind using assessment results in counseling, Zunker and Norris cover many different types of career assessments in 11 additional chapters. Descriptions of specific instruments are found within each of these chapters. Case studies are included to illustrate interpretations for some of the instruments.

Career Development Texts

Brown, D., & Brooks, L. (1991). *Career counseling techniques.* Boston: Allyn & Bacon.

This textbook, written especially for career counselors about specific techniques for assessing and interviewing, is appropriate for a wide variety of career problems. A six-chapter section describes how to use assessment techniques, such as assessing interests, values, personality and interrole relationships.

Brown, S. D., & Lent, R. W. (Eds.) (1992). *Handbook of counseling psychology,* (2nd ed.). New York: Wiley.

This comprehensive reference volume, written for counselors and counseling psychologists, includes four parts, one of which is titled "career and educational counseling." Within that group of chapters is one devoted to a review of critical issues in career assessment .

Gysbers, N. C., Heppner, M. J., & Johnston, J. A. (1998). *Career counseling: Process, issues, and techniques.* Boston: Allyn & Bacon.

This textbook emphasizes the process of career counseling. Several chapters cover techniques and instruments for gathering client information, including a chapter on standardized tests and inventories. Whole chapters are devoted to cards sorts and genograms.

Harris-Bowlsbey, J., Dikel, M. R., & Sampson, Jr., J. P. (1998). *The Internet: A tool for career planning.* Columbus, OH: National Career Development Association.

This NCDA publication covers many aspects of career planning in respect to Internet resources, including assessment. Web sites for selected assessments that are available on the Internet are provided with brief annotations. Appendix A provides the NCDA Guidelines for Use of the Internet for Provision of Career Information and Planning Services.

Herr, E. L., & Cramer, S. H. (1996). *Career guidance and counseling through the life-span: Systematic approaches* (5th ed.). New York: Harper Collins.

This text provides a comprehensive treatment of career guidance and counseling for all ages. One chapter covers assessment and is divided into four functions: prediction, discrimination, monitoring, and evaluation. Within each section, several instruments are described briefly with particular attention to scale names.

Herring, R. (1998). *Career counseling in schools: Multicultural and development perspectives.* Alexandria, VA: American Counseling Association.

This book is designed to enhance school counselor's knowledge about cultural diversity and provide appropriate interventions with special population students. Included is a chapter titled Appraisal from a Multicultural Focus in which sources of biases are treated separately.

Isaacson, L. E., & Brown, D. (2000). *Career information, career counseling, and career development* (7th ed.). Boston: Allyn & Bacon.

This is a general textbook about facilitating career development processes. One chapter contains extensive treatment of assessment procedures including qualitative and quantitative/objective assessment instruments. Several specific interest, values and personality inventories, multiple aptitude tests and career diagnostic instruments are described briefly.

Peterson, G. W., Sampson, J. P., Jr., & Reardon, R. C. (1991). *Career development and services: A cognitive approach.* Pacific Grove, CA: Brooks/Cole.

The authors describe career development and career counseling from a unique cognitive information-processing framework. They include one chapter on how to select and interpret career assessment procedures that elaborates on self and career schemata. A few instruments are described as examples.

Reardon, R. C., Lenz, J. G., Sampson, Jr., J. P., & Peterson, G. W. (2000). *Career development and planning: A comprehensive approach.* Belmont, CA: Brooks/Cole-Wadsworth.

This text is designed for use in a college-level undergraduate career development course. It uses a cognitive psychology approach to impart knowledge to the student/user. Included is a chapter on Knowing about Myself that describes various approaches to assessing values, interests, and skills, and discusses how this information would be helpful in making career decisions.

Savickas, M. L., & Spokane, A. R. (Eds.) (1999). *Vocational interests: Meaning, measurement and counseling use.* Palo Alto, CA: Davies-Black.

A collection of papers written by leading authorities about contemporary vocational interest theory, research, and practice presented in three sections: Conceptualizing Vocational Interests, Measuring Vocational Interests, and Using Vocational Interests in Career Interventions. Several standardized inventories are discussed throughout.

Savickas, M. L., & Walsh, W. B. (Eds.) (1996). *Handbook of career counseling theory and practice.* Palo Alto, CA: Davies-Black.

This volume contains 27 chapters on the relationship between theory and practice in career counseling. Part 3 contains seven chapters on Innovations in Career Assessment.

Seligman, L. (1994). *Developmental career counseling and assessment* (2nd ed.) Thousand Oaks, CA: Sage.

This book was written to help readers understand the lifelong process of career development and become better able to use counseling and assessment to facilitate that process. Two chapters are devoted to the use of assessment and examples of assessment tools.

Spokane, A. R. (1991). *Career intervention.* Englewood Cliffs, NJ: Prentice Hall.
This textbook is about how to help people improve their ability to make career decisions. It contains elaborate chapters on vocational assessment and selection and use of vocational inventories.

Zunker, V. G. (1998). *Career counseling: Applied concepts of life planning.* (5th ed.). Pacific Grove, CA: Brooks/Cole.
This is a comprehensive career counseling text intended for use in a graduate course in counseling. It includes a chapter on Using Standardized Assessment in Career Counseling that briefly describes many of the prominent standardized instruments available to assess aptitude, achievement, interest, personality, values, and career maturity. Publisher addresses are also provided.

Materials for Special Populations

Brown, C. D., McDaniel, R. M., Couch, R. H., & McClanahan, M. (1993). *Vocational evaluation systems and software: A consumer's guide.* Menomonie, WI: Materials Development Center, Stout Vocational Rehabilitation Institute, University of Wisconsin-Stout. (ERIC Document Reproduction Service No. ED 364 721).
This publication describes and reviews 18 commercially available vocational assessment and evaluation systems and nine job search software packages. The guide is an updated combination of two previously published documents on vocational assessment authored by Botterbusch at the University of Wisconsin-Stout. The primary purpose of this guide is to help those who may be potential purchasers and users of such systems. A standard format for each product reviewed includes descriptions, administration procedures, scoring, interpreting and reporting, measurement properties, and a summary and review.

Clark, G. M. (1998). *Assessment for transitions planning: A guide for special education teachers and related service personnel.* Austin, TX: PRO-ED.
The focus of this book is on assessing persons with disabilities at any age as they plan for transitions. Both formal standardized instrument and informal techniques are described and discussed. The information presented would be useful for both in-school transitions using the IEP process as well as transition to work through Individual Transition Planning (ITP).

Jones, R. L. (Ed.) (1996). *Handbook of tests and measurement for black populations, Vols. 1 & 2.* Hampton, VA: Cobb and Henry.

A two-volume compilation of tests and measures developed or modified for use with African Americans. Very few of the over 80 instruments discussed measure career behaviors exclusively, although several measures of beliefs, values, and work environments are applicable.

Harrington, T. F. (1997). *Handbook of career planning for students with special needs* (2nd ed.). Austin, TX: PRO-ED.

This practitioner's guide covers all aspects of career planning with special needs youth and adults. Topics range from identifying goals to planning for transition. The assessment of abilities and interests related to career goals is specifically addressed.

Levinson, E. M. (1993). *Transdisciplinary vocational assessment: Issues in school-based programs.* Brandon, VT: Clinical Psychology Pub.

This text is written for educational personnel working with special populations. The contents include chapters on "General considerations in assessment," "Vocational assessment techniques and strategies" and "Vocational assessment domains and instrumentation." Summaries of a wide range of tests are included as well as work samples and situational assessment strategies.

Power, P. W. (2000). *A guide to vocational assessment* (3rd ed.). Austin, TX: PRO-ED.

Written for anyone who counsels clients with disabilities, this book addresses both the intellectual and emotional needs of students in regard to vocational evaluation and rehabilitation. Specific vocational interest, intelligence, and educational achievement instruments are discussed in reference to people with disabilities.

Suzuki, L. A., Meller, P. J., & Ponterotto, J. G. (Eds.). (1996). *Handbook of multicultural assessment: Clinical, psychological, and educational applications.* San Francisco, CA: Jossey-Bass.

This text presents current research and practice in multicultural assessment as well as discussing many relevant social and ethical issues. Individual chapters deal with specific areas of assessment including vocational assessment across cultures. A second edition is due for publication in November 2000.

Test Bibliographies and Reviews

Educational Testing Service. (1992). *Test collection catalog: Vol. 6: Affective measures and personality tests.* Phoenix, AZ: Oryx Press.

This source contains descriptions of 1,560 measures of the psychological, social, and affective reactions of individuals to their environment. Some of the measures, e.g., locus of control, coping skills, apply to career development. For each instrument the following are provided: name, descriptors, availability, target audience, length of test and administration time, and a brief description.

Educational Testing Service. (1995). *Test collection catalog: Vol. 2. Vocational tests and measurement devices.* (2nd ed.) Phoenix, AZ: Oryx Press.

Among the 1,310 measures described in this second volume from ETS's Test Collection are vocational interest inventories and aptitude tests, work samples, attitude assessments, measures of career development, certification tests, measures for use with persons with disabilities, and instruments to measure organizational climate and managerial styles. Information provided for each test includes name, descriptors, availability, length of test and administration time, and a brief description.

Impara, J. C. & Plake, B. S. (Eds.) (1998). *Thirteenth mental measurement yearbook.* Lincoln, NE: Buros Institute of Mental Measurement, University of Nebraska–Lincoln.

This is the most recent volume in the most well-known source of test reviews. Previous editions published in 1995 (12th), 1992 (11th), 1989 (10th), and 1985 (9th) should also be consulted. Several critical reviews are printed for each instrument. Each test is described and technical and practical issues are addressed. Most instruments used in career guidance and counseling have been reviewed in one or more volumes of the MMY series. This volume contains reviews of over 70 tests classified for *vocations.* Reviews of a variety of career assessment instruments are included.

Kapes, J. T., & Mastie, M. M. (Eds.). (1982). *A counselor's guide to vocational guidance instruments.* Falls Church, VA: National Vocational Guidance Association.

Reviews of 40 instruments divided into appropriate categories comprise the primary emphasis of this volume. Over 70 additional tests and inventories are briefly described. A summary of the principles of choosing a test, a checklist of testing competencies, and a bibliography of testing references are also included.

Kapes, J. T., & Mastie, M. M. (Eds.). (1988). *A counselor's guide to career assessment instruments.* (2nd ed.). Alexandria, VA: National Career Development Association.

This second edition of the above-described guide contains many of the same sections as the first edition in expanded and/or revised form. Reviews of 43 of the most prominent instruments are included as well as brief descriptions of 126 additional instruments. A Users Matrix, that cross-references test names with category and level of use, is an added feature.

Kapes, J. T., Mastie, M. M., & Whitfield, E. A. (Eds.). (1994). *A counselor's guide to career assessment instruments.* (3rd ed.). Alexandria, VA: National Career Development Association.

The third edition of the guide is similar to the previous two editions, but is expanded in its coverage with reviews of 52 major instruments and brief descriptions of 245 additional instruments. As with previous editions, all reviews and several of the chapters are completely new with different authors for all reviews. For this reason, users may want to consult previous editions for additional independent opinions.

Keyser, D. J., & Sweetland, R. C. (Eds.). (1984-94). *Test Critiques. (Vols. 1-10).* Austin, TX: PRO-ED.

These volumes contain descriptive and critical reviews of measurement instruments judged by the volume editors to be the most frequently used. Included are 25 instruments used in *vocational guidance* and another 15 instruments measuring *interests*. Coverage overlaps with the Mental Measurement Yearbook series, but these reviews are lengthier and are limited to single reviewers.

Maddox, T. (Ed.). (1997). *Tests: A comprehensive reference for assessments in psychology, education and business* (4th ed.). Austin, TX: PRO-ED.

This fourth edition of Tests follows close on the heels of the first (1983), the second (1986), and the third (1991) editions. Tests is narrower in coverage than Tests in Print, but there is considerable overlap. Information is provided under the following headings: Title, Author, Copyright Date, Population, Purpose, Description, Format, Scoring, Cost, and Publisher. Eight indices cover Titles, Tests not in 4th Edition, Publishers not in 4th Edition, Foreign Language Availability, Computer Scored Tests, Authors, Publishers, and a Cross-reference.

Murphy, L. L., Impara, J. C., & Plake, B. S. (Eds.). (1999). *Tests in print V: An index to tests, test reviews, and the literature on specific tests.* Lincoln, NE: Buros Institute of Mental Measurements, University of Nebraska–Lincoln.

Nearly all commercially published test in the English language are listed her in alphabetical order by test title. Information provided includes the following: Title, Purpose, Population, Publication Date, Acronym, Scores, Administration, Forms, Manual, Restricted Distribution, Price, Languages, Time, Comments, Author, Foreign Adaptations, Sublistings, and Cross-references. Seven indices are also provided for Title, Tests out of Print, Acronyms, Subject, Publisher, Names, and Scores.

Periodicals that Publish Test Research and Reviews

Listed here are those American periodicals that, over the last few years, have published a large portion of the reviews and research articles involving career assessment instruments.

AAC Newsnotes. Association for Assessment in Counseling, 5999 Stevenson Ave., Alexandria, VA 22304 (4/yr.). (Formerly: AMECD Newsnotes and AMEG Newsnotes.)

The Career Development Quarterly. National Career Development Association, P.O. Box 2513, Birmingham, AL 35201-2513 (4/yr.). (Formerly: The Vocational Guidance Quarterly.)

The Counseling Psychologist. Sage Publications, Inc., 2455 Teller Road, Thousand Oaks, CA 91320 (6/yr.).

Counselor Education and Supervision. American Counseling Association, P.O. Box 2513, Birmingham, AL 35201-2513 (4/yr.).

Educational and Psychological Measurement. Sage Publications, Inc., 2455 Teller Road, Thousand Oaks, CA 91320 (6/yr.).

Journal of Applied Psychology. American Psychological Association, 750 1st Street NE, Washington, DC 20002-4242 (6/yr.).

Journal of Career Assessment. Psychological Assessment Resources, Inc., P.O. Box 998, Odessa, FL 33556 (4/yr.).

Journal of Career Development. Human Sciences Press, 72 Fifth Ave., New York, NY 10011 (4/yr.). (Formerly: Journal of Career Education.)

Journal of Counseling and Development. American Counseling Association, P.O. Box 2513, Birmingham, AL 35201-2513 (6/yr.).

Journal of Counseling Psychology. American Psychological Association, 750 1st Street NE, Washington, DC 20002-4242 (4/yr.).

Journal of Educational Measurement. National Council on Measurement in Education, 1230 17th St. NW, Washington, DC 22304 (4/yr.).

Journal of Personality Assessment. Society for Personality Assessment, Inc., 6109 H Arlington Boulevard, Falls Church, VA 22044 (6/yr.).

Journal of Psychoeducational Assessment. The Psychoeducational Corporation, 505 22nd Street, Knoxville, TN 37916 (4/yr.).

Journal of Vocational Behavior. Academic Press, 6277 Sea Harbor Drive, Orlando, FL 32887 (6/yr.).

Measurement and Evaluation in Counseling and Development. American Counseling Association, P.O. Box 2513, Birmingham, AL 35201-2513 (4/yr.).

Professional School Counselor. American School Counselor Association, 801 North Fairfax Street, Suite 310, Alexandria, VA 22314 (5/yr.) (Includes what was formerly published as The School Counselor and Elementary School Guidance and Counseling)

Psychology in the Schools. John Wiley & Sons, Inc., 606 Third Avenue, New York, NY 10158 (6/yr.).

School Psychology Review. National Association of School Psychologists 4340 East West Highway, Suite 402, Bethesda, MD 20814 (4/yr.).

Websites Relevant to Career Assessment

A few websites give important information about assessment instruments. Two of the most widely used are –

ERIC Clearinghouse on Assessment and Evaluation Test Locator:
    http://www.ericae.net/testcol.htm
Buros Institute of Mental Measurements:
    http://www.unl.edu/buros/

Publisher Addresses

Academic Therapy Publications
20 Commercial Boulevard
Novato, CA 94949
800-422-7249
Fax: 415-883-3720
http://www.atpub.com/
E:mail: atpub@aol.com

ACT, Inc.
2201 North Dodge Street
P.O. Box 168
Iowa City, IA 52243-0168
319-337-1566
Fax: 864-646-1250
http://www.act.org
E-mail: cps@act.org

American Guidance Service, Inc.
(AGS)
4201 Woodland Road
Circle Pines, MN 55014-1796
800-328-2560
Fax: 612-786-5603
http://www.agsnet.com/
E-mail:agsmail@agsnet.com

Arc of the U.S.
1010 Wayne Ave
Suite 650
Silver Spring, MD 20910-5638
http://www.thearc.org/
E-mail: thearc@metronet.com

Assessment Enterprises
925 Hayslope Drive
Knoxville, TN 37919
423 690 4498
E-mail: mstahl@utk.edu

Associated Consultants in Education
P.O. Box 875
Suffern, NY 10901
800-748-9073
http://www.msmall.com/parent/
E-mail: ace@misnet.com

Attainment Company
P.0. Box 930160
Verona, WI 53593-0160
800-327-4269
Fax: 800-942-3865
http://www.attainment-inc.com/
E-mail: info@attainmentcompany.com

Note: Addresses and, when available, phone numbers, fax numbers, web pages, and e-mail addresses are provided for all instruments included in either the review or additional instruments chapters. All information provided here was compiled by Linda Martinez, Department of Educational Psychology, Texas A & M University, and Edwin L. Whitfield, Ohio Department of Education.

Ball Foundation
800 Roosevelt Blvd.
Building C, Suite120
Glen Ellyn, IL 60137
630-469-6270
800-469-8378
http://wwww.ballfoundation.org./
E-mail: tonychen@Ball Foundation.org

Bay State Psychological Associates, Inc.
225 Friend Street
Boston, MA 02114
800-438-2772
http://www.eri.com/contact.html
E-mail: sales@eri.com

Behavior Science Press
P.O. Box BV
University, Alabama 35486
205-759-2089
Fax: 205-758-3222
E-mail: john.mckee@pacelearning.com

Bowling Green State University
Department of Psychology
Bowling Green, OH 43403
419-372-8247
Fax: 419-372-6013
www.bgsu.edu/departments/psych/JDI/
E-mail: jdi@listproc.bgsu.edu

Cambridge Career Products
90 Maccorkle Avenue SW
Charleston, WV 25303-0141
800-727-5507
Fax: 800-329-6687
www.cambridgeeducational.com/
E-macustomerservice@cambridgeol.com

Career Consulting Corner
1492 Cloud Lane
New Braunfels, Texas 78130
830-625-9515
www.careercc.com
E-mail: career30@careercc.com

Career Passports, Inc.
4747 Table Mesa Drive, Suite200
Boulder, CO 80303
800-321-9381

Career Center
University of Missouri
305 Noyes Hall
Columbia, MO 65211
573-882-2351
Fax: 573-882-5440
http://web.missouri.edu/~cppcwww/mocs.shtml
E-mail: coatsl@missouri.edu

Career Education Readiness Measurement and Research
University of Southern Illinois
Edwardsville, Il 62025
618-650-3708

Career Research & Testing, Inc.
2005 Hamilton Avenue, Suite 250
P.O. Box 611930
San Jose, CA 95125
800-888-4945
Fax: 408-441-9101
www.careertrainer.com/
E-mail: knowdell@careertrainer.com

Career Systems International, Inc.
900 James Avenue
Scranton, PA 18510-1548
800-577-6916
Fax: 570-346-8606
www.careersystemsintl.com/
E-mail: careerintl@aol.com

Careerware
2300 St. Laurent Blvd
Ottawa, Ontario K1G 4K2
CANADA
613-247-6802
www.can.ibm.com/ism/careerware/

**Center on Education and Training
for Employment (CETE)**
Ohio State University
1900 Kenny Road
Columbus, OH 43210
614-292-4277
Fax: 614-292-1260
cete.org/products/
E-mail: jarvis.2@osu.edu

CFKR Career Materials, Inc.
11860 Kemper Road, Unit 7
Auburn CA 95603
800-525-5626
Fax: 800-770-0433
www.cfkr.com/
E-mail: cfkrcm@foothill.net.

CHC Forecast, Inc.
4028 Williams Street - Suite 200
Fruitland Park, FL 34731
352-365-1200
Fax: 352-365-1210
www.hayesinternational.com
E-mail: mrd@hayesinternational.com

**Chronicle Guidance Publications,
Inc.**
P.O. Box 1190
Moravia, NY 13118
800 899-0454
Fax: 315-497-3359
www.chronicleguidance.com/
E-mail:
customerservice@ChronicleGuidance.c
om

COIN Educational Products
3361 Executive Parkway, Suite 302
Toledo, OH 43606
800-274-8515
Fax: 419-536-7056
www.coinep.com
E-mail: tmoore1@coinep.com

**Comprehensive Adult Student
Assessment System (CASAS)**
5151 Murphy Canyon Road
San Diego, CA 92123
800-255-1036
Fax: 858-292-2910
http://www.casas.org/
E-mail: casas@casas.org

The Conover Company
1050 Witzel Avenue
Oshkosh, WI 54902
920-231-4667
Fax: 920-231-4809
http://www.conovercompany.com
E-mail: conover@execpc.com

Consulting Psychologists Press, Inc. (CPP)
3803 East Bayshore Road
Palo Alto, CA 94303
800-624-1765
Fax: 650-969-8608
www.cpp-db.com
E-mail: mrs@cpp-db.com

Consulting Resource Group International
#386 - 200 West Third Street
Sumas, WA 98295-8000
604-852-0566
Fax: 604-850-3003
www.strategicprofitsinc.com/cgrleader/j
cart.html
E-mail: crgi@crgleader.com

Council for Exceptional Children (CEC)
1920 Association Drive
Reston VA 20191-1589
703-620-3660
703-264-9451 (LCCE)
Fax: 703-264-9494
http://www.cec.sped.org/
E-mail: service@cec.sped.org

Crites Career Consultants, Inc.
5460 White Place
Boulder, CO 80303
303-447-1639
Fax: 303-440-0434

CTB McGraw Hill
20 Ryan Ranch Road
Monterey, CA 93940
800-538-9547
Fax: 800-282-0266
http://www.ctb.com/
E-mail: tmsupport@ctb.com
E-mail: astreetman@ctb.com

Curriculum Associates (Brigance)
PO Box 2001
North Billerica, MA 01862
800-225-0248
Fax: 800-366-1158
www.curriculumassociates.com/
E-mail:
jeanm@curriculumassociates.com.

Defense Manpower Data Command (ASVAB)
Personnel Testing Division
400 Gigling Rd
Seaside CA 93955
831-583-2400 (Ext. 4282)
www.dmdc.osd.mil
E-mail: webmaster@osd.pentagon.mil

Education Associates, Inc.
8 Crab Orchard Row
P.O. Box Y
Frankfort, NY 40602
800-626-2950
Fax: 502-227-8608
www.educationassociates.com/
E-mail: stw@e-a-i.com

Educational and Industrial Testing Service (EdIts)
P.O. Box 7234
San Diego, CA 92167
800-416-1666
Fax: 619-226-1666
http://www.edits.net/index2.htm
E-mail: edits@k-online.com

Educational Technologies/Invest Learning
Computer Curriculum Corporation
P. O. Box 3711
Sunnyvale, CA 94088-3711
800-927-9997
http://www.ccclearn.com
E-mail: info@cccpp.com

Educators'/Employers' Tests and Services Associates
P.O. Box 327
St. Thomas, PA 17252
717-369-4222
Fax: 717-369-2344
www.eetsa.com
E-mail: psb@epix.net

Educational Testing Service (ETS)
Rosedale Road
Princeton, NJ 08541 USA
609-921-9000
Fax: 609-734-5410
www.ets.org/
E-mail: etsinfo@ets.org

Elbern Publications
P. O. Box 09497
Columbus OH 43209
614-235-2643
E-mail: ezbecker@compuserve.com

Emotional Learning Systems
6050 Rio Vista Drive
Corpus Christi, TX 78412-2860
361-992-3799

Employment Technologies Corporation
225 S. Westmonte Drive, Suite 1110
Altamonte Springs, FL 32714
800-833-3279
Fax: 407-788-1496
http://www.etc-easy.com/
Email: Info@etc-easy.com

Exceptional Education
P.O. Box 15308
Seattle, WA 98115
425-486-4510

Finney Company
3943 Meadowbrook Road
Minneapolis, MN 55426
800-846-7027
Fax: 612-938-7353
www.finney-hobar.com/
E-mail: feedback@finney-hobar.com

H & H Publishing Co., Inc.
1231 Kapp Drive
Clearwater, FL 33765
800-366-4079
www.hhpublishing.com
E-mail: HHService@HHPublishing.com

Hay/McBer
Training Resources Group
116 Huntington Avenue
Boston, MA 02116
800-729-8074
Fax: 617-927-5060
trgmcber.haygroup.com/learn01.htm
E-mail: trg_mcber@haygroup.com

Hawthorne Educational Services, Inc.
800 Gray Oak Drive
Columbia, MO 65201
573-874-1710
Fax: 800-542-9509

Human Resource Development Press
22 Amherst Road
Amherst, MA 01002
800-822-2801
Fax: 413-253-3490
www.hrdpress.com/home3.htm
E-mail: info@hrdpress.com

Human Sciences Research Council
Private Bag X41
Pretoria   0001
[+27 (0) 12] 302 2999
www.hsrc.ac.za/
www@ludwig.hsrc.ac.za

Human Systems Consultants
2804 Forum Boulevard, STE 4
Columbia, MO 65203-0632
573-446-5046

Industrial Psychology International
4106 Fieldstone Road
Champaign, IL 61821
217-398-1437
Fax: 217-398-5798
www.metritech.com/
E-mail: awiseman@metritech.com

Institute for Personality & Ability Testing (IPAT)
P. O. Box 1188
Champaign IL 61824-1188
800-225-4728
Fax: 217-352-9674
www.IPAT.com
E-mail: custservice@ipat.com

International Assessment Network
7600 France Avenue South, Ste 550
Minneapolis, MN 55435
888-311-0311
www.Assessment.com
E-mail: info@assessment.com

JIST Works, Inc.
720 N. Park Ave.
Indianapolis, IN 46202
800-648-5478
Fax: 800-547-8329
www.jist.com/index.htm
E-mail: jistworks@aol.com

Jossey-Bass/Pfeiffer
350 Sansome Street, Fifth Floor
San Francisco, CA 94104-1342
800-274-4434
Fax: 415-433-0499
http://www.Pfeiffer.com
E-mail: webperson@jbp.com
E-mail: support@Learning-Resources.com

Key Education, Inc.
229 Newman Springs Road
Tinton Falls, NJ 07724
732-747-0048
www.kevas.com/
E-mail: info@kevas.com

Lafayette Instrument Company
P.O. Box 5729
3700 Sagamore Parkway North
Lafayette, IN 47903
800-428-7545
Fax: 765-423-4111
www.licmef.com/products.htm
E-mail: lic@licmef.com

Lawrence Jones
North Carolina State University
P.O. Box 7801
Raleigh, NC 27695
919-515-6359
Fax: 919515-6891
E-mail: larry_jones@ncsu.edu

Learning Resource, Inc.
700 Canal Street
Stamford, CT 06902-5921
203-637-5047
Fax: 203-637-2786
www.learning-resources.com/
E-mail: support@Learning-
Resources.com

**Life Insurance Marketing and
Research Association, Inc. (LIMRA)**
P.O. Box 208
Hartford, CT 06141
800-235-4672
www.limra.com/Products/NorthAmerica
/careerpro.asp
E-mail: Selection@limra.com

**Life Office Management Association
(LOMA)**
2300 Windy Ridge Parkway, Suite 600
Atlanta, GA 30339
800 275-5666
Fax: 770-984-0441
www.loma.org/jeps.htm
E-mail: empselect@loma

Management Research Institute
11304 Spur Wheel Lane
Potomac, MD 20854
301-299-9200
Fax: 301-299-9227
E-mail: mrieaf@aol.com

McCarron-Dial Systems
PO Box 45628
Dallas, TX 75245
972-247-5945
214-634-2863
Fax: 214-634-9970
www.mccarrondial.com
E-mail: mds@mccarrondial.com

Measurement for Human Resources
83 Rougeau Avenue
Winnipeg, Manitoba CANADA R2C
3X5
204-661-6438
www.escape.ca/~mhr/
E-mail: mhr@escape.ca

Meridian Education Corporation
90 MacCorkle Ave., SW, Dept. WEB
South Charleston, WV 25325
800-727-5507
Fax: 888-340-5507
www.meridianeducation.com/
E-mail:
meridian@meridianeducation.com

**Missouri Testing and Evaluation
Service Assessment Resource Center**
2800 Maquire Blvd.
Columbia, MO 65211
800-366-8232
Fax: 513-882-8937
www.arc.missouri.edu/k12/mac.html
E-mail: bargenw@missouri.edu

Moving Boundaries
1375 Southwest Blaine Court
Gresham, OR 97080
888-661-4433
503-661-4126
Fax: 503-661-5304
www.movingboundaries.com/
E-mail: info@ movingboundaries.com

NCS Assessments
5605 Green Circle Drive
Minnetonka, MN 55343
800-627-7271
Fax: 847-292-3400
http://assessments.ncs.com/
E-mail: assessment@ncs.com

**National Association of Secondary
School Principals** (NASSP)
1904 Association Drive
Reston, VA 20191-1537
703-860-0200
Fax: 703-476-5432
www.nassp.org/
E-mail: nassp@nassp.org

**National Career Assessment Services,
Inc.**
601 Visions Parkway
P.O. Box 277
Adel, IA 50003
800-314-8972
Fax: 515-993-5422
www.ncasi.com
www.kuder.com
E-mail: ncasi@ncasi.com

**National Center on Employment &
Disability**
P.O. Box 1358
Hot Springs, AR 71902
501-623-7700
Fax: 501-624-6250
www.cei.net/~regionvi/CEDR.htm#T
E-mail: jrp@cei.net

**New Concepts Career Development
Corporation**
1854 S. Alvernon Way
Tucson, AZ 85713
800-828-7876
Fax: 520-745-8524
www.nccdc.com
E-mail: Nccdcdjw@aol.com

**National Occupational Competency
Testing Institute (NOCTI)**
500 North Bronson Avenue
Big Rapids, MI 49307
800-334-6283
Fax: 231-796-4699
www.nocti.org/
E-mail: nocti@nocti.org

Nelson Canada Limited
Measurement and Guidance Department
1120 Birchmont Road
Scarborough, Ontario, Canada
MIKSGA
800-268-2222
800-430-4445
www.nelson.com/
E-mail: rstrana@nelson.com

NFER-Nelson Publishing Co., Lt
2 Oxford Road East
Windsor, Berkshire SL4 1DF
United Kingdom
44(0)1753 858961
www.assessmentcentre.com/
E-mail: edu&hsc@nfer-nelson.co.uk

**North Carolina ONET Center
(GATB/Ability Profiler)**
700 Wade Ave
Raleigh, NC 27605
919-733-2790
www.onetcenter.org
E-mail: o*net@esc.state.nc.us

PAQ Services, INC.
Data Processing Division
1625 North 1000 East
North Logan, UT 84321
435-752-5698
Fax: 435-752-5712
www.paq.com/
E-mail: info@paq.com

Peregrine Publications
209 Harvard Street
Suite #501
Brookline, MA 02446
617-738-8819
Fax: 617-738-9783
www.careerdiscovery.com
E-mail: wba@world.std.com.

Personal Strengths Publishing
P.O. Box 397
Pacific Palisades, CA 90272-0397
800-624-7347
Fax: 760-730-7368
www.personalstrengths.com/
E-mail: john@personalstrengths.com

PESCO International
21 Paulding Street
Pleasantville, NY 10570
800-431-2016
Fax: 914-769-2970
www.pesco.org
E-mail: Ckass96219@aol.com

Piney Mountain Press, Inc.
P. O. Box 333
Cleveland, Ga 30528
800-255-3127
Fax: 800-905-3127
www.careernetworks.com
E-mail: cyberguy@stc.net

Practical Press
P. O. 455
Moorehead, MN 56561
218-233-2842
www.practicalpress.net/
E-mail: ppress@practicalpress

Price Systems, Inc.
P. O. Box 1818
Lawrence, KS 66044-8818
800-574-4441
Fax: 785-843-0101
www.learningstyle.com/
E-mail: learn@learningstyle.com

PRO-ED, Inc.
8700 Shoal Creek Blvd
Austin, TX 78757
512-451-3246
800-897-3202
Fax: 512-451-8542
www.proedinc.com
E-mail: info@proedinc.com

Prometheus Nemesis Book Company
P.O. Box 2748
Del Mar, CA 92014
800-754-0039
Fax: 714-540-5288
www.keirsey.com/
Email: keirsey@orci.com

Psychological Assessment Resources (PAR)
PO Box 998
Odessa, FL. 33556
800-899-8378
Fax: 800-331-8378
www.parinc.com
E-mail: custserv@parinc.com

Psychological Corporation (PsyCorp)
555 Academic Court
San Antonio, TX 78204-2498
800-211-8378
Fax: 800-232-1223
www.psychcorp.com/
E-mail:
customer_service@harcourt.com

Psychological Services, Inc.
100 West Broadway, Suite 1100
Glendale, CA 91210
818-244-0033
Fax: 717-369-7223
www.psionline.com
E-mail: comments@psionline.com

Psychologists and Educators, Inc
P.O. Box 513
Chesterfield, MO 63006
314-536-2366
Fax: 314-434-2331
E-mail:
Psychologistseduc@earthlink.com

Psychometric Affiliates
PO Box 807
Murfreesboro, TN 37133
615-890-6296
Fax: 615-890-6296
E-mail: jheritag@mtsu.edu

Psychometrics Canada Ltd.
7125 - 77 Avenue
Edmonton, Alberta, Canada T6B 0B5
800-661-5158
Fax: 780-469-2283
www.psychometrics.com/
E-mail: info@psychometrics.com.

Ramsay Corporation
Boyce Station Offices
1050 Boyce Road
Pittsburgh, PA 15241-3907
412-257-0732
Fax: 412-257-0732
http://www.ramsaycorp.com/index.htm
E-mail: RamTom@aol.com

R.B. Slaney
Department of Counseling Psychology
327 Cedar Building
Pennsylvania State University
University Park, PA 16803
814-865-8304
E-mail: trx@psu.edu

Research Psychologists Press
P.O. Box 610984
Port Huron, MI 48061-0984
800-265-1285
Fax: 800-361-9411
www.sigmaassessmentsystems.com
E-mail:
inforeq@sigmaassessmentsystems.com

Riverside Publishing
425 Spring Lake Drive
Itasca, IL 60143-2079
800-767-8420
Fax: 630-467-7192
www.riverpub.com
E-mail: rpcwebmaster@hmco.com
E-mail: firstname_lastname@hmco.com

Richardson, Bellows, Henry & Co., Inc.
1140 Connecticut Avenue, NW, Suite 610
Washington, DC 20036
202-659-3755
www.epredix.com/

Saville & Holdsworth Ltd USA, Inc
Flatiron Park West
2555 55th Street
Boulder, CO 80301
800-899-7451
Fax: 416-361-1114
www.shlusa.com/Contact/Contact.htm
E-mail: info.n-america@shlgroup.com

Scholastic Testing Service (STS)
480 Meyer Road
Bensenville, IL 60106-1617
800-642-6787
Fax: 630-766-8054
www.ststesting.com/
E-mail: STSLH25@aol.com

SIGMA Assessment Systems
511 Fort St., Suite 435
PO Box 610984
Port Huron, MI 48061-0984
800-265-1285
www.sigmaassessmentsystems.com
E-mail:
inforeq@sigmaassessmentsystems.com

Slosson Publishing
P.O. Box 280
East Aurora, NY 14052
888-756-7766
Fax: 800-655-3840
www.slosson.com/index2.htm
E-mail: slosson@slosson.com

SOI Systems
45755 Goodpasture Road, Box D
Vida, OR 97488
541-896-3936
Fax: 541-896-3983
www.soisystems.com/
E-mail: info@soisystems.com

SRA/London House
9701 West Higgins Road
Rosemont, IL 60018
800-221-8378
Fax: 847-292-3401
http://assessments.ncs.com/
E-mail: assessment@ncs.com

Steck-Vaughn
P.O. Box 26015
Austin, TX 78755
800-531-5015
Fax: 512-343-6854
www.steck-vaughn.com
E-mail: tlefebvre@steckvaughn.com

Stoelting Company
620 Wheat Lane
Wood Dale, IL 60191
708-860-9700
Fax: 630-860-9775
www.latanet.com/e-source/
!VENDORS.MZ/!STOELTI.HTM
E-mail: Physiology@Stoeltingco.com

**Stout Vocational Rehabilitation
Institute**
The Rehabilitation Source
University of Wisconsin-Stout
Menomonie, WI 54751
715-232-2475
www.chd.uwstout.edu/svri/
E-mail: WesolekJ@uwstout.edu

Talent Assessment, Inc.
P.O. Box 5087
Jacksonville, FL 32247-5087
800-634-1472
Fax: 904-292-9371
http://users.leading.net/~talent
E-mail: talent@leading.net

Talico, Inc.
4375-4 Southside Blvd, Suite 157
Jacksonville, FL 32216
904-642-0300
Fax: 904-642-7004
www.talico.com/
E-mail: info@talico.com

Teleometrics International
1755 Woodstead Court
The Woodlands, TX 77380
800-527-0406
Fax: 281-292-1324
www.teleometrics.com/
E-mail: teleo.info@teleometrics.com

Training House, Inc.
P.O. Box 3090
Princeton, NJ 08543-3090
800-860-1361
Fax: 609-652-2790
www.traininghouse.com/
products/products.htm
E-mail: randy@hrdpress.com

**U.S. Department of Labor
Employment and Training
Administration**
200 Constitution Avenue, N.W.
Washington, D.C. 20210
202-219-7161
http://www.doleta.gov/
E-mail: O*net@doleta.gov

Valpar International Corporation
2450 West Ruthrauff Road, Suite 180
Tucson, AZ 85705
520-293-1510
800-528-7070
Fax: 520-292-9755
www.valparint.com/
E-mail: valpar@rtd.com

Vocational Psychology Research
University of Minnesota
N620 Elliot Hall,
75 East River Road
Minneapolis, MN 55455-0344
612-625-1367
E-mail: vpr@tc.umn.edu

Vocational Research Institute (VRI)
1528 Walnut Street, Suite 1502
Philadelphia, PA 19102
800-874-5387
215-875-7387
Fax: 215-875-0198
www.vri.org/
E-mail: info@vri.org

**Vocational-Technical Education
Consortium of States (V-TECS)**
1866 Southern Lane
Decatur, GA 30037-4097
800-248-7701 Ext. 543
Fax: 404-679-4556
http://vtecs.home.mindspring.com/
E-mail: vtecs@mindspring.com

Walden Personnel Testing and Training, Inc.
4115 Sherbrooke W., Suite 100
Montreal, Quebec
Canada H3Z 1K9
800-361-4908
Fax: 514-989-9934
www.waldentesting.com/
E-mail: tests@waldentesting.com

Walter V. Clarke Associates, Inc.
Foster Plaza, Building 7
Pittsburgh, PA 15220
412-922-5661
Fax: 412-922-8693
www.wvcava.com/
E-mail: gwen@bizet.co

WestED
730 Harrison St.
San Francisco, CA 94107-1242
(415) 565-3000
www.WestEd.org/
E-mail: srabino@wested.org

Western Psychological Services (WPS)
12031 Wilshire Blvd.
Los Angeles, CA 90025-1251
310-478-2061
Fax: 310-478-7838
www.wpspublish.com/
E-mail: custsvc@wpspublish.com
E-mail: madden@wpspublish.com

West Virginia Research and Training Center
806 Allen Hall
P.O. Box 6122
Morgantown, WV 26506-6122
304-293-5314
www.icdi.wvu.edu:80/
E-mail: Walls@rtc1.icdi.wvu.edu.

Wide Range, Inc.
P. O. Box 3410
Willingtom, DE 19804-4184
(302) 658-4184
800-221-9728
Fax: 302-652-1644
www.widerange.com/
E-mail: widerange@widerange.com

Wintergreen/Orchard House
425 Spring Lake Drive
Itasca, IL 60143-2079
800-323-9540
FAX: 630-467-7192
www.riverpub.com/
E-mail: rpcwebmaster@hmco.com
E-mail: firstname_lastname@hmco.com

Wonderlic, Inc.
1795 N. Butterfield Ave.
Libertyville, IL 60048-1387
800-963-7542
Fax: 847-680-9492
www.wonderlic.com
E-mail: mike.callans@wonderlic.com

World of Work, Inc.
64 E. Broadway Road
Tempe, AZ 85282
602-966-5100
Fax: 602-966-6200
www.wowi.com/
E-mail: info@wowi.com

APPENDIX C ⸻

Testing Standards and Codes

Responsibilities of Users of Standardized Tests

I. Introduction

Background
At the 1976 AACD (then APGA) Convention, the Board of Directors requested the development of a statement on the responsible use of standardized tests to promote proper test use, reflecting the advantages of assessment along with concerns about negative effects, and to help its members employ safeguards against misuse of tests. A committee representing all AACD divisions and regions spent two years studying the issues and developed a statement, published in the October 1978, issue of *Guidepost,* titled "Responsibilities of Users of Standardized Tests." The Association for Measurement and Evaluation in Counseling and Development was charged with maintaining ongoing review of the so-called Statement. The present statement has grown out of that review.

Target Audience
The statement is intended to address the needs of the members of AACD and its David Branches, and Regions, including counselors and other human service workers. Although it may interest test developers, teachers, administrators, parents, the press, or the general public, it is not specifically designed for these audiences.

Organization and Focus
The statement is organized into eight sections: Introduction, Test Decisions, Qualifications of Test Users, Test Selection, Test Administration, Test Scoring, Test Interpretation, and Communicating Test Results. Basic to the statement is the assumption that test data are merely numbers and that guidelines can help to

Note: This 1989 revision of the 1978 RUST Statement was prepared by a standing committee of Association for Assessment in Counseling (AAC) chaired by William D. Schafer. Participating in the revision were Esther E. Diamond, Charles G. Eberly, Patricia B. Elmore, Jo-Ida C. Hansen, William A. Mehrens, Jane E. Myers, Larry Rawlins, and Alan G. Robertson. Additional copies of the RUST Statement may be obtained from the American Counseling Association, 5999 Stevenson Avenue, Alexandria, VA 22304. Single copies are free.

promote their constructive use. The statement specifies general principles and activities which constitute responsible practice. These are grouped around similar issues and are indexed for ease of reference.

II. Test Decisions

Decisions should be based on data. In general, test data improve the quality of decisions. However, deciding whether or riot to test creates the possibility of three kinds of errors. First, a decision not to test can result in misjudgments that stem from inadequate or subjective data. Second, tests may produce data which could improve accuracy in decisions affecting the client, but which are not used in counseling. Third, tests may be misused. The responsible practitioner will determine, in advance, the purpose for administering a given test, considering protections and benefits for the client, practitioner, and agency.

A. Define purposes for testing by developing specific objectives and limits for the use of test data in relation to the particular assessment purpose:
1. Placement: If the purpose is selection or placement, the test user should understand the programs or institutions into which the client may be placed and be able to judge the consequences of inclusion or exclusion decisions for the client.
2. Prediction: If the purpose is prediction, the test user should understand the need for predictive data as well as possible negative consequences (e.g., stereotyping).
3. Description: If the purpose is diagnosis or description, the test user should understand the general domain being measured and be able to identify those aspects which are adequately measured and those which are not.
4. Growth: If the purpose is to examine growth or change, the test user should understand the practical and theoretical difficulties associated with such measurement.
5. Program Evaluation: If the purpose of assessment is the evaluation of an agency's programs, the test user should be aware of the various information needs for the evaluation and of the limitations of each instrument used to assess those needs, as well as how the evaluation will be used.
B. Determine information needs and assessment needs:
1. Determine whether testing is intended to assess individuals, groups, or both.
2. Identify the particular individual and/or group to be tested with regard to the agency's purposes and capabilities.

3. Determine the limitations to testing created by an individual's age; racial, sexual, ethnic, and cultural background; or other characteristics.
4. Avoid unnecessary testing by identifying decisions which can be made with existing information.
5. Assess the consequences for clients of deciding either to test or not to test.
6. Limit data gathering to the variables that are needed for the particular purpose.
7. Cross-validate test data using other available information whenever possible.

III. Qualifications of Test Users

While all professional counselors and personnel workers should have formal training in psychological and educational measurement and testing, this training does not necessarily make one an expert, and even an expert does not have all the knowledge and skills appropriate to some particular situations or instruments. Questions of user qualifications should always be addressed when testing is being considered.

Lack of proper qualifications can lead to errors and subsequent harm to clients. Each professional is responsible for making judgments on this in each situation and cannot leave the responsibility either to clients or to others in authority. It is incumbent upon the individual test user to obtain appropriate training or arrange for proper supervision and assistance when engaged in testing. Qualifications for test users depend on four factors:

A. Purposes of Testing: Technically proper testing for ill-understood purposes may constitute misuse. Because the purposes of testing dictate how the results are used, qualifications of test users are needed beyond general testing competencies to interpret and apply data.

  B. Characteristics of Tests: Understanding the nature and limitations of each instrument used is needed by test users.

C. Settings and Conditions of Test Use: Assessment of the quality and relevance of test user knowledge and skill to the situation is needed before deciding to test or to participate in a testing program.

D. Roles of Test Selectors, Administrators, Scorers, and Interpreters: Test users must be engaged in only those testing activities for which their training and experience qualify them.

IV. Test Selection

The selection of tests should be guided by information obtained from a careful analysis of the characteristics of the population to be tested; the knowledge, skills, abilities, or attitudes to be assessed; the purposes for testing; and the eventual use and interpretation of the test scores. Use of tests should also be guided by criteria for technical quality recommended by measurement professionals (i.e., the APA/AERA/NCME "Standards for Educational and Psychological Tests" and the APA/AERA/NCME/AACD/ASHA "Code of Fair Testing Practices in Education").

A. Relate Validity to Usage:
   1. Determine the validity of a test (whether the test measures what is meant to be measured) through evidence of the constructs used in developing the test, the correlation of the test performance with other appraisals of the characteristics being measured, and/or the predictions of specified behaviors from the test performance.
   2. Determine whether a test is congruent with the user's definition of the characteristics of human performance to be appraised.
   3. Use tests for selection purposes only when they show predictive validity for the specific tasks or competencies needed in an educational or employment experience and when they maintain legal and ethical prescriptions for non-discriminatory practices in program selection, employment, or placement.
B. Use Appropriate Tests:
   1. Document tests as appropriate for the characteristics of the population to be tested.
   2. Only use tests within the level of skills of administration and interpretation possessed by the practitioner.
   3. Use tests consistent with local needs:
      a. Give attention to how the test is designed to handle variation of motivation, working speed, language facility, and experienced background among persons taking it; bias in response to its content; and effects of guessing in response to its questions.
      b. Determine whether a common test or different tests are required for accurate measurement of groups with special characteristics.
         i. Recognize that the use of different tests for cultural, ethnic, and racial groups may constitute ineffective means for making corrections for differences.

      ii. Determine whether persons or groups that use different lan-
          guages should be tested in either or both languages and in some
          instances, tested first for bilingualism or language dominance.

C. Consider Technical Characteristics:
    1. Select only tests that have documented evidence of reliability or con-
       stituency.
    2. Select only tests that have adequate documented evidence of the effec-
       tiveness of the measure for the purpose to be served and justification of
       the inferences based on the results.
    3. Scrutinize standardization and norming procedures for relevance to the
       local population and use of the data.
    4. Use separate norms for men and women or other subgroups when em-
       pirical evidence indicates they are appropriate.
    5. Determine the degree of technical quality demanded of a test on the ba-
       sis of the nature of the decisions to be made.
    6. Include ease and accuracy of the procedures for scoring, summarizing,
       and communicating test performance among the criteria for selecting a
       test.
    7. Consider practical constraints of cost, conditions, and time for testing as
       secondary test selection criteria.

D. Employ User Participation in Test Selection: Actively involve everyone who
will be using the assessments (administering, scoring, summarizing, interpreting, making decisions) as appropriate in the selection of tests so that they
are congruent with local purposes, conditions, and uses.

V. Test Administration

Test administration includes procedures to ensure that the test is used in the manner specified by the test developers and that the individuals being tested are
working within conditions which maximize opportunity for optimum, comparable performance.

A. Provide Proper Orientation:
    1. Inform testing candidates, parents, and institutions or agencies in the
       community as appropriate about the testing procedures. The orientation
       should make the test meaningful for the individual or group being
       tested, and should include the purposes of the test, the kinds of tasks it
       involves, how it is administered and how the scores will be reported and
       used.
    2. Provide persons being tested sufficient practice experiences prior to the
       test.

3. Prior to testing, check all test takers' ability to record their responses adequately (e.g., in the use of machine-scoreable answer sheets).
4. Provide periodic training by qualified personnel for test administrators within agencies or institutions using tests.
5. Review test materials and administration sites and procedures prior to the time for testing to ensure standardized conditions and appropriate response to any irregularities which may occur.

B. Use Qualified Test Administrators:
1. Acquire any training required to administer the test.
2. Ensure that individuals taking self-administered or self-scored instruments have the necessary understanding and competencies.

C. Provide Appropriate Testing Conditions:
1. Ensure that the testing environment (seating, work surfaces, lighting, heating, freedom from distractions, etc.) and psychological climate are conductive to the best possible performance of the test takers.
2. Carefully observe, record, and attach to the test record any deviation from prescribed test administration procedure.
3. Use a systematic and objective procedure for observing and recording environmental, health, or emotional factors, or other elements which may invalidate test performance. This record should be attached to the test scores of the persons tested.
4. Use sufficiently trained personnel to provide uniform conditions and to observe the conduct of the examinees when large groups of individuals are tested.

D. Give Proper Directions:
1. Present each test in the manner prescribed in the test manual to ensure that it is fair to each test taker.
2. Administer standardized tests with the verbatim instructions, exact sequence and timing, and identical materials that were used in the test standardization.
3. Demonstrate verbal clarity, calmness, empathy for the examinees, and impartiality toward all being tested. Because taking a test may be a new and frightening experience or stimulate anxiety or frustration for some individuals, the examinees should attempt each task with positive application of their skills and knowledge and the expectation that they will do their best.

E. Coordinate Professional Collaboration: In settings where skill and knowledge are pooled and responsibility shared, consider the qualifications of the testing team as a whole as more important than those of individuals. However, coordination and consistency of responsibilities with expertise must be maintained.

VI. Test Scoring

Accurate measurement of human performance necessitates adequate procedures for scoring the responses of examinees. These procedures must be audited as necessary to ensure consistency and accuracy of application.

A. Consider Accuracy and Interpretability: Select a test scoring process that maximizes accuracy and interpretability.
B. Resource Samples: Routinely rescore samples of examinee responses to monitor the accuracy of the scoring process.
C. Screen Test Results: Screen reports of test results using personnel competent to recognize unreasonable or impossible scores.
D. Verify Scores and Norms: Verify the accuracy of computation of raw scores and conversion to normative scales prior to release of such information to examinees or users of test results.
E. Communicative Deviations: Report as part of the official record any deviation from normal conditions and examinee behaviors.
F. Label Results: Clearly label the date of test administration along with the scores.

VII. Test Interpretation

Test interpretation encompasses all the ways that meaning is assigned to the scores. Proper interpretation requires knowledge about the test which can be obtained by studying its manual and other materials along with current research literature with respect to its use; no one should undertake the interpretation of scores on any test without such study.

A. Consider Reliability; Reliability is important because it is a prerequisite to validity and because the degree to which a score may vary due to measurement error is an important factor in its interpretation.
   1. Estimate test stability using a reliability (or other appropriate) coefficient.
   2. Use the standard error of measurement to estimate the amount of variation due to random error in individual scores and to evaluate the precision of cut-scores in selection decisions.
   3. Consider, in relationship to the uses being made of the scores, variance components attributed to error in the reliability index.
   4. Evaluate reliability estimates with regard to factors that may have artificially raised or lowered them (e.g., test speededness, biases in population sampling).

    5.   Distinguish indices of objectivity (i.e., scorer reliability) from test reliability.

B. Consider Validity: Proper test interpretation requires knowledge of the validity evidence available for the intended use of the test. Its validity for other uses is not relevant. Indeed, use of a measure for a purpose for which it was not designed may constitute misuse. The nature of the validity evidence required for a test depends upon its use.

    1.   Use for Placement: Predictive validity is the usual basis for valid placement.

        a.   Obtain adequate information about the programs or institutions in which the client may be placed to judge the consequences of such placement.

        b.   Use all available evidence to infer the validity of an individual's score. A single test score should not be the sole basis for a placement or selection recommendation. Other items of information about an individual (e.g., teacher report, counselor opinion) frequently improve the likelihood that proper judgments and decisions will be made.

        c.   Consider validity for each alternative (i.e., each placement option) when interpreting test scores and other evidence.

        d.   Examine the possibility that a client's group membership (socio-economic status, gender, subculture, etc.) may affect test performance and, consequently, validity.

        e.   Estimate the probability of favorable outcomes for each possible placement before making recommendations.

        f.   Consider the possibility that outcomes favorable from an institutional point of view may differ from those that are favorable from the individual's point of view.

    2.   Use for Prediction: The relationship of the test scores to an independently developed criterion measure is the basis for predictive validity.

        a.   Consider the reliability and validity of the criterion measures) used.

        b.   Consider the validity of a measure in the context of other predictors available (i.e., does the test make a valid contribution to prediction beyond that provided by other measures).

        c.   Use cross validation to judge the validity of prediction processes.

        d.   Consider the effects of labeling, stereotyping, and prejudging people (e.g., self-fulfilling prophecies that may result from labeling are usually undesirable).

e.   If a statistically valid predictor lacks both construct and content validity, analyze the mechanism by which it operates to determine whether or not its predictive validity is spurious.

3.   Use for Description: Comprehensiveness of information is fundamental to effective description, since no set of test scores completely describes an individual.

a.   Clearly identify the domain assessed by any measure and the adequacy of the content sampling procedures used in developing items.

b.   Clarify the dimensions being measured when multiple scores from a battery or inventory are used for description.

i.   Examine the content and/or construct validity of each score separately.

ii.   Consider the relative importance of each of the separate elements for interpretation.

iii.   Give appropriate weights to reflect the variabilities (e.g., standard deviations) and relationships (e.g., correlations) of scores which are to be combined.

a.   Distinguish characteristics that can be validated only empirically and those for which content specifications exist.

5.   Use for Assessment of Growth: Assessment of growth or change requires valid tests as well as a valid procedure for combining them.

a.   Specifically evaluate the reliability of differences between scores as measures of change.

b.   Establish the validities of the measures used to establish change in relation to one another as well as individually.

c.   Consider comparability of intervals in scales used to assess change.

i.   Evaluate derived or extrapolated scores (e.g., grade equivalents) or possible different meanings at different score levels.

ii.   Consider problems in interpretation and comparability of tests (e.g., floor or ceiling effects, content changes from level to level, poor articulation in multilevel tests, lack of comparability of alternate forms, inadequacy of score-equating across forms, and differences in administration and timing of tests from that of their norming).

a.   Assess potential for undesirable correlations of difference scores with the measures entering into their calculations (e.g., regression toward the mean).

      b.   Recognize the potential lack of comparability between norms for differences derived from norms and norms for differences derived from differences (i.e., mathematically derived norms for differences are not necessarily equivalent to norms based on distributions of actual differences).

   6. Use for Program Evaluation: Assessments of group differences (between groups or within groups over time) are based on research designs which to varying degrees admit competing interpretations of the results.

      a.   Use procedures in the evaluation which ensure that no factors other than those being studied have major influence on the results (i.e., internal validity).

      b.   Use statistical procedures which are appropriate and have all assumptions met by the data being analyzed.

      c.   Evaluate the generalizability (external validity) of the results for different individuals, settings, tests, and variables.

C. Scores, Norms, and Related Technical Features: The result of scoring a test or subtest is usually a number called a raw score which by itself is not interpretable. Additional steps are needed to translate the number directly into either a verbal description (e.g., pass or fail) or into a derived score (e.g., a standard score). Less than full understanding of these procedures is likely to produce errors in interpretation and ultimately in counseling or other uses.

   1. Examine appropriate test materials (e.g., manuals, handbooks, users' guides, and technical reports) to identify the descriptions or derived scores produced and their unique characteristics.

      a.   Know the operational procedures for translating raw scores into descriptions or derived scores.

      b.   Know specific psychological or educational concepts or theories before interpreting the scores of tests based on them.

      c.   Consider differential validity along with equating error when different tests, different test forms, or scores on the same test administered at different times are compared.

   2. Clarify arbitrary standards used in interpretation (e.g., mastery or nonmastery for criterion-referenced tests).

      a.   Recognize that when a score is interpreted based on a proportion score (e.g., percent correct), its elements are being given arbitrary weights.

      b.   Recognize that the difficulty of a fixed standard (e.g., 80 percent right) varies widely and thus does not have the same meaning for different content areas and for different assessment methods.

    c.   Report the number (or percentage) of items right in addition to the interpretation when it will help others understand the quality of the examinee's performance.

  3. Employ derived scores based on norms which fit the needs of the current use of the test.

    a.   Evaluate whether available norm groups are appropriate as part of the process of interpreting the scores of clients.

      i.   Use norms for the group to which the client belongs.

      ii.   Recognize that derived scores based on different norm groups may not be comparable.

      iii.   Use local norms and derived scores based on them when ever possible.

    b.   Choose a score based on its intended use.

      i.   Consider relative standing scores (e.g., percentile ranks) for comparison of individuals to the norm or reference group.

      ii.   Consider standard or scaled scores whenever means and variances or other arithmetic operations are appropriate.

      iii.   When using a statistical technique, use the test's derived score which best meets the assumptions of the analysis.

D. Administration and Scoring Variation: Stated criteria for score interpretation assume standard procedures for administering and scoring the test. Departures from standard conditions and procedures modify and often invalidate these criteria.

  1. Evaluate unusual circumstances peculiar to the administration and scoring of the test.

    a.   Examine reports from administrators, proctors, and scorers concerning irregularities or unusual conditions (e.g., excessive anxiety) for possible effects on test performance.

    b.   Consider potential effects of examiner-examinee differences in ethnic and cultural background, attitudes, and values based on available relevant research.

    c.   Consider any reports of examinee behavior indicating the responses were made on some basis other than that intended.

    d.   Consider differences among clients in their reaction to instructions about guessing and scoring.

  2. Evaluate scoring irregularities (e.g., machine scoring errors) and bias and judgment effects when subjective elements enter into scoring.

VIII. Communicating Test Results

The responsible counselor or other practitioner reports test data with a concern for the individual's need for information and the purposes of the information. There must also be protection of the right of the person tested to be informed about how the results will be used and what safeguards exist to prevent misuse (right to information) and about who will have access to the results (right to privacy).

A. Decisions About Individuals: Where test data are used to enhance decisions about an individual, the practitioner's responsibilities include:

    1. Limitations on Communication

        a.   Inform the examinee of possible actions that may be taken by any person or agency who will be using the results.

        b.   Limit access to users specifically authorized by the law or by the client.

        c.   Obtain the consent of the examinee before using test results for any purpose other than those advanced prior to testing.

    2. Practitioner Communication Skills:

        a.   Develop the ability to interpret test results accurately before attempting to communicate them.

        b.   Develop appropriate communication skills, particularly with respect to concepts that are commonly misunderstood by the intended audience, before attempting to explain test results to clients, the public, or other recipients of the information.

    3. Communication of Limitations of the Assessment:

        a.   Inform persons receiving test information that scores are not perfectly accurate and indicate the degree of inaccuracy in some way, such as by reporting score intervals.

        b.   Inform persons receiving test information of any circumstances that could have affected the validity or reliability of the results.

        c.   Inform persons receiving test information of any factors necessary to understand potential sources of bias for a given test result.

        d.   Communicate clearly that test data represent just one source of information and should rarely, if ever, be used alone for decision making.

    4. Communication of Client Rights:

        a.   Provide test takers or their parents or guardians with information about any rights they may have to obtain test copies and/or their completed answer sheets, to retake tests, to have tests rescored, or to cancel test scores.

    b.   Inform test takers or their parents or guardians about how long the test scores will remain on file along with the persons to whom, and circumstances under which, they may be released.

    c.   Describe the procedures test takers or their parents or guardians may use to register complaints or have problems resolved.

A. Decisions About Groups: Where standardized test data are being used to describe groups for the purpose of evaluation, the practitioner's responsibilities include:

  1. Background Information:

    a.   Identify the purposes for which the reported data are appropriate.

    b.   Include additional information (e.g., population characteristics) if it can improve accuracy of understanding.

  2. Averages and Norms:

    a.   Clarify the amount of meaning that can be attached to differences between groups (e.g., statistical significance should not be taken as a judgment of importance).

    b.   Qualify norms based on their appropriateness for the group being tested.

  3. Use obsolescence schedules so that stored data are systematically relocated to historical files or destroyed.

  4. Process data used for research or program evaluation to assure individual anonymity (e.g., released only in aggregated form).

  5. Political Usage:

    a.   Emphasize that test data should be used only for the test's stated purposes.

    b.   Public release of test information provides data for many purposes. Take steps to minimize those which may be adverse to the interests of those tested.

  6. Agency Policies:

    a.   Advocate agency test-reporting policies designed to benefit the groups being measured.

    b.   Advocate the establishment of procedures for periodic review of test use.

IX. Extensions of These Principles

This statement is intended to address current and emerging problems and concerns that are generic to all AACD divisions, branches, and regions by formulating principles that are specific enough to serve as a template for more closely focused statements addressed to specific situations. Individual divisions, branches, and regions are encouraged to elaborate upon this statement to reflect principles, procedures, and examples appropriate to their members.

Code of Fair Testing Practices in Education

Prepared by
The Joint Committee on Testing Practices

The Code of Fair Testing Practices in Education states the major obligations to test takers of professionals who develop or use educational tests. The Code is meant to apply broadly to the use of tests in education (admissions, educational assessment, educational diagnosis, and student placement). The Code is not designed to cover employment testing, licensure or certification testing, or other types of testing. Although the Code has relevance to many types of educational tests, it is directed primarily at professionally developed tests such as those sold by commercial test publishers or used in formally administered testing programs. The Code is not intended to cover tests made by individual teachers for use in their own classrooms.

The Code addresses the roles of test developers and test users separately. Test users are people who select tests, commission test development services, or make decisions on the basis of test scores. Test developers are people who actually construct tests as well as those who set policies for particular testing programs. The roles may, of course, overlap as when a state education agency commissions test development services, sets policies that control the test development process, and makes decisions on the basis of the test scores.

Note: The Code has been developed by the Joint Committee on Testing Practices, a co-operative effort of several professional organizations, that has as its aim the advancement, in the public interest, of the quality of testing practices. The Joint Committee was initiated by the American Educational Research Association, the American Psychological Association, and the National Council on Measurement in Education. In addition to these three groups, the American Association for Counseling and Development/Association for Measurement and Evaluation in Counseling and Development, and the American Speech-Language-Hearing Association are now also sponsors of the Joint Committee. This is not copyrighted material. Reproduction and dissemination are encouraged. Please cite this document as follows: *Code of Fair Testing Practices in Education.* (1988). Washington, DC: Joint Committee on Testing Practices. (Mailing Address: Joint Committee on Testing Practices, American Psychological Association, 1200 17th Street, NW, Washington, DC 20036.)

The Code presents standards for educational test developers and users in four areas:

A. Developing/Selecting Tests
B. Interpreting Scores
C. Striving for Fairness
D. Informing Test Takers

Organizations, institutions, and individual professionals who endorse the Code commit themselves to safeguarding the rights of test takers by following the principles listed. The Code is intended to be consistent with the relevant parts of the *Standards for Educational and Psychological Testing* (AERA, APA, NCME, 1985). However, the Code differs from the Standards in both audience and purpose. The Code is meant to be understood by the general public; it is limited to educational tests; and the primary focus is on those issues that affect the proper use of tests. The Code is not meant to add new principles over and above those in the Standards or to change the meaning of the Standards. The goal is rather to represent the spirit of a selected portion of the Standards in a way that is meaningful to test takers and/or their parents or guardians. It is the hope of the Joint Committee that the Code will also be judged to be consistent with existing codes of conduct and standards of other professional groups who use educational tests.

A. Developing/Selection Appropriate Tests

Tests developers should provide the information that test users need to select appropriate tests.

Test users should select tests that meet that purpose for which they are to be used and that are appropriate for the intended test-taking populations.

Test Developers Should:

1. Define what each test measures and what the test should be used for. Describe the population(s) for which the test is appropriate.

2. Accurately represent the characteristics, usefulness and limitations of tests for their intended populations.

Test Users Should:

1. Define the purpose for testing and the population to be tested. Then select a test for that purpose and that population based on a thorough review of the available information.

2. Investigate potentially useful sources of information, in addition to test scores, to corroborate the information provided by tests.

3. Explain relevant measurement concepts a as necessary for clarity at the level of detail that is appropriate for the intended audience(s).

3. Investigate potentially useful sources of information, in addition to test scores, to corroborate the information provided by test.

4. Describe the process of test development. Explain how the content and sills to be tested were selected.

4. Become familiar with how and when the test was developed and tried out.

5. Provide evidence that the test meets its intended purposes(s).

5. Read independent evaluations of a test and of possible alternative measures Look for evidence required to support the claims of test developers.

6 Provide either representative samples or complete copies of test questions, directions, answer sheets, manuals, and score reports to qualified users.

6. Examine specimen sets, disclosed tests or samples of questions, directions answer sheets manuals, and score reports before selecting a test.

7. Indicate the nature of the evidence obtained concerning the appropriateness of each test for groups of different racial, ethnic, or linguistic background who are likely to be tested.

7. Ascertain whether the test content and norms (groups or comparison groups) are appropriate for the intended test takers.

8. Identify and publish any specialized skills needed to administer each test and to interpret scores correctly

8 Select and use only those tests for which the skills needed administer the test and interpret scores correctly are available.

Many of the statement in the Code refer to the selection of existing tests., However, in customized testing programs test developers are engaged to construct new tests. In those situations, the test development process should be designed to help ensure that the completed test will be in compliance with the Code.

B. Interpreting Scores

Test developers should help users in-
terpret scores correctly.

Test users should interpret scores cor-
rectly.

Test Developers Should:

Test Users Should:

9. Provide timely and easily understood score reports that describe
test performance clearly and accurately, Also explain the meaning
and limitations of reported scores.
10. Describe the population(s) represented by any norms or comparison groups(s), the dates the data
were gathered, and the process
used to select the samples of the
test takers.

9. Obtain information about the scale
used for reporting scores, the
characteristics of any norms or
comparison group(s), and the
limitations of the scores.
10. Interpret scores taking into account any major differences between the norms or comparison
groups and the actual test takers.
Also take into account any differences in test administration practices or familiarity with the specific questions in the test.

11. Warn users to avoid specific, reasonably anticipated misuses of test
scores.

11   Avoid using tests for purposes not
specifically recommended by the
test developer unless evidence is
obtained to support the intended
use.

12. Provide information that will help
users follow reasonable procedures for setting passing scores
when it is appropriate to use such
scores with the test.
13. Provide information that will help
users gather evidence to show that
the test is meeting its intended
purpose(s).

12. Explain how any passing scores
were set and gather evidence to
support the appropriateness of the
scores.
13. Obtain evidence to help show that
the test is meeting its intended
purpose(s).

C. Striving for Fairness

Test developers should strive to make
test that are as fair as possible for test
takers of different races, gender, ethnic
backgrounds, or handicapping condi-
tions

Test users should select tests developed
in ways that attempt to make then as
fair as possible for test takers of differ-
ent races, gender, ethnic backgrounds,
or handicapping conditions

Test Developers Should:

14. Review and revise test questions and related materials to avoid potentially insensitive content or language.
15. Investigate the performance of test takers of different races, gender, and ethnic backgrounds when samples of sufficient size are available. Enact procedures that help to ensure that differences in performance are related primarily to the skills under assessment rather than to irrelevant factors.
16. When feasible, make appropriately modified forms of tests or administration procedures available for test takers with handicapping conditions Warn test users of potential problems in using standard norms with modified test or administration procedures that result in noncomparable scores.

Test Users Should:

14. Evaluate the procedures used by test developers to avoid potentially insensitive content or language.
15. Review the performance of test takers of different, races gender and ethnic backgrounds when sample of sufficient size are available. Evaluate the extent to which performance differences may have been caused by inappropriate characteristics of the test.
16. When necessary and feasible, use appropriately modified forms of test or administration procedures for test takers with handicapping conditions. Interpret standard norms with care in the light of the modifications that were made.

D. Informing Test Takers

Under some circumstances test developers have direct communication with test takers.   Under Other circumstances, test users communicate directly with test takers.   Whichever group communicated directly with test takers should provide the information described below.

Under some circumstances test developers have direct control of tests and test scores.   Under other circumstances, test users have such control. Whichever group has direct control of tests and test scores should take the steps described below.

Test Developers or Test Users

17. When a test is optional, provide test takers or their parents/guardians with information to help them judge whether the test should be taken, or if an available alternative to the test should be used.

18. Provide test takers the information they need to be familiar with the coverage of the test, the types of question formats, the directions, and appropriate test-taking strategies. Strive to make such information equally available to all test takers.

Test Developers or Test Users

19. Provide test takers or their parents/guardians with information about rights test takers may have to obtain copies of tests and completed answer sheets, retake tests, have tests rescored or cancel scores.

20. Tell test takers or their parents/guardians how long scores will be kept on file and indicate to whom and under what circumstances test scores will or will not be released.

21. Describe the procedures that test takers or their parents/guardians may use to register complaints and have problems resolved.

Note: The membership of the Working Group that developed the Code of Fair Testing Practices in Education and of the Joint Committee on Testing Practices that guided the Working Group was as follows:

Theodore P Bartell
John R. Bergan
Esther E. Diamond
Richard P Duran
Lorraine D. Eyde
Raymond D. Fowler
John J. Fremer
    (Co-chair, JCTP and
    Chair, Code
    Working Group)

Edmund W. Gordon
Jo-Ida C. Hansen
James B. Lingwall
George F. Madaus
    (Co-chair, JCTP)
Kevin L. Moreland
Jo-Ellen V. Perez
Robert J. Solomon
John T. Stewart

Carol Kehr Tittle
(Co-chair, JTCP)
Nicholas A. Vacc
Michael J. Zieky
Debra Boltas and Wayne Camera of the American Psychological Association served as staff liaisons.

Rights and Responsibilities of Test Takers: Guidelines and Expectations

Preamble

The intent of this statement is to enumerate and clarify the expectations that test takers may reasonably have about the testing process and the expectations that those who develop, administer, and use tests may have of test takers. Tests are defined broadly here as psychological and educational instruments developed and used by testing professionals in organizations such as schools, industries, clinical practice, counseling settings and human service and other agencies, including those assessment procedures and devices that are used for making inferences about people in these settings. The purpose of the statement is to inform and to help educate not only test takers, but also others involved in the testing enterprise so that measurements may be most validly and appropriately used. This document is intended as an effort to inspire improvements in the testing process and does not have the force of law. Its orientation is to encourage positive and high-quality interactions between testing professionals and test takers.

The rights and responsibilities listed in this document are neither legally based nor inalienable rights and responsibilities such as those listed in the United States of America's Bill of Rights. Rather, they represent the best judgments of testing professionals about the reasonable expectations that those involved in the testing enterprise (test producers, test users, and test takers) should have of each

---

Note: The Rights and Responsibilities of Test Takers: Guidelines and Expectations was developed by the Joint Committee on Testing Practices (JCTP), a cooperative effort of several professional organizations, that has as its aim the advancement, in the public interest, of the quality of testing practices. The joint committee was initiated by the American Educational Research Association, the American Psychological Association, and the National Council on Measurement in Education. In addition to these groups, the American Counseling Association, American Speech-Hearing Association and the National Association of School Psychologists are now also sponsors of the joint committee.

other. Testing professionals include developers of assessment products and services, those who market and sell them, persons who select them, test administrators and scorers, those who interpret test results, and trained users of the information. Persons who engage in each of these activities have significant responsibilities that are described elsewhere, in documents such as those that follow (American Association for Counseling and Development, 1989; American Speech-Language-Hearing Association, 1994; Joint Committee on Testing Practices, 1988; National Association of School Psychologists, 1992; National Council on Measurement in Education, 1995).

In some circumstances, the test developer and the test user may not be the same person, group of persons, or organization. In such situations, the professionals involved in the testing should clarify, for the test taker as well as for themselves, who is responsible for each aspect of the testing process. For example, when an individual chooses to take a college admissions test, at least three parties are involved in addition to the test taker: the test developer and publisher, the individuals who administer the test to the test taker, and the institutions of higher education who will eventually use the information. In such cases a test taker may need to request clarifications about their rights and responsibilities. When test takers are young children (e.g., those taking standardized tests in the schools) or are persons who spend some or all their time in institutions or are incapacitated, parents or guardians may be granted some of the rights and responsibilities, rather than, or in addition to, the individual.

Perhaps the most fundamental right test takers have is to be able to take tests that meet high professional standards, such as those described in Standards for Educational and Psychological Testing (American Educational Research Association, American Psychological Association, & National Council on Measurement in Education, 1999) as well as those of other appropriate professional associations. This statement should be used as an adjunct, or supplement, to those standards. State and federal laws, of course, supersede any rights and responsibilities that are stated here.

References

American Association for Counseling and Development (now American Counseling Association) & Association for Measurement and Evaluation in Counseling and Development (now Association for Assessment in Counseling). (1989). *Responsibilities of users of standardized tests: RUST statement revised.* Alexandria, VA: Author.

American Educational Research Association, American Psychological Association, & National Council on Measurement in Education. (1999). *Standards for educational and psychological testing.* Washington, DC: American Educational Research Association.

American Speech-Language-Hearing Association. (1994). *Protection of rights of people receiving audiology or speech-language pathology services.* ASHA (36), 60-63.

Joint Committee on Testing Practices. (1988). *Code of fair testing practices in education.* Washington, DC: American Psychological Association.

National Association of School Psychologists. (1992). *Standards for the provision of school psychological services.* Silver Spring, MD: Author.

National Council on Measurement in Education. (1995). *Code of professional responsibilities in educational measurement.* Washington, DC: Author.

The Rights and Responsibilities of Test Takers: Guidelines and Expectations

As a test taker, you have the right to:
  1. Be informed of your rights and responsibilities as a test taker.
  2. Be treated with courtesy, respect, and impartiality, regardless of your age, disability, ethnicity, gender, national origin, religion, sexual orientation, or other personal characteristics.
  3. Be tested with measures that meet professional standards and that are appropriate, given the manner in which the test results will be used.
  4. Receive a brief oral or written explanation prior to testing about the purpose(s) for testing, the kind(s) of tests to be used, whether the results will be reported to you or to others, and the planned use(s) of the results. If you have a disability, you have the right to inquire and receive information about testing accommodations. If you have difficulty in comprehending the language of the test, you have a right to know in advance of testing whether any accommodations may be available to you.
  5. Know in advance of testing when the test will be administered, if and when test results will be available to you, and if there is a fee for testing services that you are expected to pay.
  6. Have your test administered and your test results interpreted by appropriately trained individuals who follow professional codes of ethics.
  7. Know whether a test is optional and learn of the consequences of taking or not taking the test, fully completing the test, or canceling the scores. You may need to ask questions to learn these consequences.
  8. Receive a written or oral explanation of your test results within a reasonable amount of time after testing and in commonly understood terms.
  9. Have your test results kept confidential to the extent allowed by law.

10. Present concerns about the testing process or your results and receive information about procedures that will be used to address such concerns.

As a test taker, you have the responsibility to:
1. Read and/or listen to your rights and responsibilities as a test taker.
2. Treat others with courtesy and respect during the testing process.
3. Ask questions prior to testing if you are uncertain about why the test is being given, how it will be given, what you will be asked to do, and what will be done with the results.
4. Read or listen to descriptive information in advance of testing and listen carefully to all test instructions. You should inform an examiner in advance of testing if you wish to receive a testing accommodation or if you have a physical condition or illness that may interfere with your performance on the test. If you have difficulty comprehending the language of the test, it is your responsibility to inform an examiner.
5. Know when and where the test will be given, pay for the test if required, appear on time with any required materials, and be ready to be tested.
6. Follow the test instructions you are given and represent yourself honestly during the testing.
7. Be familiar with and accept the consequences of not taking the test, should you choose not to take the test.
8. Inform appropriate person(s), as specified to you by the organization responsible for testing, if you believe that testing conditions affected your results.
9. Ask about the confidentiality of your test results, if this aspect concerns you.
10. Present concerns about the testing process or results in a timely, respectful way, if you have any.

The Rights of Test Takers: Guidelines for Testing Professionals

Test takers have the rights described below. It is the responsibility of the professionals involved in the testing process to ensure that test takers receive these rights.
1. Because test takers have the right to be informed of their rights and responsibilities as test takers, it is normally the responsibility of the individual who administers a test (or the organization that prepared the test) to inform test takers of these rights and responsibilities.
2. Because test takers have the right to be treated with courtesy, respect, and impartiality, regardless of their age, disability, ethnicity, gender, national origin, race, religion, sexual orientation, or other personal characteristics, testing professionals should –

a.   Make test takers aware of any materials that are available to assist them in test preparation. These materials should be clearly described in test registration and/or test familiarization materials.

b.   See that test takers are provided with reasonable access to testing services.

3. Because test takers have the right to be tested with measures that meet professional standards that are appropriate for the test use and the test taker, given the manner in which the results will be used, testing professionals should:

a.   Take steps to utilize measures that meet professional standards and are reliable, relevant, useful given the intended purpose and are fair for test takers from varying societal groups.

b.   Advise test takers that they are entitled to request reasonable accommodations in test administration that are likely to increase the validity of their test scores if they have a disability recognized under the Americans with Disabilities Act or other relevant legislation.

4. Because test takers have the right to be informed, prior to testing, about the test's purposes, the nature of the test, whether test results will be reported to the test takers, and the planned use of the results (when not in conflict with the testing purposes), testing professionals should:

a.   Give or provide test takers with access to a brief description about the test purpose (e.g., diagnosis, placement, selection, etc.) and the kind(s) of tests and formats that will be used (e.g., individual/group, multiple-choice/free response/performance, timed/untimed, etc.), unless such information might be detrimental to the objectives of the test.

b.   Tell test takers, prior to testing, about the planned use(s) of the test results. Upon request, the test taker should be given information about how long such test scores are typically kept on file and remain available.

c.   Provide test takers, if requested, with information about any preventative measures that have been instituted to safeguard the accuracy of test scores. Such information would include any quality control procedures that are employed and some of the steps taken to prevent dishonesty in test performance.

d.   Inform test takers, in advance of the testing, about required materials that must be brought to the test site (e.g., pencil, paper) and about any rules that allow or prohibit use of other materials (e.g., calculators).

e.   Provide test takers, upon request, with general information about the appropriateness of the test for its intended purpose, to the extent that such information does not involve the release of proprietary information. (For example, the test taker might be told, "Scores on this test are useful in predicting how successful people will be in this kind of work" or

"Scores on this test, along with other information, help us to determine if students are likely to benefit from this program.")

f.   Provide test takers, upon request, with information about retesting, including if it is possible to retake the test or another version of it, and if so, how often, how soon, and under what conditions.

g.   Provide test takers, upon request, with information about how the test will be scored and in what detail. On multiple-choice tests, this information might include suggestions for test taking and about the use of a correction for guessing. On tests scored using professional judgment (e.g., essay tests or projective techniques), a general description of the scoring procedures might be provided except when such information is proprietary or would tend to influence test performance inappropriately.

h.   Inform test takers about the type of feedback and interpretation that is routinely provided, as well as what is available for a fee. Test takers have the right to request and receive information regarding whether or not they can obtain copies of their test answer sheets or their test materials, whether they can have their scores verified, and whether they may cancel their test results.

i.   Provide test takers, prior to testing, either in the written instructions, in other written documents or orally, with answers to questions that test takers may have about basic test administration procedures.

j.   Inform test takers, prior to testing, if questions from test takers will not be permitted during the testing process.

k.   Provide test takers with information about the use of computers, calculators, or other equipment, if any, used in the testing and give them an opportunity to practice using such equipment, unless its unpracticed use is part of the test purpose, or practice would compromise the validity of the results, and to provide a testing accommodation for the use of such equipment, if needed.

l.   Inform test takers that, if they have a disability, they have the right to request and receive accommodations or modifications in accordance with the provisions of the Americans with Disabilities Act and other relevant legislation.

m.   Provide test takers with information that will be of use in making decisions if test takers have options regarding which tests, test forms or test formats to take.

5. Because test takers have a right to be informed in advance when the test will be administered, if and when test results will be available, and whether there is a fee for testing services that the test takers are expected to pay, test professionals should:

    a.   Notify test takers of the alteration in a timely manner if a previously announced testing schedule changes, provide a reasonable explanation for the change, and inform test takers of the new schedule. If there is a change, reasonable alternatives to the original schedule should be provided.

    b.   Inform test takers prior to testing about any anticipated fee for the testing process, as well as the fees associated with each component of the process, if the components can be separated.

6. Because test takers have the right to have their tests administered and interpreted by appropriately trained individuals, testing professionals should:

    a.   Know how to select the appropriate test for the intended purposes.

    b.   When testing persons with documented disabilities and other special characteristics that require special testing conditions and/or interpretation of results, have the skills and knowledge for such testing and interpretation.

    c.   Provide reasonable information regarding their qualifications, upon request.

    d.   Ensure that test conditions, especially if unusual, do not unduly interfere with test performance. Test conditions will normally be similar to those used to standardize the test.

    e.   Provide candidates with a reasonable amount of time to complete the test, unless a test has a time limit.

    f.   Take reasonable actions to safeguard against fraudulent actions (e.g., cheating) that could place honest test takers at a disadvantage.

7. Because test takers have the right to be informed about why they are being asked to take particular tests, if a test is optional, and what the consequences are should they choose not to complete the test, testing professionals should:

    a.   Normally engage in testing activities with test takers only after the test-takers have provided their informed consent to take a test, except when testing without consent has been mandated by law or governmental regulation, or when consent is implied by an action the test takers have already taken (e.g., such as when applying for employment and a personnel examination is mandated).

    b.   Explain to test takers why they should consider taking voluntary tests.

    c.   Explain, if a test taker refuses to take or complete a voluntary test, either orally or in writing, what the negative consequences may be to them for their decision to do so.

    d.   Promptly inform the test taker if a testing professional decides that there is a need to deviate from the testing services to which the test taker initially agreed (e.g., should the testing professional believe it would be wise to administer an additional test or an alternative test), and provide an explanation for the change.

8. Because test takers have a right to receive a written or oral explanation of their test results within a reasonable amount of time after testing and in commonly understood terms, testing professionals should:

   a.   Interpret test results in light of one or more additional considerations (e.g., disability, language proficiency), if those considerations are relevant to the purposes of the test and performance on the test, and are in accordance with current laws.

   b.   Provide, upon request, information to test takers about the sources used in interpreting their test results, including technical manuals, technical reports, norms, and a description of the comparison group, or additional information about the test taker(s).

   c.   Provide, upon request, recommendations to test takers about how they could improve their performance on the test, should they choose or be required to take the test again.

   d.   Provide, upon request, information to test takers about their options for obtaining a second interpretation of their results. Test takers may select an appropriately trained professional to provide this second opinion.

   e.   Provide test takers with the criteria used to determine a passing score, when individual test scores are reported and related to a pass-fail standard.

   f.   Inform test takers, upon request, how much their scores might change, should they elect to take the test again. Such information would include variation in test performance due to measurement error (e.g., the appropriate standard errors of measurement) and changes in performance over time with or without intervention (e.g., additional training or treatment).

   g.   Communicate test results to test takers in an appropriate and sensitive manner, without use of negative labels or comments likely to inflame or stigmatize the test taker.

   h.   Provide corrected test scores to test takers as rapidly as possible, should an error occur in the processing or reporting of scores. The length of time is often dictated by individuals responsible for processing or reporting the scores, rather than the individuals responsible for testing, should the two parties indeed differ.

   i.   Correct any errors as rapidly as possible if there are errors in the proc ess of developing scores.

9. Because test takers have the right to have the results of tests kept confidential to the extent allowed by law, testing professionals should:
   a.   Ensure that records of test results (in paper or electronic form) are safe-guarded and maintained so that only individuals who have a legitimate right to access them will be able to do so.
   b.   Should provide test takers, upon request, with information regarding who has a legitimate right to access their test results (when individually identified) and in what form. Testing professionals should respond ap-propriately to questions regarding the reasons why such individuals may have access to test results and how they may use the results.
   c.   Advise test takers that they are entitled to limit access to their results (when individually identified) to those persons or institutions, and for those purposes, revealed to them prior to testing. Exceptions may occur when test takers, or their guardians, consent to release the test results to others or when testing professionals are authorized by law to release test results.
   d.   Keep confidential any requests for testing accommodations and the documentation supporting the request.
10. Because test takers have the right to present concerns about the testing proc-ess and to receive information about procedures that will be used to address such concerns, testing professionals should:
   a.   Inform test takers how they can question the results of the testing if they do not believe that the test was administered properly or scored cor-rectly, or other such concerns.
   b.   Inform test takers of the procedures for appealing decisions that they be-lieve are based in whole or in part on erroneous test results.
   c.   Inform test takers, if their test results are under investigation and may be canceled, invalidated, or not released for normal use. In such an event, that investigation should be performed in a timely manner. The investi-gation should use all available information that addresses the reason(s) for the investigation, and the test taker should also be informed of the information that he/she may need to provide to assist with the investiga-tion.
   d.   Inform the test taker, if that test taker's test results are canceled or not released for normal use, why that action was taken. The test taker is en-titled to request and receive information on the types of evidence and procedures that have been used to make that determination.

The Responsibilities of Test Takers: Guidelines for Testing Professionals

Testing Professionals should take steps to ensure that test takers know that they have specific responsibilities in addition to their rights described above.

1. Testing professionals need to inform test takers that they should listen to and/or read their rights and responsibilities as a test taker and ask questions about issues they do not understand.

2. Testing professionals should take steps, as appropriate, to ensure that test takers know that they:
   a.   Are responsible for their behavior throughout the entire testing process.
   b.   Should not interfere with the rights of others involved in the testing process.
   c.   Should not compromise the integrity of the test and its interpretation in any manner.

3. Testing professionals should remind test takers that it is their responsibility to ask questions prior to testing if they are uncertain about why the test is being given, how it will be given, what they will be asked to do, and what will be done with the results. Testing professionals should:
   a.   Advise test takers that it is their responsibility to review materials supplied by test publishers and others as part of the testing process and to ask questions about areas that they feel they should understand better prior to the start of testing.
   b.   Inform test takers that it is their responsibility to request more information if they are not satisfied with what they know about how their test results will be used and what will be done with them.

4. Testing professionals should inform test takers that it is their responsibility to read descriptive material they receive in advance of a test and to listen carefully to test instructions. Testing professionals should inform test takers that it is their responsibility to inform an examiner in advance of testing if they wish to receive a testing accommodation or if they have a physical condition or illness that may interfere with their performance. Testing professionals should inform test takers that it is their responsibility to inform an examiner if they have difficulty comprehending the language in which the test is given. Testing professionals should:
   a.   Inform test takers that, if they need special testing arrangements, it is their responsibility to request appropriate accommodations and to provide any requested documentation as far in advance of the testing date as possible. Testing professionals should inform test takers about the documentation needed to receive a requested testing accommodation.

b. Inform test takers that, if they request but do not receive a testing accommodation, they could request information about why their request was denied.

5. Testing professionals should inform test takers when and where the test will be given, and whether payment for the testing is required. Having been so informed, it is the responsibility of the test taker to appear on time with any required materials, pay for testing services and be ready to be tested. Testing professionals should:

a.   Inform test takers that they are responsible for familiarizing themselves with the appropriate materials needed for testing and for requesting information about these materials, if needed.

b.   Inform the test taker, if the testing situation requires that test takers bring materials (e.g., personal identification, pencils, calculators, etc.) to the testing site, of this responsibility to do so.

6. Testing professionals should advise test takers, prior to testing, that it is their responsibility to:

a.   Listen to and/or read the directions given to them.

b.   Follow instructions given by testing professionals.

c.   Complete the test as directed.

d.   Perform to the best of their ability if they want their score to be a reflection of their best effort.

e.   Behave honestly (e.g., not cheating or assisting others who cheat).

7. Testing professionals should inform test takers about the consequences of not taking a test, should they choose not to take the test. Once so informed, it is the responsibility of the test taker to accept such consequences, and the testing professional should so inform the test takers. If test takers have questions regarding these consequences, it is their responsibility to ask questions of the testing professional, and the testing professional should so inform the test takers.

8. Testing professionals should inform test takers that it is their responsibility to notify appropriate persons, as specified by the testing organization, if they do not understand their results, or if they believe that testing conditions affected the results. Testing professionals should:

a.   Provide information to test takers, upon request, about appropriate procedures for questioning or canceling their test scores or results, if relevant to the purposes of testing.

b.   Provide to test takers, upon request, the procedures for reviewing, retesting, or canceling their scores or test results, if they believe that testing conditions affected their results and if relevant to the purposes of testing.

    c.   Provide documentation to the test taker about known testing conditions that might have affected the results of the testing, if relevant to the purposes of testing.

9. Testing professionals should advise test takers that it is their responsibility to ask questions about the confidentiality of their test results, if this aspect concerns them.

10. Testing professionals should advise test takers that it is their responsibility to present concerns about the testing process in a timely, respectful manner.

A Counselor's Guide User's Matrix:
An Alphabetical Listing of Career Assessment Instruments
By Category and Type of Use

Jerome T. Kapes
Professor Emeritus

Linda Martinez
Doctoral Student

Department of Educational Psychology
Texas A & M University

The User's Matrix is an alphabetized listing of all 326 instruments either reviewed or briefly described in the fourth edition of *A Counselor's Guide*. These instruments are identified by *Characteristics* assessed, Level of *Use*, and whether or not the instruments are particularly appropriate for *Special Populations*. Instruments in boldface type (56) are reviewed and may be located using the Table of Contents. All other instruments (270) are briefly described in the *Additional Career Assessment Instruments* chapter under the appropriate category. The exact page number for either reviewed or briefly described instruments may be obtained from the Index.

The *Characteristics* used to describe the instruments do not exclusively correspond to those used to group them for either the reviews or brief descriptions, because many instruments fit more than one category. However, they are categorical descriptions of what the instruments are intended to measure. The Values category includes instruments that assess Job Satisfaction and Environments.

The *Use* categories are based on level of schooling or setting for those uses beyond four years of college. The Adult Education/Training category includes instruments used with adults who are receiving counseling for education, training or job change outside the traditional college environment. The Business & Industry/Employment category describes instruments that would be administered by or for employers who would typically use the results to make hiring or advancement decisions.

The *Special Populations* Category is listed separately from those that designate either characteristics assessed or level of use. Instruments identified here may be appropriate for individuals with particular disabilities or academic, economic, or social disadvantages.

The reader may find the matrix useful to provide a quick overview of the instruments, by name, which are available to assess particular characteristics. Furthermore, an initial judgment about an instrument's fit for an intended population can also be made.

INSTRUMENT NAME	CHARACTERISTICS						USE						
	Achievement	Aptitude	Interest	Values/Satisfaction/Environments	Career Development/Maturity	Personality	Elementary School	Junior High/Middle School	Senior High School	2-Year or 4-Year College	Adult Education/Training	Business & Industry/Employment	Special Populations
Ability Explorer		*						*	*	*			
ACCU Vision - Workplace Success Skills System	*								*		*	*	
Activity Vector Analysis (AVA)	*				*	*						*	*
Adaptability Test		*							*			*	
Adult Basic Learning Exam (ABLE)	*									*	*		*
Adult Measure of Essential Skills (AMES)	*									*	*		*
Adult Personality Inventory (API)						*				*	*	*	
Applicant Review		*	*			*						*	
Apticom	*	*	*						*	*	*	*	*
Aptitude Interest Inventory (ABCD/IBCD - Computer based)		*	*						*				
ARC Self-Determination Scale (ARC-SDS)					*	*			*		*		*
Armed Services Vocational Aptitude Battery (ASVAB - CEP)		*	*	*						*			
Armed Services-Civilian Vocational Interest Survey			*					*	*	*	*		
Ashland Interest Assessment (AIA)			*					*	*	*	*		*
Assessing Specific Competencies					*			*	*	*	*	*	

INSTRUMENT NAME	CHARACTERISTICS						USE						
	Achievement	Aptitude	Interest	Values/Satisfaction/Environments	Career Development/Maturity	Personality	Elementary School	Junior High/Middle School	Senior High School	2-Year or 4-Year College	Adult Education/Training	Business & Industry/Employment	Special Populations
Assessment of Career Decision Making (ACDM)					*				*	*			
Ball Aptitude Battery (BAB)		*			*				*	*	*	*	*
Barriers to Employment Success Inventory (BESI)					*				*	*	*		*
Barsh Learning Styles Inventory - Revised						*					*		*
Basic Skills Locater Test	*								*				*
Becker Work Adjustment Profile (BWAP)					*				*		*		*
Bennett Hand Tool Dexterity Test (BHTDT)		*							*		*	*	*
Bennett Mechanical Comprehension Test (BMCT)		*							*	*	*	*	
Brigance Employability Skills Inventory (BESI)	*				*				*		*		*
Brigance Life Skills Inventory (BLSI)	*				*				*		*		*
Business Careers Interest Inventory			*							*		*	
California Life Goals Evaluation Schedules				*					*	*	*	*	
California Psychological Inventory (CPI)						*			*	*	*	*	
Campbell Interest & Skills Survey (CISS)			*						*	*		*	
Campbell Organizational Survey				*								*	

INSTRUMENT NAME	CHARACTERISTICS						USE						
	Achievement	Aptitude	Interest	Values/Satisfaction/Environments	Career Development/Maturity	Personality	Elementary School	Junior High/Middle School	Senior High School	2-Year or 4-Year College	Adult Education/Training	Business & Industry/Employment	Special Populations
Candidate Profile Record		*										*	
Career Ability Placement Survey (CAPS)		*						*	*	*	*	*	
Career Action Inventory					*					*	*	*	
Career Anchors: Discovering Your Real Values				*							*	*	
Career and Vocational Form of the SOI-LA Basic Test		*	*					*	*	*	*	*	*
Career Assessment Battery (CAB)									*	*			
Career Assessment Inventory (CAI)			*					*	*	*	*	*	
Career Attitudes and Strategies Inventory (CASI)					*					*	*	*	
Career Awareness Inventory (CAI)					*		*	*	*				
Career Beliefs Inventory (CBI)					*			*	*		*	*	
Career Compass			*					*	*	*			
Career Decision Profile					*				*	*			
Career Decision Scale (CDS)					*				*	*	*		
Career Development Inventory (CDI)					*			*	*	*	*		
Career Development Profile					*							*	

INSTRUMENT NAME	CHARACTERISTICS						USE						
	Achievement	Aptitude	Interest	Values/Satisfaction/Environments	Career Development/Maturity	Personality	Elementary School	Junior High/Middle School	Senior High School	2-Year or 4-Year College	Adult Education/Training	Business & Industry/Employment	Special Populations
Career Directions Inventory (CDI)			*						*	*	*		
Career Exploration Inventory (CEI)			*					*	*	*	*		
Career Exploration Series (CES)			*		*				*	*	*		
Career Factors Inventory								*	*	*	*		
Career Finder			*				*	*	*	*			
Career Guidance Inventory			*					*	*	*	*		
Career Interest Inventory (CII)			*					*	*	*	*		
Career Inventories for the Learning Disabled (CILD)		*	*			*			*				*
Career IQ and Interest Test (CIQIT)		*	*					*	*	*	*		
Career Key			*						*	*			
Career Leverage Inventory					*								
Career Mastery Inventory (CMAS)					*			*	*	*	*	*	
Career Maturity Inventory (CMI)					*			*	*	*	*		
Career Occupational Preference System Interest Inventory (COPS)			*					*	*	*	*		
Career Orientation and Planning Profile (COPP)			*					*	*	*	*		

INSTRUMENT NAME	CHARACTERISTICS						USE						
	Achievement	Aptitude	Interest	Values/Satisfaction/Environments	Career Development/Maturity	Personality	Elementary School	Junior High/Middle School	Senior High School	2-Year or 4-Year College	Adult Education/Training	Business & Industry/Employment	Special Populations
Career Orientation Placement and Evaluation Survey (COPES)				*				*	*	*	*		
Career Planning Survey		*	*					*	*	*	*		
Career Planning System (CPS)		*	*					*	*	*	*		
Career Profile Assessment		*	*					*	*				
Career Profile System	*				*	*						*	
Career Programs Assessment Test (CPAT)								*	*	*	*		
Career Scope		*	*					*	*	*	*		
Career SnapShot 2001		*			*			*					
Career Suitability Profile						*		*			*	*	
Career Technical Assistance Program (C-Tap)	*							*	*		*		
Career Thought Inventory									*		*		
Career Values Card Sort Kit				*						*	*	*	
Career Values Scale				*				*	*	*	*	*	
Career/Personality Compatibility Inventory						*				*	*	*	
Chronicle Career Quest (CCQ)			*					*	*				

INSTRUMENT NAME	CHARACTERISTICS						USE						
	Achievement	Aptitude	Interest	Values/Satisfaction/Environments	Career Development/Maturity	Personality	Elementary School	Junior High/Middle School	Senior High School	2-Year or 4-Year College	Adult Education/Training	Business & Industry/Employment	Special Populations
CITE Learning Styles Inventory						*	*		*		*		*
Clerical Abilities Battery (CAB)	*	*							*	*	*	*	
Clerical Skills Test Series	*	*							*	*	*	*	
COIN Basic Skills and Career Interest Survey		*	*						*	*	*		
COIN Career Targets			*					*	*				
COIN Clue					*			*					
COIN Educational Inventory			*						*	*			
College Major and Vocational Program Selector			*							*			
College Major Interest Inventory (CMII)			*						*	*			
Comprehensive Ability Battery (CAB)		*							*	*	*	*	
Comprehensive Personality Profile						*						*	
Computer Operator Aptitude Battery (COAB)		*								*	*	*	
Computer Programmer Aptitude Battery (CPAB)		*								*	*	*	
Crawford Small Parts Dexterity Test (CSPDT)		*							*		*	*	*
Curtis Interest Scale			*						*	*	*		

INSTRUMENT NAME	CHARACTERISTICS						USE						
	Achievement	Aptitude	Interest	Values/Satisfaction/Environments	Career Development/Maturity	Personality	Elementary School	Junior High/Middle School	Senior High School	2-Year or 4-Year College	Adult Education/Training	Business & Industry/Employment	Special Populations
Customer Service Skills Assessment Program	*								*	*	*	*	
Deal-Me-In/It's In the Cards		*	*					*	*	*	*		
Differential Aptitudes Test (DAT)		*						*	*	*	*		
Dole Vocational Sentence Completion Blank			*					*	*	*	*	*	
Dvorine Color Vision Test		*							*	*	*	*	
Educational Interest Inventory, Revised Edition (EII)			*						*	*	*		
Edwards Personal Preference Schedule (EPPS)						*			*	*	*	*	
Emerging Occupations Interest Inventory			*					*	*	*	*	*	
Employability Inventory					*					*	*	*	*
Employability Maturity Interview					*				*	*	*	*	
Employee Aptitude Survey (EAS)		*									*	*	
Employee Competency Scale (ECS)	*					*			*	*		*	
Employee Effectiveness Profile												*	
Employee Reliability Inventory						*					*	*	*
Employment Barrier Identification Scale (EBIS)	*				*				*		*	*	*

INSTRUMENT NAME	CHARACTERISTICS						USE						
	Achievement	Aptitude	Interest	Values/Satisfaction/Environments	Career Development/Maturity	Personality	Elementary School	Junior High/Middle School	Senior High School	2-Year or 4-Year College	Adult Education/Training	Business & Industry/Employment	Special Populations
Endorale Seversen Transition Rating Scale	*	*			*				*		*		*
ETSA Tests (Employers' Tests and Services Association)	*	*	*		*				*	*	*	*	*
Evaluating the Participant's Employability Skills	*	*							*	*	*		
Explore								*					
Explore the World of Work (E-WOW)	*	*	*								*		*
Flanagan Aptitude Classification Test (FACT)		*							*	*	*	*	*
Flannagan Industrial Tests (FIT)		*							*	*	*	*	*
Fleishman Job Analysis Survey (F-JAS)				*								*	
Forer Vocational Survey: Men-Woman	*				*	*			*	*	*		
Functional Assessment Inventory	*										*		*
Fundamental Interpersonal Relations Orientation-Behavior (FIRO-B)					*	*			*	*	*	*	*
Gains I & II							*	*					
Geist Picture Interest Inventory			*					*	*	*	*		*
General Clerical Test (GCT)		*								*	*	*	*
Gordon Occupational Checklist II			*					*	*	*	*		

INSTRUMENT NAME	CHARACTERISTICS						USE						
	Achievement	Aptitude	Interest	Values/Satisfaction/Environments	Career Development/Maturity	Personality	Elementary School	Junior High/Middle School	Senior High School	2-Year or 4-Year College	Adult Education/Training	Business & Industry/Employment	Special Populations
Gordon Personal Profile-Inventory (GPP-I)						*			*	*	*	*	*
Group Interest Sort			*				*	*					
Group Test of Musical Ability		*					*	*					
Guide for Occupational Exploration (GOE) Inventory			*					*	*	*	*		
Guilford-Zimmerman Interest Inventory			*	*									
Guilford-Zimmerman Temperament Survey (GZTS)						*					*	*	
Hall Occupational Orientation Inventory (HALL)			*				*	*	*	*	*	*	
Harrington-O'Shea Career Decision-Making System (CDM)			*					*	*	*	*		
Hay Aptitude Test Battery		*									*	*	
High School Career-Course Planner			*					*	*	*	*		
How Well Do You Know Your Interests?			*							*	*		
Individual Career Exploration (ICE)				*			*	*	*				*
Individual Style Survey (ISS)		*							*	*	*	*	
Industrial Reading Test (IRT)	*								*	*	*	*	
Insight Inventory						*				*	*	*	

INSTRUMENT NAME	CHARACTERISTICS						USE						
	Achievement	Aptitude	Interest	Values/Satisfaction/Environments	Career Development/Maturity	Personality	Elementary School	Junior High/Middle School	Senior High School	2-Year or 4-Year College	Adult Education/Training	Business & Industry/Employment	Special Populations
Interest Explorer	*		*						*				*
Interest, Determination, Exploration & Assessment System (IDEAS)		*	*					*	*		*		
Intuitive Mechanics		*							*	*	*	*	
IPI Aptitude-Intelligence Test Series		*				*			*	*	*	*	
Jackson Personality Inventory (JPI)						*			*	*	*	*	
Jackson Vocational Interest Inventory (JVIS)			*						*	*	*		
Job Choice Decision-Making Exercise	*				*	*			*	*			
Job Descriptive Index, Revised (JDI-R)	*			*							*	*	
Job Effectiveness Prediction System (JEPS)	*				*							*	
Job Search Attitude Inventory								*	*	*	*		
Job Search Inventory								*	*		*		
Job Seeking Skills Assessment									*	*	*		*
Job Skills	*								*		*	*	
Job Skills Tests	*	*								*	*	*	*
Job Style Indicator (JSI)				*							*	*	

INSTRUMENT NAME	CHARACTERISTICS						USE						
	Achievement	Aptitude	Interest	Values/Satisfaction/Environments	Career Development/Maturity	Personality	Elementary School	Junior High/Middle School	Senior High School	2-Year or 4-Year College	Adult Education/Training	Business & Industry/Employment	Special Populations
Judgement of Occupational Behavior-Orientation (JOB-O)	*		*				*	*	*	*	*		*
Keirsey Character Sorter		*				*				*	*	*	
Keirsey Temperament Sorter II						*				*	*	*	
Key Educational Vocational Assessment System (KEVAS)	*	*	*			*					*		*
Kuder Career Search with Person Match			*					*	*	*	*		
Kuder General Interest Survey (Kuder E)			*					*	*	*	*		
Kuder Occupational Interest Survey (Kuder DD)			*						*	*	*		
Learning Skills Profile	*	*						*	*	*	*	*	
Learning Style Profile						*		*	*	*	*		
Learning Styles Inventory - Price						*	*	*	*		*		*
Learning/Working Styles Inventory						*			*		*		*
Leisure to Occupations Connection Search (LOC)			*				*	*	*		*		*
Leisure/Work Search Inventory			*						*		*		
Life-Centered Career Education Competency Assessment (LCCE)	*	*						*	*				*
McCarron-Dial System (MDS)	*	*				*		*	*		*		*

INSTRUMENT NAME	CHARACTERISTICS						USE						
	Achievement	Aptitude	Interest	Values/Satisfaction/Environments	Career Development/Maturity	Personality	Elementary School	Junior High/Middle School	Senior High School	2-Year or 4-Year College	Adult Education/Training	Business & Industry/Employment	Special Populations
Mechanical Movements		*							*		*	*	*
Meyer-Kendall Assessment Survey (MKAS)		*	*			*						*	
Microcomputer Evaluation of Career Areas (MECA)		*							*	*	*	*	*
Minnesota Clerical Test (MCT)		*							*	*	*	*	*
Minnesota Importance Questionnaire (MIQ)				*									
Minnesota Job Description Questionnaire (MJDQ)				*									
Minnesota Paper Form Board-Revised		*											
Minnesota Rate of Manipulation Test, 1969 Edition (MRMT)		*						*	*	*	*	*	*
Minnesota Satisfaction Questionnaire (MSQ)				*								*	*
Minnesota Satisfactoriness Scales (MSS)					*							*	
Minnesota Spatial Relations Test, Revised Edition (MSRT)		*							*	*	*	*	*
Missouri Aptitude and Career Information Inventory (MACII)		*	*						*	*	*	*	
Missouri Occupational Card Sort (MOCS)	*	*	*	*				*	*	*	*		
Motivated Skills Card Sort (MSCS)	*	*	*					*	*	*	*	*	
Motivational Approach of Personal Potential						*							

INSTRUMENT NAME	CHARACTERISTICS						USE						
	Achievement	Aptitude	Interest	Values/Satisfaction/Environments	Career Development/Maturity	Personality	Elementary School	Junior High/Middle School	Senior High School	2-Year or 4-Year College	Adult Education/Training	Business & Industry/Employment	Special Populations
Multidimensional Aptitude Battery (MAB)		*					*		*	*	*		*
Musical Aptitude Profile		*						*	*				
My Vocational Situation (MVS)					*				*	*	*		
Myers-Briggs Type Indicator (MBTI)			*			*			*	*	*	*	
Neo Personality Inventory (NEO-PI-R)						*				*	*	*	
NOCTI Occupational Competency Tests	*									*	*	*	
Occupational Aptitude Survey & Interest Schedule-2 (OASIS-2)		*	*					*	*	*	*		*
Occupational Clues			*	*				*	*	*	*		
Occupational Interest Card Sort (OICS)			*					*	*	*	*	*	
Occupational Personality Assessment						*					*	*	
Occupational Personality Questionnaire						*					*	*	
Occupational Preference Inventory		*	*			*			*	*	*	*	
Occupational Stress Inventory (OSI)						*		*	*		*	*	
O'Conner Finger Dexterity Test		*						*			*	*	*
O'Conner Tweezer Dexterity Test		*						*	*		*	*	*

INSTRUMENT NAME	CHARACTERISTICS						USE						
	Achievement	Aptitude	Interest	Values/Satisfaction/Environments	Career Development/Maturity	Personality	Elementary School	Junior High/Middle School	Senior High School	2-Year or 4-Year College	Adult Education/Training	Business & Industry/Employment	Special Populations
Office Skills Test	*	*							*	*	*	*	
Ohio Vocational Interest Survey II (OVIS II)			*					*	*	*	*		*
Pennsylvania Bi-Manual Worksample		*							*	*	*	*	*
Perceptual Speed		*								*	*	*	
Personal Audit						*					*	*	
Personal Skills Map (PSM)						*	*	*	*	*	*	*	
Personal Style Indicator (PSI)				*		*					*	*	
Personality Research Form (PRF)						*						*	
Personnel Tests for Industry (PTI)		*						*	*	*	*	*	*
PESCO 2001 System	*	*	*		*	*					*		*
Phoenix Ability Survey System		*							*	*	*		
Pictorial Inventory of Careers (PIC)			*					*	*	*	*		*
Plan	*		*						*				
Position Analysis Questionnaire (PAQ)				*								*	
Position Classification Inventory (PCI)				*								*	

INSTRUMENT NAME	CHARACTERISTICS						USE						
	Achievement	Aptitude	Interest	Values/Satisfaction/Environments	Career Development/Maturity	Personality	Elementary School	Junior High/Middle School	Senior High School	2-Year or 4-Year College	Adult Education/Training	Business & Industry/Employment	Special Populations
Practical Assessment Exploration System (PAES)	*	*	*		*			*	*				*
Preliminary Diagnostic Questionnaire	*	*			*	*					*		*
Prevocational Assessment Screen (PAS)		*						*	*		*		*
Professional Employment Test		*										*	
Program for Assessing Youth Employment Skills (PAYES)	*	*	*		*				*		*		*
PSI Basic Skills Test for Business, Industry, and Government	*	*										*	*
Purdue Pegboard		*						*	*		*	*	*
Reading-Free Vocational Interest Inventory:2 (RFV2)			*					*	*		*		*
Responsibility and Independence Scale for Adolescents	*				*			*	*		*	*	*
Retirement Activities Card Sort			*								*	*	
Revised Beta Examination–Second Edition (BETA-II)		*								*	*	*	*
Rokeach Value Survey				*				*	*	*		*	
Sales Attitude Checklist						*						*	
Sales Personality Questionnaire						*						*	
Salience Inventory (SI)				*				*	*	*	*	*	

INSTRUMENT NAME	CHARACTERISTICS						USE						
	Achievement	Aptitude	Interest	Values/Satisfaction/Environments	Career Development/Maturity	Personality	Elementary School	Junior High/Middle School	Senior High School	2-Year or 4-Year College	Adult Education/Training	Business & Industry/Employment	Special Populations
Satisfaction Research Questionnaire (SRQ)		*		*							*	*	
Scholastic Level Exam (SLE)		*							*	*	*	*	*
School to Work Career Survey			*					*	*	*	*	*	
Schubert General Ability Battery (GAB)		*							*	*	*	*	
Self Directed Search (SDS)			*					*	*	*	*	*	*
Self-Motivated Career Planning						*			*	*	*	*	
Short Employment Tests (SET)		*							*	*	*	*	*
Short Tests of Clerical Ability (STCA)		*							*	*	*	*	*
Singer-Loomis Inventory of Personality (SLIP)						*			*	*	*	*	
Sixteen Personality Factors (16PF)						*			*	*	*	*	
Skills Assessment Module (SAM)		*							*	*	*		*
Skills Confidence Inventory (SCI)		*							*	*	*	*	
Slaney Vocational Card Sort			*		*		*		*	*	*	*	
Social & Prevocational Information Battery (SPIB)	*						*	*	*		*		*
Space Relations (Paper Puzzles)		*							*		*	*	*

INSTRUMENT NAME	CHARACTERISTICS						USE						
	Achievement	Aptitude	Interest	Values/Satisfaction/Environments	Career Development/Maturity	Personality	Elementary School	Junior High/Middle School	Senior High School	2-Year or 4-Year College	Adult Education/Training	Business & Industry/Employment	Special Populations
Space Thinking (Flags)		*							*		*	*	*
SRA Clerical Aptitudes		*								*	*	*	
SRA Mechanical Aptitudes		*							*	*	*	*	
SRA Pictorial Reasoning Test (PRT)		*						*	*	*	*	*	*
SRA Test of Mechanical Concepts		*						*	*	*	*	*	*
Strategic Assessment of Readiness for Training (START)	*				*						*	*	
Street Survival Skills Questionnaire (SSSQ)						*		*	*	*	*	*	*
Strength Deployment Inventory						*						*	
Stromberg Dexterity Test (SDT)		*						*	*	*	*	*	*
Strong Interest Inventory (SII)			*					*	*	*	*	*	
Student Styles Questionnaire (SSQ)						*		*					
Styles of Teamwork Inventory						*						*	
Success Skills 2000	*	*					*		*	*		*	
SureHire	*			*					*	*	*	*	
Survey of Interpersonal Values (SIV)						*			*	*	*	*	

INSTRUMENT NAME	Achievement	Aptitude	Interest	Values/Satisfaction/Environments	Career Development/Maturity	Personality	Elementary School	Junior High/Middle School	Senior High School	2-Year or 4-Year College	Adult Education/Training	Business & Industry/Employment	Special Populations
Survey of Personal Values (SPV)	*			*		*			*	*	*	*	
Survey of Work Styles (SWS)						*					*	*	
Survey of Work Values				*					*	*	*	*	
System for Assessment and Group Evaluation (SAGE/C-A-M)	*	*	*			*			*	*	*		*
Talent Assessment Program (TAP)		*						*			*		*
Technical Test Battery	*	*							*	*	*	*	
Technology and Internet Assessment	*	*			*			*	*	*	*	*	
Temperament Comparator (TC)						*		*				*	
Test of Adult Basic Education (TABE)	*								*	*	*	*	*
Tests for Everyday Living (TEL)	*					*		*	*				*
Thurstone Temperament Schedule						*				*	*	*	
Training House Assessment Kit	*	*										*	
Transition Behavior Scale					*				*				*
Transition Planning Inventory (TPI)					*				*				*
UNIACT IV			*						*	*			

INSTRUMENT NAME	CHARACTERISTICS						USE						
	Achievement	Aptitude	Interest	Values/Satisfaction/Environments	Career Development/Maturity	Personality	Elementary School	Junior High/Middle School	Senior High School	2-Year or 4-Year College	Adult Education/Training	Business & Industry/Employment	Special Populations
USES Basic Occupational Literacy Test (BOLT)	*								*		*	*	*
USES Clerical Skills Test		*							*	*	*	*	
USES General Aptitude Test Battery (GATB)		*						*	*	*	*	*	
USES Interest Checklist			*								*	*	*
USES Interest Inventory (USESII)			*								*		*
USES Non-reading Aptitude Test Battery (NATB)		*							*	*	*	*	*
Valpar 300 Series Dexterity Modules		*							*	*	*	*	*
Valpar Aviator	*	*	*						*		*		*
Valpar Component Work Sample Series	*	*	*						*	*	*		*
Valpar Pro 3000	*	*			*				*	*	*		*
Valpar System 2000	*	*			*				*	*	*		*
Valpar Test of Essential Skills (VTES)	*										*	*	*
Values Preference Indicator				*				*	*	*	*		
Values Scale (VS)				*				*	*	*	*	*	
Viewpoint						*						*	

INSTRUMENT NAME	CHARACTERISTICS						USE						
	Achievement	Aptitude	Interest	Values/Satisfaction/Environments	Career Development/Maturity	Personality	Elementary School	Junior High/Middle School	Senior High School	2-Year or 4-Year College	Adult Education/Training	Business & Industry/Employment	Special Populations
Vocational Adaptation Rating Scales (VARS)	*				*			*	*		*	*	*
Vocational Assessment & Curriculum Guide	*				*				*		*		*
Vocational Behavior Checklist (VBC)					*						*		*
Vocational Decision-Making Interview		*	*		*			*	*		*		*
Vocational Evaluation System		*	*					*	*		*		*
Vocational Evaluation Systems (Singer)								*	*				*
Vocational Implications of Personality (VIP)			*			*		*	*	*	*	*	*
Vocational Insight and Exploration Kit (VIEK)										*		*	
Vocational Interest Assessment System (VIAS)			*					*	*		*		*
Vocational Interest Exploration (VIE) System			*					*	*		*		*
Vocational Interest Inventory & Exploration Survey (VOC-TIES)			*					*	*		*		*
Vocational Interest Inventory (VII)			*						*	*			
Vocational Interest Temperament and Aptitude System (VITAS)		*						*			*		
Vocational Learning Styles						*			*		*		*
Vocational Preference Inventory			*			*			*	*	*	*	*

INSTRUMENT NAME	Achievement	Aptitude	Interest	Values/Satisfaction/Environments	Career Development/Maturity	Personality	Elementary School	Junior High/Middle School	Senior High School	2-Year or 4-Year College	Adult Education/Training	Business & Industry/Employment	Special Populations
	CHARACTERISTICS						USE						
Vocational Research Interest Inventory (VRII)			*						*		*		*
Vocational Training Inventory and Exploration Survey (VOC-TIES)		*	*					*	*				*
Vocational Transit		*	*					*	*		*		*
VOC-TECH Quick Screener (VTQS)									*		*		*
V-TECS Assessments	*								*	*	*	*	
Watson-Glaser Critical Thinking Appraisal		*										*	
Wesman Personnel Classification Test (PCT)		*										*	
What - Where - How?				*			*					*	
Wide Range Achievement Test (WRAT)	*								*	*	*		*
Wide Range Interest Opinion Test (WRIOT)			*					*	*	*	*		*
Wiesen Test of Mechanical Aptitude		*						*	*	*	*	*	
Wonderlic Basic Skills Test (WBST)		*							*		*	*	*
Wonderlic Personnel Test										*		*	
Work Adjustment Inventory					*	*			*		*		*
Work Adjustment Scale					*				*	*			*

INSTRUMENT NAME	CHARACTERISTICS						USE						
	Achievement	Aptitude	Interest	Values/Satisfaction/Environments	Career Development/Maturity	Personality	Elementary School	Junior High/Middle School	Senior High School	2-Year or 4-Year College	Adult Education/Training	Business & Industry/Employment	Special Populations
Work Environment Scale	*			*								*	
Work Exploration Checklist			*					*	*		*		
Work Keys									*	*	*	*	
Work Motivation Inventory (WMI)				*								*	
Work Performance Assessment					*	*			*	*	*		*
Work Personality Profile					*	*					*		*
Work Preference Questionnaire			*									*	
Work Skills Development Package (WSD)	*	*			*	*		*	*		*		*
Work Temperament Inventory				*							*	*	*
Workmate								*	*	*	*		
World of Work Inventory (WOWI)	*	*	*	*					*	*	*		*

INDEX

A

A Counselor's Guide User's Matrix, 549
Ability Explorer, 74
ACCU Vision – Workplace Success Skills, 436
ACT Staff Members (developer), 109, 139, 141, 183
Activity Vector Analysis, 436
Adaptability Test, 468
Additional Career Assessment Instruments, 433
Addresses of Publishers, 489
Adult Basic Learning Examination, 82
Adult Measure of Essential Skills, 87
Adult Personality Inventory, 463
Applicant Review, 463
Apticom, 436
Aptitude Interest Inventory, 436
Arc's Self-Determination Scale, 386
Armed Services Vocational Aptitude Battery Career Exploration Program, 93
Armed Services-Civilian Vocational Interest Survey, 448
Artese, Victor (developer), 178
Ashland Interest Assessment, 468
Askov, Eunice (reviewer), 83
Assessing Specific Competencies, 460
Assessment & Counseling Competencies & Responsibilities, 65
Assessment of Career Decision Making, 460

B

Ball Aptitude Battery, 102
Barriers to Employment Success Inventory, 460
Barsch Learning Styles Inventory – Revised, 468
Basic Skills Locator Test, 436
Becker Work Adjustment Profile, 468
Becker, Ralph L. (developer), 412
Bennett Hand Tool Dexterity Test, 443
Bennett Mechanical Comprehension Test, 443
Bennett, G. K. (developer), 123
Betz, Nancy (developer), 289
Biggs, Shirley (developer), 87
Blair, Ellen (reviewer), 394
Boggs, Kathleen (reviewer), 195
Borgen, Fred (developer), 289
Borman, Christopher (reviewer), 76
Botterbusch, Karl (reviewer), 426
Brigance Life/Employability Inventories, 393
Brigance, Albert (developer), 393
Briggs, Katherine (developer), 363
Brolin, Donn (developer), 405
Brown, Clarence (reviewer), 118
Brown, Michael (reviewer), 311
Buki, Lydia (reviewer), 243
Business Careers Interest Inventory, 448

C

C.I.T.E. Learning Styles Inventory, 468

California Life Goals Evaluation Schedules, 455

California Psychological Inventory, 463

Campbell Interest & Skill Survey, 194

Campbell Organizational Survey, 455

Campbell, David (developer),194

Campbell, Vicki (reviewer), 230

Candidate Profile Record, 443

Card Sorts, 458

Career Action Inventory, 460

Career Anchors: Discovering Your Real Values, 455

Career & Vocational Form of the SOI-LA Basic Test 436

Career Assessment Battery, 449

Career Assessment Inventory, 202

Career Attitudes & Strategies Inventory, 310

Career Awareness Inventory, 460

Career Beliefs Inventory, 316

Career Compass, 449

Career Decision Profile, 460

Career Decision Scale, 460

Career Development Inventory, 323

Career Development Profile, 461

Career Development/Maturity Measures, 309

Career Directions Inventory, 449

Career Exploration Inventory, 449

Career Exploration Series, 449

Career Factors Inventory, 331

Career Finder, 449

Career Guidance Inventory, 449

Career Interest Inventory, 202

Career Inventories for the Learning Disabled, 468

Career IQ & Interest Test, 436

Career Key, 450

Career Leverage Inventory, 461

Career Mastery Inventory, 461

Career Maturity Inventory, 336

Career Orientation & Planning Profile, 450

Career Planning Survey, 109

Career Planning System, 450

Career Profile Assessment, 437

Career Profile System, 461

Career Programs Assessment Test , 437

Career SnapShot 2001, 437

Career Suitability Profile, 463

Career Technical Assistance Program, 437

Career Thoughts Inventory, 343

Career Values Card Sort, 218

Career Values Scale, 455

Career/Personality Compatibility Inventory, 463

CareerScope Assessment & Reporting System, 116

Carr, Darrin, 47

CASAS, Foundation for Educational Achievement, (developer), 132

Cattell, Heather (developer), 369

Cattell, Karen (developer), 369

Cattell, Raymond (developer), 369

Chartrand, Judy (developer), 331

Chronicle Career Quest, 222

Chronicle Guidance Staff (developer), 222

Ciechalski, Joseph (reviewer), 282

Clark, Gary (reviewer), 420, 425

Clerical Abilities Battery, 443

Clerical Skills Test Series, 443

Clonts, Winifred (developer), 178

COIN Basic Skills & Career Interest Survey, 437
COIN Career Targets, 450
COIN Clue, 461
COIN Educational Inventory, 450
College Major & Vocational Program Selector, 450
College Major Interest Inventory, 450
Comprehensive Ability Battery, 437
Comprehensive Personality Profile, 350
Computer Assisted Career Assessment , 47
Computer Operator Aptitude Battery, 443
Computer Programmer Aptitude Battery, 443
CopSystem, 210
Craft, Larry L. (developer), 350
Crawford Small Parts Dexterity Test, 444
Crites, John D. (developer), 336
CTB/McGraw-Hill (developer), 170
Curtis Interest Scale, 451
Customer Service Skill Assessment Program, 444

D

Daly, Joe (reviewer), 344
Daniel, Larry (reviewer), 223
Deal-Me-In, 458
Defense Manpower Data Center (developer), 93
Differential Aptitude Test, 123
Dole Vocational Sentence Completion Blank, 451
Dvorine Color Vision Test, 444
Dye, D. A. (developer), 164

E

Educational Interest Inventory, 451
Edwards Personal Preference Schedule, 464
Emerging Occupations Interest Inventory, 451
Employability Competency Scale, 131
Employability Inventory, 461
Employability Maturity Interview, 461
Employee Aptitude Survey, 437
Employee Effectiveness Profile, 464
Employee Reliability Inventory, 464
Employment Barrier Identification Scale, 469
Endorele Seversen Transition Rating Scales, 469
ETSA Tests, 438
Evaluating the Participant's Employability Skills, 462
Explore, 139
Explore the World of Work, 451

F

Feller, Rich (reviewer), 344
Flanagan Aptitude Classification Test, 438
Flanagan Industrial Tests, 438
Fleishman Job Analysis Survey, 455
Forer Vocational Survey: Men-Women, 464
Freitag, Patricia (reviewer), 134
Functional Assessment Inventory, 469
Fundamental Interpersonal Relations Orientation-Behavior, 464

G

Gains I & II, 462
Gardner, Eric (developer), 82
Garfield, Nancy, 65
Geist Picture Interest Inventory, 469
General Clerical Test, 444
Glutting, Joseph (developer), 377
Gordon Occupational Checklist II, 451
Gordon Personal Profile-Inventory, 464
Gottfredson, Gary (developer), 310
Group Interest Sort, 451
Group Test of Musical Ability, 444
Guide for Occupational Exploration Inventory, 452
Guildford-Zimmerman Interest Inventory, 452
Guilford-Zimmerman Temperament Survey, 464
Gysbers, Norman, 35

H

Hall Occupational Orientation Inventory, 455
Hall, Michael (reviewer), 318
Hanna, Gerald (reviewer), 179
Harmon, Lenore (developer), 289
Harrington, Joan (developer), 74
Harrington, Thomas (developer), 74, 228
Harrington-O'Shea Career Decision- Making System-Revised, 228
Harris, Jeffrey (developer), 116
Hay Aptitude Test Battery, 438
Healy, Charles (reviewer), 364
Henderson, Patricia (reviewer), 143

Hendrix-Frye, Helena (developer), 399
Herr, Edwin, 15
High School Career-Course Planner, 452
Hill, Stephen (reviewer), 351
Holland, John (developer), 276, 278, 279, 281, 310
Hollingsead, Candice (reviewer), 152
Horton, Connie (developer), 377
How Well Do You Know Your Interests?, 452
Hughey, Kenneth (reviewer), 179

I

Individual Career Exploration, 452
Individual Style Survey, 455
Industrial Reading Test, 438
Insight Inventory, 464
Instruments for Special Populations, 385
Interest & Values Inventories, 193
Interest Determination, Exploration & Assessment System, 242
Interest Explorer, 235
Interest Inventories, 448
Intuitive Mechanics, 444
IPI Aptitude-Intelligence Test Series, 438

J

Jackson Personality Inventory- Revised, 357
Jackson Vocational Interest Survey, 250
Jackson, Douglas N. (developer), 250, 357
Jepsen, David (reviewer), 359, 475

Job Choice Decision-Making Exercise, 465
Job Descriptive Index, 456
Job Effectiveness Prediction System, 438
Job Search Attitude Inventory, 462
Job Search Inventory, 452
Job Seeking Skills Assessment, 462
Job Skills, 444
Job Skills Tests, 439
Job Style Indicator, 456
Johansson, Charles (developer), 202, 242
Jordaan, Jean (developer), 323
Judgment of Occupational Behavior-Orientation 2000, 452
Juhnke, Gerald, *xii*

K

Kapes, Jerome, 1, 433, 475, 535
Karlsen, Bjorn (developer), 82
Kass, Charles (developer), 158
Kass, Joseph (developer), 158
Keirsey Character Sorter, 464
Keirsey Temperament Sorter II, 465
Kelchner, Kathy (developer), 386
Kelly, Kevin (reviewer), 269
Kernes, Jerry (reviewer), 219
Key Educational Vocational Assessment System, 469
Kinnier, Richard (reviewer), 219
Kjos, Diane, *xii*
Knapp, Lila (developer), 210
Knapp, Robert (developer), 210
Knapp-Lee, Lisa (developer), 210
Knowdell, Richard (developer), 218
Krumboltz, John (developer), 316
Kuder Career Search With Person Match, 267

Kuder General Interest Survey, Form E, 257
Kuder Occupational Interest Survey For DD, 265
Kuder, Frederic (developer), 257, 265, 267

L

Lapan, Richard, 35
Learning Skills Profile, 458
Learning Style Profile, 469
Learning Styles Inventory, 469
Learning/Working Styles Inventory, 399
Leconte, Pamela (reviewer), 388
Leisure to Occupations Connection Search, 453
Leisure/Work Search Inventory, 453
Lenz, Janet (developer), 343
Life-Centered Career Education Competency Assessment, 405
Lindeman, Richard (developer), 323
Linkenhoker, Dan (developer), 418
Loch, Chuck (developer), 158
Long, Eliot (developer), 178
Lumsden, Jill, 47
Lund, Jeffrey (reviewer), 426
Lunneborg, Patricia (developer), 303
Luzzo, Darrell (reviewer), 332
Lynch, Patricia (reviewer), 407

M

Martinez, Linda, 433, 535
Matrix, 535
McCarron, Lawrence (developer), 418
McCarron-Dial System, 470
McDivitt, Patricia Jo (reviewer), 337

McGlashing, Jennifer (reviewer), 401

McKenna, Molly (reviewer) 378

Measures of Work Values, 454

Mechanical Movements, 445

Mehrens, William, 27

Meyer-Kendall Assessment Survey, 465

Microcomputer Evaluation of Career Areas, 469

Miller, Robert (reviewer), 152

Miner, Claire Usher (reviewer), 204

Minnesota Clerical Test, 445

Minnesota Importance Questionnaire, 456

Minnesota Job Description Questionnaire, 456

Minnesota Paper Form Board – Revised, 445

Minnesota Rate of Manipulation Test, 445

Minnesota Satisfaction Questionnaire, 456

Minnesota Satisfactoriness Scales, 462

Minnesota Spatial Relations Test, 445

Missouri Aptitude & Career Information Inventory, 439

Missouri Occupational Card Sort, 459

Moinat, S. M. (developer), 164

Morrill, Weston (developer), 331

Motivated Skills Card Sort, 459

Motivational Approach of Personal Potential, 439

Mueller, Ralph (reviewer), 134

Multidimensional Aptitude Battery, 439

Multiple Aptitude, Achievement, & Comprehensive Measures, 436

Musical Aptitude Profile, 445

My Vocational Situation, 462

Myers, Isabel Briggs (developer), 363

Myers, Roger (developer), 323

Myers-Briggs Type Indicator, 363

N

Neopersonality Inventory-Rev. 465

Nevil, Dorothy (developer), 298

Newsome, Deborah (reviewer), 292

NOCTI Occupational Competency Tests, 439

O

O'Conner Finger Dexterity Test, 445

O'Conner Tweezer Dexterity Test, 446

O'Shea, Arthur J. (developer), 228

Oakland, Thomas (developer), 377

Occupational Aptitude Survey & Interest Schedule, 2nd Ed., 150

Occupational Clues, 453

Occupational Interest Card Sort, 459

Occupational Personality Assessment, 465

Occupational Personality Questionnaire, 465

Occupational Preference Inventory, 465

Occupational Stress Inventory, 465

Office Skills Test, 446

Ohio Vocational Interest Survey II, 453

P

Parker, Randall, 150

Parrish, Linda (reviewer), 394

Patrick, John (reviewer), 104

Patton, James (developer), 425

Pennsylvania Bi-Manual Worksample, 446

Perceptual Speed, 446

Personal Audit, 466

Personal Skills Map, 466

Personal Style Indicator, 456

Personality Assessments, 349, 462

Personality Research Form, 466

Personnel Tests for Industry-Oral Directions Test, 470

PESCO 2001, 158

Peterson, Gary (developer, reviewer), 343, 351

Phoenix Ability Survey System, 439

Pictorial Inventory of Careers, 470

Plan, 141

Pope, Mark (reviewer), 258

Position Analysis Questionnaire, 456

Position Classification Inventory, 457

Practical Assessment Exploration System, 470

Preliminary Diagnostic Questionnaire, 470

Prevocational Assessment Screen, 470

Professional Employment Test, 439

Program for Assessing Youth Employment Skills, 471

PSI Basic Skills Test, 164

Publisher Contact Information, 483

Purdue Pegboard, 446

R

Raiff, Gretchen (reviewer), 230

Rayman, Jack (reviewer), 318

Reading-Free Vocational Interest Inventory, 412

Reardon , Robert (reviewer), 110, 343

Responsibility & Independence Scale for Adolescents, 471

Retirement Activities Card Sort, 459

Revised Beta Examination - 3rd Ed., 440

Riverside Publishing Staff (developer), 235

Robbins, Steven (developer), 331

Rogers, Jeff (reviewer), 95

Rogers, Bruce (reviewer), 173

Rojewski, Jay (reviewer), 159

Rokeach Value Survey, 457

Rounds, James (reviewer), 378

Ruch, W. W. (developer), 164

S

Sackett, Sharon (reviewer), 237

Sales Attitude Checklist, 466

Sales Personality Questionnaire, 466

Salience Inventory, 457

Sampson, James (developer), 47, 343

Satisfaction Research Questionnaire, 457

Saunders, Denise (developer), 343

Savickas, Mark (developer), 336

Schafer, William (reviewer), 304

Schoenrade, Patricia (reviewer), 299

Scholastic Level Exam, 440

School-to-Work Career Survey, 453
Schubert General Ability Battery, 440
Seashore, H. G., 123
Selecting a Career Assessment Instrument, 27
Self-Directed Search, Career Explorer, 281
Self-Directed Search, Career Planning, 279
Self-Directed Search-E, Fourth Edition, 278
Self-Directed Search-R, Fourth Edition 276
Self-Motivated Career Planning Guide, 466
Sellers, Steven (reviewer), 204
Short Employment Tests, 446
Short Tests of Clerical Ability, 446
Shub, A. N. (developer), 164
Shute, Robert (reviewer), 252
Singer-Loomis Inventory of Personality 466
Sitlington, Patricia (reviewer), 301
Sixteen Personality Factor Questionnaire, 369
Skills Assessment Module, 471
Skills Confidence Inventory, 288
Slaney Vocational Card Sort, 459
Smith, Jo (developer), 87
Smith, Juliet (reviewer), 83
Social & Prevocational Information Battery, 471
Sources of Information About Testing & Career Assessment, 475
Space Relations, 447
Space Thinking, 447
Special Populations , 467
Specific Aptitude & Achievement Measures, 442
SRA Clerical Aptitudes, 447

SRA Mechanical Aptitudes, 447
SRA Pictorial Reasoning Test, 447
SRA Test of Mechanical Concepts, 447
Strategic Assessment of Readiness for Training, 466
Street Survival Skills Questionnaire, 418
Strength Deployment Inventory, 467
Stromberg Dexterity Test, 447
Strong, E.K., 288
Strong Interest Inventory, 288
Student Styles Questionnaire, 377
Styles of Teamwork Inventory, 467
Success Skills 2000, 440
Sundre, Donna (reviewer), 324
Super, Donald (developer), 298, 323
SureHire, 467
Survey of Interpersonal Values, 457
Survey of Personal Values, 457
Survey of Work Styles, 467
Survey of Work Values, 457
System for Assessment & Group Evaluation/Compute-A-Match, 440

T

Talent Assessment Program, 471
Tanguma, Jesus (reviewer), 88
Technical Test Battery, 440
Technology & Internet Assessment, 448
Temperament Comparator, 467
Testing Standards & Codes, 503
Tests for Everyday Living, 471
Tests of Adult Basic Education, 170
The Ball Foundation (developer), 102
Thomas, Stephen (reviewer), 413
Thompson, Albert (developer), 323
Thompson, Bruce (reviewer), 165

Thompson, Donald (reviewer), 104

Thurstone Temperament Schedule, 467

Townsend, John (reviewer), 186

Training House Assessment Kit, 440

Transition Behavior Scale, 2nd Ed., 471

Transition Planning Inventory, 425

Trends & Issues in Career Assessment, 15

U

UNIACT IV, 453

USES Basic Occupational Literacy Test, 472

USES Clerical Skills Test, 448

USES General Aptitude Test Battery, 441

USES Interest Checklist, 453

USES Interest Inventory, 454

USES Non-Reading Aptitude Test Battery, 472

User's Matrix, 535

Using Assessment for Personal, Program, & Policy Advocacy, 35

V

Vacc, Nicholas (reviewer), 292

Vacha-Haase, Tammi (reviewer), 243, 433

Valpar 300 Series Dexterity Modules, 448

Valpar Aviator, 441

Valpar Component Work Sample Series, 472

Valpar Pro 3000, 441

Valpar System 2000, 441

Valpar Test of Essential Skills, 441

Values Preference Indicator, 458

Values Scale, 298

Vansickle, Timothy (reviewer), 371

Vernick, Stacie (reviewer), 110

Viewpoint, 467

Vocational Adaptation Rating Scales, 472

Vocational Assessment & Curriculum Guide, 472

Vocational Behavior Checklist, 472

Vocational Decision Making Interview, 472

Vocational Evaluation System, 441

Vocational Evaluation Systems, 472

Vocational Implications of Personality, 467

Vocational Insight & Exploration Kit, 459

Vocational Interest Assessment System, 454

Vocational Interest Exploration System, 454

Vocational Interest Inventory & Exploration Survey, 454

Vocational Interest Inventory, Revised, 303

Vocational Interest Temperament & Aptitude System, 473

Vocational Learning Styles, 473

Vocational Preference Inventory, 468

Vocational Research Interest Inventory, 454

Vocational Training Inventory & Exploration Survey, 473

Vocational Transit, 473

VOC-TECH Quick Screener, 441

V-TECS Assessments, 442

W

Wang, Lin (reviewer), 125
Watson-Glaser Critical Thinking Appraisal, 442
Wehmeyer, Michael (developer), 386
Wesman Personal Classification Test, 442
Wesman, A. G., 123
What – Where – How? 462
Whitfield, Edwin, 1
Wickwire, Pat Nellor (reviewer), 212
Wide Range Achievement Test, 473
Wide Range Interest-Opinion Test, 473
Willson, Victor (reviewer), 88
Wisen Test of Mechanical Aptitude, 448
Wonderlic Basis Skills Test, 178
Wonderlic Personnel Test, 442
Work Adjustment Inventory, 474
Work Adjustment Scale, 462
Work Environment Scale, 458
Work Exploration Checklist, 454
Work Keys, 183
Work Motivation Inventory, 458
Work Performance Assessment, 474
Work Personality Profile, 474
Work Preference Question- naire, 454
Work Skills Development Pack- age, 474
Work Temperament Inventory, 474
Workmate, 458
World of Work Inventory, 442

Z

Zytowski, Donald (developer), 267